W9-DIS-277

Black Jack Logan

John A. Logan in 1884.
(COLLECTION OF THE AUTHOR)

Black Jack Logan:

AN EXTRAORDINARY LIFE IN PEACE AND WAR

Gary Ecelbarger

THE LYONS PRESS

Guilford, Connecticut
An imprint of The Globe Pequot Press

For Carolyn

———————————

Copyright © 2005 by Gary Ecelbarger

ALL RIGHTS RESERVED. No part of this book may be reproduced or transmitted in any form by any means, electronic or mechanical, including photocopying and recording, or by any information storage and retrieval system, except as may be expressly permitted in writing from the publisher. Requests for permission should be addressed to The Lyons Press, Attn: Rights and Permissions Department, P.O. Box 480, Guilford, CT 06437.

The Lyons Press is an imprint of The Globe Pequot Press.

Printed in the United States of America

ISBN 1-59228-566-X (trade cloth)

Contents

Acknowledgments   vii

Introduction   1
Chapter One: His Father's Son   9
Chapter Two: Prince of Egypt   32
Chapter Three: Patriots and Traitors   69
Chapter Four: Promotion   107
Chapter Five: Earned Faith   127
Chapter Six: Saving the Union   168
Chapter Seven: Victory   208
Chapter Eight: Memorial Days   233
Chapter Nine: Tainted in the Gilded Age   252
Chapter Ten: Rise of a Candidate   276
Chapter Eleven: Coronation   302
Epilogue   318

Notes   325
Bibliography   361
Index   375

Acknowledgments

P. MICHAEL JONES of Murphysboro, Illinois, has been an indispensable asset to this book. As director of the General John A. Logan Museum in Murphysboro, Mike has dedicated himself to preserving the memory of the town's most famous citizen. He contributed letters, memoirs, photographs, and courthouse research to the book. Mike's previous friendship with the late Barbara Burr Hubbs has produced material previously never considered before and the historical context necessary to understand those records. Mike also read the entire manuscript and provided valuable historical edits. As a pure "Logan-phile," he took away any guilt I would otherwise feel in constantly contacting him with nagging questions about the various aspects of the subject's life.

Steven Woodworth, associate professor of history at Texas Christian University, generously took time away from his own writing projects to review the select chapters and lend his expertise on the Civil War, particularly with the Army of the Tennessee and its campaigns. Several friends from the Washington, D.C. metropolitan area also contributed to the project. Bill Scheid read the entire manuscript and provided advice from the perspective of a biography aficionado. Cyndi Abbott, Martha Betts, and Bill Stott read chapters as well. All of their efforts are sincerely appreciated. Norman Dasinger, Jr., of Dallas, Georgia, was particularly helpful to guide me on a private tour of the Dallas battlefield; his generosity and his family's hospitality will always be remembered.

Researcher B. J. Ross of Springfield, Illinois, was instrumental in procuring copies of letters and newspapers from her city's libraries and archives. Her prompt service filled in gaps that still existed after my own visits to the same facilities. James Pickett Jones, the previous biographer of John A. Logan, also deserves recognition for laying the foundation and sparking the interest to recapture that life story. Professor John Y. Simon of Southern Illinois University was instrumental in republishing Jones's books; his interest and advice in my version of the life story was helpful to initiate this work.

I am indebted to Farley Chase for his faith in the manuscript to represent it. That appreciation extends to George Donahue of The Lyons Press for supporting the work, and to Lisa Purcell for her dedicated attention to editing the manuscript and polishing it for publication.

My most heartfelt gratitude is reserved for Carolyn M. Ecelbarger, oft-published assistant professor of physiology, runner of five marathons, coach of youth sports, and mother of three. Her patience and understanding nature through fifteen years of marriage to support my literary efforts have earned a dedication for this book, and my love and respect for a lifetime.

New York City
June 10, 1885

SENATOR JOHN A. LOGAN came here to visit a dying friend.

Three weeks after securing his third term in the United States Senate, he had departed Washington on a train bound for New York. Here he found himself staring at a four-story brick mansion trimmed with brownstone. The mansion— Number 3, on the north side of East Sixty-Sixth Street—nestled in the center of New York City's best residential quarter, near the corner of Fifth Avenue and within sight of Central Park. Behind its heavy front doors rested Logan's friend, a man he had known for twenty-four years. Members of the press and concerned New Yorkers milled on the sidewalk in front of the building, keeping a vigil on its resident. The dying man was the most popular American of the past two decades, a former president and the highest-ranking U.S. officer in the history of the nation. He was Ulysses S. Grant.

Logan sidestepped the gathering, and was invited inside. He greeted Grant's wife, Julia, and her son, Frederick, and then followed a family member up the carpeted stairway to Grant's room. He found his friend resting upon an immense brass bedstead, complete with a huge canopied overhead. Perhaps they shook hands, but without touching him Logan could see the ravages of cancer upon Grant's body. Grant had weighed 180 pounds during his White House years, but this day he was at least 40 pounds lighter. The extensive graying of his hair and beard somehow complemented his gaunt and grizzled face, making him appear older than his sixty-three years.[1]

Conversely, Logan's appearance did not surprise Grant, for the senator looked much the same in June 1885 as he had five summers earlier. Logan was a shorter man than Grant, giving up an inch to him. Though not fat, he was much thicker than he had ever been before, yet his signature features still shone through. His complexion, which had earned him the sobriquets "Black Jack" and "Black Eagle," remained swarthy as ever, and the ends of an impressive walrus mustache still drooped below the corners of his mouth. His whiskers now appeared more than a quarter gray, giving away his fifty-nine years of life. The rest of his face was clean-shaven, accentuating his spectacular eyes. Black and animated, they seemed to blaze with passion. A newsman had once rated them "the finest pair of eyes ever possessed by a man." Logan's other noteworthy feature was his hair. He still wore it long, as he had done twenty years earlier. Unlike his mottling mustache, His crown had only begun to sprout gray, visible only upon close scrutiny, and he still had a full head of hair, a mane so dark that one observer described it as "blue-black." It was so unnaturally black that it raised debate in Washington's social circles over whether he dyed it or not. Those who insisted that he blackened his hair never considered the family trait of raven locks that began with Logan's father and carried on to a third generation to his son.[2]

After the cordial greeting, the two old friends talked, but Logan understood the effects of throat cancer upon the president. Decades of cigar smoking likely precipitated Grant's fatal disease. On this June day he could speak (in a few weeks he would be mute), but did so with noticeable effort and difficulty. His voice was weak; Logan needed to sit right next to him to hear him clearly. Still, Grant gave no indication to Logan that he wished to preserve his voice. Each friend had kept tabs on the other, following newspaper reports and occasionally writing. No doubt Grant congratulated Logan on his remarkable Senate victory, his third win to the upper house of the U.S. Congress.[3]

Both men understood the importance of retaining that Senate seat. Logan had run for president in 1884. Grant had endorsed him, but Logan still came in second for his party's nomination, and his party came in second in the presidential race. The disappointment of 1884 strengthened his resolve; he would run again in 1888. He was the best-known candidate seeking the presidency since General Grant twenty years earlier. Unlike Grant, he had a power base of influence and the experience of four terms in the House of Representatives and two full terms in the Senate—twenty years in the U.S. Congress—to buttress his reputation as a war hero.

Logan also benefited from previous endorsements and alliances. He had the backing of the Grand Army of the Republic, the influential organization of Civil War veterans who had steered elections in the past and were more powerful than ever in 1885. More than one quarter of a million former soldiers belonged to the G.A.R. They and all the other Union veterans received $800 million in pensions; one out of every four dollars spent by the federal government went to these soldiers. Logan had championed their cause. As a three-term president of the organization, he organized the veterans as a powerful lobby and used that power to elect Grant for his first term. He also designated a national commemoration day for fallen comrades. Celebrated every year since 1868, it was an event marked by decorating graves with flowers and wreaths. By 1885 the end-of-May ceremonies were more popular than ever. Logan rightfully claimed Memorial Day as the proudest act of his life.

African Americans also hailed Logan as their candidate. This was a most unusual alliance because he had persecuted blacks throughout the 1850s. But the Civil War was an epiphany that completely altered his social and political philosophy, so much so that since the war had ended in 1865, he had fought long and hard for suffrage and education rights for former slaves. Logan's Saul-to-Paul conversion was so impressive that Frederick Douglass, America's most famous African American, not only forgave him for his past sins against his people but had also officially endorsed him for president in 1884, and was expected to repeat the endorsement for the upcoming campaign. "As for us," proclaimed an African-American newspaper, "we are for Logan every time, so long as he remains a friend and advocate of popular education and equal rights for all American citizens, regardless of race, color, or previous condition of servitude." That endorsement ran off the presses in 1884. Logan was still a friend; he was still an advocate and would continue to fight for those rights until the day he died.[4]

Logan and Grant would have naturally discussed politics and Logan's upcoming bid for the presidency. The conversation flowed, for they had much in common. They had lived in Illinois in the 1860s, shared similar interests, and excelled in politics and war. The Civil War had made each of them an American hero. Whereas Grant was the most successful career army man since George Washington to turn to politics, Logan not only was considered the best political general of the era, he had also been dubbed the best volunteer soldier in the country. Civil War veterans idolized them both during the 1880s. If Grant was the Union soldiers' father, then Logan was their best friend. They were so identified with the war—now twenty years past—that they were both honored with the title "General" rather than "President" and "Senator." Both men preferred it that way.

They talked away the remainder of the morning, the conversation seamlessly transitioning to the present, and then to the past. Near noon, Logan let Grant rest a while and headed downstairs where he was escorted to the dining room toward the back of the residence. It would have surprised no one if Julia quizzed her guest during lunch about the health and happiness of Mary Logan—the senator's wife of thirty years—and his son and daughter. Other topics made their way to the table. Logan learned during his visit that the Grants would relocate in one week to a cottage at Mount McGregor, a village nestled in the foothills of the Adirondacks above Saratoga.[5]

Colonel Frederick Grant, Ulysses' oldest son, who had followed in his father's footsteps to West Point and the U.S. Army, had known Logan since he was twelve. No doubt the two relived those memories of Mississippi during the spring and summer of 1863. Fred had tagged along with the Army of the Tennessee to witness what would become his father's signature campaign, and Logan had been Grant's favorite tool to accomplish his strategy at the Battle of Champion Hill, the key contest of the campaign. More than twenty years after the battle, he could not purge from his mind the image of General Logan directing his troops while perched on his war horse. "I believe that could a picture be made of Logan for exhibition as I saw him at Champion's Hill on that bright afternoon, May 16, 1863, every youth and maiden in the land would be his devoted admirer and follower," he insisted, adding, "He was magnificent."[6]

Logan would also never forget those moments. He always considered himself a soldier. Perhaps a day never went by in his life where he did not flash back to when he led men on battlefields. Unable to recapture the past, Logan compensated by fighting postwar battles for his men, particularly in pension legislation. His soldiers, who worshipped him during the war, remained dedicated to him. "To know him was to love him," wrote one of them in 1884. "He was my ideal soldier, and my ardor and love for him have not abated one iota in the years that have intervened while leaving the service."[7]

When Logan climbed the stairs back to Grant's room, he took those memories with him. The two picked up where they had left off late in the morning. They talked briefly that afternoon, reminiscing over the heroic and humorous aspects of the war. They shared many battles and campaigns in Illinois and Missouri, Tennessee, and Mississippi. Their past service conjured up the surnames of Civil War legends they both knew—Lincoln, Sherman, Sheridan, McPherson, and Thomas.

The "soldier speak" was natural for them, but it also had a purpose. Both were writing books. Logan's, titled *The Great Conspiracy*, was a castigation of the South for starting the Civil War. This theme was consistent with his "spread-eagle" oratory. Although some had advised him to modify his stance, the senator held steadfast to his convictions, and his near-daily work on the book reinforced them even more strongly. Grant was penning his *Personal Memoirs*—and he was racing against time. Advance orders for his reminiscences were outstanding, but Grant needed to complete the work before the cancer had consumed his strength and memory. Both men had suffered financial setbacks since the war's close, but Grant had literally gone broke in recent years. His book was necessary to pull his family out of debt.

Grant's book was also therapeutic; it kept his thoughts active and diverted during his rapidly waning days. He was writing at an impressive clip, and had been well into the Civil War period of his life during the time of Logan's visit. Grant freely allowed Logan to view that portion of the manuscript dealing with the senator. He read Grant's version of their first meeting, back in 1861 when Grant was a new colonel and Logan was a congressman. Likely more amused than offended, Grant's words reminded Logan about the time when his loyalty to the country was under question.

Pressing on, he perused Grant's handling of the battles they fought together: Belmont, Forts Henry and Donelson, the five battles and the siege that comprised the Vicksburg Campaign. In addition to his memoir, Grant had nearly completed an article about Vicksburg and he asked Logan if he would read and comment on it before it was published in *Century Magazine*. Logan, of course, agreed. Grant's literary work impressed him, for he subsequently told a reporter, "His physical suffering seems to have nerved his mind for its best efforts."[8]

In the middle of the afternoon, as Grant grew weary, the three-hour conversation dwindled to its awkward conclusion. The two proud soldiers worked their way through the sorrowful and poignant acknowledgment that they were parting for the last time. Logan said his final goodbye and took his leave. Returning to the main floor, he bid adieu to Julia and Fred Grant, exited the house, and returned to the railroad station. As the train hissed, creaked, and then lurched from the station to carry him back home to Washington, he realized the next time he would be back in New York would be for Grant's funeral—and that was likely to be before the summer was over.[9]

During the 250-mile trip to the nation's capital, Logan reflected upon the daylong visit with Grant. Perhaps it forced him to contemplate his own mortality. He was still eight months shy of his sixtieth birthday, but his failing body convinced him he would not celebrate the ripe old age his grandfather had enjoyed. His father had died in his sixties. John Logan shared his father's name, his enjoyment of horses, his love of family, and his passion for politics. Would he also share his father's fate?

With time to contemplate the past, Logan's thoughts may have drifted to his roots. No one could fault him if the image of Dr. John Logan crept into his mind. It was not the first time, nor would it be the last time he reflected with fondness on the life of his father.

Courage is one of God's noblest gifts to man.

It is a high, brilliant, and commanding quality of man's nature.

It is incapable of being imparted by education.

Those who do not inherit it can never have it.

But it rarely leaves a family line to which it belongs.

—JOHN A. LOGAN

CHAPTER ONE

His Father's Son

JOHN ALEXANDER LOGAN descended from a Northern Ireland family. His father, born in 1788 and christened "John Logan" by his father before him, set the stage for one of nineteenth-century America's most ostentatious personalities to act upon, producing a performance rewarded by poems and paintings, songs and statues, and an American holiday that became his legacy.

In 1793, five-year-old John Logan boarded a wooden ship with his parents and his five siblings, sailing away from the home and country where his ancestors had toiled for centuries. A weeks-long ocean voyage ended on the shores of America, and they soon migrated to Ellicott Mills, Maryland, twenty miles northeast of the capital city of Washington. In 1802, the Logan family—now expanded to nine children—trekked across the Alleghenies to the state of Ohio, persuaded to move there by a cousin. The new Logan home was Scioto County, the hill country resembling their homeland of Monaghan, Ireland. John spent his teenage years as an Ohioan. He experienced the birth of another sister, the death of his mother, and the proliferation of the new aunts, uncles, and cousins produced by the marriages of his oldest siblings.[1]

John nurtured a passion for horse breeding as he grew to manhood. His father had raised a fine stock and encouraged him to become involved in the business of trading them so he abruptly quit school and devoted himself to the horse trade. While still a teenager, he bought a boatload of horses and floated them down to New Orleans. He swiftly sold off the stock at the wharves to Northern merchants who unloaded their goods and needed transportation back to their homes. Buoyed by the quick sale and recognizing lucrative possibilities, John repeated the venture several times over the next few years, enjoying tidy profits each time he reached New Orleans.[2]

Before he turned twenty, John had formed a partnership with an Ohio neighbor. The two entrepreneurs bought a huge boat and crowded it with the largest lot of horses John had ever dealt with before. They had no problems selling off the immense load, turning in a greater profit than John ever had enjoyed from his solo ventures. He pocketed his share and started for home. But his life turned in a new direction when he stopped in Vicksburg, Mississippi. There he met Dr. Lem Claiborne, and the two struck up a friendship. Dr. Claiborne proved to be as good a salesman as he was a physician, for he persuaded John to stay in Mississippi and apprentice under him in the field of medicine. John agreed, and the two new partners headed to Natchez, where Dr. Claiborne practiced his trade.

Barely 150 miles north of New Orleans, Natchez was the oldest city on the Mississippi. Situated on a 200-foot bluff towering over the river, it boasted a wealthy intellectual class that exerted a significant political and social influence throughout the lower Mississippi Valley. Cotton was king in Natchez, as any traveler could discern when he viewed sprawling plantations run by slave labor. Not affected by the oppressive heat, John chose to stay for four years, shunning the lucrative horse trade while learning the art and science of medicine. Early in the second decade of the 1800s, he departed Natchez with a new title: Dr. John Logan.[3]

Dr. John Logan also left Natchez with a large debt, a financial dungeon he could not escape while trying to establish his Ohio practice. He headed back to New Orleans in 1813 to parlay another huge horse deal—and was relieved to find the trade there as prosperous as ever. As he made his way back North, he kept a couple of $1,000 horses with him. At the junction of the Mississippi and Ohio rivers, he continued northward on the former water route, diverting from the normal path home to Ohio. Several miles up the Mississippi, he disembarked at the port town of Cape Girardeau. He had planned to exercise his horses there for a while and then attempt to sell them off. Then he met Marie Berthiaume Lorimier, the widow of a prominent landowner and military post commander who died early in the year. "Mary" was the half-French, half-Shawnee daughter of a former gunsmith for the Indian tribe who kept a store at the mouth of Apple Creek. She was well educated and beautiful, charming potential suitors from far and wide. John was immediately smitten by her, and she felt the same about him. The two married in February 1814. John gained a wife and a windfall, for Mary's late husband left her a wealthy estate. He also inherited a claim originally staked out by her first husband—all the horses and ponies ranging in the woods near his Apple Creek homestead.

John set up his medical practice, added to his horse stock, and erected a water mill near the village of Dutchtown. He successfully coaxed most of his Ohio family to move close to Apple Creek. Extended family members followed in this massive transplant of the Logan clan—eight Ohio families resettled in the trans-Mississippi territory. Mary bore the doctor a daughter in 1815, but the little girl died as an infant. A second daughter, Louisa Villars Logan, was born in November 1816. She survived.[4] The next five years were satisfying ones for John. He ran a mill, raised and sold horses, and practiced medicine in a region teeming with family members. The Logans strengthened their faith in the Methodist Church. Their settlements became a portion of a new state in 1821 when the U.S. government established Missouri as the twenty-fourth state. In a compromise plan that established Maine as a free state, Missouri came in as a slaveholding state. Desensitized to slave labor from his New Orleans and Natchez days, John inherited, bought, and owned thirty slaves at Cape Girardeau.[5]

His idyllic life crumbled away from him in 1821. While he negotiated a stock sale in New Orleans, Mary fell gravely ill. Despite all the best efforts of doctors who came from Jackson, they could not cure her. She died before John could return home. Widowed and left caring for a six-year-old daughter, he underwent a thorough life upheaval. He scouted out and purchased several hundred acres of prime farmland along the Big Muddy River in Illinois in October 1822. He sold off his Missouri mill lands, much of his stock, and most of his slaves. Late in 1823 he crossed the Mississippi River into Jackson County, Illinois.[6]

Illinois was the fifth and final state John would call home. Carved out of the Northwest Ordinance, Illinois had achieved statehood in 1818, but did so with a constitution challenged by the slave-preferring residents in the southern portion of the state. Like John, many residents brought their slaves with them. The 1818 Constitution outlawed slavery except for the property of the French inhabitants and those working in the salt-producing section of the state. The document also allowed indentured servitude of black workers. The new governor, Edward Coles, challenged the entire institution, calling for the complete abolition of slavery in Illinois. Early in 1823 slavery advocates coaxed the state legislature to pass a resolution to have a referendum to allow the citizens to hold a convention for the prospect of converting Illinois into a slave state. This would violate the 1787 Northwest Ordinance from which Illinois was created, and would nullify the 1818 state constitution. Two out of every three Jackson County residents—

John's neighbors—voted to hold the slavery convention. Their numbers matched well with the southern counties of Illinois, but this proslavery faction could not win the statewide vote. When the votes were counted, Governor Coles won his victory by routing the proslavery forces 6,640 to 4,972. There would be no convention to turn Illinois into a slave state, but restricted slavery still stood, as did indentured servitude.[7]

John boarded with his youngest sister, Margaret, and her husband, Reverend Philip Davis (a Methodist minister), in Brownsville, the small town serving as the Jackson County seat, four miles from the Logan farmland. His daughter attended school in Brownsville and he worked as one of only three practicing physicians in the entire county. The first state legislature had passed a bill to divide Illinois into five districts, regulating physicians to keep detailed records of their activities, and logging all births and deaths within their district. Although he was one of several physicians practicing in his district, by 1824, John conducted the greatest share of the practice in Jackson County, traveling in a radius that exceeded thirty miles from his home. He was identifiable by his plaited, foot-and-a-half-long hair and his easygoing personality. The more educated sectors of the region appreciated his style, never seeming to mind his limited education, which became apparent to his neighbors when he scrawled the word "medasin."[8]

By the nature of his work, John hobnobbed with the county elite. They included Alexander Jenkins, the state representative. Jenkins had settled in Brownsville several years earlier when he and his sister escaped an abusive father in Tennessee. Since then, Jenkins had worked as a carpenter and later as a lawyer, before being elected to represent Southern Illinois in the state legislature. After the annual Illinois convention, he headed back to Tennessee to bring another sister to live with him. When he returned to Brownsville he introduced his sister, Elizabeth, to his friend. Love struck the new acquaintances almost instantly. John could not help but admire the tall, elegant, and modest Southerner. Though retiring in a crowd, Elizabeth Jenkins shone with cheerfulness when conversing in comfort. Margaret Logan Davis considered her "very fascinating in looks and appearance," and so did her brother. John courted Elizabeth in Brownsville; by the summer of 1824, she consented to be his wife.[9]

Buoyed by Elizabeth's acceptance of his proposal, John labored on his Big Muddy River land, building a two-story house on the property for his daughter and his future bride. In February 1825, Justice of the Peace Joel Manning, the bride's brother-in-law, married Dr. John Logan and Elizabeth Jenkins in Brownsville. That spring John and Elizabeth rode to Missouri on a mission—to persuade the family to move with the doctor once again. The campaign continued by mail after the newlyweds returned to the Logan farm, and by the summer they convinced several Logans to liquidate their Missouri assets and move to Illinois. By fall 1825, the Logan clan was well aware that a new member would be joining them as Elizabeth glowed in her pregnancy.

On February 9, 1826—nearly one year to the day after their marriage—John and Elizabeth celebrated the birth of their first child, a son. Reverend Philip Davis, who had moved his family to a neighboring farm, baptized his new nephew. For at least two previous generations, tradition held that a Logan son carried the name of his father. John would not break the tradition, choosing his brother-in-law as the source of the baby's middle name. Thus, the Logans announced the arrival of John Alexander Logan to all of their family and friends in Southern Illinois.[10]

Called "Jack" or "Johnny" by family members, baby Logan's world for the first years of his life was his father's sprawling farm. Beginning in the summer of his second year, he shared the home with a baby brother, Thomas. The two Logan boys would be nearly inseparable throughout their childhoods. Yet, visitors to the Logan farm took immediate notice of Jack. Daniel Brush, several years older, saw him in 1829. Brush remarked that Jack "was a pert little fellow of three years, blackeyed, blackhaired, and dark skinned, straight-built and Indian-like, as his father was before him." Young Logan also began to mimic his father's hairstyle. He wore it long, enhancing his wild appearance.[11]

One of Jack's first trials of life would be the brutal winter of 1830–31. Those who survived it would refer to it as "the winter of the deep snow" whenever they discussed it, and all knew the year to which the expression referred. Jack celebrated his fifth birthday in the midst of nine weeks of seemingly incessant snowfall. Thirty-one snows fell in Illinois that winter, hampering travel and livelihoods. The combination of drifting snow crusted by layers of freezing rain and sleet had forced most Southern Illinois residents indoors.[12] One legacy of that frigid season may have been the region's new name—"Egypt." Local legend attributes the similarities with the Bible story of Jacob's sons, who were forced to travel to Egypt to buy grain so they could survive a famine, as the name's source. Northern Illinois residents—their crops destroyed by the snow—were forced to travel to Southern Illinois to buy their seed corn for the upcoming planting season on the prairies. The delta-like character of the state's southernmost portion may have also justified the name.

Jack's father and uncle were among the region's movers and shakers. John's practice flourished and he continued to engage in horse breeding. He also helped establish McKendree College, a new Methodist school in the town of

Lebanon, having been elected one of thirty-three managers of the institution in 1828. Although John gained prestige in Southern Illinois, "Mother" Logan's family, the Jenkins clan, was more prominent. Shortly after becoming a lawyer, Uncle Alexander Jenkins was elected as state representative to Illinois' Seventh General Assembly, He won reelection in 1832, and subsequently served for a time as speaker of the house, but not before he temporarily left his legislature seat to captain a company in the Black Hawk War of 1832. (John accompanied his brother-in-law in their one-month service—first as a corporal, then as surgeon.) Another uncle, Joel Manning, was a prominent Brownsville lawyer and clerk of the courts of Jackson County. Mrs. Manning, Elizabeth's sister, was considered the belle of Brownsville at the time of her marriage. The Jenkins-Logan-Manning clan was known as the "royal family" of Southern Illinois.[13]

While John gained prestige in Jackson County, his children remained on the Logan acres and its environs. John had mimicked his own father's Ohio estate. His land had everything a boy desired: room to run, trees to climb, a river in which to swim and fish, and playmates close by. In addition to the lads neighboring the Logan farm, Jack and Tom also played with the "help." James "Wilkinson" Dumbaly, three and a half years older than Jack, was the son of a slave woman owned by the doctor. Once he moved to Illinois, Wilkinson immediately converted to an indentured servant, deeded to work for Dr. Logan until his twenty-first birthday. (His father, Monday Dumbaly, labored on a neighbor's farm.)[14]

As the only town in the region and the county seat, Brownsville was the focal point of Jackson County industry, government, and commerce. Nearly one third of county residents lived in Brownsville in the 1830s; approximately 500 men, women, and children made the town their home, sheltered in log and frame houses. Brownsville also benefited from its location on the Big Muddy River. The river gave the townspeople an outlet to the Mississippi and opened the way to sell produce at New Orleans and St. Louis. The riverbanks held huge coal reserves to help the community thrive in a land surrounded by hills and wilderness.[15] John's quandary was that Brownsville limited the educational opportunities of his children. Established schoolhouses were nonexistent in Jackson County, so the Logan children attended schools wherever they popped up and whenever an itinerant schoolmaster was available to teach them. Jack began his formal education at the age of seven, attending a new school in Brownsville. After a very short stint there, he went to Tuthill's Prairie, twelve miles from his home, where Daniel B. Tuthill established a private school in the mid 1830s. Noted as a fine Greek and Latin scholar, Tuthill imparted his knowledge to the sons of Southern Illinois' most prominent men. Jack absorbed his teacher's lectures and—according to Tuthill—he showed great capacity for rapid assimilation of his lessons. He also displayed natural leadership when among the other boys. But Tuthill also confessed some difficulty keeping Jack focused on his studies for long stretches—despite his scholarly abilities, he was too active and full of energy.[16]

Throughout the first half of the 1830s, John's medical account books teemed with notations of all of his activities. The doctor's "inventive" spelling underscored why he considered it so important that his children receive a better education than he had. He administered "tonic Biters," a "viel of coff drops," and other "doases." He charged one neighbor three dollars for treatment with "madison for 2 children with worms," while another paid him half that sum for "Madison and proscription for his son." Although John spent a great deal of time on the road making house calls, county residents sought him out at the Logan farm. During these visits, Jack helped treat patients. He would mix concoctions in a big mortar by grinding it with a pestle. He also watched how his father treated people and quickly grew cynical about the practice of medicine. "People would come round, and father would feel their pulses and look at their tongues and tell me to mix up some pills—put in a lot of stuff that wouldn't hurt anybody," he recalled. "They'd take the medicine and go off and imagine it cured them. They would have got well just as quick if they hadn't taken anything." Dr. Logan forced his preteen son to learn all the bones, organs, and muscles of the body. "I didn't take to it very kindly," Jack later confessed, as he recalled how he prodded his father over the forced anatomy lessons. He asked him, "Father, why don't you make a man?" Once he grasped his father's curious attention, Jack explained that since he knew how to put all the bones together and knew where all the flesh, muscle, and other body parts went, "Why can't you build a man and then turn in the blood and set the machine a going?" His father gave up. "John," he conceded, "I don't think you've got sense enough to make a doctor."[17]

Although medicine clearly was not his calling, Jack inherited the doctor's passion for politics. His uncle's career also influenced him. In 1834, Alexander Jenkins ascended from speaker of the house to lieutenant governor of Illinois. Political success came even closer to the Logan home in 1836, when John won the election for the legislative seat formerly occupied by Jenkins. Throughout this period Jack met many prominent politicians of the region as well as in the state. He absorbed their stories and grew more fascinated with the political arena.

The Logan and Jenkins families thrived during the presidency of Andrew Jackson and were devoted disciples of his doctrine. President Jackson cast himself as a man of the people who led by the will of the people; this kept Logan and

Jenkins as loyal adherents. The president's ascent and widespread popularity provided a lesson for John to teach Jack and other members of his family. "We all share alike in our government," he told them, pointing out that it is possible that even an "obscure young man may be brought up in our government. He may aspire even to the Presidential chair." John instilled in Jack the notion that a man rises on merit or falls on demerit; "this is great incouragement for young men of our government to try to inform themselves and qualify themselves for high stations in life."[18]

Jack absorbed and lived by the Jacksonian ideals into adulthood. His father was an unrelenting partisan of these political beliefs. When Martin Van Buren, Jackson's vice president, ran for president in 1836, John supported him with fervor because he considered this an extension of Jackson's philosophy and principles. A young Whig in the region, embittered by John's enthusiasm, called him "a most bigoted incompetent, and zealous partisan for Van Buren democracy . . ." The Whig well realized he was a minority in the region. "This county was largely democratic at the time," he recalled years later, "and I doubt whether 100 votes at that election were cast for the Whig electors." John celebrated another Democratic victory by naming his seventh child James Vanburen Logan.[19]

John left during the last weeks of 1836 to serve in the legislature at the state capital in Vandalia. Before he departed, he corrected a problem he found with his sons' education. Tuthill's school was adequate, but Mr. Tuthill was too sick and weak to continue as a teacher. John believed his boys were better off working at home while he was away on long stints in the legislature. He took Jack and Tom out of the Tuthill Prairie school after seven weeks of education there and hired a private tutor, David C. Lynch. The strict and accomplished educator continued to strengthen Jack's command of Greek and Latin, as well as the rudimentary subjects. "He proved to be all he professed to be: a splendid teacher," admitted one of Jack's aunts, who frequently visited the homestead to see him reading Caesar and Virgil. Lynch was described by a contemporary as "a crabbed man who firmly believed in the efficacy of the rod as an excitant auxiliary to books and slates." Notwithstanding his toughness and strict demeanor, "Old Man Lynch" reportedly took an immediate liking to Jack. John gave Lynch a comfortable upstairs room for teaching his lessons; he also kept Lynch employed on the farm maintaining its upkeep while he was away.[20]

During his father's legislative term Jack became a teenager, one who was clearly uninterested in his father's medical profession but drawn to his political one. Power and influence fascinated the youth, who fortified his political interests whenever he talked to his father's and his uncle's influential friends who visited their Jackson County homesteads. Jack visited his father's friends too, if not for any other reason than to serenade them with his fiddle. His ambitions exceeded those of his father, although he cloaked those desires with his casual and carefree style. The wife of one of John's friends quickly tired of the younger Logan's loafing. When Jack climbed atop her fence and fiddled a tune (he had become adept with the instrument), she ran out to reprimand him. "John Logan, what do you expect to be when you are a man?" she asked. "Congressman of the United States," he answered her as he sawed away at his fiddle.[21]

By the end of the 1830s, Southern Illinois no longer dominated the state's population and influence. Nearly 500,000 residents lived within the state borders, more than treble what the census takers tallied ten years earlier. But the population boom concentrated in the state's northern and central portions. The Erie Canal enhanced commerce and travel across the Great Lakes and the Cumberland Trail deposited Conestoga wagons into the Great Plains across the middle and upper reaches of the state. Since the end of the Black Hawk War, no obstacles challenged settlers from claiming the rich Illinois soil in the state's upper two-thirds, and business and industry in Chicago accelerated its growth and importance. This uneven growth in the northern sections forced a complete transition in state functions, so much so that even the capital moved northward from Vandalia to Springfield.[22]

The migration into and settlement of Illinois divided into cultural layers. Settlers of its middle and upper portions generally hailed from New England and the Middle Atlantic; the southern reaches consisted of Carolinians, Tennesseans, Virginians, and Marylanders. Traditionally, Southerners avoided the prairies, preferring to remain in the wooded and hill-clustered land between the Mississippi and Ohio Rivers. Egypt became more identifiable by its culture than its topography, which set the stage for political clashes and prejudices between Southern Illinois and its fellow state residents to the north.[23]

Jack never noticed these distinctions growing up in Jackson County, but his prominent father and uncle certainly did. Amicable debates in the state legislature gave way to partisan and vitriolic disputes as the rural and village-dominated Egypt fought against having its voice drowned out by the Chicago and Springfield crowd, as well as from the overwhelming numbers across the prairies. The Jacksonian Democrats from Egypt no longer represented the political philosophy of the entire state as they had in the first decade of Illinois history. Whig voices grew more powerful in the legislature. Despite their political differences, John reached out and befriended a young Whig from Springfield. The reward for the friendship was christening a newly created county with the physician's name. Logan County was formed from legislative action in the Illinois General Assembly in 1839. Carved out from Sangamon County, it was named for Dr. John Logan by his Springfield friend, a thirty-year-old lawyer and legislator named Abraham Lincoln.[24]

Lincoln and a group of legislators known as the "Long Nine" were instrumental in moving the state capital from Vandalia to Springfield. In 1840, fourteen-year-old Jack accompanied his father to Springfield and gazed upon the capitol building, under construction while his father toiled in the General Assembly at a local church. He also met state politicians, both Democrats and Whigs. Other legislators brought their sons, too. The boys formed the early connections of what would become lifelong acquaintances and friendships as they followed in the footsteps of their fathers.[25]

The Springfield experience provided Jack with a firsthand look at the function of state government, albeit an informal one. After completing his second legislative term, John sought to formalize the education of his children. Daniel Lynch, the tutor who worked with some success at the Logan household, was gone; he had started his own school twenty-five miles from the Logan homestead. John now experimented by enrolling Jack into a boarding school in Perry County established by Benajah G. Roots. Known as "Father Roots," he became a pioneer in the early years of the Illinois education system by advocating the graded school approach to replace the reader-to-reader approach to student advancement. Jack attended one spring season, not long enough to fully benefit from Roots's prowess. Nevertheless, the Roots school also left a lasting impression on Jack, not so much for what was taught but for whom he met there. He befriended William Joshua Allen, who was three years his junior, but like Jack hailed from a prominent family. "Josh" was the son of Willis Allen, a fellow state representative with political views similar to those of John, whom he met in Vandalia in the late 1830s. The Allen family had recently moved to Marion, the seat of Williamson County, twenty miles east of the Logan farm. After boarding together for the spring term, Jack and Josh parted, destined to meet again.[26]

In the summer of 1840 John was back at his farm. In his fifties, the physician showed no signs of slowing down. His passions and interests remained strong. Although it was clear to John that his firstborn would not be following in his career footsteps, he must have been pleased by his teenager's interest in politics. But more than that, father and son teamed up in a shared passion they turned into profit—horse racing.

In his early teenage years, Jack was still small and wiry—the perfect build for a jockey. In the saddle from the time he could talk, his horsemanship as a youth had few peers. His brother Tom was also a good horseman, but he was too excitable in racing conditions. Conversely, Jack was an even-tempered, cool-headed rider. Neighborhood boys called him "Indian racer," a moniker that captured the long-haired boy with skin and hair much darker than any of the white boys around.[27]

John and Jack breathed, ate, and slept horses. John took out one of his wheat fields to build a 1,000-yard, straightaway racetrack and Jack practiced upon it routinely. His favorite horse was Walnut Cracker, a racer he was astride so often as to appear a centaur. With his head up and always snorting defiance, Walnut Cracker was a confident and intimidating animal. Not surprisingly, Jack often rode him to victory. John reaped huge rewards for the audacious bets he placed on the success of his favorite jockey. After running Walnut Cracker for years, though, Jack knew the horse was getting too old to race. His father would not hear of retiring him. In the summer of 1840 he accepted Lieutenant Governor Stinson H. Anderson's challenge to a race on the Logan track. John bet $1,000 — against Jack's recommendation. But the race was on. Walnut Cracker jumped out to a quick lead and, with Jack riding him hard, he gained several lengths on Bill Anderson, the governor's son. But with 200 yards to go, old Walnut Cracker began to peter out; the rival horse closed the gap and pulled into the lead. Jack lost the race, something he rarely experienced on any horse. Appearing more infuriated than his father, who was $1,000 poorer after the event, the teenaged jockey jumped off Walnut Cracker and ranted, "Father, I told you this damned old horse couldn't run a thousand yards."[28]

Father and son carried their passion into the 1840s. John was reelected to the legislature for the third time in 1840. He returned to Jackson County in 1842 devoted to his horses and his son—his favorite jockey. He had sold property he owned in Vicksburg, Mississippi, for $1,800, giving him money to spend in horse trading and race betting. Father and son took Dr. Logan's string of thoroughbreds to Kentucky, winning four-figure bets. They then went to Jackson, Missouri, where Jack continued his string of victories, while his father made more money by selling off some of his stock. The connections across state lines brought Kentucky and Missouri horse breeders to the Logan farm, where Jack continued to ride to impressive victories on his home turf. These were effective word-of-mouth Saturday spectator events, attended by folks across Jackson County and other points of Egypt. One witness to several races on the Logan track insisted he never saw Jack lose a race there. Rampant gambling also marked these events, resulting in occasional arguments and fistfights. The more devout members of the Logan family frowned on John's income-earning interest, and believed it was also corrupting his jockey son. "You speak of Dr. Logan havin run a horse race," wrote a nephew to his sister in the summer of 1842. "What a shame for a man who once was a member of the Church." He clumsily attempted to invoke the word of Jesus when he wrote, "He won the race—But 'what proffet have wee if we gain the whole world and lose our soul.'"[29]

John's "proffet" rose with an impressive streak of victories by his son. But Jack was not so corrupted as to shun his religious beliefs. The Logan children were raised in the Methodist faith, and although their parents were active members of the church, the one who kept the faith strong was John's fire-and-brimstone sister Margaret, who lived nearby. Jack oftentimes visited the Davis farm, primarily to play with his cousins who were fairly close to his age. His Aunt Margaret relished when he also took part in the evening prayer meetings at her house. He also escorted her to prayer meetings at neighbors' houses, and occasionally conducted the group worship at these gatherings.[30]

But Jack did not make a habit of practicing what he preached. His gambling continued, now including poker and other games of chance as well as horse racing. His fistfights also continued—he had that Southern Illinois tendency to never back down from a fight. And as they aged through their teen years Jack and Tom attracted controversy and trouble. Jack had the defender's instinct, which overtook him whenever bullies provoked his younger brother. Jack once pummeled a youth who challenged Tom. He learned soon afterwards that he had beaten up a widow's son. According to one of his neighbors, "John went up to her and apologized for giving the boy the licking he deserved, because he felt sorry for his mother." Jack also protected his brother from nonhuman threats. On one of their walks home from Brownsville, the boys detoured onto a footpath through the woods. Jack found an empty black bottle, picked it up, and twirled it in his hands as they strolled. Suddenly, they stopped—a panther crouched on the trail in front of them. Jack gripped the bottle and—as soon as the panther pounced at them—he swung the makeshift club, striking a perfect blow across its skull. It fell to the ground, twitching in a fit. The boys then finished it off with a combination of large sticks and Jack's bottle. They headed home from there with quickened steps and a feeling of accomplishment through camaraderie as both brothers and best friends.[31]

As he advanced into his mid-teen years, Jack became leader of his circle of friends. He would never be physically imposing, but his bravery—oftentimes reckless—was admired by them. His companions included his brother Tom, his Davis cousins, and boys that lived on farms near the Big Muddy River, which was itself a prime attraction for the boys. On one occasion, Jack oversaw the construction of a flatboat. Once completed, the other boys shuddered at the thought of steering it into the swift-running current. Without hesitation, Jack jumped aboard and poled his boat into the churning waters for a wild, solo ride. He was also an accomplished prankster, and his antics became local legends. Cash Pond, in Williamson County, was the source of one of these legendary pranks. There some of Jack's friends found him struggling to haul in a huge catfish. His catch became a nine-day wonder, for it was the largest of its kind ever seen in the pond. Soon several fishermen living near the pond could be seen casting their lines, attempting to duplicate Jack's feat. This was impossible—he had purchased the catfish from the net of a nearby Ohio River fisherman, and planted it on his line to fool his friends into thinking that it actually came from the pond.[32]

As the son of an active and partisan Democrat, Jack naturally became more vocal in his politics. As John's sons matured adhering to his ideals, his political opponents lamented that there were too many of them. By 1842 nine children filled the Logan home (another child, born in 1832, died in infancy), but one of those children was not a Logan. Diza Glenn was the daughter of Elizabeth's sister. When her parents died early in the 1830s, John took in his orphaned three-year-old niece. She grew up more as a sister of Jack than as a cousin. Gone from the homestead was John's indentured servant, James Wilkinson Dumbaly. By state law Dumbaly was bound to John until his twenty-first birthday in 1843, but John released him in 1837 to Monday Dumbaly, the boy's freed father. The early release was magnanimous *and* pragmatic; Monday paid John $175 for his son's early freedom, a reimbursement John had calculated to offset the loss of Wilkinson's labor.[33]

The twenty-foot-by-fifty-foot Logan house was hardly large enough for a family of eleven, but until John built a larger home, he alleviated his problem by sending his oldest children off to a new school on Shiloh Hill. Chartered in 1840, the two-year-old school was called Shiloh College, a misleading name, for it was merely a little country school converted from a church. But it was taught by Daniel C. Lynch, the former Logan tutor. Obviously satisfied with Lynch, John saw to it that his oldest boys—Jack and Tom—receive a quality education from him in a formal setting. Jack sharpened and honed his oratory skills while attending Shiloh; one of his chosen topics was drunkenness, which he defined in a speech as "loathsome leprosy."[34]

He remained at the school for three years, with infrequent trips home from 1842 to 1845. But home changed dramatically while he was gone. The Brownsville courthouse succumbed to fire in 1843, leaving Jackson County and its 3,500 residents without its most important government building. Brownsville had fallen out of favor as the county seat, so John immediately stepped in and offered to set aside a twenty-acre tract of his vast acreage accumulated four miles east of the town to form a new one. His political enemies fought against the offer, sure he would derive power for what they considered a gesture more opportunistic than magnanimous. Alexander Jenkins, currently living with one of his children at the Logan farm, sided with his brother-in-law to fight the opposition. After an appreciable period of debate among the commissioners and populace, the offer was accepted. The new county seat was named Murphysboro in honor of a popular commissioner. As this new town sprung up in 1844, John built a new, ample frame house, two lots from the corner of the designated public square. He suffered significant damage on his acreage when the Big Muddy River flooded over, covering some of his fertile land in a freshet. He also lost a close race for reelection to the state legislature, but in 1844 he reclaimed his seat and went back to Springfield for his third term.[35]

When nineteen-year-old Jack completed his studies at Shiloh College in 1845, he returned to the now-roomier Logan home. His father still hoped that his oldest son and namesake would become the second "Dr. Logan" in the family, but Jack still wanted no part of medicine. His enviable education failed to point him in a clear direction, though. While he made up his mind, he bided his time at home, where on October 9 of that same year, he witnessed a friend of his become family when Lindorf Ozburn married Diza Glenn. Nearly three years Jack's senior, "Doff" Ozburn and his family had been mainstays in the county and always remained close to the Logan family, so much so that John addressed Doff as his "nephew." The groom was twenty-three years old; the bride was still three months shy of her sixteenth birthday.[36]

Although the Ozburn-Glenn wedding was a festive event for Jack that October, the month turned sour for him exactly one year later. He continued to partake in gambling — against the statutes of the state — and he and two friends were caught doing this on October 10. They had pitched dollars to win a pint of whiskey worth about ten cents. Jack was found guilty of the petty crime and paid a fine. He obviously regretted the gambling imbroglio. If it was up to him he would have been fighting for his country instead of idling away bored in his hometown. He was consumed with the topic of the day — Mexico. The United States declared war with Mexico back in May 1846. President James K. Polk called for 50,000 volunteers; Governor Augustus C. French responded by authorizing three Illinois regiments to fill his quota. In twenty days 1,000 more Illinois volunteers enlisted than were called for. Jack came late onto the scene — too late. When he and Squire Davis applied for service, they were both rejected because a Jackson County company had already been raised.[37]

Jack's legal troubles did not taint his father's political campaign; Dr. Logan handily won his fourth election to the Illinois General Assembly. Jack and John Logan spent some time together in St. Louis after the election. Jack saw his father off to Springfield from there early in December 1846, promising him that he would not enlist before the close of the winter legislative sessions. Jack returned to his family in Murphysboro to the saddest Christmas he ever endured, for scarlet fever had invaded the Logan home and infected two of his brothers. Four-year-old George died on Christmas Eve and five-year-old Philip succumbed three days later. They were the fourth and fifth Logan children to die, and the first of those to do so after infancy. Jack continued to be blessed with good health, but endured the sorrow of seeing three brothers die in less than twenty months.[38]

The disease spread through Murphysboro, seemingly claiming a member of every family that winter. Some households lost every child to scarlet fever. By spring the scourge was over, but Jack prepared himself to endure more deaths, and to give up his own life, if necessary, for his country. He could no longer resist the call to arms and, with Doff Ozburn and Squire Davis, he gathered young men in Jackson County to form a company to enter the war against Mexico. They recruited thirty-six eager volunteers.

Unable to make them a Jackson County company, they took their would-be soldiers over to Williamson County where they learned that two prominent citizens, Captain James Hampton and Captain John M. Cunningham, were actively recruiting. Jack used his family connections to gain the best advantage possible. Uncle Alexander Jenkins knew Captain Cunningham, a client of his law practice, and he wrote a letter supporting his nephew. Cunningham's company was full, but Captain Hampton's company had only forty-three recruits. Jack added his men into the unit and accepted a second lieutenancy for his recruiting efforts.

The volunteer soldiers stayed in Marion a few days before heading out to their rendezvous site at Alton. There Logan and Cunningham struck up a friendship. The twenty-one-year-old had an easygoing way, Cunningham learned. Perhaps his continual associations with friends of his father enabled Jack to connect with the thirty-three-year-old family man. Among Cunningham's four children was Mary, a precocious and pretty eight-year-old. Shortly before the young men marched from Marion, Jack called on Cunningham at his home, not surprised to find him with little Mary resting on his knee. The proud father was planning for his daughter's future. "John, if you distinguish yourself in the war," he teased, "I'll let you marry Mary here."[39]

Jack took the friendly ribbing in stride. He officially enlisted on May 9, 1847, mustered in the staff of Company H, First Illinois Infantry under Colonel Edward

W. B. Newby. Captain Cunningham's Williamson County recruits came into the same regiment as Company B. The troops organized at Camp Dunlop at Alton and in the middle of June, the regiment boarded steamers and headed down the Mississippi and up the Missouri to Fort Leavenworth in Nebraska Territory. From there they marched to Santa Fe. Jack and Captain Cunningham strengthened their friendship during their service in the same regiment. Jack drifted over to Company B to converse with Cunningham, who had stories to tell about his previous work as sheriff of Williamson County and as the representative of the region in the Illinois General Assembly. Their politics were compatible and their discussions never seemed forced. Cunningham continued to tease his young friend about the wedding he had arranged. Receiving a letter from little Mary one day, Cunningham handed it to Jack to read, saying, "Here's a letter from your sweetheart, John."[40]

At Santa Fe Jack drilled his men, learned a little Spanish, and served as the quartermaster for a time, but the boredom continued as the regiment was held in a reserve position at the northern rim of the theater of operations. A deadly bout of measles infected the company, killing nine members and debilitating several more, including Jack, who recovered without complications. As the summer of 1848 approached, all in Santa Fe awaited orders to head southwards to engage the Mexicans on the field of battle. The orders never came. Logan's company suffered not a single battle casualty, for the troops never left Santa Fe. The Treaty of Guadalupe Hidalgo ended the Mexican War in 1848, a victory for the United States that added new territories to its boundaries. The companies of Captains Hampton and Cunningham stepped off the steamers onto Alton soil, where they were mustered out of the service in October 1848. Lieutenant John A. Logan returned to Murphysboro from Alton as a Mexican War veteran who never saw a battle. This did not detract from the prestige he gained with his rank and responsibilities. Squire Davis, a lifelong friend, recalled, "We were proud of the young soldier, and the whole county was proud of him."[41]

With the war over, Logan decided that a law career was his calling. Perhaps in tribute to his father, the hopeful future lawyer altered his name. Friends like Doff Ozburn and John Cunningham were already calling him by his given name; soon everyone else would do the same. He unofficially dropped the nickname "Jack" in favor of John A. Logan. The name change was his transition to adulthood and independence.

Logan sought the aid of his middle namesake, Uncle Alexander Jenkins. After holding several state positions, Jenkins had returned to his law practice. He invited his nephew to apprentice in his office. There, Logan read Jenkins's law books and received a firsthand view of a lawyer's work. The law appealed to him, as did the natural transition to politics it offered. It convinced him to get experience in the county clerk's office. Beginning in February 1849, he served as the deputy to the elected county clerk for three months. The position suited him, and he decided to run against the sitting clerk in the autumn election. On November 6, 1849, Logan won his first election to political office: clerk of Jackson County commissioners.[42]

Horse thieves briefly interrupted his career plans. They seized a neighbor's stock and headed out to Missouri. Logan headed a committee of vigilantes to hunt them down. The justice seekers never caught the thieves, but they found the stolen horses in the swamplands of eastern Missouri and returned home with them. But on the way back Logan went down from a devastating attack of pain radiating through his joints. After reaching his parents' house in Murphysboro, he was bedridden with pain and fevers. Dr. Logan diagnosed the malady as rheumatic fever; he proceeded to administer to his son, who through his father's doctoring skills and his mother's nursing efforts, regained his health and strength. Nonetheless, his rheumatism would haunt him for the rest of his life.[43]

After his recovery, Logan took the office of county clerk in December. In 1850 he scrawled his name to the marriage records of two of his sisters. In March, he authenticated the second marriage of his half-sister, thirty-three-year-old Louisa Garner, to Charles Cummins. Three months later he issued a marriage license for his nineteen-year-old sister, Dorothy. She married Cyrus Thomas, a new Murphysboro resident who was noted for his love of "bug-hunting." Thomas hailed from eastern Tennessee where he received a law-based education, but he wanted to pursue a career in entomology. Until he realized that dream, the first position he took after his marriage was deputy clerk—to his new brother-in-law—in October 1850. A third Logan sister also married in 1850, but this one did so against her family's wishes. Annie Logan, all of sixteen, eloped that summer, submitted a false affidavit claiming her age as eighteen, and subsequently was married in Benton, the seat of neighboring Franklin County. "I was not at home at the time, nor did I see them," wrote Benton friend Sam Casey, who sympathized with Dr. Logan by adding, "I regret very much that your daughter should have married in opposition to the wishes of her best friends."[44]

Logan and Cyrus Thomas were merely six months apart in age, and they got along well as family, friends, and employees. The brothers-in-law also lived under the same roof at the Logan home. By then, Dr. Logan had finished his fourth term as representative in the Illinois General Assembly, and he wanted to continue as a state politician, this time as a senator. But his oldest son did not witness his father's election defeat that November. Instead, Logan, who already called himself a lawyer (at least that's what he told the census taker in 1850), saved the money to formalize his law education. He resigned as county clerk after serving in the position for less than a year, and Cyrus took his duties. Logan headed to Kentucky, where he enrolled in a course of lectures for the autumn school session of 1850 in the Law Department at the University of Louisville. He breezed through the course. Despite sitting in a large class, his Shiloh College–honed oratorical skills and experience in his uncle's office helped him to stand out. Another student recalled, "He was a chivalrous, studious young man, and in the moot court he was the best debater in the class." He vied with two others for class valedictorian, but lost the prestigious ranking to R. T. Durrett, who confessed, "Although I secured the valedictory, I think he left the school the best lawyer in the class." Logan graduated early in 1851 and was subsequently admitted to the bar.[45]

The new attorney returned to Southern Illinois that spring, in time to congratulate his friend Doff Ozburn on his newest baby, a boy named John Logan Ozburn. He also stepped into a new Logan home. Dr. Logan constructed a Jackson County rarity—a brick house. The three-story structure stood next to the frame building he had built seven years earlier. The house served as both a home and a business, for Dr. Logan used it as a hotel, dubbing it the "Logan House." There Dr. Logan worked more as a hotel proprietor and a little less as a traveling physician. John A. Logan settled into these new surroundings. He took the time to become a mason, riding to the closest lodge out at Pinckneyville to take his degrees. He also teamed up with Alexander Jenkins in a law partnership, a lucrative practice for uncle and nephew. He gained courtroom experience and also resumed as county clerk, while Cy Thomas returned to his deputy position. It was in this position that he issued a marriage license to another family member; this one went to his brother Tom, who married the daughter of a county judge.[46]

Logan remained with his uncle for only a few months. He threw his hat in the ring for the summer elections for prosecuting attorney of the Third Judicial District. He won the four-year position and packed his bags to move into the heart of the region where he would prosecute. Sam Casey, the Benton lawyer who had been unable to stop Annie Logan's marriage, had remained a close family friend. He convinced Logan to move to Benton, the seat of Franklin County. He also proved to be an influential contact outside of Jackson County, which represented the center of the judicial district. By the spring of 1852, Logan was paying rent in Benton, but he rarely could be found in the town. He continually worked his district, attending the courts in the county seats throughout his judicial circuit.[47]

Politics had been an integral part of his life for the length of his memory, so it surprised no one when he officially entered the political arena in 1852 by running for representative to the Eighteenth General Assembly in Illinois, the same state legislature seat formerly held four times by his father and once before him by his uncle. "Politics is a trade," he told his family, "and if my few fast friends in Jackson will stand by me, the day is not far distant when I can help myself and them to pay ten fold." He stumped the Fifth District of Illinois, which encompassed both Jackson and Franklin counties, throughout the late summer and fall, attending militia days, mass meetings, and other public events. Despite his young age, he was very familiar to the residents of the counties, particularly in Jackson where the Logan and Jenkins names had prevailed for three decades. His father and uncle aided him in the contest, relying upon their skills and experience to strengthen his campaign. Logan also linked his campaign with William A. Denning, a district judge and family friend running for a U.S. congressional seat. Denning lost, but Logan won.[48]

He was off to Springfield, the town he knew well from his visits with his father in the 1840s. Many faces in the Eighteenth General Assembly were familiar to him, for he had seen them in his numerous excursions through the middle and southern parts of Illinois. Adding to his comfort was sitting with a vast majority. Democrats outnumbered Whigs by a nearly four-to-one margin. This enhanced Logan's prospects to accomplish much in his term. He had campaigned about several issues on the stump, and the legislature would feel this new member from Egypt's winter whirlwind of conviction. One of the first orders of business was the election of a U.S. senator, a seat the U.S. Constitution authorized to be decided not by the popular vote of state residents, but by the legislators at the state capital. Logan had campaigned to reelect Stephen A. Douglas, the compact and polished Chicago politician who was seeking his second congressional term. Logan's vote was one of seventy-five for Douglas, who easily distanced his opponent who received the endorsement of only nineteen legislators. The "Little Giant" was back in the Senate.[49]

Logan's winter days of 1853 were spent in the capitol; his nights were spent at one of the primitive hotels in Springfield, marked by drafty rooms separated by thin partitions. Early in the legislative session, Logan had befriended William H. Snyder, a St. Clair County representative. The two young attorneys chaffed at the inactivity of a Springfield winter. When they stayed indoors at night they bided their time by sharpening their oratory skills, using John Reynolds's *Pioneer History of Illinois*. Taking turns with the book, they read selections aloud, but too loud for other hotel guests. Unfortunately for the two orators, the room adjacent to theirs was occupied by General Assembly Speaker of the House John Reynolds—the sixty-four-year-old former governor and author of the book. Believing that Logan and Snyder were mocking his literary style, Reynolds took his revenge during the House sessions. He conveniently failed to recognize them whenever they attempted to get the floor, making it exceedingly difficult for either Logan or Snyder to distinguish himself.[50]

Logan began to work himself free from Reynolds's vengeance during polarizing legislation. His most noteworthy role in the Eighteenth General Assembly became his most notorious one when he took the lead in sponsoring an act that exposed his hostility to African Americans. "It was never intended that whites and blacks should stand in equal relation," he maintained in a debate on a bill to enable blacks to testify in court. But his views went beyond trial rights—far beyond. The revised constitution of Illinois, crafted in 1848, contained a provision for the legislature to make it state law to prohibit blacks from settling in the state. The Illinois legislatures of 1849 and 1851 failed to act on this provision. As a member of the judiciary committee, Logan made sure that the 1853 legislature would not adjourn without a vote on the issue. On January 6, he proposed a bill to prevent free blacks from migrating into Illinois. Four weeks later the bill was reported out of committee to be debated on the floor.[51]

Here again the young legislator well represented the views of his constituents, as well as those of his family. His mother grew up in the slave culture of North Carolina. His father, although raised for nearly a decade in Ohio, spent the subsequent decade surrounded by slavery in the South, a culture that induced him to buy slaves to complete his labors in Missouri. Other family members had criticized Dr. Logan for this. A nephew claimed that his father—Dr. Logan's brother-in-law—refused to associate with his influential relative, "for Father said that he didn't want any thing to do with a man that bought and sold human beings like they were a cow or a horse." This sentiment was not shared by the vast majority of Egypt. The racist views of John A. Logan dovetailed with those of his neighbors. He railed against abolitionists, partly because he did not approve of them judging those who did not share their beliefs and partly because he failed to see how blacks could be treated as equal to whites. He even referred to African Americans as subhuman. He wrote a friend "that a monkey is the latter end of the human family—this [might] be offensive to some of those 'abolitioners' . . ." Indeed, it was.[52]

The rest of the state was predominately in lockstep with Egypt in preventing freed blacks from calling Illinois their home. When this section of the revised Constitution of 1848 was separately submitted to the state residents for ratification, they approved it by an overwhelming vote of 50,261 to 21,297. Logan took advantage of public sentiment to convert the statewide ratification into law. Here he displayed his racism to counter the more abolitionist members of the legislature. Using history as a lesson that black Americans are "not suited to be placed upon a level with white men," Logan ranted about what he perceived as the legislature's lack of support for white supremacy. "It has almost become an offense to be a white man," he said. "Unfortunate were these gentlemen in their birth that they could not have been ushered into existence with black skin and a wooly head." He assured his opponents he would see this issue through to the conclusion he supported: "Unless this bill shall pass you will hear it again next session and again until something shall be done to protect those people from the inundation from the colored population."[53]

Logan's threat to his fellow legislators never materialized; it did not have to. The bill easily passed through the bicameral legislature. Although blacks already living in the state were exempt, the law was one of the most draconian ever enacted in Illinois. It imposed fifty-dollar fines on any interloping Negro or mulatto (defined as one who has at least "one-fourth negro blood") who stayed in Illinois longer than ten days. Those unable to pay were to be sold as indentured servants in public auction to the person who offered the shortest term of service in return for paying the fine and trial costs. The bill was identified by its sponsor's name: "Logan's Black Law." It made Logan both noteworthy and notorious throughout the state, depending on the region. The law was denounced in Chicago and northern sectors, while Illinois' southern portion endorsed it. Joseph H. Barquet, an African American living in Chicago, cleverly belittled the law by claiming that it would force exempted black men to marry white women—a concept absolutely abhorrent to most in the Prairie State. "Well sir," wrote Barquet, "I wish to annex myself to a wife, but the commodity in colors is scarce in our market! What shall we do? If we go from home to import one, the dear creature will be sold to some heartless Logan . . ., and if Mr. Logan shuts out the black girls, why we must taker the white ones, that's all."[54]

The chief advocate of Logan's Black Law was its author. Logan rankled northern Illinois legislators and newspaper editors with the legislation, but he endeared himself to Southern Illinoisans who considered themselves more allied with those living below the Mason-Dixon Line than those above it. A Franklin County paper took an us-versus-them approach to an analysis of Logan: "Mr. L. has demonstrated to the north by his tact, talent and eloquence in the halls of our legislature, that we, the south, have interests to foster, guide and protect, and that we have men who are able to do it." Logan, who celebrated his twenty-seventh birthday during the session, returned to Egypt during the late winter of 1853 as one of its chief spokesmen and rising stars. "Mr. Logan is quite young, but already gives evidence of the possession of a very high order of talents, which if properly cultivated, will make him one of the ornaments of the country," wrote the *Alton Weekly Courier* under one of the first headlines ever dedicated to John A. Logan. The newspaper was unrestrained in its praise: "Possessing a very attractive personal appearance, splendid voice, and great energy of delivery, with a mind very evenly balanced, he commanded individual attention whenever he addressed the Legislature, and was very successful in the measures he advocated."[55]

He stayed in Benton and teamed up with fellow attorney William K. Parish to form a law partnership in March 1853. The town was proud that Logan planted stronger roots in Benton. "We are . . . happy to learn, that Mr. Logan has since fitted up his law office in this place, and that he intends to make Benton his home for the present at all events," raved the *Benton Standard*, which went on to advertise Logan as a prized, eligible bachelor: "And as John is young, good-looking, talented and witty, we should not be surprised if an extensive practice, which he no doubt will enjoy, and a pair of 'bright eyes' might be an inducement to him to remain here permanently."[56]

No one was prouder of John A. Logan's accomplishments than the man for whom he was named. Dr. Logan kept close tabs on the rising career of his oldest son. He had not followed him into a medical career (a younger son would take up this mantle), but he had blazed his own trail, one that Dr. Logan had mapped for him years earlier in his own political career. But by 1853, Dr. Logan had realized that not only was his influence waning in the region, so too was his life. The sixty-five-year-old Logan family patriarch drew out his will in September. He suffered from an abscessed liver and from progressive heart failure, both of which sapped his strength and vitality. He had toiled for decades to save the lives of his neighbors and his children, but Dr. Logan could not cure his own failing body.

Although he lived thirty-five miles east of Murphysboro, Logan oftentimes conducted business in Jackson County, offering him the frequent opportunity to check up on his ill father. He prosecuted cases in Murphysboro and also worked as a commissioner for a newly created railroad company. In November Logan sped to Murphysboro. There he joined his large family to be with his father in his final moments. Dr. John Logan died on November 4, 1853, at the age of sixty-five.[57]

The Logan family buried their patriarch in a cemetery in Murphysboro, the town he had helped create. His passing closed perhaps the most influential period of John A. Logan's life. He had modeled his early life after his father's, and although he had become independent, no doubt exists that the death of Dr.

Logan cut him deeply. Most of his passions, his sense of duty, and his political ideals could be traced to his father. Most important, Dr. Logan had provided his son an education—both formal and through life's experiences—that equal-aged young men in the county could only envy. Logan either attended school or was tutored for twelve years—sometimes sporadically—but nevertheless he was an educated young man who benefited from his father's wealth, prestige, and influence. Logan could take solace that his father witnessed the beginning of a promising career, one that he helped to forge for him.

CHAPTER TWO

Prince of Egypt

LOGAN OPENED THE YEAR 1854 by working with his family to settle his father's affairs. After each family member received a portion of his estate, Dr. Logan had stipulated that a public sale be held for the rest of his personal property; this occurred on February 6. Family members purchased most of the late physician's belongings. His widow, Elizabeth, bought several medical books and supplies. Tom Logan and Cyrus Thomas also purchased items. Outside the immediate family, the most frequent buyer of Dr. Logan's supplies was a Jackson County newcomer: Israel Blanchard, a physician from western New York who settled with his brother in Carbondale, six miles east of Murphysboro in 1852.[1]

While Logan was back at work, both in his Benton law partnership and in his second term as prosecuting attorney for the Third Judicial Circuit, Blanchard continued to ingratiate himself in Jackson County. He had married the widowed sister-in-law of Daniel Brush, the region's prominent Whig and Logan family antagonist. Blanchard had met her while boarding in her Carbondale home with her six fatherless children, apparently charming her into a quick wedding. Brush despised Blanchard, denouncing him not only as "a man without means or honor" but also as "an oily tongued, unprincipled scoundrel who married the widow to get a home, and the means she possessed."[2]

Logan soon learned that Brush's charges were not altogether baseless. The young attorney prosecuted Blanchard twice for minor charges, cases that carried into 1854. Blanchard's new wife died that very winter, and when Daniel

Brush took her six children into his home, he landed into a legal argument with Blanchard over the rights to her property. The argument turned so contentious that Blanchard was arrested a third time—for hurling a rock at Brush's five-year-old son.[3]

Blanchard continued to sink himself into legal quagmires and hired Logan to defend him on at least two occasions. Logan must have been struck by the irony of defending the same man he had prosecuted in the past, but Blanchard became more than Logan's client. Another widow had attracted him—Logan's spirited sister Annie, who lost the husband she had eloped to marry back in 1850 when the young man died of smallpox on a return trip from New Orleans. Although no longer living in the same county, Logan was assured he and Israel Blanchard would be acquaintances for years to come.[4]

Logan had many more clients than just Blanchard. He worked in his private practice throughout 1854 whenever he was not tied up in the county courts as the states attorney. But his elected position kept him as busy as ever, taking him away from his new home for several weeks at a time. His cousin, Squire Davis, considered Logan as energetic a prosecuting attorney as he was a jockey. Logan needed the energy; his private practice became a one-man business. William K. Parish was forced to give up his attorney career by springtime when he donned the robes of a district judge.[5]

Ironically, Judge Parish presided over Logan's most important case of 1854. Logan prosecuted Decatur Campbell of Metropolis, one of Illinois' southern-most towns. Campbell, a black man, had killed Goodwin Parker of the same town. In the dead of night, Parker—armed with a hatchet—and three companions had walked to Campbell's home and called him out. Ahead of his three friends, Parker assaulted Campbell with the hatchet and Campbell retaliated by stabbing his assailant to death. Logan lost his murder charge, but won the case, primarily because Parish instructed the jury that they "are bound to find the defendant guilty of manslaughter," regardless of the self-defense circumstances. (Parish had also disallowed the fact that Campbell had a hatchet wound on his head to be admitted as evidence.) The defense attorney appealed this case to the Illinois Supreme Court; they accepted it later in the year. Their landmark ruling went against Logan, although nothing was found errant in his prosecution of the case. The justices cited seven errors in the Metropolis trial, and wrote a decision that not only defined self-defense, but also stipulated that in a murder trial, "the law makes no distinction in its principles as to the color of the accused." Logan's philosophy that whites took precedent over blacks in trials was squelched by the highest court in his state.[6]

With his reputation as a tough opponent growing from his string of victories, Logan worked his district, hobnobbing with Southern Illinois' preeminent litigators and defenders. His most prominent friend was Samuel S. Marshall, who had recently moved to McLeansboro from Benton and was widely considered to be at the pinnacle of his profession. In 1854 Marshall was running for U.S. Congress as representative of Southern Illinois, more specifically the southernmost eighteen counties that comprised the Ninth District. Since Logan's judicial circuit covered nearly two-thirds of Marshall's territory, he stumped for Marshall to elicit his vocal support for himself. Marshall liked Logan and appreciated his efforts on his behalf. The two remained close friends for years.[7]

Marshall's campaign likely reinvigorated Logan's passion for politics, as did one of the most significant and controversial legislative measures of the 1850s—the Kansas-Nebraska Act of 1854. The chief proponent of the measure was Democrat Stephen A. Douglas, the "Little Giant," whom Logan helped to reelect as U.S. senator from Illinois in January 1853. Douglas championed the concept of "popular sovereignty"; that is, that western territories would become free or slaveholding states based on the will of its people as drawn up in their respective state constitutions. This measure was controversial enough, but Douglas, the Senate chairman of territories, stirred the pot further when he was forced to cave in to pressure from Southern senators to convert the Territory of Nebraska into a slaveholding one even prior to statehood. Additionally, Douglas endorsed the division of the vast territory in question into two distinct territories: Kansas and Nebraska. A slave-labored Nebraska Territory directly violated the Missouri Compromise of 1820, which banned territorial slavery north of 36 degrees, 30 minutes. But even if the people of Nebraska turned their slaveholding territory into a free state, proslavery legislators were still guaranteed that half of the original territory would become the slaveholding state of Kansas. It was no coincidence that Kansas's southern boundary ran across the same coordinate.

Forced into the compromise, Douglas predicted that it would "raise a hell of a storm." It certainly did. During spring 1854 there was little life in the proposal; all but one of the ten Northern state legislatures in session early in 1854 denounced it (only the Nineteenth General Assembly of Illinois endorsed it). But the five-foot-four-inch Douglas proved to be a parliamentary giant and won Senate passage of the bill in March by a surprisingly wide margin, 41 to 17. The subsequent House of Representatives vote was predictably close, but the proslavery advocates won out late in May. The House vote killed off the fledgling Whig Party, which split on the Kansas-Nebraska issue. Lesser parties, such as the

American Party and the Free-Soilers, were weakened by divisions within their ranks over the new law. Although they were the dominant political force in the country, the Democratic Party became more polarized as a result of this measure. Of the fifty-nine House Democrats from the North who voted for the measure, only seven of them won reelection to their seats in 1854. This guaranteed that the freshman Northern Democrats would be more opposed to measures by the slave-supporting Southern Democrats. The Kansas-Nebraska Act proved to be the end of the era of compromise legislation.[8]

"I feel as if the mission of my life was performed," pronounced Senator Douglas. His bill brought Abraham Lincoln—dormant for years—back into politics and induced him to run for the Senate. In an October speech Lincoln claimed that Douglas's Kansas-Nebraska legislation split up the Democrats throughout the state.[9] This included Egypt, where opponents feared that wealthy and powerful slaveholders planting roots in Kansas would dissuade if not prevent small farmers—like themselves—from spreading out across the fertile Kansas prairie. Logan, however, following his South-against-the-North ideals, began and remained an advocate of the bill. As far as he was concerned, one need only to gaze at a U.S. map to understand his philosophy, that of his father, and the majority of his family, neighbors, clients, and constituents. His judicial district existed in the southernmost extension of any state north of the Ohio River or the Mason-Dixon Line. Egypt cut deep into the body of the South like a bowie knife; its V shape penetrated to a point nearly in line with the Virginia–North Carolina border. Murphysboro and Carbondale were geographically as southern as Richmond.

Although not a slaveholder, Logan was more than sympathetic to Southern principles; he adopted them as his own. His political affiliation was part of it. "John is of the right sort; a pure patriot and unflinching Democrat," crowed a like-minded newspaper editor. Logan shared another ideal with most influential Southern politicians; a former General Assembly colleague pinpointed it afterwards: "John was a flaming Democrat, and no man hated an abolitionist more than he." Logan despised the haughty condescension of Northerners—particularly New Englanders—who frowned upon the Southern lifestyle, a way of life he did not practice himself, but clearly accepted. So did his neighbors. Sam Marshall won his election to the House in November 1854. In doing so he joined a group of freshmen congressmen from the North who repudiated his views. Marshall's allies would be found in the Southern Democrats and his constituents from Egypt. When Marshall submitted the names of his most "intimate acquaintances" in November, Logan's name prominently graced the top of the list.[10]

Three months later Logan's name received statewide attention. When the Illinois legislature cast its votes for U.S. Senator in February of 1855, Abraham Lincoln led after the first ballot, but with too few votes to win the seat. Five ballots later Lincoln's support dropped and three legislators cast their votes for someone who never officially entered the race—John A. Logan. The attempt to create a groundswell by entering Logan's name never took root, but Lincoln was also forced to concede to a different "dark horse" candidate. On the tenth ballot, the Nineteenth General Assembly of Illinois elected Lyman Trumbull to the U.S. Senate.[11]

William J. Allen was a member of that General Assembly, and shortly after it adjourned, he became Logan's new law partner. Josh Allen's career ran parallel with Logan's. Both men were sons of influential fathers, both were highly educated in a rather primitive region of the country in the 1830s and 1840s, both were elected as prosecuting attorneys in Southern Illinois judicial districts, and both completed stints in the Illinois legislature. It was only natural for them to pair up in the Benton law practice. That Allen held the same political views as Logan made their partnership even more amicable.[12]

Logan's work generally involved small claims, but his work on murder cases garnered the most attention. In one of these trials, he benefited from planned and unplanned oratory. The accused was a prominent Union County resident, but also a controversial one who provoked so much hostility from his neighbors that Logan wisely and successfully argued to move the trial from Jonesboro (the seat of the county) to Pope County. The courthouse stood in Golconda, a town so rural that the building shared a field with grazing sheep. After the prosecution opened with a strong case against the man, Logan began his initial defense statements. But his speech was interrupted by a lamb that burst into the courtroom, spooked by a yelping dog that had chased it. Logan scooped it up and quickly used the moment to his advantage. He likened his defendant's case to the "Paschal Lamb," which had come in to offer itself as a sacrifice to save the life of his innocent client. He immediately hooked the jury with his on-the-spot metaphor.[13]

He went on to surgically dissect the case with a spirited, effective defense. The murder victim had been stabbed through the back. Logan called up the physicians who examined the man *post mortem*. Their testimony isolated the only wound to a back wound, caused by a sharp instrument that penetrated the spleen. Naturally the prosecuting attorney had no cause to stop Logan's defense—it seemed he was solidifying his own case for murder. But what happened next defies belief, save for the universal assessment that Logan was a most powerful orator ("He was a talker those days, don't forget it," remembered a cousin several years later). Hearkening back to medical discussions with his father, Logan fought the case on a progression of facts: (1) that the spleen was the only significant wound on the body, (2) that no one was certain of its function, and (3) that no professional physician deemed it a vital organ. Therefore, concluded Logan, the lone wound on the victim's body could not have caused his death. His argument proved persuasive to the jury. They ruled his client guilty of a lesser charge of "assault to kill," but could not convict him of murder. The thankful defendant went to the penitentiary for a short sentence. According to one of Logan's relatives, "The man got off on a quibble when he should have been hung."[14]

Logan left most of his defense work to Allen during much of 1855 because Allen could devote more time to the practice. Logan had a heavy docket of work as prosecuting attorney. He traveled the circuit much as he did the previous two years, but his popularity throughout his district attracted larger crowds to his trials. The cases in each county were known throughout the land as "Court Week." The name was a misnomer, however, for in many instances the event transpired in a few days. It was a semiannual event, particularly for the small towns with sparse county populations. The prominent judges, states attorneys, and defense lawyers helped to turn each week into a memorable round of activities, rivaled only by a traveling circus or a county fair. Crowds thronged to the courthouses, jostling for seats to witness the spectacle of a spectrum of cases—from mundane disputes to thrilling murder trials. Reporters also gathered in the towns to record the events, assuring the host community that their county seat was a headline news story at least two times per year.

Still in his twenties, Logan was a savvy veteran of court week. He gained his first experience with his uncle in Jackson County, and he traveled for his third full year of court cases. But unlike the residents of the towns he traveled to, Logan's court "week" spanned almost three months, repeated each spring and autumn. It took ten weeks to complete his circuit, followed by a summer lull, and then the circuit duty repeated, beginning in September. The routine followed a rhythmic pace: a long buggy ride to the town; greeting the locals and the dignitaries as he entered the county seat; determining where to sleep during his stay; sharing a bed—or at least a room—with several other attorneys; preparing his cases before and after the first night's sleep; performing in court on the first day; making a formal speech near the courthouse immediately after the close of court duty; meeting with fellow attorneys, judges, and townsmen at a local tavern to share ribald stories, jokes, and anecdotes; prepare cases for the next day; and sleep a few hours to start the routine anew the following morning. When the work closed, Logan and the other traveling judges and lawyers formed a caravan to ride on to the next town on a circuit, a trip that featured several-mile stretches without glimpsing a soul along the rough roads.

Politics permeated court week. Not only was it discussed in the evenings and mornings, it was also featured as a separate event after the completion of each workday at the courthouse. One of the lawyers delivered a speech that either defended his party, harangued the opposing party, or both. The following day, as soon as court adjourned, another lawyer from the opposite party would respond. This continued daily for the length of the service. Politics in Southern Illinois not only was the source of news, it was also a history lesson, a sporting event, a major source of entertainment for all, and something even more serious to most. As one witness to these events recalled, "These discussions were of the most fervid character as there were but few men whose politics were not akin to their religion."[15]

Logan understood that his job was not only to perform his assigned duties, but it was also to give a memorable performance. Crowds thronged the courthouse to see him as much as to hear the trial. "There was a majesty about his figure, a magnetic influence issuing from his person, that seemed to both awe and fascinate the audience," said a spectator. Logan also excelled outside the courthouse, particularly in the political speeches that followed each trial day. By 1855, his name was recognized throughout Southern Illinois, and reporters were quick to record portions of his speeches in shorthand.[16]

Growing weary from prosecuting cases in eight counties since early spring, Logan rode out to Shawneetown in Gallatin County for his final cases. Over the previous year, while there, he had lodged at Captain Cunningham's house rather than pack himself in an uncomfortable room with the other court professionals. Captain Cunningham had moved his family from Marion to Shawneetown earlier in the decade after suffering financial hardships, and had taken the appointed position of registrar in the U.S. Land Office there. Logan's last four visits to the Cunningham home were spent with fewer members of the captain's family on hand, compared to his first trip there in 1852. Missing from the household was teenaged Mary, who had been attending school at a convent in Kentucky. Logan and Captain Cunningham still shared their running joke that Mary was his promised bride. Prior to his 1855 early summer trip to Shawneetown, Captain Cunningham notified Logan that Mary would be home, the first time Logan would see her in nearly three years.

Mary turned Logan inside out the moment his eyes lit upon her. Her beauty stunned him, catching him off guard more than any opposing lawyer could expect to do in the courtroom. She was petite—weighing only ninety-five pounds—and carried her lithe figure with grace. Long, dark, curly hair cascaded over her shoulders, and her captivating eyes mesmerized him. If he didn't fall in love at first sight, he did so by the end of the evening. The two strolled along the Ohio River, stealing glances when side by side, and gazing at each other by moonlight when face-to-face. They talked for long periods, and other times they said nothing at all. Logan was as taken by her intellect as he was by her looks. In the past she had stepped forward to help her mother care for her family when Captain Cunningham unsuccessfully tested his luck in the California gold rush, and she had aided her father during his federal appointments while he was home. She was educated and she was smart—traits that were not always one in the same. She seemed very mature for her age.

The problem, however, was her age. Mary was just sixteen, and although she was attracted to Logan—his handsome, dark complexion, his professional status, his intelligence, and his mien—she was not immediately as devoted to him as he was to her. She had never had a suitor as mature as the twenty-nine-year-old Logan, and she reacted to him as she would to a teenaged boy. Since his circuit work was not slated to begin again until the end of August, Logan made frequent visits to Shawneetown that summer, not just to win her over, but also to win over her parents. He seemed completely unconcerned about the twelve-and-a-half-year difference in their ages; he knew only that he had to be with her. In the summer of 1855, John A. Logan was determined to make Mary Cunningham his wife.

When July turned to August Logan made sure that Captain Cunningham understood that the years-long joke was over. "Captain, you promised to give me Mary," he reminded him, this time with all seriousness, "and I expect you will be a man of your word. I want to marry her." Cunningham liked and respected his daughter's suitor, a friend for many years, but still had reservations at losing his oldest daughter at such a young age (she celebrated her seventeenth birthday in August). He consented, provided Mary felt the same way about Logan as he did about her. Logan proposed to her, ostensibly on the bank of the Ohio River, at a place they indistinctly called "our favorite point." She was taken by how he poured out his feelings to her, but she was not prepared to give him an answer.[17]

Although he did not hear it come from her lips, Logan left Shawneetown confident that she was committed to him. He wrote to her within a week. He reiterated his commitment to her in closing, "Be assured of my sincerity, and after mature reflection say that you will be mine. Then I am content." But Mary would not say it. She wrote back revealing that she visited the site of his proposal to reflect on it. "I have not so yet come to a permanent answer to your question," she responded, ". . . I think and hope you will not expect an answer in this [letter]."

Logan had signed his missive off "Yours truly"; she closed hers with "your sincere friend." He fired back an immediate response: "I hope you will continue to visit the same spot until you shall be inspired with love sufficient to say to me that on that point our happiness had its origin."[18]

Logan panicked; his insecurities consumed him with each passing day without a note from Mary. Finally he received a letter in her handwriting. His heart broke upon reading it. She told him that they were to regard each other only by the way she had signed off her letters—as friends. "Oh Heaven!" he lamented, "Was ever man's fate so hard as mine? Is there no one on earth whose heart beats sympathetically with mine? . . . I *am miserable*." He would not let her rejection stand, not without hearing it from her lips. He wrote back, telling her he would travel to Shawneetown after court duty to see her again in a week, and closed his letter with unabashed angst: "Alas; how sudden the scene is changed. Mary, the very thought that when we next meet that you will only regard me as a friend is a torture to my very soul. My feelings will not allow me to say more. I remain Your Distressed, John A. Logan."[19]

He rode with determination from the courthouse at Carmi during the middle of the week, arriving at Shawneetown as promised on Thursday, August 23. Another stroll along the Ohio River followed, one that took them back to "our favorite point." There Logan delivered his most heartfelt and important oration—exceeding any that he had delivered in a courthouse—to convince Mary that he was the man for her. He tempted the fates and proposed to her again, not knowing how he would survive a second, crushing rejection. His spirit soared when he heard the word "yes" sing from her lips. It was a night both would cherish and remind each other about in future correspondence.

Logan's poignant letters had certainly moved Mary, but she was equally impressed by her beau's extraordinary determination to win her over. She later revealed that she was as indifferent to him as she was to others who displayed their affection for her. "Consequently, I was not infrequently chided by father, mother, and Mr. Logan for being too much inclined to flirtation," she confessed, finally comfortable "that my happy-go-lucky days were over." They set a late-November wedding date since Logan had another ten weeks of circuit duty to complete.[20]

Logan left Shawneetown on August 25 a new man, unburdened by doubts and insecurities. The fall court session was the most satisfying work he ever did, not so much for the cases as for his own self-rejuvenation. "To know that I am loved by one that I love with pure devotion is such a reflection as fills my heart with joy not circumscribed by any bounds," he wrote. During the subsequent courtship they exchanged love letters so frequently that three would arrive at one time because the postal service could not keep up with the pace of their correspondence combined with Logan's constant circuit travels. They exchanged "miniatures" in the mail, small photographic images that each would gaze upon as they limned their love for each other in every letter they penned.

Mary called this "a happy time" with good reason. Her fiancé continued to open his soul to her. Enduring trips hampered by broken buggy wheels, mosquito infestations, and uncomfortable sleeping quarters, Logan was too consumed by "my own Mary" to be bothered by it all. "Just when the spark that at 'our favorite point' first fell from the fire of love and lodged in our hearts was fanned into a flame," he gushed, "there to glow warmer and more brilliant." Mary also invoked the spot where he proposed. "'Tis now evening," she informed him in a September 9 letter, "and I am sitting near the window. The shades of nightfall are stealing over the earth producing the most beautiful effect upon nature. . . . I remember a similar evening *we* were strolling along the mighty Ohio; but alas! Where are you now?"[21]

Their letters persisted throughout the autumn court season. He wrote from Marion, longing to return to the spot "where I first breathed the whispers of love to you and you to me, where I first learned that for the first time in my life I truly loved and found a heart that properly appreciates it and duly reciprocates it." When Logan rode into Murphysboro for a visit home prior to another court session, he told his large and extended family about the woman he was going to marry. Mary was playfully more secretive about her engagement, delighting in the gossip that pervaded her neighborhood about her dark, mysterious suitor. "Every body's curiosity is up to the utmost pitch," she wrote "My Dear Logan" on October 27. "I think they will die or commit some awful deed if they continue as they have commenced. I am watched on all occasions and asked innumerable questions about 'My Spaniard' and some say 'Injun.' I have been in perfect bliss for the last three weeks."[22]

Logan completed his circuit in mid November, rode back to Benton, and subsequently followed his well-worn path to Shawneetown for his wedding. The distance was too great for his Jackson County family to travel, but Logan promised that he and his new wife would visit them soon afterwards. He did have many of his friends on hand to witness the end of his bachelorhood. Beautifully fitted in a lavender silk dress, Mary Cunningham became Mary Logan in her father's home on November 27, 1855. John Logan brought his Benton friends to the Cunningham house. His former law partner, Judge William K. Parish, performed the ceremony, while his current law partner, Josh Allen, stood by his side as best man. The house teemed with Logan and Cunningham associates, most of them known by Logan only since 1850, but still good, close friends. Congressman Sam Marshall, Sam Casey, and a host of other attorneys, judges, and circuit clerks, celebrated Logan's big day with him.[23]

Bidding adieu to the throng of well-wishers, the newlyweds rode back to their home in Benton. From there, it was off to Murphysboro to visit the Logans. Mary was taken by the simple scenes of the town, including an organ grinder in front of the Jackson County courthouse. She then endured the overwhelming process of meeting her husband's numerous family members. Mother Logan and the rest quickly accepted her as one of their own. Logan's Aunt Margaret was most awestruck by Mary's beauty. "Her dark, fine silken curls hung negligently around her white neck," she remembered. "I thought she was loveliness without the aid of ornament; her eyes sparkling with youth and intelligence, and with all she was a beautiful figure." She assessed her nephew's bride as "almost or quite a perfect beauty." Her son offered a folksier accolade about her intelligence. "Mary's just about as sharp as they got 'em up," claimed Squire Davis.[24]

Logan's career forced the newlyweds to spend their first Christmas apart. While Mary remained in Benton, he spent the holiday in the Jonesboro court-house running through twenty cases tied to Union County. He wrote her a let-ter, promising to return to her as soon as possible. Upon reading it, Mary scrawled "My Christmas Gift" across the top of it. She had a gift of her own to share with her husband—she was bearing a child.[25]

Mary Logan was the best thing that ever happened to her husband. Not only did she brighten John A. Logan's life, she also proved an invaluable partner in his law practice. Logan needed her assistance, for despite his prominent family name, and his double duty in an educated profession, he had little to show for it. The Logans stayed with Judge Parish and his wife in Benton while a new home was prepared for them. Logan had few items to clutter the Parish household. Mary assessed her husband's worldly goods at the time of their marriage as a horse and buggy, fifty law books, and $300 in cash. Although he was far from wealthy, Logan clearly did not marry his bride for money. Months earlier, when Logan informed his cousin, Squire Davis, that he was about to get married, Davis asked to whom. "To a girl that's as poor as poor," Logan replied. "She aint got a thing, but she's got a bushel of sense."[26]

Mary employed her keen sense and organizational experience to assist her husband on his circuit run during the spring of 1856. Her bookkeeping for her father in the general land office gained her a feel for business matters, which she employed to the machinations of attorneys. She developed a new skill—writing blanks for her husband's indictments. Logan need only insert the names on her template, and then submit them to the court official at the end of the session. She also studied law reports and highlighted important points from appropriate cases for her husband to streamline into his prosecutions and defenses. The skills his wife developed saved Logan countless hours of night work, and kept Mary busy during the day while her husband performed in the courtroom. Logan insisted she accompany him on the circuit. Notwithstanding the poorly furnished taverns, the occasional disagreeable meals, the bone-rattling roads, and the mundane routines, she confessed her adoration of the life of a circuit attorney. Viewing court week from the perspective of an attorney rather than a townsperson particularly enthralled her. Logan's popularity enhanced the experience, as did the now familiar names and faces she encountered at each county seat and on the roads between the towns. The Logan-Allen partnership added more clients and cases, offsetting the expenditures of the business.[27]

The year 1856 was Logan's final one in his elected term as prosecuting attorney of the Third Judicial District. Traveling to the region where he grew up, Logan was kept busy by his former neighbors. In March he wrote out an indictment in Marion for twelve defendants—including the county treasurer, drainage commissioner, and a prominent lawyer and politician—for violent behavior that began as a traditional serenade of a new bride and groom of the town. Mary must have been struck at how cavalier her husband was at setting bail at $100 for each of the twelve men, most whom she would have known as associates of her father. But Logan had a knack for separating his legal work from his personal association with family and friends. This trait was stretched to its limit early in the year when one of his clients became a member of his family. Dr. Israel Blanchard, the physician whom Logan prosecuted and later defended at least two times in his dual roles, married his offbeat sister, Annie, in January. Other family news was more welcome. Logan's youngest brother, Bill, took an interest in the study of law. Logan took him under his wing and allowed him to clerk for his and Allen's practice, just as Alexander Jenkins had done for him. Bill took on a second function when Mary informed her husband that she was pregnant. She left the circuit during the spring and remained in the new Logan house in Benton. Logan convinced his brother to keep her company while he completed his circuit duties.[28]

The presidential election campaign of 1856 dominated the political discussions of the day. A new party formed from disaffected factions of Whigs, Free-Soilers, Know-Nothings, and lesser affiliations, none of which alone could compete with the Democrats. The new organization called itself the Republican

Party. They nominated John C. Fremont, the explorer and abolitionist, as their first presidential candidate. The Whig Party was extinct, but the Know-Nothings stayed in for the fight and nominated former President Millard Fillmore at its convention. Logan stumped throughout the spring for Democratic Party leaders to nominate Stephen Douglas. Instead, James Buchanan from Pennsylvania won the nomination. Sam Marshall ran for reelection in Illinois' Ninth Congressional District. Logan also gained an honor in the district; he was chosen as its presidential elector. He added a second duty. Knowing his term as prosecuting attorney was about to expire, he decided to run again as a legislator for the General Assembly of Illinois.

Logan campaigned hard and strong during the summer and fall. While stumping for the Democrats across the ticket, his modus operandi was to demonize the new party candidates he dismissed as "Black Republicans." The Know-Nothing Party also caught his ire; he called it "the dark lantern party plotting treason." This election year was extremely active for Illinois voters, for they would be choosing a new governor. William Richardson, a Logan friend, was running against William Bissell, a former Democrat who dropped the party over Senator Douglas's "popular sovereignty" stance. Logan considered Bissell a turncoat. For the first time in his career as a public speaker the tone of his speeches hardened into partisan rhetoric.[29]

His addresses were only softened by participating in group speaking events, where other prominent Democrats and opposing party members spoke before and after him. Logan attracted extensive regional coverage with his overly partisan delivery. At Tamaroa in the heat of July, Logan and Josh Allen returned to the town where they first met as schoolboys. They joined Sam Casey there to oppose a St. Louis speaker for the Know-Nothing Party in a public meeting attended by 15,000 citizens. Logan stepped up as the third speaker that afternoon to an audience beginning to wear from long addresses and a diminishing water supply. He ranted and raved for two hours. His strong denunciation of the Know-Nothings provoked a heated reaction. An incensed spectator jumped onto the stage, only to be struck down by a blow to the forehead—delivered by a walking cane carried by another in the crowd. Impressed that Logan performed the entire time without notes, a reporter considered it "worse than useless" to try to define his style. "If any one ever heard thunder, argument, and sarcasm dealt out by the wholesale, they have an idea of Mr. L's speech," he concluded in his coverage of the event, published in a paper Mary could read in Benton two weeks later.[30]

But Mary was not in Benton in the middle of August. Her parents had moved back to Marion and she stayed with them for the duration of her pregnancy.

Almost nine months to the day after her wedding, Mary delivered a baby boy. He was given the name John Cunningham Logan. Buoyed by this most welcome addition to his family, Logan campaigned with greater vigor on the circuit. U.S. congressmen from Illinois accompanied Logan later on the speaking tour. Sam Marshall, John A. McClernand, and James Robinson added more prominence to the stage. Logan, however, was the one who stuck out, but not favorably for many. He denounced Bissell so severely that one witness to his vitriol became convinced that Logan had disgusted Democrats as well as Know-Nothings and Republicans.

It turned out to be mere wishful thinking for Logan's adversaries. He easily won his election to the General Assembly and gained the opportunity to cast his vote for James Buchanan, who claimed Illinois with a mere 9,000-vote majority out of nearly a quarter million cast within the state. Egypt carried the state for Buchanan, filling Logan's chest with pride. In fact, Logan's two home counties of his legislative district—Franklin and Jackson—overwhelmingly endorsed Buchanan with an incredible vote tally of 2,172 to 7. Predictably, Sam Marshall easily won reelection to his U.S. House of Representatives seat, but Logan suffered the bitter disappointment of seeing Bissell beat Richardson and claim the gubernatorial seat.[31]

Before he headed to Springfield, Logan wrapped up his four-year term as prosecuting attorney in a most unusual way. With less than convincing evidence to present, he still successfully convicted a horse thief, a victory that slapped the accused with a seven-year penitentiary sentence. The judge must have thought the evidence was shaky, for he granted the guilty man's motion for a new trial. The convicted man learned that Logan's term as circuit prosecutor had ended; therefore, he hired him as his defense lawyer. Logan moved the new trial to Marion and won his acquittal there. It was indeed a singular feat for one lawyer to win twice, on opposite sides of the same case. When asked by a bemused witness which one of the two verdicts was correct, Logan smugly responded, "Both of 'em."[32]

In December Logan returned to the General Assembly, representing the two-county Fifth District, the most partisan district in the state, based on the vote totals in the previous November's presidential election. It irritated him to the core that the man holding Illinois' highest office was a Republican. Logan considered him a traitor, and he had the confidence of his overwhelming support in Southern Illinois to back his opinion. In 1853, he had turned heads immediately in the Eighteenth General Assembly when, with clench-jawed determination, he pushed through "An Act to Prevent the Immigration of Negroes into the State." He was prepared to stir the pot of controversy again.

Logan was selected as a member of six committees, serving as chairman for one of them (Elections). He introduced the first bill of the session, to incorporate Carbondale College. The bill passed easily, as did several others. During his forty-six days of service, Logan introduced twelve bills; nine of them passed through the bicameral legislature and subsequently received Governor Bissell's signature. But Logan's partisanship overshadowed his leadership in the 1857 session. On January 12, he displayed his pettiness by moving to print 10,000 copies of Governor Bissell's address, half the customary print run established in previous General Assemblies. (Fifteen thousand copies, one third in German, eventually ran off the presses.) Logan did not conceal his contempt for Bissell, but the day's session closed before he could present his case against him.[33]

Logan's motion set the stage for a verbal explosion the following day. He became the spokesman for the more extreme sect of his party. They had learned that former Secretary of War Jefferson Davis, a proud Mississippian, had challenged Bissell, a former Mexican War officer, to a duel after an argument about what they did or did not do in the Mexico Campaign. The revised state constitution of 1848 forbade a duelist from holding office. With charges of perjury to back him, Logan tore into Bissell on January 13 as the chosen respondent to the governor's address. He attacked him on his position against popular sovereignty, accused him of perjury over his undisclosed dueling matter, and labeled him unfit for his position. "I warn young men and old against the example set," declared the fired-up Logan; "I pray God that we may never again witness such an occasion; Virtue and Truth bereft of all their charms, while the hideous and hateful gods of vice hold dominion over the people." He invoked the spirit of "my aged and venerable father" to continue his venom-spewing harangue: "Shall I stand quietly by, as one of the people's representatives, and see her public morals corrupted, her constitution violated, her honor tarnished, and give no sound of alarm?"

The historian documenting it rated it as the most severe speech Logan ever uttered, noting that "It shocked the better sense of all considerate men not wholly devoured by partisan malignity." Logan stirred the ire of the Republicans and the Know-Nothings; members of both parties allied to denounce him and defend Governor Bissell. It polarized the Twentieth General Assembly, a body still able to complete its legislation, but it did so with anger and resentment against the opposing party. What the Republicans and Know-Nothings were oblivious to was that this was a preplanned attack. Logan let loose upon the legislature on a signal and tore Bissell's character apart using letters uncovered and handed to him by other Democrats in the General Assembly. For his performance, Logan was subsequently honored by his party with a gold-headed cane inscribed "To John A. Logan from his friends for the advocacy of our rights on the 13th of January, 1857."[34]

Logan returned to Southern Illinois as a more respected spokesman than ever before. His brazen willingness to tackle a murky issue endeared him to his constituents. But in doing so he was painting himself into a corner. His extreme positions, and his ostentatious presentation of them, had restricted his appeal to regional; he was unable and unwilling to garner statewide support for any of his beliefs. Yet he endeared himself to the southernmost counties with each controversy he created.

After a springtime stay at the Benton cottage with his wife and son, Logan returned to his practice at the courts. He and Josh Allen took on a case at Shawneetown that gained interest throughout Southern Illinois, but one that consumed most of his spring and summer. They were hired as prosecutors on behalf of John E. Hall's associates, who sought justice for the man's murder. Hall was killed by a gunshot wound, fired by Robert Sloo, the son of a political opponent. Sloo overreacted to an attack against his father that Hall apparently published in a Marion newspaper. Logan had a personal interest in the case. Hall was the clerk of the Gallatin County and circuit courts, a close friend of Captain Cunningham, and one of the guests who attended his wedding; his daughter had been Mary's maid of honor. Logan did not expect a difficult case. Hall had died in the arms of an unimpeachable witness, Robert Ingersoll, who had been taking dictation from Hall when Sloo burst in the office and fired the fatal shot. Sloo did not flee, and Logan was confident he would not have a self-defense claim to counter.

The trial began in May but was interrupted by a hiatus and did not reconvene until midsummer. By July there seemed to be no early end in sight. But the defense team shocked Logan and Allen by bringing four Northern physicians to Shawneetown to provide expert testimony that Sloo was insane. Logan fumed in a letter to Mary, deriding the doctors as "abolitionists," his favorite pejorative for the most partisan Republicans, particularly the New Englanders. Temporary insanity had precedent in the country, but had rarely succeeded in Illinois. Notwithstanding state history, the twenty-three-day trial ended on August 14 with the jury finding Robert Sloo not guilty by reason of insanity. For the second time in three years, Logan lost a landmark case in Illinois. Sloo went to the insane asylum, where he made a "miraculous recovery" and was released after four months.[35]

The trial had been especially grueling for Logan, who was forced to increase his workload when Allen took sick shortly after the first week of testimony. Issues on the home front also burdened him. Throughout the summer he learned from Mary's letters that she had sickened with increasing severity. The baby was sick, too. Wracked with guilt, Logan wrote to her on August 4, "We are nearly through this week and God knows I will not leave you again." By the time the verdict was read ten days later, Mary had assured him that both she and Johnny were on the mend. Soon after, Logan boarded his buggy, tugged on the reins, and rode back to Benton, irritated at the verdict but relieved about his family's improving health.

Logan's relief was short-lived, however, for Mary's pronouncement proved premature. She indeed had recovered, but Johnny's rally was cut short by a return of his illness a few days after his father came home. Both parents fretted as his condition deteriorated. In desperation, they took him to the Logan House in Murphysboro, hoping against hope that someone in the family could treat their dying baby. Those hopes were dashed on September 6. John Cunningham Logan died just two weeks past his first birthday.[36]

The Logan family, both immediate and extended, buried the infant in Murphysboro and mourned their loss. Mary, still a teenager, was experiencing the heartache that Mother Logan had endured at the deaths of four of her young children. Logan agonized from the loss and his guilt associated with it. He had missed his baby's birth, and was absent for most of the year of his life. Yet, the passage of time helped to numb the pain of both parents. Logan stayed with Mary through the remainder of the year, but both understood that the nature of his profession required him to break the angst-driven promise he had made to her back in August. They celebrated Christmas together, and then Logan headed off for his court cases. He also looked forward to an active year of politicking, preparing to stump for Stephen Douglas to keep his Senate seat in the election of 1858.

Mary was more at ease with her husband's departure than she had been in the past, and not only because her brother-in-law Bill remained in the Benton cottage to look after her. She occupied herself with joyous thoughts, for she also looked forward to another Logan who would be coming to stay with her in June. The question that repeatedly danced through her mind was, "Would it be a baby girl or a baby boy?"

Logan and Allen closed the year 1857 by tending court cases in Logan's hometown. Judge Parish joined them there, reportedly presiding over the cases. Logan brought in the new year of 1858 in the courthouse again. Under most circumstances he would have brought his wife with him to visit his Murphysboro family while he and Allen handled their court work, but both of them agreed not to risk winter travel with Mary beginning her fourth month of pregnancy. He reasoned that he would be home soon enough to care for her in Benton. On New

Year's Day, Logan informed his wife that he would be delayed. "There was a murder committed last night about ten miles from town," he wrote from the Logan House in Murphysboro; "One of the Sorrels shot one of the Cheatham's dead." Concerned about her fragile state, he advised her, "If anything should get the matter, send for me immediately."[37]

Because it was not a district-prosecuted case, the trial would take place in Carbondale, six miles east of the county seat. Judge Parish returned to Springfield to begin work at the annual session of the General Assembly, but Logan and Allen stayed to handle the case, a trial judged by a justice of the peace. Logan somehow made the trial a family affair. He reached out to his Uncle Alexander Jenkins, who agreed to assist, as did his brother-in-law Cyrus Thomas. Two other lawyers outside of Logan's family joined the other attorneys in Carbondale. John Dougherty, Logan's constant foil in the courts, rode up from Jonesboro. Leonard Kean, a Carbondale attorney, also came aboard.

The Sorrell trial began with a most unusual partition of lawyers. The Sorrell family hired Logan to defend the accused, and Jenkins joined him as his assistant, a reunion of the short-term practice they began in 1852. Allen, Dougherty, and Kean were set to prosecute the case. Not only were partners Logan and Allen opposing each other for this trial, but Logan also found himself in familiar territory, pitted against Dougherty. Both sides employed the pinnacle of talent and experience in Southern Illinois, including two former lieutenant governors (Jenkins and Dougherty). Given the normally dull winter season, Jackson County citizens would attend, remember, and reminisce about the trial as a major event in their neighborhood.[38]

The defense deposed scores of potential witnesses, while the prosecution did the same for the Cheatham family. No fewer than seventy-five witnesses were scheduled to testify, guaranteeing a longer-than-usual trial. The case swayed strongly to the prosecution side, based on the evidence at hand. No one could dispute that Sorrell fired the shot and—unlike Logan's notorious "spleen defense" of four years earlier—no one could dispute that the gunshot wound caused the fatality. The prosecution presented an extremely powerful case toward the close of the first week of January. Writing to his wife on January 8, Logan confessed, "It is a bad case but what will become [of it] I can not tell."[39]

The defense did not counter many of the prosecution witnesses, and after Dougherty and Allen rested their case, Logan began his presentation of the defense, weakened by the peppering interruptions of Kean of the prosecution, who jumped up frequently throughout the defense and exclaimed, "May it please the court, I object." Logan saved his best for last. His closing left no doubt that he had earned every dollar paid to him by the Sorrell family. He presented an emotional close, insisting that Sorrell was convinced that his action was predicated on the firm belief that Cheatham and his friends were about to kill him. Sorrell fired the fatal shot in self-defense, argued Logan, who went on to describe the hardships his family would suffer should the jury find him guilty. His speech exuded pathos, reducing many in the courtroom to tears. The most hardened residents of Carbondale could not escape the effect of his words. "I remember old Eph Snyder sat with tears running down his face," recalled one of the townsmen nearly thirty years after the trial, "indeed; half the people in the court were crying." Logan's "pity" strategy worked to perfection. Sorrell was acquitted of murder.[40]

Back at Benton early in the third week of January, Logan found a letter from Congressman Sam S. Marshall waiting for him. The two had been friends for nearly four years, but their steady stream of correspondence since the fall of 1857 was driven by politics as much as friendship. Marshall and Logan had plotted together to install Democrats as postmasters of Jackson County towns. Doff Ozburn received the nod for Murphysboro, and Logan's former commander, Captain James Hampton, had taken over at Carbondale. They also planned the upcoming senatorial campaign to reelect Stephen A. Douglas, who both realized was in for a tough fight to win the state in the aftermath of the Kansas-Nebraska Act. It had enhanced his reputation in the lower counties of Illinois, but had rankled voters in the northern cities. The state legislature had a strong edge in Democrats—the representatives who would actually elect the U.S. senator in one year—but voters in the autumn campaign could alter the makeup of the General Assembly on pure discontent with Douglas, or rising content with a yet-to-be named contender.[41]

The most important point not addressed in the wintertime letters exchanged between Logan and Marshall was the latter's future plans. Late in 1857, Marshall had informed Logan in confidence that he would not seek a third congressional term. Logan seized upon the opening and plotted that winter to construct the campaign for the person he deemed most qualified for the position—himself. He and Mary discussed his desire, and she appears to have given it her tacit approval. Early in March Logan announced that he was in the race to become the Ninth Congressional District of Illinois' representative to the U.S. Congress.

The battle for the seat would essentially end when the Democratic nominee was chosen in the Illinois Democratic convention. The rest of the race was regarded as a formality. There was no immediate concern that a Republican could possibly capture the southernmost eighteen counties of Illinois, as strong a Jacksonian Democrat hotbed as could be found anywhere in the country above the Ohio River and the Mason-Dixon line. Whoever won the nomination would gain the seat, rightly believed Logan, who felt his name recognition and popularity in nine of those counties—his Judicial Circuit from 1853 to 1856—well positioned him to claim this prize. But he needed help, and he went quickly to work to get it. His battle was to convince the most influential Democrats in the state to throw their support to him.

The looming issue in 1858 for Democrats in Egypt was a split in the party rent by the antagonistic relationship between Senator Douglas and President Buchanan. The Kansas Territory's controversial new Lecompton Constitution (named for the town in which it had been drawn up) had heightened their rivalry. As expected, the document authorized slavery and provided for its continuance once Kansas became a state. What was unusual about the territorial administrators of the Lecompton Constitution is that they called for a popular referendum, not on the entire document, but merely on the slavery provision. In an attempt to settle the Kansas-Nebraska controversy, Buchanan endorsed the Lecompton Constitution and tried to strong-arm other Democratic leaders to do so, too. But Douglas refused. His opponents derided his anti-Lecompton position as insincere; his supporters lauded him for consistency by attacking the constitution as a fraud against popular sovereignty. The question of Douglas's sincerity—was this political expedience or principle?—polarized Illinois Democrats.[42]

Logan stayed in the Douglas camp and adopted the anti-Lecompton position. His goal was to gain support early. Since Sam Marshall had not made his decision official, Logan gingerly sought the support of other party leaders in Southern Illinois. He sent letters out to the most influential men of the county seats within the district, and officially placed his name for nomination at the convention. The planning consumed his days and evenings. When Logan and Allen headed out early in March to prosecute and defend clients, he continued to solicit support in person during the day and through letters written at night.

Mary was overwhelmed by it all. The implication and consequences of her husband's ambition sunk in by early March. She was into her sixth month of pregnancy, and she grew troubled about the prospect of her husband's absences becoming more protracted with national duties ahead. Not feeling that she could discuss the matter face-to-face with him, she poured out her concerns on paper. "I know that you are so situated that I must give you up to a great extent, yet my Dear when you are here I hope you will not allow yourself to become so much excited that you will cease to engage a quiet evening at home with your wife," she admonished him. "Politics, if you will allow, can destroy our happiness together. It will rob you of all domestic feelings. . . . My Dear, do not think this unkind of me, for I can not bear to think of sacrificing all our enjoyment together, and live in a continual excitement when together and then be separated the remainder of our time."[43]

Traveling to the courts throughout March and April, Logan labored on three fronts to perform his duties, assuage his wife's concerns, and solicit endorsements from the influential in Egypt. He tried to placate Mary through the mail, informing her that he could not get home and risk speaking engagements. "I must not allow myself sacrificed now since I am in the race," he informed her in response to her March 8 letter; "I hope you will appreciate my reasons for so doing." His toughest work was gaining support, for many were reluctant to endorse him unless Congressman Marshall officially bowed out of the race.[44]

"The Lord is on our side," hailed a Logan supporter in April. Everything began to fall in place for Logan that month. Marshall notified the *Illinois State Register*, the organ of the Democratic Party, that he would not be seeking another term, thus opening the door for Logan and others to walk through and claim his seat. Logan aided his cause immensely with a speech at Cairo on April 13. He wisely toned down his sarcastic, bellicose tone to deliver a calm and reasoned argument that was hailed by a cheering audience as well as an appreciative press. The power base of Southern Illinois, hesitant to speak out for him in March, sent a stream of endorsing letters in April. One of them saw Logan's clear path to win the nomination at the Thebes convention later that spring. "I will willingly insure you a seat in Congress," he initially wrote, but he crossed out the word "will" and replaced it with "would."[45]

Indeed, his supporters could not guarantee his victory. Throughout the early spring, it looked to Republicans that they had no chance to win the Egypt seat; however, they saw an opening as the summer campaign heated up throughout Illinois. The Democrats split into two camps, those who supported Douglas and those who supported Buchanan. The latter, anti-Douglas faction were dubbed "Danites" by the pro-Douglas camp to link them with what the Douglas men considered Buchanan's lack of success against the Mormon Rebellion of the previous year (Danites was a Mormon society known as "Daughters of Zion"). Each faction held conventions in Southern Illinois to select a candidate for the November election. At Thebes near the southern tip of Illinois, the pro-Douglas Democrats selected Logan; the anti-Douglas camp chose John Dougherty, Logan's opponent in the courts.

Logan's blood was up to campaign against Dougherty, but he took a break early in the summer to hustle home to Benton. Mary delivered a baby girl on June 25. The Logans named her Mary Elizabeth, after her mother and her paternal grandmother. They nicknamed her "Lizzie" and "Dollie," the latter for the baby's doll-like appearance. After a hiatus to attend to his wife and newborn, Logan returned to the campaign trail.[46]

The two adversarial attorneys squared off against each other politically to kick off the summer of 1858. "Dougherty and Logan are quarreling like dogs," gleefully reported David L. Phillips, a rare but prominent Republican in the Ninth District. Phillips saw the splitting apart of the Democratic supporters in Egypt. Doubtful back in March about any chance of success for Republicans, he was much more confident by summertime. With hopes that two additional Democrats would also jump in to further cloud the muddy waters, he crowed, "If this should turn out to be the Case we will carry the district." Not only did Phillips see congressional chances improve, but he also saw an opening for the Republican senatorial candidate to steal the region from Douglas by converting the legislature there in the fall election. He pleaded with the candidate that "we must have your help to revolutionize this dark corner of Illinois."[47]

That Republican candidate for the senate seat was Abraham Lincoln. He and Douglas scheduled a series of debates to cover most of the congressional districts of Illinois. Douglas had originally considered Egypt safe, but the Danite uprising changed his mind. Distressed at the vocal opposition within the Democratic Party, he complained, "The Hell-hounds are on my track." He scheduled a debate with Lincoln at Jonesboro, Doughtery's hometown, and solicited help to win the district. Sam Marshall came in from Washington to reinforce Douglas's efforts in Southern Illinois. "It will never do to let the Opposition get a foothold in Egypt," he warned Charles Lanphier, the editor of the *Illinois State Register*. "If they do, the State is gone beyond redemption."[48]

Marshall teamed up with Logan to stump the region for both Logan and Douglas. Logan was pleased, for Marshall epitomized partisan politics. Marshall was incredulous that the Danites had been plotting "to secure the success of the Black Republican ticket in Illinois." He informed Logan, "Such men professing to be Democrats ought not only to be damned but doubly damned." He considered Logan's race as important as the senate contest. "It is a terrible ordeal which the Democracy of our state [has] to pass through in the approaching Congress," he continued; "but if we are successful as I trust we shall be it will be the most glorious and memorable political victory on record."[49]

Logan welcomed the assistance from his esteemed friend, who joined him early in August. They barnstormed throughout the Ninth Congressional District. Josh Allen joined his law partner, working with him to harangue Republicans. An offended member of the attacked party wrote Lincoln that they "professedly hate Abolitionism about as bad as they do the Democracy." Logan's campaign overwhelmed Dougherty and effectively eliminated him as serious competition. By August Dougherty dropped out. William K. Parish, Logan's former law partner, replaced him on the ticket. Logan did not learn who his Republican opponent was until late in August, when Ben Wiley campaigned briefly against him, but Wiley was out one month later, replaced by David L. Phillips who had already been carrying the mantle of the Republican Party in Egypt by countering Logan at every speaking site in the district.[50]

His opposition's lack of organization sealed the congressional election for Logan. He now pressed his campaign to win for Douglas. All the opposing participants congregated at Jonesboro in the middle of September where Lincoln and Douglas debated on the fifteenth. The 2,000 people who attended made Jonesboro the smallest of the debate series between the two senatorial candidates. Although Phillips spoke after Lincoln and Douglas, Logan did not address the crowd. His moment came a day later, when Douglas stopped at Benton on the way to the fourth debate at Charleston. There he was greeted by a large audience. Logan presided at the mass meeting, and Mary hoisted a flag she created over the previous night to honor the senator. The next day Logan and the rest of the Douglas team planted themselves at the state fair in Centralia. Sam Marshall spoke before Logan and reportedly "got graveled" by the Buchanan men and the Lincoln supporters. Logan followed the congressman and was wise enough not to invite questions as his speech took off with a grand rush. His voice spent from the heavy campaigning, he rested in Benton while Douglas and his supporters trained up to Charleston for another debate.[51]

"I am well and in [a] better fix for speaking than heretofore," he wrote his wife early in October. He had missed the final debates between Lincoln and Douglas, but he was back on the speaking trail and putting all of his energy into the campaign. Mary's letters revealed her continued anxiety over his long absences, but for the first time she exuded the partisan rhetoric that had become her husband's trademark. "I flatter myself you would not be afraid of any man, *even old Abraham* himself," she wrote, "and I should feel very much hurt to have any Northerner over reach one of our gallant Democrats and I do pray that you may gain enough of [Lincoln's] speech from your friends to cool the *enthusiasm* that he may fancy that he has excited."[52]

Neither Logan nor his wife ever expressed any concern about his own race in the final month of the canvass. The election results of November 2 proved that they had good reason to maintain their confidence. Logan trounced David L. Phillips, 15,878 to 2,796, while William K. Parish took a mere 144 votes with an additional 37 votes scattered to other candidates. A breakdown of the eighteen counties in the Ninth Congressional District showed Logan why his political phi-losophy ruled in Egypt. He lost only one county (Edwards) to Phillips—by 127 votes—but three counties alone guaranteed the outcome. Johnson, Hamilton, and Saline County men cast more votes for Logan than Phillips received in the entire district. His margin of victory in those three counties was an incredible 3,455 to 16. John A. Logan was elected to the U. S. House of Representatives.[53]

Logan's efforts on the behalf of Douglas provided him more recognition throughout the state. He also contributed to the election of a legislature guaran-teed to secure Douglas's Senate seat over Lincoln. Overall, more Illinois voters cast their votes for Lincoln-supporting legislators, but when the statewide results came in, Democrats in the Illinois legislature outnumbered Republicans in the Illinois House and Senate. The year 1858 was a good one for the anti-Lecompton Democrats in Illinois.[54]

Logan's teenage ambition, from the day he played the fiddle on a neighbor's fence and told the lady of the house that he would be a U.S. congressman, was now realized. He would not occupy his house seat for a year, for the Thirty-sixth U.S. Congress would not go into session until December 1859. Until then, Logan would earn his living on the court circuit. By the summer of 1859 he was often forced to work alone. Judge Willis Allen, Josh Allen's prestigious father, died during a court session in June. Allen left the practice to mourn the loss, and was then appointed as the circuit court judge to replace his father.[55]

In mid November, after an active and lucrative season in the courts, Logan bade his family farewell and headed eastward to Washington to sit on the Demo-cratic side of the aisle in the Thirty-sixth U.S. Congress. He picked up the Balti-more and Ohio line at Wheeling, Virginia, and took in the rugged Allegheny landscape that surrounded the train as it steamed along the Mason-Dixon Line. He also took note of U. S. soldiers stationed all along the rail line. The train halted temporarily at Harpers Ferry, a town nestled in a bowl-shaped valley formed by the junction of the Shenandoah and Potomac rivers. One month earlier John Brown, a long-bearded, fire-and-brimstone abolitionist, led two dozen men on a raid into the town to initiate a slave insurrection. It failed miserably. Brown and his disciples killed several citizens, including a freed black man and the town mayor, stirring up retaliation against them. Brown and five of his followers were captured while other raiders escaped and several were killed. Brown stood trial at Charlestown, a Virginia town close to the raid site, was found guilty, and sched-uled to die at the gallows with his cohorts on December 2.[56]

From the train window, Logan could easily see the bullet holes pocked in buildings near the train—battle scars left behind by John Brown's raid. As the train's steam engines revved up and carried him away from the site, he reflected on the deeper scars the raid had inflicted on the country. The 1850s had begun with a congressional act to keep the expanding country united. The decade was ending with that compromise jeopardized, and the North and South splitting further apart. Political, social, and economic issues polarized the country, but the overriding issue of the decade was slavery. The Compromise of 1850 staved off threats of secession by placating slavery advocates and abolitionists with a plan to bring in a portion of the new territory acquired from the fruits of the Mexican War as slave-labored land and California as a new slavery-free state. The compromise had only delayed what now appeared inevitable.

As an advocate of two early 1850s policies—the Fugitive Slave Act and the Kansas-Nebraska Act—Logan lamented that the former spawned the Underground Railroad movement, a clandestine, informal operation to shuttle runaway slaves to safe Northern locales. Debates over the location to run a proposed transcontinental railroad predictably polarized the proponents along the same lines. Then came the Dred Scott decision by Chief Justice Roger Taney in 1857, declaring that slaves were to be treated as property of human beings more than as human beings themselves. One year prior to Taney's controversial decision, the fanatical abolitionist John Brown and four of his sons retaliated against border ruffians in Lawrence, Kansas (a free center of the territory), by hacking to death five proslavery advocates along Pottawatomie Creek. Brown's encore at Harpers Ferry closed the decade, but no one believed for a minute that it was the end of violence in the less-than-united states of America.[57]

Logan stepped off the train in Washington and made his way up Pennsylvania Avenue, the first time he trod in the U.S. capital. He secured boarding at Brown's Hotel, and appropriately obsessed over his finances. The previous year's cases failed to swell his wealth and with rent alone costing $25 per month, Logan had tallied that it would cost $1,500 per year—nearly a third of his annual government salary—to serve his district in the House of Representatives.[58]

That service officially began on December 4, 1859, with the Illinois caucus, followed by the first floor debates on December 5. Logan was a member of a very important Congress, the thirty-sixth two-year session in the nation's history, one charged with doing all that was necessary to keep the country together. It was a tall order based on recent history. Statesman such as Daniel Webster and Henry Clay had put aside partisanship to draw a gray line between black-and-white issues in 1850, but they were dead and gone. Men like Logan made up the new Congress, those more noted for their partisanship than for their statesmanship. James Buchanan demonstrated his executive impotence, the fourth president in the decade whose weak leadership failed to stanch the nation's ever-widening wound. Buchanan would be out in a year and the nation would elect a new president. Logan wanted Stephen A. Douglas in that role. His rock-solid adherence to Douglas inspired his memorable maiden speech on the House floor.

After two days of rancorous debate over the house speakership, Republican William Kellogg of Illinois changed topics by attacking Senator Douglas. He dusted off an old rumor that he had forged a deal with influential *New York Tribune* editor, Horace Greeley, to diminish the Republicans' clout in the 1858 election. Logan chomped at the bit for recognition to respond; two days later he got the nod and took the floor. He was familiar with the protocol from two terms in the Illinois legislature; now he was on the national stage. Every word he uttered would be reproduced in the *Congressional Globe* to be studied and reported upon by newspaper reporters, colleagues, and constituents.

He began his address by taking Kellogg to task for his remarks, stressing that they had been uttered only to destroy Douglas's political career. He berated Kellogg for not furnishing any proof to support his claim. Kellogg's frequent interruptions failed to throw the freshman off balance; Logan deftly brushed them off, confident that his own verbal cannonballs were hitting their targets. He reminded his colleagues of his stand against Governor Bissell three years earlier, noting that the difference between his critique and Kellogg's current one was that Logan had documents to support his statements in the Illinois legislature. He continued, "I stood up and did prove it, when called upon for proof, and did not shrink from responsibility, and like a spaniel, cower . . ." The less-than-manly reference to "spaniel" was enough for Kellogg, who—believing that Logan had called him a "coward"—flew from his seat, halting Logan in mid-sentence with his charge. "Does the gentleman call me a spaniel coward?" he shouted. Logan did not back away; instead he rushed toward Kellogg with equal fervor. The entire House floor then burst into chaos with dozens of congressmen leaping from their seats amidst a cacophony of bellicose shouts from the gallery and the repeated calls for order matching the cadence of the banging gavel. Colleagues intervened between Logan and Kellogg before either threw a punch.

The melee did not end for several minutes. Logan tried to quell the turmoil before him as he continued to speak. Even as he promised to soften his temper, he still seethed with defiance. He bellowed, "If I am to be hissed; if I am to be clapped down or if I am to be intimidated in this Hall, allow me to say that I have as many rights, whether they be respected or not, as any man on this floor." Order finally ruled the House and Logan continued with his speech, fed and broadened by questions from the floor. He clearly enjoyed the center-stage attention and took full advantage to voice his views—seemingly all of them. He defended popular sovereignty, harangued abolitionists, and loosed his opinions about Democrats *and* Republicans. Yes, he differed from his fellow Democrats on certain issues, but his affiliation with the party would not waver. Referring to the Republicans, he declared, "God knows that I have differed with the other side from my childhood, and with that side I will never affiliate so long as I have breath in my body."

Proud of his history with the Fugitive Slave Laws in Illinois, he called for the strict enforcement of the national law to return escaped slaves to their owners, long on the books but by and large ignored by citizens living outside his congressional district. He pointedly expressed his shame at Northerners over this issue, preferring Illinois to be called a "Western" state and not a "Northern" one. Noting that Republicans considered it "dirty work" to catch runaway blacks and return them to servitude, Logan haughtily announced that the Democrats "are willing to perform that dirty work." He closed the issue declaring, "I do not consider it disgraceful to perform, dirty or not dirty, which is in accordance with the laws of the land, and the Constitution of the country."[59]

The speech ended before the morning did, but Logan's words reverberated for weeks. "I intend to have my speech published in a few weeks and send it to the people," Logan informed Mary, complaining that only the *Congressional Globe* correctly captured the debate. Other sources claimed eye-popping scenarios; one went so far as to report that in the heat of the exchange on the floor, Logan drew a pistol and seethed, "By God, if I can't talk, I can do something else." Given other similar incidents, this claim was not so preposterous. In a separate debate over the House speaker, another anti-Lecompton Democrat dropped his pistol on the floor during his speech. A North Carolinian challenged a Pennsylvania Representative to a duel, causing both men to be arrested. Indeed, the House floor consisted of armed members, while several spectators in the galleries also carried pistols, adding even greater danger to an already charged atmosphere.[60]

His rancorous exchange with Kellogg attracted considerable attention. He was widely denounced by pro-Republican newspapers and hailed by Democratic ones. The *Chicago Tribune* officially launched a years-long antagonistic relationship with him by dubbing him "Dirty Work" for his proudly professed willingness to snatch fugitive slaves and return them to their owners. Illinois Democrats delighted in his stance; one gibed that he "wanted to make his marks on a Kel-log."[61] Most noteworthy was that Logan attracted considerable attention outside his home state. Prominent Eastern papers covered him to a depth and degree rarely given to a freshman congressman, particularly one from the West.

The *New York Times* had a field day with Logan, featuring him in a piece published two weeks after his floor performance. Considering him "one of the most rising members" of the Democratic Party, the *Times* went on to describe Logan's striking appearance:

> Very Indian in his appearance ... Mr. LOGAN has blue-black hair, profuse, glossy and of a thick fibre; regular features and white teeth, shown to good advantage by a brown skin; and a form of head singularly high and long from brow to base, though not quite broad enough to be in good proportion. His voice is a strong clear tenor—its fault being the Western one of monotonous vigor.[62]

Although his maiden speech caused a considerable stir and garnered him notoriety, Logan dropped back to endure the difficulties experienced by all House freshman, including getting recognized. He argued with John Farnsworth, another Illinois Republican, shortly before Christmas over slavery issues. Logan's retorts clearly illustrated his contempt for those who did not denounce John Brown and abolitionism. He accused Farnsworth of being a disunionist, not realizing the charge would soon be hurled back at him.

These controversies erupted against the backdrop of the longest battle to select a speaker to that date. The battle ended on February 1 when Republican William Pennington, a New Jersey anti-Lecompton congressman, won the vote tally. Logan had worked to support his fellow Illinois Democrat, John A. McClernand, but was at least satisfied to remove the original Republican favorite, John Sherman of Ohio, the brother a West Point–trained army officer named William Tecumseh Sherman.[63]

When he wasn't ranting against abolitionists on the House floor, he worked to defend Douglas against all of his accusers. When the Douglas-Greeley rumor reared up again in March, Logan rose to protect his candidate against the charge, which prompted the *Illinois State Journal* to recognize his effort, but with the derogatory description: "Your Grecian orator, dirty-work Logan." As 1860 entered the spring season Logan had been placed on one committee (Revisal and Unfinished Business) and introduced one bill—to reorganize Southern Illinois district courts—which was soundly defeated. He voted with the vast majority to pass the Homestead Bill, which turned out to be his most significant vote of the early session.[64]

Consumed with the desire to elect Stephen A. Douglas as the sixteenth president of the United States, Logan worked tirelessly after hours in Washington.

He struck up a friendship with Congressman McClernand and James Robinson, both allied with him in their Douglas support. The three of them labored on Pennsylvania Avenue each evening in "Douglas Rooms," offices set up to frank pro-Douglas literature throughout the states. The trio also received Douglas delegates for the upcoming Democratic Convention in Charleston, South Carolina. Logan moved out of Brown's Hotel and into a room at a private boardinghouse, shared with Jim Robinson and Phil Fouke. The relocation not only saved him money, but fostered the Illinois Democrats' camaraderie.[65]

The business of politics and government kept Logan from home for the longest stretch of his life. Mary's letters made him feel more at ease about his absence. She assured him she was fine and well taken care of by family and friends. She also placated him about the professional life he had chosen. He had informed her he would run again to retain his seat. "It will I know sound rather strange to you to see me so much interested about your being a candidate who I have always felt so much opposed to your being in politics," she confessed in March, "but I am satisfied you will not be contented to lead a quiet domestic life for a few years at least . . ." But Mary labored to hide her real concerns—ones she used to spill out so effusively two years earlier—away from him in 1860. She had written Mother Logan just a few weeks before her confession of resolve to her husband, despairing, "He has now been away nearly three months and when I reflect that three more months must pass away before I shall see him, my very soul aches."[66]

Ignorant of his wife's heartache, Logan rode south to Charleston in the third week of April for the National Democratic Convention of 1860. Although he was not a delegate, reporters did not overlook his presence. On the eve of the convention he could be found sitting on the steps of Hibernia Hall, his back against a pillar, his hands tucked into his pockets, and the cheeks of his usually thin face puffed out with a wad of chewing tobacco. The other Illinois congressman appeared equally flat as they sat scattered on steps nearby. According to a Cincinnati reporter, the collective demeanor of the Prairie State congressmen befit their mournful prospects, for he felt that their candidate's political stock had been dropping throughout the day.[67] Their lethargy was justified by the next day's events. Called the "Demagogue of Illinois," Douglas was a lightening rod for Southern Democrats, who made it their mission to strike him down. The convention split the Democrats into Northern and Southern adherents; the Northerners coalesced around Douglas and the Southerners lined up to block his nomination. The latter succeeded; after fifty-seven ballots, Douglas failed to capture the necessary two-thirds. The convention broke up early in May, both sides returning home with a burgeoning contempt for each other that rivaled each side's hatred of "Black Republicans." Logan was disgusted by it all. "I can assure you that the world has never witnessed such infamy as was perpetrated at that convention in order to defeat one man," he ranted.[68]

The only thing that both sides agreed to in Charleston was to meet again six weeks later in Baltimore and attempt to unite against a common opponent. In the middle of May, Logan learned that the opponent would be Abraham Lincoln, who upset the front-running New York senator, William H. Seward, to win the Republican Party nomination in Chicago. Lincoln's nomination electrified him to campaign harder to make the election a contest of Illinois candidates. On May 22, he stepped inside the Cooper Institute in New York, the new education center that had launched Lincoln as a national candidate after a speech he delivered there in February. Logan was the third of eighteen speakers at a pro-Douglas demonstration to rally support for the national candidate. He was in fine form and gave a short but effective address. The audience erupted in laughter and applause with his closing quip, one that mocked the Republicans who favorably characterized Lincoln as "The Rail Splitter" to appeal to the common man: "I have one proposition to make to the friends of Mr. Lincoln, that when Mr. Douglas is nominated each candidate shall be sent back to his original employment, Lincoln to making rails, and Douglas to making *cabinets*."[69]

The outcome of the convention in Baltimore was just as disastrous as Charleston for Douglas supporters. The South Carolina firebrands had walked out of the Charleston convention in protest six weeks earlier. They did so again in Baltimore, but they were joined by a third of the delegates. The anti-Douglas men subsequently formed their own convention where they nominated the current vice president, John C. Breckinridge of Kentucky. Logan witnessed Douglas's nomination, meaning the Democrats had split their ticket for the upcoming election. Although old-line Whigs reformed to call themselves the Constitution Party and put up slaveholding John Bell of Tennessee as their candidate, the four-way split all but secured the outcome for the Republicans. The election was now Lincoln's to lose.

Logan returned to Southern Illinois in June. He did not consider his Republican congressional opponent, David T. Linegar, a serious threat to his re-election, so he devoted much of his campaign speeches to the Democratic ticket. Egypt's vote tally would be critical to secure the Electoral College votes of Illinois. Logan headed off to Springfield in the middle of July to counter Lincoln's "Wide Awake" supporters—devotees who campaigned for him late into the night. Logan and other prominent Illinois Democrats addressed the most zealous of their partisans in near-nightly meetings in Springfield, railing against what they considered the radical proclivities of Republicans, especially Lincoln, the Rail Splitter.[70]

He was back in his congressional district immediately after his Springfield trip, stumping Egypt. As they had been in 1858, Logan's speeches were part of larger events where he shared the stage with other Democrats canvassing the region. These were well-advertised, marked by loud and festive fanfare. At Cairo, for example, discharging cannons heralded the meetings. (Unfortunately for one citizen, the cannon blast was his death knell.) Other interruptions were less deadly, but more troublesome for Logan. He knew he was a lock in Egypt, but could not say the same for Douglas. "Egypt is almost wiped out, as a Democratic stronghold," a letter writer predicted in the *New York Herald* in August. Logan need only look at his hometown of Benton to heed such a warning. The *Franklin Democrat*, like all area papers, had placed the names of the candidates it supported on its masthead. In the first days of September Logan was back home in Benton for a stopover before he returned to the stump. He picked up the paper, his shocked eyes widening when he scanned the masthead. Rather than highlighting "Stephen A. Douglas" for president as had been the custom for several months, the paper inconceivably replaced the Democrat with the Abraham Lincoln/Hannibal Hamlin ticket.[71]

Logan sped to the newspaper office where he learned that the publishers switched their support after they decided that Douglas had no chance to win. They supported Lincoln in an effort to assure that Breckinridge—backed by the South Carolina and Baltimore convention bolters—did not gain any foothold in the election. Logan found this unacceptable, and offered to buy out the paper for $550. The publishers refused, but a rabid and dangerous crowd congregated at the newspaper office throughout the night, forcing them to accept an offer they felt they no longer could refuse. Forced out of Benton, the newspapermen fled to Springfield where they spoke out in the *Illinois State Journal* on September 20. "Go on, Mr. Logan, put down free speech," they bitterly ranted, "close up the avenues of free thought, gag the press if you can, trample under foot the sacred guarantees of the Constitution, but you can never stop the march of truth." With their accusation circulated throughout Illinois in newspaper excerpts and follow-up reports, "Dirty Work" Logan had become increasingly notorious. His appeal as a celebrity and congressman was strictly regional—isolated to a dismissed corner of the state.[72]

As the new owner of the Benton newspaper, Logan returned home in October and attempted to churn out issues in his vision. His wife became the bookkeeper; two others aided in the printing process. By the end of October, Logan's ungrammatical editorials stopped running from the presses. With Lincoln's election a *fait accompli*, neither his heart nor his head was focused on the project, and the paper subsequently faded into oblivion.[73]

Abraham Lincoln easily won the four-way race for president on November 6. He distanced himself from the rest of the pack by 250,000 votes, sweeping all the electoral-college-rich Northern states. He edged Douglas in Illinois with a plurality of 5,000 votes out of 350,000 cast. Logan's district, despite predictions of political change, proved to be comparably as united as in previous contests. Logan trounced Linegar with nearly 80 percent of the votes. An unprecedented 28,000 residents of the Ninth Congressional District voted that day; all but 7,500 of them voted for Douglas, who took 75 percent of the votes. Lincoln received only 5,219 votes—a mere 17 percent of the total.[74]

Logan returned to Washington late in November. Mary came, too, taking up residence with him in Brown's Hotel. Logan stepped back into the House chambers on December 3 to start the second session of the Thirty-sixth Congress. Although he would be returning for the Thirty-seventh Congress, many faces in his aisle and across from it would not. No one could predict the state of the country, for all looked ahead to South Carolina's planned secession convention. Set to begin in two weeks, the state firebrands found Lincoln's election unacceptable. Although Lincoln had never threatened to end slavery in states where it already existed, he had campaigned on stopping its spread into territories west of the Mississippi. Many sympathized with South Carolina's plans; others saw this as an unfathomable response to the election in which their candidate (Breckinridge) did not win.

Logan voted with the majority to create a commission to investigate the state of the Union. He also amended a resolution that passed unanimously, stating that all men should obey the Constitution. He did not give a speech that registered an opinion if secession was in violation of the Constitution but off the record, Logan's words and actions were somehow interpreted as antithetical to Douglas. Douglas's camp suggested that Logan was breaking with the Little Giant. Although his district gained 14,000 votes for Douglas in Illinois—the highest number of any congressional division in the state—rumors spread that Logan was rumbling with resentment over a speech Douglas had delivered in Norfolk in August 1860, an address in which he promised, if he was to lose the election, to lend his full support to the Lincoln administration in maintaining the Union. According to one of the politicians campaigning at the time, Logan was "ugly and full of fight," assailing Douglas's Virginia speech in a furious rampage against him.[75]

Another witness used the same terminology to describe Logan in the halls of Congress in December, but with opposite meaning. Joseph Medill, the *Chicago Tribune* editor and a Lincoln confidant, wrote the president-elect from Washington in mid December with his observations about the mood of those in government. He informed Lincoln that all Republican senators and representatives were in favor of maintaining the Union "at whatever cost." He felt the Northern Democrats, with a few exceptions, felt the same by pointing out that the Illinois delegation favored coercion of the South to maintain the nation's unity. "Logan is full of fight," Medill pointedly stated, but for a reason far different from the summer accusations: "Hang, shoot and kill the traitors are his words, spoken without disguise or concealment."[76]

In Springfield, the president-elect absorbed the words of his Washington contacts. Shortly afterwards Lincoln and Judge Joseph Gillespie warmed themselves by a stove as they talked politics together over a winter evening. Lincoln told Gillespie that if he had his way, he would form a cabinet out of Illinois politicians, including Democrats. "I know where every man would fit and we could get right down to work," he asserted. Gillespie was incredulous at Lincoln's statement. "Do you mean, Mr. Lincoln, you'd take a Democrat like Logan?" asked the judge. "Yes sir, I would," came Lincoln's emphatic reply; "I know Logan. He's [against] me now and that's all right. You can count on Logan to do the right thing by the country, and that's the kind of men I want—them as will do the right thing by the country." Speaking in the third person, Lincoln concluded, "Taint a question of Lincoln, or Democrat or Republican, Judge; it's a question of the country."[77]

The winter of 1861 was cold, disappointing, and frustrating for Logan. He opened the year by circulating a letter for publication. He wrote it on New Year's Day to Isham N. Haynie, a friend, lawyer, and judge who he met on the circuit in the 1850s. Logan explained the genesis of the controversy leading to secession, but shortsightedly brought it back only to Lincoln's election. He denounced Lincoln and his supporters and asserted that "flushed and drunken with victory [they] are plunging deeper into their fanatical orgies, the nearer our beloved country is undone." He compared the incoming administration to the fanatical Nero, who sawed on a fiddle while Rome burned. His harsh words about Lincoln did not absolve the Southerners and their ultimate act. Calling secession "deplorable" for overthrowing the republic, Logan hoped—as did most—that other states would not follow South Carolina and that cooler heads would prevail in the seceded state to return it to the Union. He closed his letter firmly positioning himself if his hopes were not realized. "[We] of the Northwest having as much, if not more, at stake than any other section can not stand silently by while the joint action of extremists are dragging us to ruin."[78]

Logan had chosen his words with care and deliberation. Refusing to call Illinois the "North," he appeared to proclaim himself as state spokesman in his dual denunciation of secessionists and abolitionists. But the Illinois Democratic press did not universally denounce the secessionists. "The sympathies of our people are mainly with the South," wrote the editor of the *Cairo City Gazette*, while the *Joliet Signal*, seeing a statewide movement to organize the militia in the face of the growing crisis, declared, "As Democrats, we claim exemption from service in this Black Republican war."[79]

Haynie circulated the letter, but most Illinois papers did not publish it. The pro-Lincoln, *Illinois State Journal* dismissed it as "partisan pique and party hatred." Logan's party also took a hit from the *Chicago Tribune*, which reported unfavorably on the January Democratic state convention held in Springfield. The *Tribune* branded the Democrats as "semi-secessionist" for passing pro-Union resolutions while concurrently opposing coercion to bring back the disgruntled South Carolinians, recently joined by Mississippi, Florida, and Alabama, who voted to secede with them. Other states were sure to follow. Although Logan was not present at the convention, one of the attendees told his wife that Logan's earlier assault on Douglas's prowar "Virginia Speech" had "caused a rumpus" at the convention.[80]

Back in Washington, congressional debates grew more rancorous. A committee had been formed to produce a report for compromise with the secessionists. Floor debates tied up the session so much that night sessions commenced to allow for more representatives to put their words on record. During the evening session of February 5, Logan was recognized and took the floor, commanding the stage for an hour. His presentation varied little from his letter of January 1, but here he was seeking broad coverage to clarify his position. He opened by praising the unbounded prosperity of the nation throughout its history to contrast it with the disintegration of Union bonds beginning with South Carolina's secession on December 20, 1860. "Revolution exists in six States," he declared that cold February night, "with the chance that it will spread ere long, as a fire on the prairies, over many more of the slaveholding States. What a sad change, Mr. Speaker, a few short weeks have wrought!"

He went on to dissect the causes of the crisis, repeating his denunciation of Southern and Northern extremists. He drew a painstaking analogy to the revolution that gave birth to the United States, one that likened the Republicans to King George III. He then called upon his colleagues on both sides of the aisle to put aside politics, a plea without weight since he had just castigated the opposing party in the harshest of terms. He looked to compromise, but specified measures that essentially conceded all to the slaveholding states. He called for noninterference with the interstate slave trade, the opening of the territories to slavery if so desired by the citizens of the territories, and for the consideration of all the compromise proposals, particularly the Crittenden Compromise, set before them to reunite the country. He declared his vehement opposition to war as a means to bring the seceding states back into the Union. He denounced draconian measures, opposing those who wished to hang the secessionists. "They [secessionists] are not our enemies, with whom we should be willing to measure swords, but a part of our people," Logan declared. "They are our kinsmen, and should be dealt with kindly. Their return from their wanderings may be looked for at some future day, if our action shall be tempered with forbearance and moderation; but if you 'let slip the dogs of war,' never! never!"[81]

Logan's pacifist and compromising approach to settle the crisis contradicted what *Chicago Tribune* reporter Joseph Medill had insisted to Abraham Lincoln six weeks earlier. Back then the reporter believed Logan was bellicose, wishing to do what he since had denounced: hang the traitors. Up to four days before the address, the *Tribune* hailed Logan as a Unionist, stressing his courage and patriotism and claiming he had broken all political ties for the sake of the country. The hourlong speech of February 5 did not contradict his pro-Union stance, but his conciliatory words toward the Southerners dominating over his strident critique of the prowar sect of the Republican Party induced fellow Illinois Democrat John A. McClernand to deride him as a "compromiser."[82]

While in Illinois, Abraham Lincoln had openly praised Logan's desire to do what was right for the country. He did not comment on Logan's speech to indicate if his opinion of Logan had changed. During the dark morning hours of February 23, friends secretly escorted him into the nation's capital, long considered a Southern-sympathizing town, to Willard's Hotel. Later that morning, Logan stepped into the hotel with other members of the Illinois delegation. They visited the tired president-elect, ostensibly offering encouraging words to him.[83]

Logan worked in Congress to complete the second session. The House of Representatives debated and voted on their final legislation, including the enforcement of the fugitive slave law, a measure highly supported by "Dirty Work" Logan. Congress adjourned on March 4, the same day Abraham Lincoln was inaugurated as the sixteenth president of the United States. The Logan family returned to Benton shortly after Congress adjourned. Logan's days in Franklin County were numbered. The Illinois General Assembly had been active in redistricting procedures. Logan had been warned that he was a target because the Ninth Congressional District was about to lose Franklin County to the neighboring Eighth District, represented by James Robinson, the popular Democrat who Logan would not be able to unseat in the next state Democratic Convention. Although the gerrymandering proposals varied and would not go into effect for a couple of years, Logan used foresight to prevent his future displacement.[84]

Logan no longer called Benton "home." He moved his family twenty miles south to Marion, the seat of Williamson County. The decision was a wise one. He had been a familiar and popular visitor there for nearly a dozen years, frequently visiting friends and engaging in business in the law circuit. For Mary the move brought her closer to her parents—much closer. The Logan family moved into the Cunningham house until the transaction to secure their own home was completed. They also split time by living with the Marion "Curt" Campbell family in Marion. (Hannah Campbell, Curt's wife, was Mary's sister.) Logan settled in Marion as March turned to April. His new surroundings included some of the strongest supporters of secession throughout the North. A few weeks before he arrived, one of the prominent citizens delivered a speech in the courthouse; in it he declared, "Our country must be saved." But by his hand motion gestured during the declaration, everyone in attendance understood he referred to saving the South. Once settled in Marion Logan rode out to work in his second profession as a practicing attorney. After Allen left the practice to ascend to judgeship, Logan formed looser associations with a few attorneys he had met on the Egypt circuit. They included Cy Thomas, but his brother-in-law was more actively pursuing his naturalist interests. Logan teamed up with a Franklin County attorney in 1860 and in 1861 he and Massac County friend, William H. Green, worked closer together on cases in Southern Illinois. But in the early spring he rode out alone, handling cases in neighboring county seats.[85]

With his first session of the Thirty-seventh U.S. Congress three months away, Logan toiled exclusively as a lawyer, his money concerns never abating from the time he left his father's care. A more pressing concern overtook the financial ones. It also dominated the thoughts and discussions of everyone he would greet at county courthouses. Everyone was obsessed with Charleston, South Carolina, more specifically with Fort Sumter, deep in the city's harbor. The U.S. fort was threatened by the first seceded state; South Carolina's state militia cannons pointed directly at the besieged fort, occupied by U.S. soldiers commanded by Major Robert Anderson. The threat materialized on April 12, 1861, when South Carolina batteries bombarded Fort Sumter. The aggressive act by a state against U.S. soldiers on U.S. property closed the book on decades of compromise. The event—both anticipated and feared at the same time—materialized into a national crisis. All eyes redirected their focus to Washington. Abraham Lincoln's response to South Carolina would decide the fate of a nation.

Fort Sumter's bombardment and subsequent surrender on April 13 sent shock waves from the Atlantic Coast to the Mississippi River. Telegraph operators deciphered the dots and dashes clicking off their machines, providing them with the biggest news story they had ever witnessed. President Lincoln wasted no time in reacting to South Carolina's capture of a U.S. enclave. Beginning on Monday, April 15, newspapers across the country published his call for 75,000 troops to suppress the rebellion. Civil war had begun.

CHAPTER THREE

Patriots and Traitors

THE REACTION TO LINCOLN'S PROCLAMATION came swiftly as the Northern states promised to fill the administration's quotas for volunteer soldiers. Sumter invigorated the Northeast in other ways. New England abolitionists found new life in the news and quickly spread their fervor. The reaction was similar across New York and Pennsylvania, where "War Meetings" in big cities and small villages produced unified, if not frenetic, support for the Union. In New York City, renowned as a haven for Southern sympathizers, 250,000 people turned out for a Union rally.[1]

Although some observers predicted that the West would be slower to respond, the region from Ohio to the Mississippi and beyond shook the East with "one great Eagle-scream." Flags waved everywhere, hailed by a populace with a seemingly united sentiment to put down the rebellion. "There is something splendid, yet terrible, about this roused anger of the North," noted Lincoln's secretary shortly after the fall of Sumter; "The North will not have mercy, for mercy is cruelty now. The Government must die or crush its assailants. Freedom and Slavery stand in the field, like the hosts of good and evil in the Apocalypse, for a final fight on Armageddon's plain."[2]

The eagle did not scream in Logan's new hometown. Immediately after the news of Sumter's surrender permeated Marion several influential townsmen met at a local saloon in the town square. They called a meeting for the public safety, one that commenced at the courthouse on Monday, April 15. James

Manier organized the group by appointing a committee to draft pro-secessionist resolutions, drawn up prior to the courthouse gathering. Protesting what they considered Lincoln's overt aggression, Manier's panel unabashedly threw their support for the independence of the rapidly forming Confederate States of America. Calling themselves "loyal citizens," they drew up a document with one key line that resonated throughout Lincoln's home state: "We heartily pledge ourselves to use all means in our power to effect the [division of the state] and attach ourselves to the Southern Confederacy."[3]

The crowd zealously applauded the announcement. John M. Cunningham helped draft the set of resolutions and signed it, as did ten others (one man refused). News of the event and the document spawned from it spread through Illinois, but common sense prevailed immediately in Marion when a Carbondale resident rode into town the next day to tell them to quickly revoke the resolutions. General Benjamin Franklin Prentiss, concentrating a volunteer army in Cairo, had received the document by telegram. If the resolutions were not repealed, war could be waged in Egypt. A new meeting was instantly called, predominantly attended by residents absent from the earlier meeting. Josh Allen addressed the group, advising repeal. This was done and the new document was sent to General Prentiss, who told the messenger, "I am glad to see them. The resolutions of secession would have caused your folks trouble; but now I hope all will be right."[4]

Logan did not take part in either proceeding, for he was not home. Circuit duties carried him away from Marion and out of Williamson County at the time of Fort Sumter's surrender. Marion was not the only town in Egypt that displayed pro-secession demonstrations, and no one in northern Illinois appeared very surprised about it. Governor Yates—keeping tabs on these activities—received several letters warning him of secessionists who plagued the region. Not in sync with the sentiments of the northern counties, Egypt had more in common with the border states that surrounded it. Those noncommitted states—Kentucky and Missouri—housed rivaling factions in their towns, citizens determined to fight for and against the United States.

Both extremes struck Logan as he rode through his circuit. Issued a quota to supply six volunteer regiments, Illinois quickly raised the equivalent of ten. Mass meetings of Union support were held in every town. But towns in Egypt expressed antithetical points of view. In April's fourth week, while attending court at Pinckneyville, Logan learned of a potential standoff between citizens and soldiers near Carbondale. On April 22 U.S. troops passed through in boxcars en route to Cairo, cheered on by the Unionists at Carbondale while secession sympathizers kept a wary eye on events, seemingly stationed at every street corner.[5]

General Prentiss dropped off a company of soldiers and two cannons at the bridge that spanned the Big Muddy River north of Carbondale, instigating the most partisan citizens of Jackson and Williamson counties to form an armed posse, declaring that "the men at the bridge must be whipped away." Logan quickly headed to Carbondale to put a stop to it. He met with several Marion men and convinced them to go back home. Isham Haynie, John Dougherty, and other prominent Egyptians also quelled the rabid crowd with speeches. The armed resistance dissipated; everyone returned home without incident. The Marion citizens cursed all the way back home from Carbondale, insisting that they could have cleared out the soldiers and cannons.[6]

Although he believed he had lent a hand in preventing a firestorm, Logan realized how difficult it would be to quell a mass uprising against the policies of a very unpopular president in the region. When he returned home to Marion he learned of the resolutions passed on the fifteenth and his father-in-law's role in them. Logan respected Captain Cunningham's opinions; he even sympathized with them, but he did not agree with them. And here was his quandary. Insomuch as he despised anything supporting secession, Logan was conflicted by a balancing animosity directed at the abolitionist sect that he felt was driving the Lincoln administration.[7]

Letters from associates supporting Logan's peace position came in, including one from fellow Illinois congressman, James Robinson, and one from William H. Green, who wrote Logan from Springfield. While Logan held tightly to a pacifist position, other congressmen—John McClernand in particular—were outwardly hawkish in their denunciations of the South. Although he had not spoken with him for quite a long time, Logan believed he and Senator Stephen Douglas remained of the same mindset. Logan and Douglas were not nearly as close as they were in 1858, when they campaigned together throughout the Ninth District. As Douglas groomed himself as a presidential candidate, he had softened some of the most partisan positions he and Logan once shared. Nonetheless, there appears to have been an understanding among Illinois Democrats—both national and state representatives and senators—to publicly express a unified position on the potential of war. Logan rode to Springfield late in April to observe a special session of the state legislature. It was also an opportunity for him to help solidify the position of the state Democrats.[8]

Logan entered Springfield on April 28 and soon realized that he held a minority position. Three days earlier Senator Douglas had delivered a rousing pro-Union speech to the General Assembly in Springfield. In that speech Douglas urged the prosecution of the war to suppress the rebellion. He was endorsing

President Lincoln's position—anathema to the most partisan of Democrats. Logan read Douglas's words and flew into a rage. Douglas was the most influential Democrat in the state, and he was espousing a position that was certain to sway other not-so-resolute legislators. Logan's anger exploded; he denounced Douglas within earshot of anyone who paid attention to his rants. He seethed that Douglas had "sold out the Democratic Party." So incensed was he at the address that when he bumped into Douglas on Springfield's streets during the last days of April, he refused to shake his hand. They ended up on the same train to Joliet—Douglas rode it to give another pro-Union speech while Logan was heading there to visit Sam Casey and other friends. Logan stewed at an apparent line in Douglas's Springfield address that characterized his current position on the crisis as unpatriotic. When a Douglas associate diplomatically attempted to persuade Logan to make a speech from the rear car platform at their Bloomington dinner stop, Logan retorted with a childish rant: "I'll be damned if I will. I'm a traitor and I will not speak."[9]

Choosing not to reconcile with Douglas, Logan returned to Marion during the first days of May, appalled at true acts of traitors in his new hometown. Marion remained a hotbed for secessionists. Logan saw "Notices to Organize" hung in and around the town. He was informed that the disloyal factions were disgruntled over the repeal of their resolutions of April 15, 1861. They met again on April 27 to put forth a motion to "seize the money in the hands of the sheriff to defray the expenses of arming and equipping the soldiers of the Southern Army." This time, cooler heads prevailed. The motion was voted down and the meeting broke up in disorder. Incensed at what citizens in his town had attempted, Logan told the parties involved that this motion, as well as the resolutions passed on April 15, were treasonous. For this, they would all be hanged. Instilled with more fear than brain power, the rabid partisans quickly tore down the signs to remove any vestige of treason. Satisfied that he saved his new neighbors from arrest, Logan returned to the law circuit in neighboring counties.[10]

On May 1 Douglas delivered perhaps his most memorable speech in support of the Union. Speaking to a large throng of legislators in Chicago's Assembly Hall, he denounced the secession of Southern states. "Every man must be for the United States or against it," insisted the senator. "There can be no neutrals in this war, only patriots and traitors." Logan read those words a few days later in a newspaper. Douglas had taken what Logan had considered a gray issue and broadcast it starkly in black and white. Was Logan's silent neutrality Douglas's inspiration? If the answer was "yes," then Douglas had brazenly challenged Logan to declare himself on the side of patriotism or of treason.[11]

Douglas's patriot-or-traitor speech failed to stir Logan from his public silence. But what he refused to say in public, he revealed in private. While attending court in Murphysboro on May 9, he wrote to a Quincy constituent. Still smarting over Douglas's address to the Illinois legislature, he bristled when the constituent accused him of conspiring to "put down" Judge Douglas. He denied the charge, stating, "The only crime that I am guilty of in the crisis I suppose is being consistent. I opposed war upon the south & invasion last winter as being certain disunion forever, I am still of the same opinion." He also noted that Douglas had shared the same belief back then. "Now he tells me that he is for capturing Richmond and prosecuting a war of subjugation if necessary to compel obedience," Logan complained, "I can not nor will not agree to it. As a question of Policy, it is very wrong."

Where Douglas was changed by the reality of Fort Sumter, Logan remained steadfast in his belief. The abolition movement haunted him; it remained the driving force that kept him allied with Southern sympathies. "I am no secessionist and have made bitter speeches against [it] here and elsewhere, tho it being common for every man to be called a rebel & traitor that does not sustain Lincoln and his policy," declared Logan. "The attempt now is being made to transfer the democracy to the tail end of an infamous abolition disunion party. I for one shall not be transferred . . ."[12]

Logan soon learned that his constituents "transferred" in opposite directions. Discordant philosophies prevailed, so unlike unified Union sentiments in New England. Neighbors, friends, and families now pitted themselves against each other in Egypt's small towns and farm regions. The effect of all of this struck Logan close to his heart. While he was attending the courts away from home, his family suffered the greatest calamity of the secession crisis. When two secessionists in the region began organizing a company of troops to join the Confederate army, Hybert Cunningham—Logan's youngest brother-in-law—cast his lot with them. Mary and the rest of Hybe's family pressured him not to go through with it, but their pleas fell upon deaf ears. Union support was beginning to prevail in Southern Illinois; the first Egyptian regiment was nearly completed while other state recruits headed to the southern tip of Illinois at a large Union training camp. On May 25, the rebel company claimed only thirty-five new volunteers and headed into Kentucky to report for Confederate duty. Private Hybert Cunningham left with them, choosing to bear arms against his country.[13]

His decision devastated his sister. Shortly after Hybert headed south, Mary lamented, "No one could tell what I would give to have him restored again to our once unbroken circle around the dear fire side at home; yet, alas. That can never be. War has separated us forever. I have no hope of again beholding him this side of eternity and I give him up as . . . dead and gone forever. Oh life! How full of sorrow." Overwhelmed by it all, she could not hide her feelings about President Lincoln and his cabinet. "The administration and his advisors have already begun their work of invasion," she seethed; "their arrogance and power have hurried them on in their progress. . . ." She wrote to her husband on May 25 that "one can not honestly and honorably or justly endorse the course of the president."[14]

For his part Logan studied the tide rippling across the nation. Union forces had entered western Virginia to seize the B&O Railroad from a small Confederate army holding control of it in Grafton. A large army was collecting in Washington that would inevitably march into Northern Virginia to battle a Confederate force threatening another railroad junction. The coastal regions of Virginia and North Carolina also showed activity with opposing armies destined to battle each other. Closer to home, 4,000 U.S. volunteers encamped in Logan's district at Cairo—the southern tip of Illinois, preparing to head southward.

Logan persistently remained mum on the issue, shunning the opportunity to air his views with the local press. He took note of the effects of secession, Sumter, and slavery on the citizens who had overwhelmingly landed him in office two years earlier. Although it was clear that there was a rabid pro-secession movement in Egypt, it was offset by strong fervor to suppress the rebellion. Logan no longer could sympathize with the South, for their citizens were preparing to kill U.S. soldiers in order to tear away from their country. As much as Logan despised the abolition movement—he coined it a "dis-Union Party"—he could not support the alternate extreme. He still sought the middle ground, attempting to support the preservation of the Union without any appearance of aligning with the abolitionists. But his silence painted him neutral—a position that Senator Douglas resoundingly declared was impossible to maintain.

Others agreed. Logan's silence was soon no longer deemed a neutral position. The rumor mill was up and running, grinding out reports that Logan was active in the April Marion resolutions, had tried to suppress the raising of Egypt's first volunteer regiment, had tried to tear down American flags, and, more recently, had helped raise the company that Hybert Cunningham joined. The latter rumor—like the others—had no basis in truth, for Logan was conducting business outside Williamson County when the Confederate company was swiftly raised and departed. "I know you will be accused of having something to do with this thing," Mary predicted to her husband on May 25, "but I thank God that you were not even here."[15]

But Logan's absence mattered not at all, for this rumor caught fire and spread swiftly to the most influential Illinoisans. One of Governor Yates's confidants in Marion wrote him on May 28, naming Yates and his father-in-law as two of several coconspirators who helped support and form the rebel force. "The company so organized departed rejoicing in their treacherous mission of blood," he insisted, "and the men above named are making efforts for another company." Logan said nothing publicly, and again his silence was interpreted as support for secession. In fact, members of the Confederate company admitted no involvement from Logan in their organization, but they too inferred from Logan's previous speeches sympathizing with the South that he still supported them and might lead them in battle against the North.[16]

Logan's discomfort escalated into the first week of June. He was shocked to learn of the sudden death of Stephen Douglas, whose health had been poor during the past year. He died in Chicago from throat and liver maladies on June 3. A day later, Logan's brother-in-law, Israel Blanchard, was arrested by orders of Brigadier General Benjamin M. Prentiss, who ran the Union soldier training camp in Cairo and was fed up with Dr. Blanchard's rebel rousing. Blanchard was escorted to Springfield.[17]

Close to the time Blanchard was arrested the authorities also nabbed James D. Pulley of Marion, a vociferous—most would say rabid—critic of the Lincoln administration. Logan had indicted him back in 1856 for a disturbance, but this time Pulley was charged with treason. "He is so mean and desperate that I cannot command language to describe him," wrote a U.S. authority keeping a close eye on his activities. "He hurrahs for Jeff. Davis publicly and dares any one to say a word for the Union." Pulley was one of two men who ran the postmaster out of Marion at the end of April. He was also suspected of escorting the Illinois Confederate company into Kentucky. Arrested in Carbondale, he joined Blanchard on a trip to Springfield.[18]

Logan had recently returned to Marion from his court duties. The town was walking a tightrope, flaunting its disdain for federal authority. After Douglas had delivered his pro-Union speech, the residents cut down his liberty pole with much ceremony. Most recently, on June 1, the Confederate flag waved over one of Charley Goodall's barbecues, east of town. The arrest of James D. Pulley in Carbondale the next day set the stage for another display against the government—one in which Logan would participate.

He had barely settled in when he received a warning that he was a target for capture. The warning came from a panicked Carbondale resident who witnessed

Pulley's arrest and rode eastward to Marion to warn Logan that a hostile group was coming up from Big Muddy Bridge to seize him and Josh Allen. It was an odd claim (the messenger may have been referring to U.S. troops coming to arrest him), but Logan later recalled that he was at his father-in-law's house when the man came in telling him that "a crowd of people" was on its way to burn the town and arrest the citizens. Logan decided to gather some locals to resist the attempt. Thirty men reported to Marion's public square that night, but when one asked Logan the whereabouts of Josh Allen, Logan replied, "I guess he is at home under the bed, Go and bring him out."

After Allen arrived in the square, Logan's impromptu company marched out to the old fairgrounds west of town, armed with more whiskey jugs than guns. The whiskey was gone by 10:00 P.M., so they fell back to town to replenish their supplies. Moving to a creek bridge southeast of Marion, Logan and his drunken volunteers formed small parallel lines of six men each, armed with clubs and bottles (the rest of the men collapsed near logs and stumps, unable to arise from their stupors). A driving rainstorm pelted them throughout the night. Another resident found them all the following morning fast asleep on a bed of water and covered with blankets of mud. Awakened and informed that no enemy was coming after all, Logan and Allen returned to Marion with their hungover recruits.[19]

Logan enhanced the camaraderie with his friends in Marion, but in doing so he unwittingly risked his reputation by potentially resisting the actions of the U.S. government in Southern Illinois. As it turned out, there was no planned advance upon Marion by either soldiers or a fanatical crowd. The night of armed watch was the first suspect action in which Logan truly participated. Newspapers never picked up on the story, but the next day another Marion meeting became infamous to the Union-loyal portions of Illinois. Josh Allen led this gathering, crafting more resolutions designed to denounce the formation of Brooks's company of Illinois rebels in the county and pledging their support for the Union. But the preamble of the resolutions denounced secession in a way to rankle the Unionists—by "placing it upon the same ground we have heretofore placed Abolitionists."

These resolutions ended up in an early June issue of the *Illinois State Journal*, under the unfortunate title of "The Traitors of Williamson County." The paper printed the name of seemingly every male Marion resident as signers of the document—ninety-two names in all, including Josh Allen. But Logan's name was nowhere to be found. He had left for Benton immediately after his night of unreported armed resistance. The *State Journal* quickly denounced the resolutions for the balancing act between secession and abolition in the preamble, ". . . the time having come when there can be no neutrals, is not treason, and levying war upon the Government the legitimate result of such a position." The editorial went on to blame John A. Logan and Josh Allen for teaching the residents that the neutral position was a just one.[20]

Here Logan was guilty by association, for this had been his philosophy. By the end of the second week of June, it was becoming apparent to him that his stolid silence had gone on far too long. Rumors swirled with greater intensity. Unfortunately for Logan, newspapers published in his district continued to suggest that his allegiance tilted to the secession's side. Centralia's *Egyptian Republic* left no room for guessing with an article in their June 13 issue. It reported that a captain stationed at a Big Muddy River bridge to protect the railroad structure from destruction by Illinois secessionists "told us that he did not think the people would keep quiet until LOGAN, the chief traitor among them was arrested. Said [Logan] was so smart that he covered his tracks and there would be nothing to get a hold of him by."[21]

Logan returned to Springfield during June's third week having yet to publicly declare himself as a patriot or traitor. In the state capital, Logan read, to his dismay, how detrimental his silence had been throughout Illinois. The *State Journal* ran a column on June 18, reporting on a pro-Union meeting held in Carbondale. "We . . . are glad to record all such meetings as this," stated the paper, "but the question frequently comes up, in the midst of these Union demonstrations, where is John A. Logan . . . Why does he never figure in these gatherings?" To emphasize the question further, the paper excerpted three other papers that reported on the same issue.[22]

This is where Logan learned that the greatest political mistake he had ever made was not leading his constituents in this time of peril. Most damaging was an excerpt from the *New York Herald*, whose Cairo correspondent named Logan, Captain Cunningham, Josh Allen, and brothers-in-law Israel Blanchard, Hybert Cunningham, and Curt Campbell as coconspirators in a plot to cleave a portion of Southern Illinois from the Union and "set up a separate State government, to be confederate with the other slaveholding states." Another excerpt included a series of resolutions passed by the Egyptian Home Guard, a company recruited near Logan's boyhood home. Their series of resolutions were formed against their representative—"The Hon. John A. Logan." They stated that they had previously been warm supporters of their congressman, but they considered his handling of the crisis to "call forth the indignation and censure of patriots and Union loving men." The Home Guard therefore resolved to request Logan's resignation.[23]

The power of the press had effectively conspired against Logan. Notwithstanding the false rumors about him, he well understood that this was his fault; he should have spoken out sooner. Determined to right his wrong, he sat down to make his first formal statement since February. He crafted a long letter to counter the accusations hurled against him throughout the spring season. For the first time he defended himself, not only denying, but also ridiculing the charges that he had aided the secession movement. Insisting that he had never uttered an expression of disloyalty to the government, he pointed out that no evidence of proof existed to substantiate any of the rumors about him. He also exposed the Egyptian Home Guard and its resolution as the creation of a newsman who opposed his point of view. He punctuated his final sentence and sent the letter to a St. Louis and Springfield newspaper for publication.

Logan pounced on the opportunity to publicly clarify his views the very next day. On June 19, while on the streets of Springfield, Logan and John A. McClernand met a mutual acquaintance walking with an officer whom neither had seen before. The man was a newly appointed colonel, placed in command of the Twenty-first Illinois. Though born in Ohio, he was considered one of Illinois' own, spending the past two years of his life in Galena near the northwest corner of the state. His presence was far from commanding; he was average looking and perhaps a bit disheveled with a slight 135-pound build covering a five-foot-eight-inch frame. The acquaintance introduced him to the congressmen and for the first time, Logan shook hands with Colonel Ulysses S. Grant.

Logan later described Grant as "looking very badly" that day. It was a fair assessment. Grant's pressing problem in June of 1861 was his new regiment. The Twenty-first Illinois was transitioning from three-month's state service to a three-year volunteer federal service. Colonel Grant was concerned that grumbling members of the unit would walk away from their duty. The time to muster the men into protracted service was just a few days away. The unit was already down to 600 members, and Grant feared he would not be able to retain half of them in the coming week. Their mutual friend asked Grant if Logan and McClernand could help him by speaking to his disaffected troops. Grant hesitated a moment. He had never met either of the congressmen before. He had heard much about Logan, but his opinion of him was based primarily on negative reports from Illinois' partisan newspapers. Grant admitted that his impressions of Logan "were those formed from reading denunciations of him." (No doubt he read the devastating article about Logan the previous day in the *Illinois State Journal*.) Grant fretted about Logan breaking his silence with an address to his men. "I had some doubt as to the effect a speech by Logan might have," remembered Grant about the moment; "but as he was with McClernand, whose sentiments on the all-absorbing questions of the day were well known, I gave my consent."[24]

With that, Logan and McClernand followed Grant to Camp Yates in the Springfield Fairgrounds. Officers and men gathered in front of the grandstand to hear the addresses. McClernand spoke first and after a fairly short performance, he introduced Logan to the troops. Grant paid very close attention to Logan's words; he was still concerned that Logan would harangue the North in his first public address since February. Logan rendered Grant's trepidation unnecessary. He began by lightheartedly teasing the men about returning home without fighting a battle, done so in a way to capture their attention rather than alienate them. From there, he seized the moment with a forceful and eloquent two-hour speech, one that worked him up so much that he needed to peel off his coat and handkerchief. "You never saw a man work harder in your life," remembered a mesmerized witness twenty-five years afterwards; "He related stories which made them laugh, and then he described a soldier's life in such beautiful language that one would think no other life had so many charms." His words exuded pure patriotism as he spilled his passion about preserving the Union to Grant's unruly regiment. His appeal penetrated the souls of the three-month troops; almost to a man they mustered in as three-year soldiers. An officer of the regiment rated it "a ringingly loyal speech."[25]

The most affected member of Grant's regiment was Grant himself. He credited Logan's impassioned address as the impetus for near-unanimous enlistment. "It breathed a loyalty and devotion to the Union," wrote Grant, "which inspired my men to such a point that they would have volunteered to remain in the army as long as an enemy of the country continued to bear arms against it." Logan downplayed his acclaimed performance: "Whether my speech was good or bad, it had the desired effect." He did not realize that he had wiped away a poor first impression from one of the most influential people on his subsequent career. No doubt Colonel Ulysses S. Grant offered his most sincere thanks to Logan as the two clasped hands that June afternoon. Logan left a new admirer at the campsite of the Twenty-first Illinois to oversee an invigorated regiment.[26]

Logan's political instincts proved perfect in timing his sentiments. "John Logan at Last Heard From" trumpeted the *State Journal* on June 20, crediting Logan for coming out as strongly as he did, while crediting itself for succeeding "in making Mr. Logan define his position."[27] The press provided Logan with a windfall. His impassioned letter of June 18 was published in the St. Louis *Missouri Republican* on June 20 and the *Illinois State Register* the following day. The letters were subsequently picked up as excerpts by other papers in the North.

Editorials responded with praise. In their eyes, Logan had reemerged as a staunch Union supporter.

The secession-sympathetic sectors of Southern Illinois surprisingly displayed no animosity to Logan when he returned a few days after his speech to Colonel Grant's regiment. Logan's position, although publicly stated, still had not satisfied the extreme political wings fluttering in Illinois. Most were now convinced that Logan was a Unionist and not a secessionist; however, no one was sure of his position about fighting a war to decide the issue. Logan's constituency had no idea that he had been plotting to raise a regiment of Southern Illinois soldiers to help suppress the rebellion.

After Hybert Cunningham and his rebel mates marched out of Marion to join the Confederacy, Logan had toiled behind the scenes to recall his wayward brother-in-law's enlistment. He recruited Curt Campbell, married to Mary and Hybert's sister, to use his influence to get Cunningham back to Illinois. When Campbell's attempt failed, Logan broached the topic of helping him to raise a Union regiment. Campbell refused, as did Captain Cunningham, who was solicited by John A. McClernand to help him raise a brigade out of Egypt. Both influential Marionites were too sympathetic to the South to dare lead men against it.[28] Campbell did help Logan in this endeavor by suggesting the name of John H. White, clerk for Williamson County. White would make a sound lieutenant colonel, insisted Campbell, and would be of great benefit to him. Logan used his own influence to convince his father-in-law that if he could not bear arms against the South, he could use his past Mexican War leadership and experience to help him raise troops out of Williamson and neighboring counties. Logan found a third source of aid in the form of George W. Goddard, the young and well-connected Williamson County circuit clerk.

Logan and his three recruits secreted themselves at John H. White's office in Marion. The quartet solemnly pledged each other their honor that they would stand by the Union. The four decided that if a prolonged war—one that extended beyond the three-month enlistments—was inevitable, Logan would complete his session of Congress and return to Egypt to raise a regiment of Union soldiers. He would command as colonel, John White would serve as lieutenant colonel, and Goddard would captain a company of the regiment. Cunningham would be deputized to run White's county clerk office and Goddard's circuit clerk office. They agreed to keep their plan secret, but they never revealed how they would obtain the commissions necessary to run the regiment.[29]

Logan received his notification to return to Washington to attend a special session of Congress called by President Lincoln concerning the rebellion. As hot and hazy weather closed out the last days of June, two friends, Isaac Clements and Ike Kelly, escorted Logan to the Carbondale railroad depot. There they chatted about the events swirling around them as they waited for Logan's eastbound train. Kelly asked Logan what he would do in Washington. "I'm going to do my utmost for peace," came Logan's reply. "I'm going to help quiet down the trouble, but I tell you, Ike, if we can not have peace I'll come home and go soldiering." As the train carried Logan away, Clements was struck by the word "soldiering;" it was the first time he had heard the word. He should have been more taken in by who delivered the odd verb—the same man who one month earlier was accused of organizing a force to aid the rebellion.[30]

Logan wrapped up business in Springfield before heading eastward. There he met up with George Rearden, a Cairo friend whom he had known for nearly a dozen years. The two discussed the war and Logan revealed to Rearden that he was heading to Washington, but when he returned he would do all that was necessary to help suppress the rebellion. Rearden was also struck by Logan's words: "I will raise a regiment, go into the war, and fight them, to the bitter end."[31]

Logan arrived in Washington on July 3, just in time for the initiation of the special session. As the legislators entered the congressional chambers, they could see the galleries sporting a martial look as blue-clad volunteer soldiers watched American democracy in action. "You have no idea [of] the excitement here," noted Logan, deducing the utter folly "for northern men to sacrifice themselves by standing out against the storm." Logan continued to spew venom at the antislavery movement in his private letters home. "Thus it seems that the devil's perverseness has seized upon these infernal abolitionists and they would rather see us in a revolution than to modify their fanatical notions," wrote Logan to his father-in-law. By July's second week Logan considered war a foregone conclusion. All attempts at compromise had failed and battles were inevitable. A campaign deep in western Virginia's hill country had been progressing for weeks while closer to Logan, Union troops crossed the Potomac and had encamped in Virginia. Everyone in the nation's capital was certain a battle in Virginia would develop before the end of the month.[32]

On July 15 Logan and several of his colleagues took advantage of a break in the session to visit the Union camps. The martial display chipped away at Logan's shell, continuing a process that had begun almost from the instant he arrived at the capital. He had been denying himself the opportunity to fulfill a desire that had grown too fast to hide any longer. He finally let his wife peek into his intentions. "I am and intend to vote for men and money to carry on the war as it appears that nothing but war will do both sides," he wrote to Mary the following day.

"I intend to give them a chance to preserve the Govt. if it can be done. I do not think it can," he continued. "I can not reproach myself that I was not willing for a trial."[33]

What he didn't tell his wife would have stunned her. Logan not only supported the prosecution of war, he wanted to shoulder a rifle and fight in it. He proved that the caucus he formed with Mary's father, Goddard, and White in Marion was not idle chatter. Logan was so serious about commanding a regiment that he took his notion to the top. Logan met with Abraham Lincoln at the White House. This was Logan's second visit with the president; the first was a hotel greeting in February. The two chatted briefly about the war. Logan quickly broached the topic of raising a regiment to lead in battle. Lincoln was lukewarm about his request, suggesting that as an effective orator, he could be more effective off the battlefield by swaying enough Democrats to support the war by legislative measures. The less-than-enthusiastic response from Lincoln failed to quell Logan's spirit. He wrote to Captain Cunningham on July 16, "I feel very much inclined to go into the army, not for the heart in the contest, but that if the Govt. is to be preserved, to help do it."[34]

Thirty miles west of Washington, Confederate forces had seized and controlled Manassas Junction, a vital crossroads for two rail lines that could feed troops and supplies into and away from Northern Virginia. It was no secret that U.S. troops, under the command of General Irvin McDowell, had begun to advance westward from the capital to battle them. Uneasy about the prospect of sitting out a one-battle war, Logan obtained permission to witness it. Accompanied by Congressman William Richardson, he called upon General Winfield Scott on July 16. Scott granted his request to head out as a special envoy.[35]

Ignorant about war, but excited to view a real battle, a gathering throng of Washington's citizens and government representatives followed the tail of a snaking U.S. Army attempting to negotiate the dusty roads that led them to Manassas Junction. Logan and a small cortege of government witnesses marched near the front of General McDowell's army. The permission granted him from General Scott guaranteed he would get a "front seat" view of the battle. The other Washingtonians would never see the outcome, but nevertheless would mark the occasion with grand picnics on the hills a few miles east of the railroad junction.

Logan's "uniform" consisted of the clothes of a congressman: a dark long coat with a tall black silk hat to top it off. Dressed in conspicuous and similar fashion, William Richardson and four other Illinois congressmen accompanied him. Together they rode horses alongside Colonel Israel Richardson's regiment as it slowly lurched westward in fits and starts as green soldiers tried to learn to march in unison. The troops bivouacked at Germantown on the night of July 17. Logan shared a campfire with the soldiers and chatted with them—all excited about the grand event perhaps a day away from them. The next morning all awoke early, ate a bacon and cornbread breakfast, called the rolls, and trudged westward.[36]

At a Virginia crossroads hamlet called Centreville, Logan followed behind soldiers from Michigan, New York, and Massachusetts. Suddenly, Logan could hear sporadic fire south of Centreville near Blackburn's Ford, one of several crossings of Bull Run—the dominant tributary of the region. As the Michigan troops rushed toward the sound of the skirmishing, all of the congressmen followed on horseback. It was Friday, July 18, 1861, a sweltering morning portending another typically hot Virginia summer day.

As they cleared the woods on high ground overlooking the ford, Logan could see the enemy force ahead of him. A Confederate battery crowned the height across Bull Run while Southern pickets posted themselves at intervals near the water. U.S. infantry and artillery briskly moved to positions in the woods and open regions on the Centreville side of the river. Two cannons under the command of Captain Romeyn Ayres opened fire upon the Confederates, and Logan observed the result. "No sooner does Ayres open fire on the enemy than he awakens a rebel hornet's nest," he noted. "Volley after volley of musketry shows that the Bull Run bottom fairly swarms with rebel troops, while another rebel battery, more to the rebel right, opens . . . a concentrated crossfire upon him." The war was technically three months old and had experienced battles in other regions of Virginia, but for Logan, it was all opening in front of his eyes at that very moment.[37]

Massachusetts and New York soldiers opened the fight by sparring with Virginians on the other side of Bull Run. The fight dragged on into the afternoon, neither side gaining any advantage as casualties mounted along the riverbanks near the ford. Discharging muskets and booming artillery rent the air, inundating it with sulfurous smoke. American citizens, who labored in the first weeks of spring as farmers, artisans, and city workers, now littered the battleground as lifeless soldiers. Wounded men screamed in pain, their tortured shrieks convincing their three-month comrades that nothing was glorious about war.

No man can be certain how he will react when he faces death for the first time in a battle, for when adrenaline kicks in, the response is to fight or flee. No doubt Logan witnessed the diverse reactions in the three-month volunteers fighting in front of him. But while scores of soldiers prayed to live long enough to return home and resume their peaceful civilian lives, Logan craved the opposite. What he witnessed at Blackburn's Ford neither disgusted nor frightened him. It invigorated him.

The knot of congressmen waited at the wood line off to the side of the road. Screaming artillery rounds crashed all around them. Logan, now dismounted, watched in contempt as a corporal walked by, leading five privates from the field—apparently without orders. Logan stepped up to one of the timid privates and barked out his first order of the war: "Give me your gun." The private complied; Logan took the weapon and rushed forward. Following in the heels of the charging Twelfth New York Infantry, he crouched into position and fired several rounds. Committing himself as a soldier, he spent most of the battle carrying off wounded soldiers, his face blackened by powder and his hands reddened by the blood of others. By the end of the afternoon, the action produced more than fifty dead and wounded soldiers on each side but no one gained a toehold on the opposite side of Bull Run. Logan retired with the Union troops toward Centreville.[38]

The other congressmen went back to the capital while Logan stayed with the troops the following day. He had participated in a skirmish that marked the prelude of a much larger battle that was certain to begin in the next two to three days. But Logan would not bear witness to this battle. While the U.S. troops remained in Centreville, Logan made his way back to Washington on July 20. Passing more than 30,000 blue-clad soldiers as he worked his way eastward, the skirmish at Blackburn's Ford consumed his thoughts. He could not erase from his mind all that he had seen and felt on the banks of Bull Run that day.

He went back to his room at Brown's Hotel, where he read a letter from Mary, who expressed her concern about his plan to observe the fighting in Virginia. He immediately wrote a response. "I see that you are alarmed about my going out to the battle at Manassas," he said. "You need not be. I have just returned from three miles this side which is Bulls Run, and was in the fight with a musket for 4 hours and came out without a scratch." He went on to describe the battle as he had observed it, recounting briefly his role in the contest. "I am not hurt," he assured her, "and can safely say that no man who saw me on the field will [ever] say that I wanted courage." He went on by expressing his trepidation that U.S. troops could be driven out of Virginia.[39]

Logan's concern was realized the day after he penned his letter. On Sunday, July 21, Logan witnessed an immense exodus of sightseers heading over the Potomac bridges into Virginia. Picnic lunches were at a premium, as were carriages, saddle horses, and wagons to transport the citizens and government officials to the scene of battle. By the afternoon, the streets were quiet, save for the low rumbling of distant cannon. War was treated like a holiday this hot summer Sabbath.

The holiday atmosphere disintegrated at nightfall. Early reports of Union success proved premature. People had been trickling back into town since 8:00

P.M. They were casual, for they returned before the battle's conclusion and had not witnessed what others in Virginia were enduring. As the clock ticked toward midnight, traffic over Long Bridge was heavier, swifter, and panic driven. Carriages and wagons trundled in—army vehicles intermixed with civilian ones. Soon the rumors they spread were verified by the telegraph. General McDowell's army had been routed at the Battle of Bull Run. Citizens and soldiers scrambled back into Washington overnight and into the following Monday. Angry senators and congressmen were incredulous that the United States had lost the battle. McDowell's army trickled back into the city throughout the day. Some regiments maintained a semblance of order; many did not. A driving rainstorm that day made the experience more sullen and miserable.[40]

Based on his warning in the last line of his July 20 letter to Mary, Logan sensed that the United States could lose this battle. But the degree of panic he witnessed must have surprised him. More stupefying were the tallies of casualties. It would take days to sort out factual reports from erroneous ones, but it was clear that more than 5,000 dead and wounded Northern and Southern soldiers littered the battlefield. The resounding Confederate victory assured their continued presence in northern Virginia and their direct threat to the U.S. capital. It also guaranteed a protracted war. Abraham Lincoln issued a new call for troops—three-year men instead of the previous three-month commitment. Logan could not resist the opportunity to lead some of the new recruits. He must fight; he must lead. His decision was sure to create turmoil in Egypt and within his own family. He thought of Mary and her fears.

Four days after the Union fiasco at Manassas, Logan penned another letter to Mary. He reported that the panic in Washington was abating and how the "Forward to Richmond" talk was seldom heard. "I think that Genl. Scott will hereafter be allowed to pursue his own course," he predicted. If so, it will be much better for the country. I want to say a great deal to you tho can not write it all and therefore will defer until we meet." But he could not hold all his thoughts before he reunited with her. "Now my dear wife I want to join the army," he told her. He promised her he would not make it official until he came home to discuss it with her, although he was sure she would consent when he explained his position to her. "I am desirous that our noble little daughter shall be known as the daughter of an honorable and brave man. The stain upon our family must be wiped out." Logan remained tormented about his irresolute actions of the previous spring. "It may be that I am somewhat responsible for this," he reasoned about the pro-secession perception that had plagued him, "I don't think so tho [it] may be and I ought to correct it."[41]

Obviously, his concern about public perception was but one of several reasons that weighed into Logan's ultimate decision. He could not suppress his strong pro-Union sentiments, nor could he deny his passion for war. Clearly not a factor in his reasoning was abolition. Logan's views on slavery may have been changing, but in the summer of 1861 he continued to throw gibes at the abolitionists. He was still "Dirty Work" Logan, but he suppressed most concerns about his sectional proclivities.

Logan scrambled to complete his business in Congress before returning to Southern Illinois. Seeking all means necessary for peace, Logan's votes supported efforts at negotiating a compromise rather than fighting for the result. He also made clear his intentions to return home to raise a regiment, writing to several contacts in Illinois to help raise companies, apparently unconcerned about "double promises" made for potential future officers within the ranks. He apparently assured both John H. White and Isham Haynie that they would be the lieutenant colonel of his regiment. Other friends, such as Doff Ozburn, George Goddard, and George Rearden were promised captaincies. (The latter position had ten openings, the former only one.) President Lincoln granted Logan the sole command he sought. On August 11, he was commissioned a colonel of volunteers. He was still officially a U.S. congressman, but no longer would he be wearing a silk top hat on the battlefield.[42]

Less than a week after receiving his commission, Logan boarded a train and rode back home. He had sent word back to John White and his other associates in Egypt to advertise a speech he would deliver in Marion. Logan had already planned to utilize his greatest known asset—the stump speech—as a tool to garner recruits into his new regiment. Posters were printed announcing the speech and word spread throughout Egypt of Logan's planned appearance. The event was scheduled for August 18, but he missed a connection and did not arrive until early the following morning, leaving a raucous and expectant crowd of nearly 4,000 citizens shouting his name in the center of town. A brawl broke out, prompting the sheriff of Williamson County to disperse the throng, telling them to come back the following day.[43]

This time Logan did not disappoint. He was back in Marion by the late morning of August 19. The day sweltered in a typical summertime heat wave. The boisterous throng had returned to the town square; many had been there for hours. "The very crowd was enough to alarm one; they were so excited—seemingly on the verge of violent demonstration," recalled Mary. A witness in the square estimated 2,000 people surrounding him, "not so much to hear him as in the expectation of a row." Logan warned Mary not to intermix with the crowd for her own safety, but she was afraid that his message might stir the most rabid secessionists to resort to violence. Leaving his wife behind, Logan made his way through the unpredictable mass of citizens into Marion's public square.[44]

Now in the middle of the throng, Logan mounted a wagon, waved a greeting to his constituents, and began to speak. His booming voice, well trained by frequent stump speeches, served him well here, each word thrown from his lips energized with passion and conviction. Logan's message quieted the crowd almost immediately. His audience enraptured, he used that wagon as his rostrum. He spoke for two hours that hot afternoon, a slice of time that the people of Southern Illinois remembered for years. He began by invoking the principles fought for by the patriots of the American Revolution. He detailed the importance of the Union, and stressed the consequence of chaos if the Union was dissolved, with liberty replaced by anarchy. He gesticulated with every sentence uttered by his sonorous voice, underscoring his earnestness. Logan sensed that he conquered his audience in the first minutes of his address; those that were disappointed were neutralized enough to protest in silence. No longer fearing a riot, he emphasized his message with no trepidation.[45]

He closed his speech that afternoon choosing words reminiscent of the theme presented by Stephen Douglas a month before his untimely death. That was a speech Logan hated so much that he ended his friendship with the esteemed senator, but now he had come around to realize that Douglas had been right. Perhaps in tribute, Logan repeated a few of Douglas's phrases verbatim at his Marion pulpit:

> The time must come when a man must be for or against his country, not for or against his state. How long could one state stand up against another, or two or three states against others? The Union, once dissolved, we should have innumerable confederacies and rebellions. I, for one, shall stand or fall for this Union, and shall this day enroll for the war. I want as many of you as will to come with me. If you say "No," and see your best interests and the welfare of your homes and children in another direction, may God protect you.[46]

A spectator at many of Logan's addresses both previous and subsequent to the Marion performance rated his presentation, "The most powerful speech I ever heard John make." Another considered it "the most stirringly loyal speeches of his life." Some could not help the emotion they felt; Logan's words made their eyes swim in tears. "I'm blessed if he hadn't nearly every man in the square crying before he got half through," insisted one who was there. He must have been exaggerating, as was Mary who concurred with him: "There was scarcely a dry eye in the whole crowd."[47]

The speech was inspiring, but Mary left no room for chance. By a previous arrangement, she convinced an old fifer to attend the event, the same man who fifed for Logan's regiment in the Mexican War. A drummer from the same regiment also stepped forward with his instrument. Their martial cadence added to the excitement and emotion of the experience. Logan jumped down from the wagon. He was now one with his crowd; scores of men of all ages and sizes stepped forward to enlist. People considered pure rebels, like Dan Pulley and Sol Mooninghan, enlisted for the preservation of the Union. Jimmy McKeegan, one of the most threatening-appearing participants throughout the speech, had stood there for hours with a hod full of brick hoisted upon his shoulder. Consumed by patriotism, McKeegan threw the bricks into the street and shouted, "I'm with you, John." By the end of the afternoon, more than a hundred new recruits were with Logan.[48]

Eradicating all questions about his loyalty, Logan stumped Egypt to garner recruits for his regiment. He cut a path through his district like a patriotic hurricane. As he gathered momentum and support, his Union position cost him several members of his family. His brother Thomas, a lifelong companion, opposed him in the most overt way—by toiling to raise another company of Illinois Confederates. His rebel recruits never materialized into a company, but their boisterous displays under the Confederate flag raised eyebrows in the region. John A. Logan tried to recruit his brother Bill to captain a company. Bill refused, choosing to remain another Logan critic of the war.[49]

Most devastating to Logan was his mother's rejection. Mother Logan embraced her birth and heritage, and could not stand to have anyone in her family hold any animosity toward the South. Logan rode to Murphysboro late in August to visit her at the Logan House. She blocked his path at the doorstep. "Go away from my house, John Logan," she coldly upbraided him, "I never want to see your face." Heartbroken, he turned around and headed back to his recruiting mission, determined to reconcile with her at a future time. But she was equally determined never to speak with him again.[50]

Logan's youngest brother, James, was the only sibling to openly support him by helping to recruit a company of volunteers from Jackson and Perry counties. Logan's men, decked out in uniforms made of red-and-white-striped bed ticking, collected at the public square in Murphysboro. From there they marched out in unsynchronized steps—green soldiers through and through—past the Logan House. Mary Logan and Annie Logan Blanchard watched the display from the upstairs window of the brick house as Colonel Logan—Mary's husband and Annie's brother—led his men to battle the secessionists.[51]

Annie Blanchard was notorious in Murphysboro for her uneven temperament. Logan had professionally defended her husband during his legal troubles in the late 1850s, but this did not mitigate Annie's anger at seeing him lead troops in a cause she abhorred. Overcome with rage, she shouted down to him, "Damn you, I hope you will be killed before you get to Cairo." Mary was stunned that a sister could yell such a thing to a brother, let alone *her* husband. Spurred to defend her spouse, Mary likely surprised herself as she struck Annie a blow. Annie retaliated—she never could back down from a confrontation—and within seconds Mrs. Logan and Mrs. Blanchard waged their own battle—complete with punching, scratching, and hair-pulling. Mary ended the fight by picking up a chair and smacking her sister-in-law over the head with it. Dazed and defeated, Annie retreated. The fisticuffs had ended, but her open opposition to her brother had just begun.[52]

Logan's failure at uniting his family was offset by his tremendous effort to recruit patriots among his constituents. The result was astounding, and could not escape the notice of the Illinois press, which kept a close eye on Egypt's activities. As August waned to September, the *Crawford Bulletin* reported that within the Ninth Congressional District, "there has been a complete revolution among the people on the war question. Hon. John A. Logan, Congressman from that district, has been appointed Colonel, and has his regiment about ready to take the field. Many who a few days ago were of the compromise stamp, are now enthusiastic for the war." The paper indicated that all looked to Logan for leadership. "Logan declared their intention is to fight, and calls upon all Democrats to rally around the old flag, and thwart them in their diabolical efforts to destroy the Government."[53]

Logan took his men to Jacksonville in Central Illinois, at a temporary training ground dubbed "Camp Dunlop." There recruits from other regions of Illinois coalesced into the embryonic state of a regiment. The volunteers were soldiers in name only at Camp Dunlop. With no uniforms or firearms, the sons of farmers and small-town merchants slept in the open, practiced rudimentary drills, and underwent physical examinations. Early in September, Logan and his soldiers entrained at the railroad depot. Their destination was Cairo, where they disembarked and settled in Camp McClernand in the lowland at the southern end of town.

Although Logan considered himself a natural leader, his officer skills were as raw as the soldiering skills of his men. Logan found that he was too familiar with the young men he commanded. For example, his recruits regularly addressed him as "John" rather than "Colonel." In order to clear the barriers of discipline and protocol, he knew it was essential to be versed and confident in regimental leadership. His Mexican War experience—now nearly fifteen years past—was generally useless, for he was only a company officer back then. Forced to study the ubiquitous manual of army training, Logan and his fellow regimental and company officers devoured page after page of *Hardee's Tactics*, ironically a text authored by an army officer who had recently joined the Confederacy. Its information was all new to Logan. Perhaps too proud to exhibit his neophytic training abilities, he turned them over to his second-in-command, Lieutenant Colonel John H. White, Logan's former Marion neighbor who helped hash out the plan to organize the regiment. White's assistance freed up what little time Logan had to handle the piles of paperwork that confronted him.[54]

Cairo sat on a crooked V-shaped jut of land at the confluence of the Mississippi and Ohio Rivers. Although railroad systems would eventually rob Cairo of great-city status, water transportation in 1861 was vital for transporting men and supplies into contested military theaters. Major General George McClellan, commanding the Department of the Ohio, recognized Cairo's strategic importance back in May and ordered the mass concentration of U.S. troops there. By the time Logan and his men settled in their camp in the late-summer season, Cairo's original population of 2,200 swelled to treble that number with the influx of blue-clad soldiers. Thousands of them were Logan's constituents. Fellow Southern Illinois congressman John McClernand was already there when Logan detrained. Although he was his political peer, by rank, McClernand was Logan's superior. Commissioned a brigadier general, McClernand was in charge of four Illinois regiments, including Logan's Thirty-first Illinois. Across the Ohio from Cairo, an additional Illinois regiment encamped on Kentucky's northern rim. Four additional Illinois regiments occupied Bird's Point, Missouri, directly across the Mississippi from Cairo.[55]

The entire U.S. force constituted a small army, whose commander—a new general—arrived in Cairo on September 2. The commanding general of the military district of Southeastern Missouri was charged with the daunting task of controlling southeastern Missouri, southern Illinois, western Kentucky, and Tennessee. Logan recognized him immediately; it was Ulysses S. Grant.[56]

Grant headquartered himself at the St. Charles Hotel on the levee and immediately went to work. Ordered to gain a toehold in the neutral state of Kentucky, he immediately plotted to take Columbus, a Kentucky city on the eastern bank of the Mississippi eighteen miles below Cairo. Before he could put his plan in motion, a Confederate force, under the command of General Leonidis Polk—

an Episcopal bishop—seized the river town, and in so doing, captured the ire of Kentuckians who labeled the occupation an "invasion." Legislators in Frankfort, the capital of Kentucky, had the U.S. flag raised over the state capitol and re-solved that "the invaders must be expelled."[57]

Grant quickly worked to prevent other Confederate occupations of key Kentucky cities. He sent out detachments to occupy Paducah, a city at the mouth of the Tennessee River. Grant kept a line of continual correspondence with his superior officer, Major General John C. Fremont, stationed at St. Louis. To sup-port Fremont's detachments and drive Confederates from eastern Missouri, Grant agreed to send out several small infantry details into that state to seize goods and supplies he believed were en route to Southern forces.[58]

Logan's regiment was officially mustered in to service on September 18, 1861. It was designated the Thirty-first Illinois Volunteer Infantry, a mostly Egyptian unit, consisting of ten companies of recruits from Logan's congres-sional district. Two companies fielded men from northern Illinois and beyond. In addition to the infantry regiment, Logan was authorized to raise a company of cavalry. This he did, mustering them in at approximately the same time. The colonel made a speech after the flag was presented to the Thirty-first after the official muster. Highlighting the importance of the Union and the expected re-gion in which the regiment would fight, Logan stirred his men with an address teeming with resolute patriotism. He made one statement that rose above all: "Should the free navigation of the Mississippi River be obstructed by force, the men of the West will hew their way to the Gulf with their swords." Logan's adamant promise was captured by the press and reproduced throughout the North. "His speech," penned an officer several years later, "will never be forgot-ten so long as the history of this war is read." Logan's words of September 18 would find their way into Civil War literature right into the twenty-first century.[59]

Familiar faces met Logan's gaze daily at camp. John H. White took his role as lieutenant colonel of the regiment. Doff Ozburn served as the quartermaster. He was familiar with scores of company recruits, many who served as officers. Conspicuous among them was Captain Edwin S. McCook of Company E. Logan had known Edwin's father, Daniel, who had suffered the tragedy of witnessing the death of his seventeen-year-old son, Charley, at the Battle of Bull Run (Daniel had served there as a Union Army nurse). Edwin and his six remaining brothers joined their father as volunteers. Edwin's uncle, John, and his five sons also donned blue uniforms. In all, there were fifteen "Fighting McCooks"—nine from Daniel's family and six from his brother's. No other family in the United States could top the McCook claim for patriotism.[60]

Not present at the camp was Mary Logan. She had pleaded with her husband to join him but Logan insisted that she and Dollie stay home. He spouted off several reasons for her not to come, including the belief that other members of his unit would insist that their wives join them. Chief among Logan's concerns was his fear that Mary and Dollie would contract an illness that spread through his regiment or from those in neighboring camps. The death of Logan's firstborn child still haunted him; he would insist on all precautions to keep from losing his daughter. Mary had insisted that he write to her every Wednesday and Sunday at the minimum, but the overwhelming responsibilities of converting nearly 1,000 men and boys into soldiers forced Logan to break that agreement. He sent his first letter to her nearly ten days after he stepped off the train at Cairo. He promised to steal away to see her as soon as possible, and also suggested that he would work out an arrangement for her to come down and stay in a hotel when he freed himself from the burdensome training of his regiment.[61]

None of that satisfied Mary. Logan had yet to learn of his wife's brawl with his unstable sister in the upper floor of the Logan House, but Mary made sure that he was aware of the difficulties of remaining at home, of the open bitterness expressed by anyone within earshot of her. She wrote her husband late in September, pleading once again to join him at Cairo. She promised to keep herself and Dollie hidden from his command—"entirely from the society of men or any man with you"—assuring him that he should "have no fear as to the effect upon our health." This adamant stance was rooted in an issue she knew her husband did not want to face. She revealed that "the unnatural and piercing feelings our families feel about you being in the service" made it difficult to live near them. "I can trace the foundation of their feelings," she wrote, reminding him how strongly he had spoken against the war earlier in the year. "They will never feel right the fact of your having to join the Republicans under Lincoln's administration to fight the South." Perhaps in response to the heartfelt letter, Logan consented to have Mary join him. She and Dollie did so later in September.[62]

He had witnessed the effect of war on his family, his neighbors, and on much of the populace in his congressional district. Still, Logan—speaking for himself and his fellow soldiers stationed at Cairo—was forced to admit, "The strength of the feeling in the South and with the South, we didn't appreciate in the beginning." Dauntless, the colonel brushed off any trepidation he felt about the issue. He realized that he was part of an army destined and determined to advance into the neutral "Border States" to perch itself into position to invade the South. More Southern supplies were sure to be taken—not to oppress the citizenry, but to prevent it from fueling Confederate armies. Southern cities were marked as destination points to place Union armies in the best positions to control the Mississippi River Valley and the western theater of operations. These measures were necessary to assure the preservation of the Union.[63]

Early in November Logan learned that he would be penetrating into Missouri as part of the largest attacking force to leave Cairo to date. General Grant received instructions to drive the rebels to Arkansas and to demonstrate against Columbus. Accordingly, he sent out two expedition forces into the border state to clear it of its Southern occupiers. Grant would take his remaining force, consisting of two brigades of slightly more than 3,000 men, on a mission to threaten Columbus from the opposite shore of the Mississippi.

As one of the four regiments in General McClernand's brigade, the Thirty-first Illinois would be joining Grant. Logan learned that the destination was Belmont, a small hamlet of fields and a few houses on the Missouri side of the Mississippi. Grant knew the town was occupied by a small Confederate force. Destroying that army would not only remove a threat from the Mississippi River, but would also pressure General Polk and perhaps force him to remove his army from Columbus.

The Belmont expedition would accomplish a third objective—it would create activity for the Cairo soldiers who had remained untested in their camps for two months. During the night of November 6, Grant's force boarded four transports docked at the Cairo levee. Logan and the Thirty-first stepped aboard the *Aleck Scott*, a paddle-wheel riverboat that a few years earlier had been worked upon by Samuel Clemens, prior to changing his name to Mark Twain. Two gunboats, the *Lexington* and the *Tyler*, advanced ahead of the steamers to protect them and to mask Grant's landing. At Columbus, Polk had taken full advantage of the towering Kentucky bluffs looming above the Mississippi by planting 154 cannons on them. Early on the morning of November 7, Grant's transports completed a nine-mile journey and moored on the Missouri shore at Hunter's Farm, a little more than three miles above Belmont and tucked safely around the bend of the river, out of the view of the Confederate artillerists on the Columbus bluffs. The two-gunboat convoy then headed down the river to engage Polk's batteries and divert his attention away from Grant's land assault.

Eight A.M. passed. Indian summer basked the region with warmth as well as color. Half an hour later, McClernand's brigade was on the march down a farm lane surrounded by harvested cornfields. At the intersection of the lane and the road leading north to Bird's Point, McClernand deployed his men from a packed marching column into a line of battle. Logan complied, converting his men from approximately 140 four-man rows into a double line of troops—more than 200 men in each line—with two of his ten companies advanced forward across a slough. Lieutenant Colonel White commanded the two companies of skirmishers; Logan sent him out to draw fire from the hidden enemy force in the woods. This was a textbook procedure, likely practiced several times at the regiment and brigade level at Cairo. Not surprisingly, the tactic did not appear so well rehearsed for these raw soldiers in their first battle. Logan's men found themselves clustered in one portion of the line and spread out well beyond regulation distance in another. Still, the jagged double column must have impressed all who partook in the advance for it extended nearly three quarters of a mile from end to end.

The ribbon of blue swept in eastward toward Belmont, the boat landing one mile away from them. Into the woods and over the dry slough they marched, the cadenced steps of the soldiers marked by the crunching of dried leaves underfoot. Initially, Logan rode in front of his line, somehow trotting his horse slightly to the right, which irritated the colonel of the Twenty-seventh Illinois, pompous Kentuckian Napoleon B. Buford. Colonel Buford rode up alongside Logan and rebuked him, "Colonel Logan: remember, if you please, that *I* have the position of honor!" Without turning his head to face Buford, Logan gruffly retorted, "I don't care a damn where I am, so long as I get into this fight!"[64]

Crackling musket fire from Arkansas and Tennessee soldiers announced that indeed Logan was getting into the fight. Without orders to do so, the two Union regiments marching on the left of the Thirty-first Illinois maneuvered behind them and shifted to the south (right) flank of the line. This repositioning placed Logan and his regiment on the far left, anchoring the northern sector of Grant's advance. Logan's skirmishers attracted heated counterfire emanating from the defoliating trees in front of them. He ordered out a third company to assist them, but then called back all three companies to his main line, determined to head his men into the Confederate line in united strength.

Near noon General Pillow's Confederates struck Grant's advancing troops. The Thirteenth Arkansas Infantry planted themselves in front of him and the Twelfth Tennessee harassed his left flank. "The enemy opened a heavy fire on my whole line," Logan reported. Within minutes soldiers dropped to his left and right; two fell dead and several wounded. With woods surrounding him, Logan countered with instructions for his men to take cover from trees, logs, and underbrush—"Indian fashion," as defined by a member of his regiment. When not loading and firing, the Thirty-first Illinois flattened themselves upon the ground. Colonel Logan and Lieutenant Colonel White continued to ride up and down the lines, assuring discipline in the ranks. White claimed, "I am satisfied that over a thousand balls passed within a foot of me during the day."[65]

Grant put a temporary halt to Logan's aggressive enthusiasm. He ordered him to cease firing to conserve ammunition. The Southerners continued to fire, their bullets ripping through the brown, dried leaves that tiled the battlefield. But the bullets also found bodies: Logan lost another twenty men in this prostrate position. To counter the pressure on his flank, Logan wisely shifted his regiment to the left. The resistance slackened considerably, for the Southerners had run out of ammunition and began to retreat toward their camps near the riverbank. McClernand sent orders to his entire brigade to pursue.

Still holding the right of the Union line, Logan attacked the now-depleted enemy force in front of him. The Thirty-first Illinois steamrolled over the Twelfth Tennessee, and then smashed into the Thirteenth Arkansas, inflicting scores of casualties upon the Razorbacks. Throughout the offensive, Logan saw to the needs of other units as well as those of his regiment. He had detached a company to lend support to four cannons that had rolled past him. When an aide to the battery found Logan and informed him that the company had disappeared from their support, Logan personally rectified the situation. He found the wayward company and led it to the cannons. According to the lieutenant in charge of the battery, Logan "exprest himself not in polite language commanding them not to leave me again."[66]

After a brief respite to reform battle lines, Logan participated in what he thought would be the final assault of the battle, which drove the Confederates from their riverside camps. Logan claimed that his men captured the Confederate flag waving over their camp, but was unable able to keep the evidence to prove it because the Illinois captain who cut it down from the pole fell wounded. A member of the Seventh Iowa took the prized trophy and retained it. The Thirty-first Illinois did seize and retain a Confederate cannon, one of four that fell into Union hands. The remainder of the Southern force fled toward the river.[67]

It appeared that this battle was over—at least it did to McClernand who took the opportunity to convert instantly to a politician to make a victory speech. He later downplayed his harangue, claiming, "I gave the word for 'Three cheers for the Union', to which the brave men around me responded with the most enthusiastic applause." Others noted that McClernand did more. He brought a band forward into the center of the captured camp. Near the flagpole—now adorned with an American flag—the band struck up spirited renditions of "Yankee Doodle," "The Star Spangled Banner," and even a version of "Dixie." McClernand then delivered what one called "a spread-eagle speech." Others joined in delivering their own unpolished speeches and cheered themselves hoarse. Those not speaking and cheering were engaged in ransacking what had not been set to the torch, gathering up souvenirs of their first victory.[68]

Grant appeared to be the only one who kept his wits about him at this moment. His medical director soon pointed out that Pillow had not given up—far from it. Looking toward the river, Grant spied two transports packed with Southern soldiers crossing to the Missouri shore. He immediately ordered the Confederate camp and all of its baggage to be set afire. This was done quickly, under a canopy of raining artillery fire from those ominous batteries ensconced on the Kentucky bluffs near Columbus. The soldiers began to panic, fearing that they were about to be cut off from the paths leading back to their transports. "We are surrounded," they cried with utter discouragement.[69]

Their fears were realized in minutes. A Louisiana regiment circled in from the north, seized the only road leading out of Belmont and faced eastward toward the Union troops that would be forced to break out. Coming to the aid of the Confederate regiment were three more, hustling southward through the woods north of the road. If they reached their position before Grant's men, they would have him blocked directly and by flank, a deadly combination. "I announced that we had cut our way in and could cut our way out just as well," remembered Grant in revealing his solution to the predicament. "It seemed a new revelation to officers and soldiers."[70]

Several hundred yards east of this building Confederate stopgap, McClernand ordered his brigade onto the road. He placed the Thirty-first Illinois at the head of the potential breakout column, rode up to Logan and ordered him and his regiment to "cut their way through them." Aiding him would be Colonel Ezra Taylor's battery, the same four cannons and Chicago artillerists Logan supported late in the morning. "I must confess that I thought it a pretty hard task," he admitted, "though I felt complimented in getting the job, inasmuch as I was outranked by every colonel on the field."[71]

Obviously, McClernand trusted Logan's leadership more than he did that of those who outranked him, and for Logan's part, he did not disappoint. Up to this point Logan's superiors, peers, and subordinates had watched a competent colonel commanding a regiment on the offensive. For the rest of the afternoon they would witness, in its embryonic state, the hallmark of Logan's leadership— an inspirational commander who rose above the crash and commotion of battle to carry men through panic and despair.

Logan grabbed his regimental flag, stuck it in Captain Edwin McCook's hands, and bellowed to him to "carry it to the head of the column, and die with it in [your] hands." Positioning the battery on an elevation to cover an enemy flanking assault against his troops, he ordered his infantry forward, to follow him and the flag-bearing McCook. Logan led the breakout, riding in front of the flag-bearer. The artillery cut an opening through the blockade of Southern troops to give the infantry a chance to pass through.

Conspicuous at the helm of his regiment, Logan quickly captured the attention of the Confederates, many who directed their fire at him. A bursting shell sent shrapnel into his horse, and the animal crumpled beneath him. Logan extricated himself from his disabled mount, and survived a second close call when Confederate lead shattered the pistol holstered to his hip, cutting his belt away in the process. Still, he advanced, showing no effect of the near-death experiences to the men under his command. "Logan's personal presence cheered us on there," raved one of the cannoneers. Even his opponents grudgingly praised the performance playing out in front of them; an Arkansas soldier confessed that Logan and his men attacked "in good order, which was done, well done. Their bravery alone accomplished the feat."[72]

With Logan at the helm, the Thirty-first Illinois spearheaded the breakthrough with great success, a relief to Grant. Following McCook (who Logan claimed "was as cool as an icebox during the whole engagement"), the Thirty-first Illinois threw back the Louisiana regiment in front of them and whizzed by the Confederate regiments before they could plant themselves staunchly in the woods north of the column to enfilade them. Logan never realized who opposed him at that point, for racing through the woods to aid the Louisiana soldiers was the Fifteenth Tennessee infantry. Within that regiment marched the unit partially raised in Williamson County, Illinois. One of the company officers was Lieutenant Hybert Cunningham, Logan's wayward brother-in-law, determined to aid in the destruction of Grant's entire force.

The Confederates would be sorely disappointed, although they would be rewarded with more than 100 wounded Union soldiers Grant had to leave behind. Logan successfully recaptured some of the wounded bluecoats and placed them in a mule-driven wagon to cart them to Hunter's Landing. The Thirty-first charged through essentially unmolested, passing back through the woods and into the open cornfields, where sparse brown stalks stood as silent spectators to the Battle of Belmont.[73]

Now at Hunter's Farm, the Confederates had begun to harass Grant's rearward troops. Both Grant and Logan were conspicuous, exhorting in vain to rally troops around Taylor's Battery in a cornfield. But the troops sped by; their destination was the transports and neither Grant nor Logan could stop them. Soldiers discarded their weapons to rid themselves of an eleven-pound encumbrance.

Others added weight to their retreat by carrying wounded comrades. Logan turned his attention to the transports moored at Hunter's Landing. Men jumped aboard unimpeded, but the battery cannons proved to be problematic. A panicked captain of the steamer made matters worse by failing to keep his craft still while the men attempted to load the cannons on board. Disgusted with the captain, Logan stepped up to him, stuck the barrel of a borrowed pistol to the man's ear, and threatened to shoot him if the vessel was not stilled. The captain obeyed and the guns were safely aboard when the transport pulled away and entered the middle of the river. Logan's regiment was short 18 men who were left behind. Of more than 600 men he led into the five-hour battle, 10 were killed outright and 63 more were wounded (8 of those eventually died due to their injuries). Every officer, it seemed, had lost his horse; Lieutenant Colonel White claimed that two animals were shot from under him. Logan's 90 casualties in the Thirty-first Illinois were emblematic of Grant's entire force. Of the 3,000 U.S. forces engaged at Belmont, nearly 20 percent (600 men) fell dead, wounded, or captured.[74]

"The Victory or Defeat I will leave for the papers to decide," wrote Doff Ozburn after the battle. Newspapers from both sides claimed a victory for the battle, using evidence to support each declaration. Logan defiantly scoffed at Confederate boasts: "If this were a Confederate victory, there could scarcely be too many of them." The same could be offered up by the Confederates about the Union army, although Logan maintained that the battle steeled the green troops for combat. "It inspired confidence in their own abilities as soldiers, as well as in the skill of their officers," he wrote. "It taught a lesson concerning the value of discipline which our men remembered and repeated to others upon almost every subsequent battle-field."[75]

Logan received accolades from his subordinates, peers, and superiors. "We have got the best Regt. in the service and the best Col.," announced an obviously biased member of the Thirty-first Illinois. General McClernand also praised Logan for his "admirable tactics" and his ability to inspire his men "with kindred ardor." While McClernand was bombastic in his written reports and in his manner, Grant was his antithesis. At Cairo the reserved commanding general walked up to Logan after some time had lapsed after the battle. "Colonel, you handle your men well," Grant said to Logan—perhaps the most outward praise one would expect from him. "Were you educated at a military school?" Logan answered "no," and then remarked that he was a lawyer. "I am very sorry for that," responded Grant to end the conversation, and then he walked away.[76]

Logan remained pained about leaving the dead and wounded behind on a field that the Union could not hold. Under a flag of truce, an unarmed Colonel

Logan participated in burial detail on the battlefield the following day. Gazing upon mangled bodies began to harden him to the realities of war, but his most frustrating experience of the day occurred when an old Missouri farmer of the area—whose slaves fled his farm to join the Yankees—confronted Logan, calling him a "nigger thief," among other things. A witness to the confrontation saw Logan's rage build: "But, under a flag of truce and unarmed, all the Colonel could do was to take it; but his eyes flashed, and I felt sure that if he ever met that old farmer again under different conditions he would repay him with interest for the abuse."[77]

Logan returned to Cairo and greeted Mary there. As his men settled in at Camp McClernand, Logan sought to rectify a critical problem he discovered in the battle. In his official report of the battle written on November 11, Logan stated, "Many of the guns of my command choked and burst while in battle." Frustrated that he could not procure decent arms in Illinois, Logan decided to fix his problem by heading back to Washington. This he did early in December, accompanied by fellow Congressman Philip Fouke, himself the colonel of the Thirtieth Illinois Infantry. While in the capital Logan attended sessions of Congress, but he realized that he would have to decide between representing his district and fighting the war. He wrote to Mary, revealing to her where his loyalties lay, "To be candid with you, I had rather fight anyhow now. . . . Only for you and 'Dollie' do I want to live. I have no other friends outside my Regiment and with them I shall cast my fortune, either death or glory shall be mine."[78]

Logan and Fouke rode the rails to New York; they then returned to Washington to complete the mission to arm their men. Succeeding in getting guarantees for a timely shipment to Cairo, Logan stopped at the White House for a long visit with President Lincoln. He returned to Camp McClernand on January 23. Logan slept alone, for Mary had left Cairo and split her time between Marion and Murphysboro.[79]

General Grant was set to embark upon another campaign. Unlike the major army in the east, which rested out the winter in their Washington D.C., camps, Grant had sent small detachments of his burgeoning army on forays throughout December and January, and had plotted a campaign to wrest control of the Tennessee and Cumberland Rivers away from the Confederates, who manned strongholds near the junction of both waterways in the northwest corner of Tennessee—just south of the Kentucky state line. Two Confederate bastions stood eleven miles apart from each other: Fort Henry on the Tennessee and Fort Donelson, hugging the Cumberland. New, built on suspect ground, and undermanned, both forts served as objective points for Grant's campaign.

Logan received orders on the night of February 1 to prepare his regiment to head out at 2:00 the following morning—destination unknown (campaign plans were not relayed to regimental officers). The early departure caught him off-guard; he had promised his wife to notify her in time to train down to Cairo to see him off. It was too late. At 10:00 P.M. he sat down with paper and pen to write her a letter, the second one in three days. But this letter would be so unlike the others. For the first time, Logan expressed his doubts about surviving the campaign.

> My dear wife, God only knows my fate. I want your prayers—never before did I know how to love my own dear wife and child. I would give the world to see you once more. I may never have such pleasure again. If I should fall … take care of our child, raise her right, and learn her to love the memory of her father. Tell mother and all the family good bye for me. I have no un-kind feeling toward any one of them. Your father is here [and] will take this letter to you. Tell your mother and all good bye for me. I can write no more. My dear, I cover this with tears.[80]

Grant launched his campaign against Fort Henry on February 3, 1862—a day later than originally planned. Logan's role remained the same as in 1861—colonel commanding the Thirty-first Illinois. McClernand's had been elevated to division command. Logan now served in Colonel Richard Oglesby's brigade with three other Illinois regiments, all who fought with him at Belmont. Grant had labeled Belmont a "skirmish." The upcoming campaign was destined to be a bloodbath.

Several steamers transported Grant's army, convoyed by seven gunboats, including the *Lexington* and *Tyler*—the two ships employed against the Columbus batteries back in November. The transport moored ten miles from Fort Henry on February 4. Logan's efforts late in 1861 bore fruit at the landing. Waiting for his regiment were new weapons—Enfield rifles. Logan's men were finally equipped with a weapon considered standard issue for a U.S. soldier.[81]

Grant's plan for the destruction of Fort Henry called for two columns of infantry and cavalry advancing up each side of the Tennessee River while the gunboats attacked the fort directly. On the morning of February 6 Grant's men initiated the marches. Logan and his regiment moved with McClernand's two brigades on the Dover Road—merely "a rough cart path," according to a Cincinnati newspaper correspondent—along the west side of the Tennessee River. Marching four abreast, the column of troops stretched more than two miles, front to rear. This blue snake twisted back and forth as it followed the ever-turning road, softened by rains and the continuous kneading of hundreds of foot soldiers tramping upon it. Halfway to their destination, they heard the booming of the gunboats opening upon Fort Henry. "Our boys started on the run, cheering, all anxious to get the first shot at them," wrote a member of the Thirty-first Illinois.

By the time Logan reached the outer embankments of Fort Henry, he realized that he would not have to fight for it after all. Grant's gunboats had effectively reduced the fort and persuaded its commander, Brigadier General Lloyd Tilghman, to evacuate it by sending his Southern defenders up the Dover Road eleven miles to Fort Donelson and the Cumberland River. Tilghman, his staff, and sixty Confederates remained in Fort Henry and they quickly surrendered it.

At the vanguard of McClernand's force, Logan and the Thirty-first Illinois were the first to penetrate Fort Henry's earthworks on the evening of February 6. Logan sent out a cavalry detachment assigned to him to the Dover Road to run down the retreating Confederates. They returned later that night, Logan insisted, with ten rebel cannons (others claimed anywhere from two to eight captures). Soaked to the skin, many in the Thirty-first Illinois shed their Union blue and donned, albeit temporarily, gray Confederate uniforms found stacked within the fort. Other discoveries inside the fort were not nearly so pleasing. "It was a sickening sight to see the blood and brains of the poor fellows scattered around at every gun," wrote a subdued soldier to his parents the following day. Logan and his regiment stayed in Fort Henry for the next few days, awaiting their next orders from General Grant.[82]

Grant's next move was to take Fort Donelson, although he never informed his superior until he had taken Fort Henry. "I shall take and destroy Fort Donelson on the 8th, and return to Fort Henry," dispatched Grant to Major General Henry W. Halleck, who had replaced General Fremont to command the department. It would not be nearly so easy. Whereas Fort Henry was vulnerable on a river bottom, Fort Donelson stood on higher ground, protected on its flanks by flooded creeks. Two miles of fortifications protected its front, while the Cumberland formed a formidable moat behind it. Batteries outside the fort commanded the river while those within the fifteen acres of breastworks covered the front and flanks. More than 20,000 Confederate soldiers manned Fort Donelson, led by three generals—including General Pillow who opposed Grant at Belmont.[83]

Grant remained resolute. He turned his gunboats around, sent them down the Tennessee and over the Ohio River, and then up the Cumberland. Troop movements commenced late on February 11, emanating from Fort Henry on two roads that converged near Fort Donelson at the Tennessee town of Dover. February 12 was their first full-day march. The day grew so warm that soldiers cast off their overcoats and blankets, leaving them strewn along the roads running between the two rivers. That night, they struck the outer defenses but could go no farther. The next day proved the same—sporadic fire across the lines produced smoke and noise, but nothing else. Men would have to die in order to take Fort Donelson.

Logan and the rest of the troops in Oglesby's brigade massed on the Confederate left and inched their way to the first set of earthworks, marked by fallen timbers. Nature frowned upon the Union soldiers that night. A two-hour torrent of rain changed over to snow as temperatures plummeted below freezing. Wet uniforms hardened as ice interlaced the fabric. No tents and few blankets were available to provide them succor. A brisk north wind tortured them even more, particularly since they had orders not to light fires so close to the enemy works. Thousands of fingers and toes froze overnight and scores of men in the ranks sickened from the exposure—several mortally so. Logan survived the wicked exposure, but the night of February 13–14 marked the end of a robust, pain-free life.[84]

Valentine's Day followed the brutal night without incident. "We came here to take that fort, and we will take it," declared Colonel Oglesby to his men. Oglesby, Logan, and the rest of McClernand's division had no idea that the Confederate high command within the fort had planned a breakout—directly against Oglesby's brigade and the brigade of William H. L. Wallace, the troops that extended across the Forge Road leading southward from the fortress. Within the ranks of the Thirty-first Illinois, word arrived that several U.S. gunboats had been struck during the day and would not force Confederate capitulation like had been done so smoothly at Fort Henry.[85]

Logan had continued to suffer since the previous night. Stiff, sore, and unable to shake the bone-chilling temperatures from his body, he endured another brutal night of rain, sleet, and snow. Neither he nor most of his troops slept. To keep from freezing to death, they huddled in squads and walked around trees, yearning for the light of day to end the misery. To Logan, the suffering "was something almost indescribable.[86]

Before dawn exposed the contested field on February 15, Logan conducted the rote duties of his command. He likely conferred with Lieutenant Colonel White; perhaps he shared a few observations with Captain McCook as the regiment prepared breakfast. Logan was proud of the Thirty-first Illinois. Adept at turning phrases, he used a derogatory prewar sobriquet bestowed upon him as an honorable one for his regiment, which he dubbed "The Dirty-first." It was a fitting tribute, for they had been a hardy clan. An Illinois soldier from another regiment described them as "the hardest set of men I ever saw . . . all the time quarreling with each other and the hardest set of swearers in the Army." But they fought as well as they quarreled and swore. At 5:45 A.M., as the smell of morning coffee permeated the predawn air already dotted by hundreds of miniature clouds of human and horse exhalations, Logan looked upon the 600 officers and men of his regiment—his "Boys"—unaware that this would be the last day he would command them on a battlefield.[87]

Sporadic fire broke through the frigid air before appreciable light could do so. Although this was nothing unusual, what followed certainly was. Murderous infantry fire whizzed through the blue-clad ranks, followed by earth-shaking booms and a storm of iron hail from Confederate batteries. This was the Confederate breakout, one the Union force was entirely unprepared for. General Grant was nowhere to be found (he was actually across the river, conferring with one of his gunboat commanders and would be oblivious to the right flank assault for nearly an hour). Rebel yells announced the Confederate thrust as it assailed McClernand's thin line off to the front and right of Logan and his troops. The breakout was led by General Pillow, supported by General Simon Bolivar Buckner—a friend of Grant's prior to the war. The attacking force numbered nearly 10,000 determined Southern soldiers. This was the deadliest and most determined infantry fire Logan had ever seen.

"To arms! To arms!" yelled the officers as the ranks of all of the division scurried to form battle lines. Logan mounted his horse and looked for a positional advantage for his men. He found it right in front of him—a small hillock, forty paces away. He dashed along his ranks, waving his hat for emphasis while yelling, "Suffer death, men, but disgrace never. Stand firm!" Logan led his men to the hill where they dropped to their knees in the snow and fired their first volley at the desperate troops opposing them—less than 200 yards away. Southern counterfire tore through the ranks of the "Dirty-first," dropping several members. The smoke hovering around trees and underbrush concealed the opposing forces. Flaming musketry and the red glare of cannon fire lit up the killing ground with a lurid tint. Through it all Logan and his staff remained on horseback, barking orders and maintaining cohesion amidst the soup of smoke that choked the air around them.[88]

The time approached 8:00 A.M. with Logan and his men holding their ground, but running low on ammunition. The heaviest fire was thrust to their right, where two other Illinois regiments of Oglesby's brigade held the Forge Road—the Confederate escape route south to Charlotte, Tennessee. An advanced Union battery became a magnet for Confederate lead; all of its infantry support had melted away. Logan rushed his men forward to protect the cannons, but they were instantly staggered by the weight of General Pillow's attack. The white snow around them took on a crimson hue as bleeding bodies in blue lie strewn on top of it.

Regiments filed in and out in a desperate attempt to stymie the Confederate surge. Near 10:00 A.M., Oglesby ordered his brigade to retire, but either Logan did not hear him or refused to yield. All of the regiments of William W. H. Wallace's brigade on Logan's left had pulled back, except for the Eleventh Illinois Infantry. Through the din of battle and the smoke-filled air, Wallace could still see the silhouette of Logan's fierce form and hear him yell to his "Boys" to hold their position. Logan was called "The Murat of Illinois bravery," and he earned that sobriquet on the Donelson battlefield. As horrendous scenes of death and agony confronted him in front, Logan was startled at the sudden threat from behind. This was friendly fire, volleyed from a Union brigade coming in on the left-rear of the Thirty-first. Logan galloped to the confused force and commanded three regiments in the brigade to hold their fire.[89]

Riding back to his regiment, Logan pulled his depleted men back to attempt to find ammunition and reload. In the meantime he rushed up to inspire the Eleventh Illinois, the only other active obstacle holding the Forge Road. "Stepping over some of the dead men, Col. Logan, hatless, and with sword in one hand and pistol in the other came up cheering us to hold our position," recalled a private in the Eleventh Illinois. Logan found Colonel Thomas Ransom, leading his regiment. There the two quickly secured a gentleman's agreement to stand by one another. Indeed, these were the only two units on the line.[90]

Logan pulled back the right side of his regiment, a textbook maneuver called "refusing the flank." He was conspicuous on horseback, miraculously escaping harm for more than four hours. The luck ran out early in the fifth hour. A confederate ball tore into his thigh, ripping through his flesh and breaking his saddle bow. He refused to yield. A brief lull allowed his surgeon to dress the wound. As he ordered assistance to place him back in the saddle, his surprised doctor told him to seek a hospital—not the contested front, but Logan refused. He galloped back to the two-regiment line. Logan and Ransom coordinated a strategy to maximize their strength in the face of depleted ammunition. Logan stretched out the Thirty-first Illinois in front of Ransom's men, who would conserve their fire until the last rounds of Logan's regiment were depleted. Then, as the Thirty-first fell back, the Eleventh Illinois would fill in their position to buy time until reinforcements and ammunition arrived.[91]

The Thirty-first was in dire straits. Nearly 200 men had been bled out from its ranks, and those remaining had fired all of their available ammunition. Colonel Logan and Lieutenant Colonel White rode to and fro, holding the men in their position. White managed the right wing of the regiment, now hard-pressed by Pillow's Confederates slamming into his flank. In an attempt to change position for the renewed assaults, he was unhorsed by a devastating shot. White's lifeless body tumbled to the snow.

Logan became the target of the Second Kentucky Infantry's focus on the Confederate line of advance. For the second straight battle, a musket ball struck Logan's pistol, but unlike the glancing shot at Belmont, this ball slammed the gun into his side, shattering the wooden pistol handle while bruising his ribs and his hip. Wincing from the pain, he clung to the helm of his command. He seethed when he witnessed one of his captains cower in the rear rather than lead his men. He well recognized that February 15 was a watershed, "a day that tried men's nerve." Watching his line waver, Logan's stentorian voice boomed, "Boys! Give us death, but not dishonor!"[92]

Logan's men's stiffened with resolve, but the colonel had clearly kept them in place too long. A teenager in the Confederate Kentucky regiment had fired at him three or four times from a point less than 200 yards. Logan gave him another opportunity; this time, the boy did not miss. The leaden ball penetrated the upper corner of his left breast and passed through his shoulder joint. Reeling from the bloodiest of his three wounds, he still refused to yield command. Blood poured down his left side as he directed his men to fall back as Ransom and the Eleventh Illinois moved in to fill the void. By then Logan could no longer hold the saddle. His legs softened beneath him. Losing focus, the surrounding battle dulled to a blur; then all went black. A summoned surgeon pulled up Logan's sleeve to quickly determine if his heart was still beating. Logan had lost too much blood; no pulse could be detected.[93]

General Pillow's Confederates eventually drove the Eleventh Illinois back and overran the position, capturing prized cannons in the process. Occupying the hillock where the Thirty-first Illinois had stood in support of the Union battery, the Second Kentucky bore witness to the evidence of the staunch defense presented against them. Scores of dead and wounded littered the wind-whipped field. One of the Confederate Kentuckians spotted a Union officer's cap and sword on the ground. He picked them up and presented them to his colonel, Roger Hanson. "Ah! Col. John A. Logan!" responded Hanson, identifying the accoutrements. As Hanson and his men hustled forward, they passed by a body that Hanson identified as Colonel Logan. So did Captain Anson Maderia of the same Kentucky regiment, who had known Logan from law school in Louisville. The Kentuckians left him on the field. Minutes later, the Southern force was ordered back to the fort—a mistake by Confederate high command that General

Grant would seize upon and use to make history. Union troops reclaimed the contested ground, including the blood-drained bodies strewn upon it.[94]

The day after the battle, Mary Logan wrote a letter to her husband from Murphysboro. All of Egypt's populace had nervously awaited news of Grant's campaign. She had last heard from Logan two days earlier, in a letter he wrote from Fort Henry a week before. In it, he revealed that it might be a "great while" before he could meet his family again. Mary responded that late-winter Sunday. She revealed her fear "to think that meeting may never come." Her angst controlled her pen. "It chills my very blood. I feel almost heart broken. My heart rises in my throat it seems and chokes down the screams of despair . . ." She closed with: "May God save you and return you to me."[95]

Like her husband's letters, newspaper accounts were delayed in providing information about the ongoing campaign. The *Jonesboro Gazette* had recently run a short piece about Logan at Fort Henry, but nothing about the continuation of the expedition had filed in over the next few days. The local paper made it into her hands on February 17; it provided her the first glimpse of the battle of Fort Donelson. "The Day is Ours" ran a column headline, detailing the surrender of Fort Donelson and 15,000 of its Confederate defenders to General Grant. But Mary did not read on. She was too focused on the adjacent column to the right, more specifically the seven-word headline that reached out and stabbed her in the heart: "The Death of Colonel John A. Logan."[96]

The following day, Mary Logan left for Tennessee to bring back home the body of her martyred husband.

CHAPTER FOUR

Promotion

AIDES CARRIED THE BATTERED BODY of Colonel John A. Logan to the *New Uncle Sam*, General Grant's floating headquarters on the Cumberland River. The colonel was one of 2,800 men who fought and fell during the three-day battle for Fort Donelson. Contrary to what his wife had read in the newspaper, Colonel Logan was incorrectly placed on the "killed" list. The body of John Logan was alive and breathing.[1]

The surgeon who had failed to detect Logan's pulse successfully resuscitated him. He was, however, in grave condition. The three wounds he sustained—through the shoulder, into the thigh, and against the hip—missed vital organs, but the shoulder wound was serious. The musket ball that tore through it missed bone, but severely damaged soft tissue, apparently nicking an artery. Logan had anointed the snow-covered battlefield with a substantial pool of his blood. Although weak from blood loss and the consecutive days of exposure to the unforgiving winter elements in northwestern Tennessee, he still clearly understood the inspecting surgeon's diagnosis—his arm had to be amputated at the shoulder. He refused the deforming procedure, but any initial improvement detected in his health quickly gave way to a new concern. An infection had taken him down with a burning fever. The wife of another Illinois colonel nursed Logan in the immediate Donelson aftermath. She performed heroic work on him, but he continued to weaken.

A new nurse stepped aboard the *New Uncle Sam* on February 20, charging herself with the sole duty of caring for Colonel John A. Logan. Her mere presence lifted his spirits, as well as hers, although she nearly suffocated the sick and wounded officer with hugs and kisses. His new nurse had a personal interest in her patient, for he was her husband.

Mary Logan had boarded a train at Carbondale two days earlier, heartbroken and despondent. As soon as she reached Cairo she was informed that the crushing newspaper report about her husband was erroneous. Logan was alive but severely wounded—news that infused life into her sapped spirits. This elation quickly gave way to impatience and despair when she was denied a pass to see him. She parted company with her two escorts, Tom Logan and Captain Cunningham, shortly before she was introduced to a former client of her husband— Logan had previously won the man an acquittal for manslaughter. Freed from a certain imprisonment, he committed himself to deliver his former attorney's wife to him. He captained a small stern-wheel steamer that was currently on a mission to take the governor of Indiana and his staff to Fort Donelson. Mary hopped aboard on Tuesday and found herself alongside the *New Uncle Sam* on Thursday morning.

Notwithstanding the heroic attention paid to him prior to Mary's arrival, Logan was so thin and wan that she admitted he "looked like death." The doctors continued to advise amputation of his entire left arm, and the Logans continued to refuse. Blanched from blood loss, and beset with a scorching fever, Logan required twenty-four-hour attention. Day and night she fed and hydrated him; she cooled him with cold compresses when his fever spiked and she kept him warm when the fevers gave way to chills.[2]

Slowly and steadily Logan perked and strengthened. His replenished blood supply nourished his muscles and organs, and his wounds sported healing tissue. No longer did the Logans hear the word "amputation" tumble from the lips of the doctors. Logan had also cleared the fog from his head and assisted in resuming limited command duties from bed. He barked out orders for aides to deliver to the Thirty-first Illinois. The losses in his regiment reflected the perilous position they had defended. His friend and lieutenant colonel, John H. White, was dead as were several others from Marion—the recruits of Company C Logan had signed up that memorable August day. Other companies had been decimated. Initial claims that half of his command were killed and wounded proved exaggerated, but the amended body counts were still devastating. Logan's name topped the list of 176 casualties in the Thirty-first Illinois; of those, fifty-eight men were killed outright or would die from their wounds. Day-to-day improvement signaled that Logan's name would not join the latter list.[3]

The *New Uncle Sam* served as Grant's headquarters for the remainder of February. Dispatch-carrying orderlies continually entered and exited the general's cabin, their dangling swords giving the impression of a third, steel leg. The Logans had marveled at how the unpretentious commander had transformed into an American hero. Grant's capture of Fort Donelson and its 14,000 trapped Confederate inhabitants (including 2 generals, 48 cannons, 20,000 rifles and more than 2,000 horses) had given rise to a new *nom de guerre*, borrowing from his first initials "U. S." The man formerly derided as "USeless" Grant was hereafter hailed as "Unconditional Surrender" Grant, honored for his resolute order to the Confederate General Simon Buckner: "No terms except an unconditional and immediate surrender can be accepted."[4]

Grant and Logan held a stronger bond than ever expected between a general and a regimental commander in the midst of a campaign. Logan had displayed courage and a raw talent for command and control of troops in desperate circumstances, both at Belmont and at Fort Donelson. Added to this was Grant's sincere appreciation of Logan's patriotism—displayed for the first time in front of the unruly Twenty-first Illinois in Springfield—to make Logan a favorite of the general. The admiration was reciprocated from Logan's side.

Grant recorded his assessment and appreciation of Colonel Logan in a February 22 letter written to reward his friend for his dedicated service to the country. Grant sent the missive to Elihu Washburne in Washington, who was an influential congressman with close ties to President Lincoln and a favorite sounding board for the general. "Allow me to call your attention to a fact that has just been known to me to day for the first time," opened Grant, who was clearly disturbed when studying a list of appointed generals from the state of Illinois. He noted that "not a single Brigadier General has been made from Illinois south of about the Central part of the state." He went on to explain the injustice, for Southern Illinois "had contributed not only her proportion of troops, but a more gallant set of men cannot be found to day batteling [sic] for the preservation of the Union." Grant continued, "Among these Cols. commanding these regiments, or any others, a braver or more gallant man is not to be found than Col. John A. Logan. To him perhaps more than to any other man is to be attributed the unanimity with which south Illinois has gone into this war. . . . Col. Logan I consider eminantly [sic] qualified and equally deserving of promotion his gallantry having stood the test of Belmont and Fort Donelson, at the latter of which he was severely wounded." So pleased was Grant with Logan's leadership that he made an additional request: "Should Col. Logan be promoted I want him left with the Division of the Army I may have the honor of commanding, nor do I believe such a disposition would be disagreeable to him."[5]

Mary escorted her husband to Murphysboro to recuperate, where the former colonel learned of his new rank. Congressman Washburne wrote Lincoln on March 1, sending a list for promotion of those officers acting in capacities greater than their rank at Fort Donelson. "I also enclose you a letter I have received from Major General Grant," noted Washburne, "asking that Jack Logan be appointed a Brigadier which I hope will be done." Lincoln followed up with the request to Secretary Edwin Stanton two days later. The Senate completed the process by confirming the appointment on March 21. John A. Logan was a commissioned brigadier general of U.S. volunteers.[6]

To make his generalship official, Logan needed to be sworn into service by a superior officer, but he also had to relinquish his seat in the House of Representatives, one he had committed ten years of his life to gain and hold. The highest rank a sitting U.S. congressman could hold in the army was colonel. He never appeared to anguish over the decision; late in March Logan unceremoniously retired from the House of Representatives.

Logan chafed to put his rank into effect in the field. He was no longer comfortable in the cozy confines of home, knowing that the troops were advancing into the Confederacy. He left Mary in Illinois and headed back to Tennessee, joining up with the Thirty-first Illinois at Fort Donelson in the first week of April, in time to see the regiment unanimously promote Doff Ozburn from quartermaster to colonel. Logan was pleased at the promotion of his years-long friend, but pressing matters changed his focus. A huge battle was being waged between Grant's army and that of Confederate General Albert S. Johnson, fifty miles up the Tennessee River from Fort Henry. Logan raced to help out in the action, but he disembarked at Pittsburg Landing too late to participate.

Logan had missed the Battle of Shiloh, the last and largest battle waged in the first year of the war. More than 100,000 soldiers had participated—62,000 Union soldiers versus 44,000 Confederates. It was a two-day contest with opposite results for each day. Day one appeared to be a decisive Confederate victory when Grant and Sherman were surprised by a massive rebel assault that by day's end had pushed Grant's beaten army—now called the Army of the Tennessee—to the banks of the river for which the army was named. But reinforcements from General Don Carlos Buell's Army of the Ohio and from a previously wayward division in Grant's own army gave the Union the numbers to reclaim all their lost ground.

Furthermore, the Confederates had cleared the route to the important Southern rail hub of Corinth, Mississippi. The cost had been staggering: nearly 25,000 American soldiers, North and South, fell dead, wounded, or captured in those two days, equivalent to nearly one-tenth of one percent of America's population.[7]

Illness and battle casualties had taken their toll on the ranks of all active regiments in the western army. Logan noted that his new command consisted of five Illinois regiments, with "no Regt. numbering over 500 at this time." He wrote Mary often during the spring of 1862. Her letters of that spring and summer were hallmarked by the query, "Where is Bub?" (Her pet name for her younger brother). Logan suspected that Hybert Cunningham had fought against Grant's army at Shiloh, but he had no news to share with Mary about his fate. Nonetheless, the couple's tenderness spilled out in their letters to each other, and daughter Dollie served as the vehicle to express the loving nature of each parent to her and to each other. Logan closed one letter, "A thousand kisses to 'Dollie' and yourself," which prompted Mary to illustrate the same in her response. In an early May letter, Mary informed her husband that Dollie "has named the left side of my face 'papa's side' and she will kiss it thousands of times and pat my cheek and say 'bless his soul'!"[8]

Logan had time to regularly write home because he was not nearly as active in field command in late April as he was in early February. The turnaround Union victory at Shiloh opened the door for the siege of Corinth, Mississippi. To Logan's dismay, Grant would not lead the Northern army in the campaign. Halleck took personal charge of this operation (Grant still held a district command within Halleck's army). Halleck's plodding operation, replete with cautious advances and daily construction of field fortifications, reduced the army's rate of advance southward to ten miles in eighteen days. Only halfway to Corinth, Halleck's pace slowed further once his army entered Mississippi. "This advance was, perhaps, the most ludicrous feature of the whole war," growled Logan, who considered Halleck "recklessly over-cautious." After his brigade once again fell into the routine of improving fortifications and constructing rifle pits, Logan fumed, "My men will never dig another ditch for Halleck except to bury him."[9]

The tedious campaign carried on to the end of May. Halleck's force, consisting of the Army of the Tennessee, the Army of the Ohio, and the Army of the Mississippi, now exceeded 110,000 soldiers pitted against 65,000 Confederates who were led by General Pierre G. T. Beauregard. Realizing he was vastly outnumbered, General Beauregard retreated from Corinth by foot, wagon, and railroad. By the time Halleck's force probed into the junction, they found it evacuated. The U.S. flag flew over the courthouse by midmorning of May 30. Halleck was satisfied at seizing the junction, a key strategic initiative; but many

in the Army of the Tennessee—especially those who witnessed the "Unconditional Surrender" of nearly all the troops and supplies at Fort Donelson—saw
this much differently. An Iowa soldier confessed "an indescribable feeling of
mortification that the enemy with all his stores and ordnance had escaped."
Logan shared the private's sentiments. Never exhibiting any pride for participating in the "Siege of Corinth," Logan decided, "All that we had gained, apparently, was the barren honor of occupying an abandoned position."[10]

Shortly after Corinth was secured, Logan received orders to seize another
railroad hub—this one at Jackson, Tennessee. Trusted with the responsibility to
lead the operation, he organized his brigade for this assignment and by June 7,
the general led his men into the town after a brief and bloodless defense was offered by its Confederate protectors. Logan massed his troops in Jackson's courthouse square where he addressed the pro-Union crowd that he and his men
were there to liberate and protect. Confronted with the realities of an occupying
force, the populace of Jackson met Logan and his men with suspicion. Logan
characterized the area as "all hot 'sesech' and look daggers at us all."[11]

Although he still was subordinate to General McClernand, who headquartered twenty miles from him, Logan claimed the responsibility of a large division
of troops consisting of fifteen infantry regiments, one cavalry regiment, and
twenty cannons. The town of Jackson formed the apex of a railroad triangle; it sat
at the junction of the Mobile and Ohio Railroad and the Mississippi Central Railroad. A spur of these two adjoining lines ran ten miles northward to Humboldt,
where it joined the northeast-southwest Memphis and Ohio Railroad. Logan positioned troops, as instructed, to focus mainly on the Mobile and Ohio line. Troops
guarded the region from Jackson thirty-five miles southeast to Bethel on the railroad, and Purdy, a hamlet five miles east of Bethel and ten miles west of the Tennessee River near Pittsburg Landing and the Shiloh battlefield.

Logan never expressed regret over his decision to retire from Congress, although he must not have been pleased that Josh Allen won his vacated seat in a
mid-year election runoff. Logan only read about the political upheavals tran-
spiring in Illinois without showing any desire to comment on it, let alone partake
in it. A vote of the people had authorized a convention to revise the Illinois constitution. In November of 1861, state residents elected delegates to amend their
constitution. Although the Illinois legislature had small Republican minorities in
both the house and senate, Democrats outnumbered Republicans in the constitutional delegation by a huge two-to-one margin. The Democrats prevailed on
crafting changes to the constitution. Those alterations, packaged in six provisions, required another vote of Illinoisans to become final.

The changes put forth to the people early in the summer were far-reaching; some clearly overreached. Opponents derided the legislative session as the "Copperhead Convention." The reworked constitution was soundly defeated, as were some individual amendments to the original document. An attempt to stack electoral apportionment toward Democratic Egypt failed, as did an attempt to crush the free-bank economy. What did win approval in the popular referendum was barring blacks from settling in the state and blocking any voting and office-holding rights for those who did live there—essentially an endorsement of Logan's 1853 "Black Codes." Doff Ozburn, Logan's replacement as colonel of the Thirty-first Illinois, claimed 95 percent of his regiment favored all the provisions. "I thought that the adoption of the new Constitution in Illinois . . . would put under foot that black hearted 'fanatical' Abolition party, to which the State of Illinois [is] about to fall a victim—'God forbid'—under the guise of Republicanism," he vented to a friend back in Egypt. Surprisingly, Logan provided no commentary on an issue that would have dominated his thoughts less than two years earlier.[12]

The general and his men bore witness to the brutal realities of a slave-driven economy, both on the march to Jackson and during their sojourn in the city. This part of Tennessee was cotton country. The slave populace numbered in the thousands, and the troops found out they were sometimes purchased for reasons other than to work in the fields and in the homes. A planter's young mulatto slave girl named Zela escaped her master and found protection within Logan's ranks. "Her tender years and great beauty of face and figure made her an object of pity as well as of attraction," recalled an Ohio soldier. According to the same volunteer, Zela told the troops that she had been purchased by a local planter to satisfy his lust, making her desperate to escape him and find comfort and solace behind Union lines. She gained self-esteem from her blue-clad protectors by working for the provost marshal at the courthouse. Her cunning former owner put an end to this by feigning a mortal illness in his home. When Zela received a message from him that he wanted to see her one last time before he died, she took the bait and returned to his home unescorted. The planter seized her and drove her out of town undetected. Zela was sold at Holly Springs to a Georgia planter, forced to yearn for the freedom she tasted so briefly at Jackson.[13]

Zela's plight underscored the oppression of blacks in Tennessee. The situation there did not convert Logan into an abolitionist, but it appears to have affected his belligerent and often-unprovoked criticism of their cause. Logan emphatically disavowed politics, so much so that when a Bloomington, Illinois, newspaper claimed that he gave a pro-abolition speech to his troops in Jackson,

Logan fired off a rapid response. "I have never, during my connection with the army, made a political speech to soldiers or citizens," he insisted. "I shall continue in the discharge of my military duties, honestly, and faithfully; (entirely ignoring politics) hoping that my feeble efforts may somewhat assist in restoring the country to its former strength and glory." Perhaps for the first time, Logan did not vent against the abolition movement when the newspaper's accusation would normally goad him to do so.[14]

His military duties proved arduous; when Mary complained that he was not writing to her frequently enough, Logan tersely responded, "You do not know what I have to do. I am almost worked to death." He groaned at how indefensible his region was. Victimized by rebel cavalry raids that succeeded in burning railroad bridges within fifteen miles of his headquarters, his leadership was criticized by a superior for the first time in the war when McClernand sent a series of testy dispatches admonishing Logan for his troop placements.[15]

Logan also caught criticism from those subordinate to him—and in one case, insubordinate. Colonel Frank Rhodes of the Eighth Illinois Infantry was far from awed by his commanding general. When Logan sent instructions that the colonel was to follow specific orders, Rhodes responded in defiance, "The general can kiss my ass." Instead of following Rhodes's colorful advice, Logan arrested him. Other soldiers were displeased when Logan exerted discipline in the district of his command. Fed up with the general's insistence to guard citizens' property and not to confiscate it, a member of the Twelfth Wisconsin questioned Logan's patriotism. Noting that their own colonel had no problem with the troops taking produce from the Tennessee locals, the soldier derisively dubbed Logan's policy, the "Vegetable Order." The private complained to his father that Logan was "a traitor at heart" for the enforcement: "I hope that those of our Gen'ls who have had such tender conscience towards rebel property may be promptly relieved of their command and more honest patriots succeed them."[16]

The combination of guerrilla warfare, a rabidly secessionist segment of the populace, and the overly scrutinizing tendencies of commanding officers wore him down so much that he submitted a request for a leave of absence to visit home on August 8. Nearly three weeks after filing the request, Logan still remained at Jackson without permission to leave. The threats had diminished and Logan was able to manage affairs without the setbacks he suffered in late July. He was cheered at the presence of his old regiment, the "Dirty-first." Company C was now commanded by George Goddard, commissioned captain after the resignation of the previous officer in June. Goddard had seethed about not having the captain's commission back in 1861, as was hashed out in the Marion meeting between himself, Logan, Captain Cunningham, and John White. Now he had the position he desired.[17]

If Logan took the opportunity to reflect, the events of one year before must have seemed so distant. Then it was Congressman Logan, and lawyers Goddard, White, and Allen sharing the camaraderie of overnight civilian picket duty— with one gun and a bottle of whiskey—shortly before Logan boarded a train to Washington for the special session of Congress. One year later White was dead, Josh Allen held Logan's congressional seat, Goddard commanded overnight picket duty in life-and-death circumstances, and Logan was responsible for the welfare of several thousand men covering more than 700 square miles of enemy territory, rather than "commanding" a dozen neighbors outside the town square of Marion, Illinois.

Equally thought-provoking was seeing Captain Goddard in Union blue; barely fifteen months earlier the same man was involved in drafting the infamous Marion resolutions. Now, all was forgiven, partly due to Logan's efforts on his behalf. Much more effort from Logan would be required on the home front. Logan's influence was tested again late in August when he received word that U.S. Marshall David L. Phillips, the Republican Logan crushed in 1858 to win his congressional seat, conducted a large sweep of Confederate sympathizers in Southern Illinois. On August 14 he netted several Peace Democrats accused of affiliations with the Knights of the Golden Circle. The K.G.C. was a secret society pledged to support the Confederacy. Phillips was convinced their means of support in Egypt included plans to congregate and attack Union supporters.

Logan reportedly saw the list of fiery Democrats arrested and sent to Cairo, scheduled to be detained in Washington. Heading the list was U.S. congressman Josh Allen, who had grown distant from his former law partner since the war began. Circuit judge Andrew Duff of Benton, another outspoken critic of the Lincoln administration, joined Allen in prison. But the name that struck Logan the most was that of a member of his family. Israel Blanchard had been arrested for the second time in sixteen months. Despite the oaths spewed at Logan by his sister Annie and his growing disdain for those who openly dissented against the Union, family duty dictated his response. Logan pressed Grant for a six-day leave of absence. "I have been compelled to ask this on account of family troubles that are of serious nature," he stated, too chagrined to elaborate. Granted the request, Logan secured a worthy subordinate to command in his stead; he then sped to Egypt.[18]

When Logan stepped off the train at Carbondale, he remained in the town since he had previously purchased a home there. Mary and Dollie had occupied the residence earlier in the summer. Carbondale was the third community in fifteen months that the Logans called "home." The Logan house stood half a mile west of the town square. Mary considered Carbondale as home to "the very best society south of Springfield." Carbondale also freed her from the uncomfortable relationship with her husband's family in Murphysboro and the unstable environment of Marion.[19]

Carbondale also proved the optimal locale for General Logan because the Illinois Central Railroad depot and the telegraph office were located there. This trip required him to head back to Murphysboro to get a handle on Dr. Blanchard's alleged activities that led to his arrest. Waking up on the twenty-eighth, perhaps Logan had intended to do just that, but his day would be interrupted by a more uplifting diversion. Courted by his oldest of friends, who were now his newest of neighbors, to deliver a speech, Logan complied. The address—his first to his non-military constituents since the Marion speech more than one year earlier—captured more attention than he could have imagined. It also lent credence to the hope that the words of one man can move thousands to patriotism—even to those not present to hear those words.

Hundreds gathered in Carbondale's town square on that late-summer afternoon, many hearing their former congressman's fervid eloquence for the first time. Although unable to capture Logan's oratory—described as "a beautiful combination of musical words, in a voice of silver harmony"—a shorthand reporter for the town paper recorded the lengthy address, nearly in its entirety. "These are times that demand the most heroic energy and undaunted bravery," pronounced the Black Eagle from his perch. "Every patriot in the land is called upon to come to the rescue of his country, to do his part in this struggle, and the man who fails to lend his influence and energies in this crisis, who lingers while liberty bleeds at every pore, is a traitor, and deserves a traitor's doom." With his relentless, sledge-hammer style, Logan pounded this theme into the minds and souls of his audience throughout his address, shaming any able-bodied resident for not donning Union blue. "Why object to filling the place of the brave boys who fell at Belmont, Donelson, and Shiloh," he pointedly asked, "whose bodies sleep in soil contaminated by the footsteps of rebels." Disavowing politics with marked consistency, Logan insisted, "Party lines and partisan feelings should be swallowed up in patriotism."

Carbondale's newest and most famous resident also addressed his evolving views on slavery. "But there are some who say, 'I can't go, this is a war to free the niggers!'" Logan belittled the excuse, announcing that so many slaves were escaping their masters, that none will be left if the war drags on for five years. He then purposely created a ridiculous scenario to add another reason to enlist. "If you wish slavery to continue, join the army and help us to whip the rebels quick, and there will probably be a few more stumps left," he mocked, but then ended the scenario with reality: "If not, then slavery must go." He completely reversed his opinion about fugitive slaves, obliterating the "Dirty Work" moniker by admitting "if the master is engaged in the attempt to overthrow this government . . . and the slave runs away and gets free, it is none of my business. It is a family quarrel in which I shall not interfere." He then loosed a volley that resonated throughout the state in the form of excerpts published in several newspapers:

> If the question were presented to me as to which should live, the Union or slavery, I would say the Union with my latest breath. The Union is worth everything. If the sacrifice of a million of men was necessary to the salvation of this government and nothing else would save it, and I was the arbiter of its destinies, I would consign the millions to death—and die with them. I am for a vigorous prosecution of this war.[20]

Indeed, he was. The Carbondale speech, in total and in excerpts, was reprinted in the *Illinois State Journal* and other smaller newspapers in the state. Pro-Union editorials and letters to the editor hailed him. "The ground he takes in this speech will be approved by patriots everywhere," read one, which went on to credit him for his "earnest, unconditional patriotism, rising above all considerations of party or selfish ambition." Egypt's *Grayville Independent* praised Logan for the "noble and patriotic path you have chosen and bravely traveled." Although Logan had shunned politics, his stance did not stop the movement to run him for congressional representative, using the state's at-large seat. The Carlinsville *Free Press* announced its endorsement—without consulting the general.[21]

Imbued with patriotic fervor, nothing could destroy Logan's zeal more than what he read in the issue of the *Carbondale Times* that fell upon his gaze. "Exposition of the K. G. C.," read the taunting headline. It was a detailed expose, reproduced from the August 26 issue of the *Chicago Tribune*, which described the activities of the Knights of the Golden Circle in Southern Illinois. The account drew a sharp outline around the nebulous organization and partially filled it in with affidavits and a detailed account by an agent of the U.S. marshal who infiltrated the K.G.C. and attended a meeting of up to 400 determined Confederate sympathizers. Logan already knew that Blanchard's name was among those who attended, but it must have struck him to see him erroneously listed as living in Washington County, and not contributing an opinion in the meeting (something that Dr. Blanchard usually could not resist).

The K.G.C. operatives and attendees had secretly gathered on August 10 near Pinckneyville, where they allegedly engaged in a conspiracy to induce hordes of Southern sympathizers to enlist in the Union army, obtain arms, and subsequently desert to the Confederacy in droves. Josh Allen was not present at the meeting, Logan read, but he was deemed a "general" in command of the organization. Three columns of the article were replete with examples of Congressman Allen's quotes from speeches deemed subversive to the Union cause. This apparently led to Allen's arrest. The only arrested members in attendance of the 400 near Pinckneyville were Judge Duff and Dr. Blanchard. "Every person who graces this column could have been arrested," the article claimed, "but it was thought better to secure the leaders . . . and let the dupes remain unmolested for the present."

That Blanchard was deemed "a leader" perhaps was not shocking to Logan. What stunned him to the core were the names of two of the "dupes" that did grace the column. Phillip Davis, his first cousin, was one of them; the other was a closer relative—Tom Logan. Not only was his brother in attendance, he also spoke out. With understandable pain and disgust, John A. Logan read his brother's contribution to the event:

> Thomas Logan then arose and said he had a brother in the Federal army, and nothing pained him so much as to be hear him called "General Logan" when he came home. They might call him "dirty work Logan," "secessionist," or what not, so long as they do not call him "an abolitionist." For himself, he [Tom] resolved to support Jeff Davis and the Southern Confederacy.[22]

Logan rode out to Murphysboro to settle the issue. Mary had already written the governor on Dr. Blanchard's behalf. She had yet to hear Yates's response. David L. Phillips, the marshal who arrested Dr. Blanchard, worked for the federal government, out of Yates's jurisdiction. Nevertheless, he assured Governor Yates that Blanchard "is a gambler and a bad man," claiming to have the resolutions drafted at the Pinckneyville meeting in Blanchard's handwriting.[23]

If true, these would be charges Logan could not defend, particularly considering his strengthening abhorrence of the peace faction of the Democratic Party. But this time Logan was convinced of his brother-in-law's innocence. In Murphysboro he collected evidence to prove it. He confirmed that Dr. Blanchard tended a sick child in town the very day of the Pinckneyville meeting, and was witnessed in Murphysboro the day afterward. No rail communication linked

Murphysboro with Pinckneyville; therefore, Blanchard would have had to magically travel twenty-eight miles after his visit to the child to be present at the August 10 anti-Union meeting, and then return at the same breakneck speed to be back in Murphysboro where he was seen on the eleventh. Impossible, Logan concluded, recognizing that David L. Phillips was overzealous in his quest to eradicate traitors from the home front.[24]

Assured of Blanchard's innocence, Logan turned his focus to his brother. The published exposé on the K.G.C. was fraught with errors and appears to have been the product of embroidered reporting. Logan could not tell if his brother said the quotes attributed to him, or if he was even present at the Pinkneyville meeting. Tom would likely deny any of his alleged activities, but the general had another reason to visit him. Once the best of friends as well as the closest of siblings, John and Tom Logan had drifted apart, chiefly from diverging interests and ambitions that had weakened the bond between them. Logan carried something long absent in his brother—a passion or a purpose in life. He saw how former secession-supporter George Goddard benefited from the status of an officer; perhaps Tom would reap the same reward. Logan convinced his brother to enlist in the Thirty-first Illinois, hoping it would cure him of the discontent that lurked within him. He also persuaded Phillip Davis to agree to enlist with his cousin.[25]

Logan returned to Carbondale at the end of August, forced to wire General Grant again. "My family & affairs generally are now in such a situation that if an extension of my leave is not granted, deleterious result will follow," he stated, pointing out that if he was forced to return within the six-day limit, "an injustice will be done me." Grant approved of the additional days Logan requested; Logan received his wire at Carbondale on August 31: "You can remain a week longer, but your services are much needed."[26]

Logan labored during his additional time to settle the issue. He sent a letter to Abraham Lincoln, who held the ultimate jurisdiction on the actions of U.S. marshals. "Dr. Blanchard is said to be en route to the Old Capitol Prison, charged with the crime of . . . attending on August 10, a meeting of subversive nature," wrote Logan. "Herewith, I append evidence proving that he could not have been there. Please act promptly in accordance with this information." To keep this less-than-flattering family matter under wraps Logan never revealed any information about Israel Blanchard and Tom Logan's alleged association with the K.G.C., nor would he or Mary ever register the incident in their future writings and memoirs.[27]

With growing impatience to return to his military duties, Logan turned down his extra granted time and on September 3 he was back in command at division headquarters in Jackson, Tennessee, greeted once again with a burning bridge set upon by rebel raiders. He stanched this wound and prepared his department for an advance into Mississippi that Grant had planned. In October, Logan learned that his efforts on behalf of his sister paid off. Lincoln informed his war secretary, Edwin M. Stanton, "I strongly incline to discharge Dr. Blanchard." Stanton took it from there and released him. Blanchard parlayed the incident to tell many of his patients, "You have reason to be thankful that I picked the right brother-in-law." Logan could not say the same.[28]

Logan's family continued to be an impediment to him. The most egregious offense committed by a Logan in Egypt was one that the general may not have been apprised of until well after the fact—if at all. It occurred just days after he left Southern Illinois to return to his post. His brother was beset with problems—likely linked with a dependence on the bottle—and Logan attempted to cure him with a position in the Union army. Tom dutifully enlisted in the Thirty-first Illinois on September 2, but for unexplained reasons, he did not immediately join the regiment, which was stationed with his brother near Jackson, Tennessee. Tom (a married man) became obsessed with a young woman, Esculane A. Phillips. Late on the night of September 6, he disrupted Miss Phillips and her parents by creating a ruckus—apparently a drunken one—at their Murphysboro home. They filed a complaint, but that failed to stop him. Tom continued to stalk her and on October 7 he allegedly broke into the Phillips house and tried to rape her. To make matters worse, he abused her family and threatened to kill her mother. Authorities drew a warrant for his arrest, but somehow Tom evaded the law and stepped off the train in Jackson, Tennessee, later that month to take his place as the dirtiest member of the Dirty-first.[29]

The Logan family troubles, for the time being stayed "in the family." For General Logan, this was fortunate, for he had continued to garner only positive press from the pro-Union newspapers. He also put an end to the clamor to run again for Congress. Amazingly, the Republican Yates administration asked lifelong Democrat Logan to represent a new Illinois district. Logan declined the request to fill the at-large seat, but his passionate explanation stirred the Illinois Union Convention in September, where it was read to the delegates. His words clearly revealed a man who had swung completely away from the sympathetic views he held for the South fourteen months earlier:

> I express all my views and politics when I assert my attachment for the Union. I have no other politics now, and consequently no aspirations for civil place and power. No! I am to-day a soldier of this Republic, so to

remain, changeless and immutable, until her last and weakest enemy shall have expired and passed away.[30]

That Logan's address was read at the Republican convention and not the Democratic one indicates that had he returned to Congress in 1863, he could have occupied the side of the aisle that he despised so passionately eighteen months earlier. His letters home, however, had been and continued to be void of political discussions. Still, the politics and events of Illinois and America in the summer and fall of 1862 had been influential on the course of the war and dramatic on the course of the home front.

Everything appeared to resolve around President Lincoln's intention to issue an emancipation proclamation to free all the slaves existing in the Confederacy. His planned measure was hailed as a humanitarian effort by the abolitionist sect, for it added a new cause for the North to fight the Civil War: to free the slaves as well as preserve the Union. Others hailed it as a necessary military measure to prevent the antislave European nations from recognizing and granting aid to the Confederacy, a direction in which they had been leaning due to the months-long success of Confederate General Robert E. Lee and his Army of Northern Virginia against Union armies east of the Alleghenies. Lee was turned back after the bloody Battle of Antietam in western Maryland. At about the same time, the U.S. Army of the Cumberland turned back Confederate forces (led by General Braxton Bragg) from northern Kentucky. With these dual Confederate threats removed from the borderlands of the North, Lincoln's proclamation, planned for months, was now publicized in the autumn of 1862. Lincoln would sign it into law on the upcoming New Year's Day.

News of emancipation erupted throughout Illinois. Anti-abolition feelings trumped pro-Union ones at the polls, where Democrats took both bodies of the legislature away from the Republicans. Voters also retained Josh Allen as Logan's replacement in the Ninth Congressional District—despite the fact that Allen was sitting in Old Capitol Prison (he was released and took Logan's old seat). Buoyed by their House and Senate gains, the Democrat-controlled Illinois legislature selected a committee to put forth a new resolution to counter the president's proclamation.

The preliminary emancipation proclamation set off a firestorm within regiments recently recruited in Logan's old district. Two new regiments—the 109th Illinois and the 128th Illinois Infantry—suffered so much unruliness and desertion that the units had to be disbanded before they took the field. Those supporting emancipation seemed to be in the minority in the Illinois regiments.[31]

Despite the turmoil, Logan's military life eased a bit from army reconstruction as General Grant pieced together a plan to capture Vicksburg, Mississippi, the key Confederate stronghold that hugged the Mississippi River and prevented the Union from gaining control of the most important and heavily contested waterway of the war. Grant placed Logan in command of the Third Division of the new Seventeenth Corps, Army of the Tennessee. Grant remained army commander, and General James Birdseye McPherson took the helm of the corps. Fourteen regiments in three brigades constituted Logan's 7,000-man division; most of these regiments hailed from Illinois and had served under Logan since the late spring. Receiving orders early in November, Logan departed Jackson and marched his men into the state of Mississippi.

The division shifted positions three times in less than one month. Logan found little time to write home. Mary received a letter from him in the middle of December. In it Logan claimed satisfaction with his command, but disappointment in the failures of the eastern armies closer to Washington. He deemed Lincoln's pending Emancipation Proclamation as "foolish." Missing from the letter was a denunciation of the abolition movement, which would naturally follow the statement.[32]

Logan did not express any charitable opinions during the Christmas season of 1862 toward abolitionists and their cause. But he had noticeably refrained from castigations of the movement. Perhaps he had warmed to the necessity of Lincoln's proclamation as a necessary war measure; or perhaps what he witnessed day after day in Tennessee and Mississippi for the previous nine months gave him pause on the issue. Two days before Lincoln signed his proclamation into law, a private in the Thirty-first shot a black boy. Delivered information about the "incident," Logan went through the chain of command to deal with the matter by writing Lieutenant Colonel John A. Rawlins (General Grant's assistant adjutant general) to request a military commission to try the soldier. Rawlins replied instantly requesting the name of the boy. Logan confessed he did not know the boy's identity. Perhaps for a moment, it struck the general that he was more likely to know the boy's name if he had been white instead of black.[33]

During the third week of 1863, Logan received and complied with Grant's directive to move his division into Memphis, upriver from Grant's target of Vicksburg. Logan complied and in a driving rainstorm, he moved his men by foot and rail to Memphis. The dreary winter weather mimicked and directed Logan's mood. He was enduring his greatest "low" since entering the service. So depressed was the general that he wrote Mary, "I shall hold on to my command a while yet and see if all will not become sane again. If not I shall probably leave the army."[34]

More than one factor led Logan to believe that he was surrounded by insanity. Nearly a year had passed since Fort Donelson and the war was slogging so slowly that no end seemed to be in sight. Desertions were bleeding dry the Army of the Tennessee, including Logan's division. A soldier in the Eighty-first Illinois recorded in his diary entry of February 10, "Last night, fourteen men deserted from the regiment.... Dissatisfaction prevails to an alarming extent, both here and in the North. Many are losing all hopes of putting down the Rebellion, and are talking of going home. Many of them received letters from home, encouraging them to desert."[35]

Logan was convinced that the home front wielded a heavy hand in driving the desertions. To him it was treason, directed by newspaper editors who painted a fictional picture of sentiment in the hometowns of the soldiers. He also was convinced that the Knights of the Golden Circle was exacerbating the problem, spurred by Lincoln's Emancipation Proclamation, which was made official on New Year's Day. He was not alone in the sentiment. Lincoln had been apprised of the same accusations by Union-loyal citizens of Southern Illinois. One of them warned the president, "The Spirit, the fierce and bloody Spirit of opposition to you Sir, and to the Govt. of the Union, that exists in our midst, is I think more to be dreaded than an army of Rebels in the field."[36]

Most disconcerting to Logan was the spirit of opposition within the "Dirty-first" Illinois. Desertions were rampant in Logan's old regiment, and Colonel Ozburn shared the helplessness of his fellow regimental commanders at putting a stop to it. But Logan was suspicious that Doff sympathized with the deserters. When he heard a report that Ozburn complained that he was unwilling "to fight to free the niggers," he called his old friend to headquarters to test the veracity of the rumor. When Doff unabashedly repeated the statement in front of him, he responded in a way that his staff would never forget. "Logan roared with rage like a lion," recalled a witness in the room, "I cannot repeat his language, but his words came hot and thick from an outraged heart." Logan demanded the colonel's resignation. "I want nothing to do with him," he informed his wife. Within weeks of the confrontation, Lindorf Ozburn was out of the service.[37]

Ozburn was not alone in leaving the Thirty-first Illinois for suspicious reasons. Tom Logan's life as a soldier also ingloriously ended in February. Lieutenant Logan initially had taken well to his duties. But he could not escape the demon of alcohol, which in Memphis was as prevalent around the soldiers as were the prostitutes. According to members of the Thirty-first, Tom drank to intoxication and rode up and down the street shouting, "Hurrah for Jeff Davis." Logan had apparently pulled strings to enter Tom in as an officer; he did the same to arrange for his brother's resignation and send him home. No sooner did Tom Logan step foot into Jackson County than he was arrested for the late-night surprise he pulled on his Murphysboro neighbor.[38]

The only refreshing family-related reward Logan received at this time was the arrival of Mary in Memphis. The Logans stayed at the Lanier Mansion in the city and for most of Mary's visit the general stayed confined to his bed. Her arrival was timely, for he was struck down with a flareup of rheumatism, a debilitating malady he traced back to those tortuous nights in front of Fort Donelson. As she had done on the *New Uncle Sam*, Mary nursed her husband back to health.

As Mary worked to eradicate the illness from Logan's body, he had to shake himself from his despondency. This he did on February 12, but without his usual flourish. Still too weak to saddle his horse, he addressed his division from the balcony of the mansion where they had bivouacked to serenade him. One of his division commanders spoke first, pledging the loyalty of his command in the up-coming campaign against Vicksburg. Logan followed, holding an order he had dictated to Mary, too weak at the time to write it out himself. Although more subdued in his delivery, Logan's words still struck home. Notwithstanding the devastating number of desertions infecting his division, Logan assured his men that "your General still maintains unshaken confidence in your patriotism, de-votion and ultimate success of our glorious cause." Logan's address compared deserters to cowards, condemning them as traitors in strong and persuasive lan-guage. "Patriot Soldiers!" trumpeted Logan in closing, "This great work accom-plished, the reward for such service as yours will be realized; the blessings and honors of a grateful people will be yours."[39]

The address found its way into newspapers throughout the North. The phe-nomenon of covering Logan in the press turned ironic—nearly all supportive newspapers prior to the war had turned on him, while those that vilified him early in 1861 were quickly warming to his words and deeds. The *Jonesboro Gazette*, a career-long supporter of Logan, had yet to repudiate him, but it did find the reason for such a supportive speech of the Lincoln administration. "We have it from an officer associated with Gen. John that Gen. John is as ardent a democrat as he ever was, and he hates the Abolitionists as much as he ever did— but that Gen. John wants to be promoted a Major General, and that he intends to bid high enough, in *words*, to secure the position." The paper suggested an ul-terior motive for Logan's patriotism: "He is sharp enough to make tools and fools of the Abolition humbuggers, and as this is his object, we can't resist the in-clination to wish him all sorts of good luck in his new enterprise."[40]

The accusing papers were absolutely correct—but only in respect to Logan's desire to become a major general. Unfortunately, his name did not appear on the list drawn up by the president for promotion. Lincoln never specified a reason for this, but it appeared obvious in the record of events for the past year. Since his gallant action at Fort Donelson, Brigadier General Logan had led a brigade, then a division in remote areas of Tennessee and Mississippi. But in a most active and bloody year of campaigns and battles, John A. Logan had not commanded any action beyond skirmishing. The president and his cabinet were satisfied to keep him as a brigadier general.

Ulysses S. Grant was not. He and his staff seethed when they saw Brigadier General Napoleon B. Buford's name for promotion to major general instead of Logan. Lieutenant Colonel Rawlins saw this as a detriment to the soldiers if Buford received his unworthy commission. In a letter to Congressman Washburne, Rawlins maintained, "Logan deserves promotion for his unflinching patriotism and desire to whip the enemy by any rout or means practicable." Grant went further to correct what he considered to be a gross injustice. "I see the name of N. B. Buford for Major General," wrote Grant to Abraham Lincoln on February 9. "He would scarcely make a respectable Hospital nurse if put in petticoats, and certain—is unfit for any other Military position. He has always been a dead weight to carry, becoming more burdensome with his increased rank."[41] Setting up a stark contrast, Grant continued:

> There are here worthy men to promote who not only would fill their positions with credit to themselves and profitably to their country, but whose promotion would add weight to our cause where it was needed and give renewed confidance [sic] to a large umber of brave soldiers. Conspicuous among this latter class is Brig. Gen. J. A. Logan. He has proven himself a most valuable officer and worthy of every confidence. He is entitled to and can be trusted with a command equal to what increased rank would entitle him to. There is not a more patriotic soldier, braver man, or one more deserving of promotion in this Dept. than Gen. Logan.

Logan never saw Grant's February 9 letter to the president, but it turned out to be the most valuable birthday present he had ever received. Twice in the span of a year Grant stepped in to promote Logan's value to the president. The Senate list now had Logan's name on it. Nominated at the end of February, Logan was confirmed in mid March.[42]

Logan's promotion would have been at the least delayed and may never have occurred without Grant's intervention, a remarkable occurrence given that Grant had witnessed him only once on a battlefield prior to 1863. Major General Logan had much to prove in the upcoming campaign to justify Grant's faith in his leadership.

CHAPTER FIVE

Earned Faith

"UNCLE ABE HAS AT LAST SENSIBLY CONCLUDED to arm the darkey and let him fight." So wrote Jacob Bruner, a member of the Sixty-eighth Ohio, to his wife from Camp Logan in early April 1863. Bruner's opinion had personal meaning—he was an African American aiding the regiment's quartermaster, ready to march as a soldier in one of the new black regiments the president intended to create. Others in Camp Logan were clearly hostile to the notion. Like the Emancipation Proclamation, Lincoln's edict was likely to stir controversy and spark desertion. As a preemptive strike, the administration sent Adjutant General Lorenzo Thomas to inspect General Grant's army and address the troops about the decision to create black regiments to help prosecute the war.[1]

General Thomas arrived by steamer and in the afternoon the Third Division of the Seventeenth Corps, Army of the Tennessee, gathered at the military camp nestled near Lake Providence, Louisiana. The Camp Logan force numbered 7,000 men in Thomas's estimate. He addressed the division and detailed the policy of raising twenty regiments of black troops. He closed his short speech listing the proper treatment of blacks who come into the ranks in subsequent camps and campaigns: "They are to be encouraged to come to us; they are to be received with open arms; they are to be fed and clothed; they are to be armed."[2]

Thomas's "demands" elicited hisses and boos from scores of Union soldiers who stood before him, many who considered his speech nothing but a harangue to force each camp to issue "a series of threatening resolutions" to support the Lincoln administration. Thomas hid an ace up his sleeve to counter the anti-Negro sentiments: he followed up by offering, with the authority of the War Department, to fill up the officer rolls of these regiments with white soldiers currently in front of him. This helped ameliorate the initial hostile reaction, but the mood changed more favorably and dramatically when Logan stepped up to address his men. Completely recovered from the illnesses he had suffered throughout the winter, the reinvigorated general fully endorsed Thomas's theme. Thomas raved about his eloquent remarks, informing the War Department that Logan stated "most emphatically that he would never return to his home, from which his wife and child had been driven by an unnatural father, until this wicked rebellion shall be utterly crushed."[3]

Logan voiced overwhelming support of the policy. A soldier in the Eighty-first Illinois recorded in his diary that Logan admitted his prejudice over the slavery issue at the commencement of the war, believing that it should not be disturbed. "But now, he thanked God that he had got over all that, and was ready to sacrifice slavery and everything else to preserve the Union, and put down the rebellion," recorded the observer. Logan's address indicated that he applauded the policy more as a war measure than as a humanitarian movement; at least that was the impression he wanted to leave on his soldiers. According to a member of the 124th Illinois, Logan roared, "Slavery had struck at the life of the Republic, and there remained no alternative but to strike slavery. . . . We must hurt the rebels in every way possible. Shoot them with shot, and shells and minie balls, and damn them, shoot them with 'niggers'. . . . So we'll unite on this policy, putting the one who is the innocent cause of this war, in the front rank and press on to victory." The soldiers responded to the speech with throaty cheers resonating across the placid lake. Subordinate commanders followed Logan to address their commands and carry on the momentum. Jacob Bruner summarized the entire event with an assessment that few would dispute: "It was a great treat."[4]

The speech underscored Logan's development from "Dirty Work" to an advocate of the Emancipation Proclamation and its inevitable side effect of converting former Southern slaves to Northern soldiers. Logan also demonstrated that the unique bond that he formed with the Thirty-first Illinois as their colonel had been expanded and repeated as a division commander of fifteen infantry regiments, cavalry, and artillery units. He took to calling the troops "My Boys" again, as he had with his former regiment. Representative Elihu B. Washburne, a daily observer of Grant's entire army, was impressed by his former fellow congressman and the three brigades he commanded. In April, Washburne informed

President Lincoln, "Logan has a magnificent division, and I think he is the most popular division commander in this army. There is certainly no man whose heart is more earnestly in the cause than his."[5]

After expending an unusual amount of energy in the attempt to penetrate Vicksburg from late in 1862 to the spring of 1863—including weeks of digging a canal to divert the flow of the mighty Mississippi—Grant made a gutsy call. He decided to transport his army southward and cross the Mississippi to threaten Vicksburg from that direction. After Rear Admiral David Porter surged down the river past Vicksburg by running the gauntlet with a flotilla of eight gunboats and seven transports (Porter succeeded with the loss of two steamers to the tremendous Confederate artillery barrage), Grant transported two corps south of the target city by marching them over the Louisiana bottomlands.

During the movement, he confused the Confederate commander at Vicksburg, Lieutenant General John C. Pemberton, by running simultaneous assaults by two divisions, as well as ordering a daring raid by Colonel Benjamin H. Grierson to damage railroads from LaGrange Tennessee, entirely through Mississippi to Baton Rouge, Louisiana. With all these operations running smoothly, the Thirteenth and Seventeenth Corps of the Army of the Tennessee crossed into Mississippi at the river town of Bruinsburg. Two of Logan's brigades ferried across on the night of April 30; his final infantry brigade crossed the following morning. The river crossing proved tragic. Two steamers collided at 3:00 A.M. on May 1; one of them carried Battery G, Second Illinois Light Artillery. The steamer carting Logan's cannons, artillery horses, and cannoneers, sank. The guns were lost, as were most of the horses. Two artillerists drowned. Logan shrugged off the disaster, refusing to let it foreshadow the pending campaign in Mississippi. But he was forced to enter the theater down 25 percent of his firepower.[6]

Surrounding Logan was a talented staff, a crew of eleven officers untiring in the discharge of their duties. He had looked to his old regiment for some of the aides. Major Robert R. Townes, a son of a former Benton neighbor who enlisted as a lieutenant in the Thirty-first Illinois, served as Logan's assistant adjutant general—essentially his chief of staff. Logan was pleased and comfortable with Townes, who had recently earned his second promotion under his old colonel. Another aide plucked from the "Dirty-first" was John S. Hoover, an Indiana native who sold clocks in Decatur at the start of the war. Lieutenant Hoover was one of five aide-de-camps on the staff. The most recent addition to that quintet was Captain John R. Hotaling. The thirty-eight-year-old New Yorker was perhaps Logan's most intrepid aide, bearing a sabre scar tattooed upon him during the Mexican War. Like Colonel McCook in the Thirty-first Illinois Volunteer Infantry, Hotaling prided himself on being a member of a fighting family; six Hotaling brothers fought for the preservation of the Union.[7]

Most striking about Logan's staff was its youth. Not only were the aides-de-camp young, but so were the talented members with more specialized duties. Captain Lloyd Wheaton, formerly of the Eighth Illinois, was a twenty-four years old acting inspector general; Major John C. Fry was an even younger provost marshal, all of twenty-three. The senior staff member at division headquarters was Major Carlos John Stolbrand, a forty-one-year-old Chicago resident and Logan's most colorful staff member. A native of Sweden, Stolbrand was an excitable sandy-haired officer, one who was easy to anger. His ruddy complexion turned even more sanguine with rage, matching his artillery uniform. Back in Memphis, Stolbrand had flown into fury when he found that someone had freed his clerk, whom Stolbrand had tied to a tree to discipline him for a drunken spree. His anger was not satisfied, for he could not find who countermanded his punishment. (Days later the culprit stepped up to confess: it was Mary Logan.) Major Stolbrand had commanded Battery G, Second Illinois Light Artillery, before Logan promoted him to chief of artillery. It was his guns that sunk with the transport, no doubt darkening the mood of the surly Swede.[8]

After the river accident, Logan ferried across to Bruinsburg, left Major Towne to bring his final brigade to join the other two, and then galloped out on the road to Port Gibson. He overtook his two leading brigades near a running brook and ordered them to fill their canteens. From there Logan rode at their helm. The sun sat in the noonday sky, overlooking a two-mile bobbing blue column, now more than ten miles from their starting point. "It was the most rugged country we have yet seen," observed a member of the 124th Illinois infantry, a regiment participating in its first campaign of the War. The landscape teemed with round-topped hills and their shallow valleys, stunning canebrake and the sweet fragrance of magnolia blossoms. Joyous birds serenaded the troops with their chirpy songs. But dull, distant, desultory booms miles ahead of them grew louder and sharper with each mile they marched. By 2:00 P.M. the perfume of magnolias gave way to the sulfurous stench of fired gunpowder; the chorus of birds could no longer compete with the cacophony of yelling, shouting, screaming men and boys. It was time to battle.[9]

At 2:00 P.M. General Logan and his 4,500 soldiers crested a ridge called Thompson's Hill. They were begrimed with dusty sweat, but the men's adrenaline kicked in, overtaking the fatigue they would have normally suffered from a fifteen-mile march under a hot sun. "All were weary, but when we saw them carrying off the dead and wounded, we forgot our weariness," remarked an Illinois soldier. From the summit of the ridge, Logan and his two brigades watched a panoramic view of a battle that had been roaring for several hours. Major General John McClernand had thrown the four divisions of his Thirteenth Corps into his opponent, one Confederate division commanded by Brigadier General John S. Bowen. McClernand was fully engaged, but Bowen's 7,000 men offered stiff resistance and had thus far checked the 17,700 officers and men opposing them.[10]

Outmanned more than two to one and outgunned by Union artillery by four to one, Bowen benefited from the headlong assaults of his unimaginative opponent, as well as from the thick vines and canebrake that protected his men. But since noon, Bowen had no more reinforcements to feed into the fray. Anticipating the Union troop crossing south of him on April 27, while he commanded at Grand Gulf, Bowen had pleaded with General Pemberton for more troops. Pemberton, commanding in Vicksburg, would spare no more troops for his subordinate. He was paralyzed by Union penetration into the delta north of Vicksburg, and by the success of Colonel Benjamin F. Grierson's railroad raid—just as Grant had planned. Logan's arrival, therefore, was timely; his soldiers boosted the Army of the Tennessee to 22,000 men.[11]

Now enjoying a three-to-one advantage, it was only a matter of time for Grant's men to win this contest. Logan deployed General Smith's brigade to the left, sending them northward to extend McClernand's flank. Logan personally moved with the other half of the force—General Stevenson's brigade—to the opposite flank. Logan's flank extensions widened McClernand's battle front to 2,000 yards. Bowen clung on for nearly two more hours after Logan deployed; at one point he counterpunched Stevenson's advance.[12]

With one battery out of commission, and two others near the Mississippi River, Logan's firepower was reduced to four rifled cannons and two howitzers of the Eighth Michigan Light Artillery. But these six guns were manned by one of the most talented artillery officers in the Army of the Tennessee, Captain Samuel De Golyer. The redoubtable Frenchman unlimbered his guns below the crest of a hill and ordered them loaded with canister and shell. Firing these deadly close-range rounds, the battery routed out Southern sharpshooters and sent the infantry line in commotion. With the creek bottom cleared of opposition, McClernand's and McPherson's infantry lines surged forward, and the rout was on. By sunset the Battle of Port Gibson (also named Thompson's Hill) was over—a necessary victory for General Grant to open his campaign in Vicksburg. Grant's army suffered 875 casualties (4 percent of their engaged strength) while

General Bowen's losses approached 800 men and boys (10 percent of his engaged force). Logan's First and Third Brigades suffered 43 casualties (the late-arriving Second Brigade claimed three wounded men).[13]

Although lightly engaged, Logan's division—at least two brigades of it—made an appreciable contribution to the battle of Port Gibson. For Logan, commanding ten regiments of infantry, a battery, and a cavalry company was far removed from his experience at Fort Donelson fifteen months earlier. He now led a force eight times what he then commanded. By the accounts of those who witnessed him, Logan led them well. Edward Newsome, a Carbondale soldier in the Eighty-first Illinois, noted how calm the mounted general looked as bullets kicked up dust under the horse's hooves. Congressman Washburne wrote a synopsis of the battle to the president, noting, "McClernand did bravely and Logan was magnificent inspiring everywhere the most unbound enthusiasm among his troops." Not surprisingly, the general's men cheered him as he rode by them at battle's end. No greater example of the spell Logan had on his "Boys" can be found than in a letter from Corporal W. W. Span to a Carbondale newspaper. After describing Logan's undaunted coolness while constantly exposed to whizzing bullets, Span informed his readers that if they ever read of a defeat of this division, "You may then examine the newspaper for a long list of slain and wounded, and for a good portion of rebel country stained deeply with the blood of true Unionists and Logan-loving heroes."[14]

Logan's entire division united outside Port Gibson on the night of May 1, prepared to carry on Grant's campaign on the morrow. Early on May 2, 1863, Logan put his men on the unimpeded march to Port Gibson. Singing "The Battle Cry of Freedom" the conquerors entered the city. They did not stay; Logan marched them the rest of the day and into the next one—through woods and fields, and over waterways. By the night of May 3 they had moved on to the Big Black River, twenty miles north of Port Gibson. There at Hankinson's Ferry, he remained for the next three days.[15]

Logan's advance at the head of McPherson's corps placed his command twenty miles from the southern fortifications of Vicksburg. But General Grant would not attack Vicksburg from the south. His objective was much more than driving Generals Pemberton and Johnston from the defense of Vicksburg, for if it was, Grant would move northward toward the city on a series of road networks. Grant chose to remain on the southern side of the Big Black River and head eastward, following conjoining roads toward the Mississippi capital of Jackson. Once Jackson was in the hands of Union troops, Grant planned to turn westward and approach Vicksburg from the east. If successful Grant's strategy would not only control the city and free the Mississippi River, it was destined to force the annihilation or surrender of the Confederate troops defending it.

This was an intricate plan, one impeded by logistics. Grant took over Grand Gulf, which he intended to use as his base for supplies. He ordered General William T. Sherman to bring his Fifteenth Corps and fifty tons of foodstuffs into Mississippi. Sherman's troops would swell Grant to peak strength nearing 40,000 men. Until Sherman joined him, the 24,000 troops, plus hundreds of mules and horses of Grant's army already in Mississippi, were ordered to subsist off the countryside.[16]

Logan made frequent visits to Grant's headquarters as the commanding general labored to concentrate his army and secure his base of supplies. Not only did he find Illinois Governor Richard Yates, Congressman Washburne, and Assistant Secretary Charles Dana in Grant's entourage, he also noted a newspaper reporter watching Grant's every move. Sylvanus Cadwallader, the war correspondent for the *Chicago Times*, had been reporting on the campaign. Logan may have looked upon him with suspicion, for the *Times* had been suspected of Copperhead reporting; Cadwallader himself believed that the newspaper "delighted in seeing how near it could approach the line of disloyalty without incurring the penalty." But the reporter showed none of the proclivities of which his paper was accused. Swarthy and slender, with dark eyes and a noticeably wrinkled face, Cadwallader endeared himself to Grant and enjoyed greater access to the general during the campaign than any other field reporter struggling for a "scoop" to send to their bosses.[17]

Logan impressed Cadwallader, who was familiar with the former hard-drinking and swearing congressman from Egypt. Logan had grown with his military responsibilities, so much so that Cadwallader insisted that Logan had become a temperate man. Although Logan had sworn off drunkenness, Cadwallader witnessed that he did not abstain from frivolity. He saw the general out of uniform on one occasion with a shirt and hat, next to a table adorned with a whiskey bottle and cup, fiddling a tune for a small party of blacks, who danced to it with great joy.[18]

Cadwallader was one of several newspaper reporters covering the Vicksburg Campaign. Logan permitted one to join him and his division. His name was Joseph B. McCullagh, and he wrote for the *Cincinnati Daily Commercial* under the pen name of "Mack." A diminutive but burly Dublin urchin, McCullagh began his war reporting for the *Commercial* while still a teenager. He and Logan rapidly formed an admiration for each other, and Logan allowed "Mack" to record the events of the Third Division of the Seventeenth Corps.[19]

The war correspondent moved with Logan's division as it pulled back from Hankinson's Ferry beginning on May 7; two days later Logan's entire division was leading the advance of the Army of Tennessee northeastward on the Clinton Road toward Jackson, Mississippi. The capital was Grant's new objective. Although it took him farther away from Vicksburg, Grant had learned that thousands of Confederate reinforcements had rushed into the city, under the command of Joseph E. Johnston. Originally Grant wanted to move his men northward to the Southern Railroad (which ran westward to Vicksburg), but Johnston's presence threatened the rear of Grant's force if he conducted this move. Quick to improvise, Grant split his army into four sections marching on converging roads toward Jackson.[20]

By the morning of May 12, Logan was ten miles southwest of Jackson and three miles from the hamlet of Raymond. His division led on the road with Crocker's men pacing well behind. General McPherson rode with Logan that morning while the Second Brigade, commanded by Brigadier General Elias Dennis, scaled a hill, and then deployed as they headed down to the bottomland formed by Fourteenmile Creek. A surprise awaited them. Seven Southern infantry regiments from Tennessee, Texas, and Mississippi, and three cannons, all commanded by Brigadier General John Gregg, lined the creek in position to attack.

Attack they did; 3,000 Confederates caught Dennis's brigade by surprise and before the Union soldiers could adequately react, the rebels were pounding them in front and slipping behind the Yankees to destroy them. Saving the Union brigade in the early going was the terrain. Thick creek vegetation and a dense wood surrounding it helped to obscure the position; the obstructed view also confused Gregg into believing he outnumbered his opponent. He either failed to send, or failed to receive an adequate reconnaissance that morning, one that would have indicated that 12,000 Northern soldiers were in striking distance of Raymond. Still, Gregg's initial concern was Logan's leading brigades.

The woods and underbrush also served to confuse Logan's second advancing brigade. Hearing the artillery but not knowing that Dennis's men were engaged, General John E. Smith's regiments deployed expecting to find the enemy well in front of them, closer to Raymond. Marching since 3:00 A.M. without breakfast, Smith's infantry and DeGolyer's artillerists headed to the creek. Smith deployed his regiments—without skirmishers—to the left of Dennis's soldiers. Exiting the woods and entering a field in front of the creek, the Union infantry was clearly caught off guard. "Then came the 'Rebel Yell'," recalled a member of the Twentieth Illinois. The Seventh Texas charged over the creek and forced two regiments to fall back as well as the battery, which had been watering its horses in the creek.

Gregg's Confederates seemingly were everywhere; one Union soldier insisted that "the timber were swarming with them."[21]

All was confusion as Logan's leading brigades struggled to deploy in the woods and open areas to return fire. Rifle and musket fire cut forest leaves from their stems, producing an autumn-like scene devoid of its color. Colonel Manning Force of the Twentieth Ohio watched as the Texans gained control of the nearly dry bed of Fourteenmile Creek and used it as an effective, natural breastwork. Displeased at the lost opportunity, Force asked an officer of the Twentieth Illinois next to him why they did not anchor themselves at the creek. "We have no orders," came the response.[22]

Logan and McPherson share the blame for the surprise sprung on the advance. The two brigades currently struggling at Fourteenmile Creek outnumbered Gregg's brigade, but one would never know it by the early results of the battle. Missing from the action on the Union side was leadership. At least a mile behind the opening action, Logan heard the artillery fire, followed by the rattle of musketry, and double-quicked his final brigade (General John D. Stevenson's regiments) toward the action. Members of the Second Illinois Cavalry (Company A) galloped back from the bottomland in front of Raymond and found Logan rushing Leggett's brigade to the contest. "What is the matter," Logan called out. "A hornet's nest," shouted back his horse soldiers. Logan wheeled to Stevenson's men and spurred them on by bellowing, "Go in boys and lift them out of that with cold steel."[23]

Logan galloped ahead to restore order to the chaos. He reached the battle just as the ragged blue lines began to waver. He quickly caught sight of the Twenty-third Indiana retreating from the field. He rode to the Hoosiers and, "with the shriek of an eagle," turned the soldiers to face the enemy again. "For God's sake men, don't disgrace your country," he snorted; "see how they're holding them!" At the same time he sent back aides to rush forward Stevenson's brigade and the leading brigades of Crocker's division behind them. In the meantime he moved forward to restore his battle lines. Passing by Colonel Edwin S. McCook of the Thirty-first Illinois, hobbling from a bullet to his foot and using two rifles as crutches, Logan pulled his hat from his head and waved it as he slammed his heels into his horse's flanks, instilling his own enthusiasm in the men.[24]

"Mack" bore witness to Logan's mien that afternoon, and in every subsequent battle of the Vicksburg Campaign. "The air of a battle seemed to mount his brain like the fumes of wine, and with the same outward effect," he fondly recalled. "He kept his command under absolute control always, and seemed gifted with the power of omnipresence while his troops were in action." Theodore Davis, a special artist for *Harper's Weekly Illustrated Newspaper*, sketched Logan at this point with a steady hand—a difficult task given that the artist's horse was shot beneath him moments before.[25]

Logan's lines had begun to rally by the time Stevenson's regiments reached the field. Logan made sure they entered where they were needed. With bullets flying thick around him, he shouted to the Eighty-first Illinois, "Turn back, go to the right and flank them." They complied. "The scene at that time was highly exciting," recalled a member of the regiment; "the volleys of musketry were incessant, the loud mouthed cannon were thundering continually, and the air was filled with the hiss of the rifle balls and the shriek of the grape and shells, while as the rebels were partially successful against our left, their deafening and [exultant] shouts were anything but pleasant to hear."[26]

Logan's fire finally began to take its toll on Gregg's regiments. "I fired 17 shots that time, and I am sure I made one rebel bite the dust," proclaimed a Prairie State soldier. Logan also enjoyed a large advantage in firepower; by midafternoon he deployed sixteen cannons against the three Confederate pieces. Outnumbered two to one and outgunned five to one, Gregg was not going to win the battle.[27]

But the Southerners still held on. McPherson, extremely slow to reinforce Logan, brought Crocker's division to assist him. But by the time they deployed, Gregg gave up the contest and slowly pulled back. By 4:00 P.M. he headed through Raymond and marched to Jackson. Logan claimed the field and slowly moved his men into the town. The Battle of Raymond was a Union victory—attributed to McPherson although he had little influence on the outcome. Logan and his men bore the brunt of the battle, taking all but 10 of the 440 casualties. Gregg's tenacity was more costly to him. One out of six of his soldiers was killed, wounded, or captured—500 in all.[28]

The Battle of Raymond convinced Grant that Jackson was strongly reinforced. Still, he pushed on with his plan to capture the capital. This was accomplished during a driving rainstorm on May 14. McPherson's corps entered from the northwest on the Clinton Road. Logan's division was not engaged in the light action. Unable to resist an assault with a force of 6,000 soldiers, General Johnston had evacuated Jackson after he realized he could not muster the 12,000 men he originally believed he could; he also found that Grant's force well outnumbered what he had available. Before he evacuated the capital, Johnston wrote out a set of orders to deliver to General Pemberton, instructing him to march eastward from Edwards Station (a depot fifteen miles west of the Vicksburg defenses) and, with Johnston's men north of him, converge upon the Union army near Clinton, a road junction approximately twenty miles from Edwards Station. Jackson stood less than ten miles east of Clinton.

Johnston had no idea that one of the couriers to whom he handed those instructions was a Union agent; he delivered the important dispatch to Grant. It was an intelligence coup; not only did Grant know that Johnston and Pemberton had yet to combine their forces, but he also knew to expect to clash with most of Pemberton's army somewhere along the direct road to Vicksburg. With more than 44,000 men at hand, Grant left General Sherman with most of the Fifteenth Corps to tear up the railroad and industrial facilities in Jackson. One division of the Fifteenth Corps and the entire Thirteenth and Seventeenth Corps—32,000 officers and men—would head west on somewhat parallel roads to battle Pemberton's men between Vicksburg and Jackson. Grant saw this as the opportunity to destroy the bulk of an army out of its meticulously prepared entrenchments; the least he expected was to interpose the Army of the Tennessee between Pemberton's and Johnston's armies and prevent them from ever combining their strength.[29]

Encamped two miles west of Jackson, Logan moved his division early on May 15, marching westward on the road to Vicksburg. Accompanying the headquarters' staff was Joseph McCullagh and Sylvanus Cadwallader. Cadwallader rode with Logan, expecting his division to be the first to clash with the enemy. This was Logan's expectation as well, but when he reached the intersection of the Vicksburg Road and the Edward's Depot Road, he was forced to halt his men. Colonel Alvin P. Hovey's division had already taken the latter road in front of them. Logan, according to Cadwallader, "gave one of the finest exhibitions of single-handed swearing that was ever listened to by mortal ears. The entire vocabulary was exhausted, new expletives coined by scores and hundreds, and the changes rung upon all of them until he was physically worn out." Or so Cadwallader thought. When General McPherson rode up a few minutes later, Logan repeated his tirade. After Logan settled down, the march resumed and the men moved another seven miles before they halted at a creek bed near Bolton.[30]

The Army of the Tennessee sported a new look as its available seven divisions advanced on parallel roads at 5:00 A.M. on May 16. Two divisions advanced on the Raymond Road (the southernmost road), including Major General Frank Blair's division of the Fifteenth Corps, now attached to fellow politician John A. McClernand's Thirteenth Corps. McClernand rode with two more of his divisions (Generals Carr and Osterhaus) on the next road north—appropriately named the Middle Road. Logan marched his men as part of the largest advance, moving from Bolton on the Jackson Road. Logan rode his horse in the middle of the column led by General Hovey's division of the Thirteenth Corps (temporarily attached to the Seventeenth), followed by Logan's division, with Brigadier General Isaac F. Quinby's division (the Seventh Division of the Seventeenth Corps) following in the rear. Quinby had just returned from sick leave but was still in poor health; therefore, he left his subordinate, Marcellus Crocker, in charge of his men that morning. Logan's division also returned a commander when General Mortimer D. Leggett came back from his leave of absence to resume command of the Second Brigade, displacing General Dennis from this temporary duty.[31]

Grant's decision to move with these seven divisions still pitted a force of greater strength against an opponent, but military doctrine favored Pemberton and his Confederates if the Confederate chose good ground—a height with sufficient artillery to defend it. This Pemberton did, as Grant learned by midmorning of May 16, 1863. But even before he knew, he had sent orders to Sherman to send another division from Jackson to Grant's current position.[32]

By 7:00 A.M. Hovey's men in front of Logan engaged Pemberton's skirmishers six miles east of Edwards Station. The Confederates had begun to execute Pemberton's plan to link forces with Johnston north of Jackson when the Army of the Tennessee put an end to that plan. Although disorganized and confused in the early going, the Confederates planted themselves on ground deemed strong for the defense. One division of Confederate infantry, commanded by General Carter Stevenson, covered the Crossroads—the junction of three roads, two that carried Union troops. McClernand moved northward on the Middle Road, and McPherson advanced with the divisions of Hovey, Logan, and Crocker on the Jackson road, which swung from northwest to due west as it ran through the intersection. At the point where the Jackson road diverted stood the house of Sid Champion, a local farmer serving in Pemberton's army. Across from his house the road negotiated over a portion of a seventy-foot rise that bore the name of the farmer and of the battle fought on his land—Champion Hill.

Three Confederate brigades of Stevenson's division, with a battery, successfully defended Champion Hill and the crossroads just west of it against nine Union brigades in the four divisions that converged upon the crossroads. By the time Grant arrived on the field at 10:00 A.M., he saw only Hovey's division deployed and heavily engaged. McClernand had not fought his opponent—consisting of only two brigades—on the Middle Road, following Grant's earlier instructions not to bring on a general engagement. Earlier Grant attempted to supersede those orders with attack instructions, but the courier failed to deliver the message to McClernand until after noon. Farther south, on the Raymond Road, Grant's other two divisions had not made contact with the bulk of two divisions of Confederates blocking their advance toward Edwards Station.

McPherson, to this point, had moved his troops as if they all had been marching in quicksand. He was not impressive at Raymond, where he failed to concentrate his available force, thus permitting one brigade of Southerners to slow his advance for several hours. In front of Champion Hill, two divisions were immediately at hand, but an early advantage was lost because it took McPherson two hours from the opening volleys by Hovey's division to begin to deploy the next force in his command. That force was John A. Logan's division. Hovey's men lay prone to escape the fuselage of lead fired at them. McPherson brought up Logan's men and began to lead the division to the right of Hovey's position. The steamy, dense air magnified the weight of the soldiers' accoutrements as they hustled to get into position. By 11:00 A.M. Logan and McPherson deployed two of the three brigades and their attached batteries. Leggett's brigade extended Hovey's left, followed by Smith's brigade. Stevenson's brigade would be last in line.

Logan was ready to battle. When an aide to Grant rode up to him and asked where he could be found, Logan haughtily replied, "Where the bullets fly the thickest, by G—d."[33] The bullets flew the thickest around his brigades and Hovey's division. To escape them, the deployed soldiers received orders to lie down. A Buckeye in the Twentieth Ohio recorded the action in his journal, "The command was obeyed with alacrity, for bullets were already whizzing over our heads. I never hugged Dixie's soil as close as I have today." Colonel Manning Force, commanding the Ohio regiment, recalled the firing as so heavy that a staff officer talked while unconsciously screening his eyes with his hand, as he would in a driving rainstorm. Southern artillery also wreaked havoc along Logan's line; a member of the 124th Illinois likened the buzzing shells to a swarm of bees.[34]

Before Stevenson's brigade moved into position on Logan's right, the entire division came under attack from Confederate infantry—Alabama soldiers—moving from the crest of Champion Hill. Aiming for Smith's brigade and Major Stolbrand's batteries, the Southerners rent the air with the rebel yell as they approached in tight marching formation. "Sheneral Schmidt, dey are sharging you mitt double column," declared the excited Stolbrand. "They vant mine guns." Smith expressed more confidence than did the Swedish chief of artillery. "Let 'em come," he replied, "we're ready to receive them." Logan and McPherson cantered up to the position to steady the men. McPherson bellowed, "Give them Jesse, boys, give them Jesse." Logan rose in his stirrups and announced the import of the moment: "We are about to fight the battle for Vicksburg."[35]

Logan then turned to the Thirty-first Illinois. He was accustomed to spending time with his old regiment in the intervals between battles to talk with his former regiment. Logan usually offered words of encouragement to his "Boys" and the promise to write home to tell their mothers what good soldiers they were. The overt favoritism appears to have produced no backlash from the other regiments in the division. But this day, Logan's appeal to the "Dirty-first" carried out to the rest of Smith's brigade: "Thirty onesters remember the blood of your mammas. We must whip them here or all go under the sod together. Give them hell!"[36]

The "Boys" and men responded as Logan had intended. In minutes, the attacking Alabamans marched into a sheet of flame volleyed by Yankee rifles. But Logan's artillery—DeGolyer's Michigan battery in particular—inflicted the greatest destruction upon the Southerners. As the Confederates attempted to climb a rail fence to continue the charge, the big guns opened upon them at close range. An Ohio soldier remarked, "It seemed as if every shell burst just as it reached the fence, and rails and rebs flew into the air together."[37]

As the Confederate formation loosened and broke up in front of him, Logan saw his opportunity for a counterpunch. McPherson had moved well off to his right to position Stevenson's brigade; Grant was also out of reach back at headquarters at the Champion House. On his left, Hovey's men were exhausted; Logan believed they were about to retire. His opportunity was ripe, but he had no time to find a superior officer to grant the request. Without second guessing, Logan ordered Smith to charge. "Boys, give them hell," Logan declared as he rode along the brigade front.[38]

The troops carried out Logan's order in spectacular fashion. "It was a sight that I shall never forget, when those thousands of brave boys, in perfect order, swept across the field!" raved a cavalryman escorting Logan and his staff. Those "thousands of brave boys" referred to 4,000 men in Smith's and Leggett's brigades, nine regiments bearing down on their retreating opponent. Stevenson's brigade launched off from their flank position and added four more regiments and nearly 2,000 more infantry into the fight. Stevenson's regiments turned the left flank of the Confederate infantry, at the same time driving them into the path of Smith's and Leggett's charging infantry. The combination crushed the Confederate flank. Logan's assault also rejuvenated the hard-pressed members of the two engaged brigades of Hovey's division; they surged forward along each side of the Jackson Road and roared toward the crest. In all, five brigades of Union infantry rolled up the Confederate defenders on the height. Years later a member of the Forty-fifth Illinois in Smith's brigade assessed this 10,000-man assault "as one of the finest charges of troops that I witnessed during the war, and I was in nine different battles."[39]

Logan was in peak battle form at Champion Hill. He sparked passion in his troops, offering words of encouragement as well as staying with them at the front. He bolstered wavering troops whenever he saw them by getting the attention of Major Towne, Captain Hotaling, and other staff officers. "Stick a flagstaff in the ground," Logan bellowed to his aides, "and see if the boys won't rally round it." Joseph McCullagh had reported on Logan in battle at Raymond, and watched him at Champion Hill. From his observations, "Mack" concluded that Logan was "the radiant incarnation of war." Assistant Secretary of War Charles Dana watched Logan inspire his men with his enthusiasm during this cacophonous battle, and deemed him "splendid in all its crash and commotion." Fred Grant, the commander's twelve-year-old son, watching Logan pass by as he addressed and positioned each regiment, planted the general's gallant image into his mind. He had accompanied him several times during the campaign, but never did he witness what Logan displayed in this battle. It was an image he would never forget.[40]

Fred Grant's father held Logan in the same high regard, and was willing to put his faith in him. Sensing the impact of Logan's counterpunch back at headquarters at the Champion House, General Grant—while chomping on a cigar—turned to an aide and said, "Go down to Logan and tell him he is making history to-day." Grant also instructed the messenger to ask Logan if he needed reinforcements. Logan responded with swashbuckling bravado: "Tell General Grant there are not rebels enough outside of hell to drive back the Third Division."[41]

Grant's and Logan's pronouncements proved premature. Logan's men succeeded in driving the Confederate resistance from Champion Hill, claiming the capture of hundreds of Confederates and eleven cannons (nearly every regiment in Hovey's two brigades also claimed a stake in half the artillery captures). But the hard-fought action on the hill did not chase Pemberton's men into a retreat. Since he had little resistance from McClernand's divisions on his right, Pemberton ably shifted these men toward the heavily pressed left flank. By the time Logan's men ascended Champion Hill, they faced the results of Grant's failure to have simultaneous assaults against the wings of the Confederate defense. A member of the Thirty-first Illinois noted, "Those who mounted the hill could see to their left, dense masses of infantry, the bulk of Pemberton's army."

Despite the Confederate reinforcements, Logan's division not only commanded the flank, but Stevenson's brigade, after seizing seven cannons, also had control of the Jackson Road behind the Confederate line. In other words, they blocked Pemberton's escape route. Unfortunately, no one seemed to realize this at the time. Rounding up prisoners also appeared to have sapped some of the momentum from the assault. The time passed 1:00 P.M.; McClernand's four divisions on the Union left had yet to commit to the battle. McClernand perversely stuck to the letter of his early-morning instructions not to engage his opponent, even though the raging sound of battle to his right should have convinced him that instructions handed to him several hours before were now woefully outdated. A two-brigade division of Confederates, commanded by General Bowen, arrived on the Confederate left in time to throw back the outmanned brigades of General Hovey, and sent them back toward Champion Hill.

Grant had one more division in this sector to commit—the 5,000 men in Quinby's division (still commanded by Colonel Crocker). He threw these brigades forward to support Hovey, but Bowen's division tossed them back with a crushing counterassault. Logan and Grant were conferring behind the infantry flanking the Confederate left when one of Hovey's aides delivered his general's plea to salvage his position. Desperate for reinforcements, Grant peeled off Stevenson's brigade from the far right of the Union line and sent them closer to Hovey's position toward the center. "Neither Logan nor I knew that we had cut off the retreat of the enemy," he confessed, admitting that the repositioning of Logan's brigade "uncovered the rebel line of retreat, which was soon taken advantage of by the enemy."[42]

While his other brigades staunchly clung to their position, Logan moved to the scene of the heaviest action toward the left of his line. The Missouri troops in one of Bowen's brigades had pummeled the right of Crocker and Hovey's position and thus had exposed the left flank of Logan's line. One regiment from Crocker's division, the Thirty-fourth Indiana, was especially hard hit, and they fled the field in panic—just to the left of Smith's brigade. Right there a member of the Thirtieth Illinois in Smith's force looked out and remembered what caught his line of vision: "We saw Gen. Logan, a half mile off to our right, approaching with the speed of a cyclone."

Logan had seen this happen at Raymond, ironically, with another regiment of Indiana troops. He charged toward the fleeing Hoosiers and shouted, "Men, for God's sake, don't disgrace your state." He shamed them, pointing out that he had been injured several times in this war and had never turned his back to the enemy. He lectured them like a fire-and-brimstone preacher—"every word weighed a pound," recalled one who heard him at that moment—and succeeded in getting the regiment to stop. Logan wheeled toward the adjutant of the Thirty-fourth Indiana and insisted that he get his men together. When Logan heard the adjutant's response—"General, the rebels are awful thick up there"—he spat out a succinct, homespun pearl on the secret of winning a battle. "Damn it," cursed Logan, "that's the place to kill them—where they are thick."[43]

The Hoosiers spun about and reentered the fray. Logan seized one of their flags and led them forward. Finally, McClernand received positive instructions to attack Pemberton's right flank. He did so, and with the combination of the rejuvenated Union troops near Champion Hill, Pemberton's Confederates were sent fleeing in retreat at 4:00 P.M. After the hours-long skirmishing in the morning, the Battle of Champion Hill turned out to be a five-hour fight. Pemberton lost 3,800 men; Grant took 2,400 casualties in his ranks. Logan tallied 400 killed, wounded, and missing soldiers in his three brigades. Grant's losses were not in vain. Pemberton had no chance to link with Johnston, and Grant could now surround him at Vicksburg. Indeed, this was a decisive battle for the campaign with a clear result—Pemberton lost.[44]

But Logan apparently refused to believe this conclusion. His confident leadership on the battlefield gave way to equivocal second-guessing in the immediate aftermath. Assistant Secretary Dana and Colonel Rawlins (Grant's assistant adjutant general) came across Logan shortly after 4:00 P.M. He was beside himself, according to Dana, claiming that the day was lost. Despite Dana's attempt to correct him, Logan could not be swayed. He countered, "Don't you hear the cannon over there? They will be down on us right away! In an hour I will have twenty thousand men to fight." Dana was incredulous at Logan's attempt to convince him that Grant's army lost the Battle of Champion Hill. He brushed it off as "an intellectual peculiarity."[45]

Logan recovered his senses quick enough to aid in the pursuit of Pemberton's fleeing army. The Confederates fought a delaying action at the Black River Bridge on May 17; they then nestled behind the protection of their elaborate field fortifications encircling Vicksburg. Grant's three corps (Sherman and the Fifteenth Corps had come in from Jackson) quickly outlined the Confederate earthworks with a blue crescent teeming with sun-glared steel and iron, locking Pemberton in a besieged city with a river at his back and all roads blocked by the Army of the Tennessee. Two other corps of Grant's army sealed the regions across the river. In all, Grant had concentrated more than 70,000 soldiers in the Vicksburg region. For Pemberton and his 35,000 men stuck in Vicksburg, there was no escape.

Believing in a quick end to the campaign, Grant was not initially satisfied to resort to siege tactics. Sherman and the Fifteenth Corps covered the north and northeastern sector of Vicksburg; McClernand controlled the southern and southeastern region, marked by the Southern Mississippi Railroad. This left McPherson and the Seventeenth Corps to operate across the most easterly approach. Logan's third division manned the Jackson Road; Smith's brigade covered north of the road while Stevenson's brigade covered the southern side. Leggett's brigade held a rearward position behind Smith's brigade. Smith's regiments faced a redan, a triangular-shaped fortification with the apex facing the Union soldiers. A Confederate battery and the Third Louisiana Volunteer Infantry manned the redan. Stevenson's regiments stood across and somewhat north of the rectangular-shaped fortification called Great Redoubt, the most formidable work in the Confederate defense line. Sherman's corps attacked the fortifications without success on May 19. Undaunted, Grant called upon a three-corps assault three days later. On May 22, the fateful movement commenced.[46]

"The regiment started forward, as usual, with a yell under the hottest fire I have ever been under before (and I was at Shiloh)," recounted a member of the Forty-fifth Illinois to his parents. "The air seemed filled with bullets, which whistled with spiteful fury, like the winds around our Northern homes, in winter." Generals Smith and Stevenson participated, while General Leggett held a reserve position. Leggett's regiments were fortunate, for Logan's charging brigades took a ferocious beating with no appreciable gain. The soldiers called it "Forlorn Hope" with ample justification. More than 20,000 soldiers charged against Pemberton's defenses. When it ended, Grant gained no real estate and lost more than 3,000 soldiers. Logan's two active brigades suffered nearly 360 killed and wounded in the ill-fated attack. Pemberton's fortifications proved formidable; the Confederates suffered fewer than 600 casualties that day.[47]

Making matters worse was the inability to clear the bodies between the lines for two days. Blackened and bloated in the Mississippi sun, the Union dead induced a Confederate soldier to complain, "The Yanks are trying to stink us out of Vicksburg." A brief truce on May 25 allowed time to perform the gruesome task of clearing the decaying dead from the no-man's-land region between the lines.[48]

The results of May 22 guaranteed the inevitable—a siege. The respite along the lines allowed the news of the campaign to catch up to loved ones at home. Newspapers throughout Illinois, Indiana, Ohio, Wisconsin, and the trans-Mississippi states reported extensively on the Vicksburg Campaign throughout the late spring and early summer of 1863. Logan's status was rising in the eyes of his most influential enemies. No greater example than the *Chicago Tribune* illustrated that "bygones are by-gones." In a column headline titled "Gen. John A. Logan," a late-May edition of the paper proclaimed "we may in all truthfulness and sincerity declare that since this war broke out, and since Gen. Logan assumed the patriot's part, and pushed gallantly into the thickest and hottest of the fight, we have conceived and expressed admiration for his qualities as a man and a lover of his country that we have never felt before."[49]

Letters from family and friends also caught up with the ever-moving army, and Mary's letters found their way to Logan. She complained about former neighbors in Marion "picking your bones severely . . ." in an early May letter, but then acknowledged that the news was all positive about his efforts for the Union. Logan had written his wife one short letter since he stepped onto Mississippi soil back on May 1. He updated her on the last day of May, informing her that he was well and that they captured Bob Kelly, the son of a Carbondale neighbor who had joined Thorndike Brook's company with Hybert Cunningham two years earlier. "The final struggle will be a desperate one," he admitted with thoughts of the week-old failed assault on his mind, "tho I feel confident of our success." He must not have felt as confident about his own success when he closed, "I will come home if alive as soon as the struggle is over. . . . Kiss 'Dollie' and a thousand for yourself."[50]

He had good reason to be unsure of his survival. Logan continuously flaunted his courage to the Confederates around Vicksburg. He placed division headquarters in the foremost position of the Union line. Behind a large Union battery designated "Battery Logan." The timber and dirt-filled structure stood approximately 250 yards from the Third Louisiana redan, the high point near the Confederate line of fortification. (The soldiers called the Confederate bastion "Fort Hill;" after the failed assault of the twenty-second, they renamed it "Fort Hell.") So close was Logan to the Southerners that when 200 duty-shirkers were escorted to him, he had them placed in an enclosure on a hill just behind headquarters, dubbed the "Bull Pen." There the men cowered in fear as spent balls from a Confederate cannonade dropped all around them.[51]

Confederate cannon fire became a routine experience for Logan and his division soldiers. Because of its distinctive hiss, soldiers took to calling the large Confederate siege gun "Whistling Dick" and "Whistling Jack," and its incoming artillery round "Whitiker." The shells arrived at intervals; one soldier timed the interval at fifteen minutes. A round spanned nearly one foot in diameter, and when one came in—loudly announced—it usually bore into the soft Mississippi earth with a *chug*. Then it exploded, kicking up dirt and dust. Sometimes a shell burst in air; when it did so, the fragments dispersed and fell with a *whir* and *buzz*. A characteristic *zip* emanated from the point of contact—sometimes against a body. Logan's guns responded with corresponding rapidity. Major Stolbrand tallied 13,500 rounds fired by his four batteries during the siege of Vicksburg—an average of 300 cannon blasts per day, or a discharge every three minutes during daylight hours.[52]

If the cannonades unnerved Logan, he never showed it. As he explained, "Sometimes it is necessary for a commanding officer to go into danger to inspire the right kind of feeling among his men." Logan felt the need to inspire at Vicksburg; a decision he later admitted was a mistake. A large Union siege gun was planted forty feet from his tent and it wasn't long before Confederate artillerists converged their fire upon it, delivering a torrent of mortar rounds. A visitor to Logan's headquarters noted that the rebel rounds not only destroyed the general's rail stable, but also had rented the earth all around the tent. "No commander in the Army of Tennessee possessed the love and confidence of his men to a greater degree than John A. Logan," concluded the dinner guest. "This was caused not only by his care for his troops, but by his uniform habit of sharing alike the hardships and danger of the campaign."[53]

Desensitized by the incessant incoming rounds, Logan displayed a macabre sense of humor to his division officers. A major entered Logan's line to visit the division and when Logan learned he was a Swede, the general pointed across the campground to a tent region that was hit by an exploding round. He told the guest that it belonged to his Swedish chief of artillery and that he had inspected the area after the cannonade and found Major Stolbrand killed by the Confederate round. "Poor Stolbrand!" he wailed. "Perhaps you would like to see the remains?" The Swedish visitor consented and Logan led him with a host of officers to the gruesome-looking tent. They stepped inside to see a blanket covering the outlines of a body on the cot. The group walked to the head of the bed where Logan solemnly lifted the blanket. Instead of Stolbrand's mangled body, the upturned blanket uncovered only a bundle of rags. The general had staged Stolbrand's death as a practical joke for his officers and visitor, who noted that Logan was so amused by it all that his whole body shook with convulsed laughter.[54]

Notwithstanding his opportune moments for levity, Logan acknowledged the danger, but more to small arms fire than to artillery rounds. Stolbrand was alive, but Confederate sharpshooters killed two of his battery commanders, including Captain DeGolyer on May 28. One day he was out on the siege line, inspecting the position, when he noticed his conspicuous appearance on horseback (he refused to conceal his uniform) attracted rifle fire from the Confederates near the redan opposing him. Logan realized this fire was too close; but instead of turning around and riding down the hill, he galloped along the length of the Union line, attracting more fire with each pace of his horse. One bullet struck his horse and another chipped the saddle. "They must have fired a hundred shots before I got out of the way," he estimated; "I suppose that looked to some people like courage. It wasn't. It was horse sense." He reasoned that if he turned and attempted to ride away from the fire rather than along it, "they would probably have bored me through the back half a dozen times. By riding as I did I made it next to impossible for them to hit me."

Logan was struck once, and he concealed the wound. He was sitting on a chair at his tent, leaning back with his right foot propped against the ridgepole, when an unannounced ball of lead flew into headquarters. The bullet struck the top of the chair and glanced up into his thigh. The surgeon removed the ball, deeming the injury a mere flesh wound. Logan never said a word about it, but the soldiers caught and spread the news about his bullet-struck chair. His headquarters was so close to the Confederate line that Grant positioned himself there on occasion to observe the enemy position and maneuvers. The commanding general did not attract fire there, but did nearby at a sharpshooter tower constructed of railroad iron. Even the direct route between Logan's and Grant's headquarters was unsafe; Southern sharpshooters had trained their weapons upon it, forcing all riders to conceal themselves in the nearby timber during their missions between the locales.[55]

The daily violence and danger appeared to immunize Logan from fear. It also usurped common sense, not only in exposing himself to the danger, but also in understanding the fears of his wife. He understandably passed along the sad news of the death of friends and neighbors to her in his infrequent letters. But he went too far. Logan sent Mary the bullet that was dug from his leg. He also sent fragments from huge shells that exploded near his headquarters, not realizing how upsetting it all was to her. "Darling I trembled with pure horror," she wrote upon receiving the rebel ball once buried in Logan's thigh. The largest souvenir of all went to Dollie. Logan sent her a pony.[56]

Logan's men were not idle during the siege. Shortly after the failed assaults of May 22, Third Division soldiers began tunneling between a point near Logan's headquarters and the Confederate redan opposing it. Many of the workers were Galena prewar lead miners in the Forty-fifth Illinois. Throughout that sultry month of June, they burrowed between and beneath the opposing lines, north of the Jackson Road. By the middle of June the diggers reached to within twenty-five yards of the redan with an eight-foot-wide trench seven feet deep; five days later they touched the outer edge of the fortress. The work was performed to cover soldiers coming across four abreast. Over the next four days, volunteers tunneled underneath the redan. Forty-five feet later the tunnel neared completion. Concurrently, Confederate workers labored on a similar mission toward the Union works. But Logan's men proved more efficient, and on June 25, they packed the portion of the tunnel directly below the redan with one ton of black powder. Waiting to attack the position after the explosion was General Leggett's brigade, lying prone.[57]

The miners detonated the gunpowder at 3:00 P.M. Twenty-eight minutes later than expected, the ground swelled, and then exploded into airborne pulverized earth, clouds of smoke, and flying dark objects. Before the debris cleared from the air, the Union charge commenced. Pioneers led the assault, clearing the path in front of the explosion for the soldiers to pass. Onward rushed Leggett's brigade, led by the Forty-fifth Illinois filing in four abreast. They soon found that Confederates had pulled back prior to the detonation, anticipating the explosion. Rending the air with a rebel yell, the Southerners charged across from the west. Opposing infantrymen from Illinois, Ohio, Louisiana, Mississippi, and Missouri clashed in and near the crater. Fists flew in the hand-to-hand combat, but the soldiers also clubbed their muskets and stabbed each other with bayonets.

The death struggle carried on into the night and the next morning. Rebels threw hand grenades into the hole, adding more terror and death into the melee. By now it was well apparent that the endeavor would not decide the campaign. Logan watched in horror as men died in front of him. "My God! They are killing my bravest men in that hole," he cried. Grant ordered McPherson to recall the troops, putting an end to the carnage. The explosion and subsequent attack thinned Logan's ranks by nearly 200 men.[58]

Undeterred, Grant ordered another mine exploded at the same redan on July 1. This detonation was equally as impressive, but all decided against committing troops into the aftermath. Seconds after the explosion, a slave named Abraham literally "dropped in" to Logan's lines. The explosion catapulted the Vicksburg worker (he was digging the Confederate mine at the time) high into the air. In seconds, he crashed to the earth—right in front of Logan's headquarters. More stunned than hurt, the man gained his senses and was escorted to safety behind the Union lines. Logan employed Abraham at his headquarters while enterprising soldiers mimicked the famous showman, P. T. Barnum, and charged an admission fee to view the man with the most unusual route to emancipation. The real P. T. Barnum seized upon the opportunity to use Abraham in his traveling American Museum. "I claim to be a great 'blower'," wrote Barnum to Logan, "but you took the wind out of me when you blew up Abraham."[59]

Notwithstanding the ineffectiveness of the mines, the siege of Vicksburg was in its last days. On July 3 General Pemberton sent Grant a missive, suggesting a contingent of appointed commissioners to meet "with a view to arranging the capitulation of Vicksburg. Logan and several other division and corps commanders joined Grant between the lines—in front of Logan's position—as he met with Pemberton that afternoon to hash out the surrender. There Logan met a new commander of the Thirteenth Corps. Given permission to fire anyone who violated regulations, Grant used it to oust McClernand back in June when the controversial subordinate claimed sole credit for his corps during the botched May 22 assaults. McClernand made matters far worse by publishing his bombastic congratulations in a newspaper. This violated policy and gave Grant the opportunity to weed out another undesirable member of his army. Major General Ord took over for McClernand and took part in the surrender negotiations.[60]

Pemberton demonstrated that he was willing to hold out longer rather than surrender unconditionally. That afternoon and evening, negotiations produced a scenario amenable to both parties. Grant decided to parole all of Pemberton's soldiers rather than ship them off to Northern prison camps. White flags popped up along the Confederate lines the following morning. Logan and all the officers were ecstatic; they proudly passed instructions down to their foot soldiers. When Logan's men received orders to march—dressed in their best uniforms—they instantly divined the meaning. "Such a rejoicing as it made in camp is seldom known," entered a soldier in his diary. Granted the post of honor for his work throughout the campaign and siege, Logan led the Third Division into Vicksburg, the first Union troops to claim a prize fought over for a year. The Stars and Stripes flickered in the wind as soldiers hoisted the tattered flag of the Forty-fifth Illinois over the courthouse. A member of that regiment captured the ecstasy in his diary: "In a single moment the excitement became so great that you scarcely heard yourself talk. The whole division belched out in one glad shout." Impetuously the soldiers belted out their most patriotic version of "The Battle Cry of Freedom."[61]

Vicksburg proved a costly investment. The forty-five-day siege alone produced 4,671 casualties within the Army of the Tennessee, most of those incurred in one day (May 22). But Pemberton lost his entire army. The Confederacy suffered 2,000 fewer combat losses during the siege than did the Union, but Pemberton surrendered ten times that number—29,500 soldiers—to top his count well beyond 30,000. Grant had effectively wiped out his second Confederate army in eighteen months. Total campaign losses from April to July fell below 10,000 Union battle casualties (less than those lost in two days of fighting at Shiloh), but those sacrifices were necessary to destroy a Confederate army of 40,000 men and seize 260 cannon, 60,000 small arms, and millions of rounds of ammunition. Considering that Grant crossed into Mississippi at the end of April and beginning of May outnumbered by his enemy, his accomplishment was truly outstanding.[62]

Pemberton's surrender occurred just one day after Robert E. Lee lost the battle of Gettysburg to General Meade and the Army of the Potomac. But this was only part of the reason for the enhanced effect of the surrender of Vicksburg. Pemberton must not have appreciated the symbolism of dates. By agreeing to the surrender when he did, he made the ceremony that much more significant and memorable for his captors. "This was the most glorious Fourth of July we ever spent, and the proudest day of our lives," penned an emotional Forty-fifth Illinois soldier to his parents. A member of the Eighty-first Illinois exclaimed, "Oh, for a telegraph or a carrier-pigeon to proclaim the glad tidings to the nation on this anniversary day!" General McPherson told his brother, "I tell you Robt it was a Glorious 'Fourth of July' for us down here, and though we did not have much time to 'celebrate' in the approved style, we enjoyed it immensely." Conversely and not surprisingly, the Southerners found no reason to celebrate — ever again. The day and event embittered Vicksburg residents so much that the city refused to commemorate the anniversary of America's birth and independence for eighty-two more years.[63]

General Logan performed so well to easily justify Grant's faith in his leadership, for Grant praised him as "a prompt, gallant, and efficient officer" who was as competent a division commander "as could be found in or out of the army." Assistant Secretary Dana recognized this, and let Secretary Stanton — Dana's boss — know about him in a July 12 letter assessing Grant's lieutenants. Despite Logan's "intellectual peculiarity" that Dana witnessed in the immediate aftermath of Champion Hill, he saw too much positive in Logan to let that stand out in his assessment of him. He sketched Logan as "a man of remarkable qualities and peculiar manner." He also pointed out Logan's paradoxes. He characterized Logan as heroic and brilliant but unsteady, instinctive rather than reflective, oftentimes cursed by "absurd" judgments balanced by "apt" opinions, and conflicted by the forces of generosity and animosity. "On the whole," concluded Dana, "few can serve the cause of the country more effectively than he, and none serve it more faithfully."[64]

As significant as it was to be recognized by members of the War Department and by the media, Logan's status also rose in the eyes and minds of his men and his superior officer — the most important people to impress. His soldiers were in awe of him even before he stepped on a battlefield with them. Immediately after Champion Hill, an Ohioan in Logan's ranks watched Logan and Grant ride by with the all the corps commanders in the Army of the Tennessee. "I wonder if they love their men as we love them," he wondered in his diary. A Michigan artillerist rhapsodized, "I have always thought if an artist wanted to paint a picture which should personify the very spirit of war, he could not find a better subject than Gen. Logan as he sat on that great black stallion of his at Champion Hills or in the midst of any fight. He looked like the Spirit of War and was a most inspiring sight to his men."[65]

Grant placed Logan in charge of the city guard in Vicksburg, and he accepted the responsibility with relish. His pride at the accomplishments of his troops could not be contained. So worn out that he could barely write, he still bubbled over when he sat down to pen a letter to his wife. "The victory is the greatest triumph of modern times," declared Logan to Mary on July 5; "My division has immortalized itself in the eyes of the army and has universal praise."[66]

Logan had no praise for the parole process of nearly 30,000 Confederate officers and men. Grant's presurrender negotiations with Pemberton gave the latter a concession of allowing his men to leave with their property. On July 6, Pemberton coyly asked McPherson if his officers would be allowed to take their slaves with them. McPherson received authorization to allow the officers to take one servant only after that servant was questioned by a U.S. officer to be assured that he or she was willing to go.

Logan watched the process turned into a farce as coercion unfolded in the parole procedures. Officers intimidated their slaves by conveniently accompanying them to headquarters, rather than allow them to be questioned alone. Logan also received word that nefarious citizens of Vicksburg were active in the streets urging other blacks—ones who were not servants of the officers—to go with the officers. This included blacks who had been forced to work on the fortifications prior to and during the siege. This violated the Emancipation Proclamation.

Logan quickly acted to fill in this loophole in the Vicksburg parole policy. "I solemnly protest, as an officer of the United States Army, against the manner in which Confederate officers are permitted to intimidate their servants in presence of officers appointed to examine said servants," he complained in a dispatch to Grant on July 7, 1863, "and also against passes worded permitting them to go out with their masters. The manner in which this thing is being done is conniving at furnishing negroes to every officer who is a prisoner in Vicksburg." Logan's alert quickly ceased the procedure; later that day, McPherson wrote Pemberton that he was withdrawing the permission "in consequence of the abuse of the privilege." The incident marked the first time that Logan acted on behalf of African Americans solely for humanitarian reasons. It would not be his last.[67]

The command responsibilities in Vicksburg were short lived. Barely two weeks after he marched his men into Vicksburg, Grant allowed Logan a twenty-day leave to recuperate from the campaign's hardships. Logan jumped at the opportunity and headed back to Southern Illinois. Naturally, he stopped off at Cairo, and just as naturally, he was welcomed by a circle of friends and acquaintances. He spoke briefly to a small crowd gathering to hear him. He talked about Vicksburg, about the efforts of the U.S. Army, about patriotism, and about his desire to crush the rebellion by any means available. No one in the throng at Cairo—including the general himself—understood that Logan was delivering remarks they would read again and again throughout the summer.[68]

Logan boarded a passenger car and headed up the Illinois Central Railroad to home. What stepped off the train at the Carbondale Depot turned heads among the citizenry of the town. Major General Logan and his visibly young collection of staff officers made their way from the boxcars to Logan's home on the west side of town, adding to the already-heightened military presence in Jackson County, where scores of soldiers were home on furlough. Out of uniform, the soldiers took upon themselves the duty of guarding the general and his headquarters personnel wherever they traveled. The gaggle caught everyone's eyes, particularly in the small town Logan now called home.[69]

Logan's furlough offered him the opportunity to relax. Dinners, excursions, picnics, balls, and parties were commonplace. Officers Townes, Hotaling, Wheaton, Hoover, and others on the staff became very sociable and—according to Mary—smitten by the Jackson County women during their leave.[70] But after a week of these events, Logan abruptly changed his itinerary. The previous summer, he had delivered a patriotic address in Carbondale that rippled up and across Illinois. He returned to service within days of that speech, squelching any opportunity for local citizens in other towns to have him speak to them. They made sure Logan's 1863 visit would not pass without the general receiving their plea for a speech. In response to the requests Logan crafted a list of towns where he would deliver a patriotic address. He worked over the speech, one he would repeat in each community. The first heavily advertised appearance was set for Du Quoin on July 31, a Jackson County town northwest of Carbondale. He also agreed to speak in Chicago as well as other smaller cities in Illinois.

Logan's dress rehearsal was, appropriately, Carbondale's town square, where a crowd numbering 3,000 gathered to hear him on July 30. Logan's neighbors, constituents, and kin were dispersed through the crowd. Scores of soldiers on furlough also came to hear him. No doubt the strongest secession supporters traveled from the outskirts to listen to the words of their chief antagonist. The setting was familiar, for Logan had spoken in the same place on August 28, 1862. Eleven months made a huge difference, one that went beyond the extra star shining on his shoulder. Major General Logan was fast becoming not only

Egypt's most successful Civil War soldier, but also an American hero with a name that resonated through the North.[71]

He spoke that Thursday to a captivated audience. His speaking style—very familiar to the constituents who had attended other presentations by him—had not changed, but it would have caught the attention of those who were listening to him for the first time. "He certainly stands alone among the public speakers of the day—knowing no paucity of words and uttering them with a wonderful rapidity," assessed a witness to Logan on the stump. "All his words are ideas and they come forth, flash! flash! flash!—till you are dazzled at the quick succession, and almost puzzled in your comprehension. In common phrase, he thinks lightening. A steam gun discharging its hundred shots in continuous succession, is not more sudden, sustained, or certain. Keep up those discharges for three-quarters of an hour unintermittingly, and you have some faint type of the physical effect of one of Logan's speeches."[72]

Logan must have been even more physically taxing to the Carbondale crowd, for he spoke for three hours, not three-quarters of an hour. Most of the breaks in his oratory came from the applause that regularly interrupted the address and lengthened its delivery. After he was introduced by General Isham Haynie, he struck upon several themes, each one detailed with care and clarity. His introduction reiterated his refrain of casting aside politics to save the Union. He next detailed the causes of the war, and reminded all able-bodied men of their duty to serve in the U.S. volunteer armies. He then delivered a vicious and calculated rant against the peace faction in the North, which devolved into the condemnation of Southern sympathizers, Knights of the Golden Circle, and the regional conspiracy he identified as the "Northwest Confederacy." When a small group shouted him down, accusing him of forgetting his party, he fired back. "I am not a politician today and I thank God for it. I am not like those who cling to party as their only hope." More than an hour flew by for this segment of the speech.[73]

The second half of the unrelenting address struck themes Logan's veteran listeners had not heard from him before. He touched upon the sufferings of pro-Union citizens stuck in the South and the oppression they faced. Then he turned his attention to the plight of the black man. He detailed the importance of the president's Emancipation Proclamation, continuing to highlight it as a war measure and downplaying its humanitarian aspect. He suggested strongly that he would continue to support Southern slavery if the war ended immediately. At one point, he called the escaped slave a "contraband" of war. "If the rebels really want to save their negroes, let them stop fighting," he declared.

From there, Logan naturally directed his words toward the abolitionists. Here, Logan continued with his evolving strategy of avoiding criticism of this movement. In doing so he moved dramatically away from the harsh statements he made earlier about slavery. He sympathized with the plight of the black populace in the South. "There are not fifteen negroes in Mississippi, outside the Federal lines, who can eat hard bread," the general insisted. "This is positively a fact, and if you were to take a vote today of the women and children in Mississippi and Louisiana, they would declare emphatically that they want no more negro property. . . . The institution of slavery is utterly worthless, whether the rebels gain their independence or not."

Logan spoke of loyalty, damning those individuals—such as Confederate President Jefferson Davis—to pay the ultimate price for leading an effort to destroy the country. He provoked his crowd by telling them that if they want "all those hellhounds and traitors" back in the government, he would oppose them. "There is where I propose to switch off," he firmly declared, his bellicosity enhanced by his martial appearance. "So help me God, I am for hanging them as soon as caught."

He showed pure compassion for the citizens and foot soldiers of the Confederacy by contrasting them with their leaders. "The officers are rich slaveholders while the privates are all poor men, and never owned a slave in their lives." Logan erroneously generalized. "They have been forced into this rebellion." He continued to cite statistics without evidence, "Nine out of ten of the people would vote today to come back to the Union if the iron heel was removed from their neck. But now they cannot vote; bayonets will not let them."

Asserting that the rebellion was on the wane, Logan voiced his support for Grant's decision to parole the Vicksburg prisoners—a controversial decision to many Northerners. "It was the best policy," he maintained, arguing that pro-Union feelings, deprivation, and scattered locations made it nearly impossible for them to bear arms as organized units again. He claimed many of the parolees returned to him and had to be arrested. "When they came to speak to me they would beg me for God's sake not to tell their officers about it."

A master of milking emotion through oration, Logan paid a glowing tribute to the Illinoisans who had fallen in the service of the country. The *Chicago Tribune* reporter was so taken by the moment that he failed to take shorthand of it. "It is impossible to do justice to this part of the speech," he wrote. "None but those who listened with streaming eyes and throbbing brows can appreciate the thrilling power and majesty of his words. I never saw an audience so completely under the influence of eloquent words."

The response as Logan closed his address justified the newsman's assessment. Deafening cheers drowned out the routine sounds within the town square; more than 3,000 pairs of hands clapped together in discordant applause. The dress rehearsal at Carbondale was a ringing success. Buoyed by the response, Logan and his entourage headed over to Du Quoin.[74]

On Friday, July 31, Logan repeated much of the Carbondale address in Du Quoin, but there were some notable expansions. On the subject of peace Logan somehow supported the notion with fierce bellicosity. He cleverly turned a phrase to vent against secession. "I am for *peace*, but not for a *piece* of the Government. ... And I tell them now they can get peace at any moment—let them lay down their arms—come and beg pardon of the Government, and beg like a whipped child, and then they can have peace. Until then I am for *offensive* warfare."

The other marked change from the Carbondale address was an unequivocal stance on charges that he was fighting for the abolition movement. He addressed the issue, both in the third and first person: "They say that John Logan and all his chaps down there are Abolitionists—straight out.—How do they know that? I have made no speeches. I tell you why we are Abolitionists. It is because we are in the army, and Abe Lincoln is President. That is all I have to say, if they call me an Abolitionist, I can't help it. If fighting rebels and traitors be an Abolitionist, I suppose I must be counted in; and if that makes the soldiers Abolitionists, there are a good many of us. We don't care. God knows we are true to our country, and that is what is wanted."

He then segued to civil rights and responsibilities during a time of war. Ironically, two of Logan's law partners spent time in prison for what were deemed treasonous activities. First it was Josh Allen in 1862; more recently, William H. Green was arrested during the spring for subversive activities (he was released shortly after taking an oath of allegiance and writing a letter confessing his guilt). Without mentioning Allen or Green by name, Logan supported Lincoln's policy of imprisoning those suspected of secession-sympathetic conspiracies, even without strong evidence. While many railed against what they considered draconian measures—calling it "Lincoln's Bastille"—Logan felt otherwise. "I have only to say this," he stressed, and then continued with Stephen Douglas's theme. "If they were wrongfully incarcerated, I am sorry for them; if they deserved it, I am sorry they were not kept there longer. No true man need be in fear. If he is a loyal man he needn't fear. Every man must be for his Government or against it. He can't be for Jeff. Davis and the Union."[75]

Three hours after his introduction, Logan closed with "I thank you very kindly for your attention." The speech was hailed again, this time by a much

larger crowd than at Carbondale. More than 5,000 showed up for the heavily advertised address. Logan spoke at other Southern Illinois towns, and stayed at his
Carbondale home between speeches. During the first week of August, his oft-
delivered address carried well beyond the 8,000 Egyptians who had heard it to
this point. Widely circulating Illinois newspapers in Springfield and Chicago delivered his words to the state's populace. Joseph B. McCullagh, the pugnacious
and popular newsman, took them even farther. Entranced by Logan in battle,
"Mack" traveled with Logan in Egypt and submitted his transcription of Logan's
Du Quoin speech to the *Cincinnati Daily Commercial*, which subsequently filled
its ten-column front page with it on August 3. "Your speech in the *Commercial*
has created quite a stir," McCullagh informed Logan that day. "It is universally
praised." Indeed it was. Immediately upon reading it, the general secretary of the
National Union Association in Cincinnati was moved to write Logan, "Cincinnati greets you as a brave Union soldier and a patriotic statesman!" They produced 5,000 copies of the Du Quoin speech as a pamphlet, printed in English
and German.[76]

Perhaps Logan's initial intent was to make nonpolitical speeches, but he realized that they could have positive political consequences. Off-year elections
were coming up, and state legislatures hung in the balance. The most watched
political race was in Ohio, where former U.S. Congressman Clement L. Vallandigham was running for governor. It was a most unusual race, for the congressman was unable to set foot in Ohio, hiding out on the Canadian side of
Niagara Falls while his minions carried out his message. The most recognized
and radical of the Peace Democrats—enemies coined them "Copperheads,"
after the poisonous snake—Vallandigham's views were considered so subversive
to the Union cause (he had once introduced a bill in Congress to imprison the
president) that he was banished from the North earlier in 1863. His political enemies feared that his win would unravel the tight pro-Union fabric they had
woven over the past year.

In Du Quoin, Logan was solicited to speak in Cincinnati, an overture to
counter the pro-Vallandigham faction. Mack asked Logan if he would travel to
Ohio. "No," he responded; he had nine days of leave remaining and had already
decided to go to Chicago. "But I would go if I thought I was needed there to assist you in defeating that Canadian chap," came his derogatory reference to the
gubernatorial candidate. "I believe, however, you will beat him by a hundred
thousand votes, without the soldiers."[77]

Logan stepped off the train in Chicago and subsequently stepped into Courthouse Square to deliver a rendition of his address to the largest crowd to date.

"We have seldom seen a larger and more enthusiastic audience," claimed the editors of the former Logan-hating *Chicago Tribune*. "The entire space between the Court House and Randolph Street was closely packed with human beings." The equivalent of one out of every ten Chicago citizens came out to see and hear Logan. The crowd of 12,000 was treated to a performance that the best newspaperman failed to reproduce.[78] One of them explained why:

> A printed report of a speech, however accurate, can not do justice to Logan There is so much in his manner of saying certain things which it is impossible to express in print, that the speech loses much of its flavor when served up at second-hand in the columns of a newspaper. Short hand can't reproduce gestures, however faithfully it may daguerreotype words and sentences. Logan's style is clear, distinct and enunciative. Every word he utters can be heard in the most remote corner of his audience, and he has the rare faculty of being able to speak three hours to a crowd without wearying a single man or woman to it.[79]

Like the Carbondale and Du Quoin addresses, Logan's Chicago speech was recorded and reported in several of the city's newspapers. After documenting the speech—including a picture and biography of the speaker—in the paper, the *Chicago Tribune* packaged it in an inexpensive packet and published it for separate distribution. Logan's "Great Union Speech" was becoming the late-summer sensation in the Old Northwest states and beyond. Witnesses of the sensation made sure that the highest government officials in Washington were apprised of the rousing reaction to it. A confidante to Secretary of War Edwin Stanton had been concerned about pro-Confederate uprisings causing unrest throughout Southern Illinois. "But since Maj. Gen. John A. Logan has delivered his patriotic speeches throughout this region of the country," he maintained, "this hostility has greatly diminished and the spirit of volunteering has, in the opinion of many, become greater than any other period."[80]

President Lincoln received the same report on Logan's patriotic push through Illinois. "He is doing much good to our cause here," wrote an observer in Springfield with direct ties to the White House. "Logan calls things by their right names and his speeches will do a world of good in this state as showing the spirit and temper of the army." Grant extended Logan's leave. Knowing well the enrapturing effect of his subordinate's oratory, Grant told him, "I have read your speeches in Illinois, and feel that you are really doing more good there than you can possibly do whilst the army of your command is lying idle." Lincoln also read the speeches, and changed his position on his former rabid adversary. On August 22, John Hay—the president's secretary—took out his diary and wrote, "The President today said John Logan was acting so splendidly now, that he absolved him in his own mind for all the wrong he ever did & all he will do hereafter."[81]

Lincoln likely had Logan on his mind four days later when he responded to an Illinois correspondent who wanted the president to retract his Emancipation Proclamation. Lincoln firmly reasoned that the combination of the Proclamation and the employment of black soldiers had dealt the heaviest blows to the rebellion. "Among the commanders who hold these views are some who have never had any affinity with what is called 'Abolitionism,' or with 'Republican party politics,' but who hold them purely as military opinions," wrote the president. "I submit their opinions as entitled to some weight against the objections often urged that emancipation and arming the blacks are unwise as military measures, and were not adopted as such in good faith."[82]

Those newspapers speaking critically of Logan charged him with stumping for local candidates; in other words, his insistence that he was disavowing politics, in their view, was disingenuous. This may have been true, and it appears to have been supported by the War Department. Logan's extended leave was officially worded to "recover your health," but all were aware that he was no longer resting as he stumped through Illinois. At the least, his speeches catalyzed a burgeoning pro-Union movement into the autumn of 1863, one that was strong enough to affect local elections in the most partisan Jacksonian Democratic segments of the North. War-supporting Democrats and Republicans had bonded together to form the National Union Party to offset the Copperhead movement.

Logan was back in command before August ended, well prior to the elections in Egypt. He met up with his division at Vicksburg, marched them on a ninety-mile reconnaissance to the terminus of the interconnected railroad system of the country at Monroe, Louisiana, and was back in Vicksburg early in September. As had occurred time and time again during his service, he received family members who visited him at headquarters. In September, he welcomed an in-law, whom he had not seen in more than two years. Hybert Cunningham entered Vicksburg, no longer serving in the Confederate army. He apparently had deserted the Confederacy during the summer of 1863. Grant permitted the prodigal soldier to enter the Union lines, where he made his way to the headquarters of his brother-in-law.[83]

Logan remained determined in his belief that service in the Union army purged any vestige of subversion from the soul. It had worked for Captain Goddard, but failed with his brother, Tom, and cousin, Phillip Davis—the latter relative deserted from the Thirty-first Illinois. Logan was sure that Cunningham (and his friend Robert Kelly, who Logan kept at Vicksburg) would repeat Goddard's positive experience. Logan employed Cunningham at the quarter-master department for $75 per month. Kelly worked as a scout for the U.S. forces. "Hybe is doing well," insisted the general to his wife, but the same could not be said for Private Kelly. "Bob is here and doing no good," he confessed. "I think he will never amount to anything." In October Logan sent Cunningham home to deliver letters and messages; Kelly remained on duty. Sadly, Bob Kelly was killed by a Confederate bullet—the same type he once fired as a member of that service—in December.[84]

Another reconnaissance into Mississippi bore no fruit for Logan and his division, but it turned out to be his last military maneuver as a division commander. At the end of October, he received General Orders Number 349: "By the direction of the president, Maj. General William T. Sherman is appointed to the command of the Department and Army of the Tennessee, headquarters in the field, and Maj. Gen. John A. Logan to the command of the Fifteenth Army Corps." It was an unexpected promotion, instigated by the Army of the Cumberland's defeat at the Battle of Chickamauga. Grant took charge of all western armies near Chattanooga as he planned to drive out Major General Braxton Bragg's Confederate force from the Tennessee border. With Sherman's elevation to army command Logan found himself in charge of Sherman's old corps.[85]

On November 13, 1863, Logan's division held a grand review for their departing commander on level parade ground below Vicksburg. It was a spectacular, emotional event. Soldiers lined up and marched across the grounds they had shed months of blood and sweat to capture. The regimental and brigade bands blared out bouncy renditions of patriotic music. Then, one regiment at a time, they passed General Logan. When the 124th Illinois marched passed their general, they belted out a rousing rendition of "The Battle Cry of Freedom." Logan's chest swelled with pride as the Illinois soldiers sang loud and clear: "The Union forever, Hurrah! Boys, Hurrah!" After every infantry, cavalry, and artillery unit marched past they stood in formation to hear Logan address them for the final time.

He spoke to them like a proud father praising his children. "He made an excellent speech to the men, calling them his 'boys'," wrote one of the soldiers to his sister. Logan made sure his boys understood that they were the reason for his promotion. "It is to you, my brave boys, that ten Generals owe their promotions," Logan declared, "and I hope to God that the Third Division will make many more, for it has the material in abundance." He went on to recount their past glories, and then exhorted them to maintain their reputation in future battles. Logan officially turned over the command to General Mortimer Leggett, a former brigade commander.

He closed the ceremony and bade his men farewell. "Logan is an eloquent speaker, and the occasion was such to draw out his best powers," wrote an impressed infantryman. He took part in an equally eloquent display, carried out by the entire division. They responded not only as soldiers, but also as friends and family members. "The crowd gathered till the streets were filled and the air rang with farewells," he wrote Mary. The scene was affecting, for the appreciation that was reciprocated by the division to him was heartfelt. "General Logan had greatly endeared himself to us all," stated one in the ranks. Logan well understood how they felt; as he told Mary, the "God blesses were enough to melt a stone."[86]

Logan exited Vicksburg, stepped aboard a transport, and headed up the Mississippi on a river and land journey that would take him up a rung higher on the ladder of promotion in the army. In November 1861 he was a colonel in command of a regiment; exactly two years later he was a major general in charge of a corps of 17,000. The responsibility was daunting, and Logan understood that the secret to his success went beyond appearance and words. He revealed what he needed to do in a letter to his wife en route to Chattanooga: "If I can only win the confidence of my new command I am content."[87]

The transport crossed over to the Ohio River and docked at Cairo for a brief stopover. Logan disembarked and made his way to the St. Charles Hotel, the major establishment of the port town. The hotel bustled with activity because several Illinois and Indiana officers who had wrapped up their leave stopped there on their way back to their commands. "Cairo was infested with refugees, Rebel spies, and Copperheads to an extent that was surprising," wrote one of the colonels returning to the front. Logan joined several officers in the hotel office to learn of the election results of the region. Logan was ecstatic to learn that seven Egyptian counties voted in the majority for the Union ticket. Logan and others hailed the results, taking the moment to rejoice in Vallandigham's thumping defeat of the previous month in the Ohio governor's race, a contest in which the disgraced former congressman lost by over 100,000 votes—just as Logan predicted during the summer.

The frivolity was more than some in the hotel office could stand. One of the ruffians in the office—"a big, broad shouldered, villainous looking fellow, whom it was plain to be seen was backed by the baser element of the crowd"—sauntered up to Logan and confronted him. Logan recognized the burly man as a notorious river bully. He also took note of the man's companions lining one of the walls of the room. The situation spelled trouble. The man assailed Logan, calling his former congressman a turncoat for abandoning the Democratic Party. "Logan did not reply," said a colonel in attendance, "although I could see the hot blood in his veins turn the color of his swarthy cheek." The ruffian repeated the remark, more emphatically than before, and more personally. Nearly everyone's attention had diverted to this escalating confrontation. Logan could now sense that the instigator and his companions were trying to goad him to react. They wanted him to throw the first punch, he surmised, so that they could satisfy their building anger with him with a response that would go well beyond words.

Both men were standing near a counter. Logan caught sight of a half-filled pitcher of water. Sensing the right moment, he seized the pitcher by the handle and smashed his antagonist with a blow that dropped him senseless to the floor. "The pals of the ruffian immediately made a rush for Logan," recounted Colonel Reub Williams of Indiana, "but they were confronted with the open muzzles of the revolvers of every officer standing near, and evidently they decided just then that 'discretion was the better part of valor.'" Williams was convinced that the river bullies provoked the general as a premeditated attempt to murder him. Logan agreed.[88]

Alive and still standing, the incident did not dampen his excitement over the election results. "What does Josh and Co. think of the elections?" Logan rhetorically wrote his wife. "Can they see it? If not they will some day soon I hope. The whole army is rejoiced at the happy result." Logan delivered another pro-Union speech in Cairo, and then he stepped onto another transport and headed to Chattanooga.[89]

As he had at Shiloh, Logan arrived in the immediate aftermath of the Battle of Chattanooga. Fought on November 24–25, the battle pitted General Grant (in his first campaign as commander of the three armies in the Military Division of the Mississippi) and his 70,000 soldiers against 50,000 Confederates under Braxton Bragg. Through a series of flanks and direct uphill assaults Grant dislodged Bragg from his stronghold in southeastern Tennessee, thus reversing the Southern gains after their victory at the Battle of Chickamauga in northwestern Georgia two months earlier. Grant had successfully conquered Mississippi and most of Tennessee, and had secured a vital railroad hub at Chattanooga to winter his western armies, supply them, and prepare them for a springtime campaign to march into Georgia and take Atlanta.[90]

The summer 1863 speaking tour in Illinois had caused such a sensation as to generate talk of Logan for governor in 1864. Richard Yates, the governor to date, was considered as a senatorial candidate. The National Union Party, formed in

1863, courted both Republicans and War Democrats. "Logan is strong from the fact that he has served with distinction in the army and is thought to have strengthened us in Southern Illinois," observed an advisor to President Lincoln. Illinois newspapers endorsed him. "The most popular man in the state of Illinois is John A. Logan," claimed the *Cairo News*. "His enemies north and south, hate and fear him, and well they may, for he is a fearless, untiring foe, and will give them no real rest till the last one among them is completely subdued.... Logan is eminently the man for the times, and we are satisfied he would be more acceptable to the Union men for the office of Governor, than any other man who can be proposed."[91]

Logan spent Christmas in Chattanooga, obviously thinking about home. He felt relieved that Mary and Dollie had settled in Carbondale, well away from the turmoil his family continued to dole out in Murphysboro. If Logan attempted to visit his mother (she still refused to talk to him), brothers, and sisters in Murphysboro during the summer, he made no mention of it. The progression of the war had not ameliorated their feelings toward him, and their own personal problems continued to plague them.

Tom Logan could not stay out of trouble. He escaped prosecution in the attempted rape case against Esculane Phillips because she had apparently vacated the county and did not show up at the Jackson County courts when his case was about to go to trial. But Tom did not take advantage of his unexpected freedom to straighten out his life. On Christmas Eve, he found a new woman in Murphysboro to torment. Rebecca Henson suffered the same fate as Miss Phillips. Tom allegedly assaulted and attempted to rape her on December 24. When Miss Henson's friend, Minerva Benoist, tried to intervene, Logan retaliated with verbal abuse. "You whore," he yelled, "You God damned whore!" He repeated the tirade, over and over. Another Logan sibling got in the act. Annie Blanchard refused to let her brother be accused by any witness to his alleged crime. Annie pelted Minerva Benoist's house with eggs, sticks, stones, and bricks.[92]

Arrest warrants were drawn up for both Logans. General Logan heard about this from another brother, Bill, and from Mary. He destroyed their letters, a sign of embarrassment about the actions of his brother and sister. The general was fed up with family matters. When Mary persisted in apologizing to him about past issues he deemed frivolous, he testily responded, "I assure you that you are forgiven and am satisfied about the matter *so let it drop*." As for family grudges, Logan demonstrated the same impatience. "I hope mother will come and spend a time with you, and forget her nonsense." He also decided to wash his hands of all the friends and family that have burdened him over the past two years. "Tom, of course, is drunk and a fool as he always was," he pointed out, "I never want anything to do with him, Doff, or Blanchard again, under any circumstances."[93]

In regards to Doff, fate intervened to grant Logan's desire, but not the way he wanted it. While on leave in Carbondale, an angry member of the Thirty-first Illinois took out his animosity on his former colonel and struck Lindorf Ozburn over the head with a brick. Doff died from the effects of the blow. Logan wrote that it was "horrible that he met such a fate." He was equally saddened to hear of other losses within his family. Uncle Alexander Jenkins passed on in February of 1864, working until the day he died as a judge in the Third Judicial District. Two of his sons—Logan's first cousins—served in the general's old division in the Seventeenth Corps.[94]

Family matters were not the only issues scrawled into Logan's letters home. For the first time since the war commenced, Logan expressed an interest in politics, albeit a vindictive one. "I understand that Josh Allen will soon be home and commence his canvass for Congress," he wrote. "I do hope that Haynie will run against him and beat him. He can do it and God knows it [will be] good to hear of his defeat." Not only was Logan wishing the worst for his former friend, best man, and law partner, he also felt no qualms about supporting a Republican over a Democrat in his old congressional district. Notwithstanding the frequent examples of dissent in Egypt, a district that voted for Democrats by large margins over Republicans for the U.S. House of Representatives, Logan felt unusually confident that a reversal could come off in the 1864 election.[95]

Logan's headquarters personnel largely hailed from Southern Illinois and served as pleasant daily reminders of home. The staff, according to an observer, was "very numerous, and as I found afterward, very efficient. Most of them were young men." Logan had added more members since the Vicksburg campaign. His most recent acquisition was an aide-de-camp, who had an unprecedented background: he was a former Confederate officer. He also was Logan's brother-in-law. Hybert Cunningham represented the most recent attempt to support Logan's philosophy that service in the U.S. Army imbued a disaffected soul with patriotism.[96]

Logan took his leave from his staff temporarily to meet Grant at his headquarters in Nashville. There he joined Generals Sherman, McPherson, Dodge, Rawlins, and Phil Sheridan. They called on Governor Andrew Johnson at the Tennessee State House, who was taken aback by the hard-looking appearance of Grant and his officers. After the generals left the State House they indulged Sherman in one of his favorite pastimes—the theater. Watching a performance of *Hamlet*, the generals sat with an audience of soldiers—equally hardened by war. During the graveyard scene when the main actor picks up Yorick's skull to delve into Hamlet's famous soliloquy, a veteran in the audience called out, "Say pard, what is it—Yank, or Reb." Logan and the rest of Grant's entourage took their leave during the uproar that followed the soldier's question.[97]

Grant informed Logan during his business that he would be heading east. On March 3 Grant crossed the Alleghenies as the new general in chief of all the U.S. armies in the field. He decided to travel with the Army of the Potomac, fully confident in his successor, General Sherman, who stepped up from commanding the Army of the Tennessee to take over all the western armies. Sherman's ranking subordinate in the Army of the Tennessee was General McPherson, who found himself in charge of the army due to Sherman's promotion. The domino effect left a vacancy in the Seventeenth Corps. Lincoln offered his opinion on filling the gap. Major General Frank Blair overturned his own decision to return to politics and wished to run the Fifteenth Corps. Sherman consented with the switch, which would place Blair with the Fifteenth Corps, move Logan back to the Seventeenth Corps, and keep the Sixteenth Corps, commanded by Major General Grenville Dodge, unchanged. Sherman recalled back in January that Logan had contemplated switching corps with McPherson, so he felt making the switch two months later would meet with no objection.[98]

The passage of two months made all the difference in the world, as far as Logan was concerned. He was clearly upset about hearing of the plan through the newspapers, and not by direct discussion. He protested quickly, loudly, and vehemently. Considering the move "an injustice," he telegraphed the president to halt the plan. His insistence had less to do with any trouble with the Seventeenth Corps, but with his full comfort and confidence leading the Fifteenth. "I fully understand the organization of the Fifteenth Corps now," he wrote to Lincoln on March 26, expressing that he "earnestly hope[d] that the change may not be made." Lincoln conferred with Grant, and the matter was settled with General Blair assuming command of the Seventeenth Corps and Logan staying where he was.[99]

A gregarious, fun-loving man when not possessed by his battle persona, Logan not only endeared himself to the officers on his staff, but also to the officers commanding divisions, brigades, and regiments of the Fifteenth Corps even before he led them in battle. He initiated an "open door" policy at headquarters throughout the winter and early spring of 1864, allowing Fifteenth Corps commanders to visit him daily. There Logan regaled his visitors with jokes, impressions, and tales. "He was full of fun," recalled a frequent visitor, who remembered that the general "could tell a story equal to the best raconteur and possessed the ability to mimic the brogue of Auld Ireland to a very great degree." His unortho-dox style instilled an ardor into those officers he would direct on the killing fields of Georgia. Colonel Reuben Williams convincingly concluded, "As a conse-quence, an intimacy grew up between them that prevailed, I feel sure, to a greater degree in the Fifteenth, than in any other corps in the Western army."[100]

The Fifteenth Corps consisted of four divisions. General Peter J. Osterhaus, an intrepid German officer, led three brigades in the First Division; General Morgan L. Smith, Logan's ranking subordinate, led two brigades in the Second; General John E. Smith, formerly the Galena colonel in charge of the Forty-fifth Illinois commanded the Third; and William Harrow replaced Thomas Ewing to command the three brigades comprising the Fourth Division. General Harrow was the only non-indigenous general under Logan. Although an Indianan, Har-row had led troops in the Army of the Potomac (he fought at Gettysburg), be-fore transferring to the Army of the Tennessee. These commanders oversaw eleven Illinois regiments, six Indiana regiments, eleven Missouri, ten Ohio, and two Iowa regiments. Minnesota and Wisconsin each contributed one regiment to the corps. It was arguably the strongest corps fighting for the North.

Logan's satisfaction with his command spilled over in his letters to Mary. "I think I have the best corps in the army," he wrote on April 6, going on to claim that the men "think well of me." He now earned $430 per month as a corps com-mander, which also buoyed his spirits. His health, threatened by a severe bout of rheumatism during the winter, was again strong and sound. All of this did not prevent him from expressing his fears in his intimate letters home. He promised Mary not to act in a way that she would ever think less of him. "If I live through these troubles you shall love me more and more," he predicted to her on April 12, "If I get through safe I will try and stay at home and live pleasantly and happy with my dear little family that I prize more than all the world."[101]

Logan did not divorce himself from the Seventeenth Corps, now com-manded by General Frank Blair. On April 4, 1864, he was one of several mem-bers of the Seventeenth awarded a Medal of Gold inscribed with all the actions (except for Belmont) in which he participated: Fort Henry, Fort Donelson, Siege of Corinth, Port Gibson, Raymond, Jackson, Champion Hill, and Vicksburg. The award honored Logan for "gallantry in action and other soldier-like qualities" which had distinguished him during the war.[102]

The citizens of Huntsville were far from admiring of General Logan's soldier-like qualities. His feelings toward them were mutual. Writing his wife about Huntsville, Logan revealed, "This place, although a pleasant looking place, is the meanest place for the complaints of citizens that I have ever seen." The citizens understandably did not appreciate Union army restrictions on their travel and the frequent house checks ordered by Logan, done so to assure no subversive activities transpired under his nose. And the Southerners were often taken aback by his swarthiness. On one occasion he entered a home with a group of soldiers sent to inspect the house. Eyeing the general up and down, the matriarch of the home demanded Logan to answer her question: "Whose boy are you?" Her daughter, gasped, seized the woman's arm and answered for him, "Why ma! That's General Logan." The mother would not hear of it. "General Logan!" she retorted in a voice laced with contempt, "I tell you he's nothing of the kind. He's black."[103]

The citizens were not alone at voicing displeasure about Logan. General George Thomas, commander of the Army of the Cumberland, was a proud Virginia officer who earned the army command for gallant and heroic generalship throughout 1863. While Sherman was away in Cincinnati conducting preparations for his spring campaign, Thomas and Logan verbally sparred over use of the Nashville and Chattanooga Railroad. Logan exploded when he learned that Thomas forced Army of the Tennessee soldiers to obtain passes from his Chattanooga headquarters, giving the impression that the Army of the Cumberland was exclusively in possession of the line. The fight blew out of proportion and forced Sherman to mediate. He sided with Logan, much to Thomas's chagrin. For his part Logan assured Thomas he had put the matter behind him, but Thomas would not reciprocate the gesture. According to Sherman, Thomas nursed a disdain of Logan that could not easily be abated. "If there was a man on earth whom Thomas hated, it was Logan," he stated.[104]

Thomas and Logan put aside their squabble in anticipation of the grand and well-planned campaign. On April 28 Logan received orders to move the Fifteenth Corps from Huntsville to Chattanooga, where Sherman planned to supply his entire district before marching into Georgia. He stripped his force by a quarter, leaving the Third Division (commanded by Brigadier General John E. Smith) in northern Alabama to guard railroads and lines of communication against Confederate cavalry raiding parties operating in the region. His remaining three divisions, numbering nearly 13,000 officers and men, headed out to Chattanooga on May 1. Four days later, they completed the march and settled in the hub city with 100,000 Union soldiers.[105]

Sherman and the three armies under his jurisdiction—McPherson's Army of the Tennessee, Thomas's Army of the Cumberland, and Schofield's Army of the Ohio—wrapped up their preparations for the pending campaign into Georgia. As general in chief of all the U.S. armies in the field, Grant had called for simultaneous movements on all fronts, four strategic areas in the eastern and western theaters. The purpose was to pressure outnumbered Confederate forces and prevent reinforcements from one theater from crossing to aid those hard-pressed in other theaters (this is one reason why the Army of the Cumberland lost the Battle of Chickamauga the previous September). Grant specifically ordered Sherman, officially commanding the Military Division of the Mississippi, to "get into the interior of the enemy's country as far as you can, inflicting all the damage you can against their War resources."[106]

"I leave here this morning for the front," wrote Logan to Mary near midnight of May 5, 1864. The letter was void of retrospection and premonitions. He did not consider the possibility of being killed or hint that it might be the last letter he would write. Three years of bloody and brutal war had hardened him, but it did not make him cynical or pessimistic. He carried a great deal of optimistic confidence on his shoulders, informing his wife that he felt strong and did not consider defeat. "I will come home," he assured her in closing.[107]

Whether it was his intent or not, he had been an effective political general throughout the previous twelve months, a successful division commander in battle who parlayed his success on battlefields to sway public opinion throughout Illinois and beyond. He had been so effective to be seriously considered for governor of Illinois. But Logan still considered himself a soldier before a politician, even though he was willing to at least discuss the latter. Lincoln's personal selections of political generals had rarely been successful ones. Those that made the military their career frowned upon the subpar abilities and accomplishments of politicians such as Generals Nathaniel P. Banks and Ben Butler, and the interference posed by General McClernand. Logan, however, earned and received praise without scorn. His success in the field was self-made. Lincoln did not handpick Logan to lead large forces; in fact, on two occasions Grant propped his prize subordinate to higher command in spite of the president's oversight. Now Lincoln was convinced of what Logan could achieve on and off the field.

In the next six months, Logan would exceed his previous year's performance with the most astounding use of politics and generalship partitioned and separately displayed by one person in the Civil War.

CHAPTER SIX

Saving the Union

"IT HAS BEEN A VERY WARM DAY, and the 16 miles between 8 A.M. and 4 P.M. counts a hard march," penned a Fifteenth Corps Illinois officer in his diary on May 5. "The dust in many places has been ankle deep."[1] Penetrating into northeast Georgia, Sherman directed Major General George Thomas's Army of the Cumberland and General John M. Schofield's Army of the Ohio to press Confederate General Joseph E. Johnston and his Army of Tennessee at Dalton. The Union's soldiers battled the Confederates in a series of engagements at Rocky Face Ridge, three miles north and northwest of Dalton. As Sherman's "whip snapper," McPherson's Army of the Tennessee hustled on a long flanking maneuver from Chattanooga to cut off Johnston from Atlanta. The movement worked to perfection; by May 9 Major General John Logan and his 13,000 soldiers in the Fifteenth Corps followed Major General Grenville Dodge's Sixteenth Corps through Snake Creek Gap. The town of Resaca lay below; seizing that locale and the Western & Atlantic Railroad would check Johnston and his army north at Dalton; it might even checkmate them. And McPherson had close to 25,000 men in his two leading corps to seal Johnston's fate.

As the Army of the Tennessee advanced eastward beyond Snake Creek Gap, Logan, Dodge, and McPherson reconnoitered from the high ground just one mile west of Resaca. The town was unexpectedly occupied by 4,000 Confederates commanded by Brigadier General James B. Cantey, although their true numbers could not be determined from the knoll. Dodge's divisions owned the heights surrounding the three generals, but Dodge deemed it impracticable to advance and attack. He expressed his concern over crossing the formidable Camp Creek that flowed southward at the base of their hill—parallel with the railroad beyond it—before emptying into the Oostanaula River half a mile to the right of the three counseling generals.

Logan disagreed—vehemently. Neither he nor Dodge and McPherson knew they held a six-to-one advantage over the Southerners defending Resaca. Logan insisted that he could carry the town with the Fifteenth Corps alone, but McPherson and Dodge disagreed. Logan pleaded to lead the assault. McPherson vacillated; he then informed Logan and Dodge that he was going to pull their respective corps back toward Snake Creek Gap. Logan refused to let the decision go unchallenged. He and McPherson engaged in a bitter discussion. An officer who was within earshot claimed, "From pleading, [Logan] advanced to protestations, and then to curses 'both loud and deep,' and these became almost bitter denunciations of McPherson . . ." Overruled, Logan fumed as he withdrew his force.[2]

Sherman concurred with Logan and criticized McPherson for his decision. "Well Mac, you have missed the great opportunity of your life," he chided McPherson upon meeting him. Without cavalry, McPherson was blind as to the strength of his opponent at Resaca. But his refusal to take a risk allowed Johnston to fall back safely from Dalton and reinforce Resaca. William Shanks, a New York newsman permitted to travel with Sherman's advance, carelessly told Logan that Johnston had been caught napping. Logan assured him that this was not the case and they would now be forced to fight hard and heavy to claim Resaca.

Logan's prediction came true on May 12. Watching from the same knob they occupied on the ninth, Logan seethed as he watched Johnston's 65,000 troops file into the town and fortify positions north and south of it. Disgusted at the lost opportunity, he planted an Illinois battery on the knoll, commanded by Captain Francis DeGress. Charles Stolbrand, the temperamental chief of artillery, joined Logan and DeGress as they fired a round at the Confederates below. "The first round of DeGress came very near being his last," remembered reporter Shanks, who watched in horror nearby as they became a well-aimed target of several Confederate cannons who suppressed DeGress's guns immediately. As it turned out, the hill occupied by Logan had been used as target practice by Southern gunners firing from the fort near Resaca. They had cleared the hill months earlier, save for one tree on the knob used to converge their practiced barrage. Now Logan, Stolbrand, and DeGress were the targets, and Shanks could not believe that they refused to run to safety. "Courage is a sort of stamp which attracts its like," reasoned Shanks; "It surrounded Logan with men of his own stamp." While all the underlings (including the reporter) hugged the ground for dear life, Logan and his two artillery officers stood their ground as exploding shells spewed shrapnel dangerously close to them, and burrowing solid shot sprayed loose earth all around them.

Rebel fire slackened by sundown. Sherman and Thomas and several other officers scaled Logan's hill. As they consulted, Logan sat aside, leaning against a stump. William Shanks described him as "looking exceedingly glum and disgusted." As Shanks approached him Logan looked up, remembered the reporter's silly prediction made the previous day, and laughed. Shanks quickly gleaned what Logan thought was amusing and continued the irony at his own expense. "Well, general, you see I was right last night. Somebody was asleep," Shanks deadpanned. "Yes," responded Logan, "but you were mistaken in the person. It was not Joe Johnston who was sleeping."[3]

Sherman concentrated his three armies west and north of Johnston. He had 100,000 soldiers pitted against Johnston's 67,000 Confederates. Despite the numerical advantage, military doctrine dictates that an attacking force requires a greater advantage than the three-to-two margin Sherman held if he expected to dislodge his opponent. Nevertheless, Sherman ordered the assault which commenced on May 13; by the end of the day, the position of the armies remained unchanged. Undaunted, Sherman renewed the assaults the following day — again to no conclusion by the afternoon.[4]

Late on May 14 Logan received orders to "carry the first range of hills" in front of his skirmish line. Camp Creek ringed the Confederate position like a moat, and was spanned by one thin bridge, but Logan desperately forced his men over the waterway. Unable to build a series of bridges over Camp Creek under a canopy of raining rebel artillery fire, Logan improvised. He called for a legion of swimmers to gain a toehold on the east side of the deep creek. Logan proved to be an unorthodox corps commander, acting this day more like a hands-on brigadier general. In an attempt to steel his soldiers against a deadly skirmish and artillery barrage, Logan peeled off his coat, vest and boots and plunged into the creek to lead the men across. Logan's skirmish line covered the advance of two of his brigades, who stormed the single bridge and waded the creek — some using logs.[5]

Logan's tactic forced back the Confederate left. The day was nearly spent with the sun dropping to the ridge line behind Logan and his advancing force. With two brigades across, Logan's soldiers rushed a Confederate-held hill on the east side of the creek. "The firing all along both lines was picturesque," waxed Logan; "As volley after volley was discharged, it reminded one of a line of

Roman candles shooting forth." Logan's regiments took the hills. With nighttime fast approaching, Confederate General Leonidis Polk ordered successive charges to reclaim his lost position, but Logan's men tenaciously clung to the real estate—representing Sherman's sole substantial success of the day. Despite heavy counterfire that flared into the night, Logan's men dug in between Camp Creek and Resaca to maintain their hard fought positional advantage. "I tell you this the most exciting show I ever saw," raved an officer in the 103rd Illinois; who informed his family, "I write under cover of a stump which a dead man of the 26th Indiana shares with me."[6]

While some soldiers brimmed with excitement, others lamented the loss of company mates. More than 500 soldiers in the leading brigades of the Fifteenth Corps fell in the desperate struggle for the Confederate works. One who brooded over the loss of one close to him was Hybert Cunningham. He had served his brother-in-law well during the fighting of May 14, bringing up ammunition trains for Logan. Logan was handed a letter from Mary during the hottest part of the fight. Reading it hurriedly but unable to pay attention to it, he handed it to Hybert who read it more carefully and immediately fell silent. Mary had announced the death of their sister Hannah. "Poor boy," Logan guiltily lamented, "it nearly broke his heart." After serving Logan throughout the day, the young aide left his general for the evening to brood over the family tragedy. Captain Cunningham returned to Logan's side the following morning, quiet and retrospective, but ready to serve.[7]

Logan's advance had rendered Johnston's Resaca defense untenable on May 15. Logan proudly and correctly reported, "I caused artillery to be placed in the most advantageous situations in the position captured the previous day, and the railroad bridge and the town were thus held entirely at our mercy." Although unable to force Johnston back by direct assault, Sherman turned his position by sending a division to pontoon the Oostanaula River three miles in the Confederate rear. Sherman's men claimed Resaca immediately after Johnston evacuated to the south. Sherman's tactical draw and strategic victory in the three-day Battle of Resaca cost him 4,000 men. Logan tallied 628 casualties in the Fifteenth Corps; most of them fell on the May 14 assault.[8]

Unlike anything he had ever experienced before, Logan's command fought nearly every day from the middle of May; his skirmishers were constantly engaged with Johnston's rearguard troops. After crossing the Oostanaula River in pursuit of Johnston, Sherman's armies plunged deeper into Georgia. By May 19 Logan and his corps reached Kingston. The Gate City of Atlanta stood merely fifty miles down the railroad tracks. Logan suffered a wholly unexpected loss that day. His talented Swedish chief of artillery, Stolbrand, was captured by Confederate cavalry at Kingston, forcing Logan to place Major Allen C. Waterhouse in his stead.[9]

Having always kept close to his supply line on the Western and Atlantic Railroad, Sherman attempted to gain the flank of his wily opponent by striking west in an effort to avoid a struggle at the well-fortified Allatoona Pass. The Army of the Tennessee remained as Sherman's right-flank force. It crossed the Etowah River on May 23. Two days and thirty-five miles later Logan's corps passed over Pumpkinvine Creek and into Dallas, a hamlet of houses on the opposite bank of the tributary. On a ridgeline on the opposite side of town, Logan's men dug in, erecting "hasty intrenchments," a new tactic employed to protect the Civil War soldier from opposing fire.

General Johnston enjoyed peak numerical strength in May's third week. With his army at peak numerical strength—75,000—Johnston detected Sherman's flanking effort and met him in battle on a ridgeline twelve miles west of Marietta and the railroad. The Confederate lines stretched five miles from Pickett's Mill to a position one mile east of the town of Dallas. Sherman had gambled to turn the flank, and now he was blocked. With seemingly no choice Sherman attacked Johnston's line without success from May 25 to 27 at Pickett's Mill and New Hope Church. The Fifteenth Corps skirmished continually while Sherman's armies probed, fought, and rushed the defensive line, but could not effectively penetrate it. Thousands of casualties produced no gain.

McPherson received orders to flank Johnston's force but the Confederates were staunchly planted in a strong line that extended across the Villa Rica Road south of Logan's corps. Logan's men fought continuously on Friday, May 27, as they solidified their own position by extending from the right flank of Grenville Dodge's Sixteenth Corps. Logan awoke early on Saturday, May 28, with skirmish fire resuming at the light before dawn at 4:30 A.M. His men spent the morning fortifying their hasty entrenchments while the trains moved away from the lines behind them. McPherson was carrying out his new orders to reposition his army on the left flank of the Army of the Cumberland.

The men stayed in position while the supply wagons began rolling from behind them. The activity behind the Union lines convinced the Confederates that Logan's men were withdrawing from their position. Johnston sent a directive through his corps commander, General William Hardee (Logan studied his tactics manual to train the Thirty-first Illinois back in 1861), to "develop the enemy" east of Dallas. Hardee passed the order through to General William Bate who was instructed to attack the position and claim the Union earthworks there. Bate misconstrued Logan's strong position and at 3:45 P.M., his attack commenced with four brigades of 5,000 men.

An Illinois soldier in the works in front of Bate's men was stunned to see huge columns of Confederates rising from the brush and rushing toward them "with a yell the devil ought to copyright." Caught completely by surprise, Logan's Fourth Division teetered toward collapse. His line of works bent from south to west across the Villa Rica Road, the route leading southward from Dallas. Seven cannons in two batteries dominated to heights directly behind the Union works. The southernmost guns, three cannons of the First Iowa Light Artillery, attracted Confederate attention as they were stuck out with the Union skirmish line. Southerners rushed to the cannons and seized them, driving back the infantry all around them. At least 200 Union soldiers fell in less than fifteen minutes, a stunning result given that these men held earthworks at the time of the attack. Confusion reigned as Union regiments gave way all across the Villa Rica Road.

Minutes before this assault, Union horse soldiers attracted skirmish fire and discerned a large-scale attack was about to commence. Cavalry officers galloped back to Dallas to inform Logan. He got the news just at the time he heard the sound of Bate's attack. Logan rushed from his headquarters tent and sprung upon his horse, a sleek, coal-black charger he named "Slasher." He spurred the horse southeastward toward the weakest and most threatened part of his line. The time approached 4:00 P.M.

What happened next was a singular moment for the Fifteenth Corps of the Army of the Tennessee, a corps that had prided themselves as Sherman's soldiers, since he had commanded them for nearly two years before Logan had taken over that duty. "The men think more of Sherman than any other general who ever commanded them, but they did not cheer him," wrote an Illinois officer two weeks earlier, emphasizing, "I never heard a general cheered in my life." General Logan broke that streak on May 28. As he rode down the one and one-half-mile line of his corps on May 28, the corps responded from one end of the line to the other. "You should have heard them cheer him," wrote an awestruck officer—the same one who previously recorded that this corps never cheered a general.[10]

Logan's presence at this crucial moment was more than inspiring; it was electric. Galloping down the line of his works, Logan bellowed, "Fall in! Forward!" When he heard his soldiers asking the whereabouts of their regiments and officers, he shouted loud and clear, "Damn your regiments! Damn your officers! Forward and yell like hell!" A cavalry officer raved, "He rode down the line hat in hand, swinging and waving at his soldiers, directing them to fall into line, and be ready for the attack. His long black hair was streaming in the wind and he was the embodiment of masterly and magnetic energy." An Iowa soldier became a Logan disciple that afternoon. "John A. Logan came riding down the line, with his hat in his hand, looking like the very god of war," he recalled; "No one can describe how Logan looked in battle, any more than he could describe the raging sea. I am satisfied that the biggest coward in the world would stand on his head on top of the breastworks if Logan was present and told him to do so."[11]

Logan considered courage, "one of God's noblest gifts to man," and insisted, "Those who do not inherit it can never have it." This did not prevent him from trying to instill it into those who found it wanting at that moment. His presence was enough for many who witnessed "in smoke and dust, in brush and plowed field, his swiftly passing form appeared and disappeared like an eagle flying low." As he rode forward rallying his men, he met an unfortunate Union artilleryman riding in retreat. Ordering a nearby officer to hand him his pistol, Logan rode down the artillerist, stuck the pistol to the man's head, and assured him, "Damn you. If you move—yes if you move even a foot further to the rear—I'll blow your brains out." To no one's surprise the cannoneer turned his wagon around and rejoined the counterassault.[12]

Logan's men responded with alacrity, sending line after line of Confederates back to their works. The Union troops recaptured their cannons and quickly reversed all of the initial Confederate gains. Watching the momentum shift in his favor, Logan shouted to the 103rd Illinois of his Fourth Division, "It's all right, damn it, isn't it?" The regimental commander responded for his men: "It's all right, General." The left flank of the Fifteenth Corps beat back spirited assaults by two brigades, inflicting 50-percent casualties upon each Confederate column. It was all over in two hours. Logan successfully repulsed Bate's attack, but it cost him 379 killed, wounded, and missing men—a high rate attributed to the surprise the Confederates sprung on Logan. His laxity cost him more men that it should, but he inflicted a great deal of pain on Bate's command, killing or wounding nearly 1,000 men and capturing 97 additional Confederates.[13]

Logan escaped harm at the Battle of Dallas, but he was not so lucky two days later. While discussing deployment with Sherman, McPherson, and a couple of staff personnel, a bullet passed through the muscle of Logan's left arm when he extended it to point out a direction. (The same bullet struck Ezra Taylor—the Chicago artillerist who fought with Logan at Belmont and currently worked as one of Sherman's staff men—square in the chest, but a thick pocket diary saved his life.) Hybert Cunningham, Logan's brother-in-law and aide de camp, bound up the general's arm. Logan missed no duty from the slight wounds.[14]

Logan stayed attuned to home and family issues. He sent Mary a three-word telegram ("I am well") to put her at ease when she would eventually read of the heavy fighting in the Georgia region the troops called "The Hell Hole." He wrote a two-page letter the next day. "I will be careful of myself," he promised, proudly proclaiming, "Since the fight of Saturday the men are all enthusiasm and think I am all they want to command them." Many in the North got a glimpse of Logan in battle when an early July issue of *Harper's Weekly Illustrated Newspaper* included a sketch of him rallying his troops in the May 28 action. The Battle of Dallas was a fountainhead for Logan as the Fifteenth Corps commander. Notwithstanding his aggressive but generally overlooked performance at Resaca, Logan's ostentatious leadership at Dallas was witnessed by too many in his corps to be ignored. Those corpsmen who had only heard of his legendary performance at Champion Hill from Seventeenth Corps soldiers now identified him as their own. The letters home no longer pointed out their association with "Sherman's corps." Logan's efforts on May 28 would never be forgotten. More then forty years after the Battle of Dallas, one of its participants exalted Logan's performance there: "It was without question the most inspiring and magnificent example of personal magnetism and personal leadership I witnessed during the war."[15]

As May gave way to June, Johnston fell back to a line of hills that formed a rim west of Marietta, Georgia. Johnston used all the heights on this ridge—Kennesaw Mountain, Little Kennesaw Mountain, Pigeon Hill, and Cheatham Hill—as the salient of his new defense. He refused his flanks to oppose Sherman's constant attempts to outflank him. By June 25, days of heavy rains and Johnston's stalwart defense had frustrated Sherman to the point where he resorted to a desperate measure. He needed to get beyond the ridge to unite his armies on ground more suited for maneuver than the rugged northwestern Georgia terrain that had impeded him for seven weeks.[16]

A siege would grind the campaign to a halt; it would offer no reward for Sherman since Johnston could easily wiggle away from the Northern forces. Sherman chose an ill-fated assault of Kennesaw Mountain to dislodge the Confederates from their strong high-ground defenses. Logan received orders to prepare three brigades "to assault the enemy's works on the south and west slope of Little Kenesaw [sic] Mountain" at 8:00 A.M. on June 27, 1864. Sherman planned to divide the Confederates into three segments with two attacking forces; he subsequently would focus on each isolated segment of Southerners to force them off the heights. Logan led one of the initial attacking forces. Representing Sherman's middle-left in the attack, he chose the brigades in Brigadier General

M. L. Smith's Division—commanded by Brigadier General J. A. J. Lightburn, Brigadier General Giles A. Smith, and Colonel C. C. Walcutt. To improve the chances for success, Sherman planned simultaneous feints upon the flanks as the two attacking forces aimed for the midsection.

Logan's attacking force numbered 5,500 infantrymen; they straddled both sides of the Burnt Hickory Road facing their destination of Pigeon Hill. At 8:00 A.M. of June 27, an artillery bombardment commenced. McPherson's Sixteenth and Seventeenth Corps forces struck in their feint to the north of Logan's attacking columns. Fifteen minutes later, Logan's seventeen regiments surged forward. Lightburn's brigade enjoyed initial success south of Burnt Hickory Road, mauling a Georgia regiment as it struck eastward. Converging Confederate infantry fire, directed from the slopes, stifled any further progress. Hugging the ground to stay alive, the Yankee regiments could advance no more. The major of the Forty-seventh Ohio illustrated the torment of "the sheeted flame filled with missiles, giving forth ten thousand shrieks and tones, intensified by the cries of agony and the torture of the wounded." With no chance for victory, Lightburn ordered his men to head back to the woods from where they started.

The two brigades attacking north of the road met the same fate. Advancing past the north-south mountain road that bisected Burnt Hickory Road at the base of Pigeon Hill, those eleven regiments fell victim to the terrain, which forced them to fight in isolated pockets with sheer cliff walls blocking their advance. As they moved forward, a murderous opposing fire destroyed their ranks. The method of choice was guns and bullets, but Mississippi troops also hurled rocks down at the trapped Union soldiers.[17]

Through it all Logan led from the front. "I saw Logan ride at full speed in front of our lines when the bullets seemed to be falling thicker than hail," witnessed one of his attacking soldiers, "Bareheaded, powder-stained, and his long, black hair fluttering in the breeze, the General looked like a mighty conqueror of medieval days." But bravery alone does not win battles. Logan met with success in the early moments: "My attacking column succeeded in taking and holding two lines of enemy rifle pits, and advanced toward the succeeding works of the enemy, situated just below the crest of the mountain." But he could go no farther. Taking an atrocious amount of casualties, Logan realized they could not penetrate the Confederate defense. He remained in the last line of works he seized, and then he eventually retired his command.[18]

Sherman's main attack was delivered by General Thomas and the Army of the Cumberland. It too achieved initial success, but the Confederate defense proved impenetrable. Sherman's total loss in the Battle of Kennesaw Mountain exceeded 3,000 men. It was his worst defeat in the campaign. Logan lost 600 men in his three brigades, including seven regimental commanders. "Sherman is a strange man," assessed Logan after the battle, "and seems only to fight a portion of the army at a time."[19]

Logan submitted a brief report of his part in the Kennesaw Mountain battle on June 28. His anger at the "forlorn hope" could not be restrained; he complained about "so many gallant men were being uselessly slain." Logan did not exhibit the confidence in and respect for Sherman as he did in Grant. Noting that Sherman refrained from pouring any praise on his corps leadership, Logan grew suspicious that the issue centered on West Point training. "My command was first on Kennesaw," Logan railed to Mary, "but that will make no difference unless I was a West Point officer." He looked to his place in the military annals of America, realizing it was up to his legions of future historians to set the record straight. "I will get no credit for anything that may be done except by the men who carry muskets," he continued to his wife; "They will make some history should they ever return home."[20]

Logan wrote Mary the letter in mid July from Roswell, a town on the north bank of the Chattahoochie River fifteen miles east of Kennesaw Mountain. Whatever Logan thought of Sherman's tactical shortcomings, he could see little fault in his commanding general's determination and logistical acumen. Sherman's loss at Kennesaw did not deter him. He continued to shift eastward. He successfully slipped around Johnston's flank and freed himself from the hill country of Georgia. With more room to operate, Grant had originally instructed Sherman to destroy the Confederate army and damage the war resources deep in Georgia. He sent Sherman a new directive, freeing him of the responsibility to destroy the Confederate army and to focus on the war resources. This gave Sherman the impetus to divide his forces as he approached Atlanta.[21]

As part of the Army of the Tennessee, Logan took a wide route of march, crossed the Chattahoochie River near Roswell, and then headed south. Taking new orders from McPherson, Logan and his corps destroyed the Georgia Railroad just west of Stone Mountain "for a considerable distance." The temperatures soared in the region during the hottest part of the year, sapping the strength and sharpness of the Union soldiers. Disregarding the heat, Logan advanced westward and ended up on the west side of Decatur on July 19, tearing up miles of track by making "Sherman's Neckties" out of the rails. The next day Logan advanced to two and one-half miles east of Atlanta, where his twenty-pound Parrotts of Company H, First Illinois Light Artillery—under the command of Captain DeGress—threw the first rounds into the city on July 20.[22]

Atlanta stirred well before Logan's rounds crashed into its buildings. Major General John B. Hood had recently replaced Johnston. Chosen by the Confederate War Department because of his aggressive nature, Hood did what all expected—he attacked. Beaten back after several assaults against Thomas's Army of the Cumberland at Peachtree Creek, west of Atlanta, on July 20, Hood immediately changed directions and devised a plan to throw back McPherson's army threatening his position from the east. Late on the evening of July 21, he sent a corps under the command of General William Hardee on a huge overnight flank march to turn McPherson's left flank, held by General Dodge's Sixteenth Corps. Hood's plan was a simultaneous assault by Hardee from the south and General Benjamin F. Cheatham from the west against Logan's corps and Major General Frank Blair's Seventeenth Corps.

Logan had prepared to advance his corps toward Atlanta on the morning of July 22, based on a false report from Sherman that Hood had evacuated the town. By 10:00 A.M., before the movement commenced, it was suspended when Hardee's flanking movement was detected. Before the Confederates sprung the attack, they began to shell Logan's position on the right flank of the U.S. line. Logan and McPherson appeared to be the target of one of the exploding shells, which startled McPherson. Turning to his commanding officer, Logan coolly remarked, "General, they seem to be popping that corn for us."[23]

McPherson rode southward toward the Seventeenth Corps position that appeared to be the target of the Confederate movement. Logan's men anchored the northern flank of a three-mile battle line. Hardee's corps smashed into the Union left flank at noon (several hours behind schedule), while Cheatham's Confederates attempted to hold Logan's men in place on the Union right. Under strength from detaching men before the noon assault, Logan's corps clung to its position, beating back the diversionary assaults against it. Logan expected the heat of battle to crank up in front of him at any time.

In the early afternoon, Logan caught sight of one of Sherman's aides galloping toward him on a foaming horse. McPherson was dead, the aide announced (He was gunned down at the southern sector), and the Union left was folding under the weight of the Confederate onslaught. As McPherson's ranking subordinate, Logan was now in charge of the army. Logan quickly turned his corps over to his senior commander, General Morgan Smith, wheeled Slasher to the south, and whirred past the entire Union line to reach the opposite flank. He leaned backwards in his saddle with his feet well to the front as he galloped Slasher southward. "At critical moments in an engagement he was wont to go at tremendous speed toward the threatened part of his line of battle," recalled an observer.

"Then he was magnificent. His hat jammed down over his eyes, his eyes bright and his long mustache waving in the air gave him an odd look, while the terrific pace of his steed was appalling. He overcame every obstacle with ease, and it was a beautiful sight to see his horse go flying over fences, ditches or fallen trees, while the rider sat in the saddle with ease and apparent reckless indifference."[24]

Whizzing balls sped about his ears and shells exploded over his head as Logan reached the contested flank. There he conferred with Grenville Dodge and Frank Blair. Hardee's Confederates had assaulted their end of the line before deployment could be completed, taking advantage of a gap that existed between the Sixteenth and Seventeenth Corps. Blair and Dodge had nearly rectified the situation, but Logan still helped out. He filled the hole by extending Blair's left flank and sealing it with men from his own corps (Colonel Hugo Wangelin's brigade) to reinforce the threatened region. The position was stronger, but a series of Confederate attacks had forced the Union army to slowly yield ground. At a fighting strength of 30,000, the Army of the Tennessee was outnumbered by 5,000 men, but Hood's army attacked with such ferocity to appear much greater than their actual strength. Logan's earlier prediction suddenly became a reality. His Fifteenth Corps on the northern flank reeled from a full frontal assault by the remainder of Hood's army—Cheatham's attack had commenced with startling success. No longer a demonstration, the Confederates were crushing the Union right, knocking it back and seizing two Union batteries. The time passed 3:30 P.M.; not since the first day of Shiloh two years earlier had the Army of the Tennessee been attacked with so much fury. Hood's assaults had not been efficiently timed, but they were delivered by a tough and tested force attempting to take advantage of a rare opportunity to destroy a Union Army in the field.

Logan heard the assault against his original position. He wheeled toward Dodge and requested a brigade to support the crushed right flank. Dodge detached Colonel August Mersy's brigade from his flank and sent them northward to help Logan. Satisfied that reinforcements would come to the right, Logan spurred his black horse northward. "McPherson and Revenge!" he shouted. He repeated the phrase again and again, turning it into his rally cry. He tore his hat off and continued past the Seventeenth Corps, which had just re-secured the left flank after driving the Southerners back to the woods. "His horse was on a dead run with two aides just behind him," witnessed an Ohioan in the corps, "In a few minutes I heard a voice saying: 'Sing out if they come again. Put the bayonet to them!' It was Gen. Logan, this time going to the right of the line."[25]

John Bosworth of the Fifteenth Iowa had just partaken in that desperate repulse as a member of the Seventeenth Corps. "Immediately after this Gen.

Logan came riding down the works giving directions, his long black hair floating in the wind and his big mustache fairly bristling with defiance," raved Bosworth, "and to hear the men cheer as they recognized the famous and well known figure of the Fifteenth Corps's celebrated commander, 'Black Jack,' showed that the very presence of this heroic man produced an effect equal to a reinforcement of a whole division; and only those who have seen the new energy infused into disheartened and outnumbered troops by a single man can appreciate the value of a leader such as was John A. Logan."[26]

Logan passed Bald Hill, renamed as Leggett's Hill for the Union commander who successfully defended the height against a monstrous onslaught. General Mortimer Leggett was within earshot of Logan as he rode by. He had served under legends of the Civil War, but they paled in comparison to the inspirational leadership he witnessed from Logan:

> When General Grant would ride down our line he commanded the most thorough respect and confidence from all of us, and it was the same when General Sherman rode down the line. But when General Logan rode down the line, every voice was heard in a shout. He seemed to have a power to awaken the enthusiasm that was in the troops, to the extent that no other officer in our army seemed to possess. He would stir up their blood in battle. The manner in which he sat his horse, the manner in which he would hold his hat . . . seemed to have the power to call out of the men every particle of fight that was in them.[27]

Cheering Logan had become a common ritual when he rode on display to rally his men in battle. On July 22, the soldiers did more than cheer him; they chanted a nickname that honored both his swarthiness and his formidable nature in battle. "Black Jack! Black Jack!" they shouted. It started out with small clusters of soldiers, but soon spread to entire regiments. "Black Jack! Black Jack!" The chants grew louder. Every particle of fight was calling out. "Black Jack! Black Jack!" As the men shouted, they rallied, reclaiming lost ground and seizing the momentum from the Confederates.

Logan galloped on, a human hurricane on horseback. "McPherson and revenge," he shouted, with unrelenting fury. Rallying men surged forward as he rode toward his Fifteenth Corps. As Logan barked out his orders and his battle cry, Mersy's brigade hustled in with him. They were greatly needed to repulse the disaster occurring at the northern flank of the line. Ten Union cannons lay in rebel hands; scores of dead and wounded soldiers had thinned the ranks.

Tremendous numbers of prisoners had reduced the fighting élan and increased the chaos in the corps.[28]

All appeared lost for the Union at this sector of the battle line. "Dismay was depicted on every countenance and defeat seemed inevitable," insisted Captain John R. Thomas, noting that the retreat had already begun when suddenly he caught sight of Logan "galloping down the ranks like a man of iron." Captain Thomas would never forget the impression Logan created that day. "Seated on a coal black horse, with head and shoulders erect, he was the most gallant and picturesque specimen of a soldier I ever saw. As he galloped down the ranks at full speed, his flashing eyes gathered in every detail of the battle, and his stentorian voice rallied the army corps from the retreat to the charge."[29]

Private William Bakhaus of the Forty-seventh Ohio had fought desperately in the melee, escaped capture, and found his way to the rear of what used to be the Fifteenth Corps battle line. Everything seemed hopeless to him. "The next 20 minutes, however brought a sudden change," recalled Bakhaus. "Logan, with fire in his eyes, came dashing down the road at the head of a fresh brigade. I and others joined them, and with bayonets fixed we charged upon the enemy."[30]

Blue battle lines reformed and surged forward, reclaiming their batteries (two cannons remained in Southern hands) and driving back the aggressive Confederates. By 4:30 P.M. the corps had completely rallied and occupied its former position. Hood made two more attempts at Logan's army; each one was beaten back. By 7:00 P.M. the Battle of Atlanta was over. When the dust cleared, the Army of the Tennessee found itself staunchly in position. It had withstood the best Hood had to offer and it won. Logan's men had escaped a disaster in one of the most dramatic single-day battles ever fought on the American continent. One out of every eight Union soldiers engaged was killed, wounded, or captured on July 22, 1864—3,700 men in all. The Army of the Tennessee was also down ten cannon, now in Confederate hands. But the Union force doled out more pain than it received—much more. Hood's Confederate army lost nearly twice as many men (one out of every four Southerners engaged became a casualty this day). More importantly, the rebels had failed to dislodge the threat to Atlanta.

"If it had not been for John A. Logan the Battle of Atlanta would in all probability be whistled now in a different tune," claimed a Buckeye in the ranks. Captain Thomas concurred. "That day was a grand victory for Logan," he said, "and every soldier thinks of him as he looked on that occasion when the Fifteenth, Sixteenth, and Seventeenth Army Corps, obedient to his electric voice, changed from disorganized forces to a victorious army."[31]

The Battle of Atlanta provided Logan the opportunity to display that special battle talent that so impressed his peers and subordinates. His most effective position was at the head of forlorn hopes—an opportunity to rally desperate men. With Logan in command, the Army of the Tennessee had for the first time promoted a commander by attrition, but as always, the new leader was a veteran of its ranks. Logan had been a favorite of soldiers in both the Fifteenth Corps and his former command within the Seventeenth Corps. Officers admired Logan, "with his great rugged soul whom we loved for the very imperfections of his nature." One New York correspondent who covered the Army of the Tennessee since the Chickamauga campaign claimed that "neither Grant nor Sherman were its representatives." He continued, "The real representative man of that remarkable army was General John A. Logan, of Illinois."[32]

General Sherman apparently disagreed. Four days after the Battle of Atlanta, Sherman informed Logan that he would replace him with Major General Oliver O. Howard, the Fourth Corps commander of the Army of the Cumberland. General Logan would return to command the Fifteenth Corps. Sherman cited several reasons for his decision, chief among them was credentials. Sherman felt more comfortable with West Pointers, writing his brother seven months earlier, "The army is a good school, but West Point is better."[33] Although Howard came from a different army, and had yet to distinguish himself during the war, he fit Sherman's West Point criterion.

Sherman also did not take to Logan's personality. "General Logan was by nature and habit, ardent, enthusiastic, vehement in action, all qualities which command the admiration of men," Sherman admitted; "but he was strongly personal, apt to exaggerate the importance of events near his person, and correspondingly to underrate the value of services beyond the reach of his vision." Sherman went on to explain the chief reason why he demoted Logan:

> The science of war is not modern; it is as old as time, and like most sciences has resolved itself into three parts: logistics, grand strategy and combat, each essential to success. General Logan was perfect in combat, but entertained and expressed a species of contempt for the other two branches; whereas a general who undertakes a campaign without the forethought and preparation involved in logistics, will fail as surely as the mechanic who ignores the law of gravitation.[34]

Logan's reaction to his demotion was predictable and understandable. He had asked Sherman to retain the command at least until the campaign had ended. This also was denied. Dodge found him totally dejected on the porch of Sherman's headquarters. Unlike General Joseph Hooker of the Twentieth Corps, Army of the Cumberland, who resigned in protest because he outranked General Howard, Logan placed duty above all and remained in the army, but his enthusiasm for his service had suddenly waned.[35]

Logan stepped back to his former command. On July 28, as the Fifteenth Corps encircled counterclockwise around Atlanta, the Confederates launched another attack. Logan reported, "Just as my command had gained the ridge upon which was situated Ezra Chapel, the enemy suddenly and with the greatest fury assaulted the right and center of my line." When Sherman heard the sound of battle, he asked a staff officer what it meant. "Logan is feeling for them and I guess he has found them," came the reply. "Good!" Sherman exclaimed, "That is fine— just what I wanted, just what I wanted. Tell Howard to invite them to attack, it will save us trouble, they'll only beat their brains out, beat their brains out."[36]

Sherman's supreme confidence—clearly fortified with his comfort at Logan's tactical acumen—was well justified by the events of the day. The battle took the name of the church, and essentially Logan's corps fought it alone, just as he had done at Dallas. General Stephen D. Lee, a former artillery commander for Robert E. Lee, led the Confederate assault. Although disjointed, Lee's thrusts nailed Logan's line, which had yet to throw up rudimentary earthworks and had no immediate artillery support. Lee's second assault penetrated Logan's defense; at least two Union regiments broke for the rear. Watching in the rear with Captain Hotaling, Logan acted swiftly to fill the breach. "Like a thunderbolt he rushed to the spot," remembered a brigade commander. Logan filled the air with oaths as he struck at least a half dozen retreating soldiers with the flat of his sword to redirect their wayward course. He then seized one of the regiments' flags and bore it forward to the Union line. The two regiments reformed and dutifully followed, taken by their general's inspiration. Colonel Reub Williams, the commander of the broken brigade, was awed at Logan's ostentatious restoration of his line: "Hence I have always claimed that the presence of Gen. Logan at that point was equal to a brigade sent to the right place at the precise moment."[37]

Dodge and Blair sent 1,000 troops from their respective corps, but the Fifteenth Corps took all but seventy of the Union casualties. The battle raged from 11:30 A.M. until sunset; night closed the contest with Logan ensconced in the same position he had when first attacked. Howard felt that Logan looked "ill and much worn," but it did not show when the musketry rattled. The Fifteenth Corps exhibited tremendous confidence and spirit with each attack it repulsed. The bond between the soldiers and Logan was never stronger; cheering him—once a nonentity with the corps—had become commonplace. "Gen. Logan feels proud of his Fifteenth Army Corps, and the officers and men that compose it feel as proud of him," claimed an Ohio soldier moments after the battle ended; "A shout went up as he passed each regiment along the lines this evening that was convincing proof of his popularity."[38]

Logan lost 560 men in the Battle of Ezra Church (also called Ezra Chapel), but he inflicted more than 3,000 casualties on General Lee, who paid the price for his impetuous and uncoordinated assaults. "The next morning, the dead of the enemy lay in front of our lines in rows and in piles," Logan remarked. Unfortunately for Logan, he proved prophetic when he wrote his wife, "On the 28th I had the hardest fight of the campaign with my corps alone and gained a great and complete victory, but will get no credit for it. West Point must have all under Sherman who is an infernal *brute*." Although the field commander in the resounding victory, the Battle of Ezra Church goes down in the history books as General Howard's triumph. Even Howard saw it differently. "I never saw better conduct in battle," he admitted, citing Logan as the reason: ". . . the success of the day is as much attributable to him as to any one man."[39]

After the Battle of Atlanta on July 22, the capture of the Gate City was hardly in doubt. Logan's second triumph six days later at Ezra Church made it all a *fait accompli*. Sherman lay siege to Atlanta and shifted his armies around the perimeter in an effort to seize all the rail lines that spoked into the hub. No one on the Union side expressed any concern that they would not emerge victorious from the campaign. For the first time in the War, Logan's attention diverted from the military effort. He grew disillusioned with the service from his demotion and from the lack of appreciation he perceived, despite his sound accomplishments as a corps and army commander. Logan contemplated the summer of 1864 as his last in a general's uniform. "As soon as this campaign is over I think I shall come home," Logan confessed to his wife; "at least I will not serve longer under Sherman."[40]

Sherman well understood the effect of his decision on Logan's demeanor. He tried to soften the blow he inflicted upon him by sending him a copy of a preliminary report he sent to the War Department. Sherman praised Logan in the missive in a manner uncharacteristic of all acknowledgments he had sent previously. In regards to his decision to demote him, Sherman claimed, "I meant no disrespect to any officer, and hereby declare that Genl Logan submitted with the grace and dignity of a Soldier, Gentleman, and Patriot, resumed the command of his Corps proper (Fifteenth) and enjoys the love and respect of his Army and Commanders."

Sherman appropriately credited him with the Ezra Church victory and spoke for General Howard to give Logan "all the credit possible." Sherman was unrelenting in pouring out his accolades. "I also beg to add my most unqualified admiration of the bravery, skill, and more yet, good sense that influenced him to bear a natural disappointment and do his whole duty like a man," Sherman effused, highlighting the fact that Logan "already holds the highest known commission in the Army, and it is hard to say how we could better manifest our applause."[41]

Sherman's letter must have lifted Logan's spirits somewhat, for he did not criticize him in his letters to Mary as he had previously. But the letter failed to restore Logan's enthusiasm for his duties. He paid more attention to politics than he ever had before. Logan fielded the most unusual political offer back in June when he had learned that he was considered as the vice presidential candidate—on the Abolition ticket! Logan chuckled at how he was now linked with a movement that he railed against so vehemently three years before. But he considered John C. Fremont, the head of the prospective ticket, a dishonest man. The party never progressed as a serious election-year player, and Logan never took the matter seriously. "I like good jokes," Logan responded to the offer, "but this one I think is rather too good."[42]

Throughout the month of August, news from home continually filtered into Logan's headquarters. He learned that his sister Dorothy had died, devastating her husband, Cy Thomas. Josh Allen wrote Logan, asking him not to support his rival for the congressional seat. Other correspondents continually wooed him to step back into politics. Charles Lanphier, the editor of the *Illinois State Register*, begged Logan to stump the state for Democrats. Another prominent Democrat wrote two letters to Logan, asking him to be the vice presidential candidate of the Democratic ticket, headed by General George B. McClellan.[43]

But by this time Logan gave the request as much regard as he did the vice presidency of the Abolition ticket. He was consistent in his support of the Republican Party, although he never named it as such, preferring to call it the "war party." He made his feelings known in an early August letter that—like many letters before this—was published in papers throughout the North. Logan updated the situation in Georgia, but clearly equated support for the Democrats as support for the Confederacy. Logan expressed his confidence that the effort of rebels will be crushed, but warned his readers in closing: "The greatest victory for them—greater than fifty Manassases and the only one that can give them a particle of hope—will be to defeat the war party at the incoming campaign."[44]

During August, as Logan shifted troops during the siege, his corps underwent changes. General William B. Hazen transferred from brigade command in the Army of the Cumberland, to command a division in Logan's corps, replacing General Lightburn, who returned to brigade command (he had led when General Peter Osterhaus was forced out temporarily from an injury). Hazen had commanded a brigade in Thomas's army before he took over one of Logan's divisions. "He was just sitting down to supper with his staff, and I joined them . . . ," Hazen recalled. "It was the first time I had met Logan, and I was most agreeably impressed by him, both as a soldier and a man . . ."[45]

If he had known how much clout Logan wielded at this point, he would have been more impressed. Among the young staff sitting down to dinner with him was Captain Hybert Cunningham, celebrating his new rank. Logan performed another unique feat—taking a Confederate commissioned officer and gaining a commission in the Union army for him. Another young officer was Logan's new aide-de-camp, Amzi White. The Marion native was the sixteen-year-old son of John H. White, the late lieutenant colonel of the Thirty-first who died at Logan's side at Fort Donelson. Logan assured his wife that he "will take care of him as best I can."[46]

Logan's paternal instincts in the summer of 1864 were matched by his humanistic ones. As his corps approached the Flint River south of Atlanta, an orderly galloped up to Logan requesting a chaplain. When pressed for the reason, the orderly responded, "a baptism." His curiosity piqued, Logan rode to a dilapidated cabin from where the request generated. As Logan dismounted, one of the physicians remarked, "General, you're just the man we're after." When Logan asked why, he was told, "For a godfather."

Logan entered the shack to see some of his corps doctors aiding a young woman (a widow to a Confederate soldier), her mother, and her newborn. He ordered soldiers with him to clean up the place. Then the baptism commenced with Logan holding the baby while the chaplain performed the ceremony. They christened her "Shell-Anna" because she was born amidst raining artillery fire. After the ceremony ended, Logan pulled a gold coin from his pocket, and presented it to the grandmother as his christening gift for his new godchild. One of the doctors always remembered the tender but surreal scene involving "that poor little 'battle born' babe of Flint River."[47]

Shortly after the christening of Shell-Anna, Logan displayed his defensive prowess in battle one more time. Sherman maneuvered his army to a position south of Atlanta to take control of the Macon and Western Railroad, the final supply line still open to Atlanta. General Hood, desperate to prevent this, attacked Logan's corps shortly after it crossed the Flint River on August 31—the first day of the two-day Battle of Jonesboro (also spelled "Jonesborough"). Like Ezra

Church, the Fifteenth Corps took the brunt of the attacks for the first day of the Jonesboro fight. Observing but inactive soldiers took the scene in from a nearby hill that afforded them a panoramic view of the battlefield. They watched incredulously as the smoke lifted like a drawing stage curtain to reveal the Fifteenth Corps members turn their backs to the attacking Confederates, not to run, but to tear off their hats, wave them, and madly cheer a lone rider recklessly galloping down the line. One of the witnesses felt a comrade elbow him asking, "Who the devil is that?" The answer came from the discernable roar from the soldiers below them: "Logan! Logan! Hurrah for Black Jack Logan! Hurrah! Hurrah!"[48]

The observant soldiers watched in awe as members of the Fifteenth Corps leapt from the trenches to view and cheer their commander, who "dashes through the storm of iron and lead as coolly as though he were reviewing his troops on a gala day, and creates a furor of enthusiasm among the men that cannot be described, and is not easily imagined." Then Logan rode off and his corps, with support from generals Dodge and Blair, turned back all that was thrown against them that day. Logan lost less than 200 men, but inflicted more than 2,000 casualties on General Hardee's corps. The Army of the Tennessee held their position on September 1, during the second day of the battle, a contest that turned into a lost opportunity for Sherman when the Army of the Cumberland could not destroy Hood's force as they jackknifed the Confederates from the North. Although the Union troops did not annihilate their Confederate foes, they did cripple them severely.[49]

With the railroads in Union hands, Hood was forced to evacuate Atlanta. Logan and the Army of the Tennessee followed the Army of the Cumberland into the Gate City. "Atlanta is ours, and fairly won," read Sherman's classic telegram to Washington on September 4. The campaign to capture the city was a necessary, and at times spectacular, hard-fought victory for the Union forces. Logan addressed his corps, a body of troops he called "the valor of Federal arms," on September 11 at East Point, a hub east of Atlanta. Logan had cemented a nine-month relationship with the corps with bonds at least as strong as the ones he held for twenty months as commander of the regiments marching in the Seventeenth Corps. Logan assured his corps of their future success. Nowhere in his speech, however, did he intimate that he would be leading them in their future endeavors.[50]

As Sherman prepared to march the Army of the Tennessee to the eastern shores of Georgia, Logan did not prepare to go with him. Hundreds of personnel acquired leaves of absences for a stint to visit loved ones at home. Abraham Lincoln planned for Logan to return home for a mission: to secure Illinois for the upcoming elections. Urged by influential members of Congress, he also reflected back on the effect of Logan's speeches in Illinois in 1862 and 1863. The president was concerned about the activities of the Knights of the Golden Circle in Illinois and Indiana. Despite the fall of Atlanta, Lincoln also fretted about his chance for victory in the upcoming November elections. He wired a message to Sherman, insisting that Logan's presence in Illinois was most important to the national cause.[51]

Logan was consumed by the fall election campaign. J. W. Sheahan, the *Chicago Post* editor and former devotee of Stephen A. Douglas, sent him a letter that Logan received in September, one that included a copy of the platform adopted by the Democratic Party at their convention in Chicago. Sheahan urged Logan to officially endorse Democrats. "In God's name, dear Logan, by all your hopes for your country and yourself, let not the Democracy ask your arm and be refused," he pleaded. Logan had no intention of complying with his request. When he read the enclosed platform, he made defeating the platform his top priority.[52]

George B. McClellan, as expected, was officially nominated at the Democratic Convention in Chicago during the last days of August; George H. Pendleton—an Ohio Peace Democrat who Logan absolutely loathed—was chosen as his running mate. The platform under which McClellan was nominated was so controversial that even McClellan refused to endorse it. Clement Vallandigham and the Peace Democrats drafted the language calling for a cessation of hostilities to a war they condemned, to be followed by an "ultimate convention" of all the states to restore peace. The language made it easy for those opposing it to deride it as "The Chicago Surrender." That the platform was adopted on August 29 made Sherman's capture of Atlanta less than one week later that much more important to counter the Peace Democrats' claim that the war was a failure.[53]

Letters quickly made their way to Logan concerning the election campaign. Elihu Washburne, representing the Union Executive Congressional Committee for the presidential campaign of 1864, congratulated Logan for his efforts in the victorious Atlanta campaign. "You can have no conception of the thrill of joy which that news sent through every loyal heart in the country." He relayed Grant's congratulations, then expressed his hope that Logan would be able to head to Illinois to attack the Copperheads and stump for Lincoln. "We want your clarion voice to echo over our state and arouse the Union and patriotic people to the salvation of the country." Isham N. Haynie sent Logan a letter of his views of the Illinois State Democratic Convention he attended in Springfield as a looker-on. Haynie claimed that "intensely Peace men" dominated the proceedings and condemned War Democrats like Logan. "It is said you are going for McClellan and Pendleton and the ticket," Haynie informed his friend, hoping against hope it was not true. "We all want to hear from you," he continued, "I feel a deep interest in knowing—as do thousands . . ."[54]

Logan yearned to get back to Illinois to support the war and counter the adverse claims about him. On September 20, General Howard notified Logan that he was granted thirty days leave of absence; Major General Peter Osterhaus would command the Fifteenth Corps temporarily until Logan returned. Logan immediately stepped aboard a train and rode the Union-controlled rails through Georgia, Tennessee, and Kentucky. Riders in the same car could not help but hear Logan's loud denunciation of the Peace Democrats. "General Logan [was] particularly severe on the Chicago Convention," relayed a Cleveland attorney who rode with him from Nashville to Louisville; "He expressed respect for General McClellan, but would as soon vote for Jeff. Davis as Pendleton."[55]

Logan detrained at Carbondale and enjoyed a tender reunion with Mary and Dollie. He then went to work to craft the address he planned to deliver on the stump. He had a tremendous task ahead of him to campaign for Republicans in a region that was a Democratic stronghold for decades. The Republican and Democratic Springfield papers each claimed that Logan was for their party. Logan's 1862 and 1863 addresses made it clear that he supported the war as a means to preserve the Union. The question Southern Illinoisans looked for Logan to answer was, as a War Democrat, would he adopt McClellan's policy of endorsing the Democratic Party without adopting the platform?

For the third time in as many years, Logan chose Carbondale as the site to initiate his speaking tour. October 1, 1864 launched another series of speeches, but this campaign was the first specifically designed to influence elections, and he only had twenty allotted days remaining to accomplish this Herculean feat. Mary later remembered her husband as haggard from the arduous Atlanta Campaign. But his weariness did not deflect from his performance that day. The crowd exceeded 10,000—the equivalent of a third of the district voters had found their way to Carbondale. Logan had seen crowds this large, but this one was vociferous; indeed it was rabid. Politics had charged the atmosphere with an energy that could not be curtailed. There were people who loved John Logan, and there were people who hated him with equal passion, if not more. This was an unprecedented political event for the region. Never before had a prominent Democrat campaigned for a rival party in Egypt. More unfathomable was that the campaigner was formerly a politician who won the region by landslides as their Democratic representative. All awaited Logan's remarks.[56]

He stood at a finely decorated stand in an elegant grove of tall shade-casting oaks. But while the trees helped to cool the crowd on this hot summer day,

Logan fired them up with a rousing speech that displayed his case that McClellan was no traitor, but he was the tool of traitors who crafted all the resolutions of the Democratic Party platform in Chicago. Logan used prowar Democrat Andrew Johnson, Tennessee's Military Governor and Abraham Lincoln's vice presidential candidate, as an example of a Union patriot who was forced from his state at the start of the War, but had returned with the Union control of Tennessee. Logan contrasted him with George H. Pendleton, McClellan's vice presidential candidate, who Logan claimed was allied with the Northern traitors "denouncing every man connected with the war, and throwing every clog in the way of the advancement of the armies."

Setting up the contrast, Logan stirred the crowd to react: "There is the difference between these men," professed General Logan; "And yet I am asked to vote for McClellan and Pendleton. Gentlemen, I won't do it." The applause that followed was wild and deafening. Induced to keep up the favorable reaction, Logan went on. "Johnson and I fought against secession and secessionists when the war first broke out. We are fighting against them now. We stood together then, and we stand together now; and for this we are called Abolitionists."[57]

Many in the audience must have been shocked as Logan denounced the Peace Democrats. Disgusted to see members of his party "wearing long faces when the Union armies are victorious and smiles when defeated," he reminded his audience that his position had not wavered in the year and two months that transpired since his last Carbondale address in the summer of 1863. "I said then, and I say now," he declared, "that although I have ever acted and voted with you as a Democrat, I will neither act with nor support any man, or set of men, no matter by what name they may be called, that are not in favor of exhausting all the men and means under the control of the government in order to put down this accursed rebellion." His words found their way into Southern newspapers: "Men who are in favor of restoring the Union by any means necessary to do it are my friends in this struggle, and those who are not in favor of this are my enemies, and I am theirs."[58]

His next target was the Chicago Platform and its architects. His message was strident but effective. He mocked "Copperhead sympathy" by posing a series of questions and answers. "Do they congratulate us because we have planted our flag in every Southern state? They say no such thing. Do they sympathize with the widows and orphans of those slain in battle? They say not that." Logan pointed out that none of the leaders of the Democratic platform "have ever come to see the army and take the hand of the soldier," while many governors and members of state and local legislatures had done so throughout the war. He continued to belittle the Peace Democrats by adding, "I am willing to sell out my interest in their sympathy for a very small price."[59]

"The General speaks as well as he fights," assessed one reporter.[60] In essence, Logan was speaking and fighting at the same time. His then uttered his most draconian statements to date, a clear reflection of his views stimulated by three-and-a-half years of unrelenting, bloody war:

> Now, I told you we could restore this country by suppressing the rebellion. There is no matter of doubt that we can destroy their armies—we can kill every man that belongs to them, and so far as I am concerned rather than see this Government destroyed, I would kill the last rebel—Jeff. Davis himself—all of them, and see their bleeding corpses stretched upon the ground, and when the last one expired, I would wave the stars and stripes over him, and cry "Heaven be blessed, we have a restored country once more."[61]

He left no doubt about his position, one that had not wavered since his address to then-colonel Ulysses S. Grant's regiment in Springfield in June of 1861. The war had strengthened his resolve, but it also had irreparably embittered him. He eventually softened his stance that afternoon to conclude the speech with his vocal support of Abraham Lincoln and the administration. The crowd response was more than enthusiastic—most of them appeared intoxicated by his blood-lust. The speech and the reaction emboldened Logan. He was prepared to barnstorm the state of Illinois.[62]

Logan stumped the state like a whirlwind. Springfield followed Carbondale. Heavy rains reduced the crowd but failed to dampen his spirit. Unlike the previous summer's tour, he altered his addresses, delivering speeches with the same theme, but not the same words. At Springfield, Logan invoked the spirit of Stephen Douglas, repeating part of his patriots-and-traitors speech. He stayed in Springfield to craft a slate of events with Republican leaders; he then delivered a second speech, one that reiterated his support for the Lincoln-Johnson ticket. "I am for these men whether I have a friend left in the Democratic party or not," he maintained. As they had in 1863, Logan's stump speeches appeared in pamphlet form. "How Douglas Democrats Will Vote" argued that the Republican Platform was ideal; the Democratic one was unacceptable: "Mr. Lincoln stands, I say, on the true Union platform, and, therefore, I am for him."[63]

Lincoln's confidants quickly notified the president about what was going on. "Genl. J. A. Logan is making the most telling speeches ever made in Illinois," raved one of them on October 6 in a letter to Lincoln. The informant insisted that Logan's leave of absence be extended until after the election. Lincoln took the advice.[64]

Logan met with Republican leaders to prepare a schedule of towns to visit on the speaking circuit. Unlike his summer stumping of 1863, Logan concentrated his efforts in Southern Illinois. Egypt had voted against Lincoln by nearly a five to one margin in 1860; while expectations were not that Lincoln would win the Egyptian vote over McClellan, Republican leaders hoped Logan could help close Lincoln's previous 23,000-vote margin of defeat to assure that he would win Illinois in November. This effort was for other candidates as well. Logan would be campaigning—with relish—against Josh Allen by supporting Andrew J. Kuykendall, the former Thirty-first Illinois officer tagged by the Republicans to run against him. Logan's brigade commander in the Fort Donelson campaign, Richard Oglesby, was running for governor to replace Richard Yates. Not only was Logan campaigning for him, but also indirectly for Yates, who was running for the U.S. senatorial seat from Illinois. This could only be achieved by tipping the state legislature to the Republican side—another mission of the speaking circuit.

The politicians planned sixteen speeches for Logan during the remainder of his leave of absence. He teamed up with his former political adversary, David L. Phillips, and with Isham Haynie and Richard Oglesby. Most of the speeches were sited close to railroad stops, the chief source of travel for the Unionist team. Logan rode into Belleville, where he spoke on October 10. From there he went on to Centralia, delivering what a local reporter called "a three hour speech of eloquence in thoughts that breathed words that burned." The tremendous crowd at Centralia was matched at Du Quoin, then at Clinton, the latter where Logan and his team spoke on the fifteenth.[65] At one of these towns, a reporter painted a word portrait of Logan for his paper's readers:

> Imagine a man, rather below the medium stature, but of whose frame every bone, muscle and swelling contour bespeaks perfection of proportion. . . . Every limb is shapely and every movement graceful. Dark, flowing locks, generally worn rather long, hewy black eyebrows, a mustache of the same raven hue; eyes as black as coal, but large full and expressive, and firm aboriginal features, stern and unrelenting in expression when under the excitement of speech, but as gentle and benevolent when kindled with a smile, as those of a maiden looking upon her lover. Imagine all these and then try to imagine—what is beyond the conception of those who have not seen it or studied it—the manly soul—the presence—the mien of the individual, and

the reader has an imperfect picture of the dashing, gallant, bold, fearless, lion-hearted John A. Logan.[66]

The speaking circuit was planned without definitive approval from the War Department to allow Logan to remain in Illinois until the election. The approval came by telegram in mid October, clearing the path to complete the ambitious schedule. At the same time, Secretary Stanton proposed that Logan take over the Department of Missouri—a chaotic politico-military region for the Union. Unaware that Stanton was thinking of Logan for the position, Grant suggested that General George Crook—commanding the Eighth Corps in the Shenandoah Valley—head to Missouri to oversee the Department. He had a plan for who should run the Eighth Corps. "I would recommend General Logan for Crook's place," Grant wrote. "He is an active, fighting general, and under Sheridan will make a first-rate commander for that department." Lincoln decided to defer any requests involving Logan until after the election; Logan's campaign was too important.[67]

From Clinton, Logan rode to the eastern border of Illinois, giving speeches on consecutive days. The crowds remained enthusiastic, leaving him optimistic about the November election. "This district is now safe," he predicted to Mary after another positive reaction to an October 18 speech in Grayville. He spoke at Phillipstown on the nineteenth before traversing the state. Campaigning energized him, but his voice was hoarsening. Logan's team solicited the president for more help in Illinois; Logan joined in a joint dispatch ostensibly to allow General John Palmer, another political general, to tour the state.[68]

The team arrived in Alton on October 20. Logan was in fine form for a largely pro-Lincoln audience, reportedly numbering several thousand strong. As usual, he spoke for three hours, but added new lines to his favorite themes, such as McClellan's accepting the Democratic nomination while rejecting its platform. He ridiculed McClellan—who ran the Illinois Central Railroad before the war—with a finely placed barb: "Perhaps as a railroad man, he has learned that it is dangerous to stand on the platform." After he closed his address, a venerable citizen of Alton paid a tribute to Logan's bravery and patriotism and then led the crowd in three hearty cheers. A crooner then stepped up to give an effecting rendition of "The Battle Cry of Freedom." When the audience joined in the chorus, they did so with overpowering voices. A witness, deeply affected by the day's events, wrote, "Thus closed one of the largest, most enthusiastic, interesting and profitable meetings ever held in the city of Alton."[69]

The uplifting Alton experience was not repeated at the speeches that immediately followed. Logan's spread-eagle oratory exacerbated the hard feelings harbored in those who once stood as his political allies. He had campaigned unrelentingly in country teeming with members of the Knights of the Golden Circle. By 1864 this clandestine organization's reign of terror gripped the region. Known Lincoln supporters, both the vocal and the reticent, suffered from the Knight's wrath. "The burning of stacks, barns and houses was frequent," claimed a Unionist, "and the killing and skinning of cattle and sheep in whole flocks was not uncommon, apparently for 'revenue only;' but only Union men sustained such losses." Such was the climate that Logan deliberately stirred in October of 1864. Knights of the Golden Circle openly threatened to kill him as well if he attempted to make speeches. An Egyptian paper reported that "the canvass now being made by Gen. Logan and others in this portion of Illinois is the most extraordinary ever made in the Northern States. It is being made amid threats of murder, assassination and violence, but the day of doom and reckoning speedily approaches."[70]

Those threats never affected Logan. He was driven by rage, a hatred of all the subversive leaders who did not support the war. The mutual hatred boiled over at a Mount Vernon barbecue on October 25. The picnic was attended by several Peace Democrats who were not there to enjoy the festive event. "General Logan then pitched into our local coppers in his own peculiar style," reported a local newspaper. He called any supporter of the Chicago platform a sympathizer of traitors. When Willis Duff Green, a leading local physician and Democrat, requested that Logan retract the inflammatory statement, Logan refused. "I say it yet, whether you like it or not," he responded. Then the doctor challenged him: "I say any man who indorses the Lincoln platform is an enemy of his country." Logan refused to back down. "I say you are a damned liar," he shouted; then he reached for a glass tumbler and hurled it at the doctor. Dr. Green dodged it; then he drew a pistol. Logan had no revolver—just more glassware. He grabbed a pitcher and charged. David L. Phillips quickly intervened and stopped the confrontation. After Dr. Green was removed, Logan returned to his address, emboldened by the incident. Amidst hoots and heckling for the next hour, Logan hurled verbal grenades at his opponents whom he derided as "peace-sneaks" and "home rebels."[71]

Ugliness pocked the next afternoon's event. Logan was shouted down in a speech at McLeansboro; later that day the crowd chucked stones at Haynie and Phillips when these two followed Logan at the dais, reportedly injuring a spectator in the process. From that moment onward, whenever Logan took his position on the platform, he laid a revolver in front of him, admonishing his audience that anyone attempting to interfere with his right to speak must take the consequences upon himself.[72]

Logan's words continued to fray nerves. Josh Allen replaced George H. Pendleton as his chief target. Logan was unrelenting in his denunciation of Allen. Logan insisted that in the summer of 1861, Allen had proposed to work with Logan to secede Egypt to the Confederacy. "I told him I'd see him in Hell first," Logan told his audiences. Although Allen vehemently denied and denounced the charge, Logan repeated it as he swept through Egypt.[73]

As October waned to November, Logan spoke at Jonesboro, Cairo, Benton, and Golconda. At his former hometown of Benton, Logan's speech was constantly interrupted by Annie Blanchard, who was unable to disrupt her energetic brother with her secession-sympathizing rants. At Golconda, Logan's appearance typified what was witnessed at several small Illinois towns, complete with a grand barbecue, large quantities of bunting, booming cannon, and firing pistols. County residents traveled scores of miles to see him; the total head count numbered in the thousands. Twenty years later, a resident rated Logan's appearance "by far the greatest event that Golconda ever knew, either before or since." Logan continued to receive mixed reviews in the southernmost regions of the state. The *Jonesboro Gazette*, such a strong ally of Logan in the 1850s, took to calling him a "mysterious compound of buffoonery and blackguardism" in a late-October edition of the paper.[74]

By Election Day on November 8, Logan had canvassed an extraordinary portion of Southern Illinois. More than 50,000 people heard him speak during his five-week tour; perhaps an equal number of voters read excerpts of his speeches in newspapers across Egypt. His speeches and the reactions to them were also picked up in newspapers of St. Louis, Springfield, as well as Indiana, Wisconsin, Iowa, and other dailies and weeklies from the Old Northwest and the trans-Mississippi West. Despite the military campaign victory in Georgia, Lincoln feared his loss at the polls. Congressman Washburne allayed the president's fears shortly before the election. "Logan is carrying all before him in Egypt," he wrote, adding that the benefit stretched beyond Lincoln: "I have just got a letter from Cairo and our friends feel quite confident of beating Josh Allen."[75]

The election results were unprecedented. Lincoln's fears were clearly unfounded in Illinois; he won the state by more than 30,000 votes. In 1860, the eighteen counties in Logan's former Ninth District barely cast 5,000 votes for him. The new Thirteenth District, consisting of all but two counties of the old Ninth District, went for Lincoln in 1864: 11,714 to 10,926. Kuykendall beat Allen, just as Washburne had predicted. Oglesby also received the majority of Egyptian votes and won the governor's race. Egypt—a bed-rock Jacksonian Democrat region—had gone Republican for the first time in its history. Statewide, the Republican Party also seized eleven out of fourteen districts for representatives to the U.S. Congress and won strong majorities in both houses of the Illinois legislature. This made Governor Yates transition to the U.S. Senate nearly certain.[76]

The grateful beneficiaries of Logan's influence let him know the value of his efforts. Newly elected Governor Richard Oglesby, once Logan's political rival, praised that "the House 'Treason' and his rider 'Josh' hath the Lord thrown in the sea—sent to the Devil." Oglesby assured Logan, "You will never be forgotten, nor ceased to be honored by all Illinois."[77] Regional newspapers also threw the credit for the remarkable political reversal in Logan's direction. The *Missouri Democrat*, a pro-Republican St. Louis paper, paid Logan a glowing tribute after the election:

> ... The Union party is indebted in a great measure to him for the glorious result. He it was who threw away party and clung to the old flag. He it was that went to the field of battle and came back covered with glory, and exposed the traitorous machinations of Josh Allen. To this fact then, more than any other, this glorious triumph over Copperheadism in Egypt is attributable. All hail, General Logan! Farewell, Josh Allen.[78]

The impact of one man on an election is difficult to assess to be sure, but Logan's influence cannot be underestimated, particularly when such an unexpected turn of events overtook a region in which he canvassed so strongly. An 18,000-vote swing was measured in Egypt in 1864 compared to the 1860 trends.[79] Although Lincoln won his home state by 30,000 votes, Logan's statewide influence in three years of speeches may have turned votes to the Republicans outside of the Thirteenth District. Thousands of pamphlets of his patriotic addresses from the summer of 1863 circulated throughout the North, and his letters and speeches were excerpted in Northern newspapers across the country.

Not to be overlooked is what Logan pulled off between the first week of May to the first week of September of 1864. He broke a tactical stalemate with his corps at Resaca; he secured the right flank of Sherman's offensive at the Battle of Dallas. He took over an army in peril and rallied it to victory at Atlanta. His defense proved decisive at Ezra Church and Jonesboro. In the three battles in which the Fifteenth Corps fought alone (Dallas, Ezra Church, and the first day of the Jonesboro fight), Logan lost 1,100 soldiers, but inflicted 6,500 casualties on the Confederates. His battlefield tactics rivaled any other corps commander in campaigns previous to the Atlanta mission.

No greater dual performance of a political general can be found in the annals of American history that would compete with what John A. Logan displayed for six months in 1864. It was a performance that has never been surpassed.

John A. Logan, circa 1855. After serving in the Eighteenth Illinois General Assembly, the young lawyer completed his four-year term as the prosecuting attorney for the third judicial circuit while working cases in a private practice he kept with numerous partners from 1853 to 1861. (ABRAHAM LINCOLN PRESIDENTIAL LIBRARY)

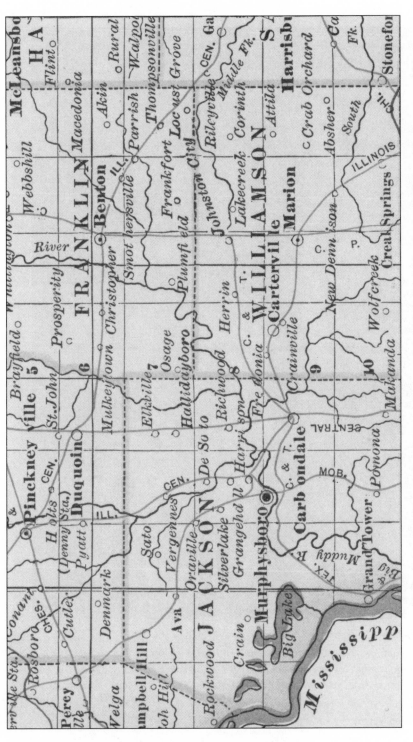

Map of Southern Illinois region known as "Egypt," showing several towns where Logan lived: Murphysboro, Carbondale, Benton, and Marion. Although north of the Ohio River, this region of Illinois was as geographically southern as Richmond, Virginia. Not surprisingly, the culture and politics of Egypt aligned with the states south of the Mason-Dixon line. (CENTURY, 1897)

Dr. John Logan (1788–1853), father of John A. Logan. The Northern Ireland immigrant was a pioneer settler of Southern Illinois. He served four terms in the Illinois General Assembly, three with Abraham Lincoln who named Logan County after him. (ABRAHAM LINCOLN PRESIDENTIAL LIBRARY)

Thomas M. Logan (1827–1907). John A. Logan's colorful and conflicted brother was weakened by suspected alcoholism, which led to felony charges and two broken marriages. His service in the Thirty-first Illinois Volunteer Infantry failed to straighten his life's course and he ingloriously left the army less than six months after enlisting. (GENERAL JOHN A. LOGAN MUSEUM)

Lindorf "Doff" Ozburn. John A. Logan's close friend, who married his cousin in the Logan home. He succeeded Logan as colonel of the Thirty-first Illinois Volunteer Infantry. After his discharge, he was murdered in Carbondale in 1864 by another Illinois soldier. (GENERAL JOHN A. LOGAN MUSEUM)

Mary S. Cunningham Logan (1838–1923). Married to John A. Logan at seventeen, she devoted her life to her husband's career for thirty-one years, and broke with Victorian Age decorum to actively solicit legislature votes during his U.S. Senate campaigns. (ABRAHAM LINCOLN PRESIDENTIAL LIBRARY)

Senator Logan addresses a political meeting in a grove at Marshalltown, Iowa. This 1880s image captures the power, prestige, and influence of the orator who could attract thousands to see him on a hastily erected platform as he discussed the issues of the Gilded Age. (ABRAHAM LINCOLN PRESIDENTIAL LIBRARY)

John A. Logan as a colonel in the winter of 1862. Close to death from wounds received at Fort Donelson, Colonel Logan was passed over for promotion by President Lincoln until Ulysses S. Grant intervened to eventually secure a brigadier general's commission in the spring of 1862, and a major general's rank one year later. (ABRAHAM LINCOLN PRESIDENTIAL LIBRARY)

Throughout the Civil War, General Logan carried this pocket case containing daguerreotypes of wife, Mary, and daughter, Mary "Dollie" Logan. These two most important women in his life frequently exchanged letters with him between 1861 and 1865. (LIBRARY OF CONGRESS)

Congressman Logan and his family in Washington, circa 1870. Manning Logan, born in July 1865, sits on his mother's knee. Manning changed his name to John A. Logan II when he reached adulthood. He was killed in 1899 as a colonel leading a charge of U.S. volunteers in the Philippines. He was posthumously awarded the Congressional Medal of Honor. (LIBRARY OF CONGRESS)

The Logan family united in New Mexico in September 1882 where they joined army officers, U.S. Geological Survey artists, and a Zuni Indian for this photograph. Logan stands fourth from the right and his seventeen-year-old son is seated at the far right; Mary is most likely standing to the right of her husband while Dollie likely appears seated in front of the tent, holding her son, Logan Tucker. (LIBRARY OF CONGRESS)

A large crowd gathers in Chicago at Logan's statue in Grant Park to commemorate the forty-third anniversary of Decoration Day on May 30, 1911. Logan nationalized this day, today celebrated as Memorial Day. The Augustus Saint Gaudens statue of Logan was completed in 1897. (DN-0056986, CHICAGO DAILY NEWS NEGATIVES COLLECTION, CHICAGO HISTORICAL SOCIETY)

Senator Logan's tell-tale features and controversial positions attracted the attention of political cartoonists. Talented artist Joseph Keppler satirized the defeated "Triumvirate"—Senators Cameron, Conkling, and Logan— hobbling away from "The Chicago Catastrophe," after their candidate, Ulysses S. Grant, was upset by James Garfield in the Republican National Convention in May 1880. (PUCK MAGAZINE)

The Atlanta Cyclorama, reportedly commissioned by Logan in 1883, was released in 1887, months after Logan's death. This image, called "Logan to the Front" was taken from the cyclorama in an advertisement to the world's largest oil painting while it was on exhibition in Minneapolis. (COLLECTION OF THE AUTHOR)

Recollections of a Soldier's Wife

By Mrs. John A. Logan

"He had shown the qualities of the born soldier which were to make him a great commander: coolness and promptness in action, quickness in taking advantage of ground and a situation, and the ability to infuse his own spirit into his command."—Mrs. Logan's tribute to her husband for his part in the battle of Belmont

EDITOR'S NOTE.—One of the hardest, and at the same time most vital, tasks confronting the Northern leaders in 1861 was to keep the southern portions of the loyal states loyal. In no state was this harder than in Illinois. Part of that state is South; Logan's task was to convince the people living there that their only salvation lay in standing by the Union. In this chapter of her "Recollections" Mrs. Logan tells the thrilling story of how he did it. She also pictures vividly the building of the magnificent army that fought so gallantly in the West and furnished the leader to checkmate Lee. We recommend the reading of this bit of history of a stirring time.

GENERAL GRANT was once asked why it was that, while southern Indiana was a hotbed of secession, southern Illinois was loyal to the Union. "Logan," was his answer.

Mr. Logan was a Douglas Democrat, and that represented in politics the overwhelming idea of the sixteen counties lying at the lower extremity of the state which he represented in Congress. The mass of his constituents had for him a genuine personal affection such as a member could win only in a frontier community. Yet if, when he started back to Washington in answer to President Lincoln's call for an extra session of Congress in July, 1861, he had announced his intention to raise a regiment for the Union, all the fat would have been in the fire. He knew his people far too well to take them into his confidence until events had reached a more acute stage.

In the preceding chapter I told how I remained at home in Marion to play in earnest his better half. I had to answer all the questions which would naturally have been put to my husband had he been at home, to mollify the fault-finders over what was being done in Washington, and to explain each new move North and South, always in an adroit effort to direct opinion into the channel which would subserve my husband's

FROM RESERVE COLLECTION

367

Although he was a subject of nine books during his lifetime, and authored three books himself, John A. Logan's nineteenth-century fame had already begun to wane early in the twentieth century. Mary Logan remained devoted to her husband's career after his death, publishing her memoirs in 1913 as a book, and in serial form in Cosmopolitan *magazine.* (FEBRUARY 1913 ISSUE, COLLECTION OF THE AUTHOR)

Logan's chair in the Senate was draped in crape in this December 1886 photograph taken during the week of his death. Today that same senate chair sits in the General John A. Logan Museum in Murphysboro, Illinois, within 200 yards of the foundation of the home where the senator was born. (ABRAHAM LINCOLN PRESIDENTIAL LIBRARY)

The body of John A. Logan lies in state in the Capitol Rotunda during the last two days of 1886, visited by thousands of spectators who file past his coffin to pay their final respects. He was only the seventh American to be honored with a State Funeral, earning the distinction for twenty-five years of national military and political service. His unexpected death the day after Christmas headlined newspapers throughout the country. (ABRAHAM LINCOLN PRESIDENTIAL LIBRARY)

CHAPTER SEVEN

Victory

THE POLITICAL BUG bit him badly.

In the latter days of his leave from the army, Logan seriously sought a reward he felt he earned for his efforts in the reelection campaign of Abraham Lincoln, the successful gubernatorial bid for Richard Oglesby, and the remarkable defeat of Josh Allen. The landslide that swept through Illinois in 1864 reversed all the gains of the Peace Democrats in 1862. Democrats had exceeded Republicans in the joint Illinois legislature by 22 prior to the election (67 to 45); afterwards, a net change of 42 House and Senate members gave the Republicans a majority of 20 legislators (75 to 55).[1]

With a preponderance of Republicans in the Illinois legislature, Logan realized that the U.S. Senate seat was safe in the hands of the Unionists. But he did not want it go to Richard Yates—he wanted that seat for himself. He considered this decision before the November 8 election. He wished to parlay the fervor, the accolades, and the tremendous ovations he experienced on the stump into the most powerful position he could hold at the national level. By the time he rode in to Mount Vernon on October 25, Logan had been swayed to have his supporters help him look to a more ambitious conclusion. He must have been confident, as he wrote to his wife on October 19, that the district (and therefore, the state) was set to trounce the Peace Democrats when the citizens went to the polls on November 8.

Logan's quandary was a complicated one. He still had to test his chances to win the Senate seat without officially declaring his candidacy. But more important: he was still in the army and on a leave of absence that would expire by mid November. To pursue the Senate seat, he would have to resign as a Major General of U.S. Volunteers. Logan never allowed his two natural gifts—politics and war—to battle each other, even when the opportunity was ripe to do so the previous winter when he was openly promoted by newspaper editors to run for governor. Back then he elevated duty above all else and refused to consider a political office during a time of war. By the end of 1864, he had changed his mind.

One man alone appears responsible for Logan considering giving up his rank and status in the army—General William T. Sherman. Logan no longer wanted to serve under Sherman and was seeking a way to avoid returning as his subordinate. His first option was to run a military department outside of Sherman's jurisdiction. He pressed this issue with Congressman Washburne. Perhaps Logan learned of Lincoln and Stanton's consideration that he run the Department of Missouri when the election was over. "Genl. Jack Logan sends word to me that he wants to go to Washington after the election to see you about certain matters that he does not wish to write about," wrote Washburne to Lincoln at the end of October; "Please give your attention to this matter of Jack's." One week later, Logan pushed another Lincoln informant in Illinois to repeat the request.[2]

By early November, Logan became convinced to take the Senate bid seriously. The man who convinced him was Isham N. Haynie. Notwithstanding their squabbles and jealousies early in the war, Logan and Haynie had always shared a mutual respect. Their friendship strengthened on the month-long speaking tour of October, a campaign in which they participated in more than a dozen events together. Watching the crowds and their response to Logan's presentations, Haynie grew more convinced that Logan—and not Richard Yates—was the ideal nominee for the Senate seat. The October experience converted Haynie into a Logan disciple. He dedicated himself to get enough endorsements for Logan to sway the newly elected Illinois legislature to elect him U.S. senator.

Logan visited Cairo early in November; reportedly he met with Haynie to discuss their plan, one that would be forced to be conducted in a truncated time frame. Logan then rode home to Carbondale to take in the election results. The campaign had been an exhilarating experience, but it physically taxed him. His body was spent and his throat was raw. So hoarse that he could no longer speak, Logan needed extra time to recover his health. On November 12, he sent a telegram to Lincoln, requesting to extend his leave a few more days to recuperate before heading back East.[3]

The president—grateful at Logan's contribution to his resounding election victory—sent the general a response later that day. Lincoln informed him that he could extend his leave up to thirty more days, provided General Sherman endorsed it. He also highlighted the planned visit Logan would be making to the White House. "If in view of maintaining your good relations with Gen'l Sherman and of probable movements of his Army you can safely come here I shall be very glad to see you," closed Lincoln in his return message. On November 15, Sherman's adjutant telegraphed Logan granting the additional leave. In the midst of a grand march from Atlanta to Savannah, Sherman stressed that it was not possible to overtake his corps until the Army of the Tennessee reached the Atlantic Ocean.[4]

Isham N. Haynie went to work for Logan soon after the election guaranteed a Republican-dominated legislature. He persuaded the editor of Mount Vernon's anti-Democrat newspaper, the *Unconditional Unionist*, to endorse Logan. Using the endorsement as a bargaining tool, Haynie contacted other prominent newspapers, including the *Chicago Tribune*, to mention Logan as a serious candidate for the Senate seat.[5] How seriously Logan considered this all remains unknown.

Despite the leave granted to him, Logan felt uneasy about his command. When Haynie arrived in Carbondale on November 19, he was disappointed to find that Logan had left for Cincinnati, where he apparently attended to military matters, and also met with a former staff officer. Before he left Carbondale, Logan did send a dispatch to Haynie, but he directed it to Mount Vernon, expecting Haynie to be there with the *Unconditional Unionist* editor. He asked Haynie to head to Chicago, but Haynie received the message at Cairo, too late to do so. Rumors of Logan's appearance at Chicago reached some of his staff. John Hotaling learned that rooms were reserved for Logan there, but he never arrived to occupy them. "He should [have] come to Chicago," complained Hotaling in a letter to Mary Logan, knowing the general lost the opportunity to enhance a Senate bid; "he has many warm friends in the North and they are anxious that he should be our next Senator."[6]

Logan's missed appearance did not stop Haynie. Logan's campaign manager used the editor of the Mount Vernon paper as the conduit to spread the "Logan for Senator" slogan throughout the state. He inserted a long editorial into his paper, and then sent a copy of it to every paper in the state. The last line of the endorsement matched Haynie's reasoning: "We are satisfied that if the matter was left to the people to be voted on, Logan would be the choice; therefore, he is *our* choice." The editor also sent a copy to every member of the legislature. By late November, other newspapers began to take up the cause of Logan for Senator in their editorials. Haynie was disappointed to learn that David L. Phillips was campaigning for Yates in Chicago and not for Logan, but this failed to deter him. "It is my design to stir things up hot," Haynie promised.[7]

By late November, Haynie was convinced that the Senate seat was ripe for Logan's taking. But the greatest obstacle for the victory was the candidate himself. Logan apparently never returned to Illinois after riding out to Cincinnati in the third week of November. He was careful not to publicly state his desire to pursue the Senate. The impression left behind was that Logan had eschewed politics for duty again. Logan's home paper believed this, considering it a persistent and admirable trait for their famous resident. "John A. Logan is our choice over all competitors, provided he was a candidate, which we do not believe he is," claimed the *Carbondale New Era* in December, "He has repeatedly said that he would accept no political office until the war was over. . . . We think it very injudicious to thrust his name forward as a candidate for United States Senator." Isham Haynie obviously disagreed, but he wished that Logan would step into Illinois to set the paper straight. "There is no question but that the senatorship was within his grasp if he had been able to be present during the contest," reasoned Haynie.[8]

Logan appears to have been conflicted about the course he should take early in November, but by the end of the month—with more and more days distancing the vivid memories and excitement of his October stump speeches—he gradually returned to his focus on military matters. He yearned to get back to the front, but had not given up on the desire to head a department or body of troops outside Sherman's jurisdiction. He left Cincinnati for Washington, still letting Haynie and others work for him to obtain the Senate seat. If Logan was to win the early January election—his expectations remained low—he would use this as an alternative to rejoining his command under Sherman. He never publicly expressed where he wanted to go, but the Department of Missouri appears to be a likely preference. General Rosecrans currently held the helm, but it was no secret he would soon be replaced.

He arrived in Washington late on the night of December 6 and made his way to the White House the following morning. Logan walked up the spiral staircase and entered Lincoln's room. There he saw the president sitting in a chair, head thrown back as a barber shaved him and his bare feet propped on a table. The two shook hands, then Logan stepped aside as the barber finished his duties. After his beard was trimmed and as the barber was working on his hair, Lincoln turned to Logan, and caught him glancing at how swollen the president's feet appeared.

"They remind me of a man in Sangamon County who made a pretty bad horse trade," he mused. "The animal was in awful condition, but the farmer got him home. About two weeks afterward one of his neighbors met him and asked him how his new horse was coming on. 'Oh, first rate,' said the farmer, 'he's putting on flesh fast. He's fat up to his knees.'" The point was clear, but the president made the final tie to his own feet. "That's my fix," he conceded.[9]

The two then moved to another room, reportedly to discuss the past election and present events. Lincoln projected an absolute conviction and supreme confidence in the outcome of the war, an air of relief and satisfaction so antithetical to how he felt the previous summer. Logan was struck by the president's focus, claiming "his ideas upon all subjects connected with it were as clear as those of any other person with whom I ever talked." Lincoln had put his faith in Grant, and was completely satisfied with his decisions and performance. "We have now at the head of the Armies a man in whom all the People can have confidence," Lincoln told Logan. Logan closed his conversation with the president just as Congressman James G. Blaine paid Lincoln a call. After a brief introduction, Logan departed. Lincoln remarked to Blaine that in a war where so many generals had fallen well below expectations, how fortunate it was for the country to have a commander such as Logan perform beyond what could ever be fathomed for him.[10]

The meeting ended late in the morning without a new command for Logan, but Lincoln would later prove that he made an effort to get him an appointment. Logan spent two more days in Washington, meeting with friends, former congressional colleagues, and other contacts. Elihu Washburne met him there and the two decided to visit Grant at City Point, the lieutenant general's headquarters near Petersburg, Virginia. The two departed Washington on the steamer *Dictator* on December 9, the same day that Grenville Dodge was chosen to head the Department of Missouri.[11]

Grant and Logan reunited at Grant's headquarters on December 9. The two had not seen each other for nearly a year, since Grant headed east of the Alleghenies to follow Meade's Army of the Potomac. In December, that army had been engaged in a months-long siege of Petersburg, locking Robert E. Lee's Confederate Army of Northern Virginia in place around the Richmond environs. Grant was seeking to capture his third army in three years. If he succeeded against Lee, the war would come to a close. Since Lincoln's election guaranteed a determined military conclusion to the American Civil War, all were confident that the outcome would be a Union victory. When it would occur and how it would end were still the major questions left unanswered.

Grant had always thought highly of Logan, and was displeased at how he was unjustly treated by Sherman in relation to the command of the Army of the Tennessee. Logan's arrival at City Point was significant, for he could not overtake his Fifteenth Corps at this time. Sherman had neared his destination of Savannah, a city he began to siege on December 10. Grant was so confident that Sherman would capture the Georgia port that he sent a steamer from City Point on December 3 filled with mail and supplies to be there when Sherman took over the city. Logan could not return to the Army of the Tennessee until Savannah fell, so he stayed with Grant for several days.

As it turned out, Grant had a place for Logan to go. As Sherman marched with the Army of the Tennessee, he had peeled off the other armies belonging to his district to send them after Hood's Confederate Army of Tennessee, now penetrating the state for which they were named. This included Thomas's Army of the Cumberland and Schofield's Army of the Ohio. Schofield planted 30,000 troops on good defensive ground at Franklin, repulsed the desperate assaults Hood thrust at him on November 30, thinning Hood's ranks by 6,000 troops at the cost of 2,300 Union soldiers. Thomas linked his available forces with Schofield and took charge of the Union forces opposing Hood.

Grant had grown impatient with Thomas's deliberate maneuvers against Hood. The Confederates had entered the Nashville environs with 25,000 men. Thomas enjoyed a two-to-one advantage, but had irritated Grant by choosing not to attack the position as quickly as Grant wanted him to, waiting for the weather to improve and for reinforcements to strengthen his position. A stream of telegrams clicked across the wires from City Point to Tennessee throughout the first two weeks of December. Concerned that Hood would threaten the Ohio River Valley, Grant ordered Thomas on December 2 to "Attack Hood at once and wait no longer for a remnant of your cavalry." On December 11, he sent another dispatch to Thomas. "I am in hopes of receiving a dispatch from you to-day announcing that you have moved," chided Grant; "Delay no longer for weather or reinforcements."[12]

Grant did not receive that awaited dispatch from Thomas that day, or the day after. On December 13 he had had enough. The solution to his problem had been in front of him for four days. "Major General John A. Logan, U. S. Vols., will proceed immediately to Nashville, Tenn.," wrote Grant by special orders on December 13. Logan and Grant had discussed the situation at great length. Logan was to train to Nashville and appraise the situation. If Thomas had not attacked Hood, Logan was to replace Thomas and take over the operation. If Thomas had indeed moved against Hood, Logan was not to act on his orders. The entire mission was not to be discussed.[13]

Logan left promptly. While stopping temporarily in Washington, a newspaper correspondent asked him about his destination. To deceive him, Logan responded that he was leaving immediately for New York, en route to Savannah to return to Sherman's army. Logan then caught a train westward, detrained at Cincinnati, and checked in at the Burnet House. Colonel Reub Williams, a former brigadier for Logan in the Atlanta Campaign, found him there. Williams was attempting to gain his release from treason conspiracy trials to get back to the front. Despite Grant's admonition not to discuss his mission, Logan did just that with Williams in his room. But he stayed in Cincinnati throughout December 15 and 16. During those two days, Thomas finally moved against Hood at Nashville and took the heart out of Hood's Southerners by routing the broken army.[14]

Logan reached Louisville, Kentucky, on December 17 and immediately notified Grant of the reaction to the Union victory: "People here are jubilant over Genl Thomas success. Confidence seems to be restored." The Confederate Army of Tennessee ceased to be a functional fighting force after the Battle of Nashville, completely vindicating Thomas's handling of the campaign. "You need not go further . . ." telegraphed Grant to Logan on December 17, "report in Washington."[15]

Knowing that Sherman had just captured Savannah, Logan was unsure of his immediate military future. He wrote Mary from Cincinnati on December 22. "I got here this morning and will leave tonight for Washington, and now suppose that I may go to Savannah from there. . . . I may be ordered differently but can not as yet tell." He had not given up the hope of gaining a command of an army or a department. Logan and his staff endured a cold and comfortless overnight train ride to Washington. He wrote to Mary an hour after he stepped off the train. Repeating his plan to leave for Savannah, Logan told her he still had one last option. "I will see the President before I leave however and do the best I can in matters."[16]

Logan visited the president the day after Christmas, the second time in three weeks he made a trip to the White House. Logan could not help but see the toll of four years of a bloody civil war on the commander in chief. Lincoln had aged considerably, the president Logan visited in December 1864 appeared much more grizzled to Logan compared to when he saw him in early January 1862. But Lincoln was far more upbeat in the post-Christmas White House this year than in previous ones. He had good reason to be. Not only had Thomas suppressed Hood and his army, but Sherman's "March to the Sea" ended in complete success. "I beg to present you as a Christmas gift the city of Savannah," wrote Sherman to Lincoln on December 22 in a dispatch Lincoln received, appropriately, on Christmas Day. In addition to seizing the city, Sherman took possession of 150 large cannons and 25,000 bales of cotton.

Lincoln responded on the twenty-sixth, "Many, many, thanks for your Christmas-gift—the capture of Savannah . . .," he wrote, confessing how anxious he felt about Sherman's decision to divide his army and march away from his supplies to the Atlantic Coast. "Now, the undertaking being a success, the honor is all yours," the president continued. "But what next? I suppose it will be safer if I leave Gen. Grant and yourself to decide." He handed the response to Logan to deliver to Sherman. Although it was established that Logan indeed was heading back to the Fifteenth Corps at Savannah; neither he nor Lincoln had given up on elevating his responsibilities in a position higher than the corps command he currently led. Lincoln promised Logan that the appointment would be made if possible. It was a promise he could not keep.[17]

The new year of 1865 opened for Logan in New York City, where he boarded a steamer to transport him to Savannah. Logan arrived there on January 6; he immediately reported to Sherman and handed him Lincoln's "thank you" letter. That same day, back in City Point, Virginia, Grant recommended Logan to Secretary Stanton as a replacement for the ailing General John G. Foster, who commanded the Department of the South, a growing army command with jurisdiction in South Carolina, Georgia, and Florida. The position instead went to General Quincy Gillmore, who took the helm of the department for the second time.[18]

The day after Logan reported for duty he reacquainted himself to his troops by participating in a large review. "It was a splendid success," reported an Iowa soldier to his hometown newspaper; "The marching, soldierly bearing and general good appearance of the corps elicited general applause from those who were fortunate enough to witness the grand pageant."[19]

The event—full of pomp and circumstance—must have infused Logan with at least some of the fervor he held for his position the previous summer. But the circumstances had changed. Gone from headquarters were several staff officers—including his reliable adjutants Hoover, Hotaling, and Townes—forcing Logan to break in a new crew of headquarters personnel. The composition of his corps had also changed somewhat. General Osterhaus no longer commanded a division in the Fifteenth Corps. The new leader of the Fourth Division was Brigadier General John M. Corse. Logan's third division, detached in Alabama for most of the Atlanta Campaign, was back, headed by Brigadier General John

E. Smith. Almost half of his eleven infantry brigades relied on new commanders as well. Logan's total force, including an eighteen-gun artillery brigade and a mounted infantry battalion, numbered 16,630 officers and men present for duty.[20]

Embedded within Logan's corps was a unique regiment, the 110th U.S. Colored Infantry, a black regiment commanded by white officers. Indications at the start of the campaign were that the African-American soldiers would have to prove their worth to the other fifty-five infantry regiments of the corps. "They make pretty good looking soldiers but our boys don't think much of them," admitted a Hoosier in Logan's ranks; "They still say this is a *White Mans War*."[21]

Sherman prepared for an active campaign to march his army—the Military District of the Mississippi—into and through the Carolinas. Logan was resolved to accept his role; it was his only option. He learned that, as expected, the new Illinois legislature elected Richard Yates to represent the state in the U.S. Senate. Without naming him, Logan pointed to Richard Oglesby as the leader of the influential sect of Illinois who should have been more grateful and supportive of his efforts on their behalf. "I guess my friends were not very enthusiastic," Logan shrugged to Mary, "but it is all right. I do not deserve any better treatment as I was foolish enough to work for men who only had their own interest at heart." Vindictively Logan lashed out, "I hope to live long enough to help some of them again in the *same* way."[22]

Isham Haynie, Logan's strongest and tireless supporter, did not consider this election result inevitable. Haynie was dumbfounded that Logan refused to campaign in Illinois. Exasperated, he wrote Mary to admit, "I never have been so vexed in my life." Haynie also wrote Logan about the results. Logan's response indicated that he had solicited support while in Washington for the Senate seat, as well as for an appointment to head a military department or army in the field. Disappointed at not getting any solid endorsements during his two visits, Logan railed about "no feeling of thankfulness among them for anything." He lashed out at the injustice over his hard work going underappreciated. "I think that they feel as if I have already received my reward in promotions for all that I have done," Logan continued. "Grant and Washburne are the only ones who evinced any disposition to acknowledge that I am entitled to any consideration." He then changed the subject to the army, which did not brighten his outlook. "I can make no calculations for the future," he admitted. "I am not a favorite of Sherman and Howard. I am not from West Point and must always explain myself a great deal ..." Clearly, General Logan was unhappy and unsatisfied in the winter of 1865.[23]

Logan's mood did not affect his preparation for the upcoming campaign through the Carolinas. The Army of the Tennessee had been trimmed down to a two-corps force; the Sixteenth Corps was dissolved with its troops reassigned into Logan's corps and Frank Blair's corps (the Seventeenth). Howard's entire force was approximately 27,000 strong. Sherman had realigned his entire army for the march to the sea late in 1864 and kept this formation for a planned march northward through the Carolinas. The Army of the Tennessee formed the right wing, while two corps held over from the Army of the Cumberland—the Fourteenth and Twentieth Corps—represented his left wing, commanded by Henry Slocum. Brigadier General Judson Kilpatrick led a cavalry division of 4,400 horse soldiers. On February 1, 1865, Sherman's entire army numbered 60,000 on both sides of the rain-swollen Savannah River.[24]

Logan was lean, rested, and ready to embark upon the campaign. Matthew Brady photographed the general at this stage of his career—he never looked better. Logan's name was legend within the corps for how he handled the men in the spring and summer of 1864. Those experiencing him for the first time became enraptured with his style. "He is the idol of his soldiers," claimed an Ohio captain in the Fifteenth Corps. "He talks with them, and mingles with them, and shakes hands with them." Studying Logan, the observant officer limned the following image:

> Physically he is one of the finest looking officers in the army. A deep and fierce black eye, heavy black mustache, black hair and very dark complexion, give him a terrible look when aroused. Broad shoulders, well set on a muscular frame, give him the appearance of a man of great power. He usually wears a broad-brimmed black felt hat, plain Major General's coat, and blue pantaloons, stuck in his boots. He has not the prim appearance of a military dandy; in fact, he looks the citizen all over. Judging from appearance, one would suppose he left his home in a hurry, to attend some business, which he has not quite finished.[25]

The business was not finished, a point Logan well realized. It did not take him long to get comfortable with his new staff, the changes within his new command, and the role he was going to play in the campaign. The men were happy to have him back, not that they were dissatisfied with the substitute command of General Osterhaus, but Logan was the man that had won them glorious victories in the 1864 campaign for Atlanta. Indeed, he had become a legend within his corps, but his fame extended beyond those directly under his command. Logan's speeches and the positive press he received as an inspirational commander rippled throughout other branches of the military. It even extended to the navy. On

January 22, a transport ship docked at Baltimore Harbor to unload 500 captured North Carolinians for delivery to Fort Delaware Prison. The name of the steamer that brought them to the north was "General Logan."[26]

By January 31, Logan's corps was on the move. One division was detached with the left wing of the army. The other three divisions advanced in two columns on the right wing. This wing was to feint toward Charleston while the left wing did the same toward Augusta. Sherman's plan was to draw enemy troops away from the interior, clearing his path to Columbia. Sherman accompanied Logan as the men distanced themselves from Savannah and pushed northward into the Palmetto State. They marched into McPhersonville, a village of summer houses nestled among the pines. The town was believed to be immune from the malaria that devastated the region twenty miles closer to the coast. But McPhersonville was not protected from the Union soldiers who entered it with vengeance on their mind. By the time the Fifteenth Corps soldiers left McPhersonville, the village was in flames. Nearly every house found along the line of march was put to the torch. All the residents had fled the region. "No citizen has been seen since leaving Beaufort," noted an Illinois soldier.[27]

For Logan, this style of warfare — total war — was a new concept, adopted while he was in Illinois and his corps marched across Georgia from Atlanta to Savannah. Additional relish was apparent in his men laying homes to the torch in South Carolina, the state they deemed symbolic with secession and civil war. A member of the Fifty-third Ohio explained, "It was remarkable how soon the soldiers realized that they had struck the state line of South Carolina, and believing that this state was largely responsible for the Rebellion, they had no mercy upon any citizen or property of the state." He went on to claim, "Our line of march throughout the state was marked by smoke in the day, and the glare of fire by night." McPhersonville was only one of several hamlets burned in the wake of Sherman's Carolina campaign.[28]

Logan regretted the incident, and said so in his report, assuming it had more to do with the town being deserted than any malicious order. Logan was forced to become quickly acquainted with other aspects of Sherman's grand marches in the "total war" scheme. He naively prohibited foraging in the early going, but was quickly corrected about this facet of advance, perfected in the previous autumn's march from Atlanta to Savannah. Logan countermanded his prohibitive orders by issuing new ones under the jurisdiction of each of his division commands. Logan insisted on using the smallest number of foragers possible with each party composed of "the best men of the command." He also insisted on commissioned officers overseeing the movement of the foragers (called "bummers") and a record kept of their activities.[29] His endorsement of the bummers, as well as his lack of prosecution of the firing of deserted homes, reflected how Logan's psyche had adapted to three years of brutal reality. Gone were the days when he left receipts for corn foraged by his men, as he did in Missouri late in 1861. A deaf ear and hardened heart immunized him to citizens' complaints about the destruction of their property.

The war also altered Logan's views on slavery. As his command advanced through the heart of the Confederacy, their ranks swelled with newly liberated slaves. On February 2, as Logan rode with his marching column past a plantation where a group of fleeing slaves rushed to them, one of the refugees turned everyone's head. His name was James Le Roach, a slave who was half French, and perhaps one-fourth Indian, although the latter was not readily apparent. What was very noticeable is that Le Roach was neither black nor mulatto—he was a white slave. The slightly built man was in his thirties, with long sandy hair and beard. Incredulous at the entire prospect of white servitude, Logan reportedly declared that this alone would have turned him into an abolitionist.[30]

Feeble resistance countered the blue-clad columns as they marched through lower South Carolina. The greatest obstacles to their advance were nature-produced ones. Incessant rains poured upon the troops. Swollen streams swamped them, forcing them to wade through the freshets. Pioneering details corduroyed the path with felled trees, a necessary but tedious procedure that oftentimes slowed the advance to a crawl. The weather was particularly detrimental to Logan, for the cold, pelting rains forced the return of what he called his "Donelson Pet." Rheumatism attacked Logan again with the same ferocity he suffered every February since he entered the war. He tried to fight his way through the pain, but the malady often won the daily battles. Logan did his best to conceal the effects, and only his staff aides appreciated how badly he felt. Amzi White, the young Marion soldier on the headquarters staff, oftentimes had to help Logan dismount at the end of a drenched day's advance and escort him to his tent where another aide rubbed liniment into his shoulder to help allay the stiffness in the diseased joint. February 9, 1865, marked Logan's thirty-ninth birthday, an anniversary he likely spent in considerable pain in South Carolina.[31]

The corps crept closer to Columbia during the second week of February. Perhaps due to his absence, Logan had not paid attention to the corps identity system adopted by every other like unit marching in South Carolina. He corrected his oversight on February 14 with General Orders Number 10, which officially adopted the Fifteenth Corps badge: "a miniature cartridge-box, one-eighth of an inch thick, fifteen sixteenths of an inch wide, set transversely on a field of cloth or metal, one and five-eighths of an inch square. Above the cartridge-box plate will be stamped or worked in a curve 'Forty Rounds.'" The badge infused even greater pride into the chests of an already proud corps. After naming twenty-nine engagements in which the Fifteenth Corps participated, Logan determinedly announced that this corps "will keep on struggling until the death of the rebellion."[32]

The city of Columbia symbolized the soul of the Confederacy, and the Army of the Tennessee was within striking distance to seize that soul. Embedded in the center of South Carolina, Columbia was an ideal location for the state capital, although in the center of the city the gray granite state house was still incomplete. The Saluda River and Broad River met here to form the Congaree, which flowed southeastward along the western border of Columbia. One of the few Confederate state capitals still in Southern possession teeming with factories producing munitions, Columbia was a vaunted prize for Sherman.

On the morning of February 15, the Fifteenth Corps, recently united with all four divisions marching together, advanced to within three miles of the city. Blocking the path to capture it was Congaree Creek, an easterly flowing feeder of its parent river running on the right of Logan's corps. On the opposite side of the creek stood high breastworks protecting 2,500 Confederate soldiers and their five cannons. This was the greatest resistance Logan faced in the two-week-old advance. He sent a division forward through a soupy fog to destroy the Southern resistance. Five hours and twenty-three casualties later, the job was accomplished. Logan's men saved the creek bridge initially torched by the fleeing Southerners. By nighttime Sherman's force crept to the western bank of the Congaree River, the last natural obstacle in front of Columbia.[33]

Columbia was not captured on the sixteenth. Confederates burned the bridges over the Congaree, Broad, and Saluda Rivers, forcing Logan's engineers to spend the day pontooning the latter two since the Congaree was too wide to cross in this fashion. During the process, the corps liberated Camp Sorghum, a prisoner-of-war enclave, at one time holding more than a thousand captured Union soldiers. The foot soldiers were enraged at seeing the condition their imprisoned comrades were forced to endure. Sherman had issued an order that day that once Columbia was captured, his army was permitted to destroy the public buildings — reportedly by burning them — but to spare libraries, asylums, and citizens' homes; but Camp Sorghum had already convinced soldiers to alter these orders without the approval of their superiors. "The doom of Columbia was decided at Camp Sorghum," claimed an Ohio officer, "and neither General Sherman nor any other man could have saved it from severe treatment."[34]

Logan did not plan on exceeding Sherman's directive, but he looked forward to enacting the first phase of it: the destruction of the warehouses, railroad property, and the factories producing Confederate materiel. From the western bank of the Congaree, Logan ordered Captain DeGress to open up upon Columbia to stop Southern soldiers from removing stores from the warehouses in town. DeGress fired 325 rounds into the center of town, not limiting his fire to the warehouses; he hit the unfinished State House several times. Logan gleefully assisted the gunners, sighting an artillery piece before scaling the riverbank to watch where the round struck. Each strike upon the State House incited Logan to wave his hat and call for three cheers for South Carolina. According to one of his Ohio soldiers, vengeance was on Logan's mind. That night, the Buckeye claimed to hear him rant, "Hail Columbia, the cradle of the rebellion, you certainly will be burned tomorrow."[35]

Columbia was defended by General Pierre G. T. Beauregard, ironically the commander who had forced the surrender of Fort Sumter that started the war in Charleston Harbor in 1861. Beauregard had been compelled to cover the entire state of South Carolina—from Charleston to Augusta, Georgia—with 20,000 men. He could not concentrate this force or any other single locale. Left in charge of Columbia was Lieutenant General Wade Hampton. He had no appreciable numbers to defend the city and its inhabitants against Sherman's 60,000 soldiers. Southern citizens and soldiers alike evacuated Columbia overnight. The men in blue were disgusted that the Confederates would not resist their advance. A Hoosier in Logan's ranks believed he spoke for the entire 100th Indiana Infantry when he announced: "If there is any place they ought to fight and fight hard its right here where treason first was hatched, but so far we have been able to brush them off our path like so many flies. Our boys are getting to have an utter contempt for them."[36]

After successfully pontooning the rivers, Logan marched his corps into Columbia on February 17. The mayor officially surrendered the city as the rest of Sherman's army prepared to march in. Logan led his men down Main Street toward the State House. "We were never so well received by citizens before," remarked a member of the 103rd Illinois, "and the negroes seemed crazy with joy." The atmosphere was festive throughout the day in Columbia. Logan conferred with Howard and Sherman, issued his orders, and headquartered himself in the elegant Preston Mansion.

As dusk rolled in, trouble began to brew as the Fifteenth Corps soldiers helped themselves to whatever they could get their hands on. The citizens were all too willing to accommodate. Logan complained about the townspeople lavishing his soldiers "with bucketfuls of liquor, and the negroes, overjoyed at our entrance, piloted them to buildings where wine and whiskey were stored, and for a while all control was lost over the disorganized mass." It became nearly impossible to control them. "Whiskey and wine flowed like water, and the whole division is now drunk," recorded a member of General Charles R. Woods's First Division. The combination of hundreds of drunken and unruly soldiers, many with vengeance on their minds, a stiff wind, and stacks upon stacks of cotton bales created a recipe for disaster. "This gobbling up of things so, disgusts me much," recorded the First Division diarist; "I think the city should be burned, but would like to see it done decently."[37]

The soldier got his wish, but only the first half. Columbia burned that night, nearly to the ground. Logan, Howard, Sherman, and the division commanders were unable to instill order into the drunken mob until it was too late. More than one-third of the city—458 buildings—was destroyed during the night of February 17, 1865. The burning extended well beyond Sherman's and Logan's intent. Although the foot soldiers, particularly the ones recently released from Camp Sorghum, had no regrets, many of the officers were horrified.

Logan had drawn a fine line on his intentions about Columbia. Clearly desirous to see portions of the city associated with the Confederacy put to the torch, the horror of the night and his inability to control it left an indelible impression in his mind. One soldier claimed that Logan was as culpable in his thoughts as the soldiers were in their actions. When Illinois soldiers despoiled a home of Catholic nuns on the night of February 17, the soldier insisted that Logan expressed his regret—through curses and oaths—the following morning that he was denied the pleasure of destroying it himself. Logan's desperate actions to stop the destruction of Columbia overnight contradict the soldier's claim, and his resolve to prevent this from happening to another Southern city would render the account aberrant.[38]

But Sherman held few lingering regrets over Columbia's fate. When asked by the women in the city why he allowed his army to burn their town, Sherman coldly responded, "I did not burn your town, nor did my army. Your brothers, sons, husbands and fathers set fire to every city, town and village in the land when they fired on Fort Sumter. That fire kindled then and there by them has been burning ever since, and reached your houses last night."[39]

Planned destruction continued on February 19 as Logan's men tore up the double track of rail bed near the capital, as well as burned down more public stores. The next day, Logan moved northward; his 16,000 men formed a marching column nearly twelve miles long. His men were vulnerable to Confederate guerrilla parties, particularly at river and creek crossings where he lost soldiers to these renegade cavalrymen who harassed his supply trains and killed foragers sent out on detail. When six Southerners were captured at Lynch Creek, they were discovered wearing Union uniforms as disguise. Logan reportedly ordered the rebels to be executed, and then he moved on.[40]

Two weeks later the column, still meeting only feeble resistance, crossed the Pee Dee River and inched closer and closer to the North Carolina border. The columns of the Army of the Tennessee marched more tightly together in the early days of March. Headquarters celebrated the anticipated crossing at General Blair's tent. In the midst of a pouring rain, Sherman, Logan, Blair, and their respective staff officers raised glasses of wine. Handed a violin, Logan regaled his audience as he sang and fiddled for them.[41]

Three days later, Logan crossed his men into North Carolina. No celebrations took place to mark the moment. It had been a miserable trek. Days upon days had been marred by water above and below. He divided his four-division corps into three columns as they marched in fits and starts over a region unfit for human travel. "It was impossible to move a wagon from the direct road," Logan complained: "the country was a perfect quicksand." He ordered working parties detached to corduroy the roads. The selected men felled trees, split the logs, fastened them down to assure the passage of cannon and wagons, and then they repeated the process. Logan remained as the right wing of Sherman's advancing district. They reached Fayetteville on March 12. Logan rested the men here for a few days to reward them for the past week of tortuous work. If he bothered to check his map, he would have realized that he had advanced 350 miles since he left Savannah at the end of January.[42]

During his respite near Fayetteville, Logan inspected the corps, reduced the size of his foraging parties, and purged unauthorized animals to reduce the subsistence required to sustain them. On March 14, Logan moved out, crossed the Cape Fear River, and began his advance to Goldsboro. He continued to lighten his march by sending the freed slaves and other refugees—numbering in the thousands—to Wilmington. Logan moved on, northeastward on the Goldsboro Road. On March 17 an Illinois soldier marching toward the rear of Logan's corps penned in his journal, "I believe I have not heard a hostile shot for 27 days."[43]

Nature was a severe impediment to Sherman's advance, but throughout the winter of 1865 it was the only one. The Confederate forces in the Carolinas had yet to mount any appreciable resistance. Robert E. Lee, concerned about the growing threat of Sherman and Grant combining their armies against him, persuaded Jefferson Davis to reinstate Joseph E. Johnston to oppose Sherman's advance through North Carolina. Johnston spent the early days of March concentrating all of his available forces at Smithfield, thirty miles northwest of Goldsboro. His only hope for success lay in defeating separated portions of Sherman's army. At the same time, Sherman worked to rectify his vulnerability by keeping his wings close enough to assist each other in the event of an attack.

But Sherman's armies began to separate as Howard's right wing, under Logan and Blair, headed to Goldsboro. The left wing under Slocum strung itself out and lagged behind. Johnston pounced on the left near the town of Bentonville on March 19 with 20,000 men. The battle lasted three days. Unable to destroy Slocum's wing that day, Johnston's fate was sealed when Howard's right wing doubled back to offer assistance. They concentrated their numbers against the overmatched Confederates on March 20, and then counterattacked the following day. Logan committed three divisions to the assault. To his right, Blair advanced north of his position. Sherman's 60,000 men were not entirely united, but they still outnumbered Johnston's by more than two to one. The attack on the north began to tell on the Confederates (General Hardee's 16-year-old son was killed during the action), but Sherman refused to press his numerical advantage. Johnston retreated overnight across Mill Creek and the Battle of Bentonville was over. Johnston suffered 2,600 casualties while Sherman had 1,500 killed and wounded.[44]

Logan's corps had suffered a mere 400 casualties during the entire campaign. At Goldsboro Logan stumbled upon a potential cash cow in the form of racehorses. One year earlier, a nationally renowned owner of racehorses named Ten Broeck offered a $20,000 reward for his four horses that were stuck in the Confederacy while he worked in the North. According to a lieutenant in the Seventeenth Corps, they found the horses at Goldsboro. "General Logan captured two, Lieut. Hickenlooper captured one, and a Surgeon another," claimed the officer in a letter to a friend in Boston. The condition of the animals revealed why Logan and the other two would not be receiving a hefty reward. "I think the horses will not prove of much value to Ten Broeck," revealed the officer.[45]

Sherman's army rested two weeks in Goldsboro while he planned to move his men by transports to Norfolk to assist Grant against Lee at Richmond. On April 6, Logan learned that Grant had driven Lee from his Petersburg trenches, captured Richmond, and was now in the process of chasing the Confederates down as they headed westward through southern Virginia. Sherman ordered a 100-gun salute to celebrate the great news. No longer would Norfolk be the destination. Sherman quickly changed the plan to march his armies northward through Raleigh and assist Grant in chasing down Lee. Bentonville proved that

Johnston could merely annoy Sherman's grand advance; he could not stop it. The spectacular drama of the Civil War had entered its last act.[46]

The march to Raleigh commenced on April 10. The following night Logan heard the rumor that Grant caught Lee, forcing the latter's surrender. The rumor was confirmed the following morning and Logan passed the glorious news to his corps. "I tell you it makes this one of my brightest days," penned a member of the 103rd Illinois; "His surrender makes sure beyond any chance that what we have been fighting for is sure." The following night Logan's men closed within five miles of Raleigh. On April 14 they passed through the town where they were reviewed by Sherman. The corps settled in campgrounds east of the city of Raleigh. "Curiosity over captured cities is 'old'," insisted one of Logan's men. Flags of truce fluttered in Sherman's and Johnston's camps as the two heads of armies prepared to discuss potential surrender proceedings.[47]

On April 17 Logan awaited word from Sherman about the results of the proceedings. At headquarters his open-door policy was in effect, as it usually was, and his visitors included brigade commanders. One of them witnessed Logan receive a dispatch that day. He opened it and read it. Overwhelming emotion rapidly overtook him: tears streamed down his face and his compact form quivered in sorrow. The elation all felt about the inevitable and rapid close to the war was pushed aside by the words that leapt from the page. President Abraham Lincoln was dead, felled by an assassin's bullet on April 14 and dying from it the following morning.[48]

Logan's relationship with Abraham Lincoln had flipped from one of mutual distrust to one of mutual respect and admiration. And now Lincoln was gone. Deeply affected, Logan and the other high-ranking officers fretted over the reaction of the men under their respective jurisdictions once the tragic news reached them. "There was nothing more remarkable in this campaign than the entire change in the treatment of private property after we entered North Carolina," recalled General William B. Hazen, Logan's Second Division commander. ". . . There were lawless men in the army, and great care was taken to hold them in check, and enforce respect for private rights." Once word of Lincoln's murder bounced through the ranks, restraining those men would become more difficult.[49]

The predictable occurred. "The army is crazy for vengeance," admitted an Illinois officer upon receiving the news on April 17. That night 2,000 irate soldiers of the Army of the Tennessee left camp heading for Raleigh, hell-bent to destroy the city. But Logan was ready for them. Galloping in front of the torch-carrying mob, he ordered them to return to their camps, but they disregarded him and continued toward the city. Then they saw the artillery lined up ahead—facing away from Raleigh and toward them. They stopped in their tracks. Logan shouted a promise to them. He drew his sword from its sheath, raised himself in his saddle, and threatened that if they continued toward the city he would open on them with canister. That settled the issue; the soldiers gave up and returned to camp. "General Logan saved the City and it owes him a debt it can never repay," contended a witness to the scene that night.[50]

Logan's actions may have reflected lingering remorse over what happened at Columbia four months earlier. The near disaster at Raleigh and its precipitating events continued to weigh on his mind when he wrote Mary two days later. Confident that the war was at an end, Logan still sought divine help in Sherman's negotiations. "God grant it may soon be consummated," he wrote to his wife on April 17. He feared a repeat of the Raleigh incident would prove disastrous. Lincoln's assassination had the army tasting blood again, asserted Logan, writing to Mary that "it has very much exasperated the army and unless peace is now made, the fortunes of this war will be terrible." The soldiers confirmed Logan's concerns. "We hope Johnston will not surrender," wrote one. "God pity this country if he retreats or fights us."[51]

Sherman and Johnston alleviated Logan's concerns and quelled the army's quest for revenge. Sherman offered unusually generous terms, which Johnston agreed upon for his surrender. When Logan heard of the terms he deemed them too liberal and predicted they would never be accepted in Washington. He was correct. The War Department believed the offer was too generous and refused to sanction the deal. The press derided Sherman as a traitor. Grant was sent down to superintend renewed negotiations, but he did not intervene with Sherman's negotiations. Eventually the deal was worked out with less lenient terms, similar to the ones Grant and Lee agreed upon. The surrender became official on April 26, 1865.[52]

That night, Logan celebrated with other high-ranking commanders at the Governor's Mansion (Sherman's headquarters) in Raleigh. He spent time with Grant and Sherman, both of whom discussed Logan's future with him. They caught Logan by surprise with a most flattering offer—a brigadier generalship in the regular army when all was officially over. (Many other generals in the volunteer army would be returning to the U.S. Army with regimental ranks.) The commission appears to have been unprecedented; to no one's recollection had a volunteer without military training ever been offered a generalship without ever holding any previous position in the professional U.S. Army. Logan wrote Mary the day after the momentous surrender. Filling her in on the offer, Logan revealed,

"They want to make me a brigadier in the regular army, but I think I shall quit the business and try peaceful associations for a while . . ."[53]

For Logan, a great burden was lifting from his shoulders and he clearly recognized the import of the moment. Rejoicing that Johnston signed the surrender agreement, Logan punctuated the proceedings when he told his wife, "Thus ends the great rebellion of Jeff. Davis . . ." He received his orders to participate in one more campaign; the army was going to march northward to Washington where Logan expected it to be mustered out of the service. Logan looked forward to going home and staying there, but he confessed that leaving his corps will produce personal consequences. "I know I shall feel as tho separated from my family when I leave them and start home," he told his wife.[54]

Logan marched his corps from Raleigh on April 29. Resting on the Sabbath, they still covered twenty miles per marching day and reached the outskirts of Petersburg, Virginia, by the end of the first week of May. There the men bore witness to the end of Grant's campaign against Lee. The scene was macabre. In front of Fort Steadman, the site of a large Confederate assault in March, Logan's men endured the sight and smell of death again when they walked by the partially buried bodies of more than forty Union soldiers, the heads and feet still protruding from the few shovelfuls of earth thrown on top of them.[55]

General Logan reviewed the Fifteenth Corps in Petersburg on May 9 and then they moved on. This campaign at the close of the war culminated in the return of Logan's esprit de corps. For a man who had worked so hard not to return to his men five months earlier, his ardor for his position reflected a man who lamented the inevitable end of his service. He told his wife as much when he assessed the Fifteenth Corps: "They are good men and could I always have them under me [I] would have no desire to leave the army."[56]

Logan's improving relationship with Sherman also added to his comfort. The backbiting and complaints had ended. Sherman included Logan in his inner circle of confidants when he was discussing surrender negotiations with Johnston; he also made sure Logan attended headquarters for the celebration that followed. But since then Sherman had suffered from the stinging rebuke he received in the press. His soldiers had been stunned at the negative opinions of their "Uncle Billy." Logan—a veteran of negative press—must have sympathized with Sherman's plight. The two also shared a strong bond over their agreement that the western armies had not been given nearly enough credit for their role in winning the war.

It all came to a head when they approached Richmond, the Virginia capital burned by retreating Confederates on April 2. The charred shells of buildings reminded the Army of the Tennessee of how they left Columbia, South Carolina. Sherman's reminder of his current troubles existed in Richmond—in the form of General Henry Halleck. Formerly warm friends, Sherman now despised Halleck, whom he now considered a Brutus for openly accusing him of coercion with Jefferson Davis because of the lenient terms he had offered the Confederacy. Halleck went to Richmond shortly after Lincoln's assassination, but Sherman refused to meet with him, and would not allow Halleck to review his troops. Sherman curtly warned him that "if noticed by some of my old command [the Fifteenth Corps], I cannot undertake to maintain a model behavior, for their feelings have become aroused by what the world judges an insult to at least an honest commander."[57]

Irritated at Sherman's grudge, Halleck decided to even the score with him. He refused to allow Logan's corps to enter the city, although Confederates had been afforded the luxury. Sherman's fury flew the moment he received Halleck's edict. Sherman knew that Logan had adopted an "us versus them" philosophy concerning western soldiers and eastern ones, a mindset he shared with his corps commander. He commiserated with Logan over the Halleck and Richmond snub. "The manner of your welcome was a part of a grand game to insult us—us who had marched 1,000 miles through a hostile country in midwinter to help them," Sherman vented to Logan on May 12. "We did help them, and what has been our reward? Your men were denied admission to the city, when Halleck had invited all citizens (rebels, of course) to come and go without passes. If the American people sanction this kind of courtesy to old and tried troops, where is the honor, satisfaction, and glory of serving them in constancy and faith? If such be the welcome the East gives to the West, we can but let them make war and fight it out themselves."[58]

Sherman's army let Halleck know what they thought of him. It marched through Richmond on May 13 (Halleck allowed this because it was the only way for them to get to Washington) and tramped by Halleck's headquarters where he stood on the portico, protected by immaculately dressed guards from the Army of the Potomac, watching troops that were once under his direct jurisdiction in 1861–1862. Rather than recognize Halleck, the troops passed him at right shoulder shift, refusing to salute. The crowning moment came when one unabashed westerner peeled himself from the ranks to spit tobacco juice on the polished boots of one of Halleck's guards. Pleased at the proceedings through Richmond, Sherman hoped that Halleck would now "think twice before he again undertakes to stand between me and my subordinates."[59]

The armies marched on, passing Fredericksburg on May 17, scene of a grand battle in December of 1862. "The most shelled town I ever saw," asserted an

Illinois soldier as they marched closer and closer to Washington. Sherman had instructed Logan back at Richmond to march at a leisurely pace and take ten days to cover the 120 miles to Washington. But the pace was never slowed and with men dropping out of the ranks from the early May heat of Virginia—some dying from the exposure—Logan covered the requisite distance in seven days, arriving in Alexandria, Virginia, on May 19 at the head of a corps that marched with an army covering nearly 300 miles in three weeks.[60]

Sherman had come full circle in his treatment of Logan. A grand review was scheduled to take place with all the victorious armies of the North on May 23 and May 24 in Washington. The Army of the Tennessee currently had no head. Howard left to take charge of the new Freedman's Bureau to assist the emancipated blacks. This time Sherman did not look beyond the ranks of the army to fill Howard's place. Logan learned that Sherman sent his name up to the new president, Andrew Johnson, to command the army until it was disbanded and sent home. Sherman's gesture was consistent with his other overt examples of placating his subordinate, but Logan still harbored doubts. He informed his wife of the army command, but until it was official, "I have nothing to expect at the hands of these men."[61]

The offer became official three days later. "I hereby assume command of the Army of the Tennessee," Logan announced in acceptance on May 23. That very day the Grand Review in Washington commenced. The first day's activities focused on the eastern armies, of which the Army of the Potomac was the largest and most famous. It was also the one most familiar to the crowds who had seen these men encamped around the capital throughout the war. The chief attraction to many of them was the western armies, for they were an unfamiliar entity to the throng of parade viewers who had read much about the accomplishments of the men who marched under Grant and Sherman, but had not seen these troops, men who were more consistently victorious throughout the war than any army in the East.[62]

The day was important to all in the western armies, not only to showcase themselves but to compete with the polished boots and brass of the Army of the Potomac and other eastern forces. Unknown to Logan was that Howard had still intended to march at the head of the Army of the Tennessee in the parade. He explained to Sherman that he had earned the right to the helm. Sherman intervened, agreeing with Howard that he certainly was justified in this belief, "but it will be everything to Logan to have this opportunity." Sherman then invoked Howard's strong Christian faith to make the necessary sacrifice on behalf of Logan. Howard consented. "I do think it but just to Logan," he acknowledged.[63]

Halcyon skies smiled upon the Army of the Tennessee when it lined up for roll call on the comfortable and clear morning of May 24, 1865. "The day was beautiful, almost perfect," remembered a member of the Ninety-third Illinois. He and his comrades marched across Long Bridge, one of four spans across the Potomac River that connected Virginia and Washington. For most, this was their first venture into the capital of the country they had fought to preserve for four arduous years. Officers consolidated depleted companies to equalize them. Their guns were cleaned but not burnished. For those who went against orders and watched the Army of the Potomac march the day before, the Army of the Tennessee could never looked so polished in formation against the white-gloved and shining brass displayed by the eastern soldiers. Logan seemed not to care at all. To him, his soldiers were "the valor of Federal arms." He could not wait to show them off in the pageant awaiting them.[64]

He did not have long to wait. The signal gun fired at 9:00 A.M. Astride his favorite mount, Slasher, the beautiful coal-black charger that galloped through nearly a dozen battles, Logan commanded his men to march. The route was Pennsylvania Avenue, perhaps the most important city road in the re-United States of America. They began at the new-domed Capitol Building, where Logan had toiled in the halls of Congress from 1859 to 1861. Hanging across the face of the building was a banner with a memorable message: "There is but one debt we can never pay, the debt of gratitude we owe the Union soldiers." Upon reading those words, nervousness was replaced by pride. Logan was ready.[65]

Major General John A. Logan trotted down the avenue toward the White House, leading 30,000 soldiers hailing from the states of the Old Northwest and the trans-Mississippi regions. His "Boys" fell in with their characteristic long-swinging step, a swagger unique from the stiff and choppy step of the eastern armies. Their skin was bronzed from the campaign of Savannah to Washington; they were ragged and shoeless (the quartermaster never solved this problem); and they looked dirty. Yet, as one soldier bragged, they were "the healthiest and bravest lot of dare-devils that ever paraded in review before an American public."[66]

It seemed to Logan and his soldiers that the entire American public had come out to see them that Wednesday morning. Although the soldiers labored to look straight ahead, the scene to their periphery was overwhelming. "The sidewalks were packed with people, and my! How they cheered!" exclaimed an Indiana soldier. A constant roar reverberated across and down Pennsylvania Avenue. The *New York Times* reporter covering the event estimated 200,000 spectators. Whether true or not, it clearly was the largest crowd Logan and his soldiers had ever seen.

An event this huge attracted reporters from most of the large cities across the North. All were impressed by the swagger of the western soldier. They were taken by the sight of General Blair doffing his hat while upon his white horse, but Logan seemed to embody the appearance and spirit of the troops marching behind him. The *Times* reporter noted that his stallion "careened and plunged just enough to show the General's fine horsemanship." He also claimed that Logan's appearance and mien marked him for "the most vociferous applause from the very moment his prancing steed appeared on the avenue."[67]

At least one photographer snapped a picture of Logan at the head of his troops. He continued undaunted, too proud to exhibit any acknowledgment. He had endured more than three years of relentless artillery, screaming men, and the rebel yell in battle, but the continuous din this day was so much more powerful and entirely pleasurable. The audience looking upon this army commander recognized him as a Washington politico, but this day he appeared every inch a general and a soldier. He also showed the power of sensitivity and sensibility— riding sidesaddle in the staff directly behind him was Mary Ann "Mother" Bickerdyke. She had gained some degree of notoriety as the "calico colonel," the devoted nurse in the distinctive field dress who was always willing to speak her mind to Grant, Sherman, and Logan. Logan saw to it that she be acknowledged among his official staff officers.

A floral wreath found its way to Logan's neck as he neared the White House toward the end of the route. In front of the president's mansion was the reviewing stand filled with dignitaries, including General Grant, President Johnson, and Secretary Stanton. Sherman—riding with Howard at the front of all the western armies—had been concerned that his troops would be overwhelmed by the crowd and would not keep its formations and compare well with the eastern armies that marched the day before. When he turned back before entering the reviewing stand, he saw his columns in perfect formation, with every eye to the front, as they were greeted by a hurricane of acclamation. Sherman always remembered that moment as "the happiest and most satisfying moment of my life." In similar fashion, Logan would never forget the public reaction to Sherman. "He was greeted with cheers by men and women, by white and black," he later recalled. "Bouquets were strewn everywhere. Every heart leaped with joy; and if the dead could have spoken, they would have hallelujahs to his name."[68]

After Sherman and Howard entered the reviewing stand, teeming with nearly 40,000 spectators surrounding it, they caught the rest of the parade, starting with "Black Jack" Logan and the Army of the Tennessee. The spectacle between the ranks was orchestrated with freed slaves marching between divisions and carts and mules disarrayed behind each marching column. But the focus was set upon the soldiers and their commanders, and the tattered flags adorned with the names of Belmont, Fort Donelson, Shiloh, the battles of the Vicksburg and Atlanta campaigns, and other names to remind the audience that these men marched across half a continent and was the most victorious of all the armies in the field. As the Fifteenth Corps filed past the reviewing stand, the Prussian ambassador turned to his neighbor and declared, "An army like that could whip all Europe." A former U.S. senator agreed. "They marched like the lords of the world," he asserted.[69]

Although his part in the parade ended in the late morning hours, May 24, 1865, became a day like no other he had ever experienced. The parade and the reaction to his presence and his army's could never be effaced from his mind. If he took a moment to reflect upon how close he came to missing it, Logan would have considered himself a very fortunate man. Had he pressed Lincoln or Grant harder during the winter, he never would have ended his military career at the head of the army he loved. Had he aggressively pursued the Senate seat, he may have won it. The result would have been an unseemly stain, for the public still considered him the man who eschewed politics for duty. Not only would Senator Logan not have been able to lead his men in the parade, he would have been derided for breaking with his altruistic morals that endeared him to his public for four years.

He stepped away from the parade grounds as one of the most famous and recognized names associated with the preservation of the Union. The name "Logan" lagged behind the martyred Lincoln, and the victorious Grant, Sherman, Sheridan, and Thomas, but not far behind. The war had transformed Logan from an obscure and controversial congressman to a bona fide hero, one whose surname alone conjured up the image of the long, raven-haired general whose raised hat, flowing locks, and tremendous mustache adorned the pictorial newspapers that covered his battles. The Senate seat—and perhaps even greater rewards— were well within his grasp. The parade made it all worth the wait. As Logan explained to his wife, "We are through the noise and a grand affair it was."[70]

CHAPTER EIGHT

Memorial Days

MAJOR GENERAL JOHN A. LOGAN wound up his military career on July 13, 1865, when he mustered out his Army of the Tennessee in Louisville, Kentucky. He released his men from duty with a flourish, addressing them for the final time in an emotional ceremony. "Affections have sprung up between us during the long years of doubt, gloom, and carnage, which we have passed through together," he announced to his men, "nurtured by common perils, sufferings and sacrifices, and riveted by the memories of gallant comrades, whose bones repose beneath the sod of a hundred battlefields, nor time nor distance will weaken or efface."[1]

His soldiers stood in perfect ranks; more than 30,000 veterans who shared up to four full years of agony and ecstasy in campaigns that traversed half the country from the Mississippi River to the Atlantic Ocean. "The effect of his sudden outbursts of eloquence was thrilling," marveled a listener. "The impetuosity of the speaker—the exquisite melody of his voice—all combined to make this a fine piece of rhetorical declamation."[2]

Logan could not have been prouder than during that moment, facing his army, and he let them know it. After recounting their accomplishments, he hailed them for saving the country, assuring them that they had won renewed respect at home and abroad and were prepared to enter a new era of growth and prosperity, a by-product of peace. He implored his soldiers to become model citizens when they returned to their homes. He closed, "Let not the luster of that bright name you have won as soldiers be dimmed by any improper acts as citizens, but as time rolls on let your record grow brighter and brighter still." Those were his last words of an army commander addressing his troops, the final orders of Major General John A. Logan, an officer in the volunteer army of the United States of America.[3]

Four years of bloody conflict had made him a star, a hero, and a household name throughout the country, but it also dramatically altered his social philosophy. The war was his epiphany. It happened in stages over the previous four years but there could be no denying that the sun-bronzed general that stepped away from the parade ground was not the same man who had previously worn his moniker "Dirty Work" like a badge of honor. His next public presentation would prove that.

As his former soldiers departed Louisville, Logan remained to complete his duties, unfinished business initiated by the martyred president, Abraham Lincoln. Three months before his death Lincoln proposed a thirteenth amendment to the U.S. Constitution. This one called for the abolition of slavery throughout the country, thus correcting what the founding fathers had refused to address, the oversight that eventually led to civil warfare in America. Nine days after Logan delivered his farewell address to his army he spoke in Louisville for two and a half hours to a large audience on the amendment, one the people of Kentucky and twenty other states needed to approve for its ratification. Logan admitted that he still did not consider the black man his equal, but he solemnly vowed to fight to end his bondage. A former political colleague had once said of Logan, "No man hated an abolitionist more than he." He had now become the man he had formerly detested. He was an abolitionist.[4]

Logan returned home to Carbondale at the end of July to reunite with his family, accompanied by two staff officers, three freed blacks, and several horses and headquarters camp gear. Mary had a surprise to show her husband—a newborn baby son. The new father was undoubtedly taken by the size of his child; he was listed at thirteen pounds when he was born on July 24. The baby was christened with the name "Manning Alexander Logan," the first name derived from the surname of his maternal aunt and uncle. On August 14, Logan entered the telegraph office at the Carbondale depot to wire his final message as a member of the U.S. Volunteer Army. "I hereby tender my resignation as major-general of volunteers," Logan informed the War Department. The resignation was accepted the following day.[5]

For his battlefield exploits Logan was hailed as a hero. *Harper's New Monthly Magazine* reminded its vast national readership that Logan was the most prominent of America's citizen soldiers, marveling at his "lion-like spirit" and the principles which earned him his double stars. "Such men are the strength of the country," proclaimed *Harper's*, "and the country knows it."[6] But the feeling was not universal. Resentment choked the air around him; a thick, dark, cloud that followed him throughout Egypt. Logan's family had not reconciled with him. Only his youngest brother, James, had remained a strong advocate. Elizabeth Logan continued her protest against her oldest son, refusing him entry into her Murphysboro home. Annie Logan Blanchard was more demonstrative. Townspeople would never forget her behavior after news of Lincoln's assassination in the spring. When two young men attempted to lower the courthouse flag to half mast, Annie walked up and down Murphysboro's main street, shouting her hope that the two would fall and break their necks.[7]

Tom Logan had somehow escaped prosecution for his attempted rape charge. He and Bill Logan—the brother Logan had taken into his Benton home to study law—remained in strong opposition to the general's abolitionist views. Ironically, Bill followed in his oldest brother's footsteps into the Illinois Twenty-fifth General Assembly. There in 1865, he voted "no" on a bill to ratify the Thirteenth Amendment and "no" to House and Senate bills to repeal John A. Logan's infamous Black Law of 1853 (despite his objections, the measures passed by wide margins). Logan well realized that his family's views represented his own merely four years before and—based on the 1864 election results—those of at least 10,000 voters in his former congressional district.[8]

The strong opposing views jeopardized any future plans as a representative from his district. He previously could measure 80-percent support from his constituents, but in 1865 that support had waned. Logan realized that his epiphany was not a shared phenomenon, making it difficult for most of his neighbors to understand the complete reversal of his political and social philosophy. But this was not Logan's concern in 1865. Unfortunately for Mary, her husband refused to settle into a domestic lifestyle in Carbondale. Although she had always expressed her desire that he remain home with her and the children, a tacit agreement between the two appears to have allowed him to travel alone.

Logan left Carbondale in August and rode northward through Illinois. He attended the state fair in Springfield with great fanfare at the end of August, displayed in a carriage ride around the track with General Grant and General Benjamin Grierson. From there he was off to other towns and county fairs. The activity and public reaction to him buoyed his spirits considerably. Back in July he had assured Mary that he no longer suffered from the bite of the political bug. But that diagnosis changed less than two months later. Writing to her from Chicago early in September, he crowed, "Everywhere I have been the people seem glad to see me and unless I am very much fooled I will have but little trouble when the time comes in securing the position I may desire."[9]

His desires did not include foreign travel. President Johnson offered him the position of minister to Mexico; Logan declined. The president followed up with an appointment to Japan; Logan declined again. He began to seek and obtain backing from prominent politicos for a future Senate bid. His war-altered views aligned him strongly with the Republican Party, but strong pro-Union advocates such as General McClernand remained loyal to the Democrats, so no one knew for sure where Logan aligned. He remained close-mouthed, telling Mary, "I am saying nothing in politics nor will I until the proper time."[10]

Mary, as always, was her husband's most trusted confidant; she received numerous letters from Logan during the winter of 1865–66 while he traveled to New York and Washington to exploit the locations for political positioning. He also dabbled in stock trading and cotton speculation. He spent the entire winter in the East, which stretched Mary beyond the breaking point. Despite his insistence that the time away from her was important for their future, she saw her dream of a cozy domestic life disintegrate. They marked their ten-year anniversary in the same fashion as most of the previous anniversaries and Christmases—away from each other. In the middle of March she wrote to him, pointing out that her decade-long sacrifices for him had been for naught. She crushed him with the claim: "you have never spent *an evening* with me and made me feel you were happy . . ." Realizing there was no solution to the problem, she groaned, "Alas like all my past anticipations of pleasure, it is all over and so I will give up and do the best I can."[11]

Logan returned to Carbondale by the close of March. He once again convinced his wife that his absences were necessary for the sake of the family, promising her that they would unite in the near future. Although he was on the cusp of committing to a political future, he did not compromise his postwar military obligations. Commemoration ceremonies had sprung up in Boalsburg, Pennsylvania, in 1864, and Columbus, Mississippi, in 1865, to decorate the graves of the fallen soldiers of the Civil War. Carbondale joined these communities with a commemorative day on April 29, 1866, at Woodlawn Cemetery, the eternal resting place for sixty Civil War soldiers. Prominent Carbondale citizens planned the event and would take part in the ceremony, including Daniel Brush, formerly the colonel of the Eighteenth Illinois Infantry and the first director of the ten-year-old cemetery. Formerly a political adversary of the Logan family, Brush and Logan had warmed to each other from the Civil War service they shared as members of the Seventeenth Corps of the Army of the Tennessee. Brush report-edly asked Logan to speak at the event and he agreed.

The clear spring day—the last Sunday of the month—provided a fitting backdrop for a memorable experience. Decked out in his uniform, General Logan straddled his horse and with Colonel E. J. Ingersoll (the marshal of the ceremony) he led a procession of 219 veterans, followed by small boys and dogs. They marched with precision, for less than ten months had distanced many of them from the Carolina campaign. They advanced from the old "Blue Church" to the cemetery; the crowd gathered at the graveyard respectfully fell silent as the soldiers came into view. Once within the burial grounds, the men halted and the minister initiated the ceremony with a prayer. Other speakers offered their respectful remarks before General Logan was introduced to the assemblage.

Logan stepped up to address his neighbors. The event stirred his emotions in a manner not experienced since the grand parade in Washington back in May of 1865. Most of the soldiers buried in the ground formerly served with the Eighteenth Illinois and the Eighty-first Illinois Infantry, two regiments that fought in his division of the Seventeenth Corps during the Vicksburg Campaign of 1863. Two others were particularly close to him. Horace Bowyer captained Company H of the Thirty-first Illinois—Logan's "Dirty-first" regiment. He died in 1863. Most overwhelming was the sight of another headstone from the Thirty-first Illinois. It belonged to Lieutenant Colonel John H. White, Logan's Marion neighbor who preplanned the regiment with him back in the summer of 1861; the commander died near his side during the vicious stand in front of Fort Donelson. Logan's stentorian voice carried strong and pure that afternoon. He delivered an affecting address. Struck by the speech, a cousin wrote down its most memorable line: "Every man's life belongs to his country, and no man has a right to refuse when his country calls for it."[12]

Everyone walked away from the ceremony that afternoon satisfied that they had paid homage to their fallen friends and family members. Little did they realize the effect it had on Logan. Concurrently and coincidentally that same month, Major Benjamin Franklin Stevenson began a veteran's organization upstate in Decatur, a city thirty miles east of Springfield. He called it the Grand Army of the Republic (G.A.R.). Logan's participation in Carbondale's day of memorial to the Union martyrs and his subsequent association and involvement with Stevenson's organization would produce a lasting legacy for the United States.

Stevenson contacted Logan about the G.A.R. and he joined the organization. He was already actively involved in the Society of the Army of the Tennessee, a

fraternal organization of veterans from Logan's former army. The group was conceived in Raleigh in April 1865 when several officers met prior to Johnston's surrender. By the spring of 1866 Logan was the society's vice president, a faithful
participant, and one who relished in stories and memories of the war. The G.A.R.
further enhanced those feelings, but it accomplished much more than to reminisce
about and honor comrades both living and dead. One of the early driving forces
of Stevenson's brainchild was Richard Oglesby, a Decatur resident and the Illinois
governor who Logan helped to elect in 1864. He wished to use the power in numbers the G.A.R possessed to support members as political candidates. Senator
Trumbull learned that Oglesby would back Logan in a bid to unseat him for reelection. Trumbull understandably grew wary of Logan's future plans.[13]

Trumbull had good reason to be concerned, for Logan did desire his Senate
seat, although he had not officially declared his party affiliations. He ruled out a
run to reclaim his former district, confessing to his wife, "If I am not worthy for
something more, I want nothing." But his Senate support was not yet strong
enough; if Logan declared as a Democrat, he would lose to Trumbull in the legislature and if he declared as a Republican, he would have great difficulty in convincing convention delegates that he, as a recent convert, should be trusted to
carry the party's water over candidates who had been loyal Republicans since its
inception during the mid 1850s.[14]

Republicans in Egypt salivated at the opportunity to claim Logan as their
own. For two years they had a Republican in Congress—Andrew J. Kuykendall
(the man Logan helped beat Josh Allen in 1864)—but he had disappointed them
with a voting record that was too supportive of President Johnson's policies, ones
they felt flew in the face of Abraham Lincoln's vision. Perry County held a Republican convention in Pinckneyville early in May and named Logan as their
candidate for Congress from the Thirteenth District. Although Logan was never
consulted, the convention result spread through the state, assuming Logan's
party for him. The *Chicago Tribune* echoed the sentiments of the Perry County
officials about Logan: "He is the only Republican in the Illinois congressional
delegation whose Unionism is qualified."[15]

Logan wrapped up his business in the East and made time to vacation in St.
Paul, Minnesota, where he relaxed with his family and fished on several lakes.
The newest member of his family joined him there. Her name was Kate Logan,
a beautiful teenaged cousin from Cincinnati who Mary adopted into her family.
The trip invigorated Logan for a heavy schedule for the remainder of 1866. He
returned to Illinois at the end of June with a flourish. A three-hour address at
Cairo launched a sweep northward through his state. A lifelong Democrat,

Logan's political conversion could be traced back to speeches delivered in Illinois during the summer of 1863. Three summers later, he had not declared himself for either party.[16]

But on the Fourth of July, he allowed others to say it for him. The event was a soldiers' picnic to mark the ninetieth anniversary of Independence Day. It was held in Salem, the Marion County seat, eighty miles east of St. Louis. The small town could boast that some of the greatest war heroes congregated there—including Sherman and Logan. Governor Oglesby arrived from Decatur and Isham Haynie came in from Cairo, reuniting the team that canvassed the state in fall 1864. The event included a touching toast offered by a young Salem woman: "The young men of America; their arms our support; our arms their reward. Fall in, men—fall in."[17]

The speeches and the reaction to them turned the event into a watershed moment for Logan's political career. Sherman spoke first, a tender address to the men formerly under his command. After noon, Logan repeated his Cairo speech—all three hours of it. Governor Oglesby came in afterwards, endorsing Logan in a verbal embrace that welcomed him into the Republican Party. Disgusted at the display, Sherman telegraphed Grant from Salem, "[A]ttended here a large celebration but Logan and Oglesby spoke more politics than I think the national occasion warranted. I do not wish to be compromised by their speeches."[18]

But this was Logan's wish. Having separated his dual roles so effectively from 1861 to 1865, Logan now embraced the union of his military career and his political one, using wartime glories of the past to promote the politics of the present. His speech was an ostentatious display of provocation and bellicosity—performed in pure spread-eagle style. At that Salem Fourth of July picnic, Logan had perfected the style of blaming the ills of American society on the Democratic Party and their unpatriotic role in the Civil War. This was dubbed "waving the bloody shirt," a reminder for all audience members about who was right and who was not in regards to America's defining historical moment. "Bloody shirt" oratory would dominate political speeches for decades to come.

Logan's over-the-top presentation not only divorced him from the Democrats, but married him to the extreme wing of the Republican Party. He was vehemently anti-Johnson, denouncing the Democratic president's policies. He had previously insisted that Johnson was opposed to any strict policies against the former Confederate States. "General, there's no such thing as reconstruction," he claimed Johnson told him in 1865; "These states have not gone out of the Union. Therefore, reconstruction is unnecessary." Not only did Logan rail against the president's lenient policy toward the South, he also denounced him for his veto of the Freedman's Bureau Bill in February. The bill was restructured, but was destined to be vetoed again later in July. Logan's Saul-to-Paul conversion on the civil rights of African Americans was not shared by Lincoln's successor, and Logan berated Andrew Johnson about the policy whenever and wherever he could.[19]

Logan made it his mission to denounce Johnson face to face. Scheduled to appear at the first G.A.R. meeting in Springfield, he abruptly left Illinois and boarded a train to Washington. There, as an outsider, he supported Republican lawmakers to stand firm against Johnson's opposition to Reconstruction. When the president vetoed the Freedman's Bureau Bill for a second time, Logan headed to the White House for a verbal shootout with Johnson. They argued for an hour, the president pacing the floor as Logan remained unwavering in his conversion. Logan promised him, "I am going home, Mr. President, and I shall make a speech, and I intend to talk about that veto, and I intend to antagonize you in no uncertain language."[20]

Logan kept the promise at a landmark event in his political career. At Springfield on August 8, he attended the Republican state convention where he witnessed his own nomination for congressman-at-large, a House of Representatives' seat determined by a statewide election rather than one from a congressional district. Now an official Republican, Logan hammered away at Johnson and his policies during his acceptance speech. The convention replaced Andrew Kuykendall with Green B. Raum as the candidate for Logan's old district. Their platform endorsed Reconstruction measures that ran counter to Johnson's policies. The event was bittersweet for him. Logan actually sought the Republican Senate nomination in August, but Senator Trumbull was endorsed for reelection.[21]

Logan continued to wave the bloody shirt throughout the remainder of the campaign, already identified as a "Radical" Republican. The term identified the wing of the party that not only pushed for congressional reconstruction, but also advocated Negro suffrage and harbored a unique vindictiveness toward the South, willing to link Southern policy to their partisan hatred of Andrew Johnson. Logan perfectly fit the term.[22]

At St. Louis Logan joined Governor Oglesby and the governors of four other states at a soldiers' mass meeting on August 10. From there he headed to Chicago where he organized his campaign to stump key regions of the state for the election. There he learned that his mother-in-law, Elizabeth Cunningham, had succumbed to cholera. Mary was visiting family members in Joliet, forcing Logan to telegraph his wife the tragic news of her mother's death. Yet he did not interrupt his campaign to be with her; the very day he relayed the terrible news, he trained to Galesburg to address a crowd of 11,000.[23]

Logan's absence from Springfield took him away from the G.A.R. meeting and assured he would not be elected as the first commander of the organization (General John M. Palmer received that nod). Still, the presence of Logan and Oglesby together had G.A.R. written all over it, a point not lost upon Charles O'Beirne, an investigator sent by Johnson to monitor the movements of Radical Republicans in the West. Yet to make a mark nationally, the G.A.R. was sweeping Illinois as a political entity. In August, the fledgling organization boasted fifty-six posts, enough for the *Chicago Tribune* to believe that they directed the vote outcome in several counties. By September membership swelled to 80,000 in Illinois, nearly tripling the organized posts in the state to 141. Clearly, the G.A.R. would influence the election of 1866 in Illinois.[24]

This was good news for Logan, running in a statewide election for congressman-at-large. To counter his influence, the Democrats ran a soldier against him. His name was T. Lyle Dickey, a former Whig and a colonel of cavalry during the Civil War who turned in a noteworthy performance during the Vicksburg Campaign. But Colonel Dickey's war record withered in the shadow of Logan's exploits, and the G.A.R. was set to intensify their campaign on Logan's side. This left the Democrats with one option to have a chance to defeat him.

Throughout the late summer and autumn of 1866 Illinois newspapers espousing loyalty to the Democrats launched a concerted effort to sap Logan's strength throughout the state. The *Cairo Democrat, Chicago Times, Illinois State Register*, and the *Jonesboro Gazette* bombarded their readership with a series of reports, editorials, and anecdotes—including first and second-hand testimony—linking Logan with the secession movement during the spring of 1861. Some of the claims were ridiculous, others unsubstantiated, and some were absolutely true. Of the latter, Logan's denunciation of Stephen A. Douglas' pro-Union speech in Springfield on April 25, 1861, had come back to bite him, as did his night of armed resistance with his Marion friends in June of that year to drive off the attempt of the federal government to arrest them. Newspaper editors pummeled Logan whenever they could, with a mix of glee and venom. The *Illinois State Register* called Logan a "gross, smutty Vulcan reeking from his foul stithy." The *Chester Picket Guard* made no attempt to conceal its contempt and disdain for "that low vulgar, dirty and hypocritical Logan. Maggots would sicken on him."[25]

Newspapers friendly to Logan quickly lined up to support him. "No Illinois candidate has ever been subjected to so persistent and malignant vilification," complained the *Chicago Tribune*, a hearty defender of Logan; "It has manifested a hate and rancor perfectly fiendish." The Democratic organs had been effective, so much so that John and Mary Logan found it necessary to address the accusations rather than ignore them. They swiftly diffused two of the damaging charges—that Logan took part in the Marion meeting of April 15, 1861, where the secession resolutions were drafted, and that he was the driving force in raising the Confederate company in which his brother-in-law served. Sworn affidavits from Marion residents and members of Thorndike Brooks's company effectively countered those accusations. Included in the refutations were accounts by John Cunningham and Hybert Cunningham, each of whom came to the defense of his beleaguered in-law. Logan made sure that newspapers carried these sworn testimonies to contrast them with unsupported testimony published in the papers hostile to him.[26]

The newspaper charges, rebuttals, and countercharges formed the backdrop of a most interesting congressional race. The two candidates followed in the footsteps of the 1858 Lincoln-Douglas Senate contest by waging a series of three debates in September and October of 1866. The idea was sparked by former Logan friend, Democrat William H. Green, who firmly believed Logan's warts would be exposed in this open exchange format in front of the people of the state. Confident and comfortable, Logan had no qualms in agreeing to the proposal.[27]

At Carbondale on September 13, 1866, Logan and Dickey squared off in front of a crowd that exceeded 10,000 people. By previous agreement, each candidate spoke for ninety minutes—Logan opened for an hour, Dickey followed for one and a half hours, followed by a half hour of Logan's closing remarks. The candidates sparred with charges against each other's loyalty. They also contrasted their political philosophies; Logan left no doubt about his Radical Republican views about strict Reconstruction of the Southern states and Dickey unabashedly proclaimed his adherence to the Johnson administration's policies.

The audience helped to make the event both memorable and circus-like. Strongly divided between Democrats and Republicans, Logan's hometown advantage was disintegrated by the "outsiders" who filtered in to support Dickey. Most embarrassing to Logan was the presence of two vocal Democrats who tried to interrupt him during his remarks—his brother and sister. Tom Logan and Annie Blanchard made their presence known as Dickey supporters throughout the afternoon. But Logan's supporters came out strong, hundreds if not thousands of them former soldiers who marched with him and bled for him in Tennessee, Mississippi, Georgia, and the Carolinas. Both sides had reason to be happy with the performance of their candidates, but Logan left no room for chance. One week after the debate, he reportedly spoke for four hours at a Republican mass meeting in Carbondale, followed by Dick Oglesby and other candidates on the ticket. The *Alton Telegraph* reported a partisan crowd of 10,000 for the event, repeating the turnout of the previous week.[28]

Logan refused to lie idle before the next debate scheduled one month after Carbondale. Spurred on by the presence of President Johnson, who stumped Egypt and other Democratic-friendly parts of Illinois to garner support for his policies, Logan struck five towns in the seven days following Carbondale to wave the bloody shirt and rail against the president in his typical hours-long provocations. He steamrolled into the town of Malcomb to debate Dickey again on October 9. There in front of 15,000 Logan was in top form. He repeated the performance in Decatur one week later, the birthplace of the G.A.R. The Springfield post organized to support Logan in Decatur. Little doubt remained for the election when the opposing parties departed from Decatur.[29]

On election night Logan planted himself in the Carbondale post office with a large crowd of supporters and neighbors. Included in the latter was Eph Snyder, a die-hard Democrat and old friend of Logan's father. Snyder waged money against Logan, hoping the turncoat Republican would lose. As the returns started coming in, Snyder quickly realized his wager was in jeopardy. "How in tarnation do you come to get so many votes, John?" Reminding Snyder of the old days of betting on him when he was a jockey for his father, Logan responded, "Didn't I always run well, Eph? You used to bet on me, and never lost." Snyder took his inevitable loss in stride, suggesting that Logan return to his old profession. "And if you were riding one of your father's thoroughbreds, I'd bet on you again," insisted the old man.[30]

The election of 1866 showcased the G.A.R.'s political power. Although yet to establish its power nationwide, they proved to be a driving force in Illinois. Their organization was impressive, sponsoring reunions and picnics for the war veterans, complete with the entertainment the soldiers loved—band music, good food, and Radical oratory. Logan was a favorite of its membership and the beneficiary of its influence. Logan demolished Lyle T. Dickey by nearly 55,000 statewide votes, winning the at-large congressional seat with 57 percent of the total votes. Only three of the fourteen congressional seats were won by Democrats. The Thirteenth District, radically Democratic, surprisingly refused to return Josh Allen to the House of Representatives for the second straight election, voting for Republican Green B. Raum. The state legislature followed the same division, boasting a two-thirds majority and securing the inevitability that a

Republican would keep the Senate seat when the General Assembly convened in the winter. A decades-long bedrock for Democratic politics, the state of Illinois had suddenly become a Republican Party bastion.[31]

Senator Trumbull must have been pleased with the election results. The legislature was stacked in his favor and set to return him to the U.S. Senate for his third term. His campaign operatives finagled Logan into the at-large congressional seat, thus removing him as a threat to Trumbull in his reelection bid. At least that is what the Senator and his supporters believed. But Logan was not satisfied with his resounding victory. Buoyed by newspaper masthead endorsements, Logan sought to seize the Senate seat from Lyman Trumbull. "I do not intend to be beat for Senator," he announced to his wife on December 1. But the field got crowded on the Republican side when Palmer and Oglesby allowed supporters to fight for them. With no chance to win a four-way race, both Logan and Oglesby threw their support to Palmer, but to no avail. The legislature sent Trumbull back to the Senate in their January election.

"I came here as a Democrat . . . God knows that I have differed with the other side from my childhood, and with that side I will never affiliate so long as I have breath in my body," Logan had declared in 1859—then one of the most strident and ardent Democrats in the House of Representatives. But on March 3, 1867, Congressman Logan took the oath and took his seat—as a Republican. It was indeed a surreal moment. Logan's former enemies were now his allies; the most extreme members of the Republican Party shared his views. Conversely, those who adhered to Logan's philosophy of the 1850s found themselves across the aisle from him, including Clement Vallandigham of Ohio and Samuel S. Marshall of Southern Illinois. Marshall was Logan's former friend and confidant— and a guest at his wedding in 1855—and one of only three Illinois congressmen to claim Democratic seats in the House. The two remained cordial to each other throughout the first session of the Fortieth Congress.

Logan was uncharacteristically quiet throughout the spring session, speaking out only against a $1 million relief bill for the South. Logan's reasons highlighted the destitute state of those living in Union-loyal regions of the country, citizens ignored by the debate. Not surprisingly, he was branded as cruel and unforgiving to deny the poverty-stricken former Confederacy the necessary funds to sustain them. Logan generated no lasting impression for the remainder of the first session. Behind the scene, however, he met frequently with other Radical Republicans to consider charges of impeachment against President Johnson. The strength behind the extreme measure was nonexistent, forcing Logan and the other Radicals to bide their time.

Logan decided to pick a fight with his opponents to open the second session of the Fortieth Congress. He waved the bloody shirt at the Democrats by challenging the right for the Kentucky House members to be seated for the session. Logan maintained that the loyalty of each Blue Grass State representative must be assured before they could function in the national body. Former friend Sam Marshall took the open opportunity to challenge Logan on his own loyalty back in 1861. Logan and Marshall continually sniped at each other, but in the end the Republicans won with a vote to investigate suspected disloyal Kentuckians in the House.[32]

The new and very radical Republican chose his small battles to put himself in a leadership role. Here Logan succeeded in a summertime House session noteworthy for legislation over Reconstruction that crafted supplementary measures to remove oversight powers originally granted to the president and place them with Congress and the army, led by General Grant. Logan's words tumbled into newsprint throughout the country that summer. He spoke out loud and clear against the former Confederate states, conquered entities subject to the necessary oversight and restrictions imposed by the U.S. Army and Congress. Logan vented as only he could against the rebellion, proclaiming that he would have executed Jefferson Davis (captured and imprisoned with the fall of the Confederate government in 1865) had *he* captured him at the end of the War.[33]

The House and Senate both passed the Supplementary Reconstruction bill, as expected. Johnson vetoed the legislation, equally as expected. Before the one-month session adjourned until November Logan cast his vote to empower African Americans to hold office in the District of Columbia. Logan's vote for the D.C. legislation continued his consistent but more encompassing philosophy on extending rights for blacks throughout the country. The Thirteenth Amendment had been ratified at the end of 1865, ending slavery for all Americans except for convicts. But even with their new freedom, blacks had few rights universally guaranteed to them—including voting, education, and holding legislative offices. Logan sought to end the restrictions. The major obstacle to that quest was the unpopularity of the notion that "all men are created equal." The testing ground for that notion in 1867 was Ohio, a state entering an election for governor and a state legislature. Included on the Buckeye ballot was an amendment referendum to extend enfranchisement to African Americans.

Inundated with requests to promote Republican candidates on the stump, Logan trained to Ohio to deliver a series of speeches in the fall of 1867. He began in the western side of the state and swept eastward, delivering nine exhaustive performances in ten days. Five-figure crowds flocked wherever he spoke, events hailed with tremendous pageantry, as if he had been born and raised a Buckeye himself. Flags draped the avenues of Ohio's largest cities in anticipation of his arrival, and when he did come into view, a fired salute signified the occasion. The events were so well arranged that special trains ran veterans and other audience members from town to town to swell the crowds to 20,000 at some venues.[34]

Logan crafted a new speech for this tour, a leaner address that usually lasted two hours—half the length of some of his more rambling addresses. He continued to wave the bloody shirt, denigrating Johnson and the Democrats as stridently as he ever had. But Logan added a new twist to his Ohio stump speech, words that marked the complete transformation of his views on African Americans. The speech found its way into newspapers throughout the country in September and October of 1867:

> Now I want some Democrat to give a reason why the negro should not vote. I have read their speeches and all they say is we don't want the nigger to vote, and turn up their noses as they say it. A gentleman in Congress from your state [Clement Vallandigham] says the negro does not belong to the human species. But they are made the same as you and I; but they are black—that is all the difference. If they are not made by the hand of God, I would like to know by whom they were made . . .
>
> Years ago you had a Democratic Legislature, which decided that the man who had one half black blood in him should vote. Now, will any Democrat tell me which half of these negroes vote, the white half or the black half? If only the white half, why should he cast more than half a vote? If you won't allow a man to vote because he has a black skin, you have the same right to say I shall not vote because I have black hair. I don't care whether a man is black, red, blue, or white if he is a civilized man in a Christian community like ours . . . he has the right to say who the men shall be that control the Government.[35]

Logan's position on the rights of blacks was hardly a popular one in the states comprising the Old Northwest Territory, including Ohio. The *Defiance Democrat* reported that Logan was asked to speak at a soldier's reunion, ostensibly about the war and his soldiers. "Instead of that," complained the paper's editor, "the speech was an Abolition harangue, mainly devoted to urging them to support the Radical State ticket and to vote for negro suffrage and glorifies the nigger troops. For all this they paid an admission fee and own up that they were sold, and that Gen. Logan is a humbug—his negroes, ditto."[36]

The majority of voting Ohioans felt the same way. Logan's efforts helped to elect a Republican governor, former general Rutherford B. Hayes, but the legislature went resoundingly to the Democrats, thus following the lead of Vallandigham and repudiating Logan. The Negro Suffrage amendment lost by nearly 40,000 votes. This proved more than anything that Logan's unpopular position on civil rights was an altruistic one that represented views he knew were a political liability, not only in Ohio but also in Illinois where overt racism prevailed.[37]

The Ohio campaign proved exhausting for Logan, so much so that when he returned to Washington for the second half of the first session of the Fortieth Congress, he was too ill in the early part of the session to participate. He recuperated at Willard's Hotel, with his family there to ease his recovery. Although the remaining portion of the session did not accomplish much in regards to fruitful legislation, for Logan it continued his uphill climb to prominence. Logan was wed to the patronage system—a controversial aspect of politics in which he gained power from the support of prominent people and organizations in return for favors he would grant them from his House seat. Logging the names of those who supported him, Logan's list of Illinoisans to whom he owed favors grew to the point where he needed to divide up his names by counties. His list included state politicians, law enforcement officers, and prominent newspapermen.[38]

In addition to his influential friends, Logan derived power from his affiliations. In January 1868, Logan was elected the second commander of the G.A.R. in Philadelphia. It was a proud moment for him, but also an important one for his career. No longer considered regional, the G.A.R. boasted a burgeoning national membership, numbers that could command political influence with a leader willing to direct it. Logan was determined to be that leader. The founder of the organization, Benjamin F. Stephenson, congratulated Logan and assured him that he commanded a body with political power in the election year of 1868. "If a Republican president is elected," wrote Stephenson, "it is the G.A.R. that will do it."[39]

That January Logan also began his term in the second session of the Fortieth Congress wielding more prestige than he ever had as a Democrat prior to the war, or during his first session as a Republican. He was a vocal member of the House Ways and Means Committee, one of the most powerful committees of either body of Congress. By this time he had assumed a leadership role as a Radical Republican. The complete transformation of Logan's social and political philosophy dumbfounded his former friends, many who had turned into political enemies, since there were few areas shaded gray when associated with Logan. Sam Marshall continued to spar with Logan on the House floor; their rancor never abated. When Logan accused Marshall of altering the text of his floor speech in the *Congressional Globe* so much as to change its meaning, Marshall insulted Logan by suggesting that his irritability was caused by flatulence. When he suggested that Logan allay his ills with "Mrs. Winslow's Soothing Syrup," Logan had had enough. He roared back, blasting Marshall for his indecent language and ungentlemanly nature.[40]

Logan yearned to wield his influence against his political adversaries. Seeking a valid reason to impeach the president, Johnson granted the Republicans' wish on February 21 when he fired Edwin M. Stanton, the holdover secretary of war from the Lincoln administration. The move violated the Tenure of Office Act—grounds for impeachment according to the Radicals. They moved swiftly. Following advice from the Radicals, Stanton barricaded himself in the War Department building he had toiled in for six years. Logan joined him there, sleeping on a cot. He had sent orders to mobilize the G.A.R. forces in the event of an insurrection in Washington once impeachment proceedings were waged against the president. He had no large force of G.A.R. members at his disposal, but enough to form a guard around the War Department.[41]

The insurrection never occurred as Logan and the other Radicals tread on unfamiliar congressional territory. Impeachment had been performed on judges, but never on a president. With the Constitution offering only nebulous grounds, such as "high crimes and misdemeanors," the House would be the first body to decide if Johnson's actions met those charges. A majority vote of House members was necessary to impeach him, and then a panel of House managers would present their case across the Capitol's rotunda to the Senate. A two-thirds vote rather than a simple majority was required by the senators to remove the president from office.

The House acted with dizzying speed. They impeached Andrew Johnson merely three days after he attempted to remove Secretary Stanton with a majority of 126 to 47. Logan had delivered a half-hour speech less than forty-eight hours before the vote, answering critics that the procedures would ruin the country. Logan had cogently argued that a nation that could withstand the Civil War and a presidential assassination could handle the impeachment of a bad president. His words may have impressed fellow House members enough to include him in the seven-member panel to draw up official charges. One week later, eleven charges were rattled off one by one before the House, each one receiving a majority vote. The next procedure was to name House managers to officially present the charges before the Senate. Logan and five other panel members earned the responsibility.[42]

The Senate phase of impeachment was a trial. Logan and the other House managers presented their case not only before the fifty-four senators, but also before Johnson's team of defense attorneys. For Logan the proceedings must have felt like his prosecuting attorney days of the mid 1850s, but more than ten years removed from those days could have left him hesitant and less confident. Other House managers such as Benjamin Butler, George Boutwell, and Thaddeus Stevens had also been skilled lawyers and they presented most of the case against Johnson. They began on March 30 and presented an oft-interrupted case for more than three weeks. Logan did not present an oration, but submitted a written argument explaining why Johnson's actions rose to the level of impeachment. Logan's words received a great deal of praise in private letters and newspaper editorials.

Even with the results of the impeachment case still up in the air, Logan's star had continued to rise and shine brightly. He was constantly talked up as the man to replace the outgoing Dick Oglesby as governor of Illinois. Logan had seen the endorsement back in 1864, and his lack of ardor for the position was just as strong in 1865. "I am not a candidate, nor will I be," wrote Logan to Isham Haynie back in January, repeating the stance in subsequent letters. He had been flattered by his hometown paper's endorsement for him as president (which included other endorsements from Eastern newspapers), but did not take it seriously. Logan's eye remained focused on Congress. He wished to continue two more years as congressman-at-large. The state convention in Peoria in April named Logan as the Republican candidate for the position and Richard Palmer as the gubernatorial candidate. Considered a shoo-in for reelection later in 1868, Logan planned to strengthen his patronage base for a Senate run in 1870–71.[43]

As impeachment proceedings dragged on, Logan labored to strengthen the G.A.R. He moved headquarters from Springfield to Washington, seeking opportunities to increase its national influence. While overtly declaring the Grand Army of the Republic a fraternal, nonpartisan organization, Logan covertly admitted what was already apparent: "The organization of the G.A.R. had been and is being run in the interests of the Republican Party."[44]

Logan's most enduring act—his legacy for America—utilized his role as commander of the G.A.R. in a nonpartisan way. On May 5, 1868, Logan issued General Orders Number 11, establishing May 30 as the annual date "for the purpose of strewing flowers, or otherwise decorating the graves of Comrades who died in defense of their country." Mary Logan insisted that the notion sprung from her visit to Confederate graves in March of 1868 in Petersburg, Virginia. No doubt she described the affecting event to her husband upon her return to

Washington, but Logan's edict was not meant for Confederate graves. Logan appears to have been most influenced by his own participation in one of the earliest practices of this ceremony in the North—the event of April 29, 1866, at Woodlawn Cemetery in Carbondale. His hope in making it an event originating from the Grand Army of the Republic was to memorialize this ceremony for the Union comrades who made the ultimate sacrifice in fighting for the preservation of the Union.[45]

Logan headed to Chicago to nominate the man he thought was a surefire winner for the Republican Party. He first spoke to another veteran's group and then he headed to the Opera House; the Republican National Convention met there. Chicago was an appropriate locale for the convention since the state of Illinois dominated Republican politics. The state boasted as high a Republican contingency as could be found across the country: its governor, two senators, 75 percent of its U.S. representatives, and its state legislature. The G.A.R. was born in the state, an organization that perpetuated Republican politics. The spirit of Lincoln was in the air, as the martyred president's name rolled longingly from the lips of the party adherents. How fitting it was to nominate another presidential candidate with strong Illinois ties. On May 21, 1868, the most popular and dominant native-born Illinoisan stood up to make the nomination of the state's famous adopted citizen. After cries of "Bully! John!" resonated through the Opera House where they congregated, Logan announced to the chair, "Then sir, in the name of the loyal citizens, soldiers and sailors of this great Republic of the United States of America; in the name of loyalty, of liberty, of humanity, of justice; in the name of the National Union Republican Party; I nominate, as candidate for the Chief Magistracy of this nation, Ulysses S. Grant."[46]

The hall exploded in applause and cheers. Logan was gratified. It was Grant who advanced his stalled military career, even when Lincoln ignored Logan for promotion; it was Grant who saw the value of Logan's summertime speeches to advance the Union cause; and it was Grant who exhibited the utmost faith and confidence in Logan's abilities never before seen in a non-academy trained officer. It was fitting for him to put Grant's name up for nomination. The general accepted, setting the stage to put an Illinois resident back in the White House.

The convention victory soothed some of the sting that lingered from the impeachment proceedings. The first Senate vote took place a few days before the convention. It totaled thirty-five votes guilty and nineteen not guilty, meaning one Senate vote would have provided the two-thirds majority to remove Andrew Johnson from office. On May 26 another vote was requested for the official tally.

There was no change from the first. Johnson was acquitted of all eleven counts of high crimes and misdemeanors. He stayed in office to complete the last ten months of his presidency.[47]

Disappointed at the inability to remove Johnson from office, Logan recovered quickly enough to view the results of General Orders Number 11. The first "Decoration Day" commenced on May 30, 1868. More than 100 ceremonies were observed across the states that fielded Union soldiers in the Civil War. The *New York Times* claimed that New Haven, Connecticut, "was the only city of any note in the North which neglected to decorate the soldiers' graves." An Illinois paper gushed with admiration of the universal approach to Decoration Day: "The inauguration of this ceremony to the fallen brave; which we hope to see perpetuated, is perhaps the most beautiful and touching tribute we could give of our grateful and affectionate remembrance." It was Logan's grandest of ideas, and his enduring American legacy. In subsequent years as more towns and states participated, Decoration Day commemorated the dead from all wars where Americans died. The date eventually changed to be celebrated on the last Monday of May, and the name changed as it eventually became a national holiday, one called Memorial Day.[48]

As Logan rightfully proclaimed, "It was the proudest act of my life."[49]

CHAPTER NINE

Tainted in the Gilded Age

THE ELECTION OF 1868 returned John A. Logan to the U.S. House of Representatives. His win was achieved with a lower margin of victory than he had attained two years earlier—49,300 votes and 53 percent of the populace compared to 57 percent. Illinois Republicans rejoiced at their dominance over the Democrats. Ten out of fourteen U.S. representatives were Republicans; General Palmer won the governor's seat; and—most important—Ulysses S. Grant was elected president of the United States by carrying 26 out of 32 states, but beating Horatio Seymour by only 300,000 votes out of 5.7 million cast. Logan's plan to strengthen himself as a statewide candidate proved not only beneficial to him as congressman at large, but also enhanced the potential for a U.S. Senate bid (Richard Yates was up for reelection in January of 1871). Logan had begun to build his state political "machine," an Illinois power base driven by influential and wealthy residents allied to throw their support to him in return for his fighting to gain them their pet issues in Congress. Although Logan embraced patronage, this postwar policy polarized the country into camps that either supported this system, or stood for civil service reform.[1]

Battle lines were drawn and the fight began in January of 1869 when Logan took his seat for the final session of the Fortieth Congress. Logan, a patronage defender, sparred with Thomas Jenckes, an advocate of civil service reform. The debates were inconclusive. This was business as usual in Washington when Congress was working through a lame-duck session. The most noteworthy act of the session was the passage of the Fifteenth Amendment, guaranteeing voting rights for blacks. The issue had been soundly rejected when Logan campaigned in Ohio in the fall of 1867; therefore, its ratification was not a foregone conclusion.[2]

When he was not toiling on Capitol Hill during the winter of 1869, Logan spent time with his family at Willard's Hotel, where they had stayed when not living in Carbondale. Mary had celebrated her thirtieth birthday the previous summer and had grown more comfortable as the wife of a political and military celebrity. Her two children—Dollie was ten years old and Manning three—kept her company during her husband's busiest days, but she also reveled in the Washington social scene. She wrapped herself around the arm of her husband when he attended dinner parties and social gatherings. One night in January they attended a White House reception. Logan had a difficult time putting the recent past behind him as did Andrew Johnson, considering that impeachment proceedings had ended less than eight months ago. His resentment was thinly veiled according to Orville Browning. "Genl Jno A Logan was there," Browning told his diary on January 19. "Saw him making himself very agreeable to the President, or trying to."[3]

Mary also observed her husband in action. The day after his forty-third birthday, Logan wrestled with his colleagues in a joint session of Congress convened over restoring voting rights to states approved through Reconstruction. Georgia caused a dispute in the House after Massachusetts Congressman Ben Butler tore into Ohio Senator Benjamin F. Wade by introducing censure resolutions against Wade for the way he apparently mishandled the vote count. Logan bristled at seeing Butler chew up the venerable Wade, who was ending a long and illustrious career in the waning days of the Fortieth Congress. Logan rose to his defense with a long speech that belittled the censure plan and praised Wade's career. His magnanimous gesture was acknowledged with lengthy applause by the other House members and the gallery spectators. Most appreciative was Ben Wade. He went to Willard's that night to thank Logan personally, emphasizing his words by thumping his umbrella on the hotel floor. Logan and Wade never were strongly allied, but that night they were the best of friends as they reminisced together about Congress, Lincoln, and the war.[4]

The Civil War influenced congressional debate for nearly as long as the conflict itself, and was destined to carry over well into the next decade, and the decade after that. Logan reveled in reminding all within earshot about the war. Andrew Johnson's parting shots at Logan and the other House managers who impeached him surely stung. The outgoing president pardoned a slew of former Confederates, including Vice President Alexander Stephens. March arrived with the promise of warmer and sunnier days for Logan. Johnson departed and Grant arrived. After Grant was inaugurated, the Forty-first Congress convened with Logan trading his role on Ways and Means for a seat on the Committee on the Pacific Railroads. His earned prominence manifested itself when on March 15 Logan was named the chairman of the nine-member Committee on Military Affairs.[5]

Logan rarely stated his interest in the Pacific Railroad committee publicly, but the position (he was one of thirteen committee members) was a timely one for him. The year 1869 saw the completion of the nation's long-sought and debated transcontinental railroad, linking lines from the Atlantic to the Pacific Oceans. The committee affiliation was also consistent with Logan's interest in the West. He closed his tenure in the previous Congress by ridiculing the efforts to appropriate funds to the Plains Indians. Calling them "savages," he contended that government-purchased clothing was wasted on these "uncivilized" natives. As far as Logan was concerned, coexisting with Indians was unthinkable until they were Christianized and assured of obeying U.S. laws. His hard-edged opinions, delivered abrasively, generated complaints and sneers from House colleagues.[6]

At the same time Logan vented against Native Americans, he fostered exploration. Nepotism benefited all parties here; Logan formed a liaison with one-time law partner and brother-in-law, Cyrus Thomas. After Dorothy Logan Thomas's death, Thomas quit the law and became an Evangelical Lutheran minister, but after he remarried he returned to his first passions: natural history and entomology. Thomas parlayed his role as the founder of the Illinois Natural History Society into an appointment as entomologist for the 1869 U.S. Geological and Geographical Survey of the Territories, an exploration conducted by Frederick V. Hayden.

Logan may have influenced Hayden to include Thomas on the expedition. Back in his first year as a Republican in the Fortieth Congress in 1867, Logan formed an unofficial liaison between the scientific and political branches of the government by working with the assistant secretary of the Smithsonian Institute, Spencer Baird. The product of their working relationship was Congress's establishment of the Hayden Survey. Hayden's exploration included the discovery of a 12,000-foot mountain in the Rockies, one the explorer named "Logan's Peak."[7]

Logan spent most of the summer and fall in Illinois. In December he returned to Washington for the second session of the Forty-first Congress. His tough stance on Reconstruction softened only for an instant when he voted to readmit Georgia, Texas, and Mississippi with full state rights at the national level. But he opposed Virginia's readmission, concerned that the state would amend its constitution to oppress blacks. He acquiesced on a bill that placated him by forcing Virginians to a test oath that bound them to a vow not to change the state constitution.

Reconstruction politics dominated the times, and Logan dug in to make sure Congress also rid itself of undesirables, particularly those hailing from the South. He was equally praised and condemned for forcing the expulsion of Representative B. Frank Whittemore, a South Carolina congressman who allegedly sold appointments to West Point and the Naval Academy (Whittemore resigned before his expulsion materialized). Logan received almost no support for a pet issue he reintroduced in session—to move the capital from the District of Columbia to St. Louis. He first brought it up in 1868, arguing that the country consisted of an eastern sliver of states when the founding fathers placed the center of federal government in Washington. St. Louis better represented the center of the country and therefore should be the center for government. It only made sense to him to reconsider the issue since the United States stretched from ocean to ocean. It did not make sense to enough congressmen to bring the issue out of committee.[8]

Logan reintroduced other issues that he would not allow to die on the vine. As chair of Military Affairs, he remained active in trimming proposals that reduced the number of major generals and brigadier generals in the smaller U.S. Army, another carry-over from the lame-duck session of the Fortieth Congress. Logan noted that the number of infantry regiments was reduced nearly in half to twenty-four; therefore, he proposed that the 500 regimental officers to whom they had been assigned be dismissed from the service. The House passed these measures, but the Senate softened the blow to the career officers with modifications eventually agreed to by the House. Sherman lamented his annual salary reduced from $19,000 to $13,500—chiefly due to Logan's actions. He got even in his memoirs when he denigrated Logan for heading to Illinois "to look after politics" in the autumn of 1864 rather than participate in the March to the Sea. (Sherman conveniently failed to acknowledge that he received a request from Abraham Lincoln to send Logan back to Illinois to campaign for the election.)[9]

Logan's tough stance on military spending flew in the face of his treatment of veterans. Logan had successfully advanced the prominence of the G.A.R., both for political and altruistic reasons. With no desire to give up his leadership role in the organization, Logan thwarted an attempt to supersede him with a different commander and a shift of headquarters from Washington to New York. As its leader for the third consecutive year, and enjoying his power position in Washington, Logan led the G.A.R and introduced his grave-decorating ceremony in 1870 with orders tagging it with its permanent name: "The annual ceremonies of 'Memorial

Day' which have been firmly established by National choice and consent, will take place on Monday the 30th day of May." Logan commemorated the day with a strong and stirring address delivered at the Arlington National Cemetery.[10]

The second session of the Forty-first Congress stretched into its sixth month as it dragged toward the summer season of 1870. Logan did not always stay within party lines with his votes, defying his Radical identification. Unlike many House Republicans, Logan was deeply opposed to tariff measures. The protective tariff, proponents argued, stabilized and strengthened the economy by not only infusing more money into the country from foreign sources, but also by limiting cheaper foreign products from overwhelming the market and forcing American workers to risk unemployment. The concept was driven by New England Republicans whose concerns about foreign textiles led to the Morrill acts of 1861 and 1862. The end result was American businesses raising their prices with reduced competition. Logan considered the measure as regional and that East Coast states derived greater benefit than Illinois and its neighbors. When a fellow Republican accused him of hurting his party by his opposition, Logan retorted, "In my section of the country this is not regarded as a party question." His refusal to back down to party pressure won him praise and support in Illinois. State platforms of both parties had taken a stance against the protective tariffs. Chicago papers lauded his efforts, fortifying the congressman's belief that he could win the Senate seat in less than a year. Logan remained loyal to the Illinois congressional delegation; both Republicans and Democratic representatives adhered to this mantra, at the expense of the national party. Despite their dominance at the national level, Republican operatives lamented any breaks from the lock-step support they expected within the party. A New York Radical was so concerned over the lack of cohesiveness within his party to complain to a newspaper, "The Republican party in Congress is composed of factions in such deadly antagonisms to each other that the hate among them is more intense than that given to the Democrats."[11]

Indeed, a division deepened within the ranks of the Republican Party. The Radicals' influence had begun to be neutralized by a faction who called themselves "Liberal" Republicans. A staunch Radical during Johnson's term, Logan's voting record thus far during the Grant administration belied the extreme position he had earned during his first term as a Republican congressman. His previous "Radicalism" had been motivated by numerous factors, including true partisan emotion, political expedience, and also religion. Methodists in Illinois were generally strong supporters of Reconstruction politics due to a combination of innate antislavery fervor and fears of loss of church activity and strength with Johnson's view of Reconstruction.[12]

Logan had been a strong adherent to Methodism since his teenage years, but it appears his faith was strengthened by his membership at the "Blue Church" in Carbondale, where Logan worshipped after the war. Logan now injected Christianity into his speeches, adding a new flavor to his rhetoric. Critics accused him of pandering, but his "rebirth" was so strong that Logan was able to shed one of his most cherished and destructive vices—poker. In Washington, a former table player noticed him and said, "Jack, I hain't seen you since our game of draw poker, when you won my little two hundred." Logan informed the man that he no longer played games of chance since he received his full membership in the Methodist church. The former poker mate replied, "Jack, why warn't you received into full membership before you bagged my little two hundred."[13]

Logan never shed his proclivity for profanity, which peppered his most angry outbursts. Other vices were easier to eschew. Smoking was socially acceptable, but the senator partook of tobacco less in his postwar years than he did earlier in his life. He was fond of the pipe, but rarely indulged in it. Weeks would pass before his lips touched a cigar, but he always carried them in his pocket. Sometimes he gave them over to friends and acquaintances; Grant and Logan could often be seen relaxing, each with a Corona in his mouth. Logan often enjoyed a "dry smoke," buying a cheap brand (three cigars for a quarter). He also liked to gnaw off the ends of a Havana and chew it with relish.[14]

Captain Cunningham and Tom Logan battled alcoholism for much of their adult lives, but in comparison to these two family members, Logan was a fairly temperate man. Even an occasional drink vibrated his nerves and sickened him, so he usually abstained. He did not join the prohibition movement, for he believed the vast majority who did choose to drink did so responsibly. He once said, "The is no use in trying to law men's craving for whiskey out of existence, but the majority of decent people in a community have the right, for the sake of personal comfort, to say that the indecent minority must behave themselves."[15]

In addition to his hot temper and his penchant for profanity, Logan's next-greatest vice was his quirkiest one. Logan insisted that he was younger than his true age. He once confided to a Senate colleague that he was twenty-four years old when he was elected to the House of Representatives in 1858 and kept quiet about it, since the Constitution required him to be one year older. (In fact, Logan was thirty-two when he was elected). He kept up the charade, always insisting he was five to eight years below his actual age. His features allowed some to believe him. Logan was forty-four in 1870 with hair as ink-black as ever. While other members of Congress appeared more venerable than their chronological age, Logan appeared to be in his thirties rather than his forties. His true age, however, did guarantee greater experience, confidence, and when it was needed—independence from administration prescriptions.

One of Logan's position changes during Grant's early presidency appears to be a product of trust and a quest for power. Early in 1868 he had introduced a bill calling for the creation of a Civil Service Bureau with a purpose to evaluate candidates for government employment. His distrust of Johnson-era candidates dissipated one year later when Grant's people came in. Realizing the loss of power with a rigid oversight body, he no longer supported any civil service reform. Considering such legislation as aristocratic and anti-American, he insisted, "He who does not unite with the administration should not be trusted with its employment." Logan's reliance on the spoils system clashed with Grant's desire for civil service reform. Patronage was the bane of Grant's existence, but it was Logan's lifeline. Their difference on this issue was destined to strain the strong relationship they enjoyed during the war years and the immediate aftermath.[16]

The greatest clash between Logan and Grant in 1870 was not civil service; it was Cuba. On this issue Grant hoodwinked his former subordinate. Engaged in a yearlong armed conflict with Spain, Cuba represented a patriotic struggle to free itself from an oppressing nation—this was the opinion of the hawkish members of Congress such as Logan who wanted the United States to actively support the island's fight against Spain. Grant, on the other hand, was dead set against intervention, wishing to stay clear of the war. Back in February Logan had crafted a resolution to support the Cuban rebels by granting them belligerent rights; with the issue reemerging in late spring, the resolution was to be debated. Showing more political acumen than many career politicians, Grant staved off a challenge to his foreign policy by sending an effective message to Congress, moments before debate on Logan's resolution was to begin, that succinctly illustrated no reason to recognize the rebels. His timing was perfect. Ben Butler bolted from Logan's ranks to side with the president. Logan tore into Butler, but to no avail. The resolution went down to defeat, 70 votes for and 100 votes against. "It is the greatest triumph of the Administration has yet achieved," crowed E. R. Hoar, Grant's attorney general.[17]

Logan was clearly in a bad humor about the loss. It turned out to be poor timing for B. Frank Whittemore to take his newly elected House of Representatives seat on June 18. The South Carolinian was the same man who faced expulsion for taking pay for military appointments in February. He chose to resign rather than face the wrath of Logan at the time, but he ran again for his seat, won it, and assumed this was his mandate to return. "Whittemore will find 'Jordan a hard road to travel' while Logan is in the House," accurately predicted a newspaper correspondent. Logan lit into him with a fury, stinging him like a swarm of maddened hornets with his rapid-fire, ringing sentences. All but destroyed by Logan's vituperation, Whittemore was unable to initiate his term. Logan understood his role as did many newspaper editors covering Congress. A St. Louis daily affirmed, "When there is a disagreeable duty to be done, an over-puffed balloon to be pricked, an ugly customer to be taught good-manners, by common consent Logan comes to the front."[18]

The second session of the Forty-first Congress closed that spring with all representatives prepared to return to their respective districts to campaign for the election of 1870. Logan returned to Illinois where he delivered several rousing addresses. He also stepped across the borders to perform his skills in Iowa. His celebrity status was as high as it was in the latter years of the war. "Of all public men living to-day, there are but few whom the people of Iowa regard with equal admiration with John A. Logan," raved the *Des Moines Register*. A Democratic New York paper echoed the sentiment: "Among all the young and growing statesmen of the country there is no man who stands as high with our loyal and patriotic masses as does General Logan." Most important, Logan was in top form for Illinois audiences and editorial writers. A spellbinding speech at a packed courthouse in Cairo induced the *Egyptian Sun* to inform its readers, "We have not time now to give an analysis of his speech. But must content ourselves with saying that it was a glorious effort, worthy of the man and place." A mid-October address in Pontiac generated a similar response. The *Sentinel and Press* insisted that "never was a more thorough, candid, and eloquent defence of Republicanism heard from the lips of man."[19]

Logan's whirlwind campaign had two objectives: to win reelection to the House of Representatives in the state's at-large position, and procure endorsements from local conventions for the Senate vote in January. To win the Senate seat, his reelection bid had to be successful, but he also needed the promise of support from legislative nominees—candidates Logan felt would win their districts. His campaign strategy was so dominating that it alarmed supporters of Logan's chief Senate rival, his friend Dick Oglesby. "Logan is on the move. Look out," warned Governor Palmer to Oglesby. Independent David Davis also wanted anyone but Logan to win the seat, warning Oglesby to turn out quickly, for "Logan is canvassing." Oglesby followed the advice and stumped the state for the Senate seat, making the summer and fall of 1870 a novel one in Illinois, for Senate candidates rarely conducted campaigns so openly for the legislative vote. Newspaper editorials condemned both Republican candidates for the practice.[20]

The first objective came as predicted. Logan easily reclaimed his House seat over Democratic rival William B. Anderson. His margin of victory was less than half of what he enjoyed in his previous two runs, but his percentage of voters remained high due to lower-than-normal voter turnout. This was "Black Jack" Logan's fifth House election win in as many tries: two as a Democrat and three as a Republican. But he had no intentions of sitting in the House of Representatives for the Forty-second Congress. He yearned to take his seat at the opposite side of the rotunda—in the U.S. Senate. So dedicated was Logan to this brass ring that he abruptly left Washington in the midst of the final session of Congress. But he was there long enough to wield his chairman power to trim the navy of its top ranks as he had done to the army. Gone were the admiral and vice admiral positions after the House passed his bill.[21]

Whomever the Republicans nominated was guaranteed the Senate seat: the party controlled the Illinois General Assembly. This left the race essentially between friends Logan and Oglesby. Logan's penchant for patronage proved problematic for his rival. His docket of office holders and office seekers and his brilliance at the stump speech, combined with his clench-jawed determination, gave him a huge organizational advantage. Mary also aided her husband's campaign with an effort deemed unladylike for the Victorian era. Early in January 1871, Logan took possession of two large rooms on the ground floor of the Leland Hotel in Springfield (across from the bar). This is where the General Assembly members traditionally housed themselves for the winter session. Mary carried on his campaign in the ladies' parlor one floor above him, charming the delegates while adopted daughter, Kate, flaunted her musical talents by singing and playing the piano.

Mary Logan's efforts on her husband's behalf did not go unnoticed by his political rivals. "She is the most dangerous enemy of Gov. Oglesby," maintained a correspondent, while a liberal rival of her husband complained, "That sort of audacity deserves a square and substantial rebuke at the hands of this Legislature." When the bachelor Richard Oglesby met her on January 6, the old acquaintances exchanged pleasantries. Mary chided him for not calling on her earlier. "Well madam the fact is that I am afraid to subject myself to your blandishments," responded Oglesby. "You are making trouble here; I am afraid I might leave your presence a Logan man."[22]

To Oglesby's regret an overwhelming number of state legislators became "Logan men." The Republican caucus nominated Logan over Oglesby by a wide margin: 98 to 23 votes. Five days later, Logan basked in another election victory when the Republican-dominated General Assembly elected him U.S. senator by a 42-vote margin. A committee of seven informed Logan of the result and escorted him to the assembly. Logan delivered a short address; after the session adjourned for the day well-wishing assemblymen crowded around the speaker's stand to congratulate him. By 4:00 P.M., Logan was aboard a train, heading back to Washington.[23]

Logan spent the winter of 1871 completing a seven-year career in the House of Representatives, one that opened with the prospects of a mid-floor brawl in December 1859, and closed on March 3, 1871, with a more subdued controversy. Grant was the subtle object of Logan's criticism during the final session of the Forty-first Congress. Logan continued to be cool to Grant, while siding at times with other Republicans whose votes opposed administration policies. He spoke out on the House floor against an appropriation for a company that supplied Seneca stone (a reddish marble) for a new State Department building. Logan suspected that Grant's intimate friends benefited from the company's stock since seemingly every department in the capital was purchasing stone from the company. Bristling at what he felt was a potential scandal, Logan denounced the appropriation, which he maintained was sought chiefly to secure a contract with the company. He declared that "it would be better for the country and better for the Republican party to lay the bill on the table, and let the next Congress get up a bill which would not rob the people as this bill proposed to do." His House-floor accusations drew attention from Grant's supporters who maintained that Logan was more of a political enemy than friend of Grant. "The President has lost all confidence in him . . . when he attacked the President about Seneca stone," insisted one of Grant's informants; "I don't trust him."[24]

Logan took a rearward seat as freshman senator on March 4, 1871, the day after his marble debate in the House. He shared Illinois duties with Republican Lyman Trumbull, who was enjoying his sixteenth year in the upper house of Congress. Trumbull represented the liberal wing of the Republican Party, a faction rapidly gaining strength throughout Illinois, but yet to have a detrimental effect on party unity nationwide. Logan's position, ironically, allied more with this wing than with the Radicals. Surprised to find the junior senator more an ally than an opponent, Lyman Trumbull was pleased to inform a friend, "Logan talks and acts pretty independently."[25]

The president attributed Logan's maverick tactics to ambition, a trait that Lincoln had compared to a worm gnawing away at those who could not control their quest for something greater. With disdain Grant had observed senators such as Charles Sumner and Carl Schurz oppose him to the point where he felt they were trying to break up the Republican Party, "acting worse than any other two men." Grant felt Logan was heading in their direction in the spring of 1871. "John Logan is paving the way to be just as bad as he wants to be," Grant lamented to Elihu Washburne in May; "He is affected with that 'maggot' Mr. Lincoln used to speak of."[26]

The less-than-amicable relationship between the two former war heroes was very apparent; Trumbull noted that "there is not much love between Grant and Logan." Newspaper correspondents believed Grant's suspicion of Logan's driving ambition. A reporter for a New Orleans paper bumped into Logan in New York City during the first week of June 1871. "Among the young fellows ambitious of Presidential honors is General Logan," reported the newsman; "We know he expects to run . . . when we asked him who was his candidate he couldn't think of anybody." When given the name "Grant" as the obvious 1872 Republican candidate, Logan retorted, "Well, Grant—why, Grant has had one term in the White House . . ." As the reporter tossed up prominent names—Salmon P. Chase, Roscoe Conkling, Reuben Fenton, Charles Sumner, James Blaine, Ben Butler, and several others—Logan shot them all down with very short, unflattering assessments. Sumner was "too old"; Conkling was "too d— peacocky"; Fenton was too "oily"; and so on. The reporter concluded that Logan's inability to think of one man to run as the Republican presidential candidate in 1872 meant that by the process of elimination he was endorsing himself. His report was excerpted in big and small newspapers throughout the states.[27]

Logan never seemed concerned about his name-dropping and on-the-record criticisms of men he saw and worked with day to day. He was always a polarizing figure, dating back to the years before the war. His political transformation pulled his neighbors into camps of adoration and condemnation. On his return to his Carbondale home in the last week of June 1871, the supporters trumped the detractors by lauding him with praise. "That Senator Logan is the most popular man in the State of Illinois has been several times abundantly proved," crowed the editor of the *Carbondale New Era*. "We are proud to add that he is a citizen of Carbondale, and does not have to go away from home for his popularity . . . we also love and honor him as a fellow-citizen, a neighbor to every one in trouble, a friend of our city and all that tends to advance its interests." The editorial opinion was consistent; one week earlier the *New Era* endorsed him for president.[28]

If Logan read the words of praise in the July 1 issue of the paper, he likely did so with some discomfort. Carbondale soon learned the reason. He decided the sparse communities in his lifelong home of Southern Illinois no longer suited his future interests in politics. For several years Logan had owned property in

Chicago, on the west side of the city. He moved his family there over the late summer months. "Carbondale is in tears," gleefully reported a Democratic paper in Marion upon hearing the news that Logan "has deserted" his home. The editor surmised, "Limited poker games and unlimited Puritanism did the job."[29]

Their goods trained up to Chicago in August and by September the Logan family followed their belongings to the burgeoning city and their 300,000 new neighbors. The home sat north of the Twenty-second Street Lake Shore depot, in the middle of the Calumet Avenue block. The house fronted westward toward the Illinois Central Railroad and away from Lake Michigan, with other houses north and south of it. Broad lawns without fencing were characteristic of the neighborhood. Mary called it "a most beautiful location."

Nothing she saw early in the second week of October could be called beautiful. The Great Chicago Fire devastated the region barely one month after the Logans had settled in. The house and immediate neighborhood were spared, but the buildings ten blocks northwest of them were swallowed by flames. Some 2,600 acres of Chicago real estate were destroyed. Logan had seen cities burn during the war and well understood the devastation fire wrought. Still, the immediate effect came as a huge surprise to him. "The people were mad with fright," he reported, struggling to provide a comparison to what he saw in 1864. "I have been amid the battle-roar where armies a hundred thousand strong were struggling in fierce conflict for victory; where the smoke of the combat rose in heavy clouds above us; where the dead and dying lay thick on every side," he said three months after the Great Chicago Fire; "but never yet have I beheld such a scene of despair and wild confusion as this; and may God grant that I shall never see the like again!"[30]

The Logan home for the next two weeks housed both refugees and dignitaries. Mary estimated a hundred people occupied her home intermittently during that time—including Phil Sheridan. The diminutive, fiery Civil War general and Chicago native worked with Logan to maintain order and lead a new army of volunteers to try to ease the aftermath of those affected by the fire. The scenes of pathos touched Logan deeply. He recalled those scenes on January 16, 1872, and delivered a memorable firsthand account of his observations to the Senate in a successful effort for federal aid for the relief of Chicago. He painted a vivid portrait of the fire, followed by a tally of the destruction: 20,000 houses destroyed, 110,000 new homeless citizens, $200 million of personal and public loss. Overcome by the catastrophe, Logan begged, "Behold the spectacle! Can anyone, having witnessed this sad scene, do less than plead for the ruined city?"[31]

Logan matched his new home in Illinois with another new home in Washington. He had a somewhat nomadic existence in the capital, biding his time in

Brown's and Willard's Hotels throughout most of his congressional career. As a senator, he chose to rent homes to accommodate his family and himself. The first was a brownstone within close walking distance to the White House. This was followed by a move to Grant Place, into the home occupied by the brother and sister-in-law of Ferdinand V. Hayden, the explorer who had named Logan's Peak for the senator. There Logan stayed throughout 1872, likely fed information about the progress of the geographical survey underway in the territories, one in which Logan's own brother-in-law, Cyrus Thomas, had been participating. William B. Logan, a young distant cousin, also had been with the team as a secretary.

Logan had appointed those family members to Hayden's team without complaints from the explorer. Logan was arguably Hayden's most effective supporter when the survey was created in the late 1860s. The success of the exploration could create a windfall for Chicago, whose interests Logan represented, to tap into the resources via railroads running westward out of the city. Hayden conducted a thorough exploration of the upper waters of the Yellowstone River. His ambitious survey—the first scientific and photographic exploration of the Yellowstone basin and its unique geyser activity—aided Congress to pass the bill creating Yellowstone National Park. Grant signed the bill on March 1, 1872.[32]

The election season of 1872 rolled in with the Republican Party divided as never before. The Liberal Republican Party movement ran in full swing, particularly in Illinois where prominent members of Grant's party considered challenging him as the presidential nominee. Governor Palmer and Senator Trumbull had been successfully wooed by the Liberal movement. They held their own convention and chose newspaper editor Horace Greeley as their presidential candidate. The Democrats also backed the Republican newsman in their convention, a nomination borne more out of a desire to unseat Grant than to endorse Greeley. Logan did not attend the Liberal Republican convention, nor did he show any overt interest in joining their ranks, but his indifference to Grant's people and his unwillingness to criticize the movement rankled the president's most ardent supporters. In March his lack of support for Grant continued to upset the administration. "Gen. Logan has missed a splendid chance to make himself the leading man in Illinois, and has thrown it away," declared one of Grant's men, peeved that Logan "has allowed himself to be classed among his enemies without any particular denial."[33]

The routine was all too similar to his "silent spring" of 1861 when Logan was characterized as a secessionist for not speaking out when everyone looked his way. Eleven years later he still was plagued with a tin ear to the chorus of criticism that crescendoed around him. He appeared to patiently bide his time to gauge the support the new wing of the party had garnered. An unabashed opportunist, Logan had chosen not to criticize the reformers in the Liberal Republican movement throughout the winter and spring season. In 1861 he had burst out in dramatic fashion in front of Grant's regiment in Springfield. Logan could not repeat that drama in 1872 but he chose a more publicized and sustained forum to espouse his positions and side either with the Grant administration or with the Liberal Republicans.

He wisely chose Grant. Senator Charles Sumner, perhaps the most outspoken of the Liberals, denounced the president in a late-May speech that reiterated much of the Liberal platform. On June 3 Logan jumped to Grant's defense with a Senate-floor speech that hailed him for winning the war and effectively running the country. Logan pledged his support and proved that they were not idle promises. He stumped for the president as only he could, a canvass through seven states in the summer and autumn of 1872. A featured speaker at Republican mass meetings throughout the state of Illinois, Logan's crowds approached 20,000. He lectured several times a week that autumn with a mission: the reform advocates of the Liberal Republican faction would not get a toehold to support their cause. Grant's orators spanned the country that October to sing his praises. Logan proved to be the most adept and tireless performer of them all.[34]

Considering the bitterness of the campaign, Grant enjoyed an easy victory when he was reelected for a second term in November. Illinois gave Grant a 50,000-vote majority and seamlessly purged itself of the short-lived Liberal movement. Governor Palmer and Senator Trumbull became casualties for their alliance with this faction, the latter replaced by Dick Oglesby who reaped the reward of a large Republican majority in the Illinois General Assembly to return to the U. S. Senate after Logan deposed him two years earlier. As disappointed as Palmer and Trumbull must have been for the ill-fated decision to join the Liberals, other prominent members of the movement suffered the ultimate cost. Horace Greeley died a few weeks after the election. Charles Sumner's strength was sapped and he dwindled away to his death. The Liberal Republican movement died with them at the age of two years.[35]

Logan was back in Grant's good graces, but his hard work for his former commanding officer kept him active and away from his family. Mary claimed that the first third of his Senate term was conducted with no rest. Logan's activity could have kept him from despairing at the tragedy and ill fortune he and his family had suffered over the past five years. The death of Mary's mother was followed by that of Bill Logan. The young lawyer who followed closely in his famous brother's footsteps from law school into the Illinois General Assembly died unexpectedly from rheumatic fever in 1868. Equally surprising for the Logans was the news of Hybert Cunningham's death in July 1871. They also lost Logan's cousin and adopted daughter, Kate, eight months later from peritonitis.[36]

Tragedy intensified five days after Grant's inauguration when a telegram arrived announcing the death of Captain John M. Cunningham in Utah. Mary's father had suffered from alcoholism for years; his conflicting loyalties during the Civil War intensified his dependence on the bottle. He had remarried shortly after the death of his first wife and accepted a position as an assessor for the Internal Revenue Bureau in Provo, Utah. But his last months were unpleasant ones, wracked by the fatal effects of meningitis. Logan was tied up with his Senate duties, leaving Mary to ride the Union Pacific Railroad westward to retrieve his body. Captain Cunningham was interred with his wife in Marion.[37]

Logan had distanced himself from his birth family, in part due to longstanding friction that dated back to the summer of 1861 when he had dramatically declared his support for the Union. By 1873 he had an older half-sister and merely three surviving siblings out of an original ten; the oldest ones continued to lead colorful lives. Tom Logan's crass behavior and drinking habits were the most likely suspects for the problems with his second wife, Elvira Willis Logan. Tom escorted Elvira to a dance where too much alcohol was available to him. He got drunk and humiliated her when he lifted her skirts above her knees and made bawdy remarks to the men surrounding them. Elvira had exceeded her breaking point; she sued for divorce and won, remaining in Murphysboro as a constant reminder of his failures. Undaunted, Tom married for the third time in 1873.[38]

Annie Logan also was on her third spouse in 1873. Her first two husbands died; most recently, Israel Blanchard passed on in 1871. His tremendous bar debt revealed a troubled man who stole away from home life as much as possible. Annie had continued her reputation in town as a colorful, temperamental, and unstable woman. Uninhibited, she could loose a volley of curses with minimal provocation and had no qualms about exhibiting tasteless reactions to issues with which she disagreed. Logan saw this firsthand when Annie tried to shout him down during his speeches. One year shy of her fortieth birthday in 1873, Annie Logan Skinner was not aging well, but her spirit remained lively and unpredictable.[39]

After nearly ten years of enduring a ruptured relationship with his mother, Logan made amends with her. Elizabeth Logan had likely contributed the genes to supply some of her daughter's behavior patterns. A devout Methodist and an unreconstructed rebel, Mother Logan helped establish a branch of the controversial Southern Methodist Church in Murphysboro. Having survived the death of her husband and six of her nine children, and perhaps sensing her own approaching mortality, she warmed to her oldest son and allowed him back into her life. Logan teamed up with his brother and decided the oversized Logan House was not suitable for their mother to live out her remaining years. They selected a large lot near the family cemetery and had a smaller and more comfortable house built there and moved her in. Mother Logan no longer refused her son entrance into her home when he came into town for a visit. But the newfound relationship between mother and son never had a chance to blossom; Elizabeth Logan passed away one year later.[40]

Logan's rejuvenated faith may have precipitated his efforts to reconcile with his family. He joined the Trinity M. E. Church in Chicago shortly after moving his family there. They were active participants when in Chicago, frequently donating to the church's benevolent causes, but Logan spent little of his time in Chicago. Instead, he rented several rooms from the Strathmore Arms on Twelfth Street in Washington, a string of three boardinghouses in the Northwest sector of town run by a Mrs. Rhines and subsequently, Mary Lockwood. Logan lived there longer than any other home he owned or rented since moving from his birth home twenty-five years earlier.[41]

The unexpected deaths within his family overshadowed his own health. Logan was normally too robust to be categorized as sickly. He played as hard as he worked, priding himself on his strength and endurance. He worked out frequently with Professor Collins, a former professional fighter who taught self-defense boxing in his post-fight career. His clients included the elite of Washington, including members of the House and Senate. Logan and Collins sparred often in the rooms where Logan boarded. Collins considered Logan "the best two-handed man I ever saw in my life, amateur or professional." Logan's rough-and-tumble youth imbued him with skills he carried for a lifetime. "I never saw his like," raved Collins, pulling no punches to rate Logan as "powerful, and a hard and quick hitter."

The fighter had good reason to marvel at his student. One day they worked out in a spare room at Strathmore Arms where they boxed with laced gloves. Senator Oglesby was the lone spectator; he was treated to quite a show. Three rounds of boxing left both trainer and student winded, but they went on. Collins began to best Logan in the fourth round with telling punches, but the senator avoided his trainer's strongest blows. Growing too impatient, Collins rushed Logan, who nailed him with an uppercut, striking him perfectly under the chin. The punch sent Collins up and over a large arm chair behind him. Dazed and a bit embarrassed, Collins came back with a vengeance. A flurry of punches followed, each man trading blows with the other. Oglesby tried to stop it, but failed. Both men punched themselves out. Logan entered the Senate that day with two blackened eyes, earning the permanent respect from his teacher, who confirmed the claim of another senator that Logan could turn a handspring with ease. Collins called Logan "the best man in every respect that I ever saw, and that means a good deal when you are speaking of fighting."[42]

Logan found himself fighting off illnesses on too many occasions. Severe colds and lung ailments oftentimes kept him from speaking engagements, but it was the flareup of his "Donelson Pet" that affected him most severely. His rheumatism was dormant for several years after the war, but from his early forties onward, hardly a year went by when Logan was not laid up with the joint pain, swelling, and fever that he could trace as far back to the time in 1849 when he was struck down returning from the mission to retrieve stolen horses in Missouri. But it was those cold nights in front of Fort Donelson in February 1862 that Logan considered the real cause of his lingering rheumatism.

He was hit particularly hard in January 1875, a bout of rheumatism that locked him within Strathmore Arms for several days. He made good use of his time by writing a play. He entitled it "The Narrow Escape." Once his health improved he performed the theatrics within the boardinghouse, he himself taking on the role of the main character. Logan enjoyed writing the play and having it acted out as he wrote it. He produced a second one shortly after, appropriately titled, "The Boarding House."[43]

Logan's financial health had become worse than his physical health. In 1870 he could claim a strong estate valued at $80,000 with $3,000 cash on hand; the financial Panic of 1873 was just one of several factors that cut into that wealth to the extent that he felt destitute. He sold off land that he owned in Southern Illinois, but that money did not last. Logan's lifestyle was not extravagant; however, he clearly had lived beyond his means. Not surprisingly, he labored to increase those means. He was an outspoken proponent of the "Salary Grab," a bill debated by both bodies of Congress to raise their annual salaries from $5,000 to $7,500. That House and Senate salaries had not budged since 1853 mattered not at all to the public, who contrasted their own financial woes to Congress and hated the comparison. Making matters worse was the attempt to make the bill retroactive two years—and to provide the $5,000 in one lump-sum payment. The bill failed.[44]

Logan was tainted by other scandals during Grant's second term. Back in 1868 Logan had purchased ten shares of railroad stock for $1,000 from fellow congressman Oakes Ames. The stock was in Credit Mobilier, a limited liability finance company organized to pay the construction costs of the Union Pacific

Railroad. The railroad company itself had been unable to make a profit on the road, but large stockholders in Credit Mobilier made a large profit on the resale of the stock. The company also sold its stocks and bonds without restriction or oversight. A New York newspaper broke the scandal in 1873. It was an ugly spectacle for the public to see Congress attempt to raise its own annual salary by 50 percent while also profiting from stocks sold by a House member to a company that profited on a railroad line that Congress restricted from similar profits. Through an internal investigation, the House censured Ames for his involvement, and also investigated the dozens of congressmen who purchased stock from him. Logan was fortunate to have the good sense to not cover up his involvement. In doing so, the investigation found that he purchased the stock, but he returned the $329 dividend check—including $2 of interest—to end the transaction before the scandal broke. But a stain still existed on his reputation and Logan was out $1,000 for his involvement.[45]

The Whisky Ring Scandal of 1875 also coated Logan with unflattering colors. In an inventive attempt to avoid taxation, distillers and bottlers bribed revenue agents to look the other way when the bribers falsely measured their product, or to give them more stamp taxes than what they actually paid for. Two hundred suspects were arrested in Chicago, Milwaukee, and Illinois. An estimated $4 million was lost in liquor taxes from the fraud. Since the suspicion existed that politicians were tied in with the tax evasion, nearly every one of influence hailing from Illinois and neighboring states was investigated. This included Logan, but no evidence could be pinned to him for indictment.[46]

Logan's attempt to stop his financial bleeding led to more headline scandals at the same time as the Whisky Ring. Perhaps through his association with Ferdinand V. Hayden, Logan took an interest in Colorado, specifically the silver mines. He parlayed the proceeds from land sales near Chicago into a partial share of a mine near Georgetown, Colorado. He made two trips to the site of his investment. It turned out to be a poor choice for a business venture. Another mining company next to the one in which Logan owned shares claimed the rights to the same silver vein, leading to a heated dispute. The feud birthed endless court hearings while polarizing the mining community into partisan camps. Ambushes and murders followed. When the manager of Logan's mine met an early death in 1875, the mine was sold in a sheriff's sale. Logan's investment was a disaster.[47]

And it got worse from there. In December 1875, The *New York Sun*, the same paper that broke the Credit Mobilier scandal, began publishing sensational reports implicating Logan—without evidence—in trying to break up the neighboring mining company, which had the legal right to the silver vein, by ousting the U. S. judge assigned to the territory. The *Sun* relished any chance to take down Logan. That same month they brewed a story that he took a bribe from a pension agent in Chicago to advance his political machine. Their accusations filtered into anti-Logan newspapers throughout the North and South.[48]

The Whisky Ring, Colorado mine, and Chicago pension agent scandals all hit the papers in December. Earlier Logan was able to whisk away the Credit Mobilier scandal before it stuck to him, but the successive blows were more difficult to fend off. Making matters worse was the incredibly bad timing of his most recent attack of rheumatism, one which knocked him off his feet at the end of November. It struck him so hard that by December 1 he lay prostrate in the Palmer Hotel in Chicago. The *New York Times* called his condition "precarious" and "critical." Consumed by pain, joint swelling, and fevers, Logan lingered near death. He rallied and relapsed, then rallied again; by the second week of December his physicians no longer worried that he would die, but the two weeks Logan's voice and pen were muted proved disastrous. The scandals festered into the Christmas season, although his allies helped counter the false accusations. In addition, the Chicago pension agent wrote him a letter that absolved him of all wrongdoing in the blackmail charge. Logan published the letter in the *New York Times* at the end of December as his exoneration. He was successful; but the necessarily delayed response allowed the scandals to drip like water torture into the early weeks of 1876—Logan's reelection year.[49]

A new political upheaval was underway in Illinois, threatening Logan's chances to reclaim his Senate seat. The Republican Party ruled Illinois for ten years, but the strength of their control dwindled with each election of the 1870s. After the death of the Liberal Republican movement in 1872, a farmer's party sprouted up preaching antimonopoly values. They offered no serious challenge to the Republicans and Democrats, but they did generate 75,580 votes in Illinois for their treasurer candidate in 1874. Their supporters fused with other disenchanted citizens to form the Greenback Party in 1876, named for the paper money that drove farmers and laborers to vote during the country's centennial. Since 1866 the treasurer slowly retired greenbacks in favor of long-timer bonds to counter the depreciated paper money. The western and eastern sides of the country differed in their opinion on this issue. The East, a creditor portion of the country, favored the return of gold to pay off the war debts. The West—including the states from Ohio, Kentucky, and Tennessee westward—boomed as a debtor segment of the country. Their debt, which largely represented farm improvements, accumulated in the depreciated greenbacks that increased in work demand value as they left the market. The boom abated by 1874 and the Western states clamored for inflation to ease their difficulties, made more severe by the depression set off by the Panic of 1873. After Grant vetoed an inflation bill that would have benefited the Western economy, Illinois citizens could draw a clear distinction between Eastern and Western interests. The result was a new party, with a very narrow platform. The "Greenbackers" merged with the antimonopoly (or farmer's) party to form a new Independent Party. They held a convention in Decatur in February of 1876, calling for repeal of the National Bank acts and the substitution of paper money for the gold payments currently favored by the East. They chose Lewis Steward as their gubernatorial candidate.[50]

The new party made Illinois Republicans and Democrats nervous, for their respective parties would split on the greenback issue. Although the Greenbackers had little national strength, they could certainly affect the state legislature in 1876, the body that would elect the U.S. senator in January 1877. Logan declared his desire to continue his Senate term, but was also considered presidential timber by enthusiastic supporters at the state Republican convention in Springfield, held in May. The delegates sent to the national convention were charged with the duty to nominate James Blaine, the senator from Maine. Three weeks later, in Cincinnati, the Republican delegates nationwide chose former Ohio governor Rutherford B. Hayes. The Democrats countered with New York Governor Samuel Tilden, a former district attorney credited with sending the corrupt Boss William Tweed to jail. Although never a Civil War soldier like Hayes, Tilden fit the Democratic platform for civil service reform, the end of Reconstruction, and the installation of "honest men" in government.

Logan made sure his Illinois power base was up and running to fuel his own Senate bid by influencing the legislature results. Not only did he have prominent state citizens to drive his machine, he continued to court the press. The *Chicago Tribune* was not as reliably for Logan as they had been in most postwar elections; it had thrown its support to the Liberal Republican movement in the early 1870s. The *Chicago Times* was vitriolic. They continued to link Logan with the prominent scandals of the past three years; they also fell back on an old tactic by revisiting Logan in the months prior to the war. To counter, Logan had the *Chicago Inter-Ocean* on his side, as well as the *Illinois State Journal* in Springfield.

Logan also employed the Grand Army of the Republic. It had been five years since Logan headed the organization and when he departed as commander, his zeal waned so much that he let his membership lapse. But Logan's renewed enthusiasm coincided with a reawakening of the G.A.R. as a political powerhouse. Logan was their hero once more, stemming from his crusade for the cash-bounty equalization bill, a measure that granted each veteran eight and one-third dollars for each month of service. He promised his vacillating colleagues that he would introduce the bill every morning in Congress until it was taken up in session. Most knew Logan well enough to know this was no idle threat. He hammered the bill through the Senate, where it slipped through by one vote.

Critics condemned Logan for using the measure as a bribe to buy the soldiers vote with a bill that—if signed into law—would cost $30 million. Logan noted that this was a campaign promise from 1872's Republican Party platform. But Grant blocked it with the power of his veto. Logan countered with a slightly different version of the bounty bill, but he failed to get it through the Senate. Exasperated, he lashed out at Grant as the source of the problem, deriding his veto as "the d——dest worst thing" that could have happened to the party.[51]

The first session of the Forty-fourth Congress ended in the middle of August. Its close signaled the start of the election campaign of 1876. Logan had campaigned for Hayes for Ohio governor in 1867, and although he was not as enthusiastically for him for president as he had been for Grant in 1872, Logan campaigned long and hard. As he did for Grant four years earlier, Logan stumped several states. Like a snowball rolling down a hill, he generated power with each successive speech. He returned to his 1860s style, and waved the bloody shirt to contrast Hayes's military career as a Civil War colonel and general with Tilden's civilian one.

Republicans assailed the Tilden campaign with a common theme that "not every Democrat was a Rebel, but every Rebel was a Democrat." Exploiting this notion, they smeared Tilden with unfounded and sometimes ludicrous rumors that he praised slavery, evaded taxes, and planned to pay off Confederate debt when elected president. Existing as a Democrat was enough for Republicans in this election. One stump speech exhibited the pure bloody-shirt rhetoric: "Every man that endeavored to tear the old flag from the heavens that it enriches was a Democrat. Every man that tried to destroy this nation was a Democrat. . . . The man that assassinated Abraham Lincoln was a Democrat. . . . Soldiers, every scar you have on your heroic bodies was given you by a Democrat!"[52]

Logan was in his element with this style of campaigning. He took pride in unfolding his bloody shirt and waving it furiously wherever he appeared. At the Indianapolis soldiers' convention, Logan assailed the Southerners as he had done during the war. He exhorted his audience to prevent the rebel hordes from destroying the nation. Only when the South proved it was finished with treason and murder, shrieked Logan, would the Union veterans "shake hands across the bloody chasm."[53]

November rolled in, and with it a national political crisis. The presidential vote tallies were so close that both sides claimed victory. Democrat Tilden won the popular vote, but Republican Hayes claimed he won the electoral college, the actual decider of this contest. Tilden claimed the same. Three states' returns were in question: Louisiana, South Carolina, and Florida. Early in December their respective electors met in their respective state capitals to cast their ballots, but the Democrats split from the Republicans in each state. The result was two sets of returns sent to Washington from each of the contested states. Without these states, neither candidate carried the minimal 185 electoral votes necessary to claim the White House.

Back in Washington, Logan had an active hand in attempting to handle the election dispute. The Senate formed a committee—four Republicans and three Democrats—with the specific function of handling the electoral vote count. Logan was appointed one of the seven committee members. The committee could not settle the issue before Logan was forced to head back to Illinois with a Republican replacement on the panel. The dispute would not be resolved until the winter of 1877.[54]

As dramatic as the indecisive presidential vote had been, Logan was much more concerned about the Illinois election. He had good reason to be. Republicans would dominate the General Assembly again, but their margin was trimmed by the presence of the greenbackers of the Independent party. Of the 204 available Illinois House and Senate seats, Republicans seized 100 of them after the election, Democrats had 89, and the Independents held 15. Logan needed a majority total of 103 votes when the Thirtieth Illinois General Assembly convened on January 3, 1877. If Logan secured all the Republican votes in caucus, it would be a struggle for him to find three more from parties dedicated to not returning him to the U.S. Senate.

He tried to repeat the ingredients of success from 1871. He again rented out receiving rooms in the Leland Hotel in Springfield, and Mary occupied one of the parlors. She kept an open house, greeting and charming her guests with her daughter, still called "Dollie," at her side. Intelligent and attractive, eighteen-year-old Dollie had been considered "a fair favorite of fortune and society" in Washington. Her job was to continue the same role in the state capital as she enjoyed in the nation's capital. But the charms of the Logan women would have little influence on the legislative vote to choose the U.S. senator. The Independents who held the deciding votes quartered in a neighboring hotel and did not visit the Leland, the hotel traditionally occupied by the Democrats and Republicans. The latter caucused and chose Logan as their candidate to the surprise of no one. The Democrats chose former Liberal Republican John M. Palmer as the man to unseat him. William B. Anderson emerged as the choice for the Independents.[55]

Logan's record in the Senate included aspects that appealed to the green-backers in the Independent party. He supported inflationary measurers to counter the economic depression precipitated by the Panic of 1873. This included the production of an additional $46 million for circulation back in 1874, a bill passed through Congress but vetoed by Grant. So dedicated was Logan to their cause, that he formed an alliance with two other senators called "The Paper Money Trinity." But all the various scandals he had endured—his silver interests, the salary grab, Credit Mobilier, the Whiskey Ring—overshadowed the green-back support. Even his lack of finesse with the English language was made an issue. Political cartoonists mocked him with caricatures, and linked him with the worse of the power hungry, big-spending politicians. Mary deplored the ganging-up tactics used against her husband; she insisted that "General Logan had been sacrificed to the stupendous scheme of political demagogues."[56]

The Independents refused to budge for Logan. Ballot after ballot was taken in the legislature beginning on January 16, and Logan could not cross the threshold. At one time he received 100 votes—just three shy of the necessary margin for election. Newspaper reporters and editors watched the drama unfold with great relish as the pro- and anti-Logan forces spun each ballot for their own purposes. But Logan's support began to wane, first with the *Chicago Tribune*, followed by other newspapers. The Democrats replaced their candidate with David Davis, who had been serving in the judiciary as a U.S. Supreme Court justice. The bold measure sealed Logan's fate. The Republicans caucused on January 23 and did something Logan had refused to do—withdraw his name from contention and replace him with another. Finally, on the fortieth ballot drawn on January 25, 1877, Judge Davis received enough votes. He agreed to leave the bench and replace Logan as U.S. senator from Illinois.[57]

Logan's enemies in the press rejoiced at his political demise, not even attempting to conceal their contempt. The *Illinois State Register* hailed the result as "one of the grandest political successes ever accomplished in this state." Another Illinois paper claimed that the election result was hailed throughout the country "by all classes of people, except one class. The Illinois ring of national office-holders don't like it. And the dirty little politicians who want a senator who will get them appointed to some fat office don't like it either." Outside the state, Logan's enemies in the presses also rejoiced. The *Portsmouth* [Ohio] *Democrat* predicted sunnier days ahead for the Senate: "Gradually, a better class of statesmen are assuming the ascendancy in that august body and the Logans and 'bloody shirt' orators are marching to the rear." A small-town Missouri paper crowed in its headline, "Logan is Left! . . . Three Cheers for the Illinois Legislature. . . . Good-bye, John." Their delight carried into the following day's paper. "The retirement of the meanest Radical demagogue in the U. S. Senate, is a great Democratic victory," raved their editorial, "and let us hope auspicious of the new time coming in the immediate future when Democrats and honest Republicans shall run this country . . ."[58]

The conclusion of the Illinois Senate race resolved the presidential contested election between Rutherford B. Hayes and Samuel Tilden. Judge Davis had been sitting as one of fifteen members of a selected electoral commission to decide which set of electoral returns would be accepted from each of the three states that submitted them. When Independent Davis left the bench as a new U.S. senator, he was replaced by Judge Joseph Bradley, a rock-solid Republican. All three contested states went to Hayes by one-vote margins from the commission, giving the Ohioan the presidency over Tilden with an electoral college vote tally of 185 to 184.[59]

Logan returned to Washington to complete his final mission as a national legislator, his lame-duck session of Congress. His friends tried to get President-elect Hayes to put Logan on his cabinet as secretary of war, but to no avail. "Hayes has sold us all out," wrote Logan to his wife in March, "and the base ingratitude shown by Hayes to those that elected him has disgusted all people here."[60]

Ten consecutive years in the House and Senate were winding to a close. For the first time in his recent memory, Logan was unsure of his future, but he was sure it was one that had financial hardship in store. Many of his Senate colleagues sympathized with him—even some of them across the aisle, but many others reveled in Logan's political demise. Perhaps none of his political enemies delighted more in his loss than did a Democrat from Tennessee who took his seat as a first-term senator back in 1874. He had good reason to glower at Logan; Logan had made it his mission to end his career. The Tennessean was former President Andrew Johnson.

Logan completed his term early in March. He stepped out of the Senate chamber, exited the Capitol, descended Capitol Hill and entered an unknown future. Logan thrived on battlefields during the Civil War and on the House and Senate floor afterwards. He had lived this way for sixteen consecutive years. The spring of 1877 was his first one since the 1850s without a political battle to wage against an opponent. Outgoing President Grant looked forward to his retirement, but he knew Logan would be ill at ease in the same role. Grant had provided the most telling assessment of the paradox affecting the deposed senator from Illinois:

"Logan is never at peace, except in war."[61]

CHAPTER TEN

Rise of a Candidate

AFTER LEAVING THE SENATE in March 1877, Logan endured the toughest months of his civilian life. Fifty-one years old and wholly unprepared to pursue a private-sector career, he found himself without a job or even the prospect of an elected position for the first time in twenty-five years. He alluded to Mary that he might give up politics altogether but he never strove away from it, writing letters and making speeches whenever the door was open to do so.

What made the period most uncomfortable for Logan was his dwindling wealth. He never considered himself a rich man, even though he enjoyed a far better lifestyle that most Americans. But the spring of 1877 revealed Logan in a more desperate financial state than ever before. Back home in Chicago, he was forced to sell off property to liquidate some of his assets. At one point he was forced to borrow money to pay off a $40 debt. Mortified at the prospect of displaying his helplessness to his old neighbors, Logan consented to his wife's request to travel to Carbondale without him to sell off some of his property there.

"I am poor," he confessed to a Washington confidant in May. Still, he turned down offers made to him. President Hayes—who Logan despised—kept an ambassadorship to Brazil open for him. Logan refused it, claiming he could not afford to go abroad, but the turn-down was consistent with other refusals for foreign appointments, such as Mexico and Spain in years past. A collectorship in Chicago was also open. Talk persisted that Logan should be given the lucrative offer, one opposed by many who believed his "salary grab" proclivities opened the door to criticism and ridicule. Logan blocked the door himself, showing no overt interest in the position while recommending it for others. When a friend suggested returning to the practice of law, Logan told him that the sixteen-year hiatus was too long for him to get back into court work. "He feels badly," wrote the advisor after the early-June conversation; "says he sits all day at home and reads to keep his mind from distraction."[1]

Logan attempted to pull himself out of his doldrums by heading West with his daughter for a trip to Denver in late June. She eventually trained back to Chicago while he remained there. He spent the summer in the Rockies, looking for a get-rich-quick strike in silver. His mining interest replaced poker as a mode of testing his financial luck; he merely found such fortune wanting. He returned to Washington in October no better off than before. Ironically, Mary had expected them to spend more time together once Logan left politics. This turned out not to be the case during the middle months of 1877; she had been separated from him as much during this time than they ever had been in his congressional career.[2]

Logan finally came home to her. The family united at the Calumet Avenue house in Chicago. On November 27, 1877, John and Mary Logan marked the twenty-second anniversary of their marriage by hosting the wedding of their daughter to William F. Tucker. A Methodist minister conducted the ceremony in the house decorated with flowers and brilliant lights, the air made pleasant by soft music and sweet fragrances. The newlyweds stayed in the Chicago home immediately afterward. Twelve-year-old Manning Logan returned to the Morgan Park Military Academy where he had been receiving his education. John and Mary Logan returned to their Washington boardinghouse. With an impatience bordering on desperation, Logan resumed his profession as an attorney, taking on a few lucrative cases into the winter of 1878. His passion for the law, however, had waned considerably from the 1850s circuit duty days. Instead, Logan—and his wife—found themselves addicted to the Washington social scene. Warmly greeted at White House receptions and other functions that winter, Mary and First Lady Lucy Hayes struck up a warm friendship, one antithetical to the cold and forced pleasantries exchanged between their husbands. Reporters remarked on the Logan couple's physical appeal, from the "ripened beauty" of thirty-nine-year-old Mary to the striking features of her fifty-two-year-old husband, whose "Indian black hair and his black shiny mustache—not a mere mustache, but one of the kind switched down on his side cheek—prove him to be a handsome man."[3]

"We have passed through a fiery furnace and can begin life together on the bottom round," wrote Mary to her newlywed daughter that winter, anticipating a close to their financial woes. Logan's law work brought in an income he had not enjoyed for nearly a year, but the blandishments of the nation's capital could not divorce him from his desire to stay politically active. Rumors found their way into print by springtime, suggesting that Logan planned to run for State Treasurer of Illinois "with a view of his subsequent election to the Senate," but Logan denied "having knowledge of any such project." He chose his words carefully, for the rumor suggested reclaiming the seat he lost when it became available again in January 1883. Part of the rumor was true; he did want the Senate seat, but not in 1883. He was looking to the Richard Oglesby seat expiring in seven months.[4]

Yet Oglesby wanted a second term in the U.S. Senate. Although he and Logan had been friends and allies, Oglesby had feared Logan's ambition from the moment "Black Jack" had lost his seat to David Davis. He had lost a Senate race to Logan in 1871 and well realized Logan's ability to have his political machine up and running if he chose to run again. Oglesby had tried to land Logan a cabinet position in the Hayes Administration—to quell Logan's ambition and remove the threat to his own reelection. Illinois had not boasted a Republican bicameral General Assembly since 1872, when the revolt within the state party broke it into weaker factions. The election of 1878 saw the presence of four parties in Illinois, with Greenbackers and Prohibitionists added to the Republican and Democrat fight. Logan and Oglesby had an uphill climb to be the Republican senator from Illinois in 1879; they had to enjoy a Republican Illinois legislature if their battle against each other had any meaning.[5]

During the summer of 1878 Logan returned to Illinois, stumping the region and testing the waters to gauge his chances of winning back his lost seat. He was present at the Illinois State Republican Convention on June 26; so was Oglesby. Both men made speeches to the 500 delegates gathered in Springfield that day, but the convention endorsed no one. Logan then made waves statewide and nationally with a rousing Fourth of July speech at an unveiling of a monument to the patriotic Union dead in Aledo, a speech printed in papers from Illinois to New York. Less than three weeks later he addressed a crowd of 20,000 at an Ohio soldiers' and sailors' reunion in Newark. Three weeks after that he and Oglesby were part of a slate of speakers in Mount Vernon, at an Illinois soldiers' reunion. Logan reunited there with his former friend and legislator, William H. Snyder, a district judge in the state. General William T. Sherman was also there. Logan and Sherman's relationship had cooled from Logan's success at enforcing budget cuts in the U.S. Army, and Sherman's unkind remarks about Logan in his memoirs, published three years earlier.[6]

The soldiers' reunions essentially launched the campaign. Logan immediately came under scrutiny; his past association with scandals, his favored policy of patronage, and even the well-worn claim of 1861 secession activities were dusted off and republished as new reports. This did little to slow down his campaign. He honeycombed the state again, as he had done in 1871. But unlike the latter campaign, where Logan could claim he was running for congressman-at-large, he campaigned in 1878 for the specific goal of creating a Republican-dominated General Assembly in an off-year election. Oglesby matched him—or at least attempted to—throughout the autumn. Logan campaigned nearly every day except Sunday, keeping his stump speeches within Illinois borders, unlike years past where he entered neighboring states to deliver his messages. He either addressed soldiers' groups or Republican mass meetings. On October 25 he spoke at Delevan, Saturday the twenty-sixth he spoke at Charleston, Monday the twenty-ninth he excited a large crowd at Rossville, repeating that performance a day later at Watseka. Logan closed his campaign in Chicago on November 1, speaking at a meeting where Oglesby also attended.[7]

The heavy canvass of Illinois helped produce the desired result. Republicans seized majorities in both the house and senate of the Illinois General Assembly. Unless the lesser parties were successfully able to unite with the Democrats the next U.S. senator was likely to be Logan or Oglesby. From the election onward, Logan held the advantage, much as he had done eight years before. Oglesby was popular and less polarizing than Logan, but "Black Jack" had tremendous support, particularly from the G.A.R. Both candidates courted and relied upon newspaper support. Oglesby received strong endorsements from the *Chicago Tribune*—this paper complained that Logan was "the embodiment of the worst phase of machine politics"—and the *Illinois State Register*, but Logan had the *Illinois State Journal*, the *Chicago Inter-Ocean*, and several other newspapers supporting his candidacy.

He also had Mary. She proved a thorn in Oglesby's side as she had been in January 1871. Appearing heavier than she did six years earlier, her formerly dark mane white as flour (attributed to the trauma of her father's death), she established her receiving parlor at the Leland Hotel. There she courted assemblymen and was not above begging, pleading, and sobbing to shame new legislators to vote for her husband. All of this worked to Logan's advantage and—despite the *Tribune*'s claim that he had only 35 votes—when the Republicans caucused, Logan received 80 votes to only 26 for Oglesby. The Democrats chose John C. Black, a contestant not strong enough to stop the "Black Eagle of Illinois." Logan reclaimed his U.S. Senate seat by a margin of 22 votes out of a total of 204 cast.[8]

Logan was called up for an acceptance speech in front of the assembly. He appeased the Greenbackers when he proclaimed, "The resumption of specie payment is an accomplished fact. The Republicans will stand by the proposition that our paper currency shall be converted into coin at the option of the holder now and in the future." He dedicated most of his short speech to what was termed "The Southern Question." He revealed that he would fight not to end Reconstruction policy, officially closed by the election of Hayes. Citing the Constitution, Logan stressed equal protection under the law, "to white or black, to rich or poor, in Illinois or South Carolina . . ." He placed the onus on the federal government "to use such power as it possesses to protect citizens in the exercise of such rights."[9]

The reaction by the press illustrated the polarized extremes Logan generated in newspapers, even within the organs of the Republican Party. The opening shots against him came from a foe-turned-friend-turned-foe-again—the *Chicago Tribune*. "Is this a time to elect a burlesque on statesmanship . . . and peddler in claims and subsidies, to the Senate of the nation, and to represent the people of Illinois?" the Oglesby-supporting paper asked rhetorically. "Is this a time to elect a man to such a place on the ground he can so bellow and roar and murder the language that the Southern brigadiers, instead of laughing at the exhibition, will hold their peace, and never do any thing without his leave? Is the Senate a circus, or a show, that this man must be sent there?"[10]

"Yes!" answered the Logan-supporting rivals. "When we recall the bitter, relentless and unjustifiable warfare made on General Logan by the *Chicago Tribune* and a few other half-hearted Republicans, we feel that we are justified in terming it a 'glorious triumph'," responded the *Iowa Weekly Hawkeye*. "It is a triumph of stalwart republicanism over namby-pambyism in politics and political chicanery." The *Trenton Times* chimed in, "The country just now needs in the national councils men of decisive political convictions, who believe in the supremacy of Republican principles and are willing to work for their triumph." Even Democrat papers not supporting Logan diplomatically filled the glass halfway with his election. "The mellow rhetoric of Logan will be somewhat of a relief to the long-suffering Washington reporters," facetiously understated the *Atlanta Constitution*. The *Cairo Evening Sun* editorialized, "Because we wanted another man . . . we opposed the election of [Logan], but as our opposition does not seem to have accomplished anything for our choice, we accept the situation and congratulate the victor on his return to an office next in dignity to that of President of the United States."[11]

Logan was treated as the dignitary suggested by the latter editorial. Buoyed by his triumph, the reelected senator basked in the glow of his victory. He toured Illinois; from a reception in the Grand Pacific Hotel in Chicago at the end of

January he swept southward, speaking to huge crowds. He entered Carbondale on February 9 where he celebrated his fifty-third birthday with a crowd of 3,000. After completing a brief tour of select sites in Illinois, he entered Washington on the evening of February 20, where a thirty-seven-gun salute announced his arrival at the train depot. Frederick Douglass served as the event's marshal, and he was one of the first to greet Logan at the platform and direct him to an open carriage drawn by four sleek white horses. A grand procession escorted Logan in a blaze of pyrotechnic lights to Willard's Hotel. A brass band supplemented the fireworks, and a grandfather clock chimed with perfect timing to cue Logan to his speech. He delivered a rousing address, one which unfolded his bloody shirt and signified that he intended to wave it throughout the next six years on Capitol Hill.[12]

He waved that shirt early and often—with unprecedented consequence. Logan stepped back into the U.S. Senate chambers not as a man beaten by his earlier defeat, but as a victorious leader of that body who expected to head issues of his choosing. When Representative William H. Lowe of Alabama, a former Confederate colonel, mentioned Logan in the House of Representatives to link him with the Secession atmosphere of 1861, Logan received word of it and denounced Lowe on the Senate floor as a "poltroon and a coward." Lowe retaliated; he challenged Logan to a duel. "Black Jack" thought better of this solution to the conflict and the affair—one which garnered tremendous newspaper coverage—closed without a murmur.[13]

Logan endured the remainder of the Hayes administration with his thoughts focused on the 1880 contest. His name was conjured up more often than ever before for the ultimate political position, but for the first time in years, Logan did not hesitate to offer his political backing for the man he wanted in the oval office— Ulysses S. Grant. A "Grant boom" had been sweeping the country in 1879. The general was more popular than ever, partly due to a highly celebrated world tour he embarked upon with his family. Continuous reports of Grant's overseas activities combined with growing dissatisfaction with the Hayes presidency helped to dissipate the bitterness over Grant's previous eight years in the White House.

Logan and Grant had reconciled after enduring some tense moments in the first half of the 1870s. Grant offered nothing but praise for Logan in an interview with a reporter who traveled with him. Criticizing Sherman's treatment of Logan in his memoirs, Grant told the reporter that Logan was a tremendous asset during the Civil War. "He was an admirable soldier," he asserted, "and is, as he always has been, an honorable true man—a perfectly just and fair man, whose record in the army was brilliant." Grant's assessment reached the States about the same time Grant returned there. The two were back in each other's good graces.[14]

Skeptics who claimed to know Logan scoffed at the notion that he would openly support Grant. Six months had passed since Logan defeated Richard Oglesby for the Senate seat, but Oglesby had not recovered from his treatment by Logan and the press. He lashed out when asked about Logan's support for a third term for Grant. "Logan for Grant!" exclaimed Oglesby with overwhelming incredulity; "That's what they think, is it? Well I can tell you they don't know anything about Logan for Grant. He is for Logan and no one else. He thinks he can be made President of the United States himself."[15]

Oglesby's gauge was defective, for Logan not only was supporting Grant for a third term, he moved ahead as one of the leaders of this movement. The Society of the Army of the Tennessee held a banquet for General Grant at the Palmer House in Chicago on November 13 to celebrate his homecoming. Sitting at Grant's table, Logan was one of fifteen speakers addressing a crowd of 600 veterans. Mark Twain, attending as a friend of Grant, had apparently watched Logan address a crowd in the days before the event, and was quite dismissive of his ideas, but taken by his look and style. "Read Logan's bosh," wrote Twain to his wife hours before the banquet, "and try to imagine a burly and magnificent Indian, in General's uniform, striking a heroic attitude and getting that stuff off in the style of a declaiming school-boy."

Twain left Chicago with a better impression of Logan after his banquet performance. "I guess this was the most memorable night of my life," Twain told his wife immediately after the event; "By George, I never was so stirred since I was born." He ranked Logan's "mighty stirring" address as one of four that night that he could never forget. "All these speeches may look dull in print," he explained, "but how the lightning glared around them when they were uttered, and how the crowd roared in response!"[16]

Back in Congress for the second session during the winter of 1880, Logan fought against the passage of a bill with a vehemence never before seen by his Senate colleagues. The issue was the case of Fitz-John Porter, a major general of volunteers during the Civil War who was convicted by a court martial and removed from the service for "willful failure to obey his orders" at the Second Battle of Bull Run on August 29, 1862. A bill to restore Porter's rank and give him $60,000 of back pay came to the floor for debate and discussion. Porter, a Democrat, was supported by most Senate Democrats with little expressed Republican opposition during the winter of 1879–1880. But on March 2 Logan used the Porter case to wave the bloody shirt, declaring the deposed general a traitor and grouping him with Confederate leaders. Logan monopolized the Senate floor for much of the first week of March with his longest speech ever. He spoke for ten hours (split up into four days) against Porter's reinstatement, insisting that Porter's inaction during the battle not only lost the battle, but also prolonged the war. He reverted back to the original board that convicted Porter, pointedly stating there was no new evidence to overturn the "nine honorable officers" who weighed the same information to remove Porter from the service. Railing against the precedent the bill would establish, Logan closed his protracted argument by maintaining that reinstating Porter would foster dereliction of duty in the future. Logan returned to his seat on March 5, having completed an address that consumed forty-five pages of the *Congressional Record*. His passion polarized the Senate, but it accomplished the goal. The Fitz-John Porter reinstatement bill did not pass. "It was a powerful presentation of the case and I think it has considerably disturbed the defenders of Porter," admitted Ohio Congressman James A. Garfield, a Porter defender himself.[17]

Five months after the memorable Chicago banquet for Grant, Logan was back in the Windy City to prepare for the upcoming state Republican convention. He was surprised to learn that 3,000 people crowded in the Central Music Hall on the evening of April 16 for another General Grant meeting. Escorted to the meeting, Logan was pressed to make an extemporaneous speech. "I am for General Grant for President," he proclaimed to an audience that worshipped the former president. He went on to exalt Grant's accomplishments and standing in the world as well as the nation. Logan then played upon the "Plumed Knight" moniker bestowed upon Senator James G. Blaine, the candidate with the best chance to seize the Republican nomination from Grant, but a man who did not fight in the Civil War. "We are told we must have a plumed Knight for President this time," Logan told the crowd. "In the person of U. S. Grant we offer you the grandest knight who ever waved a plume or thrust a lance. He won his decoration on the field of battle. At the head of his brave Union legion he crushed the most audacious armies that ever waged war against their country. His plume is recognized as the symbol of constitutional liberty and equality by every man, woman, and child in the land. The orphans of the Union soldiers recognize it; the widows of Union martyrs recognize it, and the blind Union veterans touch it that they may be thrilled by the patriotic memories associated with it."[18]

Logan's passion for Grant was unmistakable that evening. Many believed that he supported a third term for Grant to enter Grant's elusive inner circle with a cabinet position. Logan could also benefit politically by strengthening himself through solid patronage. But the speech exhibited an underappreciated aspect to his support. In Grant, Logan was refighting the Civil War by relying upon the single-greatest champion of that war. The Hayes administration had ended Reconstruction against Logan's wishes. Federal troops no longer occupied Southern states; the void allowed ex-Confederates to rebuild the "Solid South," a resurgence of strength that placed former rebel soldiers and governors in the U.S. Congress and also fostered accusations of intimidation of blacks at polling places and elsewhere. Logan saw the nation leaning toward forgiveness. He could not forgive; he would never forget. Campaigning for Grant provided him the appropriate outlet to wave the bloody shirt.

Arriving back in Washington on April 26, a crowd of skeptic reporters pressed Logan on his support for Grant from the moment he stepped off the train. When apprised of rumors that Grant's name would be withdrawn after the first ballot if he did not receive the 379 delegate votes necessary to win the nomination at the national convention, slated for early June. Logan's emphatic response turned into headlines: "General Grant is in the hands of his friends, and they will not withdraw him until he is beaten, no matter how many ballots are taken. That is the whole case."[19]

Grant's "friends" to whom Logan referred were called the "Stalwarts." They were former Radical Republicans opposed to President Hayes's attempts at reconciliation with the South. Opposed to civil service reform, they embraced the patronage system and included the G.A.R. as their major machine of support. Logan was a Stalwart leader, forming a rock-solid alliance with Roscoe Conkling of New York and Don Cameron of Pennsylvania. The three party Stalwarts were dubbed "The Triumvirate," a term that harkened back to the Romans. The Republican Party split into opposing factions, much like the days of the Radicals and Liberals during Grant's administration. Those Republicans opposed to the Stalwarts adopted the name of derision placed upon them by that conservative wing: "The Half-Breeds." Their leader was James G. Blaine, the presidential candidate who supported Hayes's position on the South, mild civil service reform, and vehemently opposed the Stalwarts—particularly the men who led the party.[20]

The press crackled and cackled with excitement over the upcoming convention. Grant, Blaine, and Senator John Sherman of Ohio all sought the party's nomination. The Republican newspapers split in their support, while the Democratic papers all aligned against the Stalwarts. Logan was often the political cartoonists' target. They derisively depicted him in various scenes with Cameron, Conkling, and the other Stalwart leaders, his long hair and flamboyant mustache making him easily identifiable.[21]

Logan carried his political convictions back to Illinois in May 1880, expecting to easily secure the majority of delegates for Grant at the state convention in Springfield. But he ran into a strong anti-Grant movement in Cook County, the most populous in Illinois because Chicago stood as the county seat. Seventy delegates pledged to Grant were chosen at the county convention, while 108 others were split between Elihu Washburne and James Blaine. Logan frowned at the notion that Grant held the majority between the three, but combined forces opposed to him threatened disaster at the state convention. He craftily solved the problem two days later when the Cook County anti-Grant delegates began to investigate the credentials of the delegates pledged to Grant. Logan fumed at the insult and took the Grant men with him to the Palmer House where they deliberated separately. The staged move salvaged the Grant delegates from a state convention ban.

Two sets of Cook County delegates traveled to Springfield one week later for the state convention. "The political cauldron was at white heat," remarked a conventioneer. Combating Logan and the other "third termers" (as the pro-Grant forces were called) were the Half-Breeds, who challenged the separate sets of Cook County men. Wielding his heavy hand, Logan solved the issue by persuading the convention to form a selection committee rather than vote as a whole. The committee was chosen by friend and fellow Stalwart, Green B. Raum. His hand-picked panel accepted the Grant delegates while locking the Blaine and Washburne ones out. The next day Logan exceeded this coup by winning a unit rule vote for the national convention. This assured that all Illinois delegates would vote for Grant rather than split as they did in the state convention. The measure passed 399 to 285; thus, all forty-two of Illinois' national delegates would cast their votes for Grant in the upcoming national convention.[22]

Logan's dominance in Illinois, combined with his strong-arm tactics, entitled him to the label of party "Boss" of a state whose three million inhabitants made it the fourth most populous state in the country in 1880 (a far cry from the 55,000 state-wide residents logged in its first census of 1820). His achievement in Springfield startled the newspapers. The *Chicago Tribune* complained that Logan winked at his followers as soon as the votes were cast for the unit rule. An Ohio paper railed, "The machine manipulated by the Indian blooded Logan controlled the convention." On the other side, an Iowa paper waxed effusively on the result under the title, "Logan's Victory," while the *New York Times* followed this line of reporting with a lengthy article carrying the subtitle, "Gen. Logan's Masterly Work." Not surprisingly Logan was pleased with his effort and more than satisfied with the result, as was his chief underling at the convention, A. M. "Long" Jones, who immediately crowed, "Glory. Genl. Logan at the head of the Illinois delegation solid for Grant."[23]

Less than a week later a dissenting paper fretted about the power of the Triumvirate; they had good reason to. "You did your work nobly," proclaimed

Senator Cameron to Logan from Chicago, where he arrived as the chairman of the Republican National Committee. "Conkling, Cameron, Logan and other leaders of the conspiracy to nominate Grant are gathering at Chicago already," grumbled a paper in Ohio, while *Puck Magazine* got into the act. Cartoonist Joseph Keppler created "To the Chicago Convention." Grant's head appeared on the steam shaft of the train engine, while Logan, Cameron, and Conkling stoke the furnace of the Republican Iron Horse. Other Stalwarts appeared in the passenger car while Half-Breeds stood in the rear, mourning the victim of the Grant machine, a woman appearing as Lady Columbia and labeled "Republican Party."[24]

The Triumvirate train did not run smoothly in Chicago. The plan to secure Grant's nomination began to crumble when the national committee rejected the unit rule; thus, scores of delegate votes were "unlocked" for transfer to the five other candidates. Rancor against the Triumvirate showed in demonstrations on the south side of Michigan Avenue on May 31. A Pennsylvania attendee denounced them to a crowd of 15,000. He proclaimed, "The political trio of 'Bosses' regarded this as a rice plantation where the masters voted for the slaves, whom they could domineer." Logan roused a crowd of 20,000 at Dearborn Park on the opposite side of the anti-Grant meeting. He shared the rostrum that evening with America's preeminent civil rights leader, Frederick Douglass. The irony of America's most famous black man aligned with the former Fugitive Slave Law advocate was striking. Logan's transformation to champion of African-American rights had gained acceptance throughout the black community.[25]

Would the delegates accept him and his two partners and share their advocacy for Grant? When the polling began on June 7, Grant had a strong lead with 304 votes after the first ballot, but he was 75 votes short of securing the nomination. Sixty-three of those necessary votes were lost from the three states of the Triumvirate due to the loss of the unit rule (Illinois cast 18 of its 42 votes for candidates other than Grant). Pre-convention wisdom suggested that Grant could not win after the first ballot, which proved to bear out in successive polling. Logan, Conkling, and Cameron held firm, wearing on the convention as ballot after ballot was taken. Grant never dipped below 300, but he also never gained appreciably in subsequent rolls. Thirty-three ballots were taken to decide the contest without significant movement.

It all began to break on the thirty-fourth ballot, taken on Tuesday, June 8. Grant broke the 310 mark with 313 votes, but a dark-horse candidate, Congressman James A. Garfield, polled 18 votes, all but one came from Wisconsin, which transferred its allegiance to him. The dominoes tumbled during the next ballot; Garfield—who never declared his interest in running for the White House—

picked up thirty-three more delegates. The Triumvirate held firm, but Blaine and Sherman gave up, urging their supporters to switch to Garfield as a compromise to upend Grant. The delegates followed the advice. On the thirty-sixth ballot, Garfield crossed the 379 threshold with 399 total delegates and became the official Republican nominee for president of the United States. New Yorker Chester A. Arthur accepted the offer to run as the vice president. The Stalwarts stuck with Grant, as promised, to the bitter end, 306 of them.[26]

The anti-third-term press reveled in the result, perhaps less so for Garfield's exciting dark-horse victory and more for the defeat of the strong-arming Stalwarts. Joseph Keppler illustrated this animus in subsequent issues of *Puck*. On June 9, he released "The Chicago Catastrophe," showing the same "Grant train" he depicted in his earlier "To the Chicago Convention" now totally wrecked in the background with injured members of the Triumvirate hobbling toward the foreground. The stinging satire caricatured Logan complete with long hair and mustache, injured leg, crutch, and shaking fist.[27]

Senator Conkling stewed and sulked at the surprising Garfield victory. To his credit, Grant was magnanimous in defeat. Logan was as well, displaying an olive branch of sorts by mounting a large banner in his hotel suite, one that proclaimed a huge majority in Illinois for the nominee. For the benefit of the party Logan promised Garfield his support, but Logan thought very little of him. "After making his bitter fight for Grant . . . it was natural for him to think unkindly of Garfield," reasoned a Logan friend, "but his dislike of Garfield had a more substantial basis than that kind of prejudice. He disliked Garfield because he was an unmanly man." Logan had heard that Garfield broke down and cried during the investigation of his role in the Credit Mobilier scandal of the early 1870s; he could not purge the image from his mind. Grant must have felt the same way about him. "Garfield," said Grant, "has shown that he is not possessed of the backbone of an angleworm."[28]

Notwithstanding his personal feelings toward Garfield, Logan was loyal to the party, and he was born to campaign. He planned several appearances for Garfield throughout Illinois and Indiana for August and September. Garfield well recognized he needed Logan's support, particularly since Senator Conkling remained cold to his candidacy. He respected the fight Logan and the Stalwart Grant supporters put up at the convention, calling them "The 306" in reference to the votes that refused to peel from their candidate, even when all was lost. Logan accompanied other prominent Republicans in New York City to plan the campaign, and traveled with Grant, Conkling (who finally quit sulking), and Cameron to Garfield's home in Mentor, Ohio, as a show of support for the nominee. Garfield, a former Civil War general, ran against one selected by the Democrats to be their standard bearer—Winfield Scott Hancock. The campaign waged between the two could not compare to Garfield's rousing "dark horse" role at the convention. Garfield won the sixth consecutive Republican presidential election in November by less than 10,000 popular votes out of nearly 9 million cast, but by a wider margin (214 to 155) in the electoral college. Illinois went for Garfield by more than 40,000 votes, partly due to Logan's influence and tireless efforts on the stump.[29]

President-elect Garfield considered Logan for a cabinet position out of necessity to placate Stalwarts rather than personal desire. Logan let him off the hook through an unlikely intermediary. Joseph Medill of the *Chicago Tribune* had warmed to Logan during the autumn campaign. As Logan's new friend, the editor visited Garfield in mid November to tell him Logan did not seek a cabinet position, nor did he believe that "The 306" wanted to be treated as a separate political faction. Appreciative, Garfield called upon Logan's counsel three months later on filling out his cabinet. Logan returned to the Garfield farm in Mentor where he proposed Robert Todd Lincoln as Secretary of War. Garfield took Logan's advice and selected Abraham Lincoln's lone surviving child as a member of his administration.[30]

Garfield reciprocated the favor for Logan. In an effort to increase his stronghold as the "Boss" of Illinois, Logan recommended his friend Alfred "Long" Jones be appointed U.S. marshal of Illinois' northern district. Garfield complied to give Logan a crony that paid dividends beyond his appointed position. Jones cofounded the *Chicago Herald*, a paper designed to support Logan's brand of Republicanism.[31]

Garfield took the oath as president in March; Logan attended. He returned to the Capitol to initiate the first session of the Forty-sixth Congress. In the middle of March, as he dressed at 8:00 A.M. in his Strathmore Arms home to head over to the Senate chamber, Logan walked into his reception room and was startled by an unannounced visitor sitting in a chair by the door. The man was oddly dressed: rubber galoshes with no stockings on his feet, no coat, and very light pants for the late-winter season. The man claimed to be one of Logan's constituents and wanted him to sign a recommendation that *he* had written to become Garfield's consul-general to France. Logan brushed him off—"I treated him as kindly and as politely as I could"—only to have the strange man return unannounced into Logan's rented rooms the following morning. Again, Logan got rid of him without incident. After the man departed for the second straight day, Logan hurriedly dressed and walked downstairs to find his landlady, Mrs. Lockwood. He coaxed her to the dining room where he pointed out the man to her, eating breakfast in silence. "I do not think he is a proper person to have in your boardinghouse," Logan advised her. When Mrs. Lockwood asked why, he replied, "I think he is a little off in the head." He knew little about the man except his name: Charles Guiteau.[32]

Logan was forced to hear accusations of his prewar secession proclivities for the fourth time since the end of the war. He survived the outbursts by Southern senators and worked on his committees (Military Affairs and Indian Affairs). He also continued to invest in projects to accumulate personal wealth. He had yet to recover from the Panic of 1873. Although he traded some stocks for four-figure profits, he lost much more than that on another failed mining venture.[33]

Logan and his wife summered in Chicago where the senator received a startling telegram from Robert Lincoln. President Garfield had been gunned down in a railroad station in Washington. The man who shot him was Charles Guiteau—the office-seeker who had barged into Logan's room unannounced on consecutive days back in March. Garfield survived the initial shock of his trauma, but died from complications three months later. Chester A. Arthur succeeded Garfield in the White House to complete the term of the second assassinated president in American history.[34]

Four months after Garfield's death, Logan suffered another attack of rheumatism, one that incapacitated him so severely that he had to be conveyed to his boardinghouse rooms, where he lay for more than a month. "I do not know how soon I can possibly venture out, to take any interest in anything," Logan lamented in March. He went West to get stronger, bathing in spa waters at Hot Springs, Arkansas, and relaxing in the elegant Arlington Hotel. His health and mood vastly improved. He felt well enough to admonish a group of young men engaged in pistol shooting at bottles. They were good shots, but not perfect, and the general let them know it. Irritated, the dozen challenged him to improve upon their skill. Logan bet them boxes of cigars that he was a better shot and could hit a dozen lined bottles with better accuracy than any of them. "I'll shoot first," he told them, "and if I hit I'm to shoot again and again until I miss." The men greedily accepted. Twelve shots and twelve broken bottles later, Logan won his cigars.[35]

He headed back to Washington, where he continued to strengthen in the Senate. Flamboyant and distinguished, he had always been a gallery favorite during the sessions. But Logan was also unorthodox; despite sixteen years of legislative experience he refused to study or adhere to the details of parliamentary measures. Often reminded of the rules, Logan routinely was oblivious to the status of his own bills on the calendar. His syntax also became the subject of ridicule, particularly by unforgiving newspaper editors. This criticism cut Logan deeper than most others, and here he worked to improve his grammar. Part of the problem was regional. He grew up learning that walnuts were pronounced "warnuts" and used colloquialisms that Easterners had a difficult time deciphering. He mixed metaphors, one time speaking of "the day when the bloody hand of the rebellion stalked through the land." Sensitive to the ribbing he incurred for his grammar and syntax, Logan worked to improve both his written and spoken words. His addresses were never perfect, but by the early 1880s he had clearly improved upon his speeches so that the mechanics of his sentence structure did not detract from his sometimes-eloquent oratory.[36]

In the early years of their marriage, Mary yearned to have her husband out of politics and living a more domestic life. Her ambitions grew to challenge his as she thrived as the wife of a renowned Washington political figure. The Logans had been grandparents since the 1870s when Dollie Logan Tucker bore a son, christened George Tucker although he was called "Logan" Tucker. But Dollie lived in the Logan's Chicago home, forcing the grandparents to learn about the boy's life through letters more than observation. Manning Logan, their surviving son, changed his name to John A. Logan II. After enrolling his son in private schools throughout the boy's teenage years, Logan secured an appointment for him at West Point in 1883. Ironically, America's quintessential volunteer soldier enrolled his son into the academy he had treated as the bane of the army.

This was not the only paradox of John A. Logan. As naturally adept a lawyer, general, and politician as he was, he proved to be a poor businessman. His estate, once valued in property holdings in Chicago and Southern Illinois in excess of $150,000, was dramatically reduced from the previous decade's financial depression and Logan's failed business ventures. With their money locked up in real estate, the Logans relied upon the senator's $5,000 salary (The rate never increased during the "salary grab" hubbub) and small-time stock trading as their sources of income in an age where many in Congress enjoyed burgeoning wealth. The Logan lifestyle ate away at his salary, keeping them locked into their modest accommodations in a "dingy" Washington boardinghouse. Logan, however, had become more conscious of his expenditures and exerted efforts to curtail them. "Gen. Logan is very abstemious," observed the proprietor of the Senate restaurant on Capitol Hill. Although Logan frequented the place, he did not indulge in oysters and ale, a favorite of his Senate colleagues. He limited himself to crackers and milk for his restaurant meals; the restaurateur claimed it as a common meal—"My milk is most all cream, and they like it." The owner did go out of his way to single out the Stalwart Republican as a "liberal" tipper, "when he feels good."[37]

Books had always been Logan's obsession. Despite his shaky financial status, he could not pass up the opportunity to add a book to his home library, which approached 5,000 volumes. An omnivorous reader, Logan proudly claimed an eclectic collection of classics and historical works. Mary considered books her husband's addiction and tried to prevent him from entering W. H. Loudermilk's book shop to feed his passion. One day while Logan worked in the Capitol, Mary watched incredulously as a wagon drove up Twelfth Street to deliver a large box of beautifully bound books to their rooms. Ironically, her husband had recently lectured her about household economy, yet she found herself staring at $300 worth of histories, standard texts, and classics. Realizing that the books were delivered that day, Logan returned home late that evening, delaying the expected confrontation with his wife. When he finally came through the door, his purchase greeted him, aligned in rows on the floor with Mary standing nearby. Logan sheepishly explained, "I know I have been foolish but I could not resist them when I dropped by Loudermilks for a few moments."[38]

His love of reading and need for money directed Logan to writing for publication. Several of his speeches had previously been released as pamphlets. He delivered a speech uniquely documented in two calendar years. Another lengthy dissent against Fitz-John Porter's relief, delivered at the end of December 1882 and for two days in January 1883, was published as a 180-page book. He followed this with a shorter and less controversial piece: "National Aid to Public Schools." This defense of federal expenditure to improve public education, regardless of race, was accepted and published by the esteemed *North American Review* in April 1883. In addition to the two plays he wrote, Logan continued to pursue literary endeavors, fermenting both a fiction and nonfiction topic for a book.[39]

Logan's hobbies did not detract from his government-paid duties; he was recognized as one of the hardest-working senators in Congress. He combined both personal and government interests in the spring and summer of 1883 when he took Mary to Santa Fe, the post where Major Will Tucker had been stationed with Dollie and Logan. The senator and his wife cared for their lone grandchild that spring while the boy's parents took a trip to Chicago. All reunited briefly in June before the elder Logans departed, Mary heading back east while her husband stayed in the West.

Before he left Santa Fe, Logan had to put out the fires of another controversy—this one centered on water. Logan was accused of partnering with his son-in-law to defraud the Zuni of some of their desert reservation property by claiming land that contained their valuable water supply. Logan was further accused of plotting to deny the Zuni their water; thus, forcing them from their land, which Logan would subsequently take. Finally, he was accused of attacking a "white Indian" named Cushing, a Caucasian man who chose to live as a Zuni on the reservation with them. President Arthur forced Logan's son-in-law off the land by executive order.[40]

Logan quickly responded to the charges with a sweeping denial. He wrote a letter, published in the *Chicago Tribune* and *New York Times*, that he had no land anywhere near the reservation. He acknowledged that Major Tucker partnered with a local to lawfully purchase land thirty miles northeast from their Zuni River valley village. Calling the charges of swindling the Zunis "one of the most villainous falsehoods that could ever be uttered," he dismissed the charge against him, his son-in-law, and the major's partner. He acknowledged that he rode over the Zuni country as a visitor, "with a large party of gentleman and ladies, purely out of curiosity and for no other purposes." He also denied attacking Cushing, a man he admitted "has my contempt, and I have not now nor heretofore had time to flatter nor abuse such a subject." Despite his published denial, the charge stuck to Logan and would not wash off.[41]

Logan felt he had slipped away from one conflict, only to step into another. He hired a friend, Timothy Isaiah "Longhair Jim" Courtright, and another man to scout for him while he was in New Mexico. The pair became involved in a murder of two settlers in the American Valley on May 6. Logan was not involved in the case but the suspicion on Courtright cast Logan in a bad light, particularly since the *Albuquerque Daily Democrat* publicized the murder several times that May.[42]

Logan departed Santa Fe but could not escape confrontation in the West. The next one was with Teton Sioux chief, Tatanka Iyotake, the leader known as "Sitting Bull" who annihilated Colonel George Armstrong Custer and his Seventh Cavalry at the Battle of the Little Bighorn in the summer of 1876. Since then Sitting Bull had scattered his tribe into small clans to avoid avenging whites. His men starved, forcing the chief to surrender himself and his clan in 1881. In 1883 he was assigned to the Hunkpapa Sioux agency at Standing Rock. There Logan confronted Sitting Bull. After leaving Santa Fe, Logan rode up to the Dakota Territory to meet with the other four legislators of Senator Henry L. Dawes's commission investigating the conditions among the Sioux. The commission had interviewed Indians, soldiers, and territory residents. Logan smiled during the opening discussions when the Indians announced they were conversing with "the coming President of the United States, General John A. Logan." Sitting Bull apparently was insulted by the entire proceedings and took the opportunity to lambaste Logan and the committee members. Claiming he was created and made chief by the will of the Great Spirit, Sitting Bull accused the commission members of conducting the proceedings under the influence of whiskey. The chief then waved his hand and every Indian got up and left with him. The shocked and angered senators sent a message to Sitting Bull that he had the option of returning with an apology or going to jail.[43]

The next day, August 23, the chief returned with 300 of his tribesmen to tell the commission he was sorry for his conduct. Then it was Logan's turn to tell the chief what he felt. "I want to say to you, sir, that the Great Father has appointed you chief," he announced, reminding him that if it was not for government protection, "you would be starving to death in the mountains." Logan assured him he would be thrown in the guardhouse if he behaved the same way again. "The point I tried to make on him," he explained shortly thereafter, "was that he was not such a hell of an Indian as he seemed to think."[44]

After completing his duties with the Dawes Commission, Logan visited Yellowstone Park, the natural wonder which he helped to preserve as one of the creators of the U.S. Geological Survey. Logan was back in Chicago by September, after his longest western journey since the Mexican War. The feedback from the trip had positive and negative elements. One paper went so far as to suggest that "Black Jack's" raven hair was partially synthetic as Logan approached his fifty-eighth birthday. A California Democrat paper claimed, "Sen. Logan lost his valise at Deadwood, and during his four days' stay among the Sioux Indians, his hair turned a beautiful gray. Since his return to civilization, however, his hair regained its natural color." The paper facetiously concluded, "Some of the effects of altitude and climate are indeed remarkable."[45]

Logan generally looked good in the eyes of the press for his admonishment of Sitting Bull, but his suspicious involvement in his son-in-law's land dealing with the Zuni cast him in an unflattering light. "Gen. Logan found two things in the Zuni country," reported a usually pro-Logan Wisconsin newspaper: "a nice ranche, and a deathblow to his presidential prospects." In Illinois, Democratic papers immediately tried to quell any Logan insurgence. After learning that Logan's son was accepted at West Point, the *Bloomington Bulletin* declared, "All the Logan family by blood and by marriage are now comfortably quartered at the public crib, except Dollie's baby, which will, if it has the family instinct, make a vigorous grab for a supply from the public fountain as soon as it ceases to receive a sustenance from the source provided by nature."[46]

But the "Logan Boom" could not be quelled. At the close of 1883 and into the winter of 1884, Logan was touted for president in seemingly endless fashion by Republican newspapers. The general-senator had positioned himself as less extreme, particularly in 1882 when he voted for the Pendleton Civil Service Act, signed into law by President Arthur in January 1883. The new law created a civil service commission that in turn appointed a corps of examiners to oversee those hired to work in Washington government departments, large post offices, and customhouses. The employees in those targeted departments could not solicit campaign contributions. Logan's "aye" vote silenced his critics on the patronage issue, for the act threatened part of his power base. Perhaps as difficult for Logan was siding with the bill's sponsor, Senator George H. Pendleton of Ohio, a man he absolutely loathed. Back in 1864 the same George H. Pendleton was a Peace Democrat pegged as George McClellan's running mate in the presidential election opposing Abraham Lincoln. Logan claimed back then that he would as "soon vote for Jeff. Davis as Pendleton," but now he was forced to vote for the Buckeye's bill to preserve his political viability.[47]

The year 1884 was the most crucial one for Logan's political career. Not only was he prepared to run for president, his second Senate term would close and the Illinois legislature elected in November would determine the subsequent party and leader to sit in Logan's seat. If Logan did not succeed as president, he still cherished his Senate seat and would have to push for his reelection. His support of the year-old Pendleton Act—the result of a new Democrat-controlled Senate and House—took away a major issue against him. Pension legislation cut both ways. Logan was the champion of veterans' rights. In 1876 one out of every ten dollars expended by the U.S. government went to veterans' pensions. In 1884 the expenditure rate more than doubled, approaching one out of every four dollars. While reformers pointed this out to push for budget control, the veterans hailed Logan as a postwar general in leading Congress to increase legislation. After a brief disassociation with the G.A.R., Logan reinvigorated himself and the organization, and by 1884 he used it to build up a boom for his presidency. The *National Tribune*, a veterans' paper and an organ of the G.A.R., boasted a circulation of 80,000 in 1884; they routinely published favorable stories and editorials about Logan. "No man who served in the Union army is more popular than he with the old soldiers," claimed the *Chicago Tribune* in 1884. "He stands especially high with the Grand Army of the Republic." The *New York Herald* believed the same and published an editorial reminding Logan that the G.A.R. was supposed to be regulated as a nonpartisan entity.[48]

Logan also carried tremendous support from African Americans. He remained a strong advocate of their rights and introduced a bill to create a commission to investigate the progress of the race since 1865. His association with Frederick Douglass was strong enough for the black leader to endorse him. "He has a backbone like the Brooklyn Bridge," praised Douglass of Logan, contrasting him with other candidates who he claimed were invertebrate animals. Knowing Logan's strong attitudes toward the South, where blacks had complained of rights suppression for years, black organizations and newspapers routinely passed resolutions in favor of the Black Eagle of Illinois.[49]

Logan had a public disagreement two years earlier when Grant published his support of General Fitz-John Porter's reinstatement in *North American Review*, a piece that helped influence Porter's reinstatement. Notwithstanding their public clashes, each man respected the other and, in fact, Logan still worshipped the memory of General Grant and the Civil War. He lobbied strongly to support the financially strapped ex-president and led the easily passed bill to provide Grant with full general's pay. Grant reciprocated by publicly endorsing Logan at the close of March in 1884, an emphatic nod that swelled the "Logan Boom" that brewed throughout the previous winter.[50]

He carried those ambitions to the Republican National Convention in Chicago beginning on June 3, 1884. By this time, however, Logan's surge had subsided somewhat. His appeal was considered more regional than national. A strong Western candidate, Logan was much less so in New England. He had no chance to win any Southern states due to his notorious antagonistic stance against politicos from this region. But his strength in Illinois and neighboring states could not be dismissed, and the two other factions of the Republican Party—the Half-Breeds and the Independents—had to consider some way to pacify Stalwarts to enfold them into the ranks.

In addition to Arthur, Logan faced stiffening competition from all corners of the Republican Party. The perennially strong candidate, Maine senator James G. Blaine, entered the Windy City as the candidate most likely to win the nomination. Blaine was a Half-Breed in the 1880 convention whose delegates helped to derail Logan's efforts as a member of the Triumvirate to nominate Grant for a third presidential term. Although a same-party rival, Logan was careful not to harbor any ill will toward Blaine, realizing that if he did not win himself, he could end up on the ticket as Blaine's erstwhile running mate. The *Chicago Tribune* considered the Blaine-Logan alliance more than a possibility. Off and on for six months the paper reported a behind-the-scenes agreement between the Stalwart and the Half-Breed to widen the appeal of their ticket. Mrs. Lockwood took note of Blaine meeting with Logan in her boardinghouse the Sunday previous to the convention.[51]

By custom, Logan did not attend the convention, but kept in contact with his supporters by telegraph line run into the Twelfth Street boardinghouse. Shelby Cullom, Illinois' junior senator, officially placed Logan's name in nomination on

June 5, 1884. Five other candidates, including Arthur, Blaine, and Ohio's John Sherman, joined Logan as convention nominees. Needing 411 votes to win, Logan received 63 after the first ballot. Blaine led with 334 and Arthur trailed him with 278. Logan dropped a few and Blaine gained a few on the second attempt. Logan fell another eight to 53 after the third roll was called; Blaine climbed to 375 and Arthur stabilized close to where he was after the first ballot at 274. Whether the *Chicago Tribune* was correct or not in regards to a pre-arranged agreement, Logan calculated that his votes could push Blaine to victory. He could not win and could suffer a greater loss if another fading candidate allied with Blaine to seal the bid. Logan wired Senator Cullom to shift his votes to Blaine. This was done; others instantly followed, and Blaine won the nomination on June 6.

The convention floor converted from cheers to a ruckus immediately after the deciding roll was announced. Anticipation swelled for the vice presidential choice of the convention. The answer came swiftly: John A. Logan. For Blaine, Logan was a wise choice to balance his ticket: Half-Breed with Stalwart, East with West, new issues with past glories. But Blaine really wanted Robert Todd Lincoln, Arthur's secretary of war (a carryover from Garfield's administration). Party allies and managers wired messages before and during the roll. Logan received a message from Blaine supporters begging him to decline the nomination, hoping instead to ally with Arthur's administration supporters. Logan ignored them. His name came up for nomination and when the roll was called, Logan received all but seven votes. He was officially on the ticket, one dubbed for the nicknames of both men: "The Plumed Knight and the Black Eagle."[52]

While the convention floor exploded in acclamation of the ticket, the feeling among Republicans was far from unanimous. Independent Republicans were known as "mugwumps." Led by reformers such as Carl Schurz, this faction detested both choices on the ticket. Schurz glanced at his pocket watch and declared, "From this hour dates the death of the Republican Party." The editor of *Harper's Weekly* concurred. "I was at the birth of the Republican Party," he wrote, "and I fear I am to witness its death." The mugwumps threatened to bolt to the Democrats and support their candidate if it was a reformer. When the Democrats chose New York Governor Grover Cleveland at its convention, the mugwumps carried out their threat.[53]

Logan's life story was published in periodical and book form, the latter he shared with Blaine as a dual story sometimes authored by the same man and other times produced by two biographers. Nine books about Logan came out in the summer and fall of 1884, each one reliving Logan's role as a Civil War hero, but also embellishing other aspects of his life, including a fabrication of his Mexican War service. The misinformation did not detract from the accurate aspects of his biography, a life story of drama and triumph. Campaign coins, banners, buttons, plates, and other paraphernalia were ubiquitous in this election year.

The Blaine-Logan ticket was weakened by defections within the Republican ranks; it also suffered from the perceived lack of unity between the candidates on the ticket. Although Logan and Blaine displayed no public animus toward each other, they also failed to exhibit much cordiality. A popular ditty played on this and Logan's reputation for bad grammar in the same couplet: "We never speak as we pass by, Me to Jim Blaine nor him to I." The press thrived on the chaos the mugwump revolt had wrought. Logan's distinguishing features were a favorite subject of cartoonists throughout the summer and fall. The *Chicago Tribune* was in its anti-Logan mood again, mocking Black Jack for broad claims and faux pas made during his stump speeches.[54]

Logan did not shirk campaigning. For all the adversity the Blaine-Logan ticket faced, and the gang mentality the press seemingly displayed against it, both men and their supporters clearly expected to win that fall. Logan proved to be the strongest vice presidential candidate seen by either party in most men's memories in 1884. "His theory," recalled an aide, "was to attack, attack, attack and never retreat." He was overwhelming on the campaign trail, running his speaking schedule at a dizzying pace while maintaining his voice and energy throughout.[55]

Traveling by special train, Logan spoke every day except Sundays. He delivered six to fifteen speeches per day, none exceeded forty-five minutes and some were as short as five. Mary Logan was instrumental in keeping her husband hoarse-free and in fine spirits. She joined him by train in Warren, Ohio, in the middle of one of his sledgehammer-style addresses. The minute Logan caught sight of her, his scowl turned into a smile as he politely bowed to her in front of the cheering crowd. A witness to the instantaneous transformation remarked, "It was a wonderful contrast between the orator and fierce partisan and hard hitter and the loving husband." After this and every speech, she whisked him into the state room, sponged down his chest and shoulders with a whiskey-based ointment, and fed him hot lemonade to him to keep his throat clear.[56]

He used his veterans' appeal to full hilt. The G.A.R. was fanatically active for Logan. He canvassed the country, addressing veterans groups while reliving the glorious days of old with each speech he delivered. Each Logan event was an extravaganza, the subsequent demonstration seemingly hell-bent to outperform the previous one. In one touching scene at Madison, Wisconsin, Logan was honored by eighty one-armed soldiers marching in solemn procession, each veteran waving a lit torch in his lone hand.[57]

The Republican Party had not lost an election in twenty-four years, and all indications appeared that their streak would continue another four. Blaine proved a strong, effective, and enthusiasm-generating speaker. That he campaigned so vigorously in 1884 rankled his rivals; they thought it unseemly for a presidential candidate to campaign for himself. Blaine logged in 400 speeches delivered in a six-week span. But he showed up at one too many appearances. Days before the November election, in New York City's Fifth Avenue Hotel, Blaine attended a large rally of ministers. The presiding officer at the event, elderly clergyman Dr. Samuel D. Burchard, made an untimely and ill-fated speech. "We are Republicans," Dr. Burchard announced to Blaine and the attendees, "and don't propose to leave our party and identify ourselves with the party whose antecedents have been rum, Romanism, and rebellion." The anti-Irish comment made its way into newspaper reports just in time for New York's Irish-laden population to read the slur before they voted. New York State went to its former governor in the election and with it went the victory. Cleveland won a close election by only 23,000 popular votes out of 10 million cast, and an electoral college edge of 219 to 182. *Puck Magazine* illustrated the result with wicked satire, a cartoon entitled, "Thanksgiving Day, 1884." In it, Logan and other prominent Republicans sit stunned around a dinner table prepared to feast on crow, while outside the window, Cleveland walked past with a slung sack labeled, "Presidency."[58]

Logan quoted Abraham Lincoln to put the defeat in perspective, an anecdote about a man who stubbed his toe. "The worst of it is," declared Black Jack, "is I'm too big to cry, and it hurts too bad for me to laugh." The quotation was widely published, but Logan privately was more sarcastic, telling an associate, "If Blaine had eaten a few more swell dinners, and had a few more ministers call on him, we should not have carried a northern state." The election finished Blaine as a future contender, but Logan's stock was high. Since Illinois voted with a 25,000 Republican plurality, Logan was told that the Republicans would have won had the positions on the ticket been reversed. "Let's get ready for 1888," a friend had told Logan after the convention the previous June. Logan's associates were prepared to sound the same clarion call.[59]

But Logan could not look ahead. The November election had put his political future in jeopardy. Democrats gained House seats in Illinois and—detrimental to Logan—they also gained seats for the upcoming General Assembly.

With Logan's Senate term expiring in January, he could no longer count on a smooth reelection to his seat. He needed to face the strong possibility of losing two major elections in the span of two months.

The Illinois General Assembly convened in January 1885 with 76 Republicans, 76 Democrats, and one Independent in the House; and 26 Republicans, 24 Democrats, and one Greenbacker in the state senate. Thus neither major party had the 103 votes necessary to decide the race, making the unaligned members vital to choosing the next U.S. Senator. Predictably, Logan eased through the Republican caucus in February, winning his party's nomination by acclamation. The Democrats chose William R. Morrison as Logan's opponent. Twenty-three years earlier, the two men fought side by side as colonels commanding their respective regiments in the Fort Donelson campaign. They saw themselves at the start of 1885 as political enemies. The picks set the stage for one of the most fascinating Senate campaigns in Illinois history.[60]

The legislature deadlocked into springtime of 1885, absolutely unable to cast the necessary 103 votes for either man. As the deadlock dragged on, two Democratic legislators died, but each came from a partisan district and was quickly replaced by another Democrat each time. More than 100 ballots were cast by early April without a decision. The day after the second Democrat replaced the dead one, another one passed away in a Springfield hotel to create another vacancy. The legislator was Henry Shaw, who represented the Thirty-fourth District, consisting of four Democratic counties near Springfield. Shaw had won his election the previous November by 2,050 votes, so the special election set for May 6 to select a replacement seemed assured to seat another Democrat. Through it all Logan remained in Springfield with his son. Both men stayed in the Leland Hotel, the scene of many previous Logan victory celebrations. In mid April, Logan rode up to Chicago. When a reporter caught up with him there, he brazenly asked Logan if he planned to step aside to break the General Assembly deadlock. Defiant, Logan assured him "No Democrat shall succeed me in the United States Senate if I and my friends can prevent it."[61]

Logan had a plan to prevent it, one that likely came from one of his supporters, Henry Caske, who proposed a "still hunt" to break the impasse. The plotters—including Logan—kept the plan under wraps and carried on as if the status quo would continue. Deception was necessary to turn around 2,000 votes in a district dominated by Democrats.[62]

The Democrats chose Arthur Leeper as their nominee for the special election; the Republicans made no nomination—at least no public one. Secretly they chose William H. Weaver of Menard County. The still-hunt planners sent emissaries into the four counties of the Thirty-fourth District—disguised as stockbuyers, insurance agents, sewing machine agents, and other professions that gave them acceptable explanations to be in the region. The emissaries honeycombed all the school districts in the four counties where they handed trustworthy Republicans tickets with Weaver's name on it. Sworn to secrecy, each of these chosen Republicans magnified the vote potential several fold by selecting up to five more clandestine Republicans to carry out the plan. Thousands of tickets were quietly distributed; each recipient was fed specific instructions not to go to the polls earlier than 3:00 P.M. and no later than 5:00 P.M. on May 6. Only at that time were they to cast their votes in an effort to catch the Democrats entirely off-guard.

The "gum-shoe campaign" climaxed on the day of the election. That Wednesday Democrats merely trickled to all the polling places in the Democratic Thirty-fourth District; they never caught on to the plot. The anemic turnout was borne out of complacency—exactly as planned. Late that afternoon the selected Republicans flooded the polls to vote for Weaver. By the time the Democrats learned what was happening, it was too late to react to it. The polls closed and election officials counted the votes. Weaver pulled in 336 more votes—an astounding 2,400-vote turnaround from the previous November. The still hunt had worked to absolute perfection.[63]

Although the Republicans had their tie-breaker elected in the legislature, the Democrats attempted last-minute wrangling in an effort to prevent Logan's election by the General Assembly. They replaced their candidate Morrison with popular party man Lambert Tree. Threats that some anti-Logan Republican legislators would not vote for him caused some pre-election dyspepsia, but it all subsided at 12:40 P.M. on May 19, 1885, when Logan received 103 votes from the General Assembly—the necessary margin—and was elected to his third term in the U.S. Senate on the 120th ballot cast by the Illinois General Assembly. "It was a long and trying fight," Logan sighed to a fellow Republican afterwards, "but our success fully repays for all of it."[64]

The gallery exploded in joy as soon as the deciding vote was cast in the four-month marathon. White handkerchiefs waved wildly; hats and papers flew recklessly in the air while throaty cheers and hearty applause swelled through the assembly hall. Three Republicans were deputized to get Logan to the front for a speech. Logan complied in the most triumphant moment of his life since the first Memorial Day ceremony seventeen years before. He delivered a short address, one he closed by saying, "Thanking you again, I hope at last it will be understood that 'the wrong man' has not been chosen." He was nearly mobbed at the close of the speech by enthusiastic congratulators. The all-supporting *Illinois State Journal* displayed a large bulletin announcing the result, accompanied by a large picture of Logan.[65]

One thousand telegrams greeted Logan back at the Leland Hotel, sent by all walks of life. A citizen in Detroit sent, "Hurrah for Logan. Accept congratulations." A former governor transmitted, "Surely, 'There is a God in Israel.' Congratulations." The managing editor of the *Chicago Tribune* claimed to speak for the entire staff when he wrote, "I congratulate you on the re-election which you have so well deserved." The common thread running through many of the telegrams echoed Logan's mindset by suggesting that Logan should not remain a senator for six more years. One of his 1884 biographers spoke for all of Logan's ardent supporters when he declared, "You have won the National Republican party another Donelson. You will follow it in '88 with another Appomattox."[66]

Raucous celebrations and torchlight ceremonies generated from Logan's triumph. After a grand reception tendered to him in Chicago, on June 8 Logan returned to his new rented home in Iowa Circle, an enclave of upper-class residences in northwestern Washington. The following morning an obsessed admirer procured a cannon, rolled it across the Potomac in Virginia, and fired it 103 times to represent the votes Logan received in his victory. The man then dragged the cannon back into the district and fired it 21 more times in Logan's honor. With his drunken gunners in tow, the admirer proceeded to Logan's house to cheer the reelected senator. A more formal serenade by African Americans and a Capital City Guard were scheduled a few days later.[67]

Senator Logan took advantage of the time in between to train northward. His destination was New York City. He went there to visit a dying friend, Ulysses S. Grant.

CHAPTER ELEVEN

Coronation

IT WAS A SERENADE BEFITTING A KING. On the night of June 12, 1885, several thousand black citizens gathered in front of the home, awaiting the appearance of the man they wished to congratulate for his dramatic Senate victory and the man they would support for president of the United States in 1888. Every African-American military company in Washington formed a procession. Arthur Smith, a locally renowned orator, led off the event by proclaiming that the colored people of the District of Columbia and the United States rejoiced in Logan's victory, and looked forward to a greater victory in three years. After a few bands blared out their selections, chants for the general permeated Iowa Circle. Logan gratified the request by stepping out onto the piazza amid loud and prolonged cheering.

More than thirty years of public speaking had perfected Logan's timing, his voice inflection, and his body language to draw out the maximum response from his crowds. This night he was superb. He thanked them for the serenade. "I know no people in this country from whom I would receive a call more gratefully than from you," he insisted. "The colored people have been known in this country for long years past as a down-trodden race. Whatever I have been able to do to elevate them and give them the rights that belong to every citizen has always been done. They are men, they are American citizens, and they are entitled to all rights that any other man and American citizen is entitled to."

Logan assured the serenaders that they would always find in him a faithful and steadfast friend. He invoked the name of his friend, General Grant, and emotionally discussed his meeting with the dying former president in New York a few days earlier. As the time ticked closer and closer to the midnight hour, Logan closed his short address with a gracious gesture to his callers: "Again thanking you for this demonstration and this evidence of esteem, I now invite as many of you as will to pass through this house in which we reside for the present, that I may be gratified in giving you my hand." One thousand African Americans took Logan up on his offer. They filed in through the front door as Logan awaited them in his hallway. One by one he clasped right hands with each of them and they continued through the parlors and out the back door.[1]

Logan spent the summer of 1885 traveling to the Northeast and delivering speeches at veterans' organizations. He also gauged the reaction to a work of fiction he wrote in the winter of 1884–1885, recently released as a serial in the *National Tribune*, the Washington-based newspaper of the G.A.R. Logan published the story anonymously, naming the author "An Officer of the Union Army." He called his work "Uncle Daniel's Story of Tom Anderson and the Great Conspiracy." The first installment was published in the middle of July, with subsequent chapters stretching well into the autumn of 1885.

Logan's story was a semi-autobiographical story of the Civil War. The storyteller—Uncle Daniel Lyon—opened the first chapter by recounting to his listeners the story of his several Union-fighting sons and the heroic efforts of Tom Anderson, a colonel-turned-general who hailed from the fictional city of Allentown in Southern Indiana. "Uncle Daniel's Story" created a stir among the veterans, mainly due to his purposeful thin veiling of his characters. Daniel Lyon was Daniel McCook, the patriarch of one of the most patriotic families in the war. Seven McCook children fought for the Union and several died, including the elder McCook. But Logan changed his history by having McCook survive to old age in the form of Daniel Lyon, who delivers several of Logan's soapbox issues: the secession movement and its Northern support, the North's abandonment of Reconstruction, harsh treatment of blacks, and lack of support for veterans' causes.

Logan placed his mind and voice into the character of Daniel Lyon, but he also cast himself in the body of Tom Anderson, the colonel of a Southern Indiana regiment who fought against his brother-in-law at the Battle of Two Rivers (Belmont), was seriously wounded at Dolinsburg (Fort Donelson), and was subsequently promoted to general. Logan has Uncle Daniel tell his story on February 22, 1884, ostensibly close to the same time he began the serial. He evidently completed the narrative after his disappointing loss in the 1884 presidential campaign, for the story turns dark and disappointing. Tom Anderson and his family are murdered by a Southern mob after the war. Uncle Daniel, Tom Anderson's uncle, is so grief-ridden by retelling the entire story that he dies in his chair immediately after narrating the tale.

Veterans who read the story that summer and fall could identify Grant as the great commander, "General Silent." Sherman was easier—"Gen. Sherwood." The battles all had new names but were by and large factually portrayed. The aging soldiers could read about battling at "Pittskill Landing" and could identify it as Pittsburg Landing where the Battle of Shiloh was fought. "Antler's Run" was Antietam, "Pageland" was the Second Battle of Bull Run (Logan named it after an actual road that ran through the field), "Chatteraugus" was Chattanooga, and "Middleton's Ridge" was Missionary Ridge.

Those Logan despised were oftentimes easier to identify; he cleverly used the words of Uncle Daniel as a vehicle for unsparing criticism of individuals he associated with the Copperhead movement, thinly veiling their names so that anyone with fleeting knowledge of the history would know to whom he was referring. "Thomas A. Strider," a Copperhead leader in the early 1860s, was a leading antagonist in the story; Logan based the character on Vice President Thomas A. Hendricks. Another pro-Secession Northerner in his story was "'Dan' Bowen," the reprobate Logan wanted his readers to identify with former law-partner Josh Allen (Logan's tell-tale clue was putting Bowen's first name in quotes, as if it was a nickname). Although some of Logan's characterizations and activities were factual, he also allowed his unsupported suspicions to become showcased in his story. Hence, "Gen. McGregor" (George McClellan), "Gen. Farlin" (Fitz-John Porter), "Gen. William Cross" (William Rosecrans), and "Gen. Bowlly Smite" engage in a conspiracy discussion to overthrow the Lincoln administration before the president emancipates the slaves.

Logan was able to write the semi-factual, semi-fictitious book amid the distractions of constant travel, speaking tours, campaign speeches—all the necessities of two campaigns waged throughout 1884 and the first half of 1885. He also was tied down by correspondence. Seldom a day passed by when he did not receive at least 300 letters. Much of the mail was generated by veterans who petitioned Logan to help them with their pension claims. He also received much congratulatory mail from well-wishers spurring him on to greater achievements. After reading and occasionally answering his daily correspondence, he retained the mail from family and friends and discarded letters from those he did not know; however, he cherished some letters enough to hold them for posterity.

One in particular came from the son of a veteran of the Twenty-first Illinois Infantry, the regiment Grant raised and Logan spoke to on the Illinois fairgrounds in June 1861. What made the letter so special was the name of the child who sent it: John Logan Berry. It thrilled Logan to learn that he influenced people so dramatically that they named their children after him.[2]

Logan had been working on a second book; this one was turning into a huge tome about the causes of the war. There were no veiled intents here—Logan stripped the clever fictitious name-dropping from his narrative and approached it more in textbook fashion. The U.S. Senate was not set to convene until December; still, Logan found it difficult to find time to write it because he had promised to speak at various engagements in the Northeast. Logan kept his promise and attended the G.A.R. encampment at Portland, Maine, on June 21, followed up by a banquet in Boston and a hugely advertised Fourth of July speech at Woodstock, Connecticut. Mary traveled with her husband that summer, and dedicated herself to be with him throughout most of his speaking engagements. The Logans made arrangements to spend July in a suite of rooms in Atlantic City. There he found some time to work on his book while vacationing near the seashore.[3]

Logan's New England trek accomplished more than routine summer travel and family vacation. He knew he was the strongest Republican presidential candidate in the "Western" states, particularly those hugging the Mississippi River banks, but he was weakest in the South and the Northeast. Logan realized his upcoming book would not endear him to the citizens of the Old South, but he could establish a positive image in the New England states. Logan's positions "evolved" over the years to be more statesmanlike to strengthen his presidential timber. In Portland, he addressed his all-time favorite issue of pensions for the soldiers; in Boston, however, Logan addressed civil service reform (he had his forced support of the Pendleton Act to buttress his position). He returned to purely patriotic themes and stressed equal rights for all men in his Fourth of July address. At each occasion, Logan realized he was speaking to people who had never seen him before. He put his best foot forward. John Sherman, another presidential hopeful, had witnessed Logan's July Fourth address at Woodstock, and admitted it was "an eloquent and patriotic speech that was received by his audience with great applause." Said Sherman of Logan, "He was personally a stranger to the Connecticut people, but his western style and manner, unlike the more reserved and quiet tone of their home orators, gave them great pleasure."[4]

Logan's summer plans were cut short when he was informed of Grant's death on July 23, 1885. He had consented to be one of his pallbearers and performed the function at Grant's New York City funeral, a moving event for all of Grant's admirers.[5] The other major event for Logan in the summer of 1885 was a more uplifting one. He moved out of his rented Iowa Circle home into the first home he ever purchased in Washington, D.C.

He named his new house "Calumet Place" after the street where his Chicago home stood. By its purest definition it was a mansion, one that stood at the corner of Thirteenth and Clifton Streets due north of the nation's capital where it crowned the top of the highest circle of bluffs known as Columbia Heights. It formerly belonged to Senator John Sherman, but the locals always called the two-story, eight-room brick house the "Stone Mansion." It was Dr. Stone who built the house in 1848, importing the granite pillars from Scotland. During the war, the house was used as a hospital for a brief time. The property transferred from Stone to Sherman well after the war; the Ohio Senator built an addition and cut the original acreage from 150 to one before Logan expressed interest in it. The house cost $20,000—four years' Senate salary for Logan. He put $1,500 down on it and mortgaged the remainder at 6 percent for six years.

Although the Logans boasted a panoramic view with their purchase, along with a sturdy barn and outbuildings, the house itself was in a near-dilapidated state of disrepair. Half the locks were missing and several doors were broken into slivers. When Mary complained about where and what to use to furnish the place, her husband retorted, "At least we have the rooms." One writer assessed, "A few thousand dollars would have made it over into a palace." But Logan had hundreds to invest, not thousands. He and Mary spent the waning summer weeks working on the house, Mary taking charge of its beautification. She frequented secondhand stores, furnishing the house with Virginia and Maryland pieces that seemed a perfect fit in the half-century-old building. Dollie Logan Tucker sent New Mexico items as touches to the rooms. Navajo blankets and tapestry, Zuni and Maki pottery and other Native American beads, embroideries, and weaponry festooned the interior of Calumet Place. Black Jack added his war relics: headquarters flags, swords and bayonets, cartridge boxes and haversacks, army blankets and blankets hung in well-designed groups in nearly every room. "We have at last got a lovely place," Mary proclaimed to her daughter late in the summer.[6]

Logan's pride and joy of the house was the library, the room where he labored and received his friends and business callers. Lit by an overhead gas four-globe chandelier, the room was filled with paintings, photographs, relics, and simple furnishings. He transferred his book collection from Illinois to consolidate the ones he had in D.C. boardinghouses into this well-attended room. Logan owned more than 5,000 volumes, including one book so rare that reportedly he owned one of only three volumes in the country. He had several rare versions of the Bible and an extensive selection in theology. History and military studies comprised his next-most voluminous possessions. His guests could rightfully claim it was the finest private library they had ever seen.[7]

Logan spent most of the autumn of 1885 in his library where he labored to complete his book. He titled the work, *The Great Conspiracy*, borrowing from the last line of his serial publication in the *National Tribune*. With his writing desk and chair positioned by a window, Logan neatly penned his manuscript on square-cut, heavy amber paper beginning at 8:00 A.M. every morning, stopping after an hour for breakfast, and subsequently returning uninterrupted until noon. He returned afterwards for rather sporadic writing in the afternoon. Logan's evenings were spent perusing his previous day's work. When suffering brief stages of writer's block, he crossed his arms tightly and waited for the inspiration to pop into his head. Mary even aided her husband here. The only other person allowed to touch anything on Logan's desk, she marked chapters in her husband's reference works that she felt he could use and arranged all the items to ease his progress. He planned to submit and publish the book by the end of 1885, but as the autumn months came and passed, Mary noted to her daughter that he has extended his writing time but "has grown as nervous as a cat." Irritated at the reality of not completing the book on his timetable, Logan prepared to enter the Senate with only revisions left. He saw grammatical mistakes on his proof pages, but decided against correcting them, reasoning, "If I do the critics will say I did not write it, and whatever else they say I do not wish them to say that."[8]

The critics had much to say about *The Great Conspiracy* when it was released in the winter of 1886, but most of it was unkind. Logan's 800-page work was described as "a narrative stump speech." The text was uneven; the *New York Times* noted, "The writing, to be sure, seems to have been largely done with scissors and paste brush, and the product is rather a medley of speeches, resolutions, and newspaper clippings." Logan's sledgehammer blows, so characteristic in his speaking style, also dominated the book. The passion of his convictions came out strongly, but so did his lack of judicious oversight. He was too emotionally tied to his subject to offer the objectivity a detached historian could offer. "I don't count John Logan as company for historians," assessed John Hay months before the book's release. More upsetting to Logan than any negative review were the lackluster sales. His dream that the book would captivate the public anywhere near what Grant's memoirs had done would not be realized.[9]

Logan was too occupied with Senate duties long before he could appreciate how poorly his book had been selling. Restored to his old post as chairman of the

Committee on Military Affairs, Logan also sat on two other committees. He immediately tried to wield his influence as a thrice-elected senator to pass bills dearest to him, but he was thwarted in the early going of the session. His bill to create a committee to investigate the "Progress made by Negroes since the Civil War" failed to pass, as did his attempt to increase pension disbursal to wounded veterans. He and Indiana senator Benjamin Harrison were strong advocates to create a state out of Dakota Territory, a bill that passed through the Senate in February.

On March 3, Senate Bill 194 was up for debate—aid in the establishment and temporary support of common schools. Logan did not sponsor this piece of legislation, but he had advocated it publicly in a periodical three years earlier. The bill was crafted to fight illiteracy, and especially to support Southern blacks who grew up in slavery. Logan spoke after a series of amendments were proposed to restrict, popping up from his front-row seat. He admonished his colleagues for the provisions they were tagging to S194, ones he deemed utterly fatal to a proper use of the fund. He reminded the senators that he had introduced four similar bills in the past, the first one to disperse $50 million for illiterate children across the states and territories that was assailed because it would primarily go to black children, whose illiteracy rates were highest. He railed against proposals that he felt would weaken the intent of the legislation. "Alas!" he proclaimed in exasperation, "Northern men have always been found in this country and have always been found in the Congress of the United States to legislate in any direction that was wanted on the colored man for the benefit of the white man." Realizing that the effect was about to be diluted, Logan proposed an amendment to add $60 million more to the original proposal of $77 million, but he was voted down 30 to 12 (thirty-four senators were absent). He then proposed to add $2 million to build schools in rural district, primarily Negro schools. This amendment passed. On March 5 the entire amended bill finally came up for a vote and Logan joined the majority to pass it, but it failed to pass in the House of Representatives.[10]

The defeat of the education bill provided evidence that Logan's advocacy on behalf of African Americans was not popular, as were few of his positions taken over the past twenty years to raise blacks to an equal plane with whites. This failed to quell his untiring efforts on their behalf. Speaking at a black church in Washington that March, Logan assured his audience, "You have the ability and capacity to reach the highest point, and even go farther in the march of progress than has any people, yet. Slavery not only blighted you and stunted your growth, but it also blighted the intellect and dulled the perception of the Southern whites who dealt in it." Logan predicted that a great "Negro poet" will hail from the South. "He will come," declared Logan, "and, after him, other still greater men." He advised the black churchgoers that their advocacy will decide the outcome of their race: "The future is yours, and you have it in which to rise to the heights or descend to the depths."[11]

Logan busied himself throughout the first session of the Forty-ninth Congress by combining Senate duties and speaking engagements. He garnered mostly positive press reports of speeches delivered in Philadelphia and Detroit. He stayed home in March to focus entirely on Congress. Most of the senators attempted to unhorse him from his charge, for Logan learned that his political opponents sometimes occupied his side of the aisle. His gallant fight for the education bill was immediately followed by the fight for his legislation as head of the Military Affairs Committee to increase the efficiency of the army. Although Logan had earned a reputation as a trimmer of officers at the upper levels, he now advocated enlarging the army from 25,000 to 30,000 members to handle any strife that threatened the nation. This was an unpopular measure in Congress considering that Indian hostilities were on the wane and no approaching conflict appeared on the horizon. His bill was defeated, but Logan's support enhanced his popularity with the public. One correspondent predicted that in 1888 Logan would take the country "by spontaneous combustion."[12]

The Great Conspiracy, however, failed to enhance those predictions. The book was not gaining a strong foothold in America's reading circles, perhaps due to its release in a market glutted with Civil War studies and reminiscences by 1886. Surprisingly, the press and public was talking about *Uncle Daniel's Story of Tom Anderson and Twenty Great Battles*—the book version of the *National Tribune* serial he published the previous summer. Released again under the authorship "An Officer of the Union Army" in the late winter of 1886, Logan's semi-fictitious war story made a stir immediately after hitting the markets. Logan used the same New York publisher, A. R. Hart and Company, as he did for *The Great Conspiracy*, and he altered the original title to remove the "Great Conspiracy" reference that could blow away his anonymous status, but newsmen quickly succeeded in identifying him as the author, although Logan never admitted it. "Surely, surely we recognize in all this lurid and tempestuous eloquence our own and only Logan," ran a *Washington Post* editorial. "Critics will undoubtedly pay due notice to the purity of style of which Gen. Logan is such a well known master," predicted a New York reporter, "but the envy, the malice, the bitter passions of the past which it seeks to arouse are too glaring not to be noticed at a glance."[13]

What the paper identified were Logan's soapbox issues that he placed in the words and thoughts of Uncle Daniel, including a raging animosity against a South he clearly maintained had not been reconstructed. "Are we not apologizing every day for what we did?" an incredulous Uncle Daniel asks his listeners. "Do we not avoid speaking of the war in the North? Are not some of our great leaders to-day men who aided and sympathized with treason, while we teach kindness to our erring brethren and forgive all? Do we not find our flag despised nearly everywhere in the South? Do they not march under their State flags instead of the Stars and Stripes? Are not all their monuments to rebel leaders and Generals? Are not their school books full of Secession sentiments? Do they not teach the children that we conquered them with hired Hessians." Logan ends the soliloquy and Uncle Daniel's reaction, indicating it was just as much his own: "The tears stood like crystals in his eyes, and he ceased to speak for the present."[14]

The author somehow escaped confrontations from those who could identify their unflattering characterizations in the book. Senator Voorhees of Indiana, a suspected Copperhead during the war, was unaware that Logan wrote the story. Nevertheless, he was forced to publish an interview in self-defense after it was erroneously determined that he was the character "Dan Bowen," the Northern rabble-rouser and Lincoln critic who was one of the leading antagonists in the story (Logan based the character on Josh Allen, not Voorhees). Logan himself made sure some of his wartime antagonists read their own portrayals. He gave General Sherman a copy of the book, telling him he knew who the author was, but would not reveal it. When Sherman read about "General Sherwood" in *Uncle Daniel's Story*, particularly the passage with his discussion with General Anderson about the importance of academy-trained soldiers as heads of armies, he could easily discern not only who Anderson was, but who wrote the passage.[15]

Logan's passion for the nonprofessional soldier inspired him to dedicate the subject for his third book, one he titled *The Volunteer Soldier of America*. He began the project in the winter. He also prepared Civil War articles for the *National Tribune*. In addition, George Francis Dawson, one of Logan's 1884 biographers, kept in close contact with Logan to update his life story, particularly when he would throw his hat in the ring for the 1888 presidential campaign. Logan remained coy about officially declaring himself for the anticipated contest, but he had a tremendous "campaign advertisement" scheduled to enhance his potential future bid. Back in 1883, Logan reportedly commissioned a team of Polish, Austrian, and German artists to create a tremendous cyclorama—an enormous oil painting displayed in a circular theater to offer a three-dimensional effect—which would recreate the dramatic moments of the Battle of Atlanta, where Logan restored his collapsing lines to win the day on July 22, 1864. Logan intended the work to support his presidential run in 1884, but the artists, based in Milwaukee, did not get started until summer 1885. The delay would help Logan—the expected completion date of what would become the world's largest oil painting was 1887.

Logan clearly held several advantages over potential competitors for the Republican nomination. He also had an experienced campaign partner—his wife, who continued to march in lockstep with her husband at every event to which he was invited. Reporters had always taken an interest in Mary Logan, and she never failed to give them something about which to write. Most memorable to a reporter covering Mary and John Logan was Memorial Day. Logan had been a featured speaker at every May 30 event since he initiated it in 1868. The eighteenth commemoration was the first without Grant, the Union's ultimate war hero. Appropriately, Logan joined a celebrated cast to mark Memorial Day at Grant's Tomb in Riverside Park, overlooking the Hudson River in Manhattan. Logan delivered a stirring speech, one which commemorated General Grant as well as Memorial Day.[16]

Sitting at the speaker's stand, a reporter seemed less impressed with the address as he was with the special connection that bonded the Logans. By the newsman's assessment their thirty-year marriage produced a very noticeable "warmth and sympathy and affection" between the two. As soon as Logan finished speaking, several dignitaries and participants walked up to congratulate him on another job well done. But Logan was distracted; the reporter watched him turn back to seek out the eyes of his wife and, as soon as they connected while she stepped forward to wrap a silk scarf around his neck (her routine to protect his throat, no matter how hot it was), only then did he turn to his audience to have his hand shook and his back slapped. The reporter attributed the silent acknowledgment to "a sort of soul telegraphy flashing from her eyes to his that seemed to say more than words could have done that she was proud of her husband and satisfied with his effort."[17]

Mary helped her husband endure an unusually tough session in the Senate. Late in June Logan was unsuccessful in blocking the reinstatement of Fitz-John Porter. The Porter bill passed both the Senate and the House, ending Logan's decade-long mission to block it. This defeat was followed by his unfortunate vote against an investigation of the charges of corruption and bribery in the election of Senator Henry B. Payne of Ohio. As a member of the Committee on Privileges and Elections, Logan and two other Republicans (John Sherman and Bill Evarts) sided with the Democrats of that body, maintaining there was not enough evidence to warrant an investigation. But the Ohio press was livid and unforgiving, dogging Logan for days about his decision. Murat Halstead, the editor of the

Cincinnati Commercial Gazette, was particularly rough on Logan, as he had been to Ulysses S. Grant and Abraham Lincoln before him. But Logan made light of his criticism. Reading an editorial of his role in the Payne case from Halstead's paper on the Senate floor, Logan focused on the line, "The Presidential boom of two distinguished United States Senators can now be tenderly laid away to eternal rest." Logan, his colleagues, and the audience in the gallery knew that he and Senator Sherman were Halstead's targets, but Logan turned to Senator Evarts and deadpanned, "That means yourself and the Senator from Ohio, Mr. Sherman. It cannot allude to anybody else." The audience laughed appreciatively.[18]

Logan's hapless session of Congress mercifully closed in July, clearing the way for a summer trip to change his luck. He and his wife embarked upon a months-long trip to the Pacific Coast and back. They joined Governor Russell A. Alger of Michigan with the intent to attend the G.A.R. meeting in San Francisco. Alger's staff occupied the same private car with their governor and his most celebrated celebrity. "I never met a more agreeable man in my life," said Major George H. Hopkins upon meeting Logan for the first time. Hopkins was stunned at Black Jack's popularity in the western half of the country. Mary recalled the trip as "one continuous ovation for General Logan from the time we left Chicago until we reached San Francisco." Hopkins's version of the trip asserted that Mary was not entirely exaggerating. "We had little time for sociability in the daytime owing to the demonstrations along the road," claimed Hopkins. "The train stopped every few minutes, and at each stop a crowd of people were in waiting. Of course they usually demanded a speech and Logan gratified them when possible. His good nature in that time was almost boundless."[19]

The whistle-stop performances repeated themselves from Chicago to Omaha, and continued across the Union Pacific and Central Pacific Railroads to Sacramento, then over to San Francisco. San Francisco treated Logan like royalty; only General Sherman commanded as much attention at the spectacular event. Escorted by 10,000 grizzled veterans in the daylight parade down Market Street, a brigade of young ladies, armed with baskets of flowers, littered the street with roses for the two dignitaries to pass over. The following night at a grand festival concert, Logan entered the hall and tried to take a front-row seat near the orchestra during the performance of the chorus, but he was recognized by the audience who deafened the hall with such a din of cheers that he almost instinctively mounted the stage to bow to the acknowledgment. The young ladies of the chorus tore off their corsage bouquets and showered him with flowers. A perfect rain of petals and stems fell upon his head and shoulders at what appeared more a coronation than a convention.[20]

"They are making a great fuss over him here," wrote an attendee to his son about Logan; "I should imagine by the look of things that he will be the next Republican choice for President." The accolades for Logan were not universal. He created an undercurrent of resentment from those who felt that he was stumping too strongly in a supposed apolitical occasion. He was accused of milking the spontaneous gestures into prolonged pro-Logan moments. His spread-eagle oratory reportedly wore thin on some of the leaders, but the audience—particularly those seeing Logan for the first time—soaked it all up and appeared to have plenty of room for more.[21]

Logan never felt more alive than in front of adoring crowds. From San Francisco he took a train and stage to Portland. No fewer than 7,000 Oregonians were on hand to meet the Civil War hero and celebrated senator. Logan did not disappoint, delivering a strong oration to his fans. He even added a moment of unintentional self-deprecating humor in Oregon. At Buttesville he spied an empty and enticing hammock swinging in a grape arbor; he could not resist a moment of comfortable repose. Swinging softly and humming "Swing Low, Sweet Chariot," his respite was cut short when the hammock gave way and sent him straight down on top of several apples. "He wasn't especially injured," reported the local paper, "but his spirit was grieved."[22]

Logan's grieved spirit recovered and soared for the rest of this tour. Side trips to Nevada and a northern trek to Puget Sound completed his summer extravaganza; in five weeks, Logan and his entourage logged 8,500 miles encompassing sixteen states and territories. He called it "one of the most instructive and delightful trips of my life." Buoyed by the overwhelming response he received in the West, Logan continued his momentum by sweeping through Illinois from Chicago to Cairo in September. He also managed to slip in a speech in Pittsburg during his Illinois canvass. On October 4 he spoke at Marion, his former home and the scene of his dramatic recruiting speech for the "Dirty-first" Illinois in August 1861.[23]

The extended speaking tour essentially launched Logan's quest for the presidency for 1888, although newspapers had commented on the "Logan Boom" one year before. His speeches were infused with the issues of the time, particularly the tariff. Logan castigated the Cleveland administration for its free-trade policy and quest for lower tariffs on imports. Unlike his anti-tariff days fifteen years earlier, Logan was an economic protectionist who favored high tariffs on imports to reduce free trade. He took the time in his addresses to detail the history of tariff legislation between the two parties, attributing the gigantic growth of the manufacturing industries to the fostering care of the protective tariff laws enacted by the Republican party. His harshest critics were quick to criticize his view. "Perhaps we may have a slight preference for him because he seems to represent all that is narrow and besotted and Bourbonistic in Republicanism, and is therefore the most easily to be defeated," the *Washington Post* informed its readers.[24]

He stayed in Illinois, headquartering himself in Chicago's Grand Pacific Hotel. There he worked on his third book while finding time to speak at advertised locales. On October 21 he wowed a crowd of 8,000 in Keokuk, Iowa, speaking about the tariff, pension vetoes, and other disagreements with the Cleveland administration. One month later he spoke to a similarly large crowd at Youngstown, Ohio. He likely met his future in-laws there. His son met Edith Andrews, a Youngstown girl, during the 1884 presidential campaign; the young couple was engaged to be married early in 1887.

Logan returned to Calumet Place late in November with his family united. Major Will Logan, with his father-in-law's influence, was relocated from New Mexico to Washington, uniting Dollie Tucker and her seven-year-old son Logan with her parents and his grandparents. John Logan II also made Calumet Place his temporary home before his upcoming wedding. The united family filled the large house as the holiday season of 1886 entered its first days.[25]

Undoubtedly the happiest member of Logan's household at this stage was Mary. She had sacrificed much to support her husband's career, but had grown quite comfortable and confident in her advancing role as a leader in Washington society. One prominent member of that society ranked her as "perhaps the most popular person in Washington." She never was closer to her husband than during the past eighteen months, and she was ecstatic to have him back home, although she fretted how the previous tour had worn him out.[26]

They were together for their thirty-first wedding anniversary and the following day, the Sunday after Thanksgiving, they attended the Metropolitan Church together, their Methodist house of worship, to hear their pastor, John P. Newman. The last time he was at the church, Logan had received the sacrament from Reverend Newman for the first time. After the sermon the Logan couple accompanied the pastor to his study where they engaged him in a long discussion about religion and relationships, among other things. Newman was impressed with Logan's intellect, but even more so with the mellowing of the caustic opinions he held against those that disagreed with him or did him an injustice. Logan's statesman-like approach in his policies and speeches in recent months, therefore, was a product of both political expediency and of an altruistic amelioration of his partisanship.[27]

Logan returned to his library at the end of November, writing furiously to complete the *Volunteer Soldier of America*. Some had discouraged Logan from his current project, explaining that his personal memoirs would sell much better, but Logan was dedicated to his thesis that America would be better off with a volunteer army rather than a professional one. He decided to include a brief section of his Civil War memoirs in an effort to entice a publisher to take on his project.

Knowing how important Samuel Clemens (Mark Twain) was to the sales success of the late Ulysses S. Grant's *Personal Memoirs*, Logan solicited Clemens for his two-year-old publishing company to take on his current book. Clemens was prepared to offer Logan 40 percent of profits. Having turned down an offer of $10,000 for his memoirs from A. R. Hart, Logan could breathe easier with the prospect of earning more with the pending deal of Clemens's company. The book deal was vital, for Logan had accumulated substantial debt from previous business dealings gone awry. His lifestyle was more extravagant, although he usually had his train trips and speaking engagements completely covered by others. Still, he needed to offset a total debt that approached $40,000, a price tag his Senate salary alone could barely dent.[28]

Logan completed his manuscript just as the Senate convened in December. He returned to Capitol Hill on December 4. But four days later he suffered from another attack of rheumatism, one that struck him in the hip and hand. It worsened so much by December 9 that he wrapped his sore hand in a handkerchief as he toiled in his committee room. The rheumatism forced Logan to retreat to his bed at Calumet Place after this day in the Senate. As in Chicago in 1875 and more recently in Washington in 1883, Logan grew stiff, feverish and swollen from the flareup of his disease. He agonized over the pain and his mood turned surly. He and the family discussed a return to Hot Springs, Arkansas, since the trip there three years before had been such a panacea for him. By the middle of the month he recovered enough to sit for long spells in his easy chair. Although he was not getting progressively better, he did not worsen either, so talk of traveling westward was put off for the holidays.[29]

A parade of well-wishers visited Logan at this time and found him a pleasant conversationalist. He would greet them in his favorite chamber on the second story of Calumet Place. The room offered a distant view of the Capitol. He sat in his easy chair next to the fireplace with a cotton-wrapped right arm swollen to twice its normal size. As pains shot through his arm, Logan would growl in agony, but he filled in the time between these painful episodes with interesting and lively tales. "The harder the twinge, the better the story," reported a newspaper; "One standing just outside the chamber door and hearing the peals of laughter would [hardly] imagine there was any suffering going on within."[30]

Logan's talkative proclivities proved a benefit to a reporter for a St. Louis newspaper who stopped by for an interview. Logan gave the newsman a stellar column to write about the Civil War, filled with opinions of leading generals, causes, what-if scenarios, and previously unknown campaign details. Logan loved to engage in war talk; rather than consider the reporter a nuisance, he conducted the interview as an early Christmas present for both men. Inside one and a half years from the presidential conventions of 1888, the reporter evidently sought Logan for his topic believing him to be the top candidate for the Republican Party.[31]

As the days ticked off closer to the anticipated holiday, Logan and his family looked forward to their first family Christmas together in years. But cautious joy turned to worry and despair on December 22 when Logan took a turn for the worse. He lapsed into semi-consciousness and grew noticeably weaker. Visitors still called upon him when he was lucid enough to talk, but Mary restricted the number and the time they spent with him. "This is one of the worst attacks I have had for a long time," Logan told Senator Cullom, the junior senator of Illinois, during the afternoon of December 23. "It's hard work to pull through it."

Logan's condition took a more dangerous downward turn on Christmas Eve. He became incoherent, confused, short-tempered with his grandson, and suffered from lapses into semi-consciousness. That Friday night, his attending physician horrified the family when he announced that the disease had invaded his brain. He called it "cerebral rheumatism," the deadliest form of the malady. He was not optimistic. As stoic as she could be, Mary told Chicago reporters that night, "I fear we cannot conceal it from ourselves much longer, and the General's friends at home should know it. He is a very sick man. We hope for a turn for the better tomorrow, but the doctors give us little encouragement."[32]

It all happened too fast, and at the absolute worst time. Christmas Day was a death watch at Calumet Place. Logan survived the day, only to have his pulse weaken dangerously after midnight. He rallied by daylight, but when his doctors consulted at 9:00 A.M., they sadly informed the family there was absolutely no hope for him. By noon they expected death to overtake him before the day's end.

Washington's residents read of Logan's critical illness in the morning papers. They immediately thronged to Columbia Heights, scaling the hill on foot or riding up by carriage to stand in vigil outside Calumet Place. Logan's closest friends had been invited inside; most were isolated to the first floor. A dozen people, including his family, Reverend Newman, Dr. Baxter, General Henderson, and General Sheridan surrounded the unconscious patriarch. Logan lay propped up against a plain mahogany bedstead in the second-story chamber in the southwest corner of the house. He was comatose; his slow and steady breathing his only visible movement. Perhaps he contracted the fatal condition chasing horse thieves in the 1840s, but exposure during the Civil War flared up eruptions that would never cease. The War that made his life was killing him.

At 2:00 he opened his eyes and locked gazes with his wife, who had been kneeling at the head of his bed for hours, one arm encircling his neck while she soothingly talked to him. For a moment, the "soul telegraphy" flashed from her eyes to his before he wearily closed his eyes again and lapsed back into complete unconsciousness.[33]

Dark and ominous clouds formed a thick ceiling over the winter sky throughout the day, but no precipitation fell from them for several hours. At 2:56 P.M., as a few feathery flakes finally floated past the windows of Calumet Place, Logan suddenly produced two sharp, guttural exhalations in rapid succession—someone in the room likened it to a salute. Then his body was consumed by peace. The Reverend Newman immediately divined what was happening and offered up a prayer commanding Logan's soul to the Father Almighty. Three minutes before three o'clock on Sunday, December 26, 1886, General John A. Logan dutifully complied with his orders and reported for duty.

"He is dead," Dr. Baxter whispered at his bedside, "He is dead."[34]

Epilogue

NEWS OF THE DEATH OF JOHN A. LOGAN stunned a nation. "Since the death of Abraham Lincoln, the people of the whole country have not received such a shock as that caused by the brief message which flashed over the wires yesterday afternoon: 'Logan is dead,'" announced an Illinois newspaper; "No one asked 'What Logan?'" A Wisconsin paper hailed, "Logan was a truly great man," and the *Washington National Intelligencer* proclaimed, "A HERO has fallen. John A. Logan has joined the silent majority."

Every city and county newspaper from Maine to California reported Logan's death as a front-page headline. "Logan!" announced the *Washington National Republican* with its one-word headline; "'Black Eagle' Gone" and "'Black Jack' Gone" headlined the *Philadelphia Press* and the *St. Louis Post Dispatch*. Readers of the *Illinois State Journal* were perhaps most struck by their headline. The paper's entire front page contained the image of an unscrolled banner with Logan's face in the center, the names of all his battles aligned toward the bottom of the banner, and the word "Logan" splashed at the very bottom of the page.[1]

"I admired Logan, and his death depresses me," one of his friends told a reporter. Sharing the man's grief were thousands of Americans from all walks of life. Logan's life course and decisions inspired them to praise him wherever and whenever they could. Particularly affected was the African American community, one of whom noted that Logan, "like Saul of Tarsus, was convicted of his error in persecuting the people of the Lord, and buckled on his sword and went forth to lead the volunteer hosts in freedom's fight, pausing not until struck down at his post of duty by the angel of death." Another black orator asserted, "I think I voice the sentiments of my colored friends when I say that his name will be honored and revered by them—second only to that of the immortal Lincoln." Samuel R. Lowery, a black lawyer and editor in Huntsville, Alabama, wrote of Logan, "We have lost a true friend of the colored race, whose speech in our behalf was as fear-less as his life as a soldier and patriot." Not surprisingly, Frederick Douglass also had something to say about the man he endorsed in 1884. "Of John A. Logan," assessed Douglass many months after his death, "it is only needed to say that he was the dread of traitors, the defender of loyal soldiers, and the true friend of the newly-made citizens of the Republic. Much was predicated for our cause on this man's future. But he, too, in the order of Providence, has laid off his armor."[2]

Most big city papers featured articles about him that carried into January 1887, acquainting the public with stories of his life told by family and friends, an-ecdotes of the Civil War as recalled by fellow soldiers, and political tales re-counted by fellow state and national legislators. Logan's body lay in state in the rotunda of the Capitol for the final two days of 1886. Only the seventh person to receive such an honor, Logan's coffin was the endpoint for lines of citizens who came out in adverse December weather to pay their final respects to a man who appropriately was coffined in the same government institution of democracy where he had labored since 1859.

Notwithstanding a pounding storm of sleet, Logan's funeral on December 31 attracted tens of thousands of people on January 1. He was laid to rest tem-porarily in the tomb of a family friend in Rock Creek Cemetery adjacent to the park of the same name in northwest Washington. He subsequently was removed to his own specially crafted granite memorial chapel erected by his wife at the southeast corner of the National Cemetery of the Soldier's Home near the Rock Creek burial ground.[3]

Logan's book, *The Volunteer Soldier of America*, was released in March 1887. Samuel Clemens's company did not publish it; a less renowned company took the project as well as a book of Logan's life that also came out that year. Neither book sold well, but a substantial fund was raised to pay off Logan's debts and support his widow. Both legislative bodies of the U.S. Congress con-vened and produced a memorial tribute to their deceased colleague. Even staunch Democrats from the Solid South—including ex-Confederate soldiers—

put away their animosities and offered only words of praise. Their sessions were published by the government in a 200-page book and released to the public. The Atlanta cyclorama, depicting Logan during his most dramatic moment in the Civil War, also came out that year and traveled the country under the title: "Logan's Great Battle." The legend of Logan was ubiquitous in 1887.

Logan had expected the near simultaneous releases of his book, his biography, and the cyclorama to bolster his presidential boom. He had forecasted that the tariff and Cleveland's free-trade policies would become major issues in the campaign in 1888; it was. The Republican National Convention met in Chicago in June to select their candidate to challenge the president on these issues. Senators Blaine and Sherman, perennial Republican candidates, returned to vie for the crown, but it was former Indiana senator and Civil War colonel Benjamin Harrison who won the nomination on the eighth ballot. The Republicans were better organized and had more funds than the Democrats, but Cleveland still won the popular vote over Harrison in November by a mere 90,000 votes out of 11 million cast. Notwithstanding the popular vote disparity, Benjamin Harrison won the presidency with his large win in the Electoral College: 233 to 168. His victory was partly achieved on the same tariff views Logan had espoused throughout 1886. Harrison's 55-vote Electoral College win was achieved despite Cleveland's capture of every state below the Mason-Dixon Line. Had Logan been the Republican candidate, he would likely have repeated Harrison's failure to take one state in the Solid South, but he was just as likely to win the other regions that Harrison claimed to become the twenty-third president of the United States.

John A. Logan's brother and sister had been colorful nuisances throughout his adult life. Dorothula "Annie" Logan, the acerbic thrice-married sister, continued to carry herself with shaky stability after her famous brother's death. Unable to shake off her demons, Annie committed suicide by overdosing on morphine in September 1894. Conversely, Tom Logan turned his life around after divorcing his second wife. He swore off the bottle and somehow became a respected citizen in Jackson County Illinois until his death in 1907.[4]

John A. Logan II straightened out his life after he married Edith Andrews in the spring of 1887. Forced to resign from West Point in 1884 for a boyish prank, young Logan had tried several occupations before settling on a farm in Youngstown where he—like his father and grandfather before him—became enamored with blood horses. (He was the first to import the Hackney breed to the United States.) Also like his father, Logan proved the volunteer military was his calling. In 1898 he participated in the Spanish American War on the staff of

Major General John C. Bates and took part in the battles at El Caney, San Juan Hill, and Santiago. After the war he returned to Cuba in the Army of Occupation until malaria forced him to return to the States. He recovered and reentered the service in 1899, commissioned a major in command of a battalion of the Thirty-third U. S. Volunteer Infantry. They were sent to the Philippines. Sailing from San Francisco, Major Logan announced, "If it is ordered that my life goes out on the battlefield, I hope it will be leading my men against the enemy."[5]

Ironically, Major Logan's regiment was attached to General Lloyd Wheaton's command. Thirty-six years earlier, Wheaton worked on the staff of General John A. Logan during the Vicksburg Campaign. General Wheaton made sure that the son of his former boss worked under him; he allowed Logan to reconnoiter and then to lead the advance to San Jacinto on the morning of November 11, 1899. Major Logan assailed an entrenched position and—while tending to a wounded sergeant in his command—he was shot and killed by a Filipino sniper. He was posthumously awarded the Congressional Medal of Honor. President McKinley assured Mary Logan that her late husband would have been proud of their son. John Hay wrote her, "It should be some consolation to you that few women have had such a husband and such a son to lose."[6]

Few men have had such a wife and mother as did John A. Logan and John A. Logan II. Mary Logan never married again after John A. Logan died, but she dedicated much of her remaining life to preserving his memory. It began with Calumet Place; she turned an entire wing of the house into a shrine to him. Her "Memorial Hall" was adorned with relics, portraits, documents, and souvenirs to show to her visitors. Joseph Pulitzer and his wife stayed with her and dubbed the doleful arrangement "The Mausoleum." She sold the house to William Jennings Bryan in 1913 but the Memorial Hall apparently remained a constant. A visitor to Calumet Place in 1914 complained about "that gaunt house with the piratical face of John A. Logan staring at you from stained-glass windows, frescoes, canvases, and marble carvings."[7]

Mary remained a favorite of the G.A.R. and was often invited as a special dignitary at their events, particularly their national encampments. She contributed articles to the *National Tribune*, highlighting some of her firsthand accounts of the Civil War. She traveled extensively overseas and hobnobbed with Washington dignitaries (she remained in the capital after selling her house). She and her daughter organized the District of Columbia society of the Dames of the Loyal Legion of the United States (DOLLUS). She also was an active writer, editing the *Home Magazine* for seven years, writing syndicated columns for the newspapers of

William Randolph Hearst, and writing four books. Her *Reminiscences of A Soldier's Wife*, published in 1913, attracted widespread readership, partly due to its concurrent abridged publication in serial form in *Cosmopolitan Magazine.*[8]

A lifelong activist, Mary represented the precursor of the women's suffrage movement. It was likely her influence that piqued her husband's interest in the right to vote for women. Senator Logan had voted to organize a select committee to investigate women's suffrage in 1881, and he corresponded with Susan B. Anthony the year before he died. Mary continued her advocacy of the cause, living long enough to see the Nineteenth Amendment—ratified in 1920—guarantee that right. Mary Logan died in February of 1923, and with her went the strongest defender of the memory of John Alexander Logan.[9]

Logan's name can be found sporadically into the second century after his death. A fort in Colorado, and a college and museum in Southern Illinois bear his name. Five statues have been erected in his honor, including one in Murphysboro, near his birthplace, one at John A. Logan Community College in Carterville, one in the Vicksburg National Military Park in western Mississippi, one in Grant Park off Michigan Avenue in Chicago, and one in the center of Iowa Circle (renamed as "Logan Circle") in northwestern Washington, D.C. The Atlanta Cyclorama, housed in another Grant Park in Atlanta, no longer bears Logan's name, but highlights his outstanding moment of generalship at the Battle of Atlanta. The state song of Illinois has only three surnames in it: Lincoln, Grant, and Logan; only the latter was born in the state.

The Logan Mausoleum at the Soldiers Home National Cemetery houses the remains of the general and his wife and daughter (his son is buried in Youngstown, Ohio). In front of the stone mausoleum stands a gold-lettered placard dedicated verbatim to Logan's General Orders Number 11: the original Memorial Day decree. The tribute, delivered by John P. Newman on the last day of 1886, captures the legend of John A. Logan, the causes he championed, and the legacy he created:

> Today 350,000 veterans in the Grand Army of the Republic, from 6,000 posts, feel that they have lost a friend. Today 622,000 pensioners bless his memory. Today 230,000 widows and orphans breathe a prayer to heaven for the peace of his soul. And now the spirits of 350,000 patriot soldiers, slain in the war, gather around the great soul of Logan, and thank him that on each returning 30th day of May their graves are not forgotten, but are covered with flowers. The designation of that day for memorial service was

suggested by Logan, and he was wont to say: "It was the proudest act of my life." And today, could the 350,000 patriot dead rise from their graves, each with a memorial flower in his hand, there would rise a floral mountain to the skies, the perfume of which would ascend in gratitude to the god of battles. Logan deserves such a monument of flowers. He himself is a martyr of liberty.[10]

Notes

INTRODUCTION

1 A newspaper report placed Grant's weight at 135 pounds in mid June. See "Gen. Grant's Summer Trip," *NY Times*, June 16, 1885.

2 "Logan's Raven Locks," *Indianapolis Daily Journal*, January 1, 1887; W. F. G. Shanks, quoted in "Recollections of General Rosseau," *Harper's New Monthly Magazine* 31 (Nov. 1865): 763.

3 George F. Dawson, *Life and Services of Gen John A. Logan as Soldier and Statesman* (Chicago & New York: Belford, Clarke & Co., 1887), 363–71.

4 "Colored Men for Logan," *NY Times*, April 1, 1884.

5 Dawson, 373; "Gen. Grant's Summer Trip."

6 Col. Fred. D. Grant, quoted in "Gen. Ulysses S. Grant," *The National Tribune*, February 3, 1887.

7 A. S. O. "Logan and McPherson: The Two Heroes of the Memorable Battle before Atlanta," *The National Tribune*, July 10, 1884.

8 Mrs. John A. Logan, *Reminiscences of a Soldier's Wife: An Autobiography* (Carbondale: Southern Illinois Univ. Press, 1997), 426; Dawson, 373; Mark Perry, *Grant and Twain: The Story of a Friendship That Changed America* (New York: Random House, 2004), 154–55. Fred Grant reported on June 9 that his father had completed the preface to the first volume of the memoirs (*NY Times*, June 10, 1885).

9 "Gen. Grant's Gifts," *Washington Post*, June 11, 1885. The New York correspondent places Logan in Grant's house on June 10 and confirms a three-hour conversation between the two.

CHAPTER ONE: HIS FATHER'S SON

1 Margaret Logan Davis Phelps, Family Record—Logan Family (1883), Typescript, General John A. Logan Museum, Murphysboro, Illinois (Hereinafter cited as GJALM), 1–3, 6.

2 Family Record, 6.

3 Family Record, 6; James H. Brownlee, *History of Jackson County, Illinois* (Philadelphia: Brink, McDonough & Co., 1878), 72; Dr. John Logan File, Barbara Burr Hubbs Papers, Southern Illinois University, Carbondale, Illinois (Hereinafter cited as HP).

4 Louis Houck, *A History of Missouri*, vol. 2 (Chicago: R. R. Donnelley & Sons, 1908), 179–80, 186; Family Record, 6. The author is indebted to H. Meyers for analyzing the timeline of the Logan family and their transmigration from Ohio to Cape Girardeau.

5 Family Record, 6–9. Number of slaves obtained from Typescript of Logan Family at GJALM.

6 Family Record, 9–10; Dr. Logan File, HP.

7 Theodore Calvin Pease, *The Frontier State, 1818–1848* (Springfield: Illinois Centennial Commission, 1918), 70–90.

8 "Logan Reminiscences," *Cincinnati Commercial Gazette*, January 2, 1887; "Logan Whips the Widow's Son," http://www.iltrails.org/Jackson/jchis.htm; Dr. Logan File, HP.

9 "Logan Reminiscences," *Cincinnati Commercial Gazette*, January 2, 1887; Description of Elizabeth Jenkins provided in Dawson, 4 and Family Record, 10.

10 Family Record, 10; "Logan Died Not a Pauper," *Chicago Tribune*, December 31, 1886; "General Logan's Courtship, *Chicago Tribune*, January 1, 1887; "Logan Reminiscences," *Cincinnati Commercial Gazette*, January 2, 1887.

11 Logan Family Bible Records, Logan Family Papers, Abraham Lincoln Presidential Library, Springfield, Illinois (Hereinafter cited as ALPL); Milo M. Quaife, ed., *Growing Up with Southern Illinois, 1820 to 1861, from the Memoirs of Daniel Harmon Brush* (Chicago: R. R. Donnelley & Sons, 1944), 61–62.

12 George Washington Smith, *A History of Southern Illinois: A Narrative of its Historical Progress, its People, and its Principal Interests*, vol. 1 (Chicago and New York: Lewis Publishing Co., 1912), 182; Kenneth Winkle, *The Young Eagle: The Rise of Abraham Lincoln* (Dallas: Taylor Trade Publishing, 2001), 28.

13 Dr. Logan, Alexander Jenkins, and Joel Manning files, HP; Barbara Burr, "Letters From Two Wars," *Journal of the Illinois State Historical Society* 30 (1937): 136.

14 Dr. Logan, letter to Monday Dumbaly, Quit Claim, July 3, 1837, Jackson County Deed Book D, 460–61, Murphysboro, IL. Farm description from several sources, including Quaife, 61 and James Green Memoir, Typescript in GJALM.

15 *Jackson County, Illinois: Formation and Early Settlement* (Murphysboro: Jackson County Historical Society, 1983), 17; Burr, "Letters From Two Wars," 135.

16 R. S. Tuthill, "Recollections of Gen. John A. Logan," 1884, Wisconsin Historical Society Archives, Madison, Wisconsin.

17 *Washington Evening Star*, December 27, 1886.

18 Dr. Logan, letter to "Dear nephew," July, 1847, Ozburn Papers, Southern Illinois University.

19 Quaife, 99, 132; Logan Family Bible Records, ALPL.

20 "Teachers of Jackson County," http://www.iltrails.org/jackson/teachers.htm; Woodson W. Fishback, *History of Murphysboro, Illinois, 1843–1982* (Brandon, MS: Quail Ridge Press, 1982), 74; Family Record, 10; Dr. Logan, letter to "my dear little sons," December 8, 1836, Logan Family Papers, ALPL; Dr. Logan File, HP.

21 "At Logan's Old Home," *Iowa State Register*, January 2, 1887.

22 Ed Hasse, *Southern Illinois: A Glimpse at the Past and Present in the Land of Contrasts* (Carbondale: Southern Illinois Univ. Communications, 1966), 15.

23 Winkle, 24.

24 Dr. Logan File, HP.

25 "Address of Mr. Henderson, of Illinois," in W. B. Taylor, comp., *Memorial Addresses on the Life and Character of John Alexander Logan (A Senator from Illinois), Delivered in the Senate and House of Representatives, February 9 and 16, 1887* (Washington: GPO, 1887), 81.

26 Barbara Burr Hubbs, *Pioneer Folks and Places: An Historical Gazetteer of Williamson County, Illinois* (Herrin, IL: Press of the *Herrin Daily Journal*, 1939), 50–52; Newton Bateman and Paul Selby, eds., *Historical Encyclopedia of Illinois*, vol. 1 (Chicago: Munsell Publishing Co., 1908), 458; "Roots Generation 6," http://www.eroots.net/generation6.htm.

27 "Tales About His Youth," *Chicago Tribune*, December 30, 1886; Daniel Brush recollections of Logan published in the *Chicago Tribune*, January 2, 1887.

28 J. W. Buel, *The Standard Bearers. The Authorized Pictorial Lives of James Gillespie Blaine and John Alexander Logan* (St. Louis: Historical Publishing Co., 1884), 315–16; "Tales About His Youth," *Chicago Tribune*, December 30, 1886. A similar version of this story in John A. Wall, *History of Jefferson County, Illinois* (Indianapolis: B.F. Bowen & Co., 1909, 58) but makes the embroidered claim that each man bet all of his property on the outcome, which resulted in Logan losing all of his stock "except Walnut Cracker, and the Governor said that he didn't want him."

29 Dr. Logan, letter to Elizabeth Logan, April 7, 1838, LFP; "Tales About His Youth," *Chicago Tribune*, December 30, 1886; Quaife, 62; Dr. Logan, letter to Elizabeth Logan, August 5, 1842, Logan Family Papers, ALPL. The "derived" Gospel quote can be found in Matthew 16:26.

30 "Tales About His Youth," *Chicago Tribune*, December 30, 1886.

31 "The Deposition of Witnesses in the Thomas Logan Case and John Logan Case," Logan Family Papers; "Logan Whips the Widow's Son," http://www.iltrails.org/Jackson/jchis.htm; "At His Old Home," *Chicago Tribune*, December 29, 1886. The panther story was provided by Tom Logan.

32 Thomas W. Knox, *The Lives of James G. Blaine and John A. Logan* (Hartford, Conn.: The Harford Publishing Co., 1884), 266–67; Hubbs, *Pioneer Folks and Places*, 86–87.

33 Barbara Burr, "Letters From Two Wars," 136; James Wilkinson Dumbaly Quit Claim, Jackson County Courthouse; Dr. Logan, letter to Elizabeth Logan, December 10, 1846, Logan Family Papers.

34 The anti-drinking composition is in Logan Family Papers.

35 Quaife, 124–35; James Pickett Jones, *Black Jack: John A. Logan and Southern Illinois in the Civil War Era* (1967; reprint, Carbondale: Southern Illinois Univ. Press, 1995), 5–6; *Jackson County*, 25, 75; Brownlee, 13, 25.

36 Burr, "Letters from Two Wars," 135–37.

37 "The People vs. John A. Logan," Jackson County Courthouse, Murphysboro, Illinois; George Washington Smith, 1: 228–29; "Tales About His Youth," *Chicago Tribune*, December 30, 1886.

38 Dates of death on tombstone inscriptions in Murphysboro city cemetery; Family Record, 10, Quaife, 147–48.

39 "Gen. Logan's Courtship," *Cincinnati Commercial Gazette*, January 8, 1887.

40 Ibid.

41 "Tales About His Youth," *Chicago Tribune*, December 30, 1886.

42 John Alexander Logan File, HP.

43 "Logan's First and Last Illness: Rheumatism," *Chicago Daily Inter-Ocean*, December 27, 1886; Family Record, 11.

44 Louisa V. Logan and Cyrus Thomas Files, HP; Casey, letter to Dr. Logan, August 31, 1850, typescript at GJALM.

45 Cyrus Thomas File, HP; [Dr.] John Logan to the Voters, October 22, 1850, *Alton Telegraph and Democratic Review*, November 1, 1850; 1850 Census of Jackson Country Illinois, National Archives, Washington, D.C.; Knox, 269; "Logan in Louisville," *Chicago Tribune*, December 29, 1886.

46 George Washington Smith, 2: 611; "About John Logan," [Carbondale] *Freepress*, July 29, 1899; Thomas M. Logan File, HP.

47 "General Logan's Courtship," *Chicago Tribune*, January 1, 1887. Several case file transcripts of the Jenkins–Logan team are housed in John Alexander Logan Papers, Manuscript Division, Library of Congress, Washington, D. C. (Hereinafter cited as LP).

48 Dawson, 9; Denning, letter to Dr. Logan, September 1, 1852, LP.

49 The Seventeenth Amendment, passed in 1913, changed the election of U.S. senators from the legislature to a popular vote of the state populace.

50 "Stories of Logan's Life," *Chicago Tribune*, January 3, 1887.

51 John A. Logan File, HP.

52 Memoir of James Green, Typescript in the GJALM; Quaife, 125; "'Black Jack's' Candid Comments," *The Egyptian Key*, March, 1947, 19.

53 Arthur C. Cole, *The Era of the Civil War* (Springfield: Illinois Centennial Commission, 1919) 225; Manuscript of Logan's speech in LP.

54 Eighteenth General Assembly, *General Laws of the State of Illinois* (Springfield: Lanphier & Walker, Printers, 1853), 57–60; Cole, 225; Roger D. Bridges, "The Illinois Black Codes," www.lib.niu.edu/ipo/iht329602.html.

55 "Hon. John A. Logan," *Alton Weekly Courier*, April 1, 1853 (also quotes Franklin County's *Benton Standard* within article).

56 "Hon. John A. Logan," *Alton Weekly Courier*, April 1, 1853.

57 Logan Family File, HP; *Daily Alton Telegraph*, August 23, 1853; Jackson County Circuit Court Files, 1853, Murphysboro; Family Record, 15.

CHAPTER TWO: PRINCE OF EGYPT

1   John A. Marshall, *American Bastille: A History of the Illegal Arrests and Imprisonment of American Citizens During the Late Civil War*, 24th ed. (Philadelphia: Thomas W. Hartley, 1880), 174; "The People of the State of Illinois vs. Israel Blanchard," Jackson County Circuit Court Files, Murphysboro; John Logan estate sale, HP.

2   Quaife, 190.

3   Quaife, 193–94; "The People of the State of Illinois vs. Israel Blanchard," Jackson County Circuit Court Files, Murphysboro.

4   John Logan law account book, Logan Family Papers; Dorothula Angeline (Annie) Logan File, HP; Family Record, 13.

5   "Tales About His Youth," *Chicago Tribune*, December 30, 1886.

6   "Decisions of the Supreme Court of the State of Illinois November Term, 1854 at Mount Vernon," HP.

7   Cairo *City Times*, November 1, 1854.

8   James M. McPherson, *Battle Cry of Freedom: The Civil War Era* (New York: Oxford Univ. Press, 1988), 121–25; David Herbert Donald, *Lincoln* (New York: Simon & Schuster, 1995), 167–69. Professor McPherson is convinced that "this law may have been the most important single event pushing the nation toward civil war."

9   McPherson, 125–28.

10   Cairo *City Times*, November 1, 1854, Usher F. Linder, *Early Reminiscences of the Bench and Bar* (Chicago: Chicago Legal News Co., 1879), unnumbered pages in HP.

11   "Senatorial Election," Galena *Weekly Northwestern Gazette*, February 9, 1855.

12   Cairo *City Times*, May 2, 1855.

13   Dawson, 9. ML, *Reminiscences*, 52.

14   "Logan Reminiscences," *Chicago Tribune*, December 29, 1886; Buel, 325–26.

15   John M. Palmer, *Bench and Bar of Illinois*, vol. 1 (Chicago: Lewis Publishing, 1899), 15; Harry Edward Pratt, "David Davis," in *Transactions of the Illinois Historical Society* (1930), 163; Donald, 104–106; "Recollections of Mrs. John A. Logan," Typescript monograph in LP.

16   Buel, 331–33.

17   Mary Logan (Hereinafter cited as ML), *Reminiscences*, 37–39; "Gen. Logan's Courtship," *Chicago Tribune*, January 1, 1887; John A. Logan (Hereinafter cited as JAL), letter to ML, ML, letter to JAL, September 9, 1855, LP.

18   JAL, letter to ML, August 6 and 10, 1855, ML, letter to JAL, August 9, 1855, LP.

19   JAL, letter to ML, August 15, 1855. Mary's letter is missing from the collection, although it appears she saved every other one from him. Logan likely destroyed her letter soon after reading it. But his response indicates what she likely told him.

20   ML, *Reminiscences*, 38–39.

21   JAL, letter to ML, August 28, 1855, ML, letter to JAL, September 9, 1855, LP.

22   JAL, letter to ML, August 20 and October 9, 1855; ML, letter to JAL, October 27, 1855, LP. The response from Mary to Logan's letters make it clear that many of his correspondences were predated by one full month. This must have been purposeful, as Logan clearly must have known the correct date for court appearances, from

reading newspapers, and from reading hers and others' letters to him. He reverts back to the correct date beginning in his October headings.

23 "Gen. Logan's Courtship," *Chicago Tribune*, January 1, 1887.

24 "Recollections of Mrs. John A. Logan," Typescript monograph in LP. Family Record, 11; "Tales About His Youth," *Chicago Tribune*, December 30, 1887.

25 JAL, letter to ML, December 25, 1855, LP.

26 Mary Elizabeth Logan Tucker, "Sketch of Life of John A. Logan," February 1929, Typescript at GJALM; "Tales About His Youth," *Chicago Tribune*, December 30, 1887.

27 ML, *Reminiscences*, 50–55.

28 Hubbs, *Pioneer Folks and Places*, 174–75; Annie Logan file, HP; ML, *Reminiscences*, 57–58.

29 *Southern Illinoisan*, July 25 1856; excerpted in John A. Logan File, HP.

30 "Jefferson," letter to the editor, published in the *Benton Standard*, August 15, 1856.

31 Gustave Koerner, *Memoirs of Gustave Koerner*, vol. 2 (Cedar Rapids: Torch Press, 1909), 29.

32 "Logan Reminiscences," *Chicago Tribune*, January 2, 1887.

33 John A. Logan File, HP.

34 Alexander Davidson and Bernard Stuve, *A Complete History of Illinois, from 1673 to 1873* (Springfield: H. W. Roker, 1884), 660–63; Jones, *Black Jack*, 27–29; JAL, letter to ML, February 7, 1859, LP.

35 JAL, letter to ML, July 28, 1857, LP; Henry Binmore, *Trial of Robert C. Sloo of Shawneetown, for the murder of John E. Hall, Late Clerk of the Circuit Court of Gallatin Co., Ill.* (St. Louis: George Knapp & Co., 1857), 153; *Alton Weekly Courier*, January 14, 1858.

36 JAL, letter to ML, August 4, 1857, LP; Logan Family Bible, ALPL.

37 W. K. Parish, letter to W. J. Allen, January 17, 1858, LP; JAL, letter to ML, January 1, 1858.

38 JAL, letter to ML, January 8, 1858, LP; Edmund Newsome, *Historical Sketches of Jackson County, Illinois* (Carbondale: Edmund Newsome, Publisher, 1882), 169–70. JAL, letter to ML, January 8, 1858, LP.

39 JAL, letter to ML, January 8, 1858, LP.

40 "Logan Reminiscences," *Chicago Tribune*, January 2, 1887; Newsome, *Historical Sketches*, 170.

41 Marshall, letter to JAL, January 13 and May 2, 1858, LP; JAL, letter to Marshall, January 21, 1858, in "'Black Jack's' Candid Comments," *Egyptian Key*, vol. 2 (March, 1947), 19.

42 Cole, 157.

43 ML, letter to JAL, March 8, 1858, LP.

44 JAL, letter to ML, April 2, 1858, LP; Thomas Cooper, letter to JAL, March 22, 1858, Logan Family Papers.

45 William S. Hacker, letter to JAL, April 11, 1858, LP; Cairo *Times and Delta*, April 14, 1858; J. S. Robinson, letter to JAL, April 26, 1858, LP.

46 Logan Family Bible, Logan Family Papers; Family Record, 11.

47 Phillips, letter to Abraham Lincoln, June 9 and July 24, 1858, Lincoln Papers, Manuscript Division, Library of Congress, Washington, D. C.

48 George Port Milton, *The Eve of Conflict: Stephen A. Douglas and the Needless War* (New York: Octagon Books, Inc., 1963), 346.

49 Marshall, letter to JAL, June 21, 1858, LP.

50 Jones, *Black Jack*, 36.

51 George Washington Smith, 1: 300–301, 467; "Little Dug Entered at the State Fair," *Chicago Daily Press and Tribune*, September 20, 1858.

52 JAL, letter to ML, October 3, 1858 and ML, letter to JAL, October 4, 1858, LP.

53 Horace Greeley and John F. Cleveland, comp., *A Political Text-book for 1860: comprising a brief view of Presidential Nominations and Elections* (New York: Tribune Association, 1860), 247.

54 Greeley and Cleveland, 247.

55 John W. D. Wright, *A History of Early Carbondale, Illinois 1842–1905* (Carbondale: Southern Illinois Univ. Press, 1977); Hubbs, 50–52.

56 JAL, letter to ML, November 27, 1859, LP; McPherson, 201–206.

57 McPherson, 152–53, 170–80.

58 JAL, letters to ML, November 27, December 1, December 6, 1859, LP.

59 The speech and on-the-floor reaction it caused can be found recorded in the *Congressional Globe*, 36th Congress (1st Session), pt. 1, 83–86.

60 JAL, letter to ML, December 10, 1859, LP; Hugh C. Bailey, *Hinton Rowan Helper: Abolitionist-Racist* (Birmingham: Univ. of Alabama, 1965), 77.

61 *Quincy Daily Whig and Republican*, December 19, 1858; Milton, 400; Jones, *Black Jack*, 44.

62 "Characteristics of Congressmen," *NY Times*, December 19, 1859.

63 *Congressional Globe*, 36th Congress (1st Session), pt. 1, 237–40, 611–12.

64 Jones, *Black Jack*, 50–51.

65 JAL, letters to ML, December 10 and 13, 1859, LP.

66 ML, letter to JAL, March 4 [1860], LP; ML, letter to Elizabeth Logan, February 9, 1860, Typescript in GJALM.

67 William B. Hesseltine, *Three Against Lincoln: Murat Halstead Reports the Caucuses of 1860* (Baton Rouge: Louisiana Univ. Press, 1960), 12–13.

68 McPherson, 213–15; JAL, letter to ML, May 5, 1860, LP.

69 "National Politics. Great Douglas Demonstration in New-York," *NY Times*, May 23, 1860.

70 JAL, letter to ML, July 19, 1860, LP; Paul M. Angle, *Here I Have Lived: A History of Lincoln's Springfield, 1821–1865* (Springfield: The Abraham Lincoln Association, 1935), 244.

71 Newspaper Scrapbook, LP; *Chicago Press and Tribune*, September 7, 1860.

72 Cole, 200–201; *Illinois State Journal*, September 20, 1860.

73 *Cincinnati Commercial Gazette*, January 2, 1887.

74 George Washington Smith, 1: 314–15.

75 Milton, 493.

76 Medill, letter to Lincoln, December 18, 1860, Lincoln Papers.

77 Emanuel Hertz, ed., *Lincoln Talks: A Biography in Anecdote* (New York: Viking Press, 1939), 164.

78 JAL, letter to Haynie, January 1, 1861, LP.

79 *Cairo City Gazette*, December 6, 1860; *Joliet Signal*, January 15, 1861, cited in Cole, 258–59.

80 *Illinois State Journal*, February 14, 1861; Jones, *Black Jack*, 70; *Illinois Historical Journal*, October 1933, 252.

81 Jones, *Black Jack*, 69–71; "State of the Union. Speech of Hon. John A. Logan, of Illinois," *Congressional Globe*, 36th Congress (2nd Session), appendix, 178–81.

82 *Chicago Tribune*, February 1, 1861; McClernand, letter to Charles Lanphier, February 8, 1861, Lanphier Papers, ALPL.

83 *Illinois State Register*, February 26, 1861; John A. Logan, *The Great Conspiracy, Its Origin and History* (New York: A. R. Hart, 1886), 142. With 25 years of reflection, Logan claims only one other member of Congress went with him. More untrustworthy is his claim that he urged Lincoln to suppress the rebellion "no matter at what cost in men and money." See Jones, *Black Jack*, 74.

84 Jones, *Black Jack*, 70, 75.

85 *Illinois State Register*, April 9, 1861; "Logan Reminiscences," *Chicago Tribune*, December 29, 1886; Milo Erwin, *The History of Williamson County, Illinois* (Marion, 1876), 257.

CHAPTER THREE: PATRIOTS AND TRAITORS

1 McPherson, 274.

2 McPherson, 274; Michael Burlingame, ed., *Lincoln's Journalist: John Hay's Anonymous Writings for the Press* (Carbondale: Southern Illinois Univ. Press, 1998), 35–58, 355 (n. 27).

3 JAL, letter to the editor, June 18, 1861, *Illinois State Register*, June 21, 1861; Erwin, 258; *Chicago Tribune*, April 25, 1861.

4 Erwin, 259–60.

5 Victor Hicken, *Illinois in the Civil War* (Urbana: Univ. of Illinois Press, 1991), 1–2.

6 Erwin, 262–64; "The Times' Slanders Upon General Logan," *Chicago Evening Journal*, October 4, 1866; Quaife, 246–48.

7 Quaife, 248–49; Erwin, 258.

8 James Robinson, letter to JAL, April 18, 1861 and W. H. Green, letter to JAL, April 25, 1861, LP; Shelby M. Cullom, *Fifty Years of Public Service: Personal Recollections* (Chicago: A. C. McClurg, 1911), 81.

9 Koerner, 11, 124; Linder, 345; Charles Lanphier, letter to "a gentleman in Washington," published in the *Chicago Times* on October 31, 1876. The account of the failed "diplomat" can be found in "Conversion of John A. Logan from Secession to Union," St. Louis *Daily Republican*, April 6, 1902.

10 Erwin, 261–62.

11 Robert W. Johannsen, *Stephen A. Douglas* (Urbana: Univ. of Illinois Press, 1973), 867–68.

12 JAL, letter to James Loomis, May 9, 1861, GJALM.

13 ML, letter to JAL, May 25, 1861, LP.
14 ML diary, n.d., LP 143:5; ML, letter to JAL, May 25, 1861, LP.
15 ML, letter to JAL, May 25, 1861.
16 Patrick Lang, letter to Yates, May 28, 1861, Yates Papers, ALPL; Erwin, 264–65; F. M. Woollard, letter to E. L. Bost, April 22, 1909, Woollard Papers, ALPL.
17 Johannsen, 871–72; Centralia *Egyptian Republic*, June 13, 1861; U.S. War Department, *The War of the Rebellion: Official Records of the Union and Confederate Armies*, 128 vols. (Washington, D.C., 1881–1901) [hereinafter cited as *OR*] 2 (1): 34. Blanchard took an Oath of Allegiance to the United States and was released on June 8.
18 Erwin, 270; "Important Arrest," *Illinois State Journal*, June 5, 1862; *OR* 2 (1): 244.
19 Erwin, 270–73; "'The Times' Slander Upon General Logan," *Chicago Evening Journal*, October 4, 1866.
20 "The Traitors of Williamson County," *Illinois State Journal*, June 10, 1861.
21 "Relieved," Centralia *Egyptian Republic*, June 13, 1861.
22 "Egypt Speaks for the Union. What Position Does John Logan Occupy?" *Illinois State Journal*, June 18, 1861.
23 "Egypt Speaks for the Union."
24 Ulysses S. Grant, *Memoirs and Selected Letters* (New York: Library of America, 1990), 161–62; "General Grant's Early Experiences in the War," Petersburg [VA] *Daily Index*, July 7, 1865.
25 "How He Gave Grant a Start," *New York Herald*, December 27, 1887; "Grant's Only War Speech: Reminiscences of Major J. W. Wham," *New York Tribune*, September 27, 1885.
26 Grant, *Memoirs*, 162; Logan's self-assessment in "General Grant's Early Experiences in the War," Petersburg, [VA] *Daily Index*, July 7, 1865.
27 "John Logan at Last Heard From," *Illinois State Journal*, June 20, 1861.
28 Erwin, 274; Marion C. Campbell, letter to JAL, May 10, 1879, LP.
29 Marion C. Campbell, letter to JAL, May 10, 1879, LP; Erwin, 264. The latter history places the meeting at the end of April. Given Logan's charged remarks against coercion of the South in private letters in May, a June date for the meeting is more likely.
30 Isaac Clements interview published in the *Cincinnati Commercial Gazette*, January 2, 1887.
31 Rearden, letter to the editors of the St. Louis *Globe-Democrat*, April 29, 1879, Typescript in LP.
32 JAL, letter to ML, July 4, 1861, LP; JAL, letter to John Cunningham, July 6, 1861, LP.
33 JAL, letter to ML, July 16, 1861, LP.
34 H. W. Blodgett, "John A. Logan," in *Memorial Day, 1909*, Circular 33 (Springfield: Illinois State Journal Co., 1909), 16–17; JAL, letter to John Cunningham, July 16, 1861, LP.
35 JAL, letter to John Cunningham, July 16, 1861, LP.
36 "Logan's Unfaltering Loyalty," *New York Tribune*, December 30, 1886; Dawson, 15; *OR* 2: 312; "Conversion of John A. Logan from Secession to Union," St. Louis *Daily Republican*, April 6, 1902.

37 John A. Logan, "Bull Run." *National Tribune*, April 1, 1886.

38 "Conversion of John A. Logan from Secession to Union," St. Louis *Daily Republican*, April 6, 1902; "Logan's Unfaltering Loyalty," *New York Tribune*, December 30, 1886.

39 "Logan's Unfaltering Loyalty," *New York Tribune*, December 30, 1886; JAL, letter to ML, July 20, 1861, LP.

40 Margaret Leech, *Reveille in Washington* (New York: Carroll & Graf, 1969), 100–105.

41 JAL, letter to ML, July 25, 1861, LP.

42 Richard Yates, letter to JAL, Yates Papers.

43 *Carbondale Times* report reprinted in *Jonesboro Gazette*, August 24, 1861.

44 ML, *Reminiscences*, 94–97; "General Logan's Courtship," *Chicago Tribune*, January 1, 1887.

45 ML, *Reminiscences*, 94–97; "General Logan's Courtship," *Chicago Tribune*, January 1, 1887.

46 ML, *Reminiscences*, 98.

47 W. B., "Send Round Those Mules," *The Chicago Tribune*, January 5, 1887; ML, *Reminiscences*, 94–97; "General Logan's Courtship," *Chicago Tribune*, January 1, 1887.

48 The recruits would become Company C of the Thirty-first Illinois Infantry. Mooninghan and Pulley were commissioned as lieutenants; McKeegan does not appear on the roster. W. S. Morris, L. D. Hartwell and J. B. Kuykendall, *History of the 31st Regiment Illinois Volunteers, Organized by John A. Logan* (1902; reprint, Carbondale: Southern Illinois Univ. Press, 1998), 13.

49 Buel, 335–36; R. J. Wheatley, letter to Richard Yates, July 26, 1861, Yates Papers.

50 ML, "Sketch of General John A. Logan," LP; "Matter about Logan," *Cincinnati Commercial Gazette*, January 2, 1887, 14. Logan's differences with his family were well known by his friends and acquaintances, See R. S. Tuttle, "Recollections of Gen. John A. Logan."

51 James V. Logan obituary, newspaper clipping in the GJALM.

52 Annie Logan File, HP.

53 Crawford *Bulletin* article reprinted in the *Waukesha* (WI) *Freeman* on September 24, 1861.

54 ML, *Reminiscences*, 108; Morris, *31st Regiment*, 19–20.

55 Hicken, 12–13.

56 John A. Logan, "Military Reminiscences," in *The Volunteer Soldier of America* (Chicago and New York: R. S. Peale Co., 1887), 619–20.

57 Jean Edward Smith, *Grant* (New York: Simon & Schuster, 2001), 118.

58 Bruce Catton, *Grant Moves South*, (Boston: Little, Brown & Co., 1960), 48–49, 55.

59 Morris, *31st Regiment*, 12–15, 18, 213; "Case of John A. Logan," Box 49, LP; George W. Nichols, *The Story of the Great March* (New York: Harper & Brothers, 1865), 156–57; Byron Andrews, *A Biography of General John A. Logan* (New York: H. S. Goodspeed, 1884), 397; Carl Sandburg, *Abraham Lincoln, The War Years*, vol. IV (New York: Harcourt, Brace Co., 1939), 18.

60 Morris, *31st Regiment*, 179, 209; James Street Jr., *The Struggle for Tennessee* (Alexandria, VA: Time-Life Books; 1985), 94–95.

61 JAL, letter to ML, September 13, 1861, LP.

62 Morris, *31st Regiment*, 179, 181; ML, letter to JAL, September 1861, LP.

63 "An Interesting Invalid: General Logan in the sick room," Chicago *Daily Inter-Ocean*, December 27, 1886.

64 The exchange between Buford and Logan was witnessed by Lewis Hauback of the 27th Illinois and recorded in Dawson, 19.

65 Logan's Belmont Report, *OR* 3: 287–88; Morris, *31st Regiment*, 23; White, letter to "Dear Capt." November 8, 1861, LP. The definitive comprehensive study of the Battle of Belmont is Nathaniel Chears Hughes, Jr., *The Battle of Belmont: Grant Strikes South* (Chapel Hill: Univ. of North Carolina Press, 1991); pages 94–95 detail this advance along Logan's line.

66 Logan's Belmont Report, 288; Hughes, 102, 106.

67 Logan's Belmont Report, 288; Hughes, 19; Steven E. Woodworth, "Logan of the Dirty-First," *Civil War Magazine* 72, (1997): 25–37.

68 McClernand's Belmont Report, *OR* 3: 280; Hughes, 127, 130.

69 Brooks D. Simpson, *Ulysses S. Grant: Triumph Over Adversity, 1822–1865* (Boston: Houghton Mifflin, 2000), 100; JAL, "Military Reminiscences," 624.

70 Grant, *Memoirs*, 276.

71 McClernand's Report and Logan's Report, 280, 289.

72 Hughes, 153. Logan's close calls are not presented in any official reports, but are oft repeated in 1884 biographies of him. See Knox, 289–91 for an eyewitness account relayed to the author. The earliest reference to Logan losing his horse and pistol at Belmont comes from James Grant Wilson, *Biographical Sketches of Illinois Officers Engaged in the War Against the Rebellion in 1861* (Chicago: James Barnet, 1862), 97.

73 Hughes, 153; [JAL], *Uncle Daniel's Story of Tom Anderson and Twenty Great Battles* (New York: A. R. Hart & Co., 1886), 33.

74 Walter Scates, letter to his father, November 13, 1861, Pearce Collection, Navarro College; St. Louis *Daily Missouri Republican*, January 26, 1886; Hughes, 184; White, letter to "Dear Capt.," November 8, 1861, LP.

75 Burr, "Letters from Two Wars," 150–51; JAL, "Military Reminiscences," 625–26.

76 G. W. Goddard, letter to "Dear Capt.," December 28, 1861, LP; *OR* (3): 282; *Uncle Daniel's Story*, 33.

77 *Confederate Veteran* 16 (1908), 190.

78 JAL, letters to ML, January 3 and 5, 1862, LP.

79 *Illinois State Journal*, January 24, 1862.

80 JAL, letter to ML, February 1, 1862, LP.

81 Morris, *31st Regiment*, 30.

82 JAL, "Military Reminiscences," 633–36; Morris, *31st Regiment*, 31; Francis W. Stickney, letter to his parents, February 7, 1862, (Toulon, IL) *Stark County Union*, February 28, 1862.

83 John Y. Simon, "Fort Donelson," in Francis H. Kennedy, ed., *The Civil War Battlefield Guide* (Boston: Houghton Mifflin, 1990), 16–19.

84 "Ichabod," letter to the editor, February 22, 1862, *Carlyle Weekly Reveille*, February 27, 1862; Morris, *31st Regiment*, 34–35; Hicken, 33–35. Logan developed chronic

illness that he always attributed to his exposure at Fort Donelson. While he never ascribed a date to the cause, the night of February 13–14 is likely. See Robert Pearson Affidavit, Mary Logan Pension file, National Archives.

85 Hicken, 35.

86 *Uncle Daniel's Story*, 47.

87 *Uncle Daniel's Story*, 47; 36; Morris, *31st Regiment*, 35; Woodworth, 31.

88 *Uncle Daniel's Story*, 47; Orville J. Victor, "Incidents of the Battle Before Fort Donelson," in *Incidents and Anecdotes of the War* (New York: James D. Torrey, 1862), 340; Mrs. John A. Logan, "News From Donelson," *National Tribune*, May 31, 1888. Logan also provided a vivid account of participating in a battle. See "A Hero's Eloquence—A Brilliant Battle Picture By General John A. Logan," *Iowa State Register*, June 6, 1877.

89 Walter R. Houghton, *Early Life and Public Career of James G. Blaine, including a biography of General John A. Logan* (Cleveland: N. G. Hamilton & Co, 1884), 232–33; Davidson and Stuve, 824. The regiments Logan admonished were from Colonel Charles Cruft's brigade. (*OR* 7: 246, 248–249.)

90 Morris, *31st Regiment*, 35–36; Thomas B. Craycoft Pension Application, National Archives; Houghton, 232–33 (quotes brigade and division *OR* reports), JAL, "Military Reminiscences," 655–56.

91 Buel, 354–55; ML, *Reminiscences*, 125; Logan Pension File.

92 ML, *Reminiscences*, 125; JAL, "Military Reminiscences," 656–57; Dawson, 22; Mrs. John A. Logan, "News From Donelson," *National Tribune*, May 31, 1888; JAL, letter to "My Fellow Soldiers, March 3, 1862, LP. The captain accused of cowardice was Alexander Somersville of Company K. He was court martialed and dismissed from service. See John Y. Simon, ed. *The Papers of Ulysses S. Grant*, vol. 4, (Carbondale: Southern Illinois Univ. Press, 1967–2003), 486.

93 JAL, "Military Reminiscences," 656–57; Dawson, 22; "Who Shot Col. Logan?" *Illinois State Journal*, February 26, 1862; Silas Thompson Trowbridge, *Autobiography of Silas Thompson Trowbridge, M.D.* (Vera Cruz: Published privately, 1872).

94 "Who Shot Col. Logan?" *Illinois State Journal*, February 26, 1862; "Payne Reminiscences," http://www.rootsweb.com/~orphanhm/paynerem.htm; Houghton, 360.

95 ML, letter to JAL, February 16, 1862, LP.

96 *Jonesboro Gazette*, February 15, 1862; ML, letter to JAL, February 16, 1862; "The Death of Col. John A. Logan," newspaper clipping in scrapbook, Box 92, LP; Mrs. John Logan, "News From Donelson;" ML, *Reminiscences*, 123.

CHAPTER FOUR: PROMOTION

1 William F. Fox, *Regimental Losses in the American Civil War, 1861–1865* (Albany, NY: Albany Publishing Co., 1889), 361.

2 The sole source previously cited for Mary's odyssey to find her husband, and his recuperation on the steamer had been her 1913 autobiography, (*Reminiscences*, 123–28). A quarter of a century earlier, she provided another version, never cited in subsequent works but more reliable since it relates the incident twenty-six years later

instead of fifty-one. ("News From Donelson," *National Tribune* May 31, 1888.) The twentieth-century reference appears to add much not found in the 1888 story and appears heavily embroidered. This lends credence to critics who caution against using Mary's 1913 reminiscences as a major reference to her husband's life.

3   Casualty figures obtained from Fox, 361. This source is one of a mere few to tally those who were mortally wounded in battle and add them into the "killed" figures.

4   "News From Donelson," Catton, *Grant Moves South*, 175, 178.

5   Simon, ed., *Papers of Ulysses S. Grant*, vol. 4, 274–75.

6   Simon, ed., *Papers of Ulysses S. Grant*, vol. 4, 275–76; John A. Logan Commission File, M1064, National Archives.

7   George A. Reaves III, "Shiloh," in *Civil War Battlefield Guide*, 30–35.

8   JAL, letters to ML, April 15 and 17, 1862; ML, letter to JAL, May 3, 1862, LP.

9   JAL, "Military Reminiscences," 661–664; Last quote reproduced in Jean Edward Smith, 209.

10   JAL, "Military Reminiscences," 665–67; Catton, *Grant Moves South*, 276–77.

11   "M.," letter to the editor, June 19, 1862, published in the *Freeport* (Illinois) *Bulletin*, July 3, 1862; JAL, letter to ML, June 20, 1862, LP.

12   Davidson and Stuve, 871–77; Burr, "Letters From Two Wars," 154.

13   Ira Blanchard, *I Marched With Sherman: Civil War Memoirs of the 20th Illinois Infantry* (San Francisco: J. D. Huff and Company, 1992), 66–67.

14   JAL, letter to the editor, July 14, 1862, *Quincy Daily Herald*, July 21, 1862. Logan likely did not realize that he responded to a claim that found its way into papers outside of Illinois. See "Listen, Democrats." *Waukesha* [WI] *Freeman*, July 15, 1862.

15   JAL, letters to ML, July 15, 22, 29, 1862, LP; Simon, ed., *The Papers of Ulysses S. Grant*, vol. 5 (1973), 248–49; *OR* 17 (2): 133–138.

16   Thomas Lowry, *Tarnished Eagles: The Courts-Martial of Fifty Union Colonels and Lieutenant Colonels* (Mechanicsburg, PA: Stackpole Books, 1997), 62–63; Frank H. Putney, letter to his father, August 8, 1862, www.russscott.com/~rscott/12thwis/ltfraput.htm.

17   Simon, ed., *Papers of Ulysses S. Grant*, vol. 5, 410; Morris, *31st Regiment*, 187; Goddard, letter to Capt. [Cunningham], December 28, 1861; JAL, letter to ML, June 28, 1862, LP.

18   Simon, ed., *Papers of Ulysses S. Grant*, vol. 5; "Treason in Illinois," *Chicago Tribune*, August 26, 1862.

19   ML, *Reminiscences*, 111, 142. Mary claimed in her 1913 memoirs that she moved to Carbondale in 1861. The passage of 50 years must have affected her memory as none of her 1861 to August 1862 letters bore a Carbondale heading.

20   *Carbondale Times* report of the August 28 address reproduced in "Speech of Gen. John A. Logan," *Illinois State Journal*, September 11, 1862. Logan's speaking style described in George W. Pepper, *Personal Recollections of Sherman's Campaigns in Georgia and the Carolinas* (Zanesville, OH: Published by Hugh Dunne, 1866), 498.

21   Illinois *State Journal*, September 11, 13, 19, 23, and October 2, 1862.

22   "Treason in Illinois," *Chicago Tribune*, August 26, 1862.

23   Phillips, letter to Yates, September 8, 1862, Yates Papers.

24 Mark Neeley, *The Fate of Liberty: Abraham Lincoln and Civil Liberties* (New York: Oxford Univ. Press; 1991), 54–55.

25 Jones, *Black Jack*, 145–46. A study about subversive activities in the Civil War included an analysis of the "K.G.C. expose" that argues convincingly that the *Chicago Tribune* article was an embroidered piece written by an agenda-driven reporter named Joseph K. C. Forrest. "Forrest's fabrication of August, 1862, became the basis for the myth that Illinois was the center of K.G.C. and treasonable society activity . . ." See Frank L. Klement, *The Copperheads in the Middle West* (Chicago: Univ. of Chicago Press, 1960), 149–52.

26 Dispatches quoted in Simon, ed., *Papers of Ulysses S. Grant*, vol. 5, 331–32.

27 JAL, letter to Lincoln, August 30, 1862, in Webb Garrison, "Near-dictatorship Evoked the Wrath of 'Blackjack' Logan," *A Treasury of Civil War Tales* (New York: Ballantine Books, 1988), 124.

28 Simon, ed., *Papers of Ulysses S. Grant*, vol. 6, 16, 19; Garrison, 125, 128.

29 Oath of Esculane Phillips, October 8, 1862, SIU. It cannot be ruled out that Logan used his power and influence to ease Tom's enrollment after the incident, but a subsequent court appearance in the spring of 1863 (Tom was back in Murphysboro and out of the army by then) suggests that Logan may not have informed his sibling of this issue.

30 Logan's letter reproduced in Dawson, 26–28.

31 Hicken, 139–40.

32 JAL, letter to ML, December 12, 1862, LP.

33 Simon, ed., *Papers of Ulysses S. Grant*, vol. 6, 506.

34 JAL, letter to ML, January 21, 1863, LP.

35 Edmund Newsome, *Experiences in the War of the Great Rebellion By a Soldier of the Eighty-first Regiment Illinois Volunteer Infantry* (Carbondale: Edmund Newsome, Publisher; 1880), 30.

36 W. Holmes, letter to Abraham Lincoln, January 22, 1863, Lincoln Papers.

37 Lt. Merriman witnessed the exchange, but incorrectly believed that Ozburn was gone by day's end and that Ozburn was married to Logan's sister. See "Cashiering His Brother-in Law." *Indianapolis Daily Journal*, January 1, 1887, 7; Ozburn's correspondence suggests that poor health initiated his resignation. Burr, "Letters From Two Wars," 156–57. Logan wrote on March 2, "Doff is going home, resigned. He did not treat me very well, but it is all right." (JAL, letter to ML, March 2, 1863, LP) Given Ozburn's feelings about abolitionists, and his subsequent involvement in the Peace movement, both factors appeared to have influenced his discharge.

38 Thomas Logan File, HP; Warrant and Arrest of Thomas M. Logan, February 6 and 27, 1863, Jackson County Courthouse, Murphysboro.

39 ML, *Reminiscences*; JAL, letter to "My Fellow Soldiers," February 12, 1863, LP.

40 "Gen. John A. Logan's 'Card'," *Jonesboro Gazette*, March 14, 1863.

41 Grant, letter to Lincoln, February 9, 1863, Abraham Lincoln Papers.

42 John A. Logan Commission Branch File, National Archives.

CHAPTER FIVE: EARNED FAITH

1 Jacob Bruner, letter to his wife, April 9, 1863, Jacob Bruner Papers, Ohio Historical Society, Columbus.

2 Horace Greeley, *The American Conflict; a history of the great rebellion in the United States of America, 1860–'65: its causes, incidents and results*, vol. 2 (1866), 526–27.

3 Stephen D. Carpenter, *Logic of History. Five Hundred Political Texts* (Dahlonega, GA: Crown Rights Book Co., 1864), 265; *OR* 3: 121.

4 Newsome, *Experience in the War*, 38; Richard L. Howard, *History of the 124th Regiment Illinois Infantry Volunteers* (Springfield: H. W. Rokker; 1880), 65–66; Jacob Bruner, letter to his wife, April 9, 1863, Bruner Papers.

5 Washburne, letter to Lincoln, April 30, 1863, Lincoln Papers.

6 Bearss, "The Vicksburg Campaign and Siege," in *The Civil War Battlefield Guide*, 126–27; *OR* 24: 642–43.

7 Appointment information on each officer in commission branch files, M1064, National Archives. Also refer to the Personnel Directory of the "American Civil War Research Database" http://www.civilwardata.com; Additional biographical information on Hotaling in Samuel Fletcher, *The History of Company A, Second Illinois Cavalry* (Chicago: 1912), 65, 203; for Hoover in "Biographical Sketches of Blue Hill," http://www.rootsweb.com/~newebste/bluebios.html.

8 Personnel Directory of the "American Civil War Research Database" http://www.civilwardata.com; Although he served only briefly under Logan, Wheaton went back to the Eighth Illinois and won the Medal of Honor in Battle at Fort Blakely in Alabama in 1865; he distinguished himself after the war as a Major General in the Regular Army. See W. F. Beyer and O. F. Keydel, eds., *Deeds of Valor: How America's Civil War Heroes Won the Congressional Medal of Honor* (Detroit: Perrien-Keydel Co., 1903), 533–35; for Stolbrand story, see ML, *Reminiscences*, 132–34.

9 OR 24: 642–43; "E." and John W. Mosby (124th Illinois), letters to the editor, May 6, 1863, published in the *Keithsburg Observer*, May 28, 1863.

10 Newsome, *Experience in the War*, 42; Bearss, *The Campaign for Vicksburg*, vol. 2, 405.

11 Bearss, *The Campaign for Vicksburg*, vol. 2, 346, 402–407; Edwin C. Bearss, "The Vicksburg Campaign and Siege," 126–27.

12 Newsome, *Experience in the War*, 42; *OR* 24: 643.

13 *OR* 24: 644, 649, 651, 654.

14 Newsome, *Experience in the War*, 42; Washburne, letter to Lincoln, May 1, 1863; Lincoln Papers; Span, "Battle of Thompson's Hill," May 7, 1863, Newspaper Scrapbook, LP.

15 *OR* 24: 644–45.

16 Simpson, 193–94; Jean Edward Smith, 240–41.

17 Louis M. Starr, *Bohemian Brigade: Civil War Newsmen in Action* (New York: Knopf; 1954), 280.

18 Benjamin Thomas, ed., *Three Years with Grant as Recalled by War Correspondent Sylvanus Cadwallader* (New York: Alfred A. Knopf; 1955), vi, 66–67.

19 Starr, 61. The author misidentifies McCullagh reporting to the *Cincinnati Gazette* instead of the *Commercial*.

20 Edwin C. Bearss, "Raymond," in *The Civil War Battlefield Guide*, 139, 141.

21 Bearss, 139, 141. "E.," letter to the editor, May 28, 1863, published in the *Keithsburg* [IL] *Observer*, June 11, 1863; Henry O. Dwight, "The Affair on the Raymond Road," [New York] *Semi-Weekly Tribune*, November 19, 1886; Osborn Oldroyd, *A Soldier's Story of the Siege of Vicksburg* (Springfield: Published by the author, 1885), 15–16; Blanchard, 87–88.

22 Manning F. Force, "Personal Recollections of the Vicksburg Campaign," *MOLLUS Ohio*, vol. 1 (Cincinnati: Robert Clarke & Co.; 1888), 299.

23 Fletcher, 90.

24 Henry O. Dwight, "The Affair on the Raymond Road," [New York] *Semi-Weekly Tribune*, November 19, 1886; Oldroyd, 17; Blanchard, 88; Theodore R. Davis, "How a Battle Scene Was Sketched During the Civil War," *St. Nicholas Illustrated Magazine* 16 (2) (1889): 661–68.

25 Theodore R. Davis, "How a Battle Scene Was Sketched," *St. Nicholas Illustrated Magazine* 16 (2) (1889): 661–68; "Mack" quoted in Charles C. Clayton, *Little Mack: Joseph B. McCullagh of the St. Louis Globe-Democrat* (Carbondale: Southern Illinois Univ. Press, 1969), 37.

26 Edwin Loosley, letter to his wife, June 1, 1863, Loosley Papers, SIU; *OR* 24: 646; Hicken, 157–58; Newsome, *Experience in the War*, 45.

27 Edwin Loosley, letter to his wife, June 1, 1863, Loosley Papers.

28 Bearss, *The Campaign for Vicksburg*, vol. 2, 515–17; Bearss, "Raymond," 141.

29 Simpson, 197–98; Bearss, "Champion Hill," in *The Civil War Battlefield Guide*, 142–43.

30 *OR* 24: 646; S. Cadwallader, "Named a Big Battle: A War Correspondent's Just Claim—Champion's Hill," *American Tribune*, October 24, 1890; Cadwallader, *Three Years with Grant*, 77. The reporter believed the incident occurred on the 16th, but Logan's report makes it clear that Hovey's men were with him before the march of May 15 had been completed.

31 *OR* 24: 647; part 2, 59–60.

32 Simon, ed., *Papers of Ulysses S. Grant*, vol. 8, 228.

33 Blanchard, 92.

34 Oldroyd, 22; Force, 302; "E," letter to the editor, May 28, 1863, *The Keithsburg Observer*, June 11, 1863.

35 Morris, *History of the 31st Regiment*, 64–65.

36 Morris, *History of the 31st Regiment*, 64–65; Clayton, 38.

37 Oldroyd, 23.

38 Tuthill, "Reminiscences of John A. Logan," *OR* 24: 647; Morris, *31st Regiment*, 65, and "E," letter to the editor, May 28, 1863, *The Keithsburg Observer*, June 11, 1863; William P. LaBounty, ed., *Civil War Diaries of James W. Jessee 1861–1865* (Normal, IL: McLean County Genealogical Society, 1997), 20–21. The author is indebted to Steven Woodworth for interpreting the chronology of the charge.

39 Edward C. Downs, *The Great American Scout and Spy* (New York: Olmsted and Co., 1870), 248–49; *OR* 24: 648; Wilber F. Crummer, *With Grant at Fort Donelson, Shiloh, and Vicksburg* (Oak Park, Illinois: E. C. Crummer Co., 1915), 103.

40 Clayton, 37–38; Charles A. Dana, *Recollections of the Civil War* (New York: D. Appleton and Co., 1898), 67; Col. Fred D. Grant, "Gen. Ulysses S. Grant: His Son's Memories of Him in the Field," *The National Tribune*, February 3 and 10, 1887.

41 Recollection of Dr. William M. Beach (78th Ohio), in Robert Underwood Johnson and Clarence Clough Buel, eds., *Battles and Leaders of the Civil War*, vol. 3 (New York: Century Co., 1887), 511; Tuthill, "Reminiscences of John A. Logan."

42 Grant, 345–46.

43 R. M. Dibel, "Champion Hill: A Graphic Picture of a Most Exciting Time—Logan's Division at Champion's Hill," *National Tribune*, September 11, 1884; J. B. Harris, "An Incident of Champion Hills—Gen. Logan's Advice," *National Tribune*, July 31, 1884.

44 Edwin Loosely, letter to his wife, June 1, 1863, Loosely Papers; Bearss, "Champion Hill," 143–45; *OR* 24: 654.

45 Dana, 53–55. No other accounts of this "intellectual peculiarity" have been uncovered in previous or subsequent battles. It may have been isolated to the Battle of Champion Hill.

46 Terrence J. Winschel, *Vicksburg: Fall of the Confederate Gibralter* (Abilene, Texas: McWhiney Foundation Press; 1999), 89–90.

47 Post, 269; Simpson, 203–204.

48 Winschel, 94

49 "Gen. John A. Logan," *Chicago Tribune*, May 21, 1863.

50 ML, letters to JAL, May 3 and 21, 1863, LP; JAL, letter to ML, May 31, 1863, LP.

51 Fletcher, 100–101. The use of the name "Fort Hill" leads to confusion, for there was a Fort Hill in Vicksburg, near the river. Today it is the grounds of the National Cemetery.

52 Thomas Murphy, "At Vicksburg," *National Tribune*, December 15, 1892; Newsome, *Experience in the War*, 61; *OR* 24: 292.

53 JAL quote in Dawson, 451; W. J. Landram, "Gen. Logan's Courage," *National Tribune*, November 6, 1884.

54 Hans Mattson, *Reminiscences: The Story of an Emigrant* (St. Paul: D. D. Merrill Co., 1891), 69.

55 Dawson, 451–52; Simpson, 204–210; Cadwallader, *Three Years With Grant*, 101.

56 ML, letter to JAL, June 28, 1863, LP.

57 James R. Arnold, *Grant Wins the War: Decision at Vicksburg* (New York: John Wiley & Sons, Inc.; 1997), 273–74; Hicken, 178.

58 Hicken, 180; Jones, *Black Jack*, 175.

59 Fletcher, 106; Winschel, 117; Barnum, letter to JAL, December 31, 1863, LP.

60 Simpson, 210–11.

61 Simon, ed., *Papers of Ulysses S. Grant*, vol. 8, 464; Newsome, *Experience in the War*, 73; Jones, *Black Jack*, 176.

62 Hicken, 182; Bearss, "The Vicksburg Campaign and Siege," 135.

63 Post, 271; Newsome, *Experience in the War*, 73; James McPherson, letter to his brother, July 26, 1863, http://www.sandusky-county-scrapbook.net/McPherson/Letters5.htm; Arnold, 298.

64 Dana, letter to Stanton, July 12, 1863, in *Recollections of the Civil War*, 67–68.

65 Washburne, letter to Lincoln, April 30, 1863, Lincoln Papers; Oldroyd, 23; Tuthill, "Reminiscences of John A. Logan."

66 Grant, *Memoirs*, 331, 659; Simon, ed., *Papers of Ulysses S. Grant*, vol. 8, 464, 473–74; JAL, letter to ML, July 5, 1863, LP.

67 *OR* 24 (3): 481, 483–84; "Affairs at Vicksburgh," *NY Times*, July 21, 1863.

68 "General Logan at Cairo," *NY Times*, July 27, 1863; "What a Genuine War Democrat Says—Eloquent Speech of Maj. General Logan," *Norwalk* [OH] *Reflector*, August 4, 1863; "Gen. Logan on the Rebellion," [Chaudry, OH] *Jeffersonian Democrat*, August 21, 1863.

69 ML, *Reminiscences*, 141.

70 ML, *Reminiscences*, 142–43.

71 Crowd estimate provided in *Chicago Tribune*. Report clipped into *Illinois State Journal*, August 5, 1863.

72 Pepper, 498–99.

73 *Chicago Tribune* report of July 30 speech published in *Illinois State Journal* on August 5, 1863; quote from Houghton, 255.

74 *Chicago Tribune* report of July 30 speech published in *Illinois State Journal* on August 5, 1863.

75 "Gen. John A. Logan at DuQuoin," *Illinois State Journal*, August 5, 1863; Davidson and Stuve, 891–92.

76 ["Mack"], "Speech of Major General John A. Logan at Duquoin, Illinois on Friday, July 31, 1863," *Cincinnati Daily Commercial*, August 3, 1863; John D. Caldwell, letter to JAL, August 3, 1863, LP.

77 John A. Logan, *Speech of Major General John A. Logan on His Return to Illinois after the Capture of Vicksburg* (Cincinnati: National Union Association of Ohio, 1883), iv.

78 "Gen. Logan's Great Speech," *Chicago Tribune*, August 11, 1863; "The Great Rally For The Union," *Chicago Evening Journal*, August 12, 1863.

79 Joseph McCullagh description provided in JAL, *Speech . . . on His Return to Illinois*, iv. He refers to the Du Quoin speech, but the style was repeated in Chicago.

80 *Chicago Tribune*, August 11, 1863; "Great Union Speech of Gen. Logan. Eloquent Words of a True Patriot," [Galena, IL] *Weekly Northwestern Gazette*, August 25, 1863; George Marvel, letter to Stanton, n.d., Logan Scrapbook, LP.

81 William Dole, letter to John Usher, August 9, 1863, Lincoln Papers; Simon, ed., *The Papers of Ulysses S. Grant*, vol. 9 (1982), 176. Hay Diary, August 22, 1862, *Inside Lincoln's White House*, 75.

82 JAL, *The Great Conspiracy*, 519.

83 It cannot be ruled out that Cunningham was captured with Bob Kelly during the summer's siege. Logan's first mention of him to his wife is a mid-September letter: "'Hybe' has got a place with Capt. Fort Qr. Master at $75." (JAL, letter to ML, September 17, 1863, LP). The reference assumes that he discussed her brother with her at an earlier date. This was either in a letter that no longer exists, or perhaps Logan told her all about Cunningham when he came home on leave in July.

84 JAL, letter to ML, September 19 and October 12, 1863, LP; W. W. Williams, letter to ML, December 21, 1863, LP.

85 *OR* 31 (1): 759.
86 Thomas Christie, letter to his sister, November 14, 1863, Minnesota Historical Society, St. Paul; Newsome, *Experience in the War*, 94–95; Richard L. Howard, 158–59; JAL, letter to ML, November 16, 1863, LP.
87 JAL, letter to ML, November 16, 1863, LP.
88 Reub Williams, "Logan Reminiscences," *Warsaw Indianan*, January 1887, Newspaper Scrapbook, LP.
89 JAL, letter to ML, November 21, 1863, LP; Jones, *Black Jack*, 185.
90 Charles P. Roland, "Chattanooga," in *The Civil War Battlefield Guide*, 157–62.
91 "Candidates," *Illinois State Journal*, February 3, 1864; Joseph Gillespie, letter to Abraham Lincoln, December 29, 1863, Lincoln Papers; *Cairo News* editorial reproduced in "Gen. John A. Logan for Governor," *Illinois State Journal*, January 21, 1864.
92 "The People of the State of Illinois vs. Thomas M. Logan," File #1941 and The People of the State of Illinois vs. Dorothulia A. Blanchard," File #893, Jackson County Courthouse, Murphysboro.
93 JAL, letters to ML, February 9, 11 and 17, 1864, LP.
94 JAL, letter to ML, May 5, 1864, LP; Burr, "Letters From Two Wars," 157; Alexander M. Jenkins File, HP.
95 JAL, letter to ML, March 4, 1864, LP.
96 William B. Hazen, *A Narrative of Military Service* (Boston: Ticknor and Company; 1885), 280; Jones, *Black Jack*, 184; JAL, letter to Richard Yates, July 16, 1864, LP.
97 Incident relayed in Bruce Catton, *Grant Takes Command* (Boston: Little, Brown and Co., 1968), 137–38.
98 *OR* 32 (3): 156; Simon, ed., *Papers of Ulysses S. Grant*, vol. 10, 21.
99 Jones, *Black Jack*, 190–91; Roy Basler, ed., *Collected Works of Abraham Lincoln*, vol. 7 (New Brunswick: Rutgers Univ. Press, 1953), 248.
100 Reub Williams, "Logan Reminiscences."
101 JAL, letters to ML April 6 and 12, 1864, LP; Logan's salary in "A Statement of Payment Made to General John A. Logan," Box 49, LP.
102 John A. Logan Commission Branch File, M1064, NA; "The Roll of Honor: Awards of Army Medals in the 17th Army Corps," *Burlington* [Iowa] *Weekly Hawkeye*, April 23, 1864.
103 JAL, letter to ML, March 4, 1864, LP; Ada Sterling, comp., *A Belle of the Fifties: Memoirs of Mrs. Clay, of Alabama, Covering Social and Political Life in Washington and the South, 1853–66* (New York: Doubleday, Page & Co.; 1904), 184–85.
104 Jones, *Black Jack*, 193; Grenville M. Dodge, *Personal Recollections of General W. T. Sherman* (Des Moines, Iowa: n.p, 1902), 9; John F. Marszalek, *Sherman: A Soldier's Passion For Order* (New York: The Free Press; 1993), 279.
105 *OR* 38 (3): 90 (Hereafter all citations in this 25-page printed report will be cited as Georgia Report).
106 Jay Luvaas, "The Atlanta Campaign," in *The Civil War Battlefield Guide*, 173.
107 JAL, letter to ML, May 5, 1864, LP.

CHAPTER SIX: SAVING THE UNION

1   H. H. Orendorf, comp., *Reminiscences of the Civil War from Diaries of Members of the 103d Illinois Volunteer Infantry* (Chicago: J. F. Learning, 1904), 48.

2   Quote taken from *New York Tribune* and republished in "Logan at Resaca," *The National Tribune*, June 19, 1884; and Byron Andrews, 447–48. See also William F. G. Shanks, *Personal Recollections of Distinguished Generals* (New York: Harper, 1866), 310 for confirmation of the bitter argument.

3   Shanks, *Personal Recollections*, 311–17.

4   Georgia Report, 91–92.

5   *OR* 38 (4): 185; Andrews, 448; Georgia Report, 93–94.

6   *Uncle Daniel's Story*, 342; Castel, 166–67; Mark E. Kellogg, comp., *Army Life of An Illinois Soldier, including a Day-to-Day Record of Sherman's March to the Sea: Letters and Diary of Charles W. Will* (Carbondale: Southern Illinois Univ. Press, 1996), 241.

7   JAL, letter to ML, May 20, 1864, LP.

8   Georgia Report, 94.

9   Georgia Report, 95.

10   Kellogg, 239; Tuthill, "Reminiscences of Gen. John A. Logan;" JAL, letter to ML, May 20, 1864, LP.

11   Robert Kennedy, "General Kennedy Writes of Gen. John A. Logan," [Bellefonte, Ohio] *The Daily-Index Republican*, September 18, 1905; J. W. Long, "Flanking Johnston: The Army of the Tennessee on the Move," *The National Tribune*, September 13, 1888.

12   Russel H. Conwell, *Biography of General John A. Logan of Illinois: Childhood, Manhood, Peace and War* (Augusta, Maine: E. C. Allen & Co., 1884), 445; George Stone to the editor, January 17, 1884, republished in Andrews, 452–53.

13   Hicken, 249; Castel, 246. The campaign historian in the latter work estimates Bate's losses "at least 1,000 and perhaps as many as 1,500."

14   JAL, letter to ML, May 30, 1864, LP; Hybert Cunningham to his father, May 30, LP, William Tecumseh Sherman, *Memoirs of General W. T. Sherman* (New York: Literary Classics, 1990), 514.

15   JAL, letters to ML, May 29 and 30, 1864, LP; Kennedy, "General Kennedy Writes of Gen. John A. Logan," *The Daily-Index Republican*, September 18, 1905.

16   Jay Luvaas, "The Atlanta Campaign" and "Kennesaw Mountain" *The Civil War Battlefield Guide*, 175–76, 187–91.

17   Dennis Kelly, *Kennesaw Mountain and the Atlanta Campaign* (Atlanta: Kennesaw Mountain Historical Association, 1999), 31–35; Richard A. Baumgartner and Larry M. Strayer, *Kennesaw Mountain, June 1864: Bitter Standoff at the Gibralter of Georgia* (Huntington, WV: Blue Acorn Press; 1998), 112–14.

18   Baumgartner and Strayer, 112–14; "Logan in Battle," *Indianapolis Journal*, December 30, 1886.

19   Georgia Report, 99; Luvaas, "Kennesaw Mountain," 187–91; JAL, letter to ML, July 16, 1864, LP.

20   JAL, letter to ML, July 14, 1864, LP.

21   Luvaas, "The Atlanta Campaign," 173, 176.

22 Georgia Report, 100–102.

23 Georgia Report, 100–102; "Logan in Battle," *Indianapolis Journal*, December 30, 1886.

24 Logan Report, 103; "Generals in the Saddle," *Southern Historical Society Papers* 19 (October 1891): 172–73.

25 Dodge, 19–20; Quote from Alvers Curtis, Eighty-first Ohio, in *Echoes of Battle: The Atlanta Campaign*, 245.

26 John S. Bosworth, "July 22, 1864: Gallantry of Logan, Giles A. Smith and Others on that Terrible Day," *The National Tribune*, August 7, 1884.

27 Leggett quote in *Report of the Proceedings of the Society of the Army of the Tennessee, at the Twentieth Meeting*, (Cincinnati: Published by the Society; 1893), 541.

28 *Echoes of Battle*, 245.

29 "Several Reminiscences. Stories Told of Incidents in Gen. Logan's Career," *Chicago Tribune*, December 27, 1886.

30 Bakhaus quoted in *Echoes of Battle*, 249.

31 *Echoes of Battle*, 249; "Several Reminiscences. Stories Told of Incidents in Gen. Logan's Career," *Chicago Tribune*, December 27, 1886.

32 Gilbert A. Pierce, "Annual Oration," *Report of the Proceedings of the Society of the Army of the Tennessee at the Twenty-first Meeting* (Cincinnati: Published by the Society, 1893), 92; Shanks, *Personal Recollections*, 304–305.

33 *OR* 38 (5): 260–261; Castel, 418.

34 "Address of General W. T. Sherman," *Proceedings of the Society of the Army of the Tennessee at the Twentieth Meeting*, 471–72.

35 Dodge, 21–22.

36 Georgia Report, 104; Castel, 430–31.

37 Reub Williams, "Logan Reminiscences."

38 *OR* 38 (3): 87; R. W. Burt, letter to the editors, July 29, 1864, published in the Newark [OH] *True American*, August 19, 1864.

39 Georgia Report, 104–105; [JAL], *Uncle Daniel's Story*, 349; JAL, letter to ML, August 6, 1864, LP; *OR* 38 (3): 87.

40 JAL, letter to ML, August 8, 1864, LP.

41 Sherman, letter to Halleck, August 16, 1864, LP.

42 JAL, letters to ML, June 8 and July 5, 1864, LP.

43 JAL, letter to ML, August 6, 1864, LP (refers to Josh Allen letter); Francis Young, letter to JAL, July 27 and August 12, 1864, LP; Lanphier, letter to JAL, August 7, 1864, LP; John A. Logan File, HP.

44 The August 2 letter was originally published by the *Boston Transcript* and can subsequently be found in "Letter From General Logan," *Janesville Weekly Gazette*, September 23, 1864.

45 Hazen, 280.

46 JAL, letter to Richard Yates, July 16, 1864, LP; JAL, letter to ML, June 18 and August 6, 1864, LP. Amzi White was born on September 4, 1847. See *History of Gallatin, Saline, Hamilton, Franklin and Williamson Counties. Illinois* (Chicago: Goodspeed Publishing, Co., 1887), 954–55.

47 The physician first placed the story in *The National Tribune* in July of 1884. It was reproduced in Dawson, 76–80.

48 "Mac," letter to the [Milwaukee] *Sunday Telegraph*, n.d., reproduced in Dawson, 81–82.

49 For a detailed analysis of this battle, see James R. Furqueron, "The Finest Opportunity Lost: The Battle of Jonesborough, August 31–September 1, 1864," *North and South* 6 (September, 2003).

50 Dawson, 84–86; Georgia Report, 103.

51 Henry Wilson, letter to Abraham Lincoln, September 5, 1864, Lincoln Papers; Sherman, letter to JAL, February 20, 1883, LP. Sherman explained to Logan that Lincoln's telegram was part of a collection of military papers that burned in the Great Chicago Fire of 1873.

52 Sheahan, letter to JAL, August 31, 1864, LP.

53 Donald, 530. The platform, in its entirety, can be found in Houghton, 518–19.

54 Washburne, letter to JAL, September 12, 1864, LP; Haynie, letter to JAL, September 9, 1864, LP.

55 Special Orders No. 212, September 20, 1864, LP; "Out for Lincoln" *Burlington Weekly Hawkeye*, October 8, 1864.

56 ML, *Reminiscences*, 173–75.

57 "A War Democrat on the Political Situation: Extracts from the Speech of Gen. John A. Logan at Carbondale, Illinois," *Burlington* [IA] *Hawkeye*, October 15, 1864.

58 "General Logan Making Speeches for Lincoln," *Raleigh* [NC] *Weekly Standard*, October 26, 1864.

59 "The Copperhead 'Sympathy' for the Soldiers," *Waukesha* [WI] *Freeman*, October 11, 1864.

60 "John A. Logan Before the People," *Centralia Sentinel*, October 6, 1864.

61 "A War Democrat on the Political Situation: Extracts from the Speech of Gen. John A. Logan at Carbondale, Illinois," *Burlington* [IA] *Hawkeye*, October 15, 1864.

62 "A War Democrat on the Political Situation: Extracts from the Speech of Gen. John A. Logan at Carbondale, Illinois," *Burlington* [IA] *Hawkeye*, October 15, 1864.

63 *Illinois State Journal*, October 6 and 7, 1864; JAL, *Letters of Loyal Soldiers: How Douglas Democrats Will Vote* (New York: Loyal Publication Society; 1864).

64 Thomas J. Turner, letter to Abraham Lincoln, October 6, 1864, Lincoln Papers.

65 "Political Protracted Meeting," *Centralia Sentinel*, October 13, 1864; *Illinois State Journal*, October 17, 1864.

66 Newspaper Clipping, Logan Scrapbook, LP.

67 Edwin M. Stanton, letter to Maj. Genl. Logan, October 14, 1864, LP; Stanton, letter to Lincoln, October 16, 1864, Lincoln Papers; *OR* 41 (3): 808.

68 David L. Phillips, letter to Lincoln, October 20, 1864, Lincoln Papers; JAL, letter to ML, October 19, 1864, LP. Mary states that she, Logan, and David Phillips rode a mule-pulled carriage from town to town where Logan spoke. "For six weeks we traveled from place to place, being at last obliged to take the train, and send the mules home, as we went farther North and the distance increased." (ML, *Reminiscences*, 178–180). She appears to confuse 1864 events with his speaking tour

of 1863. John Logan left Carbondale after his October 1 speech and entrained to Springfield. Mary is never mentioned at any of the newspaper reports of the speech sites. The fact that Logan is writing to her on October 19 refutes her reminiscences.

69 "Immense Outpouring of the People! Unbound Enthusiasm! Maj. Gen. John A. Logan's Speech," *Alton Telegraph*, October 21, 1864.

70 F. M. Woolard, letter to E. L. Bost, April 22, 1909, Woollard Papers, ALPL; Tuthill, "Recollections of Gen. John A. Logan;" "The Champions of Free Speech," *Alton Telegraph*, November 4, 1864.

71 "War on the Stump," *Burlington* [IA] *Hawkeye*, November 12, 1864.

72 "The Champions of Free Speech," *Alton Telegraph*, November 4, 1864; Tuthill, "Recollections of Gen. John A. Logan."

73 "Secession of a Part of Illinois Proposed," *Burlington* [IA] *Weekly Hawkeye*, October 22, 1864; *Illinois State Journal*, October 29, 1864.

74 Annie Logan File, HP; Buel, 397–98; "John A. Logan," *Jonesboro Gazette*, October 29, 1864.

75 Washburne, letter to Lincoln, October 27, 1864, Lincoln Papers.

76 Cole, 327–28; George Washington Smith, 1: 314–315, Jones, *Black Jack*, 238.

77 Oglesby, letter to JAL, November 20, 1864, LP.

78 *Missouri Democrat* tribute published in the *Alton Telegraph* on November 18, 1864.

79 "John Logan's Old District," *Alton Telegraph*, November 18, 1864.

CHAPTER SEVEN: VICTORY

1 Davidson and Stuve, 879, 908.

2 Washburne, letter to Lincoln, October 27, 1864, Lincoln Papers; John D. Defrees, letter to Lincoln, November 2, 1864, Lincoln Papers.

3 JAL, letters to Lincoln, November 6 and 12, 1864, Lincoln Papers.

4 Lincoln, letter to JAL, November 12, 1864, Lincoln Papers; *OR* 44 (1): 465.

5 Haynie, letter to JAL, November 19, 1864, LP.

6 Haynie, letter to JAL, November 19, 1864, LP; Hotaling, letter to ML, November 20, 1864, LP.

7 Jones, *Black Jack*, 240; Haynie, letter to JAL, November 25, 1864, LP; *Unconditional Unionist* editorial excerpted in *Illinois State Journal*, November 26, 1864.

8 Carbondale *New Era* editorial excerpted in *Illinois State Journal*, January 3, 1865; Haynie, letter to ML, January 4, 1865, LP.

9 Logan intimated that his trip East was related to the opposing armies in Tennessee; he then recounted Lincoln's anecdote in *The Great Conspiracy*, 602. Logan relayed the anecdote to reporter W.B.S., who published it in a slightly different form in the *St. Louis Globe Democrat* on December 21, 1886.

10 JAL, *The Great Conspiracy*, 602; "Mr. Blaine Speaks," *Chicago Tribune*, December 27, 1886.

11 Simon, ed., *Papers of Ulysses S. Grant*, vol. 13, 321–22; Mark Mayo Boatner, *The Civil War Dictionary* (New York: Random House, 1991), 556.

12 Grant, 651–59.

13 Special Orders No. 149, LP; Horace Porter, *Campaigning With Grant* (Secaucus, NJ: The Blue and Grey Press, 1984), 348. Although the Special Orders do not state Logan's command orders specifically, Grant revealed, "I gave him an order to proceed to Nashville to relieve Thomas." See Grant, 659.

14 *New York Herald*'s Washington Correspondent report republished in the *Jonesboro Gazette*, December 24, 1864. Reub Williams, "Logan Reminiscences." Logan left an itinerary of his mileage that he submitted for reimbursement. (Box 49, LP). Logan specifies that he left Washington on December 13, confirming that he left City Point promptly after receiving his orders. He likely reached Cincinnati on December 14, one day prior to Thomas's attack, but stayed in Cincinnati as Thomas battled Hood over the next two days, ostensibly informed at the Burnet House that the Battle of Nashville had commenced. Mary claims that her husband warned Thomas that he was on his way to replace him (ML, *Reminiscences*, 187), which prompted him to battle, a sensational claim with no direct or circumstantial evidence to support it.

15 JAL, letter to Grant, and Grant, letter to JAL, December 17, 1864, LP. Logan's first line to Grant was, "have just arrived," confirming that he stayed in Cincinnati for two days prior to crossing the Ohio River.

16 JAL, letters to ML, December 20, 22 and 23, 1864, LP.

17 Logan hand-delivered Lincoln's December 26 message to Sherman, confirming that he met with the president after Christmas, but the meeting could have taken place a day or two after the president wrote it. If he met with the president that day, Logan likely did so during a White House reception given on December 26 (*New York Herald*, December 29, 1864). On January 4, 1865, Lincoln wrote Stanton, "I did promise Gen. Logan that this appointment should be made if it consistently could, and I personally carried the paper to Col. Hardie who will inform the Secretary of War all about it." The specifics of the appointment were never revealed. (See Basler, ed., *Collected Works of Abraham Lincoln*, vol. 8, 181–82, 197.)

18 JAL, letter to ML, January 1, 1865, LP; Sherman, letter to Lincoln, January 6, 1865, Lincoln Papers; Simon, ed., *Papers of Ulysses S. Grant*, vol. 13, 238; Boatner, 301–302, 778–79. Had Logan won the command, part of his responsibility would have been organizing black troops.

19 W. G. K., letter to the editor, January 11, 1865, published in the *Burlington* [IA] *Weekly Hawkeye*, January 23, 1865.

20 *OR* 47 (1): 239.

21 *OR* 47 (1): 238; Theodore F. Upson, *With Sherman to the Sea: The Civil War Letters, Diaries and Reminiscences of Theodore F. Upson* (Baton Rouge: Louisiana State Univ. Press, 1943), 149 (no apostrophe in original).

22 JAL, letter to ML, January 20, 1865, LP.

23 Haynie, letter to ML, January 5, 1865, LP; JAL, letter to Haynie, January 22, 1865, Haynie Papers, ALPL.

24 W. T. Sherman, *Memoirs*, 749–50.

25 Pepper, 500–501.

26 "Fleet Returned," *Burlington* [IA] *Weekly Hawkeye*, January 28, 1865.

27 W. T. Sherman, *Memoirs*, 753; "Civil War Reminiscences of Hugh Milton Stackhouse," http://www.geocities.com/Yosemite/6648/Civil_War_Rem.html; Harvey M. Trimble, *History of the Ninety-third Regiment Illinois Volunteer Infantry* (Chicago: Blakely Printing Co., 1898), 165–66.

28 John K. Duke, *History of the Fifty-third Regiment Ohio Volunteer Infantry, During the War of the Rebellion 1861 to 1865* (Portsmouth, OH: The Blade Printing Company, 1900), 176.

29 *OR* 47 (1): 222; Hazen, 342.

30 Henry Hitchcock, *Marching with Sherman: Passages from the Letters and Campaign Diaries of Henry Hitchcock Major and Assistant Adjutant General of Volunteers*, (New Haven: Yale Univ. Press, 1927), 258; "A White Man Held in Slavery," *Alton Telegraph*, March 31, 1865; "The White Slave," *Burlington Weekly Hawkeye*, April 1, 1865.

31 H. T. Clark, John Moore, and Amzi F. White Testimonies, Logan Pension File, NA.

32 John D. Billings, Charles W. Reed, and William L. Shea, *Hardtack and Coffee, Or the Unwritten Story of Army Life* (Lincoln: Univ. of Nebraska Press, 1993), 263.

33 *OR* 47 (1): 226–27.

34 *OR* 47 (2): 444; Pepper, 311.

35 Melvin Grigsby, *The Smoked Yank* (Sioux Falls: Dakota Bell Publishing Co., 1888), 235–36; Joseph Saunier, *A History of the Forty-Seventh Regiment Ohio Veteran Volunteer Infantry* (Hillsboro, OH: Lyle Print Co., 1903).

36 Upson, 150.

37 *OR* 47 (1): 227; Orendorf, 182–83.

38 *OR* 47 (1): 227–28; Hicken, 294.

39 Marszalek, *Sherman*, 324–25.

40 "Sherman's Grand March," *Burlington Weekly Hawkeye*, April 22, 1865.

41 Samuel H. M. Byers, *With Fire and Sword* (New York: Neale Publishing Co., 1911), 182.

42 *OR* 47 (1): 232–33.

43 *OR* 47 (1): 233–34; Orendorf, 198.

44 John G. Barrett, "Bentonville," *The Civil War Battlefield Guide*, 268–72; *OR* 47 (1): 235–36.

45 "Fast Horses," *Burlington Weekly Hawkeye*, April 15, 1864.

46 *OR* 47 (3): 111–12.

47 Orendorf, 204–207.

48 Reub Williams, "Logan Reminiscences."

49 Hazen, 376.

50 Orendorf, 208; Upson, 166–67; Dawson, 96–97.

51 JAL, letter to ML, April 19, 1865, LP; Orendorf, 208.

52 Marszalek, *Sherman*, 345–349.

53 Hitchcock, 316; "Address of General W. T. Sherman," September 14, 1887, in *Proceedings of the Society of the Army of the Tennessee at the Twentieth Meeting*, 472; JAL, letter to ML April 27, 1865.

54 JAL, letter to ML, April 26, 1865, LP.

55 Orendorf, 209–217.

56 JAL, letter to ML, April 26, 1865, LP.
57 Marszalek, *Sherman*, 352.
58 Sherman, letter to JAL, May 12, 1865, LP.
59 Orendorf, 218–19; Jones, *Black Jack*, 260; Marszalek, *Sherman*, 353.
60 Orendorf, 219–221; *OR* 47 (3): 478.
61 *OR* 47 (3): 532; JAL, letter to ML, May 20, 1865, LP.
62 *OR* 47 (3): 562.
63 Oliver Otis Howard, *The Autobiography of Oliver Otis Howard*, 2 vols. (New York: Baker & Taylor, 1907), 210–11.
64 Trimble, 199; Upson, 175–76.
65 Untitled and undated Logan speech, Container 57, folder 7, 46, LP.
66 Duke, 199.
67 Upson, 177; "Review of the Armies . . . Two Hundred Thousand Spectators Watching for Sherman, Thomas, Howard and Their Men," *NY Times*, May 25, 1865.
68 "Review of the Armies," *NY Times*, May 25, 1865; Andrews, 574.
69 Leech, 416–17; Jack Rudolph, "The Grand Review," *Civil War Times Illustrated* 19 (November 1980): 34–43.
70 JAL, letter to ML, May 26, 1865, LP.

CHAPTER EIGHT: MEMORIAL DAYS

1   Speech reproduced in Dawson, 98–100.
2   Pepper, 498–99.
3   Dawson, 100.
4   "From Kentucky: Brief of Maj. Gen. John A. Logan's Louisville Speech," *NY Times*, July 30, 1865; "Kentucky," *NY Times*, August 5, 1865; Linder, 344.
5   ML, *Reminiscences*, 201, 203; Logan Family Bible, ALPL; Jones, *Black Jack*, 268; *OR* 49 (2): 1100–1101.
6   "Editor's Easy Chair," *Harper's New Monthly Magazine* 32 (December, 1865): 123.
7   Annie Logan File, HP.
8   25th General Assembly votes in GJALM.
9   "Illinois State Fair," *NY Times*, September 16, 1865; Jones, *Black Jack*, 269.
10 Dawson, 113–14; JAL, letter to ML, December 12, 1865 and January 18, 1866, LP.
11 ML, letter to JAL, March 15, 1866, LP.
12 John W. D. Wright, 41–43; "Facts About Woodlawn Cemetery," http://www.ci.carbondale.il.us/woodlawn.htm.
13 Jones, *Black Jack*, 273–74.
14 JAL, letter to ML, May 2, 1866, LP.
15 *Chicago Tribune*, May 8, 1866, excerpted in HP.
16 ML, *Reminiscences*, 211; Cairo speech printed in full in *Chicago Tribune*, July 2 and 3, 1866.
17 Toast reproduced in "Gleanings," *Chicago Evening Herald*, April 6, 1867.
18 *Chicago Tribune*, July 6, 1866; Simon, ed., *Papers of Ulysses S. Grant*, vol. 16, 239.
19 *The Daily-Index*, July 12, 1865; "Logan and Andy Johnson," *Indianapolis Daily Journal*, December 30, 1886.

20 *Chicago Tribune*, July 13, 1866; "Logan and Andy Johnson," *Indianapolis Daily Journal*, December 30, 1886.

21 *Illinois State Journal*, August 9, 1866; *Chicago Tribune*, August 9, 1866.

22 Harris L. Dante, "Western Attitudes and Reconstruction Politics in Illinois, 1865–1872," *Journal of the Illinois State Historical Society* 44, no. 2 (Summer 1956): 152.

23 Mary Dearing, *Veterans in Politics: The Story of the Grand Army of the Republic* (Baton Rouge: Louisiana State Univ. Press, 1952), 104–106; ML, *Reminiscences*, 211–12; *Alton Telegraph*, August 31, 1866.

24 *Chicago Tribune*, August 27 and 30, 1866; Jones, *Black Jack*, 277–78; "News Items," *Alton Telegraph*, September 21, 1866; Dante, 151.

25 Cole, 398, 400–404.

26 *Chicago Tribune*, November 1, 1866; other newspaper clippings in Logan Scrapbooks, LP.

27 Jones, *Black Jack*, 280; Debate Agreement, LP.

28 "Passages of a Busy Life," *Chicago Tribune*, December 28, 1886; Cole, 402; "News Items," *Alton Telegraph*, September 21, 1866.

29 *Chicago Tribune*, October 12, 1866; *Alton Weekly Telegraph*, September 28 and October 19, 1866; "Joint Discussion at Decatur: Logan and Dickey," *Illinois State Journal*, October 17, 1866; Dante, 151. Logan's speaking schedule published in *Illinois State Journal*, September 15, 1866.

30 "Matter About Logan," *Cincinnati Commercial Gazette*, January 2, 1887.

31 Dante, 151; Cole, 403.

32 *Congressional Globe*, 40th Congress (1st Session), 471–80.

33 James Picket Jones, *John A. Logan: Stalwart Republican from Illinois* (Carbondale: Southern Illinois Univ. Press, 2001), 8.

34 "Gen. Logan in Cleveland, Ohio," *NY Times*, September 29, 1867.

35 "Speech of Gen. John A. Logan, Delivered at Hamilton, Ohio, September 12, 1867," Carbondale *New Era*, September 26, 1867, (reprinted from the *Cincinnati Gazette*).

36 "Sold Badly," The *Defiance Democrat*, September 14, 1867.

37 Ohio election results of 1867 derived from Jones, *John A. Logan*, 12.

38 Jones, *John A. Logan*, 13; undated notebook, Logan Family Papers, ALPL.

39 "Grand Army of the Republic—Gen. Logan Assumes Command," *NY Times*, January 26, 1868; Stephenson, letter to JAL, January 30, 1868, LP.

40 *Congressional Globe*, 40th Congress (2nd Session), pt. 1, 987–90.

41 *Illinois State Journal*, Feb. 22, 1868.

42 Jones, *John A. Logan*, 23; Dawson, 128–32.

43 JAL, letter to Haynie, January 30 and February 9, 1868, Haynie Papers, ALPL; "Logan for President," Carbondale *New Era*, April 11, 1867.

44 JAL, letter to William E. Chandler, September 19, 1868, Chandler Papers, Library of Congress.

45 Dawson, 123; ML, *Reminiscences*, 242–44.

46 Ely, Burnham and Bartlett, *Presidential Election, 1868* (Chicago: Evening Journal Printers, 1868), 90.

47 Sean Dennis Cashman, *America in the Gilded Age*, 3rd ed. (New York: New York Univ. Press, 1993), 212–14.

48 *NY Times*, June 16, 1868; "Honor the Fallen Brave," *Alton Weekly Telegraph*, June 5, 1868.

49 *Indianapolis Journal*, January 1, 1887.

CHAPTER NINE: TAINTED IN THE GILDED AGE

1 Cashman, 214; Robert W. Cherny, *American Politics in the Gilded Age, 1868–1900* (Wheeling, IL: Harlan Davidson, Inc., 1997), 14–16.

2 Dawson, 159–61, 176–77.

3 Orville Hickman Browning's diary entry for January 19, 1869 in Theodore Calvin Pease and James G. Randall, eds., *The Diary of Orville Hickman Browning*, vol. 2 (Springfield: Trustees of the Illinois State Historical Library, 1925–33), 235.

4 ML, *Reminiscences*, 233–35.

5 ML, *Reminiscences*, 232; Committee makeup for the 41st Congress obtained from *Congressional Globe*, 41st Congress (1st Session), 75–76.

6 Jones, *John A. Logan*, 35.

7 Marlene D. Merrill, *Yellowstone and the Great West: Journals, Letters and Images from the 1871 Hayden Expedition* (Lincoln: Univ. of Nebraska Press, 1999), 29, 222 (n. 5); Hayden, letter to JAL, September 21, 1870, LP.

8 "Proposed Removal of the National Capital," *Decatur Republican*, June 18, 1868; Dawson, 166–69.

9 Marszalek, 430–31; W. T. Sherman, *Memoirs*, 605.

10 Dawson, 181. Logan's Arlington speech printed in the *Chicago Evening Journal*, June 3, 1870.

11 Dante, 158; quotation in Cashman, 247.

12 Dante, 152.

13 Wright, 50–51; Dawson, 127–28; "The Little Game at Washington," *N.Y Sun* article clipped into the *Waukesha* [WI] *Plaindealer*, March 18, 1871.

14 "Stories of Logan," *Cincinnati Commercial Gazette*, January 2, 1887; Earle S. Kinsley, *Recollections of Vermonters in the State and National Affairs* (Rutland, VT: Privately printed, 1992), 22.

15 "Stories of Logan," *Cincinnati Commercial Gazette*, January 2, 1887.

16 "Stories of Logan"; Jean Edward Smith, 588–89, 702 (n. 51–53).

17 Jean Edward Smith, 497–99; Dawson, 184–85.

18 Dawson, 187; *Missouri Daily Democrat*, June 20, 1870.

19 All articles cited in Dawson, 188–91.

20 Jones, *John A. Logan*, 46; Ernest L. Bogart and Charles M. Thompson, *The Industrial State, 1870–1893* (Springfield: Illinois Centennial Commission, 1920), 62.

21 David W. Lusk, *Politics and Politicians of Illinois, 1856–1884* (Springfield: H. W. Rokker, 1884), 2, 5–17; Jones, *John A. Logan*, 48–49.

22 Davenport [IA] *Daily Gazette*, January 13, 1871; Bogart and Thompson, 63; ML, *Reminiscences*, 284–87.

23 "The Election of U.S. Senator," *Illinois State Journal*, January 19, 1871.

24 *Congressional Globe*, 41st Congress (3rd Session), 1917–19; "Logan and Grant," *New York Tribune*, December 28, 1886; "Gen. Grant and the 'Red Stone' Job," *Waukesha* [WI] *Plaindealer*, March 21, 1871; Simon, ed., *Papers of Ulysses S. Grant*, vol. 23, 21.

25 Trumbull, letter to William Jayne, April 9, 1871, Jayne Papers, ALPL.

26 William B. Hesseltine, *Ulysses S. Grant, Politician* (New York: Mead & Company, 1935), 251; "Grant on Logan," *Washington Post*, December 17, 1886. The article excerpts Grant's May 17, 1871, assessment of Logan.

27 "General Logan and the Presidency," [Elyria, OH] *Lorain Constitutionalist*, July 12, 1871; "Logan Would Not Decline," *Waukesha* [WI] *Plaindealer*, July 18, 1871.

28 "Logan and the Presidency," *Carbondale New Era*, June 24, 1871; "Serenade to Senator Logan," *Carbondale New Era*, July 1, 1871.

29 Marion *Friend* excerpted in *Carbondale New Era*, July 22, 1871.

30 ML, *Reminiscences*, 290–91; Dawson, 200.

31 ML, *Reminiscences*, 291–92; Dawson, 198–200.

32 ML, *Reminiscences*, 294; Merrill, 29, 31, 222 (n. 5); William H. Goetzmann, *Exploration and Empire: The Explorer and Scientist in the Winning of the American West* (Austin: Texas State Historical Association, 2000), 495–96, 507–9.

33 Simon, ed., *Papers of Ulysses S. Grant*, vol. 23, 20–21.

34 Logan's Senate speech reprinted in Dawson, 200–202. For the canvass, see ML, *Reminiscences*, 311; "Mt. Pulaski Overflowing—Grand Tanner Parade," *Decatur Daily Republican*, October 7, 1872; "Senator Logan at Mount Pulaski—20,000 Republicans Turn Out," *NY Times*, October 7, 1872.

35 Bogart and Thompson, 78–82.

36 John Logan Bible Records, Logan Family Papers; Family Record, 14; ML, *Reminiscences*, 302–303; JAL, letter to ML, July 15, 1871, LP.

37 ML, *Reminiscences*, 311, 325.

38 Tom Logan File, HP.

39 Annie Logan File, HP; Israel Blanchard Bar Bill, Typescript in GJALM.

40 "Mother Logan," *The Citizen Soldier: A Quarterly Publication of the General John A. Logan Museum* (Winter, 2003): 1–2.

41 ML, *Reminiscences*, 364; Mary S. Lockwood, *Historic Homes in Washington: Its Noted Men and Women* (New York: Belford Co., 1889), 293–95. Mrs. Logan claimed that the address of the boarding houses existed between 810–814 on Twelfth Street, but Logan's papers place his address at No. 808.

42 "Logan as a Fighter," *Indianapolis Daily Journal*, January 4, 1887; "Ready to Make Amends," *Chicago Inter-Ocean*, January 1, 1887.

43 Both handwritten plays in LP. See also "Amateur Theatricals, *Indianapolis Journal*, December 28, 1886.

44 Population Census of Jackson County, Illinois, 1870, National Archives; Allan Nevins, *Hamilton Fish: The Inner History of the Grant Administration*, vol. 2 (New York: Frederick Ungar, 1957), 612.

45 Jean Edward Smith, 552–53; Democratic Party National Committee, *The Campaign Text Book. Why the People Want a Change. The Republican Party Reviewed: Its Sins of Commission and Omission* (1876), 643–44.

46 Ernest S. Bates, *The Story of Congress, 1789–1935* (New York: Harper & Brothers, 1935), 270–71.

47 JAL, letter to ML, 1874, 1875, LP; Muriel Sibell Wolle, *The Bonanza Trail: Ghost Towns and Mining Camps of the West* (Bloomington: Indiana Univ. Press, 1953), 405–6.

48 For an illiterate interpretation of the *New York Sun* reports, see "A Shameless Peice of Scoundreling and Villiany Exposed," *New York Sun* clipping excerpted into the *Statesville* [NC] *Landmark*, December 18, 1875; "Ineffable Meaness: Senator Logan . . . Blackmailing a Soldier's Daughter," *Statesville Landmark*, December 25, 1875.

49 Ada C. Sweet, letter to JAL, December 24, 1875, in "The Chicago Pension Agency," *NY Times*, December 28, 1875.

50 Bogart and Thompson, 106–110.

51 Dearing, 219–20; *Sedalia* [MO] *Daily Democrat*, August 29, 1876.

52 Paul F. Boller, Jr., *Presidential Campaigns* (New York: Oxford Univ. Press, 1984), 134.

53 Dearing, 226, 228–29.

54 Jones, *John A. Logan*, 92–3.

55 "Viator," letter to the editor, *Chicago Daily Inter-Ocean*, January 22, 1871; "Marriage of General Logan's Daughter," *NY Times*, December 4, 1877.

56 ML, *Reminiscences*, 361.

57 *Chicago Tribune*, January 18–27, 1877; *Illinois State Journal*, January 20–24, 1877.

58 *Illinois State Register*, January 24, 1877; *Edwardsville* [IL] *Intelligencer*, January 31, 1877; *Portsmouth* [OH] *Times*, January 27, 1877; *Sedalia Daily Democrat*, January 26 and 27, 1877.

59 Jones, *John A. Logan*, 100.

60 Stanley P. Hirshson, *Farewell to the Bloody Shirt: Northern Republicans and the Southern Negro, 1877–1893* (Bloomington: Indiana Univ. Press, 1962), 27.

61 "Anecdotes of the Dead Senator," *New York Tribune*, December 28, 1886.

CHAPTER TEN: RISE OF A CANDIDATE

1 ML, *Reminiscences*, 362–63; Jones, *John A. Logan*, 103–105.

2 *Colorado Springs Gazette*, June 30, 1877; JAL, letters to ML, July 1, 24, 27, August 8, 15, 20, 1877, LP.

3 "Marriage of Gen. Logan's Daughter," *NY Times*, December 4, 1877; ML, *Reminiscences*, 364; "Society and Fashion: Some of Washington's Sociable Features," *Washington Post*, January 19, 1878; "Personal," *Washington Post*, April 20, 1878; ML, *Reminiscences*, 364–66.

4 ML, letter to Mary Tucker, LP; "Political Notes," *NY Times*, May 12, 1878.

5 Charles A. Church, *History of the Republican Party in Illinois, 1854–1912* (Rockford: Press of Wilson Brothers Co., 1912), 132–33.

6 Mark A. Plummer, *Lincoln's Railsplitter: Governor Richard J. Oglesby* (Urbana: Univ. of Illinois Press, 2001), 166–67; "The Political Campaign," *NY Times*, June 26, 1878; "For What Our Soldiers Died," *NY Times*, July 8, 1878; "The Soldier's Reunion," *Washington Post*, July 23, 1878; "The Great Reunion. Mt. Vernon Alive with Soldiers. Speeches by Gov. Cullom, Gen. Logan and Others," *Decatur Daily Republican*, August, 1878.

7 "This on Logan," *Chicago Times* article clipped into the *Edwardsville Intelligencer*, August 28, 1878; Plummer, 166–67; "Personal," *Decatur Daily Republican*, October 26, 1878; "Telegraphic Tales," *Washington Post*, November 2, 1878.

8 Bogart and Thompson, 128–29; Plummer, 167–68.

9 "Illinois—John A. Logan," *NY Times*, January 23, 1879.

10 "All of Which Refers to Logan," *Chicago Tribune* excerpt clipped into *Washington Post*, January 14, 1879.

11 "Logan's Luck," [Burlington] *Iowa Weekly Hawkeye*, January 23, 1879; Trenton *Star and Sentinel*, January 23, 1879; *Atlanta Constitution*, January 23, 1879; "Senator Logan," *Cairo Evening Sun*, January 29, 1879.

12 [Albert Lea, MN] *Freeborn County Standard*, February 6, 1879; Dawson, 238–43; "A Grand Glorification," *Washington Post*, February 21, 1879 (with editorial).

13 "Senator Logan Challenged," *NY Times*, January 26, 1879; "Outraged Southern Honor," *NY Times*, January 27, 1879.

14 "Grant and His Generals," *Chicago Inter-Ocean*, January 15, 1880.

15 "Dick Oglesby on Logan," *Washington Post*, July 18, 1879.

16 Paul Fatout, *Mark Twain on the Lecture Circuit* (Bloomington: Indiana Univ. Press, 1960), 200–201; *Chicago Tribune*, November 14, 1879; Mark Twain, *Mark Twain's Letters 1876–1885* (arranged by Albert B. Paine), vol. 3, http://www.fullbooks.com/The-Letters-Of-Mark-Twain-Vol-3.html.

17 *Congressional Record*, 46th Congress (2nd Session), appendix, 47–92; Harry J. Brown and Frederick D. Williams, ed., *The Diary of James A. Garfield*, vol. IV (Michigan State Univ. Press, 1981), 378.

18 "Grant Honored at Home. Gen. Logan's Speech at a Demonstration in Chicago," *NY Times*, April 16, 1880.

19 "A Contest to be Made for Grant: Senator Logan Announces that the Ex-President's Name Will Not Be Withdrawn Under Any Circumstances," *NY Times*, April 27, 1880.

20 Cashman, 246–47.

21 Richard S. West, *Satire on Stone: The Political Cartoons of Joseph Keppler* (Urbana: Univ. of Illinois Press, 1988), 232–33.

22 Church, 136–37; "Logan's Third Termers. They Carry the Illinois Convention for the 'Old Man'," *Washington Post*, May 22, 1880.

23 *Cincinnati Enquirer*, December 30, 1880; *Chicago Tribune*, May 22 and 23, 1880; [Cambridge, OH] *Jeffersonian*, May 27, 1880; "Logan's Victory," [Burlington, IA] *Hawk-Eye*, May 29, 1880; "Grant's Illinois Victory . . . Gen. Logan's Masterly Work," *NY Times*, May 22, 1880; A. M. Long, letter to ML, May 21, 1880, LP; "Gath," *Cincinnati Enquirer*, December 30, 1886.

24 *Sangamo* [IL] *Monitor*, May 27, 1880; [Cambridge, OH] *Jeffersonian*, May 27, 1880; West, 210–11.

25 Reports of the demonstrations in June 1 editions of *NY Times*, *Chicago Inter-Ocean*, *Illinois State Journal* and *Chicago Tribune*. The *NY Times* called Frederick Douglass "Stephen A. Douglass."

26 "The Story of the Balloting," *NY Times*, June 9, 1880. The most thorough coverage of the exciting convention is found in Kenneth D. Ackerman, *Dark Horse: The Surprise*

Election and Political Murder of President James A. Garfield (New York: Carroll & Graf Publishers, 2003), 53–133.

27 Cartoons in *Puck Magazine*, June 9 and 16, 1880.

28 Ackerman, 125; T. C. Crawford, "Logan as a Partisan," *St. Louis Post Dispatch*, January 1, 1887; Hesseltine, *Ulysses S. Grant*, 443.

29 Boller, 144. Logan's 1880 scrapbook shows newspaper clippings for all his addresses. See Container 97, LP.

30 Brown and Williams, ed., *Diary of James A. Garfield*, 462, 488–89, 543.

31 Brown and Williams, 559–60 (n. 94).

32 Ackerman, 269, 271–73; "The Guiteau Trial," *Washington Post*, November 27, 1881.

33 Z. L. W., "Anecdotes About General Logan," *New York Tribune*, December 27, 1886.

34 Jones, *John A. Logan*, 149–50.

35 "Illness of Senator Logan," *Washington Post*, February 4, 1882; JAL, letter to J. M. Dalzell, March 5, 1882, Pierpont Morgan Library; "Logan on Grant and Conkling," *Washington Post*, May 16, 1882; Z. L. W., "Anecdotes About General Logan," *New York Tribune*, December 27, 1886.

36 "As a Senator," *Cincinnati Enquirer*, December 28, 1880; Buel, 316; Slason Thompson, *Life of Eugene Field: The Poet of Childhood* (New York: D. Appleton and Co., 1927), 223–24; Z. L. W., "Logan as an Orator," *New York Tribune*, December 28, 1886.

37 Z. L. W., "Anecdotes About General Logan," *New York Tribune*, December 27, 1886; "The Senate Restaurant," *Trenton Times*, March 26, 1884.

38 Mary Logan Tucker Reminiscence, Typescript in GJALM.

39 John A. Logan, *Fitz-John Porter: Speech of Hon. John A. Logan, of Illinois . . . on the Bill (S. 1844) for the Relief of Fitz-John Porter* (Washington: n.p., 1883), 1–182; John A. Logan, "National Aid to Public Schools," *North American Review* 136, no. 137 (April, 1883): 337–45.

40 Justus D. Doenecke, *The Presidencies of James A. Garfield & Chester A. Arthur* (Univ. of Kansas, 1981), 90.

41 "Gen. Logan and a Critic," *NY Times*, May 29, 1883.

42 Larry D. Ball, *The United States Marshals of New Mexico and Arizona Territories, 1846–1912* (Albuquerque: Univ. of New Mexico Press, 1999), 149.

43 Howard R Lamar, ed. *The New Encyclopedia of the American West* (New Haven: Yale Univ. Press, 1998), 1056.

44 "The Commissioners' Pow Wow," [Butte, MT] *The Daily Miner*, August 25, 1883; "Saucy Sitting Bull. . . . Senator Logan Sits Down on Him," *Washington Post*, August 25, 1883; "Logan and Bull," *NY Times*, September 13, 1883.

45 [Placerville, CA] *Mountain Democrat*, September 22, 1883.

46 *Waukesha Freeman*, May 10, 1883; *Bloomington Bulletin* editorial clipped into the *Decatur Morning Review*, September 15, 1883.

47 Cashman, 256–57; "Out for Lincoln" *Burlington Weekly Hawkeye*, October 8, 1864.

48 Cashman, 262; Dearing, 274–90.

49 "The Progress of the Colored Race," *Washington Post*, February 9, 1884; Mark W. Summers, *Rum Romanism, and Rebellion: The Making of a President 1884* (Chapel Hill: Univ. of North Carolina Press, 2000), 129; "Douglass for Logan," *Washington*

Post, April 11, 1884; "Gen. Logan and the Negroes.: A Tribute to the Heroes who Began the Anti-Slavery Movement," *NY Times*, February 14, 1884; "A Talk with a Colored Leader," *NY Times*, March 5, 1884; "Colored Men For Logan," *NY Times*, April 11, 1884.

50 "Grant and Logan," *Cincinnati Enquirer*, December 28, 1886; "Grant and Logan," *Washington Post*, November 28, 1882; H. Wayne Morgan, ed., *From Hayes to McKinley: National Party Politics, 1877–1896* (Syracuse: Syracuse Univ. Press, 1969), 179–80.

51 Jones, *John A. Logan*, 178; Lockwood, 296.

52 Lockwood, 296–97; Jones, *John A. Logan*, 180–82; Summers, 141.

53 Summers, 141; Morgan, 203.

54 Morgan, 221; Bogart and Thompson, 148–49.

55 A. B. Hall, "Logan as a Campaigner," *Washington Post*, November 2, 1992.

56 "Logan Reminiscences," *Chicago Tribune*, January 2, 1887; "Logan in the Saddle," *Iowa State Register*, December 30, 1886.

57 Morgan, 222.

58 Summers, 290–96; *Puck Magazine*, November 26, 1884. Image of Bernhard Gilliam's "Thanksgiving Day 1884" online at http://xroads.virginia.edu/~MA96/PUCK/403.jpg.

59 Hornellsville [NY] *Weekly Tribune*, November 21, 1884; Morgan, ed., 232; Jones, John A. Logan, 196.

60 Bogart and Thompson, 154–57.

61 Bogart and Thompson, 157; Raum, *History of Illinois Republicanism*, 185–86; *Chicago Tribune*, April 18, 1885.

62 Henry Craske, *A Complete History of the Campaign in Which "The Mighty Sleeper" was Defeated in the 34th Senatorial District of Illinois, which Culminated in the Reelection of Hon. John A. Logan to the United States Senate* (Rushville, IL: One of the "fine workers," 1885), 5–9.

63 Craske, 45–47; Church, 156–57; Bogart and Thompson, 157–58.

64 "Victory at Last," *Illinois State Journal*, May 20, 1885; JAL, letter to A. Worth Spats, May 27, 1885, author's personal collection.

65 "Victory at Last," *Illinois State Journal*, May 20, 1885.

66 "Congratulations. From People Everywhere," *Illinois State Journal*, May 20, 1885.

67 "One of Logan's Admirer," *NY Times*, June 9, 1885; "Jottings About Town," *Washington Post*, June 12, 1885.

CHAPTER ELEVEN: CORONATION

1 "Logan Welcomed by Colored Men," *Decatur Daily Republican*, June 13, 1885; "Senator Logan Makes a Speech," *Washington Post*, June 13, 1885; *Decatur Daily Republican*, June 15, 1885.

2 *Waukesha Freeman*, June 26, 1885; J. Logan Berry, letter to JAL, March 14, 1885, LP. Berry told Logan in his letter that he had just read a story in a newspaper about another namesake who wrote him about his veteran father.

3 "Logan's Atlantic City Visit," *Trenton Times*, June 12, 1885; *Waukesha Freeman*, June 26, 1885.

4 John Sherman, *John Sherman's Recollections of Forty Years in the House and Senate and Cabinet*, vol. 2 (New York: Greenwood Press, 1968), 920; Hirshson, 132. Logan's speeches and newspaper reaction to them reproduced in Dawson, 374–85.

5 Sergeant-at-arms of U.S. Senate, letter to JAL, July 25, 1885, LP.

6 "Calumet Place Famous in History of Capital," *Washington Post*, March 4, 1925; "The Logan Mansion," [Washington, D.C.] *National Republican*, December 28, 1886; *Cincinnati Commercial Gazette*, January 2, 1887; ML, letter to Mary Logan Tucker, September 2, 1885, LP. Photographs of interior of Calumet Place, 1886, can be found in ALPL; Sketches of interior rooms in "His Last Review," *National Tribune*, January 6, 1887.

7 Dawson, 505.

8 "Literary Notes," *NY Times*, September 28, 1885; "The General's Literary Working Habits," *National Republican*, December 29, 1886; "Literary Labors," *Chicago Tribune*, December 27, 1886; ML, letter to Mary Logan Tucker, October 21, 1885, LP.

9 "Sen. John A. Logan's Book," *NY Times*, May 17, 1886; William R. Thayer, ed., *The Life and Letters of John Hay*, vol. 2 (Boston: Houghton Mifflin, 1908), 31; Jones, *John A. Logan*, 216.

10 Jones, *John A. Logan*, 217, 269 (n. 15). For the full two-day debate on Senate Bill 194, see *Congressional Record*, 49th Congress (1st Session), pt. 2, 1995–2001, 2033–2037.

11 Dawson, 412–13.

12 Jones, *John A. Logan*, 218.

13 "Logan As A Novelist," *Washington Post*, March 22, 1886; Untitled article linking Logan with the book in *Washington Post*, March 25, 1886.

14 *Uncle Daniel's Story*, 63.

15 *Uncle Daniel's Story*, 63; "Gen. Logan Was Its Author: He Wrote the Book that Made a Stir in 1886," *Washington Post*, December 16, 1895; *Report of the Proceedings of the Society of the Army of the Tennessee, Seventeenth Meeting* (Cincinnati: Published by the Society, 1893), 473–74.

16 "The Nation's Shrine," *National Tribune*, June 10, 1886.

17 *Cincinnati Commercial Gazette*, January 8, 1887.

18 "Logan and the Payne Case," *Indianapolis Journal*, December 28, 1886; "Ohio People Very Angry: Logan, Evarts, and Teller in Bad Odor for Helping Payne," *NY Times*, June 28, 1886; "Logan on the Payne Case," *NY Times*, July 5, 1886; Dawson, 430.

19 "Had Enough of Politics," *NY Times*, July 26, 1886; ML, *Reminiscences*, 427; "Major Hopkins Acquaintance," *Chicago Tribune*, December 28, 1886.

20 Dawson, 431–35; "'Black Jack' Receives Hundreds of Visitors," & "Arrival of Logan," *San Francisco Chronicle*, August 3, 1886; "Gen. Logan Showered with Flowers," *San Francisco Examiner* article clipped into *Washington Post*, August 13, 1886.

21 E. J. Phillips, letter to his son, August 4, 1886, http://home.comcast.net/~m.chitty/sanfrancisco.htm; "Comrade Logan," *Portland Oregonian*, August 27, 1886; "Logan and the Veterans," *NY Times*, August 25, 1886.

22 "Portland's Guest," *Portland Oregonian*, August 24, 1886; "General Logan's Hammock Experience," *Portland Oregonian*, August 24, 1886.

23 Speeches excerpted in Dawson, 436–43.

24 The Logan Boom," *Washington Post*, October 29, 1885; "Logan's Slogan. The Illinois Senator Opens the Campaign at Pittsburgh—His Tariff Views," *Waukesha Freeman*, September 30, 1886.

25 "Personal Intelligence," *Washington Post*, October 11, 1886; "Logan at Keokuk," *Defiance Democrat*, October 28, 1886; "Telegraphic Ticks," *Washington Post*, October 22, 1886.

26 "What Miss Cleveland Will Do," *Defiance Democrat*, September 30, 1886.

27 "His Connection with the Church," *Chicago Tribune*, December 27, 1886.

28 "Incumbered By Debt," *Cincinnati Enquirer*, December 28, 1886; Samuel Charles Webster, ed., *Mark Twain, Business Man* (Boston: Little, Brown and Company, 1946), 369.

29 Dawson, 447–49; "Last Days in Congress," *Chicago Tribune*, December 27, 1886; ML, *Reminiscences*, 429.

30 "Death of John A. Logan," *Chicago Tribune*, December 27, 1886; "Illness of Senator Logan," [Carbondale, IL] *Barton's Free Press*, December 25, 1886.

31 W. B. S., "An Interesting Invalid . . . A Couple of Hours with Rheumatism and Reminiscences," *St. Louis Daily Globe Democrat*, December 21, 1886.

32 "The Fatal Turn in Logan's Illness," *Cincinnati Commercial Gazette*, January 2, 1887; Dr. Baxter affidavit, Mrs. John A. Logan Pension file, National Archives; "Death of John A. Logan," *Chicago Tribune*, December 27, 1886.

33 Dr. Baxter affidavit, Mrs. John A. Logan Pension file; "Logan is Dead," *Cincinnati Commercial Gazette*, December 27, 1886; "Death of John A. Logan," *Chicago Tribune*, December 27, 1886; "Dead," *Chicago Inter-Ocean*, December 27, 1886; "Logan No More," *Chicago Times*, December 27, 1886; "The Last Scene," *Indianapolis Journal*, December 27, 1886.

34 "Logan is Dead," *Cincinnati Commercial Gazette*, December 27, 1886; "Death of John A. Logan," *Chicago Tribune*, December 27, 1886.

EPILOGUE

1 All newspapers mentioned referenced the December 27 issue of their publication.

2 "Senator Logan Dead," *Indianapolis Journal*, December 27, 1886; "Casey on Logan," *Illinois State Journal*, December 31, 1886; Robert J. Brahma and Philip S. Fonder, *Lift Every Voice: African American Oratory, 1787–1900* (Tuscaloosa: Univ. of Alabama Press, 1998), 714; [Huntsville, AL] *Southern Freeman*, January 1, 1887; John W. Blassingame and John R. McKivigan, eds., *The Frederick Douglass Papers Series One: Speeches, Debates, and Interviews*, vol. 5 (New Haven and London: Yale Univ. Press, 1992), 375.

3 "His Last Review," *National Tribune*, January 6, 1887; ML, *Reminiscences*, 430–31; "At Rest in a Chapel," *Washington Post*, December 27, 1888.

4 "Gen. Logan's Sister Dead," *NY Times*, September 17, 1894; George W. Smith, *A History of Southern Illinois*, vol. 3, 1148–49.

5 "Maj. John A. Logan," in *Youngstown* (Chicago: American Historical Society, 1920), 177; *Chicago Times Herald*, November 15, 1899.

6 *Chicago Times Herald*, November 15, 1899; ML, *Reminiscences*, 446–48.

7   Ida Hinman, *The Washington Sketchbook: a Society Souvenir* (Washington, D.C.: Hartman & Cadick Printers, 1895), 69; Don C. Seitz, *Joseph Pulitzer: His Life and Letters* (New York: Simon & Schuster, 1924), 47, 232; "Bryan Chooses a Home," *Washington Post*, March 14, 1913; Ellen M. Slayden, *Washington Wife: Journal of Ellen Maury Slayden from 1897–1919* (New York: Harper & Row, 1963), 230–31.

8   ML, *Reminiscences*, xx–xxii, 430–51.

9   Jones, *John A. Logan*, 152, 203; "Mrs. John A. Logan Dies at Age of 84," *NY Times*, February 23, 1923.

10   Dawson, 473.

Bibliography

MANUSCRIPT COLLECTIONS

Abraham Lincoln Presidential Library, Springfield, Illinois
    William Jayne Papers
    Charles Lanphier Papers
    John Logan Family Papers
    Lindorf Ozburn Papers
    F. M. Woollard Papers
    Richard Yates Papers

General John A. Logan Museum, Murphysboro, Illinois
    "'Black Jack's' Candid Comments." *The Egyptian Key* 2 (March, 1947): 19.
    Casey, Samuel. Letter to Dr. John Logan. August 31, 1850.
    Dr. John Logan's migration form Maryland to Illinois (Typescript history).
    Green, James. Memoir.
    Logan, James V. Obituary, newspaper clipping.
    Logan, John A. Letter to James Loomis. May 9, 1861.
    Logan, Mary. Letter to Elizabeth Logan. February 9, 1860.
    "Mother Logan." *The Citizen Soldier: A Quarterly Publication of the General John A. Logan Museum* (Winter, 2003): 1–2.
    Phelps, Margaret Logan Davis. "Family Record—Logan Family." c. 1883.
    Reed, Ronald D. "Bald Dillard's Story." *The Springhouse Magazine: The Journal of the Illinois Ozarks* 2. No. 3. (May/June, 1985): 5–8.
    Tucker, Mary Elizabeth Logan. "Sketch of Life of John A. Logan." February 1929.
    Twenty-fifth Illinois General Assembly votes, 1865.

Jackson County, Illinois Courthouse, Murphysboro, Illinois
   Logan, Dr. John. Letter to Monday Dumbaly. Quit Claim. July 3, 1837.
   The People of the State of Illinois v. Dorthulia A. Blanchard. File No. 893.
   The People of the State of Illinois v. Israel Blanchard. Jackson County Circuit Court
      Files, Murphysboro.
   The People of the State of Illinois v. John A. Logan. 1846.
   The People of the State of Illinois v. Thomas M. Logan. File No. 1941.

Library of Congress, Manuscript Division, Washington, D.C.
   William E. Chandler Papers
   Abraham Lincoln Papers
   John A. Logan Papers

Morris Library, Southern Illinois University, Carbondale, Illinois
   Barbara Burr Hubbs Papers
   Edwin A. Loosley Papers

Minnesota Historical Society, St. Paul
   Christie Family Letters

National Archives, Washington D.C.
   Compiled Pension Records of Civil War Soldiers.
   Letters Received by the Commission Branch of the Adjutant General's Office,
      1863–1870. 527 rolls (M1064).
   Population Schedules of the Census of the United States, 1790–1930. RG 29.
   Records of the Adjutant General's Office. Record Group 94.

Navarro College, Corsicana, Texas
   Pearce Collection of Civil War Manuscripts.

Ohio Historical Society, Columbus
   Jacob Bruner Papers

Personal Collection of Gary Ecelbarger
   John A. Logan Letters.

Pierpont Morgan Library
   John A. Logan Letters

Wisconsin Historical Society Archives, Madison
   Tuthill, R. S. "Recollections of Gen. John A. Logan." 1884.

BOOKS

Ackerman, Kenneth D. *Dark Horse: The Surprise Election and Political Murder of President James A. Garfield.* New York: Carroll & Graf Publishers, 2003.

Allen, Stephen M. *Memorial Life of Ulysses S. Grant.* Boston: Webster Historical Society, 1889.

Andrews, Byron. *A Biography of General John A. Logan: With an Account of His Public Service in Peace and War.* New York: H. S. Goodspeed, 1884.

Angle, Paul M. *Here I Have Lived: A History of Lincoln's Springfield, 1821–1865.* Springfield: The Abraham Lincoln Association, 1935.

——. *Lincoln in the Year 1854, Being the Day-by-Day Activities of Abraham Lincoln During That Year.* Springfield: The Lincoln Centennial Association, 1928.

Arnold, James R. *Grant Wins the War: Decision at Vicksburg.* New York: John Wiley & Sons, 1997.

Bailey, Hugh C. *Hinton Rowan Helper: Abolitionist-Racist.* Birmingham: University of Alabama Press, 1965.

Ball, Larry D. *The United States Marshals of New Mexico & Arizona Territories, 1846–1912.* Albuquerque: University of New Mexico Press, 1999.

Basler, Roy, ed. *Collected Works of Abraham Lincoln.* 8 vols. New Brunswick, New Jersey: Rutgers University Press, 1953–1955.

Bateman, Newton and Paul Selby, eds. *Historical Encyclopedia of Illinois.* 2 vols. Chicago: Munsell Publishing Co., 1907–1908.

Bates, Ernest S. *The Story of Congress, 1789–1935.* New York: Harper & Brothers, 1935.

Baumgartner, Richard A. and Larry M. Strayer. *Kennesaw Mountain, June 1864: Bitter Standoff at the Gibralter of Georgia.* Huntington, West Virginia: Blue Acorn Press, 1998.

Beyer, W. F. and O. F. Keydel, eds. *Deeds of Valor: How America's Civil War Heroes Won the Congressional Medal of Honor.* Detroit: Perrien-Keydel Co., 1903.

Billings, John D., Charles W. Reed, and William L. Shea. *Hardtack and Coffee, Or the Unwritten Story of Army Life.* Lincoln: University of Nebraska Press, 1993.

Binmore, Henry. *Trial of Robert C. Sloo of Shawneetown, for the murder of John E. Hall, Late Clerk of the Circuit Court of Gallatin Co., Ill.* St. Louis: George Knapp & Co., 1857.

Blanchard, Ira. *I Marched with Sherman: Civil War Memoirs of the 20th Illinois Volunteer Infantry.* San Francisco: J. D. Huff and Co., 1992.

Blassingame, John W. and John R McKivigan, eds. *The Frederick Douglass Papers Series One: Speeches, Debates, and Interviews.* 5 vols. New Haven: Yale University Press, 1979–1992.

Boatner, Mark Mayo. *The Civil War Dictionary.* Rev. ed. New York: Random House, 1991.

Bogart, Ernest L. and Charles M. Thompson. *The Industrial State, 1870–1893.* Springfield: Illinois Centennial Commission, 1920.

Boller, Paul F., Jr. *Presidential Campaigns.* New York: Oxford University Press, 1984.

Branham, Robert J. and Philip S. Foner. *Lift Every Voice: African American Oratory, 1787–1900*. Tuscaloosa: University of Alabama Press, 1998.

Brown, Harry J. and Frederick D.Williams, eds. *The Diary of James A. Garfield*. 4 vols. East Lansing: Michigan State University Press, 1967–1982.

Brownlee, James H. *History of Jackson County, Illinois*. Philadelphia: Brink, McDonough & Co., 1878.

Buel, James W. *The Standard Bearers — Official Edition. The Authorized Pictorial Lives of James Gillespie Blaine and John Alexander Logan*. St. Louis: Historical Publishing Co., 1884.

Burlingame, Michael, ed. *Lincoln's Journalist: John Hay's Anonymous Writings for the Press, 1860–1864*. Carbondale: Southern Illinois University Press, 1998.

Burt, Richard W. *War Songs, Poems, and Odes*. Peoria: J.W. Franks & Sons, 1909.

Byers, Samuel H. M. *With Fire and Sword*. New York: Neale Publishing Co., 1911.

Cadwallader, Sylvanus. *Three Years with Grant*. Benjamin P. Thomas, ed. New York: Alfred Knopf, 1955.

Carpenter, Stephen D. *Logic of History. Five Hundred Political Texts; being concentrated extracts of abolitionism; also, results, of slavery agitation and emancipation; together with sundry chapters on despotism, usurpations and their frauds*. Dahlonega, Georgia: Crown Rights Book Company, 1864.

Cashman, Sean Dennis. *America in the Gilded Age*. 3rd ed. New York: New York University Press, 1993.

Castel, Albert. *Decision in the West: The Atlanta Campaign of 1864*. Lawrence: University of Kansas Press, 1992.

Catton, Bruce. *Grant Moves South*. Boston: Little, Brown and Company, 1960.

——. *Grant Takes Command*. Boston: Little, Brown and Company, 1968.

Church, Charles A. *History of the Republican Party in Illinois, 1854–1912*. Rockford: Press of Wilson Brothers Company, 1912.

Clayton Charles C. *Little Mack: Joseph B. McCullagh of The St. Louis Globe-Democrat*. Carbondale: Southern Illinois University Press, 1969.

Cole, Arthur Charles. *The Era of the Civil War, 1848–1870*. Springfield: Illinois Centennial Commission, 1919.

Conwell, Russel H. *Biography of General John A. Logan of Illinois: Childhood, Manhood, Peace and War*. Augusta, Maine: E.C. Allen & Co., 1884.

Craske, Henry. *A Complete History of the Campaign in Which "The Mighty Sleeper" was Defeated in the 34th Senatorial District of Illinois, which Culminated in the Reelection of Hon. John A. Logan to the United States Senate*. Rushville, Illinois: One of the "fine workers," 1885.

Crummer, Wilber F. *With Grant at Fort Donelson, Shiloh, and Vicksburg*. Oak Park, Illinois: E. C. Crummer Co., 1915.

Cullom, Shelby M. *Fifty Years of Public Service: Personal Recollections*. Chicago: A. C. McClurg, 1911.

Dana, Charles A. *Recollections of the Civil War*. New York: D. Appleton and Co., 1898.

Davidson, Alexander and Bernard Stuve. *A Complete History of Illinois, from 1673 to 1873*. Springfield: H. W. Roker, 1884.

Dawson, George F. *Life and Services of Gen John A. Logan as Soldier and Statesman.* Chicago: Belford, Clarke and Company, 1887.

Dearing, Mary R. *Veterans in Politics: The Story of the Grand Army of the Republic.* Baton Rouge: Louisiana State University Press, 1952.

Democratic Party National Committee, *The Campaign Text Book. Why the People Want a Change. The Republican Party Reviewed: Its Sins of Commission and Omission.* New York: Democratic Party National Committee, 1876.

Dodge, Grenville M. *Personal Recollections of General William T. Sherman.* Des Moines: n.p., 1902.

Doenecke, Justus D. *The Presidencies of James A. Garfield & Chester A. Arthur.* Lawrence: University of Kansas Press, 1981.

Donald, David Herbert. *Lincoln.* New York: Simon & Schuster, 1995.

Downs, Edward C. *The Great American Scout and Spy.* 3rd ed. New York: Olmsted and Co., 1870.

Duke, John K. *History of the Fifty-third Regiment Ohio Volunteer Infantry, During the War of the Rebellion 1861 to 1865.* Portsmouth, Ohio: The Blade Printing Co., 1900.

Eighteenth General Assembly. *Private Laws of the State of Illinois.* Springfield: Lanphier & Walker, Printers, 1853.

Ellis, John B. *The Sights and Secrets of the National Capital: a Work Descriptive of Washington City in its Various Phases.* Chicago: Jones, Junkin and Co., 1869.

Ely, Burnham and Bartlett. *Election, 1868.* Chicago: Evening Journal Printers, 1868.

Erwin, Milo. *The History of Williamson County, Illinois.* Marion: n.p., 1876.

Fatout, Paul. *Mark Twain on the Lecture Circuit.* Bloomington: Indiana University Press, 1960.

Fishback, Woodson W. *A History of Murphysboro, Illinois, 1843–1982.* Brandon, Mississippi: Quail Ridge Press, 1982.

Fletcher, Samuel H. *The History of Company A, Second Illinois Cavalry.* Chicago: n. p., 1912.

Fox, William F. *Regimental Losses in the American Civil War, 1861–1865.* Albany: Albany Publishing Co, 1889.

Garrison, Webb. *A Treasury of Civil War Tales.* New York: Ballantine Books, 1988.

Goetzmann, William H. *Exploration and Empire: The Explorer and Scientist in the Winning of the American West.* Austin: Texas State Historical Association, 2000.

Grant, Ulysses S. *Memoirs and Selected Letters.* New York: Library of America, 1990.

Greeley, Horace and John F. Cleveland, comp. *A Political Text-book for 1860: comprising a brief view of Presidential Nominations and Elections.* New York: Tribune Association, 1860.

Grigsby, Melvin. *The Smoked Yank.* Sioux Falls: Dakota Bell Publishing Company, 1888.

Hasse, Ed. *Southern Illinois: A Glimpse at the Past and Present in the Land of Contrasts.* Carbondale: Southern Illinois University Communications, 1966.

Hazen, William B. *A Narrative of Military Service.* Boston: Ticknor and Company, 1885.

Hertz, Emanuel, ed. *Lincoln Talks: A Biography in Anecdote.* New York: The Viking Press, 1939.

Hesseltine, William B. *Three Against Lincoln: Murat Halstead Reports the Caucuses of 1860*. Baton Rouge: Louisiana State University Press, 1960.

——. *Ulysses S. Grant, Politician*. New York: Mead & Company, 1935.

Hicken, Victor. *Illinois in the Civil War*. Urbana: University of Illinois Press, 1991.

Hinman, Ida. *The Washington Sketchbook: a Society Souvenir*. Washington, D.C.: Hartman & Cadick Printers, 1903.

Hirshson, Stanley P. *Farewell to the Bloody Shirt: Northern Republicans & the Southern Negro, 1877–1893*. Bloomington, Indiana: Indiana University Press, 1962.

History of Gallatin, Saline, Hamilton, Franklin and Williamson Counties, Illinois. Chicago: Goodspeed Publishing, Co., 1887.

Houck, Louis. *A History of Missouri*. 3 vols. Chicago: R. R. Donnelley & Sons, Co., 1908.

Houghton, Walter R. *Early Life and Public Career of James G. Blaine, including a biography of General John A. Logan*. Cleveland: N. G. Hamilton and Co., 1884.

Howard, Oliver Otis. *The Autobiography of Oliver Otis Howard*. 2 vols. New York: Baker and Taylor Co., 1907.

Howard, Richard L. *History of the 124th Regiment Illinois Infantry Volunteers*. Springfield: H. W. Rokker Co., 1880.

Howe, M. A. Dewolfe, ed. *Marching with Sherman Passages from the Letters and Campaign Diaries of Henry Hitchcock Major and Assistant Adjutant General of Volunteers*. New Haven: Yale University Press, 1927.

Hubbs, Barbara Burr. *Pioneer Folks and Places: An Historical Gazetteer of Williamson County, Illinois*. Herrin: Press of the *Herrin Daily Journal*, 1939.

Hughes, Nathaniel Chears, Jr. *The Battle of Belmont: Grant Strikes South*. Chapel Hill: University of North Carolina Press, 1991.

Jackson County, Illinois: Formation and Early Settlement. Murphysboro: Jackson County Historical Society, 1983.

Johannsen, Robert W. *Stephen A. Douglas*. Urbana: University of Illinois Press, 1973.

Johnson, Robert Underwood, and Clarence Clough Buel, eds., *Battles and Leaders of the Civil War*. 4 vols. New York: Century Co., 1887.

Jones, James Picket. *Black Jack: John A. Logan and Southern Illinois in the Civil War Era*. 1967. Reprint. Carbondale: Southern Illinois University Press, 1995.

——. *John A. Logan: Stalwart Republican from Illinois*. 1982. Reprint. Carbondale: Southern Illinois University Press, 2001.

Kellogg, Mark E., comp., *Army Life of an Illinois Soldier, Including a Day-to-Day Record of Sherman's March to the Sea: Letters and Diary of Charles W. Will*. Carbondale: Southern Illinois University Press, 1996.

Kelly, Dennis. *Kennesaw Mountain and the Atlanta Campaign*. Atlanta: Kennesaw Mountain Historical Association, 1999.

Kennedy, Francis H., ed. *The Civil War Battlefield Guide*. Boston: Houghton Mifflin Company, 1990.

Kinsley, Earle S. *Recollections of Vermonters in the State and National Affairs*. Rutland, Vermont: Privately printed, 1992.

Klement, Frank L. *The Copperheads in the Middle West*. Chicago: University of Chicago Press, 1960.

Knox, Thomas W. *The Lives of James G. Blaine and John A. Logan.* Hartford: The Harford Publishing Co., 1884.

Koerner, Gustave P. *Memoirs of Gustave P. Koerner*, 2 vols. Cedar Rapids: Torch Press, 1909.

Labounty, Wiiliam P. *The Civil War Diaries of James W. Jessee.* Normal, Illinois: McLean County Genealogical Society, 1997.

Lamar, Howard R., ed. *The New Encyclopedia of the American West.* New Haven: Yale University Press, 1998.

Leech, Margaret. *Reveille in Washington.* New York: Carroll & Graf, 1969.

Linder, Usher F. *Reminiscences of the Early Bench and Bar of Illinois.* Chicago: Chicago Legal News Company, 1879.

Lockwood, Mary S. *Historic Homes in Washington: Its Noted Men and Women.* New York: Belford Co., 1889.

Logan, John A. *Fitz-John Porter: Speech of Hon. John A. Logan, of Illinois . . . on the Bill (S. 1844) for the Relief of Fitz-John Porter.* Washington, 1883.

———. *The Great Conspiracy, Its Origin and History.* New York: A. R. Hart, 1886.

———. *Speech of Major General John A. Logan on His Return to Illinois after the Capture of Vicksburg, with an Introduction by "Mack" of the Cincinnati Commercial.* Cincinnati: Loyal Publications of the National Union Association of Ohio, Caleb Clark Printer, 1863.

———. *The Volunteer Soldier of America.* Chicago: R. S. Peale Co., 1887.

Logan, Mrs. John A. *Reminiscences of a Soldier's Wife: An Autobiography.* Carbondale: Southern Illinois University Press, 1997.

Lowry, Thomas P. *Tarnished Eagles: The Courts-Martial of Fifty Union Colonels and Lieutenant Colonels.* Mechanicsburg, Pennsylvania: Stackpole Books; 1997.

Lusk, David W. *Politics and Politicians of Illinois, 1856–1884.* Springfield: H. W. Rokker, 1884.

Marshall, John A. *American Bastille: A History of the Illegal Arrests and Imprisonment of American Citizens During the Late Civil War.* 24th ed. Philadelphia: Thomas W. Hartley, 1880.

Mattson, Hans. *Reminiscences: The Story of an Emigrant.* St. Paul: D. D. Merrill Co., 1891.

McPherson, James M. *Battle Cry of Freedom: The Civil War Era.* New York: Oxford University Press, 1988.

Merrill, Marlene D. *Yellowstone and the Great West: Journals, Letters and Images from the 1871 Hayden Expedition.* Lincoln: University of Nebraska Press, 1999.

Miers, Earl S., ed. *Lincoln Day by Day: A Chronology 1809–1865.* 3 vols. Washington, D.C.: Lincoln Sesquicentennial Commission, 1960.

Milton, George Port. *The Eve of Conflict: Stephen A. Douglas and the Needless War.* New York: Octagon Books, Inc., 1963.

Morgan, H. Wayne, ed., *From Hayes to McKinley: National Party Politics, 1877–1896.* Syracuse: Syracuse University Press, 1969.

Morris, W. S., Hartwell, L. D., and Kuykendall, J. B. *History of the 31st Regiment Illinois Volunteers, Organized by John A. Logan.* 1902. Reprint. Carbondale: Southern Illinois University Press, 1998.

Neeley, Mark. *The Fate of Liberty: Abraham Lincoln and Civil Liberties.* New York: Oxford University Press, 1991.

Nevins, Allan. *Hamilton Fish: The Inner History of the Grant Administration.* 2 vols. New York: Frederick Ungar Publishing Co., 1957.

Newsome, Edmund. *Experiences in the War of the Great Rebellion. By a Soldier of the Eighty-first Regiment Illinois Volunteer Infantry.* Carbondale: Edmund Newsome, Publisher, 1880.

——. *Historical Sketches of Jackson County, Illinois.* Carbondale: Edmund Newsome, Publisher, 1882.

Nichols, George W. *The Story of the Great March.* New York: Harper & Brothers, 1865.

An Officer in the Union Army. [Logan, John A.] *Uncle Daniel's Story of Tom Anderson and Twenty Great Battles.* New York: A. R. Hart, 1886.

Oldroyd, Osborn. *A Soldier's Story of the Siege of Vicksburg.* Springfield: Published by the author, 1885.

Orendorf, H. H., comp. *Reminiscences of the Civil War from Diaries of Members of the 103d Illinois Volunteer Infantry.* Chicago: J. F. Learning, 1904.

Palmer, John M. *The Bench and Bar of Illinois.* 2 vols. Chicago: Lewis Publishing Co., 1899.

Pease, Theodore Calvin and James G. Randall, eds. *The Diary of Orville Hickman Browning.* 2 vols. Springfield: Trustees of the Illinois State Historical Library, 1925–33.

Pease, Theodore Calvin. *The Frontier State, 1818–1848.* Springfield: Illinois Centennial Commission, 1918.

Pepper, George W. *Personal Recollections of Sherman's Campaigns in Georgia and the Carolinas.* Zanesville, Ohio: Published by Hugh Dunne, 1866.

Perret, Geoffrey. *Ulysses S. Grant: Soldier and President.* New York: Random House, 1997.

Perry, Mark. *Grant and Twain: The Story of a Friendship That Changed America.* New York: Random House, 2004.

Plummer, Mark A. *Lincoln's Railsplitter: Governor Richard J. Oglesby.* Urbana: University of Illinois Press, 2001.

Poore, Ben Perley. *Perley's Reminiscences of Sixty Years in the National Metropolis.* 2 vols. Philadelphia: Hubbard Brothers, 1886.

Porter, Horace. *Campaigning With Grant.* Secaucus, New Jersey: The Blue and Grey Press, 1984.

Post, Lydia M., ed. *Soldiers' Letters, From Camps, Battle-field, and Prison.* Bunce and Harrington, New York: Published for the U. S. Sanitary Commission, 1865.

Quaife, Milo M., ed. *Growing Up with Southern Illinois, 1820 to 1861, from the Memoirs of Daniel Harmon Brush.* Chicago: R. R. Donnelley & Sons Co., 1944.

Report of the Proceedings of the Society of the Army of the Tennessee, at the Twentieth Meeting, September 14th and 15th, 1887. Cincinnati: Published by the Society, 1893.

Report of the Proceedings of the Society of the Army of the Tennessee at the Twenty-first Meeting Held at Toledo, Ohio, September 5th and 6th, 1888. Cincinnati: Published by the Society, 1893.

Report of the Proceedings of the Society of the Army of the Tennessee at the Twentieth Meeting, held at Detroit, Mich., September 14th and 15th, 1887. Cincinnati: Published by the Society, 1893.

Sandburg, Carl. *Abraham Lincoln: The Prairie Years.* 2 vols. New York: Harcourt, Brace Co., 1926.

——. *Abraham Lincoln: The War Years.* 4 vols. New York: Harcourt, Brace Co., 1939.

Saunier, Joseph. *A History of the Forty-Seventh Regiment Ohio Veteran Volunteer Infantry.* Hillsboro, Ohio: Lyle Print Co., 1903.

Seitz, Don C. *Joseph Pulitzer: His Life and Letters.* New York: Simon & Schuster, 1924.

Shanks, William F. G. *Personal Recollections of Distinguished Generals.* New York: Harper, 1866.

[Sheldon, George W.] *Artistic Houses: Being a Series of Interior Views of a Number of the Most Beautiful and Celebrated Homes in the United States.* New York: Appleton, 1883–1885.

Sherman, John. *John Sherman's Recollections of Forty Years in the House, Senate and Cabinet.* 2 vols. New York: Greenwood Press Publishers, 1968.

Sherman, William Tecumseh. *Memoirs of General W. T. Sherman.* New York: Literary Classics, 1990.

Sifakis, Stewart. *Who Was Who in the Civil War.* New York: Facts on File, 1988.

Simon, John Y., ed. *The Papers of Ulysses S. Grant.* 26 vols. Carbondale: Southern Illinois University Press, 1967–2003.

Simpson, Brooks D. *Ulysses S. Grant: Triumph Over Adversity, 1822–1865.* Boston: Houghton Mifflin Company, 2000.

Slayden, Ellen M. *Washington Wife: Journal of Ellen Maury Slayden from 1897–1919.* New York: Harper & Row, 1963.

Smith, George Washington. *A History of Southern Illinois: A Narrative of its Historical Progress, its People, and its Principal Interests.* 3 vols. Chicago: The Lewis Publishing Company, 1912.

Smith, Jean Edward. *Grant.* New York: Simon and Schuster, 2001.

Starr, Louis M. *Bohemian Brigade: Civil War Newsmen in Action.* New York: Alfred A. Knopf, 1954.

Sterling, Ada, comp. *A Belle of the Fifties: Memoirs of Mrs. Clay, of Alabama, Covering Social and Political Life in Washington and the South, 1853–66.* New York: Doubleday, Page & Co., 1904.

Strayer, Larry M. and Baumgartner, Richard A. *Echoes of Battle: The Atlanta Campaign.* Huntington, West Virginia: Blue Acorn Press, 1991.

Street, James Jr. and the Editors of Time-Life Books. *The Struggle for Tennessee.* Alexandria, Virginia: Time-Life Books, 1985.

Summers, Mark W. *Rum, Romanism, & Rebellion: The Making of a President 1884.* Chapel Hill: University of North Carolina Press, 2000.

Taylor, W. B., comp. *Memorial Addresses on the Life and Character of John Alexander Logan (A Senator from Illinois), Delivered in the Senate and House of Representatives, February 9 and 16, 1887.* Washington: GPO, 1887.

Thayer, William R., ed. *The Life and Letters of John Hay.* 2 vols. Boston: Houghton Mifflin Co., 1908.

Thomas, Benjamin P., ed. *Three Years with Grant As Recalled by War Correspondent Sylvanus Cadwallader.* New York: Alfred A. Knopf, 1955.

Thompson, Slason. *Life of Eugene Field: The Poet of Childhood.* New York: D. Appleton and Co., 1927.

Trowbridge, Silas Thompson. *Autobiography of Silas Thompson Trowbridge, M.D.* Vera Cruz: Published privately, 1872.

Trimble, Harvey M. *History of the Ninety-third Regiment Illinois Volunteer Infantry.* Chicago: Blakely Printing Co., 1898.

United States War Department. *The War of the Rebellion: Official Records of the Union and Confederate Armies.* 128 vols. Washington: GPO, 1881–1901.

Upson, Theodore F. *With Sherman to the Sea; the Civil War Letters, Diaries & Reminiscences of Theodore F. Upson.* Baton Rouge: Louisiana State University Press, 1943.

Victor, Orville James. *Incidents and Anecdotes of the War, Together with Lip Sketches of Eminent Leaders.* New York: James D. Torrey, 1862.

Wall, John A. *History of Jefferson County, Illinois.* Indianapolis: B. F. Bowen & Company, 1909.

Webster, Samuel Charles, ed. *Mark Twain, Business Man.* Boston: Little, Brown and Co., 1946.

West, Richard S. *Satire on Stone: The Political Cartoons of Joseph Keppler.* Urbana: University of Illinois Press, 1988.

Wilson, Douglas L. and Davis, Rodney O., eds. *Herndon's Informants: Letters, Interviews, and Statements about Abraham Lincoln.* Urbana: University of Illinois Press, 1998.

Wilson, James Grant. *Biographical Sketches of Illinois Officers Engaged in the War Against the Rebellion in 1861.* Chicago: James Barnet, 1862.

Winkle, Kenneth. *The Young Eagle: The Rise of Abraham Lincoln.* Dallas: Taylor Trade Publishing, 2001.

Winschel, Terrence J. *Vicksburg: Fall of the Confederate Gibralter.* Abilene: McWhiney Foundation Press, 1999.

Wolle, Muriel Sibell. *The Bonanza Trail: Ghost Towns and Mining Camps of the West.* Bloomington: Indiana University Press, 1953.

Wright, John W. D. *A History of Early Carbondale, Illinois 1852–1905.* Carbondale: Southern Illinois University Press, 1977.

Youngstown. Chicago: American Historical Society, 1920.

NEWSPAPERS

[Albert Lea, MN] *Freeborn County Standard*

Alton [IL] *Telegraph*

Alton [IL] *Telegraph and Democratic Review*

Alton [IL] *Weekly Courier*

Alton [IL] *Weekly Telegraph*

Atlanta Constitution

[Bellefonte, OH] *Daily-Index Republican*
Benton [IL] *Standard*
Bloomington [IL] *Bulletin*
Burlington [IA] *Weekly Hawkeye*
Butte [MT] *Daily Miner*
Cairo [IL] *City Times*
Cairo [IL] *Evening Sun*
Cairo City [IL] *Weekly Gazette*
Cambridge [OH] *Jeffersonian*
[Carbondale, IL] *Barton's Free Press*
Carbondale [IL] *Freepress*
Carbondale [IL] *New Era*
Carbondale [IL] *Times*
Carlyle [IL] *Weekly Reveille*
[Centralia, IL] *Egyptian Republic*
[Chaudry, OH] *Jeffersonian Democrat*
Chicago Daily Inter-Ocean
Chicago Daily Press and Tribune
Chicago Evening Herald
Chicago Evening Journal
Chicago Times
Chicago Times Herald
Chicago Tribune
Cincinnati Commercial Gazette
Cincinnati Daily Commercial
Cincinnati Enquirer
Colorado Springs Gazette
Crawford [IL] *Bulletin*
[Davenport, IA] *Daily Gazette*
Decatur [IL] *Daily Republican*
Decatur [IL] *Morning Review*
Defiance [OH] *Democrat*
[Des Moines] *Iowa State Register*
Edwardsville [IL] *Intelligencer*
[Elyria, OH] *Lorain Constitutionalist*
Fort Wayne Daily Gazette
Freeport [IL] *Bulletin*
[Galena, IL] *Northwestern Weekly Gazette*
[Gettysburg, PA] *Star and Sentinel*
[Huntsville, AL] *Southern Freeman*
[Indianapolis] *American Tribune*
Indianapolis Daily Journal
Janesville [WI] *Weekly Gazette*
Joliet [IL] *Signal*

Jonesboro [IL] *Gazette*
Keithsburg [IL] *Observer*
[Marion, IL] *Friend*
Murphysboro [IL] *Argus*
[Murphysboro, IL] *Daily Independent*
New York Herald
New York Semi-Weekly Tribune
New York Times
New York Tribune
[Newark, OH] *True American*
Norwalk [OH] *Reflector*
Olney [IL] *Journal*
[Petersburg, VA] *Daily Index*
Piqua [OH] *Journal*
[Placerville, CA] *Mountain Democrat*
Portland [OR] *Oregonian*
Portsmouth [OH] *Times*
Quincy [IL] *Daily Herald*
Quincy [IL] *Daily Whig and Republican*
Raleigh [NC] *Weekly Standard*
Rock Island [IL] *Evening Argus*
Sangamo [IL] *Monitor*
[Sedalia, MO] *Daily Democrat*
[Shawneetown, IL] *Southern Illinoisan*
[Springfield] *Illinois Journal*
[Springfield] *Illinois State Journal*
[Springfield] *Illinois State Register*
St. Louis Daily Globe Democrat
St. Louis Daily Republican
St. Louis Post Dispatch
Statesville [NC] *Landmark*
[Toulon, IL] *Stark County Union*
[Trenton, NJ] *Star and Sentinel*
Trenton [NJ] *Times*
Warsaw [IN] *Indianan*
[Washington, D.C.] *Congressional Globe*
[Washington, D.C.] *Congressional Record*
Washington Evening Star
[Washington, D.C.] *National Republican*
[Washington, D.C.] *National Tribune*
Washington Post
Waukesha [WI] *Freeman*
Waukesha [WI] *Plaindealer*

ARTICLES

Burr, Barbara. "Letters From Two Wars." *Journal of the Illinois State Historical Society* 30 (1937).

Carter, Chip. "Atlanta's Restored Cyclorama." *Civil War Times Illustrated* (January/February 1991): 18–22.

Confederate Veteran 16.

Dante, Harris L. "Western Attitudes and Reconstruction Politics in Illinois, 1865–1872." *Journal of the Illinois State Historical Society* 44, no. 2 (Summer, 1956): 151.

Davis, Theodore R. "How a Battle Scene Was Sketched During the Civil War." *St. Nicholas Illustrated Magazine* 16 (2) (1889): 661–68.

"Editor's Easy Chair." *Harper's New Monthly Magazine* 32 (December, 1865): 123.

Force, Manning F. "Personal Recollections of the Vicksburg Campaign.," *MOLLUS Ohio* 1 (Cincinnati: Robert Clarke & Co.; 1888)

Furqueron, James R. "The Finest Opportunity Lost: The Battle of Jonesborough, August 31–September 1, 1864." *North and South* 6 (September, 2003).

"Generals in the Saddle." *Southern Historical Society Papers* 19 (October 1891): 167–175.

Logan, John A. "National Aid to Public Schools." *North American Review* 136, no. 137 (April, 1883): 337–45.

Memorial Day, 1909, Circular 33 (Springfield: Illinois State Journal Co., 1909).

Pratt, Harry Edward. "Judge David Davis." *Transactions of the Illinois Historical Society*, pub. no. 37 (1930): 157–183.

Puck Magazine, 1880, 1884.

Rudolph, Jack. "The Grand Review." *Civil War Times Illustrated* 19 (November 1980): 34–43.

Shanks, W. F. G. "Recollections of General Rosseau." *Harper's New Monthly Magazine* 31 (November, 1865): 763–64.

Woodworth, Steven E. "Logan of the Dirty-First." *Civil War Magazine* 72 (1997): 25–37.

WORLD WIDE WEB

American Civil War Research Database. http://www.civilwardata.com.

"Biographical Sketches of Blue Hill." http://www.rootsweb.com/~newebste/bluebios.htm.

"Civil War Reminiscences of Hugh Milton Stackhouse." http://www.geocities.com/Yosemite/6648/Civil War Rem.htm.

"Facts About Woodlawn Cemetery." http://www.ci.carbondale.il.us/woodlawn.htm.

"The Illinois Black Codes." www.lib.niu.edu/ipo/iht329602.html.

"Letter of Frank H. Putney." August 7, 1862, http://www.russscott.com/~rscott/12thwis/ltfraput.htm.

"Logan Whips the Widow's Son." http://www.iltrails.org/Jackson/jchis.htm.

"Madison County Tennessee Letters from Forgotten Soldiers." http://www.tngenweb.org/tnletters/madi.htm.

McPherson, James. Letter to his brother, July 26, 1863. http://www.sandusky-county-scrapbook.net/McPherson/Letters5.htm

"Payne Reminiscences." http://www.rootsweb.com/~orphanhm/paynerem.htm.

Phillips, E. J. letter to his son, August 4, 1886.
http://home.comcast.net/~m.chitty/sanfrancisco.htm.

"Roots Generation 6." http://www.eroots.net/generation6.htm.

"Teachers of Jackson County." http://www.iltrails.org/jackson/teachers.htm.

Twain, Mark. *Mark Twain's Letters 1876–1885* (arranged by Albert B. Paine), vol. 3.
http://www.fullbooks.com/The-Letters-Of-Mark-Twain-Vol-3.html.

Index

A

Abolitionists, 28
  Brown, John, 55–56, 59
  hatred of, 35, 53
  Ozburn, "Doff" and, 113
Abraham, 148
Act, Pendleton. *See*
  Pendleton, George H.
African Americans, 3. *See*
  also White supremacy
  action on behalf of,
  151, 246
  death of Logan and,
  318–19
  formal serenade by,
  301–02
  hostility toward, 28
  rights, champion of, 286
  support of, 294
  voting rights of, 240, 245
Albuquerque Daily
  Democrat, 292
Aleck Scott, 93
Aledo, 278
Alger, Gov. Russell A., 312
Allatoona Pass, 172

Allen, "Josh" (William
  Joshua), 18, 76
  best man, 42
  campaign against, 192
  Congress, bid for, 163
  election loss, 195–96, 243
  election victory, 112
  imprisonment, 115
  law partner, 36
  opposition to Know-
  Nothing Party, 44
  subversiveness to
  Union, 118
  unrelenting denunciation
  of, 195
Allen, Judge Willis, 18
  death, 55
"Allentown, Indiana," 303
Alton speech, 193–94
Alton Telegraph, 243
Alton Weekly Courier, 30
American hero, 153
American Museum, 148
American Party, 35
American Revolution, 87
Ames, Oakes, 268

Anderson, Lt. Gov. Stinson
  H., 19
Anderson, Maj. Robert, 67
Anderson, Tom, 303–04
Anderson, William B., 260
  Independent opponent,
  273
Andrews, Edith, 314, 320
Anthony, Susan B., 322
Antietam, Battle of, 121
"Antler's Run," 304
Appomattox, 301
A. R. Hart and Company,
  309, 315
Arlington Hotel, 289
Arlington National
  Cemetery, 256
Army of Northern
  Virginia, 121
Army of Occupation, 321
Army of the Cumberland,
  166, 172, 176
  Jonesboro, Battle of, 187
Army of the Mississippi, 111
Army of the Ohio, 111
Army of the Potomac, 150,

164, 165, 228
fame of, 229
Army of the Tennessee,
    111–12, 131, 134, 137,
    164, 177
    Atlanta, Battle of, 181
    Harrow as leader of, 165
    Jonesboro, Battle of, 187
    leadership, lacking, 229
    Raleigh, heading for, 225
    Sherman marching
        with, 213
    Society of the, 237–38
    Vicksburg, casualties
        at, 149
Army, U.S., 278
Arthur, Chester A., 289, 292
Assassination
    Garfield, James A., 289
    Lincoln, Abraham, 226
Assembly Hall (Chicago)
    Douglas's pro-Union
        speech, 72
Atlanta, 171–78
    Cyclorama, 205, 322
    fall, 188
    flag, tattered, 232
Atlanta, Battle of, 177–82, 310
    Cyclorama and, 322
Atlanta Campaign, 189
    Smith, Gen. John E. and,
        215–16
Atlanta Constitution, 280
Atlantic City, 305
Atlantic Ocean
    campaigns to, 233
Augusta, 218
Auld Ireland, 165
Ayres, Capt. Romeyn, 83

B

Baird, Spencer, 254
Bakhaus, William, 181
Bald Hill, 180
Baltimore Harbor, 218
B and O Railroad, 74
Banks, Gen. Nathaniel
    P., 167
Barnum, P. T., 148

Barquet, Joseph H., 29
Bate, Gen. William, 172–74
Bates, Maj. Gen. John
    C., 321
"Battery Logan," 145
Battle. *See* specific name
Baxter, Dr., 316
Beauregard, Gen. Pierre
    G. T., 111–12
    Columbia, defended
        by, 221
Belleville
    speech, 192
Bell, John, 61
Belmont
    courage shown, 109
    expedition, 93–98
    flag, tattered, 232
Benoist, Minerva, 162
Benton, Illinois, 207m
    move away from, 67
    speech, 195
Benton Standard, 30
Bentonville, Battle of, 224
Berry, John Logan, 305
Bickerdyke, Mary Ann
    "Mother," 231
Big Black River, 132
Big Muddy River, 20–22
"Billy, Uncle," 227
Birth, 13
Bissell, Gov. William, 44
    acceptance of bills, 46
    opposition to, 57
Blackburn's Ford, 83
"Black Codes" (1853), 113
"Black Eagle," 116, 279,
    295–96
Black Hawk War of 1832,
    14, 17
"Black Jack," 180, 279, 281
Black, John C., 279
Black Law of 1853, 235
"Black Republicans," 44
    hatred of, 61
Blacks. *See* African
    Americans
Blaine, James G., 212, 262,
    271, 285

Grant, threat to, 283
    nomination for president,
        seeking, 284
    Republican National
        Convention, at, 320
    ticket, 295–97
Blair, Maj. Gen. Frank, 137,
    164, 178, 183, 217
    commander of
        Seventeenth Corps, 165
    conferring with, 179
    Jonesboro, Battle of, 187
    Pee Dee River,
        crossing, 223
Blanchard, Annie. *See also*
    Logan, Annie
    Benton speech,
        during, 195
    protection of brother, 162
    welcome home from, 235
Blanchard, Israel, 32–33
    arrest, 75, 115, 118
    death, 266
    K.G.C., alleged
        association with, 118–19
    marriage to Annie
        Logan, 43
"Bloody shirt" oratory, 239
Bloomington Bulletin, 293
"Blue Church," 237, 257. *See
    also* Methodist Church
Boalsburg, Pennsylvania, 236
"Boarding House, The," 268
"Boss." *See* Party "Boss"
Bosworth, John, 179–80
Bourbonism, 314
Boutwell, George, 249
Bowen, Brig. Gen. John
    S., 131
"Bowen, Dan," 304, 310
Bowyer, Horace, 237
"Boys," 103, 230
Bradley, Joseph, 275
Brady, Matthew
    photographed by, 217
Bragg, Gen. Braxton, 121
    Battle of Chattanooga
        and, 161
    Confederate force of, 159

Bravery
    Belmont and Fort
        Donelson, shown
        at, 109
    Medals of Gold for, 165
Breckinridge, John C., 61
Broad River, 220
Broeck, Ten, 224
Brook, Thorndike, 145
Browning, Orville, 253
Brown, John, 55–56, 59
Brown's Hotel
    (Washington), 60, 63,
    84, 263–64
Bruner, Jacob, 127–28
Brush, Daniel, 13, 236–37
    Logan family enemy,
    32–33
Bub. *See* Cunningham,
    Hybert
Buchanan, James, 44, 45
    antagonism toward
        Senator Douglas, 51
    executive impotence,
        56–57
Buckner, Gen. Simon
    Bolivar, 103, 109
Buell, Gen. Don Carlos,
    110–11
Buford, Napoleon B., 94
    promotion, 125
"Bull Pen," 145
Bull Run, Battle of, 83–85,
    91, 282
Burchard, Samuel D., 298
Burial, 319
Burnet House, 214
Burnt Hickory Road, 176
Butler, Benjamin, 167, 249,
    253, 258, 262

C
Cadwallader, Sylvanus,
    133, 137
Cairo
    hostility, 235
    pro-Union speech, 161, 195
Cairo (IL) *City Gazette*, 65
Cairo Democrat, 241

Cairo Evening Sun, 280
Cairo News
    praise by, 162
"Calico colonel." *See*
    Bickerdyke, Mary Ann
    "Mother"
Calumet Avenue, 263
    reunion in house on, 277
Calumet Place, 306,
    314–16
    shrine by Mary
        Logan, 321
Cameron, Don, 284, 286
Campbell, Curt, 67, 80
Campbell, Decatur
    prosecution of, 33
Campbell, Hannah, 67
Camp Creek, 169–71
Camp Dunlop, 24, 89
Camp Logan, 127
Camp McClernand, 89, 98
Camp Sorghum, 220, 222
Camp Yates (Springfield
    Fairgrounds), 79
Cantey, Brig. Gen. James
    B., 168
Cape Fear River, 223
Capital City Guard, 301
Capitol Building dome, 230
Capitol Hill, 253
    departure from, 275
    return to, 315
Carbondale, 207
    birthday in, 281
    depot, 152
    home, 115–16
    Logan-Dickey debate,
        242–43
    returning home to, 234,
        236, 262
    speech, 153–55
    Woodlawn Cemetery,
        236–37, 250
Carbondale College, 46
Carbondale New Era,
    211, 262
Carbondale Times, 117
Carr, Gen., 137
Carterville, 322

Casey, Sam, 25, 26
    attendance at
        wedding, 42
    Know-Nothing Party,
        opposition to, 44
Cash Pond, 21
Caske, Henry, 299
Catholic nuns, 222
Cemetery, Woodlawn,
    236–37
Centralia speech, 192
Central Pacific Railroad, 312
"Cerebral rheumatism," 316
Champion Hill, Battle of,
    138–43, 175
Champion House, 140–01
Charleston, South Carolina
    obsession with, 67
    speech, 279
Chase, Salmon P., 262
Chattahoochie River, 177
Chattanooga, 159
Chattanooga, Battle of, 161
"Chatteraugus," 304
Cheatham, Gen. Benjamin
    F., 178
Cheatham Hill, 175
Chester Picket Gaurd, 241
Chicago
    Great Fire, 263
    reception in, 301
    Senate campaign, end of,
        in, 279
    speech, 156–57
    summer, 289
"Chicago Catastrophe,
    The," 287
Chicago Convention, 189
Chicago Herald, 288
Chicago Inter-Ocean, 271
    endorsement for
        Senate, 279
Chicago Platform, 190
Chicago Post, 188
"Chicago Surrender," 188
Chicago Times, 133
    Democrats, loyalty to, 241
    scandals reported in, 271
Chicago Tribune

accusation in, 64, 285
antagonism of, 58
Blaine-Logan alliance
    and, 295–97
Carbondale speech, report
    of, by, 154
congratulations of, 301
defense by, 241–42
Democrats, opposition
    to, 65
G.A.R. involvement,
    reported by, 241
incorrect prediction, 66
K.G.C., discussed in, 117
letter to, 292
Liberal Republican
    movement, support
    of, 271
Oglesby, endorsement of,
    279–80
popularity with soldiers,
    according to, 294
praise by, 157
publication of speech,
    by, 157
Republican Unionism,
    report on, 238
Senate seat, candidate for,
    reported, 210
Vicksburg Campaign,
    reporting on, 144
waning support of, 274
Chickamauga, Battle of,
    159, 182
Southern victory, 161
Cholera, 240
Christian faith
Howard and, 229
Indians and, 254
Christmas gift
Savannah, capture of, 215
Cincinnati, 156
Cincinnati Commercial
    Gazette, 312
Cincinnati Daily
    Commercial, 133, 156
City Point, Virginia, 212–15
Civil Service Act, Pendleton,
    293–94, 305

Civil Service Bureau, 258
Civil War
    beginning, 68
    congressional debate,
        influenced by, 253–54
    last act, 225
    life and death from, 317
    Lincon's election and, 212
    soldiers, cemetery for,
        236–37
Claiborne, Dr. Lem, 10
Clay, Henry, 56
Clemens, Samuel. See Twain,
    Mark
Clements, Isaac, 81
Cleveland, Grover, 296
    criticism of, 313–14
Clinton speech, 192
Collins, Prof., 267
Colonel Frederick Grant, 4
Colorado interest in, 269
Columbia
    clearing path toward, 218
    Confederacy, soul of, 220
Columbia Heights, 306, 316
Columbus, Mississippi, 236
Committee on Military
    Affairs, 254, 289
    chairmain, 255, 307–09
Committee on the Pacific
    Railroads, 254
Company B, 24
Company C, 108
Company H, First Illinois
    Infantry, 23–24
Compromise of 1850, 56
Confederacy, Southern, 70
    casualties inflicted on,
        196–97
Congaree Creek, 220
Congressional Globe, 57,
    58, 248
Congressional Medal of
    Honor, 321
Congressional Record, 283
Conkling, Roscoe, 262,
    284–87
Constitution, 1818 , 11
Constitution of 1848, 28

ratification of revised,
    28–29
Constitution, U.S.
    Fifteenth Amendment,
        252–53
    impeachment, grounds
        for, in, 248
    Nineteenth
        Amendment, 322
    Thirteenth Amendment,
        234–35, 245
Cook County, 284–85
Cooper Institute, 61
"Copperhead
    Convention," 113
    sympathy with, mockery
        of, 190
"Copperheads." See Peace
    Democrats
"Corinth, Siege of," 112
Corse, Brig. Gen. John
    M., 215
Cosmopolitan, 322
    memoirs of Mary Logan,
        published by, 206
Courage, 109
Courtright, Timothy Isaiah
    "Longhair Jim," 292
Crawford Bulletin, 89
Credit Mobilier, 268–69,
    274, 287
Crocker, Marcellus, 138, 142
"Cross, Gen. William," 304
Cuba, 321
Cullom, Shelby, 295–96, 316
Cumberland River
    Grant's plot for, 99
Cummins, Charles, 25
Cunningham, Capt. John M.,
    23, 108
    alcoholism, battle
        with, 257
    death, 266
    defense by, 242
    delivery of letters by, 159
    friendship with, 24
    residence, 38
    resolutions drafted by, 70
    respect for opinions of, 71

Cunningham, Elizabeth
death, 240
Cunningham, Hybert,
73, 145
Confederacy, joining
the, 80
death, 266
defense by, 242
desertion of Confederate
army by, 158
determination to destroy
Grant, 97
loss of sister, 171
unknown whereabouts,
111
unprecedented support
by, 163
wounds nursed by, 174
Cunningham, Mary. *See also*
Logan, Mary
courtship of, 38–41
Cushing, 292
Custer, George Armstrong,
292
Cyclorama, Atlanta, 205, 322

D
Dakota Territory, 292
state, creation of, 308
Dallas, Battle of, 174, 175
Dames of the Loyal
Legion of the United
States, 321
Dana, Asst. Sec. Charles
Champion Hill, 143, 150
Grant's entourage, in, 133
Danites, 52
Daughters of Zion, 52
Davis, David, 259, 274
loss to, 278
Davis, Jefferson, 46
cheer for, 123
Confederate Pres., 154
imprisonment, 245
presidential
candidate, 189
rebellion, 227
Sherman's opposition to,
223–24

Davis, Margaret Logan, 12
Davis, Squire, 22, 23, 24
professional reputation,
33
Davis, Theodore, 136
Dawes Commission, 293
Dawes, Henry L., 292
Dawson, George Francis, 310
Deadwood, 293
Death, 318–320
media report of, 106
watch, 316–17
Decatur, 177
veteran's organization,
237
Decoration Day, 251
Defiance Democrat, 246
De Golyer, Capt. Samuel,
131, 146
DeGress, Capt. Francis,
169, 177
Columbia, in, 221
Delevan, 279
"Demagogue of Illinois," 60
Democratic Convention. *See*
National Democratic
Convention (1860)
Democratic Party
Illinois State Register, 52
polarization of party, 35
politics, 21
unpatriotic position
of, 239
Demotion, 182–83
Denning, William A., 27
Dennis, Brig. Gen.
Elias, 134
Denver, 277
Department of Missouri,
193, 211
possibility of overseeing,
209
Department of the
South, 215
Des Moines Register, 259
Detroit speech, 309
Dickey, T. Lyle, 241–42
defeat of, 243
Dictator, 212

"Dirty-first," 102–03, 114
appeal to, 140
Logan, Tom, as member
of, 120
"Dirty Work" Logan, 62,
66, 86
move away from, 128
Dodge, Maj. Gen. Grenville,
168, 172, 183
conferring with, 179
Department of Missouri,
chosen to head, 212
Jonesboro, Battle of, 187
Nashville, in, 163–64
"Dolinsburg," 303
DOLLUS, 321
"Donelson Pet," 219, 268
Dougherty, John, 52, 54
speech by, 71
Douglas Democrats, 191
Douglas Rooms, 60
Douglass, Frederick,
286, 319
Carbondale greeting, 281
endorsement by, 294–95
Douglas, Stephen A., 27, 48
antagonism toward
President Buchanan, 51
candidate, sixteenth
president, 59–60
failed Democratic
presidential candidate,
44
Kansas-Nebraska Act of
1854 proponent, 34
patriots-and-traitors
speech, 191
pro-Union speech,
71–72, 241
speech that ended
friendship with, 87
sudden death, 75
Dred Scott decision, 56
Duff, Andrew, 115
arrest, 118
Dumbaly, James
"Wilkinson," 14, 21
Dumbaly, Monday, 21
Du Quoin, 152

speech, 155–56
Durrett, R. T., 26

E

East Point, 187
Education bill, 308
Edward's Depot Road, 137
Edwards Station, 136–37
Egyptian Home Guard, 77–78
Egyptian Republic, 77
Egyptian Sun, 259
Eighteenth Illinois General Assembly, 28, 198
El Caney, Battle of, 321
Election Day, 195
Election to U.S. House of Representatives, 55
Emancipation Proclamation, 121–23
importance of, 153
request for retraction of, 158
violation of, 151
Equal protection, 280
Erie Canal, 17
Etowah River, 172
Ewing, Thomas, 165
Ezra Chapel, 183–84
Ezra Church, Battle of. *See* Ezra Chapel

F

Family disagreement, 88–89
"Farlin, Gen.," 304
Farnsworth, John, 59
Father Roots, 18
Fayetteville, 223
Fear of death, 100
Fenton, Reuben, 262
Fifteenth Amendment, 252–53
Fifth Avenue Hotel, 298
Fillmore, Millard, 44
Flint River, 186
Force, Col. Manning, 139
"Forlorn Hope," 144
Fort Delaware Prison, 218
Fort Don, 268

Fort Donelson, 99–102
capture of, 108–09
courage shown at, 109
deaths fighting for, 107
flag, tattered, 232
media coverage, 106
Morrison, William R., and, 299
"Fort Hell," 145
Fort Henry, 99–102
media coverage, 106
"Fort Hill," 145
Fortieth Congress
lame-duck session of, 253, 255
Fort Leavenworth, 24
Fort Steadman, 227
Fort Sumter, 67–68
Foster, John G.
recommended as replacement for, 215
Fouke, Philip, 99
Fourteenmile Creek, 134–35
France, consul-general to, 288
Franklin County
redistricting, 66–67
Franklin Democrat
endorsing Lincoln ticket, 62
Fredericksburg, 228–29
Freedman's Bureau, 229
Bill, veto of, 240
Free Press, Carlinsville, 117
Free-Soilers, 35
disaffected factions, 43–44
Fremont, John C., 185
Confederates driven away by, 91
first Republican presidential candidate, 44
replacement of, 101
French, Gov. Augustus C., 22
Front-page headline death, 318
Fry, Maj. John C., 130
Fugitive Slave Act, 56, 286

Fugitive Slave Laws, 58

G

Galesburg, 241
G.A.R. *See* Grand Army of the Republic
Garfield, James A., 283
assassination, 289
dark-horse candidate, 286–87
president, election of, 288
Garner, Louisa, 25
Gate City, 187
General Assembly
Democrat gain in, 298
election to, 45, 300
Republican domination of, 273, 278–79
Speaker of the House, 28
"General Logan," 218
General Orders
Number 10, 219
Number 11, 249, 322
Number 349, 159
Georgetown, Colorado, 269
Georgia Railroad, 177
Gettysburg, Battle of, 150
Gillespie, Judge Joseph, 64
Gillmore, Gen. Quincy, 215
Glenn, Diza, 21
marriage, 22
Goddard, George W., 80
Company C, commanded by, 114–15
promise made to, 86
Union army, service in, 158
Golconda speech, 195
Goldsboro, 223–24
Goodall, Charley, 75
Governor's Mansion (Raleigh), 226
Grand Army of the Republic, 3, 237–38, 240–41, 243
hero, 271–72
Logan, Mary, and, 321
loss, 322–23

National Tribune, 303
Portland, ME, attended
  encampment in, 305
prominence, 255–56
San Francisco meeting,
  312
second commander,
  247–48
strengthening of,
  249–50, 294
support of, 279, 284, 297
Grand Gulf, 131, 133
Grand Pacific Hotel
  (Chicago), 280, 314
"Grant boom," 281
Grant, Colonel Frederick, 4
Grant, Fred, 141
Grant Park, 322
Grant Place, 264
Grant Review in
  Washington, 229
Grant's Tomb, 311
Grant, Ulysses S.
  arrival in Cairo, 90
  Belmont expedition
    and, 93
  cancer of, 1–2
  Century Magazine, writing
    in, 5
  clash with, 258
  dying, 302–03, 305–06
  faith in leadership, by, 150
  fanfare with, 235
  inauguration, 266
  meeting, 78
  nomination for president,
    250, 284
  opposition to Buford's
    promotion, 125
  Personal Memoirs, 5
  plots, 99
  popularity, 281
  praise by, 98
  president-elect, 252
  retirement, 275
  reunion with, 212
  Sherman, joint forces
    with, fear of, 223
  surrender, terms of, 226

Union victory and, 106
Vicksburg prisoners,
  parole of, 154
White House and, 231
Grayville Independent, 117
"Great Battle, Logan's," 320
Great Chicago Fire, 263
Great Conspiracy, The, 4–5,
  307, 309
Great Redoubt, 144
Great Spirit, 292
"Great Union Speech," 157
Greeley, Horace, 57, 264
"Greenbackers." *See*
  Greenback Party
Greenback Party, 270, 278
Green, William H., 67
  former friend, 242
  support of peace
    position, 71
Green, Willis Duff, 194
Gregg, Brig. Gen. John,
  134–35
Grierson, Col. Benjamin H.,
  129, 131, 235
Guiteau, Charles, 289
"Gum-shoe campaign," 300

H

"Half-Breeds," 284–85, 295
Halleck, Maj. Gen. Henry
  W., 101
  caution of, 111–12
  problem of, for
    Sherman, 228
Hall, John E., 47
Halstead, Murat, 311–12
Hamlet, 163–64
Hamlin, Hannibal, 62
Hampton, Capt. James, 23
  plot for Democratic
    postmasters, 50
Hampton, Lt. Gen.
  Wade, 221
Hancock, Winfield Scott, 288
Hankinson's Ferry, 132, 134
Hanson, Roger, 105
Hardee, Gen. William,
  172–73, 178

death of son, 224
Jonesboro, Battle of,
  casualties, 187
Hardee's Tactics, 90
Harpers Ferry, 55–56
*Harper's New Monthly
  Magazine*, 234–35
*Harper's Weekly Illustrated
  Newspaper*, 136,
  175, 296
Harrison, Benjamin, 308
  victory of, 320
Harrow, Gen. William, 165
Hart, A. R., and Company,
  309, 315
Hayden, Frederick V.,
  254, 269
  home of, 264
Hayden Survey, 254
Hayes, Lucy, 277
Hayes, Rutherford B.,
  247, 271
  administration, cabinet
    position in, 278
  campaign for, 272
  dislike of, 276
  dissatisfaction with, 281
  president-elect, 275
  South, attempted
    reconciliation with,
    283–84
Hay, John, 158
  letter to Mary
    Logan, 321
Haynie, Isham N.,
  64, 188
  letter to, 249
  promise made to, 86
  Senate seat, supporting
    Logan for, 209
  speech by, 71
  stones thrown at, 194
  strongest supporter, 216
  teamed up with, 192
Hazen, Gen. William B.,
  185–86, 225
Hearst, William Randolph,
  322
"Hell Hole, The," 175

Henderson, Gen., 316
Hendricks, Thomas
A., 304
Henson, Rebecca, 162
Hibernia Hall, 60
Hickenlooper, Lt., 224
Hoar, E. R., 258
Home Guard, Egyptian,
77–78
Home Magazine, 321
Hood, Maj. Gen. John
B., 178
Jonesboro, Battle of,
186–87
Tennessee, penetrating,
213
Hooker, Gen. Joseph, 183
Hoover, John S., 129
Carbondale, in, 152
headquarters, gone
from, 215
Hopkins, Maj. George
H., 312
Horses, 19–20
Logan, John A., II,
and, 320
theft of, 25
Hotaling, Capt. John R.,
129–30, 141, 183
Carbondale, in, 152
headquarters, gone
from, 215
Hot Springs, Arkansas, 289
House of Representatives
career in, 261
election to, 252
nomination for, 240
Hovey, Col. Alvin P.,
137–38
Howard, Maj. Gen. Oliver
O., 182, 183, 189
Ezra Chapel victory,
184–85
Freedman's Bureau, in
charge of, 229
Hudson River, 311
Hunkpapa Sioux, 292
Hunter's Farm, 93
Hunter's Landing,

97–98
Huntsville, 165–66

I

Illinois
allegiance with the
South, 29
immigration of African
Americans into, 45
migration into, 17
state song, 322
Illinois Central Railroad,
116, 152, 263
McClelland, run by before
the war, 193
Illinois General Assembly,
260–61, 265–66
Logan, Dr. John, in, 199
redistricting by, 66–67
Illinois Natural History
Society, 254
Illinois State Democratic
Convention, 188–89
Illinois State Journal, 59
accusation in, 62
Carbondale speech in, 117
death, front-page
coverage of, 318
endorsement for
Senate, 279
loyalty of, 271
pro-Lincoln, 65
support of, 301
"traitors" named by,
76–77
Illinois State Register, 52,
53, 274
Democrats, loyalty to, 241
Oglesby, endorsement
of, 279
publication of letter
by, 79
Illinois State Republican
Convention, 278
Illinois Supreme Court, 33
Immigration of Negroes into
the State, An Act to
Prevent the, 45
Impeachment

Johnson, Andrew, of,
248–49, 251
Inauguration of Grant, 266
Independence Day, 239
Independent Party, 271, 295
Greenbackers of, 273
Indian Affairs, 289
Indians. *See* specific group
Ingersoll, E. J., 237
Ingersoll, Robert, 47
Internal Revenue
Bureau, 266
Iowa Circle, 301–02, 306, 322
Iowa Weekly Hawkeye, 280
Ireland, Northern, 9
Iyotake, Tatanka. *See*
"Sitting Bull"

J

Jackson County, 152
Jacksonian Democrats, 17
Jackson, Pres., 15
Jackson Road, 140–41,
144, 147
Jenkins, (Uncle) Alexander,
12, 14–15, 22–23
apprenticing for, 24–25
death, 163
law partnership with, 26
legal assistance by, 49
Jenkins, Elizabeth, 12
John A. Logan Community
College, 322
Johnson, Andrew
argument with, 240
delight of, in political
demise, 275
example of Union
patriot, 190
impeachment, 248–49, 251
Kuykendall's support
of, 238
Lincoln, running mate
for, 191
minister to Mexico,
position offered by, 236
Nashville, in, 163
president, 229
White House, at, 231

Johnston, Gen. Albert S., 110, 136–37, 168, 172, 175
Johnston, Joseph E., 223
  Bentonville, Battle of, and, 224
  surrender, terms of, 226–27
Joliet Signal, 65
Jones, A. M. "Long," 285
Jonesboro, Battle of, 186–187
Jonesboro Gazette, 106
  Democrats, loyalty to, of, 241
  mockery by, 195
  response to promotion by, 124
Jonesboro speech, 195
Jonesborough. *See* Jonesboro, Battle of

K

Kansas-Nebraska Act of 1854, 34, 56
Kellogg, William, 57
Kelly, Bob (Robert), 145
  death, 159
Kelly, Ike, 81
Kennesaw Mountain, 175
Kennesaw Mountain, Battle of, 176–77
Keokuk, Iowa, 314
Keppler, Joseph, 286–87
  political cartoon by, 205
K.G.C., 115, 117–19
  condemnation of, 153
  death threats by, 194
  Emancipation Proclamation, reponse to, 123
  Lincoln, concern about, 187–88
"Killed" list, 107
King George III, 65
Kingston, 171–72
Knights of the Golden Circle. *See* K.G.C.
Know-Nothings
  anger, 46

denunciation, 44
  disaffected factions, 43–44
Kuykendall, Andrew J.
  election victory, 195–96
  Johnson, support of, 238
  support of, 192
  undermined candidacy, 240

L

Lake Michigan, 263
Lake Shore depot, 263
Lanier Mansion, 124
Lanphier, Charles, 53
Law School, 26
Leave of absence, 189
Lecompton Constitution, 51
Lee, Gen. Robert E., 121, 183
  Gettysburg, loss at, 150
  surrender, terms of, 226
  Union forces, concerned about, 223
Lee, Gen. Stephen D., 183
Leeper, Arthur, 299
Leggett, Gen. Mortimer D., 138, 144, 160
  attack by, 148
  defense of Union, 180
Leggett's Hill, 180
Leland Hotel, 260, 273, 299, 301
Le Roach, James, 219
Lexington, 93
  transportation of Grant's troops, 100
Liberal Republicans, 264–65
  death of movement, 270
Lightburn, Brig. Gen. J. A. J., 176, 186
Lincoln, Abraham, 18
  assassination, 226
  call for troops by, 68, 85
  compared to Nero, 64
  decreased support of, 36
  Emancipation Proclamation and, 121–23
  fear of loss in election, 195

Johnson as running mate, 191
  K.G.C., concern about, 187–88
  mutual respect and, 225
  praise offered by, 66
  president-elect, 63
  response to South Carolina by, 68
  second meeting with, 82
  Senate contest, 242
  special session of Congress, 80
  visit with, 99
  vocal support of, 191
Lincoln, Robert Todd, 288–89, 296
Linegar, David T., 61
Little Bighorn, Battle of the, 292
"Little Giant," 27. *See also* Douglas, Stephen A.
Little Kennesaw Mountain, 175
Lockwood, Mary, 267, 288–89, 295
Logan, Annie, 25. *See also* Blanchard, Annie
  husband, third, of, 266
  marriage to Israel Blanchard, 43
Logan, Bill
  abolition, opposition to, 235
  death, 265–66
"Logan Boom," 293, 295, 313
Logan Circle, 322
Logan County, 199
Logan, "Dollie." *See* Logan, "Lizzie" (Mary Elizabeth)
Tucker, George, 290
Logan, Dorothula "Annie." *See* Logan, Annie
Logan, Dorothy, 25
  death, 185, 254
Logan, Dr. John, 6, 9–31, 200
  death, 30

medical supplies, 32
Logan, Elizabeth
    death, 267
    hostility from, 235
    rejection by, 88
    Southern Methodist
        Church and, 266
Logan, Elvira Willis, 266
"Logan, General," 218
Logan House, 26, 88
Logan, James Vanburen, 16
    loyalty of, 235
Logan, John A., II, 204
    birth, 234
    death, 321
    education, 277
    marriage, 320
    move to Washington, 314
    name change to, 290
Logan, "Johnny" (John
    Cunningham)
    birth, 45
    illness and death, 47–48
Logan, Kate
    adoption, 238
    death, 266
Logan, "Lizzie" (Mary
    Elizabeth), 203, 204
    birth, 52
    marriage, 277
    move to Washington, 314
    New Mexico, in, 306
Logan, Louisa Villars, 11
Logan, Manning Alexander.
    See Logan, John A., II
Logan, Mary S., 42–43,
    202–204 See also
    Cunningham, Mary
    breaking point, 236
    Carbondale, living in, 162
    death, 322
    devotion to, 99
    heartache, 60, 108
    illness, 47–48
    John A. Logan's "death"
        and, 106
    media interest in, 311
    memoirs published by, 206
    mother's death, 240–41

nursing husband to
    health, 124
    pregnancy, first, 44–45
    pregnancy, second, 48–49,
        51–52
    separation from, 92
    sister, loss of, 171
    "unladylike," 260
Logan Mausoleum, 322
Logan's Black Law, 29
"Logan's Great Battle," 320
Logan's Peak, 254
    naming of, 264
"Logan's Victory," 285
Logan, Tom (Thomas),
    108, 201
    alcoholism, battle
        with, 257
    death, 320
    K.G.C., alleged
        association with, 118–19
    marriage, third, 266
    Phillips, Escuale A.,
        obsession with, 120
    prosecution for rape,
        escape from, 235
    resignation, 123–24
    troubles, 162–63
    Union army, service
        in, 158
"Logan to the Front," 205
Logan, William B., 264
    move to Washington, 314
Long Bridge, 85, 230
Long Nine, 18
Lorimier, Marie Berthiaume,
    10–11
Loudermilk, W. H., 291
Louisville, 234
Lowery, Samuel R., 319
Lowe, William H., 281
Lynch Creek, 223
Lynch, David C., 16, 21
"Lyon, (Uncle) Daniel,"
    303–04, 309–10

M

"Mack." See McCullagh,
    Joseph B.

Macon and Western
    Railroad, 186
Madison, Wisconsin, 297–98
Maki pottery, 306
Malcomb, 243
Manassas Junction, 82
Manhattan, 311
Manier, James, 69–70
Manning, Joel, 12, 14
"March to the Sea," 214–15
Marietta, Georgia, 172, 175
Marion County
    dignitaries in, 239
Marion, Illinois, 207m
    Cunningham, John, burial
        of, 266
    move to, 67
    return to, 313
Market Street (San
    Francisco), 312
Marriage, 41–42
Marshall, Samuel S., 44, 45
    attendance at wedding, 42
    differing opinions of, 244
    "graveled" by Buchanan
        men, 54
    letter from, 50
    prominent friend, 34
    reelection to U.S.
        House, 45
    sparring with, 247–48
    support for Stephen
        Douglas, 53
Mason-Dixon Line, 29
Mausoleum, Logan, 322
"Mausoleum, The," 321
McClellan, Maj. Gen.
    George, 90
    Democratic presidential
        nomination, 188
    respect for, 189
    ridicule of, 193
McClernand, Gen. John A.,
    45, 59, 90, 137, 167
    admonition by, 114
    Belmont expedition and,
        93–96
    Confederate surge
        and, 103

Democratic Party,
   allegiance to, 236
   friendship with, 60
   hawkish position of, 71
   ousting of, 149
   praise by, 98
   retreat of Confederates
      and, 143
   superior rank of, 112
   Thompson's Hill, at, 131
   Ulysses S. Grant and, 78
McCook, Capt. Edwin S.,
   91, 102
   flag bearing by, 96–97
McCook, Daniel, 303
McCullagh, Joseph B., 133,
   135, 137
   Du Quoin speech, 156
   reporting by, 141
McDowell, General Irvin, 82
   Bull Run, Battle of, 85
"McGregor, Gen.," 304
McKeegan, Jimmy, 88
McKendree College, 13–14
McKinley, Pres., 321
McLeansboro speech, 194
McPherson, Gen. James
   Birdseye, 122, 134, 137,
      151, 176
   Army of the Tennessee,
      led by, 166
   celebration of victory
      by, 150
   death of, 178
   Nashville, in, 163–64
   Raymond, Battle of, 136
McPhersonville, 218
Meade, Gen. victory, 150
Medal of Honor,
   Congressional, 321
Medals of Gold, 165
Medill, Joseph, 64
   incorrect prediction
      of, 66
   new friend, 288
Memorial Day, 251, 255–56
   first, 322
   Grant's Tomb, visiting,
      on, 311

"Memorial Hall," 321
Mentor, 288
Mersy, Col. August, 179–80
Methodist Church, 11
   adherence to, 257
   Reconstruction and, 256
   Southern, 266
Metropolitan Church, 314
Mexican War, 22, 23
   end of, 24
   service, fabrication
      of, 297
Mexico Campaign, 46
Michigan Avenue, 286
Middle Road, 137
"Middleton's Ridge," 304
Military Affairs, Committee
   on. See Committee on
   Military Affairs
Military District of the
   Mississippi, 216
Military Division of the
   Mississippi, 161
   Sherman as leader of, 167
Military prestige, 24
Mill Creek, 224
minister to Mexico
   position offered by Pres.
   Johnson, 236
Mississippi Central
   Railroad, 112
Mississippi River, 233
Mississippi River Valley
   control of, 92–93
Missouri Compromise of
   1820, 34
Missouri Democrat, 196
Missouri Republican, 79
Mobile and Ohio
   Railroad, 112
Mooninghan, Sol, 88
Morgan Park Military
   Academy, 277
Mormon Rebellion, 52
Morrison, William R., 299
Mother Logan. See Logan,
   Elizabeth
Mount Vernon, 194
   soldiers' reunion in, 278

"Mrs. Winslow's Soothing
   Syrup," 248
"Murat of Illinois
   bravery," 104
Murphysboro, Illinois,
   22, 207
   family turmoil, 162
   home, not allowed in, 235

N
Name change, 24
"Narrow Escape, The," 268
Nashville, 163
Nashville and Chattanooga
   Railroad, 166
Nashville, Battle of, 213–214
"National Aid to Public
   Schools," 291
National Bank, 271
National Cemetery of
   the Soldier's Home,
   319, 322
National crisis, 68
National Democratic
   Convention (1860), 60
National Tribune, 303
   articles for, 310
   book, serial publication
      of, 307
   Logan, Mary, published
      in, 321
National Union Party, 158
   founding of, 161–62
National Union Republican
   Party, 250
Native Americans. See
   specific group
Natural History Society,
   Illinois, 254
Naval Academy, 255
Nebraska Territory
   slave labor and, 34
Negroes. See African
   Americans
Negro Suffrage amendment,
   247
Nepotism, 254
Nero, 64
Neutrality, 72, 74

Nevada, 313
Newark, 278
Newby, Col. Edward W. B.,
    23–24
New Haven, Connecticut, 251
New Hope Church, 172
Newman, Rev. John P., 314,
    316–17, 322–23
New Mexico, 306
Newsome, Edward, 132
New Uncle Sam, 107–09
New York City, 311
New York Herald
    editorial in, 294
    presidential election
        prediction in, 62
    reputation damaged by, 77
New York Sun, 269–70
New York Times
    attention from, 59
    Great Conspiracy, review
        of, in, 307
    letter in, 270, 292
    New Haven, criticism
        of, 251
    parade to White House,
        reported in, 230–31
    praise, 285
New York Tribune, 57
Niagara Falls, 156
Nineteenth Amendment, 322
Nineteenth General
    Assembly of Illinois, 34
Ninth Congressional
    District, 89
Norfolk, 224
North American Review, 291
    Porter's reinstatement
        and, 295
North Carolina, 223
Northern Ireland, 9
"Northwest Confederacy,"
    153
Northwest Ordinance, 1787, 11

O
O'Beirne, Charles, 241
"Officer of the Union Army,
    An," 303

Oglesby, Col. Richard, 100,
    102, 238
    Confederate surge
        and, 103
    dissatisfaction with, 217
    governor-elect, 196
    governor, outgoing, 249
    governor, running for, 192
    July 4, 1863, and, 239
    Logan, Mary, enemy
        of, 260
    Senate defeat of, 282
    Senate, return to, 265
    Senate rival, 259
    ungratefulness, 216
Ohio River, 21, 160
    Valley, threatened by
        Hood, 213
Old Capitol Prison, 119
    Allen, Josh, in, 121
Old Northwest states, 157
Oostanaula River, 169, 171
Opera House, 250
Osterhaus, Gen. Peter J., 137,
    165, 186, 189, 215
Ozburn, "Doff" (Lindorf),
    22, 23, 201
    "Black Codes" and, 113
    death, 163
    plot for Democratic
        postmasters, 50
    promise made to, 86
    promotion, 110
    quartermaster, 91
    reflection on Belmont
        expedition, 98
    unwillingness to free
        slaves, 123
Ozburn, John Logan, 26

P
Pacific Coast trip, 312
Pacific Railroad, 254
"Pageland," 304
Palmer, Gen. John M.,
    193, 241
    Democratic opponent, 273
    Liberal movement
        and, 265

    Senate race, 244
Palmer Hotel, 270
Palmer House (Chicago),
    282, 285
Palmer, Richard
    gubernatorial candidate,
        249
Palmetto State. See South
    Carolina
Panic of 1873, 268, 271,
    274, 289
"Paper Money Trinity,
    The," 274
Parish, William K., 33, 54
    marriage ceremony by, 41
Parker, Goodwin, 33
Party "Boss," 285
Payne, Henry B., 311–12
Peace Democrats, 115
    Cairo presence of, 160
    defeating, 208
    most radical of, 156
    movement, 158
    mutual hate, 194
Pendleton, George H., 188
Peace position, 71
Pee Dee River, 223
Pemberton, Lt. Gen. John
    C., 129, 131, 136–37
    Champion Hill loss, 143
    Grant, negotiations
        with, 151
    surrender by, 148–50
    Vicksburg, loss of army
        at, 149
Pendleton Civil Service Act,
    293–94, 305
Pendleton, George H., 188
    McClellan's running
        mate, 190
    presidential candidate,
        189
Pennington, William, 59
Pennsylvania Avenue, 230
Perry County, 238
Personal Memoirs, 5
    success of, 315
Petersburg, 224, 227
Philadelphia

speech in, 309
Philadelphia Press, 318
Philippines, 321
Phillips, David L., 192
  Mount Vernon, in, 194
  Yates, campaigning
    for, 211
Phillips, Esculane A., 120
  rape case, 162
Phillips, U.S. Marshall David
  L., 53, 54
  arrest of Blanchard by,
    118–19
  Confederate
    sympathizers, sweep
    by, 115
Pickett's Mill, 172
Pigeon Hill, 175, 176
Pillow, Gen., 94
  Confederate surge and,
    103, 105
  opposition of Grant
    by, 101
Pinckneyville, 238
Pioneer History of Illinois,
  27–28
Pittsburg, Illinois, 313
Pittsburg Landing, 112
"Pittskill Landing," 304
Plains Indians, 254
Playwriting, 268
"Plumed Knight,"
  283, 296
Political
  conversion, 239
  demise, 275
  interest, 185
  mistake, 77
  recognition, 231
Polk, Gen. Leonidis,
  90–91, 171
  pressure from Grant, 93
Polk, Pres. James K., 22
Popular sovereignty, 34
Porter, Fitz-John,
  282–83, 291
  reinstatement, 295, 311
Porter, Rear Adm.
  David, 129

Port Gibson, 130
Port Gibson, Battle of. *See*
  Thompson's Hill
Portland, Oregon, 313
Portsmouth (Ohio)
  Democrat, 274
Postmasters plot, 50
Potomac River, 230
Prentiss, Gen. Benjamin M.,
  71, 75
Preston Mansion, 221
Prohibitionists, 278
Promotion to major
  general, 125
  letters supporting, 125
  recommended for, 109–10
Provo, Utah, 266
Puck Magazine, 286–87, 298
Puget Sound, 313
Pulitzer, Joseph, 321
Pulley, Dan, 88
Pulley, James D., 75
Pumpkinvine Creek, 172

Q
Quinby, Brig. Gen. Isaac F.,
  138, 142

R
Radical Republicans, 240
  impeachment of Pres.
    Johnson, 244, 248
  leadership, 247
  monitoring of, 241
Radical State ticket, 246
Railroad. *See* specific name
  "Sherman's Neckties," 177
  Union-controlled, 189
"Rail Splitter," 61. *See also*
  Lincoln, Abraham
Raleigh, 224–27
  leaving, 227
  near disaster at, 226
Randolph Street (Chicago),
  157
Ransom, Col. Thomas, 104
Raum, Green B., 240, 285
  defeat of Josh Allen by, 243
Rawlins, Lt. Col. John

A., 122
  Champion Hill and, 143
  Nashville, in, 163
  opposition to Buford's
    promotion by, 125
Raymond, Battle of,
  135–36
Razorbacks, 95
Rearden, George, 81
  promise made to, 86
Recognition, 98
*Recollections of a Soldier's
  Wife*, 207, 322
Reconstruction
  Carbondale speech
    and, 242
  Johnson's opposition
    to, 240
  Methodist Church
    and, 256
  policy, continuation
    of, 280
  politics of, 254–55
Reelection campaigns, 208
Republican Iron Horse, 286
Republican National
  Committee, 286, 295
Republican National
  Convention, 238, 320
Republican Party
  alliances with, 236
  anger of, 46
  competition within, 295
  division deepening within,
    256, 264
  election victories in
    Illinois, 196
  formation, 43–44
  likened to King George
    III, 65
  state convention, 240
  top candidate for, 316
  winning streak, 298
Resaca, 168–71
Resignation, 234
Reynolds, John, 27
"Rheumatism, cerebral,"
  316–17
Rhines, Mrs., 267

Rhodes, Col. Frank, 114
Richardson, Col. Israel,
    82–83
Richardson, William,
    44, 82
Richmond
    burning of, 227–28
    Grant, victory of, 224
Riverside Park, 311
Robinson, James, 45, 67
    friendship with, 60
    support of peace
        position, 71
Rock Creek Cemetery, 319
Rockies. See Rocky
    Mountains
Rocky Face Ridge, 168
Rocky Mountains, 254
Roots, Benajah G., 18
Roots school, 18
Rosecrans, General, 211
Rossville speech, 279
Roswell, 177

S
Sacramento, 312
"Salary Grab," 268
Salem, Illinois
    dignitaries in, 239
Saluda River, 220
Sangamon County, 212
San Juan Hill, Battle
    of, 321
Santa Fe, 291–92
Santiago, Battle of, 321
Savannah, 214
Scarlet fever, 23
Schofield, Gen. John M.
    Army of the Ohio, led by,
        166, 168
    Tennessee, in, 213
Schurz, Carl, 261, 296
Scioto County, 9
Scott, Dred, 56
Scott, Gen. Winfield, 82
Secessionists
    atmosphere of 1861, 281
    family members, 88–89
Secretary of War. See also

Davis, Jefferson
    Lincoln, Robert Todd, 288
Secret society, 115
Senate Bill 194, 308
Senate victory, 282
Seneca stone, 261
Sentinel and Press, 259
Seventeeth Corps
    vacancy, 164
Seventh Iowa, 95
Seward, William H., 61
Seymour, Horatio, 252
Shanks, William, 169–70
Sheahan, J. W., 188
"Shell-Anna," 186
Sheridan, Phil, 263, 316
    Nashville, in, 163
Sherman, Gen. William T.,
    133, 166–67
    Atlanta, Battle of,
        reaction to, 182
    Bentonville, Battle of,
        and 224
    command of army, 159
    Halleck, hatred of, 228
    July 4, 1863, and, 239
    Kennesaw Mountain,
        Battle of, 176–77
    "March to the Sea,"
        214–15
    memoirs, 281
    Mount Vernon
        reunion, 278
    Nashville, in, 163–64
    Pee Dee River,
        crossing, 223
    praise by, 184
    presidential hopeful, 305
    Raleigh headquarters, 226
    Republican National
        Convention, at, 320
    residence, former, 306
    salary reduction of, 255
    San Francisco, in, 312
    Savannah, capture of, 214
    subordination to, 209
    surrender, terms of, 226
    White House, arriving
        at, 231

Sherman, John, 59
    presidental nomination,
        seeking, 284
"Sherman's Neckties," 177
"Sherwood, Gen.," 304, 310
Shiloh, Battle of, 110–11
    flag, tattered, 232
Shiloh College, 21
"Siege of Corinth," 112
"Silent, Gen.," 304
"Sitting Bull," 292–93
Skinner, Annie Logan. See
    Logan, Annie
"Slasher," 173, 178–79, 230
Slaveholding
    Carbondale speech and,
        116–17
    1818 Constitution, 11
    John A. Logan and, 28
Slocum, Henry, 217
Sloo, Robert, 47
"Smite, Gen. Bowlly," 304
Smith, Arthur, 302
Smith, Brig. Gen. Giles
    A., 176
Smith, Gen. John E., 134, 165
    railroad protection by, 166
Smith, Gen. Morgan L., 165,
    175–76
Smithsonian Institute, 254
Snake Creek Gap, 168, 169
Snyder, William H., 27, 278
Society of the Army of the
    Tennessee, 237–38, 282
"Solid South," 284
Sorrell trial, 48–50
South Carolina, 218
Southern Confederacy, 70
Southern Methodist
    Church, 266
Southern Mississippi
    Railroad, 143
"Southern Question,
    The," 280
Span, Corporal W. W., 132
Spanish American War,
    320–21
Springfield, 235
    Leland Hotel, 260

state convention, 284–85
"Stalwarts," 284–85, 288, 295
Standing Rock, 292
Stanton, Edwin M., 120
    firing of, 248
    pro-Confederate
        uprisings, reported
        to, 157
    recommendation to, 215
    White House and, 231
State Department, 261
State House (Columbia), 221
State Journal, 79
State Treasurer of
    Illinois, 278
St. Charles Hotel, 90, 160
Stephens, Alexander, 253
Stevenson, Gen. Carter,
    138, 142
Stevenson, Gen. John D.,
    131, 135
Stevenson, Maj. Benjamin
    Franklin, 237, 247
Stevens, Thaddeus, 249
Steward, Lewis, 271
St. Louis, 316
St. Louis Post Dispatch, 318
Stolbrand, Charles, 169
    death, 172
Stolbrand, Maj. Carlos John,
    130, 145
    death, 146
Stone, Dr., 306
"Stone Mansion," 306
Stone Mountain, 177
St. Paul, Minnesota, 238
Strathmore Arms, 267
"Strider, Thomas A.," 304
Suffrage
    African-American,
        240, 245
    Negro, amendment
        for, 247
Sumner, Charles, 261,
    262, 265
Supreme Court,
    U.S., 274
Surrender (April 26,
    1865), 226

"Swing Low, Sweet
    Chariot," 313

T
Taney, Chief Justice
    Roger, 56
Taylor, Ezra, 174
Taylor's Battery, 97
Tennessee, 214
Tennessee River, 99
Tenure of Office Act, 248
Teton Sioux, 292
"Thanksgiving Day,
    1884," 298
Third Division of the
    Seventeenth Corps,
    133, 149
"Third termers," 285
Thirteenth Amendment,
    234–35
    ratification of, 245
Thirteenth District, 243
Thirty-first Illinois, 102
Thomas, Adj. Gen. Lorenzo,
    127–28, 166, 176
Thomas, Capt. John R., 181
Thomas, Cy (Cyrus), 25
    death of wife and, 185
    deputy, as, 26
    Evangelical Lutheran
        minister, 254
    friendship with, 25
    geographical survey
        and, 264
    legal assistance by, 49
    legal association with, 67
Thomas, Dorothy Logan.
    See Logan, Dorothy
Thomas, Gen. George,
    166, 168
Thompson's Hill, 130
Tilden, Samuel, 271
    Republicans against, 272
Tilghman, Brig. Gen.
    Lloyd, 101
Townes, Maj. Robert R.,
    129–30, 141
    Carbondale, in, 152
    headquarters, gone

from, 215
"Traitors of Williamson
    County, The," 76
Treaty of Guadalupe
    Hidalgo, 24
Trenton Times, 280
Trinity M. E. Church
    (Chicago), 267
"Triumverate, The,"
    284–87
Trumbull, Lyman, 238
    duties shared with, 261
    election to U.S. Senate,
        36, 244
    endorsement for
        reelection of, 240
    Liberal movement
        and, 265
Tucker, Dollie Logan. *See*
    Logan, "Lizzie" (Mary
    Elizabeth)
Tucker, George
    birth, 290
Tucker, "Logan." *See* Tucker,
    George
Tucker, William F.,
    277, 291–92
Tuthill, Daniel B., 14
Twain, Mark, 93,
    282, 315
Tweed, William, 271
Twelfth Street
    boardinghouse, 295
Twentieth General
    Assembly, 46
"Two Rivers, Battle
    of," 303
Tyler, 93, 100

U
"Uncle Billy," 227
"Uncle Daniel." *See* "Lyon,
    (Uncle) Daniel"
"Uncle Daniel's Story
    of Tom Anderson
    and the Great
    Conspiracy,"
    303, 309
"Unconditional Surrender"

Grant. *See* Grant,
Ulysses S.
Unconditional Unionist,
210
Underground Railroad, 56
Union
advocates, political
affiliations of, 236
soldiers, 230–32
speech in favor of, 91
support, 71–72, 80, 88
victory, 105–06, 136
Union Executive
Congressional
Committee, 188
Union Pacific Railroad, 266,
268–69, 312
United States of America,
230
University of Louisville, 26
U.S. Army, 278
U.S. Army of the
Cumberland, 121
U.S. Colored Infantry, 216
U.S. Constitution
Fifteenth Amendment,
252–53
impeachment, grounds
for, in, 248
Nineteenth Amendment,
322
Thirteenth Amendment,
234–35, 245
"USeless" Grant. *See* Grant,
Ulysses S.
U.S. Geological and
Geographical Survey,
254, 293
artists, 204pl
U.S. House of
Representatives
career in, 261
election to, 252
nomination for, 240
U.S. Land Office, 38
U.S. Supreme Court, 274
U.S. Volunteer Army,
209, 234
U.S. Volunteer Infantry, 321

V
Vallandigham, Clement L.,
156, 188
differing opinions of, 244
Negro Suffrage and, 247
victory, 160
Van Buren, Martin, 16
"Vegetable Order," 114
Veteran's organization, 237
Vicksburg
flag, tattered, 232
National Military
Park, 322
speech, 159–60
Vicksburg Campaign, 135,
143–45, 154
Vicksburg Road, 137
"Victory, Logan's," 285
Villa Rica Road, 172–73
Virginia, 254
*Volunteer Soldier of
America, The*, 315,
319–20
Voorhees, Sen., 310

W
Wade, Benjamin F., 253
Walcutt, Col. C. C., 176
Wallace, William H. L., 102
Confederate surge
and, 104
Walnut Cracker, 19
Wangelin, Col. Hugo, 179
War Democrats, 188–89
War Department, 158, 184
recognition by, 150
resignation, letter of,
to, 234
speaking circuit, approval
of, by, 193
Stanton barricaded in, 248
surrender terms, rejected
by, 226
War Meetings, 69
"War party." *See* Republican
Party
Warren, Ohio, 297
Washburne, Elihu B., 209,
212, 285

Grant, Ulysses S., and, 133
praise by, 128–129
promotion, recommended
by, 109–10
Thomson's Hill, 132
Union presidential
campaign and, 188
*Washington National
Intelligencer*, 318
Washington politico, 231
Washington Post, 309, 314
Waterhouse, Maj. Allen
C., 172
Watseka speech, 279
Ways and Means, 254
Weaver, William H., 300
Webster, Daniel, 56
West
interest in, 254
trip to, 312
Western and Atlantic
Railroad, 168, 172
West Point, 177, 182, 255
Logan, John A., II, 290,
293, 320
Wheaton, Capt. Lloyd,
130, 152
Wheaton, Lloyd, 321
Whigs, 16
disaffected factions,
43–44
increasing power, 17
Kansas-Nebraska
disagreement, 34
Logan family antagonism,
32
Whisky Ring Scandal,
269–70, 274
"Whistling Dick," 145
"Whistling Jack," 145
White, Amzi, 186, 219
White House
parade of soldiers, 230–32
reception, 253
visit, 214
White, John H., 80, 102,
104–5
Belmont expedition
and, 94

death, 108, 115, 186, 237
lieutenant colonel, 91
promise made to, 86
"White Man's War," 216
White supremacy, 28, 33
"Whitiker," 145
Whittemore, B. Frank,
    255, 258
Wiley, Ben, 54
Willard's Hotel, 66, 253,
    263–64
Williams, Col. Reuben, 161,
    165, 183

treason conspiracy trials
    and, 214
Williamson County, 18
Williard's Hotel, 247
Windy City. *See* Chicago
Woodlawn Cemetery,
    236–37, 250
Woods, Gen. Charles R., 222
Woodstock, CT, 305

Y
Yates, Gov. Richard, 75, 120
    competition with, 208

Grant's entourage, in, 133
reelection, up for, 252
Senate, running for, 161,
    192, 196, 209
Yellowstone National Park,
    264, 293
Yellowstone River, 264
Youngstown, Ohio, 320, 322

Z
Zela, 113
Zuni Indians, 204, 291–93, 306
Zuni River, 292